| 2. Fremdsprache |

access 9

Cornelsen

Access 2. Fremdsprache | 9

Im Auftrag des Verlages herausgegeben von
Prof. Dr. Engelbert Thaler, Augsburg
Jörg Rademacher, Mannheim

Erarbeitet von
Laurence Harger, Nürnberg
Cecile Niemitz-Rossant, Berlin
Peadar Curran, Berlin
Marc Proulx , Berlin
Eleanor Toal, Liverpool, UK

unter Mitarbeit von
Dr. Annette Leithner-Brauns, Dresden
Birgit Ohmsieder, Berlin
Mervyn Whittaker, Bad Dürkheim

in Zusammenarbeit mit der Englischredaktion
Filiz Bahşi (Projektkoordination, verantwortliche Redakteurin), Ulrike Berendt, Dr. Philip Devlin, Sophie Dupiech (Medienmanagement), Ursula Fleischhauer, Bonnie Glänzer, Stefan Höhne (Redaktionsleitung), Anne Linder, Georg Raspe (Vocabulary, Dictionaries), Sophia Schneider

Beratende Mitwirkung
Thomas Bohlen, Traunstein
Gerhard Finster, Dillingen
Dr. Janina Kuhn-Deutschländer, München
Ingola Seger, Augsburg
Jörg Wunderlich, München

Illustrationen
Tobias Dahmen, Utrecht/NL
Michael Fleischmann, Waldegg
Eric Gira, Berlin
Burkhard Schulz, Düsseldorf

Fotos
Sapna Richter, Berlin

Umschlaggestaltung
hawemannundmosch, Berlin

Layout und technische Umsetzung
Eric Gira, Ungermeyer, Berlin

www.cornelsen.de

In diesem Werk wird in Form von Symbolen auf Audio-Material verwiesen; dieses enthält – bis auf die Hörverstehensübungen – ausschließlich optionale Unterrichtsmaterialien. Die Audio-Materialien unterliegen in Bayern nicht dem staatlichen Zulassungsverfahren.

Die enthaltenen Links verweisen auf digitale Inhalte, die der Verlag in eigener Verantwortung zur Verfügung stellt.

Dieses Werk berücksichtigt die Regeln der reformierten Rechtschreibung und Zeichensetzung.

1. Auflage, 1. Druck 2021

Alle Drucke dieser Auflage sind inhaltlich unverändert und können im Unterricht nebeneinander verwendet werden.

Druck: Firmengruppe APPL, aprinta Druck, Wemding

ISBN 978-3-06-034736-0

ISBN 978-3-06-036111-3 (E-Book)

PEFC
PEFC/04-32-0928

PEFC zertifiziert
Dieses Produkt stammt aus nachhaltig bewirtschafteten Wäldern und kontrollierten Quellen.

www.pefc.de

Access 2. Fremdsprache | 9 **enthält folgende Teile:**

Units	die vier Kapitel des Buches
Access to cultures	landeskundliche Informationen
Text File	eine Sammlung englischsprachiger Texte
Skills File	eine Beschreibung wichtiger Lern- und Arbeitstechniken
Grammar File	eine Zusammenfassung der Grammatik jeder Unit
Vocabulary	das Wörterverzeichnis zum Lernen der neuen Wörter jeder Unit
Dictionary	alphabetisches Wörterverzeichnis zum Nachschlagen (Englisch-Deutsch)

In den Units findest du diese Überschriften:

Background file	Informationen über Land und Leute
Looking at language	Beispiele sammeln und sprachliche Regeln entdecken
Language help	Hilfe in Form von sprachlichen Regeln
Practice	Aufgaben und Übungen
Access to words	Wortschatz systematisch ausbauen
Speaking course	nützliche sprachliche Hilfen beim Sprechen
The world behind the picture	vom Bild in den Film – Videoclips mit Aufgaben
Thinking about language	Aufgaben zur Sprachreflexion
Text	eine spannende oder lustige Geschichte
Your task	In der Lernaufgabe kannst du in jeder Unit zeigen, was du gelernt hast und dich selbst einschätzen.
Checkpoint	Auf diesen Seiten kannst du den Wortschatz und die Grammatik einer Unit wiederholen und dich auf Schulaufgaben vorbereiten.

Du findest auch diese Symbole:

	Texte, die du dir anhören kannst: *www.cornelsen.de/webcodes* (Webcode: *petese*)
www	zusätzliche Materialien, die du unter *www.cornelsen.de/webcodes* (Webcode: *tomixa*) finden kannst
	Übungssequenz: neue Grammatik intensiv üben und dann anwenden
Early finisher	zusätzliche Aktivitäten und Übungen für Schüler/innen, die früher fertig sind
More help	zusätzliche Hilfen für eine Aufgabe
You choose	eine Aufgabe auswählen
EXTRA	zusätzliche Aktivitäten und Übungen für alle
My Book	schöne und wichtige Arbeiten sammeln
Study skills	Einführung in Lern- und Arbeitstechniken
	Hören Sprechen Lesen Schreiben
	Mediation (zwischen zwei Sprachen vermitteln), Thinking about language (Sprachreflexion)
	Partnerarbeit Partnercheck Gruppenarbeit Kooperative Lernform

LIFEGUARD
RESCUE

Skill in focus: Reading

Skills in focus: Reading and Writing

London changing

A

C

B

D

1 London map and pictures

a) Take two minutes to tell each other what you already know about London.

b) Look at the map and the map key on p. 8.
Explain to each other what it tells you about London.

c) Partner A: Describe pictures A and B carefully.
Partner B: Suggest how your partner can improve his or her description.
Take turns for pictures C and D.

→ *SF 25: Describing, presenting and interpreting images (p. 175)*

d) Match the pictures to the London eras on the map key.
Make notes on the reasons for your decision.
Then discuss your ideas with another pair.

2 London eras

a) Work in groups of four.
Listen to the audio extracts 1–4 and match each one to a London era. Give reasons for your answers and check them in class.

b) Listen again and, in a table, take notes on:
- sounds (what they are, what they tell you)
- the situation (where, time of day, who, …)
- events (what happens?)
- background information (what you find out about the era, the city, the weather, people and places, …)

Each group member should concentrate on one of the table's headings.

c) Agree on what should go in each section of the table and compare your notes with another group.

3 Time traveller

Imagine you travel back in time to one of these London eras. Why are you there and what do you experience during your visit? Write a post for social media (about 200 words).

More help → *(p. 146)*

→ **Workbook** *1 (p. 2)*

Your task **EXTRA**

Your task for this unit: You will plan a class trip to London with your group.

1 Where to now?

Alyssa Robertson, from Ottawa, Canada, has arrived in London to spend six months as an exchange student at a London school. Her parents have travelled with her to introduce their daughter to the city. They have been checking out websites to decide where to go and what to do before Alyssa starts school next week.

Whispering in the City
Start your day at Sir Christopher Wren's magnificent St Paul's Cathedral, built after the Great Fire of London in 1666 destroyed the old one. Don't miss the coolest part, the Whispering Gallery, up inside the famous dome. Go with a friend and stand at opposite ends of the gallery. Whisper something and your friend will hear you loud and clear, although you're over 30 metres apart! How's that for acoustics?

Experiencing Black Britain
Head south of the river to Brixton, which has been a centre of Afro-Caribbean culture for over 60 years. Walk through the colourful indoor and outdoor markets and visit the Black Cultural Archives on Windrush Square. The Windrush was the ship that brought some of the first Caribbean workers to Britain in the 1940s. The archive tells their stories and shows how people of African and Caribbean origin have changed the UK.

Listening to history
Back in Central London from Brixton, your next destination is the Houses of Parliament and Big Ben clock tower, known together as the Palace of Westminster. Take an audio tour which brings a thousand years of history and modern British politics to life. Follow the route the Queen takes when she opens Parliament and find out how the place works. The tour ends with afternoon tea in a room overlooking the Thames.

Dancing on top of the world
When the sun goes down, finish your day with a silent disco at the top of Western Europe's tallest building, the Shard. Put on your headphones and dance to the best pop, rock and party tunes on three wireless channels. You'll be in heaven while you enjoy the most magnificent view in the city. Teenagers can go there with their parents. After dancing, enjoy dinner at one of the many restaurants in and around the Shard.

2 What about you?

a) Find the places Alyssa is interested in on a map of London.

b) Imagine you're in London. Rank the four sights/activities from 1 (most) to 4 (least) interesting. Note down your reasons.

c) Exchange your ranking ideas in a double circle activity.

d) Write a social media post (about 150 words). Explain which two places you are going to visit and why.

→ **Workbook** *2 (p. 3)*

3 At Trafalgar Square

Read Alyssa's chat.

Hey Lauren! Here I am in London! How are things back in Ottawa? *3:27 pm*

Lauren It's getting cold here. Raining a lot. Hey, your new classmates look pretty old … and a bit like your mom and dad! 😛 *3:30 pm*

Lol! School doesn't start till next week. We're wandering round the West End of London. Almost at Trafalgar Square. *3:35 pm*

Lauren Trafalgar Square! Send me pics! *3:37 pm*

Lauren 😲 I didn't mean a picture of Canada, girl. I'm the one in Canada! *3:41 pm*

No, it's Canada House, right on Trafalgar Square. *3:42 pm*

Lauren ??? Canadian tourist bureau, or what? *3:44 pm*

No idea *3:45 pm*

Lauren Ask your new classmates. They're old. They'll know. LOL *3:47 pm*

Dad says it's the Canadian High Commission. Like an embassy, only they don't call it an embassy, because of the Commonwealth. *3:50 pm*

Lauren Now explain that in English. 😉 *3:52 pm*

Hi Lauren, how are you? Alyssa gave me her phone so I could explain. Canada is a member of the Commonwealth, an organization of countries that were British colonies once. Countries like Canada, Australia, India, South Africa. Or Jamaica where Alyssa's mom's parents were from. And lots of other countries. These countries have a special relationship with each other so they don't call their diplomatic places embassies like everyone else. They call them High Commissions. All clear?
Andrew Robertson *4:00 pm*

Lauren Thanks, Mr Robertson. Clear as mud! 😖 *4:02 pm*

OK, Lauren, I want to stay here with the lions but Dad says we have to go into this huge old gallery now. Catch you later. *4:05 pm*

4 Visitors from the Commonwealth

a) Explain how the photo of the flags leads to the topic of the Commonwealth. Then say what you learn about the Commonwealth.

www Find out more about the Commonwealth.

b) Compare a) *It's raining a lot.* and b) *Raining a lot.* Say which is used in the text messages and why.

Find similar examples above.

➔ **Workbook** *3 (p. 4)*

We often make one word from another by adding a suffix like *-ful*, *-less* or *-ness*, e.g.:
noun: cloud → adjective: *cloudless* adjective: dark → noun: *darkness*
Knowing about suffixes will help you to understand words you haven't learned yet.
Using suffixes is also a good way to increase your vocabulary.

1 Adjectives from nouns (Suffixes *-ful* and *-less*)

a) Complete the sentences with adjectives. Find the best word in one of the boxes and add a suffix.

TIP
-ful means 'full of', e.g. power<u>ful</u>, help<u>ful</u>
-less means 'without', e.g. cloud<u>less</u>, heart<u>less</u>

-ful	colour · event · respect · rest · success+ · skill
-less	air · end · home · cloud · rain · sleep

1 Because of the time difference, Alyssa's first night in London wasn't very … .
2 She brought a cup of tea every day to the … woman outside the Tube station.
3 The boat tour on the Thames seemed … to Alyssa. She had never liked boats.
4 The Columbia Road Flower Market was more … than a rainbow.
5 Their most … evening was dinner and dancing at the top of the Shard.
6 Back at the hotel, Alyssa opened the window and let a breeze into the hot, … room.

b) Make adjectives from the words you didn't need in a) and use them to write your own sentences.

c) Using the phrases in your list, write six sentences.
Read your sentences to your partner.

→ **Workbook** 4 (p. 5)

2 Nouns from adjectives (Abstract nouns with the suffix *-ness*)

Nouns can be concrete or abstract. Concrete nouns describe material objects, e.g. *dog, house, tree*.
An abstract noun is a noun that does not describe a material object: e.g. *history, danger, culture*.
You can make abstract nouns from adjectives with the suffix *-ness*: e.g. *sickness*, *illness*.
If an adjective ends in *-y*, it is usually changed to an *-i* when you add the suffix, e.g. *happiness, silliness*.

Alyssa is talking about London. Rewrite her sentences using nouns with *-ness*.

1 The outdoor market in Brixton was crazy. — We enjoyed the … at the market in Brixton.
2 The people there were so friendly. — The … of the people there was special.
3 It was really quiet inside St Paul's Cathedral. — The … inside St Paul's was a real contrast.
4 Dad lost his jacket. He's so forgetful! — His … worries me sometimes.
5 It's amazing how fit my mom is. — I wonder if I can reach her level of … .
6 I hope I won't be lonely here. — I hope … won't be a problem for me here.

→ **Workbook** 5 (p. 5)

3 Your sentences (Suffixes *-ful*, *-less* and *-ness*)

bitter+ · child · clever · cloud · fair · friend · great · heart · help · ill · job · life · mad · nervous · power · shy · skill · tear · tired · rest

a) Choose five words from the box. Use a dictionary to find out which of the suffixes *-ful, -less* or *-ness* can be used with them. Sometimes more than one suffix is possible.

b) Write a sentence with each of the words you found in the dictionary:
bitter: There was a lot of bitterness when our team lost the match.

c) Compare your sentences.

d) In class, share sentences for each of the words in the box.

Language help

In English the definite article (*the*) isn't used before a noun in some cases.
Look at some examples from the texts on pp. 10–11.

abstract nouns	e.g. *culture, history, life, sport(s), pollution, ...* *... a centre of Afro-Caribbean* ***culture*** *... / ... a thousand years of* ***history*** *...*
plural nouns	e.g. *years, people, headphones, teenagers, countries, ...* ***Teenagers*** *can go there with their parents. / ... an organization of* ***countries*** *...*
certain places and meals	e.g. *school, church, hospital, breakfast, lunch, dinner, ...* ***School*** *doesn't start till next week. / ... enjoy* ***dinner*** *at one of the many ...*

We use the definite article only when we give these nouns a more specific meaning.

On the tour you'll learn about ***the history*** *of Westminster.*
We had a nice chat with ***the teenagers*** *who were dancing next to us.*
The school *isn't far from Alyssa's host family's house.*

➔ *GF 13: The definite article (p. 208)*

4 Around town (The definite article: plurals, places, meals)

a) Compare these two sentences. Say what you notice about the word 'people'.

- People from the Caribbean have lived in Brixton for over 60 years.
- The people on the Windrush were the first Caribbean workers in Britain.

b) Copy the sentence pairs. Add *the* where you need it.

1 It's popular to have ... lunch at a pub.
2 ... lunch they serve at The Fox is excellent.
3 In St Paul's, ... acoustics are especially good.
4 ... acoustics are important in a large cathedral.
5 At the silent disco everybody wears ... headphones.
6 You return ... headphones when you leave the disco.
7 ... people of London are extremely diverse.
8 ... people are really the same all over the world.

➔ **Workbook** *6 (p. 5)*

5 London's past and present (The definite article: abstract nouns)

Read about some historical aspects of London. Add *the* if necessary to complete the sentences.

In Central London there's [1]... history everywhere. In Brixton the Black Cultural Archives tell [2]... history of Afro-Caribbean culture in London. [3]... transport also has a long tradition in London. The London Transport Museum takes you back in [4]... time nearly 200 years ago when buses were pulled by horses. That was [5]... time of Queen Victoria, when [6]... life in London was very different. But some things haven't changed much. [7]... pollution was already a problem back then, and [8]... pollution that hung in London's skies was especially bad. Today, [9]... air in the city still could be cleaner than it is.

6 Abstract or concrete? (The definite article: abstract and concrete nouns)

a) Decide if these nouns are abstract or concrete and make two lists. Add more nouns to each list.

art · ball · boyfriend · chaos · education · energy · fashion · flag · friend · history · humour · illness · jeans · liberty · love · machine · meal · moon · peace · picture · pollution · power · school · skates · sport · statue · time

b) Choose at least six abstract nouns from your list and write sentence pairs.
Write one sentence with *the* and one without *the*.

➔ **Workbook** *7 (p. 6)*

7 WORDS Staying in touch

a) In a copy of the table, put the words/phrases from the box under the correct heading. Some may fit more than one heading. Check the meaning of any you don't know.

b) Add other words or phrases you know under the correct headings.

Greetings ...	Opening phrases ...	Communication channels	Communication acts	Goodbyes ...
...	...	...	...	...

blog • chat • +contact • dear • follow sb on … • +goodnight • +hi • introduce sb/sth to sb • like • phone sb • +share sth • text sb • +unsubscribe • block • +email • +how's things? • social media post • catch you later • +messenger service • friend • letter • +tweet • +feed • hey • post sth • what's up? • consult with sb • +follower • +trend on • +message • how are you? • later • call • send a text/email/… • good morning/… • +app • +subscribe • check out sth • hello

8 How do you stay in touch?

a) Think about the most common ways people communicate with each other, for example:
- with parents
- with brothers/sisters
- other family members
- with friends
- with teachers
- other adults
- …

b) Make appointments for three times with three other students. Go to your appointments and exchange your information. Discuss what the advantages and disadvantages of the communication channels for the different people are.

c) In class, share what most surprised you from your discussions.

➜ **Workbook** *8 (p. 6)*

9 EXTRA Panel discussion

a) Have a panel discussion on the topic: **A week of digital detox would be good for us.**

b) Choose three panellists and one moderator for your discussion. Everyone else will be the audience. Then prepare for your discussion:
- Panellists: make notes on your ideas about a week with no digital communication.
- Moderator: think of questions to ask the panellists.
- Audience: note down your own ideas.

c) Have your panel discussion.
- Moderator: make sure all the panellists can say what they think. Ask for questions at the end.
- Panellists: tell each other your ideas and react to the other panellists' ideas.
- Audience: note down questions or comments/ideas you have for the end of the discussion.

➜ **Workbook** *9 (p. 7) • Wordbank 1 (p. 100)*

10 Royals and politics (Subject-verb agreement)

Alyssa's dad is telling her about some of the sights in London. Complete the sentences with the correct form of the verbs. In some sentences there are two possible answers.

Buckingham Palace is where the royal family [1]… (live). The crowd outside the gates [2]… (wait) to see the changing of the guard. Here at the Houses of Parliament, British politics [3]… (get) very noisy – there's always a lot of shouting. Many people don't realize that the government [4]… (work) separately from the parliament. The news from Westminster [5]… (be) not always positive, but most Members of Parliament work hard. I've heard the palace has a fitness centre where aerobics [6]… (be) a favourite activity for a lot of MPs. Oh dear, look – the police [7]… (close) the Parliament entrance to visitors.

Language help

- **Group nouns** like *the government / the family / a band* can be followed by a singular or plural verb depending on whether we are thinking of one unit *(the government **has** been successful …)* or a group of individuals *(the government **are** arguing about …).*
  There is an important exception: the word *police* is always plural: *The police **are** looking for …*
- **Singular nouns** ending in *-s: politics / economics / the news / aerobics* take singular verbs: *Maths **is** an interesting subject.*

→ GF 12: Subject-verb agreement (p. 207)

→ **Workbook** 10 (p. 7)

11 Sounds different (Pronunciation and intonation)

a) Alyssa and her parents are at a tourist information office. Read the phrases and practise saying them aloud to each other.

1. A good view of life in the city.
2. But my advice to you would be …
3. Have you been on a London bus yet?
4. Shall I show you?
5. Show your ticket.
6. Some of the fun of London …

b) Look at the underlined words in the phrases. Listen to how these words are pronounced.
Compare that with how you pronounce them. What do you notice?

c) Listen and practise the phrases aloud again. Try to imitate what you hear as well as you can.

12 At the tourist office

a) Alyssa and her parents are still at a tourist information office. Think of questions they might ask there.

b) Look at the phrases below. Five of them are in the conversation Alyssa and her parents have at the tourist office.
Consider your ideas for a) and say which phrases you think they are. Explain why.

1. Could you help us with …?
2. Excuse me, please.
3. How can I help you?
4. How can we get to …?
5. I have this brochure here.
6. On the Tube.
7. Tower of London.
8. We'd like some information on …
9. You'll love it!

c) Listen and find out whether your ideas in a) and b) were correct. Write down the phrases that are in the conversation.

d) Complete the sentences.

1. Anyway, we … … … … … … … city … school … .
2. Who … … tour …, Dad, … … Mom, … …?

e) Listen again. Take notes on:

1. what the woman in the information office finds out about Alyssa.
2. what Alyssa wants to see/do.
3. what most of the conversation is about at the end. What details do you remember?

→ **Workbook** 11 (p. 8)

13 STUDY SKILLS Making a slide for a presentation

On this page you will make a slide with important information and effectively integrate an image.

a) Select the important information.
Read the text about some of the Harry Potter film locations in London.

These steps can help you take useful notes:

- On a copy of the text, underline or highlight key facts.
- Cover the text.
- Write down each key fact as a short note. Use your own words!

> **Piccadilly Circus:**
> - Deathly Hollows: H+H+R land there
> - one of busiest places in city
> - walk down Shaftesbury Ave
> - cafe near Tottenham Court Road tube: Death Eaters attack
>
> **Millennium Bridge:**
> - ...

A guided tour to Harry Potter places in London

Piccadilly Circus and beyond

In Harry Potter and the Deathly Hallows, when Harry, Hermione and Ron have to escape from the Death Eaters that are attacking Bill and Fleur's wedding, they land at Piccadilly Circus, one of the busiest and most crowded places in London. From Piccadilly Circus the trio walk down Shaftesbury Avenue before turning into an alley. The cafe where they are attacked later by Death Eaters is near Tottenham Court Road tube station.

Millennium Bridge

In the opening scenes of Harry Potter and the Half-Blood Prince you can see the Death Eaters flying around London. They do a lot of damage and one of the places they destroy is this bridge. The Millennium Bridge is a good place to cross the Thames when you find yourself walking along the river: on the south side of the river you see the Tate Modern museum with its lovely view over the city skyline from the top. On the north side of the river is the world-famous St. Paul's Cathedral – another Harry Potter film location.

b) Make notes for the Millennium Bridge. Compare your notes with a partner.

c) Review your notes, choose a key fact and write a one-line text for your slide.
Example:
Piccadilly Circus: Harry and his friends land here

d) Using your key fact from c), make a slide about the Millennium Bridge.

e) Choose an image for your slide or find one on the internet. It should give visual information for the text on your slide or other important facts.
Remember: Write down the source of your information and the copyright of your images.

Early finisher Follow steps c) and e) and make two or more slides about other Harry Potter places in London.

➜ *SF 27: Internet research (p. 177)*
➜ *SF 23: Making slides for a presentation (p. 173)*

➜ **Workbook** *12 (p. 9)*

1 Bike and animal

a) Look at the three film stills above. Imagine what the film might be about.

Compare your ideas with a partner.

Share your ideas with another pair.

b) Now watch the first part of the film. Describe what happens:
- Where does the action take place?
- Who are the boys?
- What are they talking about?
- Why?
- What stops their conversation?

c) Say what you think will happen next. Collect ideas in class.

d) Watch the rest of the film. How close were your ideas from c) to what actually happens? Explain why the boy no longer wants the bike. How does the boy with the bike react?

e) Choose three adjectives from the box below (or other adjectives you know) that you think describe the film well. Explain your decision.

absurd⁺ · boring · cool · excellent · funny · humorous⁺ · incredible · mad · magical · realistic⁺ · short · silly · slow · unusual · weird

f) Watch the whole film again. Take notes on the features of the bike and the animal that their owners describe.

Bike	Animal
titanium frame	can fire rainbows from its horn
...	...

g) In your group, talk about one of these aspects of the film and consider what it tells you about London as a diverse city:
1. Describe the three boys (what they look like, what they want, feelings and reactions, ...).
2. Consider the unicorn. What powers does it have? What do they stand for?
3. Think about the last scene (between the credits). What could its meaning be?

Present your ideas to the class. Why do you think the film-maker made the film?

h) The three boys have London accents and use slang words and phrases. Listen for these and say what you notice:

you can't even get 'em 'ere · Niiiice! · What you got there? · Just a unicorn, init? · on the hill it is well fast · fank you · All right · Safe

2 Making the film: Long shots and close-ups

a) The film uses **long shots** and **close-ups**. Look at the three film stills again and say what they are, long shots or close-ups. Which show the setting of the film? Which show the feelings and reactions of the characters?

b) Watch the film again and choose a long shot and a close-up. Describe them to your partner and explain what they tell you.

➔ *SF 15: Viewing (p. 167)*

EXTRA Read a short story about another 'mythical beast'. Explain how it is similar and different to the film.

1 Alyssa's photos

a) Look at the six photos below. Choose the one that interests you most.

b) Find a partner who has chosen a different photo.
Describe your pictures to each other. Talk about what the photos tell you about Alyssa, Brixton, etc.
Then tell the class.

➜ SF 25: Describing and interpreting images (p. 175)

Quelle: Imago Stock & People GmbH/ZUMA Press

Check out my photos of our trip to Brixton.

1 *This photo was taken at the outdoor market.*

2 *The snacks at this trendy cafe in the indoor market are made fresh every day. Delish!*

3 *At the Black Cultural Archives we saw an exhibition about black music in Britain with GREAT SOUNDS!*

4 *This David Bowie mural is opposite the Tube station. Bowie was born and grew up in Brixton. Every year on the anniversary of his death (10 Jan), lots of flowers are laid on the ground here by his fans. The mural is protected by a cover because too many visitors write messages on it.*

5 *This is the Ritzy. It's one of the oldest cinemas in England! What a nice building! It has 750 seats. Mom liked it a lot.*

6 *Dad is a windmill freak. He told us, "There are only 9 windmills left in London. This one was built in 1816. Wheat is still ground blah blah …" (on and on for 10 minutes!). But it was kind of cool.*

c) Read what Alyssa has written about her photos. Then find out more online about your favourite picture. Prepare and give a one-minute talk about it.

➜ SF 27: Internet research (p. 177) ➜ SF 1: Skimming and scanning (p. 156)

EXTRA Take a picture of a place from a walk around your own area.
Write a post about your photo (about 150 words).

2 Opinion piece

a) Read the text.

We have always come from everywhere

by Laurence Harger, 12 September

An exhibition at the *Black Cultural Archives* recently took me back to my childhood in Brixton. As I wandered the colourful South London streets where I grew up, my senses were treated to the sounds of many different languages and dialects, the aromas of food from all over the world. I realized how much the place had changed but also how much was still the same.

Always multicultural

When I was a child, Brixton already had an Afro-Caribbean vibe. Those white English nationalists who claim that multiculturalism has been a failure are clearly not Londoners like me. My London has always been multicultural. In fact, the city's inhabitants have always come from everywhere.

2000 years of immigrants

London – or Londinium as they called it – was founded in 43 CE by 'immigrants', the Romans who invaded Britain and made it a province of their empire. Other immigrants have been coming to the city ever since.

For centuries, foreigners have arrived here through the Port of London. Some came from not so far away: Irish, Welsh, Scots. At the time of the Great Fire in 1666 a majority of Londoners had been born abroad, like Protestant Huguenots. They were driven here by persecution in Catholic France. There were Jews who had fled pogroms in Spain or Eastern Europe. By 1800, the East End already had a Chinatown. The more the British Empire grew over the centuries, the more the Empire's peoples were attracted to its centre, London.

After the Second World War, Commonwealth people from places like India and the Caribbean islands were invited to help rebuild Britain. Many settled in London, in places like Brixton.

The free-movement policy of the European Union brought hundreds of thousands more immigrants.

Mixture makes London unique

This mixture, this diversity of peoples, religions, cultures and habits is nothing new. Those who would like a return to a mythical, nostalgic one-culture Britain of old, want something that has never existed. What makes London so wonderful is its tolerance of people from all over the world and the way it learns from their traditions and cultures and transforms them into its own, unique London brand.

b) Look at the article and find the following features:
- a byline
- a headline
- illustrations
- sub-headings

c) Then label the features on a copy of the drawing on the right.

d) Skim the article and decide which parts are the introduction, the body, the conclusion.

3 Facts and opinions

a) Read the article carefully. Take notes on the author's main points under the headings:
- facts about the writer
- facts about immigration and London
- opinions on London
- opinions on people who are against immigration

Check and agree on your results.

b) Exchange what you have found out in class.

4 Have a go

The windmill in Brixton was built in 1816. Find out and say when other buildings were built: your house/flat, your school, other buildings in your area, famous buildings in Germany or other countries.

Our flat was built in 1982. There's a sign on the front.

St Paul's Cathedral was built from 1675 to 1710.

→ **Workbook** *13–14 (pp. 10–11)*

1 REVISION The West End (Simple present and simple past)

Complete Alyssa's email to friends back in Canada about her day with her host family in the West End of London.
Use the verbs from the box and decide which tense to use: simple present or simple past.

arrive • be (x7) • buy • go • have • know • look • not have to • sit • start • take • walk • watch

Hey guys!
What's up back in Ottawa? Yesterday it ...[1] my busiest day in London so far. My host family ...[2] me to the West End. That ...[3] the fun area of the city with all the night life and it ...[4] lots of the most famous sights, like Buckingham Palace and Trafalgar Square. Trafalgar Square ...[5] just like the photos you all ...[6]. The weather ...[7] nice so we ...[8] by the big lions. We ...[9] into the National Gallery, which ...[10] also at Trafalgar Square. It ...[11] full of old paintings. A tour ...[12] just as we ...[13] so at least we ...[14] walk around on our own to find any interesting paintings. After the gallery, we ...[15] up to Leicester Square (London ...[16] full of squares!) and my host dad ...[17] cheap tickets for a musical (Les Mis), which we ...[18] in the evening. That ...[19] really cool!

➜ *GF 1.2/1.3: Talking about the present / past (pp. 181–182)*

2 REVISION Mural and windmill (Passive: simple present)

Complete the sentences about the places in Brixton with a verb in the passive.

1 Sometimes messages ... on the Bowie mural and pictures ... even on it. (write • paint)
2 Flowers ... often ... on the ground in front of the mural. (lay)
3 The Brixton Windmill ... black. (paint)
4 It ... every winter and ... again for tours at Easter. (close • open)
5 Regular events ... in the Windmill Gardens. (hold)
6 Places on the tours ... very quickly because only three or four people can go together. (fill)
7 Walks with a guide ... also ... on Brixton Hill on Sundays when the mill is open. (offer)
8 Workshops on how the windmill works ... for school groups. (give)
9 Wheat ... in the Windmill Gardens and it ... still ... in the mill today. (grow • grind)

➜ *GF 3: The passive (pp. 188–189)*

3 REVISION It wasn't founded by Britons (Passive: simple present and simple past)

Correct the wrong information about London in each sentence.
You can check the facts on pp. 18/19.

1 London was founded by Britons.
   – No, it wasn't founded by Britons. It was founded by ...
2 The city was first named London. – No, it ...
3 The food in the Brixton café is cooked the night before. – No, it ...
4 The Huguenots were driven to London from Spain.
5 London was burned by a Great Fire in 1665.
6 After World War II, Europeans were brought to London. to help rebuild the country.

More help ➜ *(p. 146)*

Early finisher Look at exercise 2 again. Make three wrong sentences about the mural and/or the windmill. Find a partner to correct your sentences.

➜ **Workbook** *15–16 (p. 12)*

4 REVISION Which is the oldest? (Passive: simple past)

a) Look at the pictures of sights in London and Berlin and read the dialogue.

A: Which one was built first?
B: I think the Chinatown Gate was built first.
A: Sorry, that's wrong. The Chinatown Gate was built in 2016. The Brandenburg Gate was built in the 18th century. OK, it's your turn.

Brandenburg Gate Berlin
Chinatown Gate London

b) Partner A: Continue on p. 154. • Partner B: Continue on p. 340.

5 REVISION *Romeo and Juliet* was written by Shakespeare (Passive with *by*)

Complete the text about Shakespeare's Globe Theatre using the passive form of the verbs in the box and *by*.

Shakespeare's Globe: England's most famous plays [1]... (William Shakespeare). Many of his plays [2]... (the actors of the Globe Theatre) in London. The Globe [3]... (a group of actors called *The Lord Chamberlain's Men*) in 1599. All actors were men in those days. Women's roles [4]... (boys). The Globe [5]... (a fire) in 1613 but was rebuilt. In the year 1642 all theatres [6]... (the British government), which was very strict at that time. The theatre was built again in the late 20th Century and [7]... (the Queen in 1997). This event [8]... (Shakespeare fans everywhere).

build • celebrate • close • destroy • open • perform • play • write

TIP With the passive, we use *by* ... if we want to say who did something.

→ **Workbook** *17 (p. 13)*

6 London Quiz

London Buildings
- The White Tower is the most famous part of the Tower of London. It was built by William I in 1078. The Crown Jewels are kept in the Tower.
- 20 Fenchurch Street is called the Walkie-Talkie. It is 160m tall and was designed by Rafael Viñoly.

London Culture
- Most of London's most famous museums are free.
- Many famous Turner paintings are kept at the National Gallery in Room 34.
- At the British Museum, special events like sleepovers are often held for families to enjoy.

London History
- The city was founded by the Romans who invaded Britain in 43 CE.
- Londinium was burned by Boudicca, queen of the Iceni, when she attacked the Roman city in 60 CE.
- In 120 CE the city was destroyed by fire again.

London Film Stars
- Some famous "American" film stars are actually Londoners.
- Rosamund Pike was born in London and became famous as a Bond girl.
- Idris Elba, aka Heimdall in the Marvel films, speaks with a strong East London accent.
- Emily Blunt: the new Mary Poppins was played by this South London girl.

a) Work in groups of four. Each student reads <u>one</u> fact box about London and makes questions.
• When was ... built/... ? • Where is/was ... ? • What/Who is/was ... in ... ?

b) Read the other three fact boxes.

c) Ask your questions to the group.

→ **Workbook** *18 (p. 13)*

7 STUDY SKILLS Reading for detail

This page will show you how to find detail information in a text.

a) Say what you remember about scanning a text.
Then compare your ideas with the points in the tip box.

b) Look at the text below.
Before you read, discuss these questions.
1 What kind of text do you think it is?
2 Will the style be formal or informal?
3 How will the structure of the text help you find information?

c) Kiran is an English boy with an Indian background.
Scan his blog post to find the answers to these questions.
1 Where did Kiran spend one month this summer?
2 What kind of Asian statue can you see in Chinatown?
3 Why is one area sometimes called 'Banglatown'?
4 What kind of barbecue is very popular in New Malden?
5 Where does Kiran say you can find the best curries in London?
6 What carnival did Kiran enjoy very recently?

TIP
When you scan a text to find information:
- think of keywords which will help you find the information you want.
- if you have to answer questions, underline keywords in the questions.
- look through the text very quickly and try to find your keywords.
- read the parts of the text around the keywords to find the information you need.

WELCOME TO MY BLOG | **MY SUMMER TRAVELLING AROUND THE WORLD – IN LONDON** | GALLERY | CONTACT ME

31 AUGUST

Hi all. I hope you've had a fabulous summer. I certainly have. I travelled around the world … without leaving London! London? Yes. My cousins Manish and Ana live there and I spent a whole month with them. I saw the famous sites, but you can read about them anywhere, so I'm going to tell you about some discoveries I made: London's most exciting multicultural districts. Read on to find out about the whole world in one city!

OLD FAVOURITES

Chinatown *OK, maybe Chinatown is one of London's most touristy places but it's still very, very cool. It really makes you feel like you are in China, with its beautiful gates and lion statues, and all the Chinese restaurants, shops and bakeries. Yum!*

Brick Lane *The street signs are in English and Bengali because so many people here come from Bangladesh. Brick Lane is also known a 'Banglatown' and it's a really fun place to visit. There are markets and street art and loads of bakeries and restaurants. There is food from all over South Asia but I've got an even better tip for you if you want a great curry – keep reading!*

NEW FAVOURITES

Barbecue in 'Little Korea'
I bet you've never heard of a neighbourhood called New Malden, right? Around 20,000 Koreans live in and around this district so if you like Korean food, it's the place to go. I love a Korean barbecue. It's a great way to eat together with friends (or cousins) so we visited often.

Indian … and everything else too
I love Tooting! It's a super-multicultural neighbourhood in South London, with the very best Indian curries outside of India! The area is lively but not touristy and you can walk around for hours discovering little shops, bakeries and restaurants from all over the world.

NOT JUST FOOD

In case you think I'm only interested in food, let me tell you about my absolute favourite London event: the Notting Hill Carnival. It brings together music, dance, costumes, theatre, art and (yes!) food from everywhere, but especially from Africa and the Caribbean. I was there just two days ago and I can't stop thinking about how much I love London, and the cultures of the world!

➜ **Workbook** 19 (p. 14)

➜ *SF 1: Skimming and scanning (p. 156)*

8 A formal email

a) Finn Lorenz from Munich is doing a project on famous people from Brixton. He wants to write an email to the *Black Cultural Archives* to ask for information that might help him. Look at the email layout (1–9) and choose the best answers for each point.

Email layout:

1 **To:** email address of the organization/ person you're writing to
2 **Cc:** anyone else you want to send your email to
3 **Subject:** what your email is about
4 **From:** your name and email address
5 **Start:** *Dear …*
Main body of email:
6 **Paragraph 1:**
6.1 Say why you are writing.
6.2 **Paragraph 2:** Explain the details of what you want.
7 **Conclusion**
8 **Finish**
9 Your contact details

Options:

1
a info@bcaheritage.org.uk
b volunteers@bcaheritage.org.uk

2
c sandra.lorenz16@gmx.de
d ——

3
e Famous people
f Help with my school project

4
g Finn Lorenz – finnlor@…
h fl5000@cool.…

5
i *Dear Sir or Madam*
j *Hi Info,*
k *Dear Archives workers*

6.2
l *I'm really glad I found your website on the internet, cos I think you can help me with my project.*
m *I am doing a project in my English class at school about famous people from Brixton. I hope you will be able to help me.*
n *I've got this project at school about Brixton so you can help me with it, right?*

6.2
o *There must be some really interesting black people I can put in my project. I mean famous people from Brixton.*
p *What I'm really looking for is someone who comes from Brixton and is a celebrity now so that I can make my project interesting.*
q *I know that Brixton is a multicultural area so I hope you can suggest someone with an Afro-Caribbean background, so that I can do some research on their life for my project.*

7
r *I would be very grateful if you could help me. Thank you in advance and I look forward to hearing from you soon.*
s *Send me some information as soon as you can. Thanks.*
t *Please let me know if you can help. Thank you very much.*

8
u *Yours sincerely,*
Finn Lorenz
v *All the best,*
Finn
w *Yours,*
Finn Lorenz

9
x T: 01622081430
y facebook: finnlorenz
twitter: @finnloM
instagram: picturefinnlo
z Kärntner Strasse 57
80686 München
Germany
T: +49 0162 208 1430

b) Compare and explain your answers in a group. Use a placemat to make a list of tips for writing a formal email.

c) Imagine you want to do a presentation on black music in Britain. Write an email to the Black Cultural Archives or *BritishBlackMusic.com* asking for help.

→ *SF 6: Writing a formal letter or email (p. 160)*
→ **Workbook** 20 (p. 15)

1 At the top of the Monument

Alyssa counted the steps under her breath: "278, 279, … How many steps did the guide say? Three hundred?"
She was walking up a spiral stone staircase that seemed to go on forever.

She looked up at her parents in front of her. "How did they get so fit?" she wondered, a frown on her face. When they had suggested this London walking tour to her the evening before, she had quickly agreed. Now, she was regretting it.
She emerged into the daylight at the top of the stairs. The tour guide smiled. "That wasn't too bad, was it? Come on. I'll show you the view and tell you some great stories. Then you'll see it was worth it."
Alyssa looked round for somewhere to sit as the guide went on talking to the group. They were shown the view. They were given all the facts and figures about this Monument to the Great Fire of London in 1666. Alyssa's mother was all ears.
"She loves this history stuff," Alyssa thought, while she herself was only half listening.

a) Look at the photos, read the text and explain:
- what the pictures show
- who the people are
- where they are and what they're doing
- why they are there.

b) Look at the last sentence of the text. Explain what Alyssa thinks and how she feels.

c) Take notes on all the facts you find out about the Monument. Check with a partner.

2 Phoenix from the ashes

a) Before you listen, consider what you have learned about the Monument and say what you think 'phoenix from the ashes' could mean?

b) Now listen to the audio. Describe the situation and say whose voices you hear.

c) Read the questions and look at the unfinished sentences. Listen again and take notes so that you can answer the questions/complete the sentences. Check the answers in your group.

1 How many steps are there to the top of the Monument?
2 The Monument commemorates …
3 Why is it exactly 202 feet high?
4 The Great Fire of London started in …
5 It lasted …
6 Why was the fire so bad?
7 What is the 'phoenix from the ashes'?
8 After the fire, new buildings and streets were made of …
9 The most famous new building was …

d) Try to remember some of Alyssa's reactions to what the tour guide says and describe them to a partner.

www Can you remember the nicknames of the three London skyscrapers in the photo above? Follow the link and find out more fun facts about them.

➜ Workbook 21 (p. 15)

You're a German exchange student in London. You read about 20 Fenchurch Street in your London guidebook and decide to go there at the weekend. Your host parents and their children have never been there but they might be interested in a visit and ask you about it.

1 What your host parents want to know

1 Is 20 Fenchurch Street worth a visit?
2 If so, what can you do there?
3 What else should you know before visiting?

2 Scan for answers.
Scan the extract and find the information you need to answer their questions.

3 Take notes
Take notes in English or German on the information that answers their questions. Make sure your notes are only on the information you need.

Sa./So. 11-21 Uhr

Compare your notes with a partner.

4 Say it in English
Discuss how to pass on the information in your notes. Don't translate from the brochure. Just put your notes into your own words.

Yes, I'll tell you why I think it's worth a visit. …

5 Role-play
Join another pair and act out the conversation. One pair plays the parents, the other the kids.

Mediation skills

This is what you need to do to find and work with the information you need:
- Scan the text for the information you need.
- Take notes.
- Translate key words if you know them in English.
- Paraphrase words that you don't know.

→ *SF 12: Finding key information (p. 165)*
SF 13: Paraphrasing (p. 166)

→ **Workbook** *22 (p. 16)*

20 Fenchurch Street

Das Gebäude

Seit seiner Eröffnung im Jahr 2014 ist dies eins der kontroversesten Gebäude der Stadt. Der 37 Stockwerke umfassende,160 m hohe Wolkenkratzer erinnert an ein altmodisches Handfunkgerät und wird deswegen im Allgemeinen *Walkie-Talkie* genannt. Viele Londoner finden das Bauwerk aufdringlich, weil es die Skyline der Stadt beherrscht.

Der Sky Garden

Der Walkie-Talkie wird aber bei London-Besuchern immer beliebter. Grund dafür ist vor allem der Sky Garden, eine außergewöhnliche Neuheit in den Wolken Londons, nämlich ein dreistöckiger Garten mit Restaurant und Café/Bar an der Spitze des Walkie-Talkie. Ein Fahrstuhl bringt Gäste in Sekundenschnelle nach oben, wo man sich inmitten exotischer Pflanzen entspannen und den 360° Panoramablick auf die Stadt genießen kann. Es sind ausreichend Sitzgelegenheiten vorhanden.

Und das Beste daran? Der Eintritt ist kostenlos. Allerdings muss man seinen Besuch vorher buchen und kann den Sky Garden dann zu dieser Zeit besuchen.

Öffnungszeiten und Anfahrt

Montag – Freitag	Samstag/Sonntag
10:00 – 18:00	11:00 – 21:00

Gut erreichbar mit öffentlichen Verkehrsmitteln
U-Bahn: Monument
Zug: Fenchurch St., Cannon St., London Bridge
Bus: Linie 40

1 REVISION London visitors (Verbs with two objects: active sentences)

Use the information and the verbs to write about Alyssa in London. Be careful with tenses.

1 our host family – me – a great tour of the city yesterday (give)
2 I – my parents – why I love London (explain)
3 I – them – my host family – when they visit me (introduce)
4 I – them – a list of things to bring me (send)
5 First, the guide – us – the view from the Monument (show)
6 Then he – us – the nicknames of the skyscrapers (tell)
7 He also – the city before the Great Fire – the tour group (describe)

➔ *GF 3.1: Active and passive (p. 188)* ➔ **Workbook** *23 (p. 17)*

2 Unhappy in London (Personal passive)

a) Some tourists in London weren't very happy with their holiday in the city. Finish their sentences.

1 We ... (promise) a quiet room.
2 Then we ... (give) a room above the hotel disco.
3 We ... (not tell) that breakfast was not included.
4 We ... (not show) how the shower worked.
5 We ... (offer) a bus tour of the city but ... (not tell) how much it would cost.
6 When we got back home, we ... (send) a bill for a tour we did not take.

Language help

The sentences below begin with *They* ....
Complete the translations. Then say what is different about how the German sentences begin.
They were shown the view.
... wurde die Aussicht gezeigt.
They were given all the facts and figures.
... wurden alle Daten gegeben.

➔ *GF 3.4: The passive of verbs with two objects (p. 189)*

b) Complete the dialogue and act it out. Use ideas from a).
Hotel staff: Oh, I'm sorry. What was the problem?
Guest: ...

➔ **Workbook** *24 (p. 17)*

3 Likes and dislikes (Personal passive)

Some tourists gave feedback on their trip to London.
Complete the feedback with verbs in the passive form.

1 I ... a trip to London by my rich uncle. Best thing I ever did!
2 We ... best holiday of our lives. We love London.
3 At the top of the Monument, we ... a view of all the modern skyscrapers. Ugh!
4 I ... the summers in London are warmer now. I didn't believe it but it's true!
5 We reserved our Sky Garden visit online and ... our ticket in seconds.

offer • promise • send • show • tell

Early finisher Use verbs from the box in the passive to write a comment about a place you have visited.

4 Pronunciation (Connected speech)

a) Some of the tour guide's words are shown in the speech bubbles as they sound in natural spoken English. Listen and repeat them a few times.

b) Write his words in normal spelling.
Listen again and repeat them in spoken English.

c) In these sentences the underlined words are spoken slowly and clearly first, then in natural spoken English. Listen and compare. Then listen to the sentences in natural speech again and repeat them.

1 So London is a brick and stone city today.
2 Lots of wonderful new buildings were built.
3 I am sure many of you have already been to see it.
4 London has been getting larger and growing upwards ever since.
5 See if you can guess which ones I mean.

➜ **Workbook** *25–26 (p. 18)*

5 THINKING ABOUT LANGUAGE Idioms

a) Look at these two sentences from p. 24 and translate them word for word into German. The drawings will help.
- Alyssa counted the steps under her breath.
- Alyssa's mother was all ears.

Now translate the sentences into *good* German. What do you notice?

b) In idioms and other common expressions in English, the *literal* meaning of the words is not the same as the *actual* meaning of the expression.

Here are some idioms that the tour guide at the Monument uses. Match them to the right meaning from the list on the right. Then check with a partner and in class.

1 Give yourselves **a pat on the back**.
2 The baker's shop **caught fire**.
3 I'm not **pulling your leg** here.

a) … began to burn.
b) Mind your backs.
c) I'm not joking.
d) Congratulations!
e) I'm not helping you here.

c) Other languages have idioms too. For example, German. Can you match these German idioms to any of the English idioms you have learned about here?

auf die Schippe nehmen · Feuer fangen · ganz Ohr sein · sich auf die Schulter klopfen

Do you know any idioms in other languages that are similar to the idioms on this page?

d) Think of a German idiom you use yourself. Make notes so that you can explain it in English.

Then explain your idiom in English to a partner. Can they guess the German idiom?

1 Growing up in London

What are some advantages and disadvantages of living where you live? Share your ideas.
Read the article from an online newspaper about what life is like for young people in London.

A city for the young? *by Isaac Patel*

London has always been a story of rich and poor, and of a constantly growing and changing population. This is especially true today for the city's young. London's youth population is bigger and more diverse than ever.

"There's a lot going on here. We can go to the outdoor markets, the West End isn't far away, there's Regent's Park, the local sports centre. It's a good place to be," says Nate. He's 16 and lives in Camden, an inner-London borough where the gap between the rich and the poor is wide.

"Some kids at our school are from poorer neighbourhoods. I don't know how they manage. I get pocket money from my parents, but it doesn't go very far. Often my friends and I just don't go out. It's too expensive. It's so unfair," Nate says.

Social worker Jill Marsden says, "The inequality in London is the worst in the UK. Fifty-seven per cent of London's young people live in low-income homes, and 37 per cent live in poverty. That's shocking. Young people see the rising cost of living and it worries them. They may not be able to live here when they get older."

To the east in the borough of Hackney, Mina, 15, wishes there was more on offer. "I used to go to the youth centre a lot, but it's closed now. They don't have the money to pay the staff," she says. Mina spends more time on social media now, often bored.

Disappearing youth programmes and services are one reason for increased gang activity. "The gang violence here is bad," Mina says. "A friend of mine was beaten for no reason. Now my mum and dad are worried about me. They even want me home before dark!"

Jill Marsden puts it in perspective: "It's worrying that more young people are 'slipping through the net' because the boroughs no longer have the money for certain youth services. There are programmes that we do still offer, but a lot of kids don't seem to know about them."

In some parts of London the situation looks different. "I go to the sports centre a lot with my friends after school," says Jack, 16, who lives in the distant borough of Richmond in south-west London. "Kids feel safe here. There's open, green space. We ride our bikes a lot," he says.

Jack's only complaint is the long Underground ride. "It takes ages to get into the city. That really sucks when you want to go out."

Looking at the big picture, Jill Marsden draws some conclusions: "We're failing a lot of our young people," she says. "They need services and safe places that allow them to learn, play, train, work and live." But Marsden is optimistic. "Our schools have improved a lot, especially the quality of education for young people from poorer families. The capital has so much to offer culturally and economically. It's becoming a hub for new technology, and that means new work opportunities for young people when they leave school."

2 Views of London

a) Scan the article and make notes about three negative aspects and three positive aspects about life for young Londoners.

Compare your answers.

b) What do you think Jill Marsden means when she says "young people are slipping through the net"?

Share your thoughts in class.

3 Expressing yourself

Use words from the box to describe the style of the article. Find examples in the text for your answers.

formal · informal · colloquial · emotional · informational · personal

4 A different London?

Talk about how the information in the article compares with your knowledge or experience of London. Does it change how you see the city? Explain your answer.

➜ **Workbook** *27 (p. 19)*

1 STUDY SKILLS Writing a comment

In a comment you express your opinion about a topic you feel is important.
- Before you write, it is important to collect ideas, form your opinion and organize your content.
- There are many expressions and phrases that can help you to organize and present the ideas.
- You should support your point of view with a clear argument, facts and statistics.

Write a comment on this issue:
Is London a good place to live for young people?

a) Brainstorm ideas to find out how you feel about the issue. Make two lists:

My own experience	Questions
– I've seen in Berlin, Germany how there aren't enough ...	– Why can't the city provide more ...?

b) Do research on the internet.
Has the information you've found changed your opinion? Write down your opinion in one or two sentences.

c) Look at the argumentative text structure and the expressions that start each paragraph.

Introduction	State your topic and opinion clearly. Keep it short.	London's youth population is huge and diverse. While some of them ...
Main body	Give reasons for your point of view.	Differences between rich and poor are worse in London than ...
	Give evidence in the form of statistics or other facts, to back up your main statement. Use one or two paragraphs.	...% of young people are from low-income families, while ...% live in ...
Conclusion	State your opinion again. Suggest a solution.	In my view, ... The city could ...

How else could you start a paragraph? Choose an alternative.

After thinking carefully about the issue, … • Although many people believe …, in reality, … • In my opinion … • It is often said that …, but … • There is really no evidence to support the idea that … • Some people think that … • I'd like to see … change. • It's my hope that in the future … • I think that it would be a good thing if … • I think all schools should …

d) Now write your text. You may need language to:
- *talk about advantages or disadvantages:* — • *A big advantage/disadvantage of … is …* • *Another/The biggest advantage/disadvantage is …*
- *make comparisons:* — • *… is more important than …*
- *give examples:* — • *For example, …* • *This is clear because …*
- *order arguments or examples:* — • *In the first place, …* • *Firstly,/Secondly,/Thirdly, …* • *Finally, …* • *On the one hand, …* • *On the other hand, …*
- *make a conclusion:* — • *I believe that …* • *I think … should / shouldn't …* • *I'd like to see …* • *I hope that in the future …* • *We need to change …*

e) Read your partner's text and give feedback.

➜ *SF 28: Giving feedback (p. 177)* ➜ *SF 7: Writing a comment (p. 161)*

➜ **Workbook** *28 (p. 20)*

Language help

Nominalized adjectives are adjectives that are used as nouns. We can say:
Young people often have fresh ideas or *The young often have fresh ideas.*

The noun 'people' disappears and 'young' becomes a noun.
- We often use the form when talking about groups of people: *the rich / the poor / the healthy / the weak / the strong* …
- We also use it for some nationalities: *the British / the Irish / the French* …
- We put ***the*** before the noun, and although we are talking about a group, we do not use a plural *'s'*.

➜ *GF 11: Adjectives used as nouns (p. 206)*

2 A young London … (Adjectives used as nouns)

a) Rewrite the sentences by using adjectives as nouns.

1 Young people in London are a more diverse population than a generation ago.
2 Old people in London can remember when it was much cheaper to live there.
3 Educated people have a clear advantage in the city's job market.
4 There should be more programmes to help homeless people.
5 With less government support, life is getting harder for poor people.
6 Rising prices make it difficult for disadvantaged people to live in the city.

b) Is it true that some groups of people have an easier life than others?
Complete sentences using nominalized adjectives.

Then write three more sentences like the ones in b) with your own ideas.
Think about *the old / the young / the rich / the educated* etc. and use your own ideas.

1 The … have a more difficult life in some ways.
2 The … should do more to help the … .
3 The … really know how to enjoy life!
4 I want/don't want to be one of the … .

➜ *GF 11: Adjectives used as nouns (p. 206)* ➜ **Workbook** 29 *(p. 21)*

3 WORDS Strong or weak? (Opposites)

a) Find the opposites in the boxes. Make a list.
strong – weak
hungry –

b) Partner A: Cover your list from a).
Partner B: Say a word from the list.
Partner A: Say the opposite.
Swap after eight words.

c) Choose six pairs from a) and write sentences about London or visiting London.
The street food at Camden Market is delicious.

advantage · entrance · above · daylight · nearby · same · curious · strong · delicious · possible · weird · fair · boring · fast · funny · lie down · lively · rude · rich · majority · unique

polite · get up · exciting · unfair · below · minority · normal · bad · serious · exit · far · slow · not interested · weak · darkness · different · impossible · disadvantage · poor · common · quiet

➜ **Workbook** *30 (p. 21)*

You've been to London as an exchange student. Now your host family is planning to come to Germany and they want to visit Munich for three days. Keira, the daughter in the family, writes to you.

a) Read Keira's email and take short notes about her questions.

b) Scan the text from a German website and find the information that you need.
Take notes in German or English.

c) Compare your notes with a partner.
Then practise paraphrasing words you can't translate into English.

- Rabatt: *You pay less for …*
- sie nehmen keine Scheine oder Karten: *they only take coins*

d) Write an email (about 120 words) to Keira in English and answer her questions.

➜ *SF 14: Cultural differences (p. 166)* · *SF 13: Paraphrasing (p. 166)*

➜ **Workbook** *31 (p. 22)*

Hey,

we're all looking forward to Bavaria and especially to the three days in Munich. My parents have some questions about transport in Munich. Here they are:

As real Londoners we're used to public transport. I think the Tube is the best! What kinds of public transport does Munich have?

London tourist buses are really expensive. You can use the number 11 bus instead, which passes a lot of sights. Do any buses in Munich go past famous sights?

To pay on London buses you need a special card because the bus driver doesn't take money. Is it the same in Munich?

How much does a bus journey cost? Are there special tickets for tourists that will help us to save money?

Can you answer our questions? That would be great!

Yours, Keira

Insider-Tipps für München

Wenn man fit ist und Zeit hat, sollte man München möglichst zu Fuß erkunden. Aber die öffentlichen Verkehrsmittel sind eine tolle Möglichkeit, wenn man in kurzer Zeit viele Sehenswürdigkeiten erreichen möchte.

Wie kauft man an einen Fahrschein und was kostet er?

In München gibt es S-Bahn, U-Bahn, Trams und Busse. Fahrkarten kann man online, per App oder am Automaten kaufen. In Bussen und Trams kann man sie auch direkt an Bord kaufen und bar bezahlen. Man sollte aber genügend Münzgeld haben, denn die Fahrer (und manche Automaten) nehmen keine Scheine oder Karten.

Eine Einzelfahrkarte für das Münchner Stadtgebiet (Zone M) kostet 3,30 € für Erwachsene und 1,50 € für Kinder bis 14 Jahre. Es gibt auch Tages- und Mehrtagesfahrkarten sowie Gruppentickets, mit denen man im Vergleich zur Einzelfahrkarte einiges an Geld sparen kann.

Zu Besuch in München?

Für Touristen und unternehmungslustige Münchner gibt es attraktive Angebote. Die **City Tour Card** kann man als Einzel- oder Gruppenticket kaufen. Mit ihr erhält man Rabatte bei über 70 Museen, Theatern, Restaurants und anderen Attraktionen. Sie ist für 24 Stunden oder mehrere Tage erhältlich. Die 24-Stunden-Gruppenkarte für Zone M kostet 22,90 €, für drei Tage kostet sie 37,90 €. Die **München Card** ist ein ähnliches Angebot mit bis zu 70% Rabatt bei über 80 Attraktionen. Das Gruppenticket für drei Tage kostet 42,90 €. Welches Angebot sich lohnt, hängt davon ab, was und wie viel man unternehmen möchte.

Ein Spartipp für Besucher: Mit dem Bus 100 erreicht man die berühmten Museen ohne umzusteigen, zum Beispiel die Pinakotheken, das Nationalmuseum oder die Villa Stuck. Man braucht nur einen gültigen Fahrschein.

Escape from Uncle Jack (abridged[1] from *The Thieves of Pudding Lane* by Jonathan Eyers)

a) These terms are in the story you are going to read: London – 1666 – Pudding Lane.
From what you have already learned in this unit, what do you think the story could be about?

b) Now read the introduction and the story. Only look up words if you really have to.
Remember: you can often guess[2] what a new word means because it looks or sounds like a German word or a French or Latin word you know.
Or you know part of it already, e.g. if it has a prefix[3]/suffix[4] like *un-*, *in-*, *re-*, *-er*, that will help you understand it. Sometimes you can make an intelligent guess and understand a word from the context.

It's the year 1666. The year before, London was struck by the plague[5] and Sam's parents and his brother, Thomas, died.
Sam lives alone on the streets until Uncle Jack, a man with a wooden leg, takes him in. Sam has to work as a thief during the day and bring what he steals back to Uncle Jack. In return he and the other child thieves, like Sam's new best friend Catherine, are given a place to sleep below Uncle Jack's pub in Pudding Lane.
When a great fire starts in Pudding Lane, a fire that will destroy 80% of the city of London, Uncle Jack makes Catherine and Sam steal from the houses that rich people have abandoned. In one of the houses, Sam and Catherine find Gideon, a young boy, who has become separated from his parents. The three of them decide to run away from Uncle Jack to find Gideon's parents. But things don't go quite as they planned …

'Samuel!' […] 'Stop! It's a trap![6]'

Samuel, Gideon and Uncle Jack all froze when they heard the voice. Uncle Jack spun as fast as his leg would let him, searching for Catherine. Samuel spotted her first, clambering[7] over the rooftops above them.

Uncle Jack snapped a look at Samuel, then followed his gaze up to Catherine. […]

Uncle Jack lunged for Gideon, ready to grab him by the neck. But Samuel was too fast for him. He yanked Gideon out of Uncle Jack's reach and stuck out his foot. Uncle Jack lurched[8] forwards, wooden leg first, right into Samuel's foot. The pain of the hard wood striking Samuel's shin felt like a red hot poker[9]. Samuel stumbled backwards, but didn't fall. Uncle Jack, on the other hand, lost his balance completely. He fell hard onto the cobbles[10] with a furious[11] cry. His hat and stick went flying. The lantern smashed on the ground.

'Run!' Samuel shouted to Gideon.

Gideon didn't need telling twice.

'Not that way!' Catherine shouted down.

Samuel grabbed Gideon by the tunic[12] and spun him around. He gave him a push in the other direction, then shot a look at […] Uncle Jack. […] Samuel kicked Uncle Jack's stick further out of reach then he ran too, leaving Uncle Jack to pull himself over the cobbles.

Samuel and Gideon ran parallel to the terrace[13] of houses that Catherine was scrambling across. Samuel glanced[14] at her frequently to make sure she could keep up.

They soon reached the end of the terrace. Catherine had nowhere left to go but down or back the way she had come. Her dark shape appeared against the moonlit cloud as she peered[15] over the eaves[16].

'There's no way down,' she cried.

'Jump!' Samuel called to her.

'I can't! It's too far.'

'We'll catch you,' Gideon shouted, lifting his arms up as if to prove it.

'Yes, we'll catch you!' Samuel echoed, reaching for her too.

Catherine disappeared for a moment, and when she reappeared she came feet first, lowering[17] herself as quickly as she could. Quicker than was safe, thought Samuel.

1 **abridged** [ə'brɪdʒd] gekürzt • 2 **guess** [ges] vermuten • 3 **prefix** ['pri:fɪks] Präfix, Vorsilbe • 4 **suffix** ['sʌfɪks] Suffix, Nachsilbe • 5 **plague** [pleɪg] Pest *(Krankheit)* • 6 **trap** [træp] Falle • 7 **(to) clamber** ['klæmbə] klettern • 8 **(to) lurch** [lɜ:tʃ] schwanken, taumeln • 9 **poker** ['pəʊkə] Schürhaken • 10 **cobble** ['kɒbl] Pflasterstein • 11 **furious** ['fjʊəriəs] wütend • 12 **tunic** ['tju:nɪk] Tunika • 13 **terrace (of houses)** ['terəs] Häuserreihe • 14 **(to) glance (at)** [glɑ:ns] kurz blicken (auf) • 15 **(to) peer** [pɪə] angestrengt schauen • 16 **eaves** *(pl)* [i:vz] Dachgesims, Dachvorsprung • 17 **(to) lower** ['ləʊə] sinken lassen, hinunter lassen

'Get ready! Quick! […] she said. […]

'We're ready!' he told her, stretching out[18] his arms and bending his knees, ready to take the impact.[19] 'Come on!'

Catherine slipped her other leg over the side and then, without its support, […] fell with a sharp cry.

Samuel braced[20] in the fraction of a second it took for Catherine to land on top of[21] them. She knocked[22] Gideon sideways and tumbled[23] Samuel onto his back. All the breath blasted out of him as he hit the cobbles. His vision went momentarily black with the pain. It felt like the cobbles had slammed into him, not the other way around.

When he opened his eyes again Catherine was climbing off him, helped by Gideon. Samuel picked himself up and Catherine threw her arms around him. The pain vanished[24]. He hugged her back.

Not to be left out, Gideon wrapped his arms around both of them. […]

For a moment they just looked at each other.

Then Gideon suddenly drew back. 'Oh no! Look!'

'No!' Samuel said under his breath.

Coming along the street towards them was Uncle Jack, his stick arcing[25] in quick strides[26] ahead of[27] him. His hat was gone, and his lank hair flew in the wind like dancing fire itself.

'Run!' Samuel cried. He clapped a hand on Gideon's back and grabbed Catherine's hand.

They ran around the corner and onto the next street.

'We can't go this way,' Catherine said as they ran.

'We have to,' said Samuel. 'It's the only way.'

'He's herding[28] us towards the fire. We'll be trapped.'

Samuel feared she was right. 'We'll find a way around. We have to.'

They followed the street around a bend[29], and all of them scuffed[30] to a stop. Samuel could feel the heat of the houses burning at the other end of the lane[31] from here. Red-hot embers[32] churned out of the smoke like a blizzard[33] of burning snow.

'We have to go back!' cried Gideon.

They got back to the corner in time to see Uncle Jack come around the last one.

'We're only one street away from the river,' Samuel said quickly. 'It's right on the other side of these warehouses[34]. Can you see that alley[35]?' He pointed towards the other end of the lane, towards the fire. 'That will lead us down to the water's edge. Catherine, am I wrong?'

She shook her head. 'You're not.'

'We've got to cover our heads. Come on.'

'Sam, I'm scared,' said Gideon.

Samuel loosened his tunic and pulled it up over his ears like a hood[36]. He gave the younger boy a smile. 'You do trust me, don't you?'

Gideon began to undo his top buttons.

Uncle Jack was gaining[37] on them. Not even on Pudding Lane had Samuel and Catherine got this close to the flames. The heat seemed to steal the breath from Samuel's lungs. It was so hot he was sure his clothes must actually be on fire. […]

But when they reached the turning into the alley that led down to the riverbank, things got much, much worse.

Gideon started saying 'No. No!' repeatedly.

Even Catherine was looking at Samuel and shaking her head.

Buildings on both side of the alley were on fire. Flames lapped up the walls. Tongues[38] of fire licked at the air between the buildings, flicking in the wind like whips[39] being cracked. The building at the far end had a jettied upper storey[40]. This too was burning.

Their escape route looked like a tunnel of fire.

'I can see the river,' Samuel croaked[41], as smoke churned around them. 'Look! It's only a short run. We can make it.' […]

'Don't do it!' a voice called from behind them.

They turned to see Uncle Jack. He stopped, an arm up to his face. Whether it was the heat keeping him back or he was trying not to scare them by keeping his distance, Samuel wasn't sure. […]

'That way lies only certain death,' Uncle Jack went on, creeping forward ever so slowly.

Gideon didn't back away from Uncle Jack. Now the old crook[42] wasn't the thing that terrified[43] him most. Samuel stepped in front of Gideon protectively.

18 **(to) stretch out (your arm)** [ˌstretʃ 'aʊt] (den Arm) ausstrecken · 19 **impact** ['ɪmpækt] Aufprall, (Zusammen-)Stoß · 20 **(to) brace** [breɪs] (sich) anspannen · 21 **on top of sth.** [ɒn 'tɒp əv] auf etwas (oben) drauf · 22 **(to) knock** [nɒk] stoßen; schlagen · 23 **(to) tumble** ['tʌmbl] stoßen; fallen · 24 **(to) vanish** ['vænɪʃ] verschwinden · 25 **(to) arc** [ɑːk] kurven · 26 **stride** [straɪd] Schritt · 27 **ahead of** [ə'hɛd] vor · 28 **(to) herd** [hɜːd] (sich) drängen, zusammentreiben *(Tiere)* · 29 **bend** [bend] Kurve · 30 **(to) scuff** [skʌf] schlurfen · 31 **lane** [leɪn] Gasse, Sträßchen · 32 **ember** ['embə] glühendes Stück Holz/Kohle; Glut · 33 **blizzard** ['blɪzəd] Schneesturm · 34 **warehouse** ['weəhaʊs] Lager(haus) · 35 **alley** (auch: **alleyway**) ['æli], ['æliweɪ] Gasse · 36 **hood** [hʊd] Kapuze · 37 **(to) gain on sb./sth.** ['geɪn ɒn] jn./etwas einholen · 38 **tongue** [tʌŋ] Zunge · 39 **whip** [wɪp] Peitsche · 40 **jettied storey** [ˌdʒetid 'stɔːri] Stockwerkvorsprung · 41 **(to) croak** [krəʊk] krächzen · 42 **crook** [krʊk] Gauner/in, Kriminelle/r · 43 **(to) terrify sb.** ['terɪfaɪ] jm. schreckliche Angst einjagen

'Come back here,' Uncle Jack implored them, reaching out a hand. 'You'll be safe.'

Even Catherine looked like she was considering it.

'You'll be safe,' Uncle Jack repeated. 'With me.'

And that was when everything changed.

'Samuel, how far is it?' Gideon asked, not taking his eyes off Uncle Jack.

'We can run it in five seconds.'

'Are you both ready to do this?' asked Catherine.

'Yes,' said Gideon.

'Yes,' said Samuel. 'Now!'

Uncle Jack roared. […].

Catherine was already running full pelt[44] into the alley, and Samuel shoved[45] Gideon after her, so hard he almost knocked the boy off his feet.

Samuel ran after them both, almost bent over, not looking where he was going, arms cradled[46] over his head. He heard Uncle Jack behind him. Over the roaring flames, the howling[47] gale[48], the creak and crack of burning timber[49], he could hear Uncle Jack's cries of fury.

Then Samuel entered the tunnel of fire. He batted away bits of burning wood falling from the jettied upper storey. He could see only his clogs kicking through ashes and embers, sending pieces of black, smoking rubble[50] flying. […]

He didn't stop, kept running, but threw his tunic back from his head. Catherine and Gideon had stopped, faces black and streaming with sweat, mouths gasping for air.

Samuel finally looked back, just in time to see Uncle Jack attempt[51] to run through the tunnel of fire. He made it halfway through before there was an almighty[52] crash. Samuel saw the look on his face. He had never seen Uncle Jack look frightened before.

Uncle Jack was still running when the jettied upper storey collapsed.

Samuel staggered[53] back as a billowing[54] cloud of thick smoke swallowed everything, […].

Catherine and Gideon were now standing on a narrow wooden wharf[55] that jutted[56] out into the River Thames. Catherine tried to drag Samuel after them.

'Come on, Sam,' she urged.

As the smoke cleared from the alleyway Samuel saw Uncle Jack writhing[57] on the ground. Daring to get closer, Samuel saw why. Uncle Jack's wooden leg was on fire. First he tried slapping at the flames, crying out as the fire seared[58] his palms[59]. Then he gave up, and tore at his breeches[60] until the stump of his knee was exposed[61]. He grabbed the cushioned[62] top of the false limb[63] and pulled it off. He threw the burning leg out of his way, but he was still surrounded by flaming rubble.

'Come on, Sam,' Catherine urged again. 'The rest of the building will collapse any moment.'

'We can't leave him like that,' said Samuel.

As if to emphasise Catherine's point, the roof of the next building suddenly burst[64] inwards, raining burning debris[65] down onto the next wharf. Some fell into the water with a loud hiss.

'We have to go,' said Gideon.

Samuel ignored them and approached Uncle Jack. He couldn't get close enough to help him. Samuel had to shout to him through the flames: 'Where's your stick?'

Uncle Jack finally stopped flailing about and locked eyes with Samuel. Yellow flames reflected in his black pupils. For a moment they just stared at each other.

'Get out of here, you stupid boy,' Uncle Jack said eventually, his voice gruff[66] and weak.

Samuel spotted Uncle Jack's stick then. It was behind him in the alley, broken in two, both parts burning.

He felt Gideon tug[67] at his arm. 'Come on, Sam. We've got to go now.'

Samuel nodded. But as he hurried after Gideon he saw a length of unburned wood lying by the side of the wharf. He grabbed it and tossed[68] it back towards Uncle Jack. He never saw whether Uncle Jack picked it up and used it as a walking stick, or whether Uncle Jack even noticed it at all.

'I can't swim,' Gideon said as they edged[69] further along the wharf, further away from the flames.

'Neither can I,' said Catherine.

44 **full pelt** ['fʊl pelt] mit Karacho *(so schnell es geht)* · 45 **(to) shove** [ʃʌv] schieben, stoßen; drängeln · 46 **(to) cradle** ['kreɪdl] halten *(schützend)*; wiegen · 47 **howling** ['haʊlɪŋ] tosend · 48 **gale** [geɪl] Sturm · 49 **timber** ['tɪmbə] Holz(balken), Bauholz · 50 **rubble** ['rʌbl] Schutt · 51 **(to) attempt** [ə'tempt] versuchen · 52 **almighty** [ɔːl'maɪti] riesig, allmächtig · 53 **(to) stagger** ['stægə] taumeln, torkeln, schwanken · 54 **(to) billow** ['bɪləʊ] aufsteigen *(z.B. Rauch)* · 55 **wharf** [wɔːf], *pl* **wharfs** *or* **wharves** Kai · 56 **(to) jut (out)** [dʒʌt] ragen · 57 **(to) writhe** [raɪð] sich winden · 58 **(to) sear** [sɪə] verbrennen *(z.B. Haut)* · 59 **palm** [pɑːm] Hand(fläche) · 60 **breeches** *(pl)* ['brɪtʃɪz] Kniehose · 61 **(to) expose** [ɪk'spəʊz] freilegen, entblößen · 62 **(to) cushion** ['kʊʃn] (aus)polstern · 63 **false limb** [lɪm] Prothese *(z.B. Bein)* · 64 **(to) burst** [bɜːst], **burst, burst** brechen, bersten, platzen · 65 **debris** ['debriː] Schutt, Trümmer · 66 **gruff** [grʌf] rau (Stimme) · 67 **(to) tug** [tʌg] ziehen *(z.B. am Ärmel)* · 68 **(to) toss** [tɒs] werfen · 69 **(to) edge** [edʒ] (sich) *(langsam)* schieben ·

'None of us can,' said Samuel. 'I thought there might be a little dinghy[70] we could take.'

'All the boats went hours ago.'

'Then we're trapped!' cried Gideon.

The windswept waters of the river reflected the orange firelight. It looked like the Thames was on fire too.

As he stood watching the water eddy[71] past, Samuel saw a large charred[72] piece of wood float by, just out of reach.

'We're not trapped,' he said.

Catherine must have realised what he was thinking a second later. 'It's the only way.'

'What is?' said Gideon.

Samuel and Catherine ran back along the wharf. Without discussion they both went for the same piece of broken wood, a large unburned beam[73] […].

'Heave!' Samuel shouted.

They both pulled at the same time. It was so heavy it didn't shift at first. Even when it did start to scrape along the deck, Samuel worried it was so heavy it would not float […].

Gideon joined[74] them, grabbing the beam near the middle, but Samuel's back still sang with pain[75] by the time they reached the end of the wharf.

'We need to jump in after it right away, before it floats off without us,' he said.

'How deep is it?' Gideon said.

'One way to find out.'

Samuel pushed the end of the beam over the edge. Its weight pulled the rest of the beam after it. As it plunged[76] into the river it shot an almighty splash into the air. Filthy, stinking water drenched[77] the three of them.

Samuel didn't hesitate. As soon as he saw the beam bob to the surface, as if it was as light as a twig[78], he leapt[79] in. Catherine and Gideon jumped in after him.

After flailing for a moment, each of them hugged their arms around the beam, and then it started carrying them down the river, away from the wharf, away from the fire.

---

70 **dinghy** ['dɪŋi] kleines Boot · 71 **(to) eddy** ['edi] wirbeln, strudeln · 72 **charred** ['tʃɑːd] verkohlt · 73 **beam** [biːm] Balken *(aus Holz)* · 74 **(to) join sb.** sich jm. anschließen · 75 **(to) sing with pain** [sɪŋ] *(jm.)* starke Schmerzen bereiten · 76 **(to) plunge** [plʌndʒ] hineinspringen · 77 **(to) drench** [drentʃ] durchnässen · 78 **twig** [twɪɡ] Zweig · 79 **(to) leap** [liːp], **leapt, leapt** [lept] springen

1 What's it all about?

a) After you have all read the story alone, work in groups of four. Each group member sums up one part of the story:

A: lines 1–67 B: lines 68–135
C: lines 136–223 D: lines 224–311

Read your part again carefully and write a short summary.

→ *SF 9: Writing a summary (p. 163)*

b) Swap what you have written with another member of your group. Read through your partner's work and give them feedback. Make corrections or changes to your own work.

EXTRA Join your work together and display it in class. Read some of the other groups' work.

2 The characters

a) Work in your group of four again. Each choose one of the four characters in the story: Sam, Catherine, Gideon, Uncle Jack. Make notes on your character so that you can:

- describe them (what they look like, how they feel, what kind of person they are, how old, …)
- say what their relationship to the other characters is.

Choose one or two short quotes from the story that support your ideas about them. Write down the lines of your quotes.

b) Use your notes to tell the others in your group about your character.

3 Before and after

You choose a) or b). Write about 160 words.

a) Write what you think happened in the story before Catherine shouted "It's a trap!" (l. 20)

b) Write what you think will happen next in the story as they float down the River Thames.

→ **Workbook** *32 (p. 23)*

Workbook Checkpoint 1 (pp. 24–27)

Planning a class trip to London

Work in a team to plan and put together a programme for a five-day class trip to London.

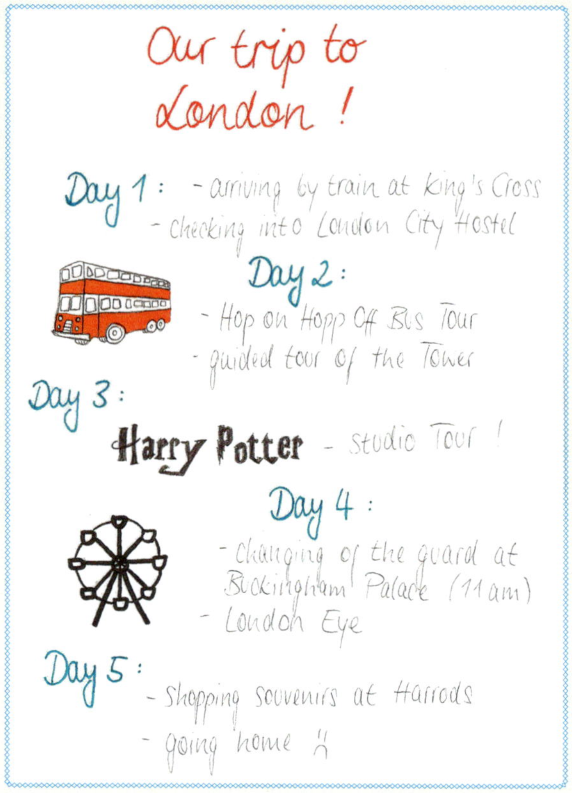

STEP 1

Discuss and agree on what needs to go into your programme. Here are some ideas:

- travel (how to get to and from London, how to travel around London, …)
- where to stay in London (where, what type, …)
- itinerary (where to go, what to see and do – mornings, afternoons, evenings)
- educational activities, entertainment
- …

STEP 2

Decide what format your programme will take:

- poster
- digital presentation
- brochure
- …

STEP 3

Agree on who is doing what (your roles) and set a realistic timetable before you begin.

- research
- graphics/layout
- …
- language
- coordinator

➜ *SF 21: Teamwork (p. 172)*

Thursday, 11am

Watching the changing of the guard at Buckingham Palace

STEP 4

Do some research and find all the information will need to put your programme together.

➜ *SF 27: Internet research (p. 177)*

STEP 5

Organize all your information and ideas and put together your programme.

➜ *SF 22: Putting a page together (p. 172)*
➜ *SF 23: Making slides for a presentation (p. 173)*
➜ *SF 24: Giving a good presentation (p. 174)*

STEP 6

Display or present your programme to your class.

STEP 7

Go to pp. 343-344 and look at some tips on how to do better. Give feedback:

a) in your group about how your teamwork went.
b) to other groups about their programmes.

➜ *SF 28: Giving feedback (p. 177)*

A

1 London quiz

Do the London quiz and see how well you know this great city.

a) Complete the missing information.

1 Do you have a T-shirt ... isn't too expensive?
2 London's tallest building is called ...
3 London was destroyed by a Great Fire in ...
4 The fire started in a street called ...
5 In Victorian London the sun was often hidden by ...
6 The financial centre of London is known as ...
7 The bridge over the Thames that opens for ships is ...
8 The church you visit to whisper to your friends is called ...

b) Name the places in pictures A–D.

c) Answer the questions.

1 Where should you sit on a London bus for the best view of the city?
2 What's the address of the Walkie-Talkie building?
3 Name a famous singer who grew up in Brixton.
4 What was built in Brixton in 1816?
5 When did lots of people from the Caribbean start coming to London?

2 Paraphrases

a) Sometimes you have to describe words: match the right words to these paraphrases and write them down.

1 It's the place where laws are made.
2 Someone who considers their country the best and better than all others.
3 A country that is owned and ruled by another country.
4 The idea that people from different cultures can live happily together.
5 A person who has come from somewhere else to live in a country.

b) Write English paraphrases for these words.

1 religion 2 foreigner 3 diversity 4 dialect 5 inhabitant 6 population

c) Use six words from a) and b) and write about your own town/area.

3 The Proms (Subject-verb agreement)

One of London's big cultural events is the season of concerts and events called the Proms. Complete these facts about the Proms with the correct form of the verbs. Some sentences have two possible answers.

The name comes from the original outdoor 'promenade concerts' of the 1800s, where the audience ...[1] (be) allowed to walk around and dance to the music. Over the years, every major international orchestra ...[2] (perform) at the Proms. The programme is mixed, so one night maybe a jazz band ...[3] (play) and the next night a choir ...[4] (perform). The different kinds of music mean that the crowd ...[5] (be) also very mixed. The BBC ...[6] (organize) and ...[7] (broadcast) the events every year. A big part is the tradition of 'promming', where people ...[8] (pay) a small price to stand and enjoy the events. During the performances the public ...[9] (be) allowed to eat and drink as well. The Proms ...[10] (be) once described as 'the world's largest and most democratic musical festival'.

4 Heathrow Airport (The definite article)

Complete the statements by a worker at London Heathrow, one of the world's busiest airports, by adding *the* where needed.

At Heathrow Airport you meet ...[1] people from all over the world, and I've met many in ...[2] time that I've worked there. The scene inside Heathrow is a bit like ...[3] time itself – it never stops. ...[4] history of Heathrow goes way back to the early 1900s. The airport today offers lots of services, for example you can go to ...[5] church. In case you're wondering, ...[6] church at Heathrow welcomes everyone. Every morning lots of passengers have ...[7] breakfast in the airport. I've eaten there and ...[8] breakfast that I had was very good. So much happens at Heathrow. I've seen ...[9] teenagers run through the airport because they were late for ...[10] school. A woman missed her boarding call because she was wearing ...[11] headphones. Believe me, ...[12] life of a Heathrow worker is not always easy. But ...[13] people I work with have a good sense of humour!

5 London culture (Personal passive)

In an online chat, Alyssa is telling her friend Lauren about another day in London with her parents. Complete her sentences.

We were on the South Bank and my mom ...[1] (hand) a rose by a street artist. He started dancing with her and it was very funny. When he finished, he ...[2] (give) a lot of money by the crowd. Later we walked over Westminster Bridge. A bike taxi came by and we ...[3] (offer) a ride, so we took it. The rider said he ...[4] (always, ask) questions about his 'real' job. He was actually a musician. He ...[5] (teach) the violin by his mother from a young age. I saw his violin case and asked him to play, but he seemed shy. He gave us an awesome tour. We ...[6] (show) sights that aren't on the tourist maps. When we finished, he said normally he ...[7] (pay) five pounds for a ride. My dad gave him ten pounds. Then we ...[8] (give) a beautiful little concert!

6 MIXED BAG Fire, fire!

Complete the text about an important event in London with the right words or phrases.

London ...[1] always been cool. After it ... ...[2] by the Romans and a bridge ... ...[3] across the Thames, it ...[4] a hub for people ...[5] all over Britannia and ...[6] bigger and ...[7]. Change was usually quite ...[8] but sometimes it came ...[9] London ... ...[10] several times ...[11] great fires. Everyone has heard of the ... ...[12] London of 1666 but ...[13] parts of the city ... ...[14] by fire much ...[15]. In 60 CE the Roman city ...[16] b...[17] to the ground ...[18] the Iceni, a tribe ... ...[19] by Queen Boudicca. Roman Londinium b...[20] again in 122 CE. ...[21] 675 the cathedral ... ...[22] by fire and f...[23] d...[24] large parts of London again in 1087, 1185 and 1212.
London ...[25] to grow steadily ...[26] all this time. After every fire, the city ... ...[27] r...[28] again, until a small Roman fort that w...[29] b...[30] on the mud next to a r...[31] r...[32] became one of the l...[33] and ... ...[34] cities ...[35] earth.

B

7 Then and now

I walk down the London streets where I grew up and wonder, "Where have the children gone?" Of course, there are not so many children now and there are none out on these streets where our lives took place.

The whole area was somewhere to play for us. We played football in winter right across the street, with the gate to our back garden as one goal and the neighbours' wall opposite the other. Summer was time for cricket and we painted a wicket on the wall and played with a tennis ball. A hide-and-seek game called *Rescue* with lots of shouting was another favourite for our gang. Our games were only seldom interrupted by a car moving slowly down the street, with just single cars parked here and there.

Today, long lines of cars are parked along both sides. No chance to play football or cricket here. On my walk up and down on a warm, sunny day, I do not meet a single kid or hear a child's voice. The only sounds are the birds in the trees and the cars that pass by every twenty seconds or so.

It isn't a school day, so where are they all? In the parks? Hanging out in the high street up the road? Or are they all at home, and if so, why?

a) Read the text and choose the right answers.

1 The writer is **a)** a child. **b)** an older person. **c)** answer not in text.

2 The streets the writer describes are now **a)** full of children. **b)** full of cars. **c)** somewhere to play.

3 The writer mostly played in the **a)** back garden. **b)** streets. **c)** summer.

4 In the streets today, the writer hears **a)** a child's voice. **b)** birds and cars. **c)** shouts.

5 It is hard to play sports in these streets now because of
a) the birds. **b)** the neighbours. **c)** the parked cars.

b) In the text, find three or four reasons why the writer thinks there are no children on the streets.

c) Complete the sentences with the correct information: **1** We played ... **2** *Rescue* ... **3** The games ...

d) Think of a good title for the text. Also think of two sub-headings for the text and write where they should go (before paragraph number ..., etc.)

C 8 Famous diaries

Du bist ein/e Austauschschüler/in in London. Deine Klasse fängt gerade mit einem Projekt an: *Famous diaries*. Ihr werdet einige historisch wichtige Tagebücher recherchieren und vorstellen.
Zuerst hat jede/r die Aufgabe, ein spannendes Tagebuch zu finden und kurz der Klasse vorzustellen.

Die Lehrerin hat folgende Anweisungen gegeben:

- Say who wrote the diary and when.
- Tell us what interesting things happened at that time in history.
- Explain why the writer himself/herself was interesting.

Du hast diesen Text in einem Reiseführer gesehen und findest ihn spannend.
Mache dir Notizen und schreibe dann einen kurzen Text auf Englisch, den du der Klasse präsentieren kannst. Dein Ziel ist es, dass das Tagebuch von Samuel Pepys Teil des Klassenprojektes wird.

Seething Lane

Diese enge Gasse kann man übersehen und sehr schön ist sie nicht, doch der Mann, der da 1666 nachts von seinem Dienstmädchen geweckt wurde, hinterließ uns eins der wichtigsten Zeitdokumente der britischen Geschichte. Das Dienstmädchen weckte ihn, um ihm zu sagen, dass ein riesiges Feuer in der Nähe brannte. Der Mann war Samuel Pepys, der das vielleicht berühmteste Tagebuch in der englischen Sprache geschrieben hat.

Samuel Pepys wurde am 23. Februar 1633 geboren. Er wurde Zeuge der Großen Pest von London im Jahr 1665 sowie des großen Brandes im darauffolgenden Jahr. Seine Aufzeichnungen sind eine unersetzliche Quelle für die Zeitgeschichte sowie für das Alltagsleben in London. Das Tagebuch führte er von 1660 bis 1669. Eine Berühmtheit oder ein großer Machthaber war er nicht, hatte aber als Staatsekretär im Marineamt und als Abgeordneter des englischen Unterhauses einen Einblick in die politischen Entwicklungen seiner Zeit. In den Tagebüchern ging es ihm vor allem um seine persönliche Geschichte. Deswegen schildert er nicht nur z.B. große politische Ereignisse, sondern auch ehrlich und unverfälscht seine Liebschaften und die Streitereien mit seiner Ehefrau Elizabeth.

Pepys Haus existiert nicht mehr, aber an der Ecke Seething Lane und Pepys Street steht seine Hauskirche Saint Olave, eines der wenigen noch stehenden mittelalterlichen Gebäude Londons. Dort ist er begraben. Ein anderer literarischer Riese, Charles Dickens, nannte die Kirche Saint Ghastly Grim (etwa „Sankt Grausig Grimmig") wegen der Totenköpfe und Knochen am Tor zum Kirchhof, die heute noch gut erhalten sind. Einige Schritte südlich der Kirche in Seething Lane Garden steht ein Denkmal für Samuel Pepys.

Guy Fawkes: Man and mask

Jigsaw

a) Work in groups of four. The parts of this text (A–D) are not in the right order.
Each student reads one part (A–D) of the text and takes notes on the important information.

b) Together find the links between the texts and decide on the best order for them.

c) Write a text (about 180 words) in English and explain how the image of someone who planned to blow up Parliament has become a symbol of resistance around the world.

A Guy Fawkes Night

Guy Fawkes wasn't the leader of the Gunpowder Plot, but he was its most famous conspirator. After all, he was caught under the Houses of Parliament with the gunpowder. That is why the November 5th tradition is named after him, although it has other names too: *Bonfire Night* or *Fireworks Night*.
The tradition started with a 1606 law. Ever since, on Guy Fawkes Night, people have commemorated the discovery of the Catholic plot. Fireworks are let off and "guys" are burned on bonfires.
In the weeks before November 5th children make these guys from newspaper, old clothes and a mask. They sit on the streets with their guy and ask for money to buy fireworks. "Penny for the guy" or "Please to remember/ The fifth of November" are the magic words which make people part with their money.
The idea is that when people burn the guy on the bonfire, they are celebrating the fact that the Gunpowder Plot was stopped. If that is true, then why has Guy Fawkes become such a popular figure of protest today?

A 'guy' waiting on a bonfire

B V for Vendetta

You've probably seen this mask before. It's like the Guy Fawkes mask that first appeared in a graphic novel called *V for Vendetta*. The story goes like this: after a nuclear war, the UK has become a fascist state under the government of Adam Susan. V, a rebel in a Guy Fawkes mask, and a young woman, Evey, use computer hacking and explosives in a plot to destroy the government. Like Guy Fawkes, V plots against the government, but it is clearly a terrible government that he wants to destroy.
The graphic novel was a great success and it became even more famous when a film of it, with Hugo Weaving and Natalie Portman as V and Evey, was made in 2005.

C Protest!

Now the V for Vendetta Guy Fawkes mask has become the symbol of protesters all over the world. The trend was started by *Anonymous,* the hacktivist (if you admire them) or hacker group (if you don't). When they first came out into the real world to protest, they needed something that would protect their identities. They chose the V for Vendetta Guy Fawkes mask.

Since then, the mask has become a symbol of resistance all over the world and is worn by people in protest movements like Occupy, Wikileaks or the Arab Spring.

Alan Moore, the author of V for Vendetta, told the Guardian newspaper that he finds it very strange that his character V has somehow escaped from his book and entered the real world.

Million Mask March, London 2015

D The Gunpowder Plot

On the night of November 4 to November 5, 1605, Guy Fawkes was discovered in a cellar under the Houses of Parliament. He gave his name as John Johnson.

Why would he do that? Well, he wasn't alone in the cellar. Below piles of wood, 36 barrels of gunpowder were hidden, enough to completely destroy the Houses of Parliament.

The attack was planned for the State Opening of Parliament on November 5. If Fawkes could blow up Parliament, he could kill King James I and many of the most important and powerful people in the country.

But – why would he do that? Well, religion was very important in Europe at that time. Protestants and Catholics had been fighting wars ever since protestants left the Catholic church during the Reformation in the 16th Century. Under King James, Great Britain was a protestant country, but Guy Fawkes was a Catholic.

Fawkes hadn't planned this alone. After he was arrested, he was taken to the Tower of London and tortured till he gave the names of the other conspirators.

Their plan was: kill the King and all the important protestants, start a rebellion and make the King's 9-year-old daughter Queen of a new Catholic Britain.

Of course, their plan did not work and things ended badly for the plotters. Some were killed when they were being arrested. The others, like Guy Fawkes, were dragged through the streets and executed. Then their heads were put on pikes for all to see.

The Gunpowder plot conspirators

➜ **Workbook** *1–4 (pp. 84–85)*

Elections in the US and the UK

1 Read about the electoral system in the USA and note down important information about the political system. Then talk about it.
Give three important facts about the system.

The electoral system in the USA uses the 'first-past-the-post' system[1]*. This means that voters must choose one candidate, and the candidate who receives more votes than any other candidate wins.*

The two houses

The US Congress consists of the House of Representatives and the Senate.
Members of the House of Representatives are elected every two years. Each state is divided into districts and each district votes for one representative. The number of districts depends on a state's population, so the most highly populated state, California, has the biggest number of representatives (53) but the huge state of Alaska, which has a small population, has only one district and therefore only one representative in the House.
Members of the Senate are also elected by the public. Each state has two senators, no matter how big or small the state is. As with the House of Representatives, the first-past-the-post system is used, so the candidates with the most votes win.

Presidential elections

Presidential elections take place every four years, and each President is limited to two terms of office[2], a total of eight years. The President usually represents one of the two main parties in the US: the Democrats or the Republicans. Each party chooses its candidate in a first round of voting[3], known as primaries[4]. The two winners of the primaries – one for the Democrats, one for the Republicans – then begin massive election campaigns, travelling across the country for months before the election is finally held in November.

The electoral college[5]

In the presidential election the people's votes are counted at state level, not at national level. Each of the 50 states has an electoral college with the same number of votes as its total number of senators and representatives. For example, California has 2 + 53 = 55 electoral college votes; Alaska has 2 + 1 = 3 electoral college votes. The candidate who gets the highest number of votes in a state gets all of that state's electoral votes. A total of 270 electoral votes is needed to win. It sometimes happens that the candidate wins 270 electoral votes, even though the other candidate received a higher total of votes nationally. This was the case in 2000 and 2016.

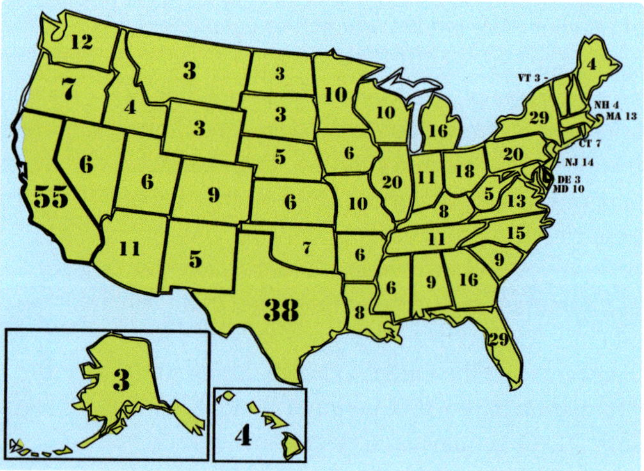

Electoral map of the USA indicating the number of electoral college votes for each of the 50 US states

2 Now read about elections in the UK and take notes about the important information. Then compare the US and UK systems. Discuss what is different and what is similar.

EXTRA Write a text (about 180 words) about the election systems in the US and the UK.

A constitutional monarchy

The UK is a constitutional monarchy (with the monarch as head of state) and a parliamentary democracy. Parliament has two houses, the House of Lords and the House of Commons (with 600-650 elected members, each representing a constituency). The Prime Minister and cabinet lead the executive. Parliamentary elections are held at least every five years but only the House of Commons is elected.

Elections

At election time, several candidates stand for election[6] in each constituency. They include members of the three main political parties, Labour, Conservative and Liberal Democrats. Other candidates represent[7] smaller or regional parties, or are independent. At the beginning of the election campaign, all parties publish statements about the policies they want to follow, and the candidates try to win public support for their party's ideas.

Election Day

On election day, the votes are counted separately in each constituency and the candidate with the most votes there wins the election (first-past-the-post system). The winner does not need to have a majority of the votes, just a higher number than any other candidate. When the counting is finished, all the candidates of a constituency[8] stand on a stage, and an official reads out the number of votes received by each candidate. He or she then declares[9] the winner. After the votes have been counted, the party with the most MPs (Members of Parliament) forms the government, and their leader becomes the Prime Minister. If there is no clear winner, a coalition government can be formed, although this has not happened very often in the UK.

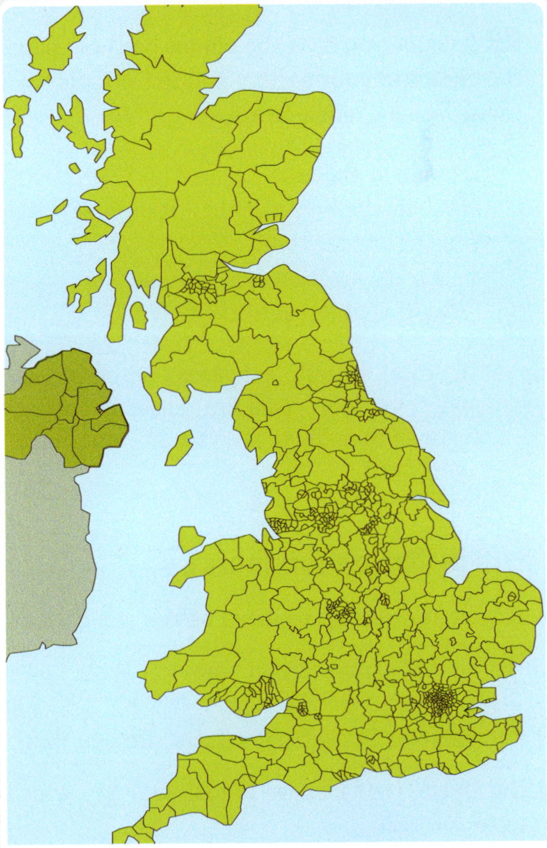

Map showing the electoral areas, so-called constituencies, in the United Kingdom

→ **Workbook** 5 (pp. 86-87)

1 **the first-past-the-post system** *wahlkreisbasiertes Wahlverfahren, bei dem der/die Kandidat/in die Wahl gewinnt, welche(r) die meisten Stimmen erhalten hat (eine absolute Mehrheit ist nicht erforderlich)* • 2 **term of office** *Amtsperiode* • 3 **round of voting** *Wahlgang* • 4 **primaries** *(pl)* ['praɪməriz] *Vorwahl(en)* • 5 **electoral college** [ɪlektərəl kɒlɪdʒ] *Wahlmänner(gremium)/Wahlfrauen(gremium)* • 6 **stand for election** *zur Wahl stehen; sich zur Wahl stellen* • 7 **represent** *repräsentieren* • 8 **constituency** *Wahlkreis* • 9 **declare** [dɪ'kleə] *bekannt geben, verkünden*

Australia, country and continent

1 Australia and me

a) Write a list of ten words you think of in connection with Australia.

b) In a double circle, use your list to tell your partners your ideas.

c) Imagine you took the photos on these pages. Describe two of the photos to your partner and the situation when you took them (noise, smells, temperature, etc).

- This photo shows …
- I took it when we were in / travelling through / …
- You can see …
- It's a tropical/coastal/… region.
- I took this photo because …

bush · coral · desert · kangaroo · outback · palm tree · rainforest · spider · wildlife · bush fire · coastal · exotic · humid · lonely · marine · remote · rocky · sandy · stunning · tropical · urban

2 Uncle Ozzie's fun facts

a) Say what these words mean before you listen.

Aboriginal · camel · convict · koala · poisonous snake

b) Comment on Uncle Ozzie's 'facts'. Do you think they are true?

c) Did Uncle Ozzie manage to fool you? Say which fact you found most surprising.

3 EXTRA A road trip

Watch the film. Which landscape/scene made the biggest impression on you?

Describe it to your partner and explain why. Name the feelings/ emotions the film triggered in you. Give reasons.

More help → p. 146

A

Western Australia

B

Northern Territory

E

Tasmania

D Queensland

C Australian Capital Territory

F New South Wales

G Victoria

Your task **EXTRA**

At the end of this unit: You will find good reasons for a six-month exchange visit to Far North Queensland.

1 On the way to Sydney

Skim the text. Say what kind of information it gives, who it is written for, and where you might find it.

A ferry at Circular Quay

Stay in **The Rocks**, the lively historical quarter where the first convicts settled in the 1790s. Or in the trendy suburb of **Woolloomooloo** with its beautiful wharf. From there it's a short walk through the **Royal Botanic Garden** into the city, to the crowds and skyscrapers of the Central Business District (CBD). On the way, you'll see the flying foxes hanging from the trees and, of course, the world-famous **Sydney Opera House**.

The best way to see Sydney's **stunning harbour** is to head for **Circular Quay** and jump on one of the ferries going to **Manly**. At the end of the half-hour ride, a five-minute walk through Manly takes you to its beautiful ocean beach.

After an ice cream in one of the cafés at Circular Quay, wander round the waterfront and enjoy all the street performers, like the great **Aboriginal didgeridoo players**. Or head for the **Museum of Contemporary Art** and go on a teen-guided tour to get a young person's fresh and honest take on the museum's works.

If you've still got some energy, don't catch the ferry back – walk the **Manly Scenic Walkway** along the water, across the northern harbour beaches and through **Sydney Harbour National Park**. Watch the sailing boats, wind and kitesurfers along the route and then catch a bus back to the city from **Spit Bridge**.

If it's night and winter and the **Vivid Sydney** festival is on, look out across the water from the museum and watch the light show transforming the Opera House and other Sydney landmarks into magical, colourful works of art changing from minute to minute.

DID YOU KNOW?

Sydney has more than 100 beautiful sandy beaches along its harbour and waterfront. So, anyone looking for the perfect wave to surf or a kitesurfing paradise, calm water for a relaxing swim, a quiet corner to read a book or a busier place to watch the people, you will find the right spot in Sydney.

Kitesurfers at Botany Bay

2 What Sydney has to offer

a) Assign each of the places mentioned in this article to one of the categories:
Natural landscapes, Cultural sites and events, Urban locations.

b) Say what you can do and see there.

3 Discovering Sydney

a) Compare and contrast Sydney to other cities you've visited or to your hometown.

b) Say which of the tips you would most like to follow. Give reasons.

➜ **Workbook** *2 (p. 28)*

4 Leon's testimonials

HOME | ABOUT US | PROGRAMMES | DESTINATIONS | TESTIMONIALS | GALLERY | HOW DO I APPLY | BLOG | CONTACT US

Leon, 16, Germany

Nearly six months ago I was on the plane flying to Sydney. I was going to spend half a year at an Australian high school and live with a family I didn't know, 16,000 km from home. From morning till night I would have to speak English. Back then I was nervous. But now I know there was nothing to worry about.

There was just one problem at first. Before I heard Australians talking, I thought I understood English. But Aussies use words I had never learned and their accent was strange, so in the first few weeks my favourite phrase was 'Sorry, can you say that again, please? Slowly.' They did – and it helped. Now I sound like an Aussie myself.

My host family are great and they immediately made me feel at home. My host dad, Brian, tells a lot of jokes, though it was hard to get some of them at first. He cooks a lot, especially on the barbie. I love the way families here eat outside together in hot weather, and I have to say Brian makes absolutely ripper snags (Aussie for "great sausages").

My host mum, Elvira, and host brother, Nick, taught me how to surf at Manly Beach, which is five minutes from their house. I fell off the board a lot at first and swallowed tons of salt water. But I'm better now ... and I love it.

At school I felt a bit lonely in the beginning. It's a private school – boys only – and sport is so important. Playing rugby is the easiest way to get accepted into a group, but it isn't my game. But Australian kids are talkative and friendly and I soon made some great friends.

At school I've been able to do subjects we don't have in Germany, like photography and drama. Now I even like the uniform – when everyone wears the same, you don't have to think about what to wear every morning.

I only got homesick once, at Christmas. It was fun to celebrate it in summer but I really missed my family and the presents on Christmas Eve.

This has been the best six months of my life and I can't believe it's almost over. I'm much more self-confident now and have learned how to do everything on my own. Sydney is fantastic and I love the easy-going Aussie way of life.

Me and a mob of kangaroos hang out near the beach.

5 Six months in Sydney

a) Make notes on:
- what Leon enjoys about his stay in Sydney
- what he finds challenging or difficult.

b) Write down questions you would ask Leon.
- Leon, when did you first see ... ?
- How often did you ... ?
- ...

c) Partner A: Ask your questions from b).
Partner B: You're Leon. Answer A's questions expanding on details from the text.
Swap roles.
- Actually, I saw a ... on my very first day.
- Usually we went ... every afternoon ...
- ...

1 Australian English (Australian English)

Like American English, Australian English is different in some ways from British English. But *no worries, mate*. Here's some help with Aussie words and Aussie pronunciation.

a) Look at these Australian words and phrases. Say what you think some of them might mean.

b) Listen to someone explaining Australian English. Note down words and phrases you hear and what they mean. Compare your results.

2 Australian sounds (Pronunciation of Australian English)

a) Australian English isn't just about words: it's also about sounds. Read TIP 1, then listen to the same eight sentences spoken by British and Australian speakers. Say what sounds different in AusE.

b) Listen to five short dialogues. Decide if the people are British or Australian. (Be careful: in two dialogues only AusE is spoken.) After each dialogue, say which sounds helped you to recognize AusE.

c) Read TIP 2. Listen to the words. Say which speaker is Australian.

d) **EXTRA** Practise saying these words with an Aussie accent: *koala, popular, prisoner, teacher, mirror, sculpture* and *humour.*

LISTENING TIP 1
Some consonants, e.g. [l] and [t], sound different in Australian English.
These BE vowel sounds are also different in AusE:

[aɪ] tried · [eə] hair · [ɪ] village · [e] text · [ɑː] car · [iː] tea

LISTENING TIP 2
Words that end with *-a, -er, -or, -ar, -our* are pronounced in Australian English with a short /a/. Make this sound by lowering your jaw and saying a quick *ah.*

3 THINKING ABOUT LANGUAGE Intonation

a) Read the text in the box below. Then listen to the dialogues in 2b) again. Using your own words, write down a definition of rising intonation.

b) Exchange definitions with a partner and compare.

AUSTRALIAN QUESTION INTONATION
In spoken AE, BE and AusE, a rise in pitch at the end of a sentence often signals a question. Australian English speakers tend to use a rise in pitch for both questions and statements.
This rising intonation – or AQI, Australian Question Intonation – has also become popular in the US and Britain, especially among young people. Some people think that AQI, or 'uptalk' as it is sometimes called, is not a positive change in spoken English since it can sound as if the person is unsure or lacks confidence. Others say that uptalk is a way of being polite or of making sure the listener is paying attention, especially since our mobile phones often distract us. What do you think?

→ **Workbook** *3 (p. 29)*

4 REVISION A first visit to Sydney (Relative clauses and contact clauses)

a) Complete the relative clauses in these sentences about Sydney with *who* or *that/which*.

1 People who are visiting Sydney for the first time want to see the most famous sights.
2 The Sydney activity ... I enjoyed the most was a ferry trip across Sydney Harbour.
3 I took a trip on a ferry ... left from Sydney Quay in the evening.
4 From the water I saw amazing buildings ... were shining in the evening sun.
5 The most famous building ... we passed was the Sydney Opera House.
6 I saw some people ... were having a barbecue on the beach. What a great lifestyle!

TIP **Relative clauses** give more information about a person or thing:
Jump on one of the ferries that goes to Manly.
You can substitute the relative pronoun and following verb with a **participle clause**.
Jump on one of the ferries ~~that goes~~ going to Manly.
You can substitute the relative pronoun and following verb with a **contact clause**.
This is the ferry (~~that~~) I take to Manly.
Contact clauses cannot be replaced by participle clauses like the one above.

b) Now make the sentences shorter using a participle clause instead of a relative clause, if you can. This does not work for every sentence.

1 People who are visiting Sydney for the first time want to see the most famous sights.
People visiting Sydney for the first time ...

➜ GF 9: Relative clauses (pp. 201–202)
➜ GF 10.2: Participle clauses instead of relative clauses (p. 203)

5 I heard the wind blowing (Participle clauses after verbs of perception)

You can also use participle clauses after verbs of perception like *see, notice*, ... ➜ GF 10.2: Participle clauses (p. 204)

a) Use the verbs to make sentences about Sydney or people living there. Use the pictures.

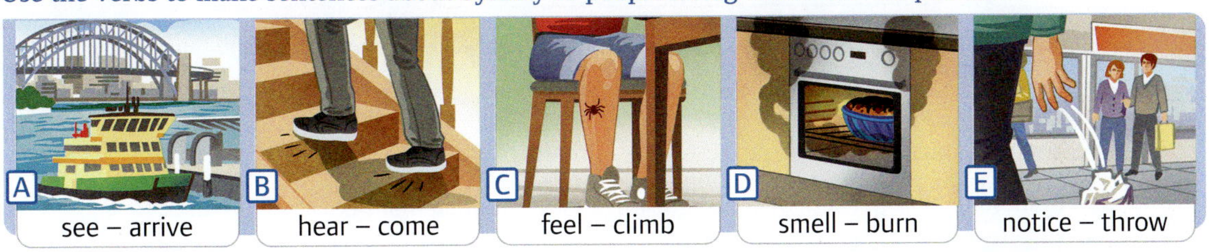

b) Imagine you are in Sydney. Describe what you see, hear, smell and feel. More help ➜ p. 146

6 The Sydney Harbour Bridge

Complete the text with the correct forms or clauses, or leave a gap if it is possible. You can use the verbs in the box if you want.

design • have • lead • look • reach • relax • see • smile (2x) • walk • wonder

My little sister Cathy and I decided to climb a bridge [1]... we had seen many times in photos and films: the Sydney Harbour Bridge. Dr JJC Bradfield, [2]... the bridge, based it on the Hell Gate Bridge in New York City, our hometown! [3]... on the catwalk [4]... to the lower arch, I noticed Cathy [5]... scared. Luckily, our guide, [6]... Cathy hesitating, whispered something in her ear. Within seconds, I saw her [7].... Together we climbed to the top of the upper arch, [8]... a staircase to the summit. Later, she told me the guide had helped her overcome the worst fear [9]... she had ever felt. [10]... what he had whispered in Cathy's ear, I asked her to tell me. [11]..., she said "Everyone [12]... the summit is a hero!"

More help ➜ p. 146

➜ Workbook 4–6 (pp. 29–30)

7 STUDY SKILLS Argumentative writing

In an argumentative text, you present arguments for and against a topic in a written form. Before you write, it is important to collect ideas, form your opinion and structure your content. There are special expressions and phrases that can help you to structure and present your arguments.

Your topic is: *An exchange year in Australia is a good idea.* Now work through the following steps.

STEP 1

Brainstorm ideas and put them in a table.

For	Against
- students can learn about Australian culture - ...	- it costs a lot of money - ...

STEP 2

Think about:

- any examples to support your arguments, e.g. A year in Australia would cost about ... euros.
- which arguments are stronger,
- whether to support or oppose the topic.

Then write down your opinion in one or two sentences.

STEP 3

Look at the argumentative text structure <u>and</u> the expressions that start each paragraph.

i Introduction 1 paragraph	You introduce the topic without giving your opinion. Use one paragraph.	Students often ask whether they should spend ...
ii Main body 1 paragraph	a) You present the arguments you oppose. Use one paragraph.	One of the main reasons why people think a year abroad ...
1 or 2 paragraphs	b) You present the arguments you agree with. Support your arguments with examples. Use one or two paragraphs. Begin each paragraph with a topic sentence.	There is, however, another way of looking at the question. In addition, people argue ...
iii Conclusion 1 paragraph	You state and explain your opinion briefly. Use one paragraph.	Personally, I believe that ...

How else could you start each paragraph? Choose an alternative.

After looking at both sides of the argument, ... · A question that people often discuss is ... · Furthermore, you could argue that ... · In my opinion/view, ... · It is often said that ... · I would first like to look at the reasons why ... · On the one hand, some people think that ... · On the other hand, people say that ... · Some people take a different view. · Some people think ...

STEP 4

Now write your text. You may need language to

- talk about advantages or disadvantages: · A big advantage/disadvantage of ... is ... · Another/The biggest advantage/disadvantage is ...
- make comparisons: · ... is much more important than ... · ... isn't quite as important as ...
- give examples: · For example, ... · This is clear because ...
- order arguments and examples: · In the first place, ... · Firstly,/Secondly,/Thirdly, ... · Finally, ...
- explain your conclusion: · Although I understand the other side of the argument, I still think ...

STEP 5

Read your partner's text and give feedback.

→ *SF 8: Argumentative writing (p. 162) • SF 28: Giving feedback (p. 177)*

 → **Workbook** 7 *(p. 30)*

8 Waltzing Matilda

a) Du arbeitest zusammen mit Kate, eurer australischen Austauschschülerin, an einem Projekt über Australien. Als du recherchierst, findest du den Blog-Eintrag über das australische Lied *„Waltzing Matilda“.*

Schreibe Kate eine E-Mail (ca. 250 Wörter), in der du auf die folgenden Punkte eingehst, um euer Projekt voranzutreiben: warum Menschen glauben, dass „Waltzing Matilda“ die australische Nationalhymne ist, die Inspiration für das Lied, den deutschen Bezug, wie das Lied zu großer Bekanntheit kam.

Leonie down under

Hi Leute! Ich bin Leonie aus Augsburg. Ich dachte, ich wüsste total viel über Australiens Kultur, weil ich sechs Jahre lang dort gelebt habe. Aber ich hatte keine Ahnung von dem Bezug zu Deutschland in dem Lied „Waltzing Matilda“.

Ich dachte immer, „Waltzing Matilda“ wäre die australische Nationalhymne. Eigentlich ist das aber „Advance Australia Fair“. Den Fehler machen aber viele, weil „Waltzing Matilda“ oft bei Sportveranstaltungen gesungen wird, und es das am häufigsten aufgenommene Lied aller Zeiten in Australien ist. Für diese Popularität gibt es viele Gründe: Es hat eine eingängige Melodie, und der Text hat viele typisch australische Wörter, wie z.B. „jolly swagman“, „coolibah tree“, „jumbuck“ und „billabong“. Falls ihr euch fragt: ein „swagman“ ist ein Wanderarbeiter, der von Farm zu Farm im Busch wanderte, um Arbeit zu finden.

Billabong: a waterhole

jumbuck: sheep

a coolibah tree

Wie ist der Text entstanden?

Banjo Paterson, ein Journalist und Anwalt, schrieb den Text zu einer Melodie von Christina McPherson, Tochter eines der größten Landbesitzers in Winton, Australien. Zuvor hatte er die Geschichte eines Streiks gehört, den unzufriedene Farmer vor einigen Jahren, 1894, in dieser Gegend begonnen hatten. Während des Streiks wurde einer der größten Schafställe von Christinas Familie niedergebrannt. Die Polizei machte einen Wanderarbeiter dafür verantwortlich, den alle Frenchy nannten. Aber Frenchy kam nicht aus Frankreich. Sein Name war Samuel Hoffmeister, und er war ein Immigrant aus Deutschland. Das war nicht ungewöhnlich, da die meisten Einwanderer im 19. Jahrhundert nach England und Irland aus Deutschland kamen.

Vor diesem Hintergrund beschreibt Paterson in dem Lied die Geschichte des Wanderarbeiters, der ein Schaf stiehlt und sich dann ertränkt, um nicht geschnappt zu werden. In Wirklichkeit wurde Hoffmeister in der Nähe eines Wasserlochs tot aufgefunden.

Aber was bedeutet eigentlich "Waltzing Matilda"? Hier ist noch eine deutsche Verbindung: „Waltzing“ geht auf den deutschen Ausdruck „auf der Waltz sein“ zurück. Und „Matilda“, ein deutscher Name, war auch die Bezeichnung für die ausgerollten Decken, die Wanderarbeiter auf ihrem Rucksack trugen. „Waltzing Matilda“ bedeutete „auf der Straße reisen“.

Man könnte denken, dass Banjo Paterson mit seinem berühmten Lied viel Geld verdient hat. Aber tatsächlich hat er es für nur fünf australische Pfund verkauft. Erst als ein Teeunternehmen das Lied für ihre Werbung nutzte, wurde es berühmt. Warum Tee? – In dem Lied wartet der fröhliche Wanderarbeiter darauf, dass sein Wasser kocht, damit er sich eine Tasse Tee machen kann.

b) **EXTRA** Höre dir das Lied an. Wie hat dir der Blog-Eintrag geholfen, die Geschichte im Lied zu verstehen?

➔ *SF 11: Mediating written or spoken information (p. 165)*

➔ **Workbook** 8 *(p. 31)*

1 Far North Queensland (FNQ)

Say what impressions Emily's pictures give you of FNQ.

CAPE TRIB KID
Hi, I'm Emily. I'm 15 and I live in Cape Tribulation – Cape Trib as we call it in FNQ. This is a great place for the outdoor life with the world's oldest rainforest (the Daintree) and biggest coral reef (the Great Barrier Reef) at our front door. I'm posting some stuff you only know about if you live up here.

Two school kids … out in the wet.

Folk at home … in the wet.

Being tropical, FNQ is always very warm and has two seasons – the "dry" and the "wet". In the wet, it rains a lot, sometimes flooding the roads. While these guys were determined to get to school, most of us (like me) were in bed, listening to the radio. But it doesn't always help to stay inside. You can also get wet while hanging out at home if an FNQ cyclone has torn your roof off.

The ants escape the water …

… and a frog comes to visit.

Insects aren't keen on wet weather either. While waiting for the flood waters to go down, the ants headed for this big stone. But green tree frogs love wet weather. So why was this guy here, sitting on the living room floor, when he could have been out enjoying the rain?

A visitor in the backyard …

… and another cool visitor.

So maybe that frog wanted to hide from the python our neighbours found in the garden. Amethyst pythons are the biggest Australian snakes and one of the longest in the world, growing to over five metres long. Luckily, they prefer frogs, possums, birds and small kangaroos to a snack of humans.
The beach is a great place for unexpected visitors too. Cassowaries are another of our exotic animals. They are the third tallest and second heaviest birds in the world. They live in FNQ's rainforest, feeding mainly on fruit. But don't provoke them – they can injure or even kill dogs or humans.

Some of our animals just look scary …

… some of them really are.

FNQ's (and Australia's) largest moth, the Hercules, might make you nervous when flying round your bedroom lamp, but don't worry – it hasn't got a mouth so it can't bite you.
Crocodiles live in rivers, right? Yes, but the monster crocs in FNQ are known as 'salties' because they don't mind salt water. They often swim out of rivers into the sea. So watch out at the beach. You don't want to bump into a six-metre-long, one-tonne saltie while enjoying FNQ's warm, tropical waters.

341 comments

2 Tropical life

a) Read the texts. Take notes about the climate, wildlife, and dangers. Say what surprised you most about FNQ.

b) My Book Write a comment to post on Emily's site. In your post, identify unique features of the environment you live in.

More help → p. 147

www Find out more about life in FNQ.

3 Have a go

a) Make sentences about what Emily was doing at the beach. Use these ideas.

look out for salties · snorkel with a friend · build a sandcastle · play frisbee · lie in the sun · watch the waves

1 Emily was at the beach, looking out for salties.
2 Emily was at the beach, …

b) Make sentences about yourself.

1 I'm at school, thinking about the weekend.
2 I'm in my English lesson, …

→ Workbook 9 (p. 32)

Looking at language

a) Find sentences on pp. 52–53 with the same meaning as these. Write them down.
   1 There is heavy rainfall, which sometimes floods the roads.
   2 So why was this guy here and why was he sitting on the living room floor?
   3 Amethyst pythons are one of the longest snakes in the world and grow to over 5 metres long.
   4 Cassowaries live in FNQ's rainforest and feed mainly on fruit.

b) Now say this sentence another way:
   We scanned the text <u>and looked for</u> participle clauses.

c) Look at your sentences. Name the form of the verb used there instead of *'and … '*.
   Explain the different functions of the present participle clauses in these sentences.

➔ *GF 10: Participles (pp. 203–206)*

1 Everyone was outside, … (Participle clauses)

Have a look at the people and animals. Match the sentence beginnings to the pictures.
Then finish each sentence with a participle clause.

1 Everyone was outside, …
2 Fluff is walking along the piano, …
3 Jake was standing in the greenhouse, …
4 Mum was in the car, …
5 Have you seen the photo of Rover, …?
6 This is Ella on her way to a party, …

More help ➔ *p. 147*

2 While waiting … (Participle clauses with *while* and *when*)

TIP
In clauses with ***while*** or ***when*** you can use a participle instead of subject and verb. Compare:
- *While they were waiting for the flood waters to go down, the ants headed for this big stone.*
- *While waiting for the flood waters to go down, the ants headed for this big stone.*

a) Use participle clauses to join each pair of sentences about people living in Sydney.
   You can use when or while in the participle clause.
   Change either sentence a) or sentence b) into a participle clause.

   1 a) I waited for my flight to Sydney. b) I read my guide to Australia.
   While waiting for my flight to Sydney, I read my guide to Australia.
   2 a) I often went surfing. b) I lived in Sydney for six months.
   3 a) I attended school in Sydney. b) I made a lot of new friends.
   4 a) I took photos of Sydney Harbour. b) I took the ferry to Manly.

b) Write two more sentences in the same format.

 ➔ **Workbook** *10–11 (pp. 32–33)*

3 Paul and Jake

Using the verbs in the box, complete the text about Paul and Jake in FNQ with the correct verb form, relative clause or participle.

bend · do · dress · feel (2x) · flood · get up give · go · hit · listen · look · make · put on · remove · ring · want

It was a January morning in Cairns, Far North Queensland, and Paul, who always [1]... early, woke up to the radio [2]... information about a big rainstorm. [3]... through the window while [4]..., he noticed the trees [5]... in the strong wind. But Paul decided [6]... to school anyway, not [7]... to miss his band practice. While [8]... his raincoat and rubber boots, he heard his phone [9]... in his back pocket. It was his best friend Jake. "[10]... you hear the good news?"

"No, what is it?"

"All the roads [11]..., so no school today, mate!" While [12]... to his friend talk about all the things he was planning to do that day, Paul watched the rain [13]... the window.

"But there's bad news too", said Jake, "when [14]... some fallen trees from the road, a workman got hurt."

"That is bad."

"Yeah, anyway, I'll call you later." said Jake.

[15]... disappointed, Paul took out his guitar. He always liked to play when [16]... frustrated. He called his song 'Rain Rebecca', [17]... him smile.

More help → p. 147

4 A trip that went wrong

a) Write a short text (about ten sentences) about a trip that went wrong.
Wherever possible use participle clauses to improve your style, to describe something you saw happening, e.g.:
While packing my bag, I forgot ... A dog ran out in front of the airport bus, forcing it to stop suddenly.

b) Hang up all your stories around the classroom for everyone to read.
Choose one text and write a comment.

More help → p. 148

5 Being new in Australia, ... (Participle clauses to give reasons)

TIP

You can use participles to give a reason. The participle clause usually comes first.
Being tropical, FNQ is always warm. (Because it is tropical, FNQ is always warm.)

→ *GF 10.6: Participle clauses instead of adverbial clauses of time (p. 205)*

Look at some sentences that people who are new in Australia have said.
Use participle clauses to explain the reasons.

1 I'm new in Australia. That's why I don't understand Aussie English very well.
Being new ...
2 We know all about floods because we live in the tropics.
3 I saw a python in the garden. I pulled out my camera to take a photo.
4 I knew that pythons are dangerous. That's why I was careful not to get too close.
5 I love the Australian outdoor life. I decided to live there for two years.

More help → p. 148

On this page you will work with words that help you to talk about a country, its landscape and towns. Then you will give a two-minute talk about Australia – the whole continent, or just a region or town.

1 Word field: Country and town (Structuring vocabulary)

a) Structure the vocabulary in the box. Add other words you know.

amazing · botanic gardens · bush · business district · central · centre · cinema · +climate · +coastline · crocodile · desert · +dramatic · +entertainment +facilities · harbour · outback · +overcrowded · rainforest · region · regional · river · +rural · shopping area · sports facilities · street · stunning · suburb · +suburban · +vast

+ = *new words*

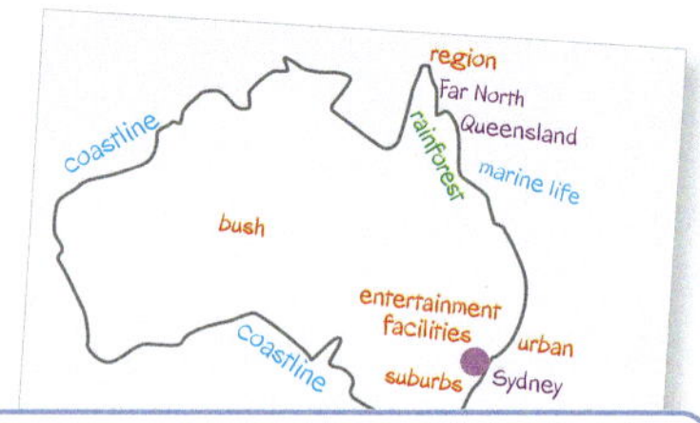

TIP
Use a map to structure geography vocabulary. Or use one of the other ways you have learned, e.g. tables or mind maps.

b) Compare your methods for structuring the words. Say why you chose your method.

2 Adjectives (Opposites)

Pairing words with opposite or contrasting meanings can make them easier to learn. Make as many pairs as you can with words from boxes A and B. Sometimes you can pair a word with two others. Sometimes it will not be possible to find pairs.

A
humid · +inland · +mild · +mountainous · nearby · northern · +old-fashioned · quiet · rural · vast · wide

B
busy · coastal · dry · flat · modern · narrow · remote · southern · suburban · tiny · tropical · urban

rural	urban, suburban
humid	...

3 Collocations (Adjectives and nouns)

a) Which adjectives from 2 go well with these nouns: *business district, climate, coastline, rainforest, region, sports facilities, street*?
Write phrases with your ideas.
– a mountainous region, a modern business district

b) Write six sentences on what you like or dislike about a place you know, e.g.
What I like about ... is the long rocky coastline.
One thing I hate about ...

TIP
Collocations are groups of two or more words that sound right together, e.g. *a tall tree*, but *a high mountain*.
When we use two descriptive adjectives, size adjectives usually come first:
a small coastal town, a vast tropical rainforest
Opinion adjectives usually come before descriptive adjectives:
a nice suburban park, lovely wide streets

EXTRA In a double circle, share your ideas from b).

Prepare your talk about Australia. Make a list of ten words or phrases you want to use.
Ask for a copy of your partner's list. While listening to his/her talk, tick the words that you hear.

→ **Workbook** *15 (pp. 34–35) · Wordbank 3 (pp. 102–103)*

For a discussion it is important to first practise agreeing and disagreeing with somebody's opinion.

STEP 1 Giving your opinion

When giving your opinion, you can say

- In my opinion, …
- In my view, …
- I'd say …
- Personally, I think …
- If you ask me, …

STEP 2 Agreeing with an opinion

To agree, you can use expressions like

- I agree.
- That's just how I feel.
- I couldn't agree with you more.
- That's so true.
- You're right.
- So do I. / Me neither.

Listen to the phrases in short dialogues. Say which three phrases you think sound the strongest. Give reasons.

Practise different ways of expressing the opinion from the cartoon.
In my view, red is …

Practise giving opinions and agreeing.
A: In my view, red is …
B: You're right.

STEP 3 Disagreeing with an opinion

Identify the tone of each statement. Say which three expressions are the strongest.

- I don't share your view.
- That's nonsense.
- I agree up to a point.
- I'm not sure about that.
- I totally disagree.
- I don't agree.
- I think that's rubbis
- You're wrong!
- That's not how I see

Access to cultures

In English, people are usually less direct than in German when they disagree with someone. So be careful: being very direct when you disagree could seem rude or be hurtful. Try not to give short answers like "No".
Be careful with strong expressions like *That's nonsense* or *I think that's rubbish!* Only use them if you're sure they won't seem rude. Be careful too when listening to someone's views. They might say what they think politely, and then you might not notice how strongly they disagree with you.

Listen and say what effect the words in orange have on the sentences.

- Sorry, I don't agree.
- I'm afraid I don't share your view.
- Actually, I think that's rubbish.

Showing understanding for someone's opinion before you disagree helps you to sound polite. When you disagree, it is polite to give your own view and explain it.

- I see what you mean, but that's not how I see it. Personally, I think blue is nicer. It's a friendly colour.
- Actually, you have a point there, but …
- You're right about that, but …

Take turns to disagree with these statements.

- Living in the country must be fun.
- Short hair looks nicer than long hair.
- It's OK to borrow something from a friend without asking.
- A gift voucher is a good birthday present.

→ *SF 17: Having a discussion (p. 169) · SF18: Agreeing and disagreeing (p. 169)*

→ **Workbook** *16 (p. 35) · Wordbank 1 (p. 100)*

1 Making a nation for all Australians

During the 18th century, the British industrial revolution drove thousands of people from the countryside into cities. Cities became overcrowded and levels of crime rose dramatically.

Faced with the problem of what to do with the growing prison population, British authorities packed prisoners onto ships. These floating prisons were known as 'convict ships'.

Sculpture of arriving convicts, Fremantle

'Happy Australia Day' Poster

'Change the date of Australia Day' protest

In 1770, the British explorer James Cook was the first European to land on the south-eastern coast of Australia. And in 1788, eleven convict ships were sent to this uncharted land to establish 'penal colonies'. The new colonies helped Britain claim Australia as part of its empire. Between 1788 and 1868, 165,000 British and Irish convicts were transported to Australia in convict ships.

The convicts were poor and uneducated. Eight out of ten had been arrested for simple theft – sometimes for nothing more than stealing a bit of food. The prisoners were kept behind bars and chained for the whole trip. The conditions were awful: one out of ten died during the arduous eight-month journey from Britain.

On 26 January 1788, the first convict ship landed in Sydney Cove. The British flag was raised and celebratory shots were fired. This was the beginning of Britain's first colony on the Australian continent – New South Wales.

Today, 26 January – Australia Day – is a public holiday celebrated with fireworks, parades, sporting events and family barbecues.

For the estimated one million Aboriginal people who had lived undisturbed on the Australian continent for sixty thousand years, the arrival of the European convicts and free settlers would prove catastrophic. For Aboriginal Australians, Australia Day is a day of sorrow and mourning.

By the mid-1800s, penal colonies and free settlements had been established in distant regions on the continent's coastline. Australia's six colonies – New South Wales, Victoria, Western Australia, South Australia, Queensland and Tasmania – were governed as separate countries, each with its own relationship to the British Crown. The colonial economy grew fast, with wool, minerals and agricultural products as the main exports. The colonists built towns in coastal regions, and roads and railways across the continent. The railway lines brought mining and agricultural products from remote areas to the ports for export. More and more colonists arrived and by the turn of the 20th century, the population had grown to about four million.

Many attempts were made to unify the colonies into one federation, and finally, on 1 January 1901, the six colonies were declared a single country: the Commonwealth of Australia. The country's parliament passed laws allowing immigration only from Europe. This became known as the 'White Australia Policy' – an attempt at keeping Asian and Pacific Islanders out of the country.

The Aboriginal people experienced the 19th century as anything but a period of growth. Their population fell to 90,000. British colonists killed tens of thousands of Aboriginal Australians, sometimes forcing whole communities off their lands. Many more died from diseases like smallpox and measles brought over by the Europeans.

Australia's constitution also established policies to control Aboriginal people. Most importantly, they were not allowed to vote. Whole Aboriginal communities were forced to leave their traditional homelands and move to various 'reserves', areas which were difficult to farm. The reserves were managed by white Australians, who often decided every aspect of Aboriginal life.

Between 1910 and 1970, the government took 50,000 Aboriginal children and children with one Aboriginal parent from their families, forcing them to live in institutions where they were not allowed to use their own languages or have any contact with their families. The children were often physically, emotionally and even sexually abused. In the words of one boy who was taken hundreds of miles from his family to a boys' home called Kinchela: *"They gave you clothes stamped with a number. They never called you by your name – they called you by your number. Kinchela was a place where they treated you like animals. All you did was work, work, work; we never went into the town – the boys' home was just a prison."* The children taken from their families became known as the 'Stolen Generations'.

After World War II, the economy was booming and there was a labour shortage. By the 1960s, the government had to change immigration laws so that people from other countries could move to Australia and be allowed to work. In 1973, the Australian government passed the Racial Discrimination Act, putting an end to the 'White Australian Policy'.

White Australia's attitude towards the Aboriginal population shifted as well. On 16 December 1976, the Australian Parliament passed a law that gave Aboriginal communities the right to reclaim land that was once theirs. And in 1998, a popular movement of Australian citizens established National Sorry Day, 26 May, to remember the suffering of the Stolen Generations. And, finally, a decade later, Australia's Prime Minister also formally apologized to the Stolen Generations.

Today, Australia's new official policy on racial diversity is "to build on our success as a culturally diverse, accepting and open society, united through a shared future."

Gate from Kinchela boys' home, National Museum of Australia

Prime Minister with members of Stolen Generation

2 A new nation

a) Answer each question about the text with at least two sentences:
   – What is meant by 'convict ships'? Who were the convicts?
   – What happened on 26 January 1788?
   – What did the Aboriginal people experience in the 19th century?

b) Identify and list the events that led to the formation of the nation of Australia.

c) Compare your list from b) with your partner. Together, make a timeline with the most important events.

3 A celebration for all Australians?

a) Describe how Australia Day is celebrated.

You choose Choose b) or c).

b) Relate this quote to historical events:

"Asking Indigenous people to celebrate January 26th is like asking them to dance on their ancestor's graves." – Karen Mundine, chief executive of Reconciliation Australia

c) Some Australians believe Australia Day should be celebrated on a different day. Choose one of these dates and write a short paragraph that explains why the date is better for Australia Day celebrations: 1 January, 16 December, or 26 May.

➜ **Workbook** *17 (p. 36)*

You are in Australia's outback, the arid and semi-arid desert that makes up 70% of the country – over five million square kilometres! You have no map and no mobile phone with a navigation app. But you do have a songline, which has a specific rhythm you tap out with a wooden stick. As you walk, you sing the song. Your walking pace is a rhythm, one among many rhythms: the wind through the grass, the hopping of the kangaroo, the call of birds and the tapping of your walking stick. Through this song you can read the land.

An aboriginal dot painting of a river splitting into two

Songlines were developed by Australia's Aboriginal people, one of the world's oldest civilizations. They settled on the continent at least 50,000 years ago, after making their way from Africa and then crossing the ocean to reach Australia. Today, 20% of Australians are Aboriginal, the original inhabitants of Australia.
For thousands of years, Aboriginal people were nomadic, lived by hunting and gathering, and developed a deep spiritual relationship with the land. There were hundreds of different Aboriginal groups in Australia, each with its own language or dialect.

In Aboriginal culture, songlines are part of the Dreamtime, the period in which life was created. The Dreaming are stories which explain how the world was made by ancestral beings. These beings often take the form of animals: crocodile, kangaroo, rainbow serpent and others. Dreamtime stories create an essential connection between Aboriginal people and their environment. These stories and the songlines were – and continue to be – passed on from generation to generation, in the form of dance, paintings, stories and songlines.

The songline is a kind of chant in which Aboriginals speak of their deep relationship with the land. Songlines also have a practical use. Imagine you live in the outback, with no roads, signs or buildings to help you know where you are. Here the knowledge of where a waterhole is, is a matter of life and death. The songline helps you read the land and, after much singing and walking, you reach the waterhole. The songline also names animals you can hunt and talks about how to make a fire that will not get out of control. Another songline will lead you to a place where you can meet people of another community with whom you can trade objects your family has made.

By singing about the terrain they passed through, Aboriginal people navigated their continent. Songlines are like maps that you sing. The melody and rhythm identify landmarks such as waterholes, rivers and stars. The whole continent is criss-crossed by songlines, some only a few kilometres long, others hundreds of kilometres. Singing the songlines in the right order helped people to travel huge distances without getting lost. Even when they crossed a language border, they could still understand the songlines because the message about the landscape is contained in the melody and rhythm. This knowledge of the landscape is also expressed in the paintings of Aboriginal artists.

a) Explain why the Dreamtime and songlines were important to the Aboriginal people. Include the picture in your explanation.

b) ▶ Watch the film and describe how the Aboriginal elder performs the songline. Say how his performance is different from his description of how the songline was originally sung.

Raging bush fires in Australia have become more common over the last 100 years because of climate change, which has caused hotter temperatures and created more frequent droughts. Recently, more than 18 million hectares burned in the Australian bush, killing millions of animals and destroying thousands of homes. Bush fires produce a great deal of air pollution, which affects people's breathing and general health. The fires in heavily-populated New South Wales burned over five million hectares, or 6.4% of the state. These are the biggest forest fires in Australian history.

A bush fire

Climate change is not the only cause of these damaging fires. For tens of thousands of years, Aboriginal people practised controlled burning, also called 'cultural burning', to effectively manage the danger of uncontrolled fires. When the government seized Aboriginal land, they put an end to cultural burning; fires were no longer managed in the traditional way and have since caused great damage.

How does cultural burning work?
Cultural burning means that small, 'cool' fires are set in certain areas early in the dry season to prevent wildfires from spreading and to help new plants grow. With cool, quick burns, no higher than your knee, animals have enough time to escape and young trees can survive. The fire goes out quickly after it burns the bush grasses, but seeds survive. In this way land is cleared so hunters can more easily travel through the outback, and bush fires have less to burn, so they don't get out of control.

Since 1992 much of the land that was taken from Aboriginal people has been returned to them, and the Australian government is beginning to support the traditional ways to manage fire. In fact, cultural burning has reduced wildfires by half in some areas. In recent years, Oliver Costello, from Firesticks Alliance Indigenous Corporation, has taught rangers and property owners how to use cultural burning and he is hopeful for the future.

"We need a three- or four-year training program [and] we need investment from whoever wants to see this country healthy again. We can work together; there is a pathway here for everybody."

Bush fires produce a great deal of air pollution.

a) Write a heading for each of the paragraphs in the text.
Compare your headings with your partner.

b) Read the text carefully. Take notes on:
- the damage/effects that recent bush fires have caused
- the reasons why these recent bush fires have occurred
- the reasons why a slow, controlled burn can be an effective way to care for the outback.

c) Read Oliver Costello's quote again. Explain why it is important that Australia uses traditional Aboriginal knowledge to preserve the natural landscape. Write a text (about 100 words).

→ Workbook 18 (p. 37)

1 Facts about Australia (Past participle clauses)

Language help

You already know how to use present participle clauses.
- *A boy carrying a surfboard appeared on the beach. (= who was carrying …)*
- *Always wear a wetsuit when surfing in cold water. (= when you are surfing …)*

You can also make participle clauses with past participles.
- *I scored in a match watched by thousands of people. (= which/that was watched …)*
- *The convicts sent to Australia were often poor and uneducated. (= who were sent…)*

➜ GF 10: Participle clauses (pp.203–206)

a) Rewrite these sentences about Australian history with past participle clauses.

1 Most of the convicts who were sentenced in Britain were arrested for minor crimes like stealing a bit of food.
2 The first convict and supply ships, which were named the 'First Fleet', landed in Sydney Cove in January 1788.
3 Australia Day, which is celebrated with fireworks, sporting events and barbecues, takes place on 26 January.
4 When they were established in the mid-1800s, the six colonies were governed as separate countries.
5 Kevin Rudd, who was elected in 2007, was the first Prime Minister to give a formal apology to the 'Stolen Generations'.
6 When they were faced with the problem of what to do with the growing prison population, British authorities packed prisoners onto boats which were known as convict ships.

b) This is a text about Jessica Mauboy, an Aboriginal pop singer. Choose the correct participle: present or past.

1 After (win) second place in the TV programme *Australian Idol*, Aboriginal pop singer Jessica Mauboy became famous.
2 (Award) the lead role in the popular TV series *The Secret Daughter*, Mauboy also created the soundtrack for the series.
3 One of the albums topped the ARIA Album Charts, (make) her the first Indigenous artist to achieve a number one album.
4 Mauboy's 4th studio album, (make) public in 2019, also hit number 1 on the ARIA Album Chart.
5 Besides (create) her own albums, Mauboy has collaborated with Snoop Dogg and Ludacris, and has toured with Beyoncé.
6 (know) for her great optimism, Mauboy is a role model for young girls in many Aboriginal communities.

2 More Aussie facts (Present or past participle clauses)

Use the present or past participle to join two sentences about Australian facts or to shorten the single sentences.

1 Aboriginal people who sang songlines were able to navigate their way around the huge continent.
2 Uluru is one of the most famous landmarks in Australia. It was called Ayers Rock by European immigrants in the past.
3 Banjo Paterson didn't expect 'Waltzing Matilda' to become so popular. He sold it for only five pounds.
4 'Neighbours' is a TV programme which is watched by millions of young people in Australia, the UK and Ireland.
5 National Sorry Day, which has been celebrated since 1998, is a day to remember the suffering of the Stolen Generations.
6 The fact that you know where a waterhole is can save your life.
7 When they are asked to name the Australian national anthem, most people say 'Waltzing Matilda'.

More help ➜ p. 148

➜ Workbook 19–21 (p. 38)

3 The Rocks

Listen to an audio guide to *The Rocks*, an old area of Sydney, then do the tasks. Your teacher will give you a copy of the page to work with.

a) Complete the sentences correctly. (Listening for gist)

The Rocks is a place in Sydney where a visitor can …

1 buy a lot of things. 2 find a job. 3 enjoy the ocean air.

The geography of *The Rocks* …

1 is very flat. 2 is very hilly. 3 was once mountainous.

b) Complete the paragraph with the correct word or phrase. (Listening for detail)

In 1790, people who had done … in England arrived in Australia.
There were no prisons in the beginning because being … kilometres away was bad enough.
These people could get married, but it wasn't easy because there were more … than … .

c) How is *The Rocks* different today than it was in the past? There is/are now …

1 a weekend market. 2 an art market. 3 a zoo.
4 carnival rides. 5 pop concerts. 6 a museum.

d) Complete the sentences with the correct word or phrase. (Listening for detail)

1 On Fridays, you can …
- buy food from … until … .
- buy food from Italy, … and … .
- buy the best … in Sydney.

2 The … are open from Fridays to Sundays.
3 The … are open from Mondays to Fridays.

e) The guide says *The Rocks Discovery Museum* got its exhibits from people who … (Sentence completion)

1 brought objects from their ancestors.
2 found them in their houses.
3 were preparing to build new buildings.

➔ *SF 20: Listening strategies (p. 171)*

1 Adam Goodes

Have a look at the picture and the title of the text. What do you think the text is about?

The story of Adam Goodes

Adam Goodes was born in Wallaroo, South Australia in 1980 to a white father and an Aboriginal Australian mother. Between 1996 and 2015, he was a professional Australian Rules Football player, playing for the Sydney Swans. During that time he played a total of 372 games, scored 464 goals and was twice winner of the Brownlow Medal, the award for the fairest and best player of the year.

Throughout his career Goodes has stood up for Aboriginal rights and has created programmes for Aboriginal youth. In 2014, in recognition of his stand against racism, Goodes was named 'Australian of the Year'. But Goodes has also been criticized for speaking out.

In May 2013, during a football match watched by tens of thousands, a fan of the opposing team called Goodes an ape. Goodes heard the jeer, turned around and pointed out the fan: a 13-year-old girl seated in the first row.

The stadium police led the girl out of the stadium. Goodes was so upset by the insult that he couldn't take part in his team's victory celebrations. When interviewed the next day, Goodes had the following things to say in reaction to the girl's comments:
"It's not her fault. She's 13, she's still so innocent. I don't put any blame on her. Unfortunately it's what she hears, in the environment she's grown up in, that has made her think that it's OK to call people names."

"I felt like I was in high school again, being bullied, being called all these names because of my appearance. I didn't stand up for myself in high school. I'm a lot more confident, I'm a lot more proud about who I am and my culture, and I decided to stand up last night, and I'll continue to stand up because racism has no place in our industry. It has no place in society."

The debate about racism provoked by this event continued for well over a year. Some people supported Goodes' reaction, while many others attacked him, saying that the girl was innocent and had not meant anything hurtful with her comment.

After this incident, Goodes was loudly booed at every game. He gave up playing professional football in 2015. He said the booing during his final season was 'one reason' he left the team.

In 2019, *The Final Quarter,* a film about the last three years of Goodes' career, was released. In making the film, director Ian Darling wanted to find out "what had provoked the crowd's behaviour and why a person who had been considered the best and fairest AFL player in the land, was now the subject of constant vitriol."

At the opening of *The Final Quarter*, the Australian Football League (AFL) issued a public apology to Goodes for not supporting him more fully during his difficult last season. The AFL said they regretted not doing more to defend Goodes and now wanted to show him how much he was appreciated.

The AFL and all of its 18 clubs stated: "Failure to call out racism and not standing up for one of our own let down all Aboriginal and Torres Strait Islander players, past and present. Our game is about belonging. We want all Australians to feel they belong and that they have a stake in the game."

2 A great career

a) Say:
- when Adam Goodes was born
- who his parents are
- what he did between the years 1996 and 2015
- what his achievements are.

b) Discuss and agree on which of Adam Goodes' achievements made him a prominent public figure in Australian society.

3 It's not her fault

"It's not her fault. She's 13, she's still so innocent. I don't put any blame on her. Unfortunately, it's what she hears, in the environment she's grown up in, that has made her think that it's OK to call people names."

a) Describe the events that led Adam Goodes to make this statement. Who do you think he was speaking to?

b) Explain what 'environment' Goodes is referring to. What or who might have influenced the girl?

c) Exchange your opinions about Goodes' reactions during the game and his public statement about the incident later on.

4 Our game is about belonging

The Australian of the Year Award honours an exceptional, highly-respected Australian, who ignites discussion and change on issues of national importance.

a) Create a timeline of the events mentioned in the text about Adam Goodes.

b) Think about how the events in the timeline reflect how public opinion about Adam Goodes changed and how these changes reveal different aspects of the relationship between European and Aboriginal Australians.

c) Discuss your ideas in your group. Then report to the class.

5 Respectful behaviour

Some professional sport leagues have come up with rules about how players and fans should behave during games.

a) Work in groups. Draft 4–6 rules for respectful behaviour during games.

b) Share your results in class.

6 Protesting racism in the US

a) Read the following text and explain what Colin Kaepernick did to protest racism in the USA.

In 2016, San Francisco 49ers quarterback Colin Kaepernick took a knee during the national anthem before an NFL game. 'Taking a knee' means kneeling while others traditionally stand, and he did this to protest racism in the United States. His actions triggered conversations about the problem of racism and what to do about it.

"I am not going to stand up to show pride in a flag for a country that oppresses black people and people of color", Kaepernick said. He lost his job but his actions made the Black Lives Matter movement known all over the world, and many players in different sports followed his example.

b) **EXTRA** Research Colin Kaepernick and note down what he said and what happened to him after he 'took a knee.' How did his story continue after 2016?

Using your research notes, compare the outcomes of Goodes' and Kaepernick's actions in both Australia and the USA. Report to the class.

1 REVISION Goodes continued to stand up against racism (Verb + gerund or infinitive)

Complete the sentences with the correct combination of verbs. Use one verb from both box A and B.

A	B
continue (2x) • prefer • try (2x)	surf • sing • visit • fall off • hunt

1 The film *The Final Quarter* shows how Adam Goodes continued to stand up for what he believed in.
2 In some parts of the outback, Aboriginal Australians … … animals the way their ancestors did.
3 "Can I … … today?" Thomas asked his mom, after he saw the surfers on Manly Beach.
4 Thomas … (not) … the surfboard when the waves broke at the shore.
5 Australians … … 'Waltzing Matilda' rather than the official anthem at sports events.
6 German tourists … (not) … Australia in the summer when the weather is cooler.

More help → p. 120

→ *GF 5, 6: The gerund, the to-infinitive (pp. 194–197)*

2 THINKING ABOUT LANGUAGE *-ing* forms and infinitives

a) Complete this advice on an anti-racism forum. Use the *-ing* form of the verb or the *to*-infinitive.

[1]… (call) out prejudice doesn't have to be hard. If you hear someone [2]… (make) a racist comment, tell them you don't want [3]… (hear) it. You might prefer [4]… (say) nothing at that moment, but later you'll feel bad about [5]… (stay) silent. If you are [6]… (sit) with a group of people, [7]… (listen) to one person's racist opinions, please speak up. If you decide [8]… (do) it, others will probably support you. You don't have to start a fight, but people who make [9]… (insult) comments should be challenged by their friends.

b) For each *-ing* form you used, say what kind of form it was. Example: This is a gerund. It is the subject of the sentence.

Language help

The *-ing* form of a verb is used in many ways. It can be a present participle or a gerund.

As a present participle, it can be used:
- in the progressive form of a verb:
  He was playing football when it happened.
- as an adjective:
  She was with a group of cheering fans.
- in participle constructions:
  While playing, he heard her shouting at him.

A gerund can be the subject or the object of a sentence:
- *Belonging to a football team is fun.*
- *People enjoy supporting you.*

Be careful! Some verbs can be followed by a gerund but others take a *to*-infinitive:
- *He enjoys helping others. / He wants to help others.*

Some can be followed by a *to*-infinitive or an *-ing* form, with a difference in meaning:
- *Remember to buy the tickets. / I don't remember seeing you yesterday.*

3 Zookeeper for a day (gerunds, participles and *to*-infinitives)

Complete the brochure text with the correct form of the verbs in the box.

be • become • eat • feed • give • help • look after • pet • receive • spend • take

Hey, animal lovers! Imagine [1]… a zookeeper for a whole day! Well, you can! The Zookeeper for a Day programme at the Australia Zoo is designed [2]… you the experience of [3]… a real zookeeper. You'll find yourself [4]… keepers [5]… the animals and [6]… different species. After [7]… lunch outdoors, you might spend time [8]… a baby zebra and [9]… photos of giraffes and alligators. Remember [10]… your zookeeper badge and cap, too. What a great way [11]… the school holidays!

→ **Workbook** *23–25 (pp. 40–41)*

1 Double Trouble: A television series

a) Yuma, a girl from Sydney, visits Alice Springs with her father. On her first day she has some strange encounters. Look at these stills from episode 1 and describe each situation.

A

B

C

D

b) Now watch part of episode 1. Say how Yuma feels when she meets the other girl, Kyanna.
What do you think their relationship is?
Explain the reactions of the women sitting on the bench and the boy to Yuma.

c) Watch another part of episode 1. Say what plan the girls make.
What problems could they have if they go ahead with their plan? What tips would you give them?

2 Making the film: Setting

E

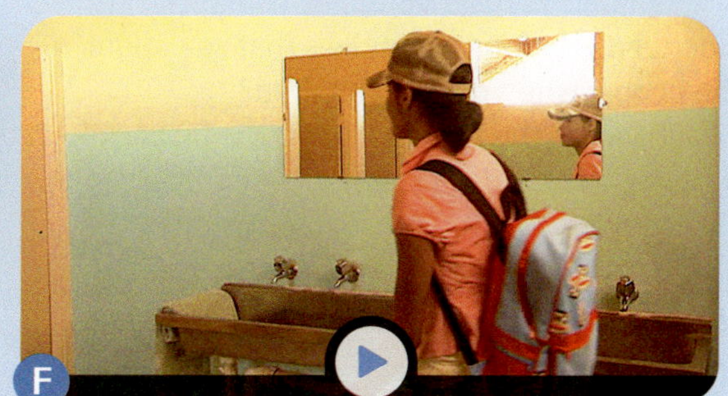
F

a) Look at these two places shown in the film. Describe each place. In what ways are they different?

b) Where did Yuma and Kyanna meet? Say why you think the film-maker chose that place.
Was it the best place for their meeting? Give reasons for your opinion.

1 Coast to coast

(from the novel by David Fermer)

Think of different reasons why people go to the beach.

Say why you like going to the beach and what you expect from a day on the beach.

When I was a kid, Dad used to say heaven is an Australian beach, and I reckon he's right. The beaches around Darwin are beautiful: the endless sky, like the promise of adventure, the breeze of the salty air, the soft sand against your feet, the border between land and sea.
We have two beaches in Darwin: Mindli and Casuarina. Mindli is where you go to party. Casuarina is where you go when you want to be alone. I go there when life is getting me down, when school is shitty, or something is bugging me – or when I have an argument with my dad. "When are you gonna stop treating school like a goddam holiday camp, Cooper?" (I've heard that a hundred times.) "Get a haircut!" (At least I've got hair, Dad.) "If you wanna throw your life away that's fine by me, but let me give you one word of advice: stop hanging around with losers like Graham Barton!"
Just some of the things he said to me when he got back from work yesterday.

Of course, I had answers like: "If Graham is a loser and his parents voted for you at the last aldermen elections, what does that say about the people who vote for you, Dad?"
Get Dad onto the subject of politics, he backs off faster than a dog caught napping by a snake. He's campaigning to become mayor of Darwin, and politics is a sensitive issue between us.
Once I've had enough of hearing about what a waste of space I am, I go to the beach to clear my head. One more year of school, then I'm out of this place. Sydney, Melbourne, Perth. There's no town north of Darwin.
I was walking along the beach as the sun went down. An orange blaze cut through the clouds, sending golden shimmers onto the water. How could anyone not feel good here? You can be at rock-bottom, the worst day of your life, but when you look at the sundown over the Timor Sea, you just know everything's going to be all right.
It was then that I saw him: a brown lump on the sand, dark against the orange of the sun. At first I didn't know what it was. A baby croc? A tree trunk? It was only when I took a few steps closer that I saw it was a person. He was huddled up like a baby, his knees under his chin, his arms around his legs, his T-shirt torn

bug sb. jn. ärgern **treat** behandeln **aldermen elections** Stadtratswahlen *(Ältestenrat)* **back off** klein beigeben **a dog caught napping** ein Hund, der beim Schlafen erwischt wird **campaign** kämpfen *(im Wahlkampf)* **a sensitive issue** ein heikles Thema **once** sobald, sowie, wenn **a waste of space** eine Platzverschwendung **blaze** lodernde Flamme **rock-bottom** Nullpunkt, Tiefpunkt **tree trunk** Baumstamm

and dirty. I had to walk around him to get a look at his face: black hair speckled with white sand; slender, Asian eyes. He looked around my age.
"Hey! Are you all right?" I put my hand on his back. He didn't move. I shook him harder. "Hey! Wake up, mate!"
No reaction.
I panicked. Jesus, this guy is friggin' dead!
I already had my phone in my hand, ready to call Triple Zero, but my fingers froze on the keys. I was shaking.

I put my phone away and got down to my knees. I took a deep breath and tried to focus. I've done a lot of First Aid courses in my time. I know the routine. First check to see if he's breathing. If not, do CPR. I bent down and put my face up to his nostrils. I could feel his breath on the skin of my cheek.
"Hey, mate, can you hear me?"
I tried to check his pulse, but I couldn't find it. I rolled him onto his back and grabbed his legs. I started shaking them like I was trying to rip them off. Get some blood back into that head of his! The brain needs oxygen!
It was then that he opened his eyes. He stared straight up at me, me standing above him, holding his feet under my arms, shaking his legs. He didn't seem in the least bit surprised.
I dropped his legs. "Are you all right?"
He turned his head and looked from left to right. "Where I?" he asked – two words that sounded like a distant dream.
"You're in Australia, mate. You're gonna be fine."

His name was Bashir, that much he could tell me. He came from Afghanistan. He spoke a few words of English, not much, but enough to say he'd been on a boat and that the boat had sunk in a storm. He'd held onto a life jacket and must have drifted around in the sea for hours. It's a miracle the sharks didn't get him. Or the crocs on the beach.
We sat there together on the sand for a while, watching the sun disappear behind the sea, and I knew from the moment I met him that I liked this guy. There was something intelligent in his eyes. He didn't say much, but I understood him. Occasionally he smiled, a dreamy smile, as if he couldn't quite believe what was going on, as if he was surprised to be alive. A couple of his front teeth were missing. He looked like a little kid or an old homeless guy. His face kept changing, sometimes young, sometimes old, like two people moving between two different worlds. I figured he was both at the same time – young and old. I guessed that was why he was here.
...
What now? I kept thinking. What am I going to do with this guy? What do you do with an illegal immigrant washed up on a beach in Australia?
"Are you hungry?" I asked him.
He didn't understand. I used my hands to show him what I meant.
He nodded. "Yes. Hungry," he said.
I took him to Joey's near the university and bought him some spare ribs and chips with lots of ketchup. He ate the stuff like he hadn't eaten for days. I guess he probably hadn't.
People kept looking at us.
"Slow down, Bashir," I told him. "Take it easy."
He seemed to understand. He saw the people staring.
After he'd finished his meal, we headed back to Rapid Creek. It was getting late. I told him to wait for me on the footbridge. "I'll be back in fifteen minutes." I gave him my watch and showed him when I'd be back.
I walked home and took the back door into the house. I went upstairs quietly, making sure no

torn zerrissen **triple zero** 000 *(australische Notrufnummer)* **key** Taste **First Aid** Erste Hilfe **CPR** kardiopulmonale Reanimation *(Herz-Lungen-Wiederbelebung)* **nostril** Nasenloch **skin** Haut **cheek** Wange **brain** Gehirn **occasionally** gelegentlich **figure** glauben, annehmen **spare ribs** Spareribs *(gegrillte Schweinerippchen)*

one saw me. Dad was out. Mum was in the living room, working on her laptop with the TV on. My little sister was in bed.
I put some fresh clothes into a bag, took some soap and deodorant out of the bathroom.
A toothbrush, toothpaste, my old sleeping bag.
I went back downstairs and took some milk out of the fridge, a can of spam, a tin opener, some biscuits. Don't ask me how I did it without Mum seeing me, but I did. I guess I can be pretty sneaky at times.
I was back on the footbridge in no time. Bashir looked relieved to see me.
"Come with me," I told him.

I took him to the hut where Dad keeps his canoe and fishing gear. It's around the back of the Surf Life Saving Club on Casuarina beach where Dad is a member. They let him build it when I was a kid, back in the days when we used to go canoeing together. It's not really official, but they let him build it anyway. It's kind of hidden away in the mangroves. No one in the Club has ever really noticed it. You can't even see it from the beach. It was the perfect place for Bashir.
I opened the hut and told Bashir he could stay here. I gave him the sleeping bag and showed him what I'd brought with me. He didn't say anything. He just nodded and flashed that dreamy smile of his that was fast becoming familiar to me.
It was hard to leave him there that night alone, but I guess anything was better than lying half-dead on a beach. I told him I would come around after school the next day. I told him not to go out. "You have to be careful," I said. "No one can see you here." I think he understood.
I went home and slipped back into the house. Dad was home. I could hear him talking to Mum in the living room. I called out to them, saying I was going to bed. I didn't want them asking any awkward questions.
Up in my room I realized how tired I was.
I went straight to bed, but I couldn't sleep.
My mind was racing, a thousand questions shooting through my head like a pinball machine. It was strange. Bashir and I were complete strangers, but now we were connected: me in my bed, the TV humming downstairs, my sister fast asleep in the room next door, and Bashir down at the beach, sleeping on the floor of our hut.

2 Understanding the text

a) Explain who Bashir is and say what Cooper does to help him.

b) Explain what Cooper means in these lines:
1. Get Dad onto the subject of politics, he backs off faster than a dog caught napping by a snake. *(ll. 26–27)*
2. I figured he was both at the same time – young and old. *(ll. 105–106)*
3. Kate is straighter than the Stuart Highway. *(ll. 231–232)*

3 Cooper's relationships

a) Read lines 1–34 and 146–156. Say what they tell us about Cooper's relationship with his dad now and as a kid.

b) Describe the ways in which Cooper's and Bashir's lives have been different. Then read lines 176–183. Say why you think Cooper feels connected to Bashir.

c) Explain why you think Cooper decides to tell Kate about Bashir and what that tells you about their relationship.

soap Seife **fridge** Kühlschrank **can of spam** Dose Frühstücksfleisch **pretty sneaky** ziemlich raffiniert **relieved** erleichtert **familiar** vertraut **awkward** peinlich, unangenehm **pinball machine** Flipper(automat)

I was still awake when my parents turned off the TV and came upstairs. I heard them walk past my door. One of them stopped, I guess Mum, to listen for a moment. I didn't move a muscle until I heard her walk away.

School next day was like a waiting game. Waiting for the day to end, waiting to get to the beach. I'd left my watch with Bashir the night before, so I spent all day discovering clocks on the walls that I'd never even seen before, watching their hands creep slowly by, checking my phone under the shadow of desks. Time can be your worst enemy when you want it to go by quickly.
I couldn't concentrate on anything that day. The teachers' voices sounded like faraway echoes. Everything I wrote was like someone else was writing it for me. Me? I was somewhere else. The only person I spoke to was Kate.
"I need to talk to you," I told her in the morning.
"Sure. What's up?"
"Not now. At break. Alone."
I didn't mean to scare her, but I know I did. God knows what she thought. Trouble with my dad? Trouble with the law? Trouble was written all over my face. She kept looking at me during lessons, sneaking glances between heads and shoulders, trying to read what had happened from my eyes, but I know how to keep my face blank.
We met at break around the back of the school. It stinks around there because of the trash cans, so you can usually count on being alone.
"What is it?" Kate asked me.
I've known Kate all my life. We went to the same kindergarten, the same primary school, now we attend the same secondary school. We're like brother and sister.
I told her about finding Bashir the night before, about how I'd given him food and let him sleep in the hut. I told her the few things I knew about him, that he came from Afghanistan, that his family lived in Pakistan, that he was on the boat that had sunk off the coast near Darwin.
Kate listened to me with that listening face of hers, the way she does when things are serious. When I finished, she turned to me and said, "Are you crazy?"
It wasn't quite the response I was expecting, but it didn't surprise me. Kate is straighter than the Stuart Highway.
"You have to talk to your dad," she said.

4 Telling a story

Coast to coast is a first-person narrative.

TIP
If one character tells a story from his/her point of view, we call this a **first-person narrative**.
We see this character's world and the whole story through his/her eyes.

a) In groups of three, each student takes one of these sections and rewrites it from Bashir's point of view: *ll. 43–61* · *ll. 62–84* · *ll. 146–183*

b) Read out each narrative.
Say what changes when the story is told from Bashir's point of view (e.g. the focus on key events, emotions, impressions, language, …).
Give reasons for your opinion.

My Book Keep a copy of your narrative.

hand Uhrzeiger **faraway** fern **sneak glances** einen schnellen Blick werfen **secondary school** weiterführende Schule

→ **Workbook** *27 (p. 41)*

Workbook Checkpoint 2 (pp. 42–45)

Six months in Far North Queensland

The Queensland government is offering $5,000 to students from Germany to help them to finance a six-month exchange in Far North Queensland. Applicants have to write and say why they think FNQ is the best place to spend six months in Australia. Your task is to prepare good arguments for your application to the Queensland government.

STEP 1

Work at separate tables in groups of four.
Think of arguments for staying in FNQ (climate, landscape, wildlife, marine life, sports and other free-time activities, towns and cities, etc). Decide which of your arguments is the strongest. Find photos (in this unit, on the internet) to support your strongest argument.

STEP 2

Each student takes one large sheet of paper.

On your sheet of paper, write down a statement with your strongest argument for going to FNQ.

> I think the strongest argument for going to FNQ is the marine life because ...

Then pass your sheet of paper to another member of your group.
Read the statement on the sheet you get and write down your comments.

> I see what you mean about marine life in FNQ, but in my view ...

Then pass the sheet on again so that the other people in the group can add their comments.
You can comment on the original statement or on the other comments.

> I agree with the statement!

> I don't quite agree with the statement, but I don't agree with Alex's comment either.

➔ *p. 57: Agreeing and disagreeing with people's opinions • SF 18: (p. 169)*

STEP 3

Compare all four sheets of paper. Choose the two sheets with the most positive comments.
Hang them up on the classroom wall.

STEP 4

Walk around and read what the other groups have written.
Write down any good ideas that you don't already have. Then return to your table.

STEP 5

Discuss the arguments of the other groups. Are they similar or different, stronger or weaker?
Then decide on the four best reasons for going to FNQ. Review all the photos you have looked at.
Try to decide on a good photo to go with each point.

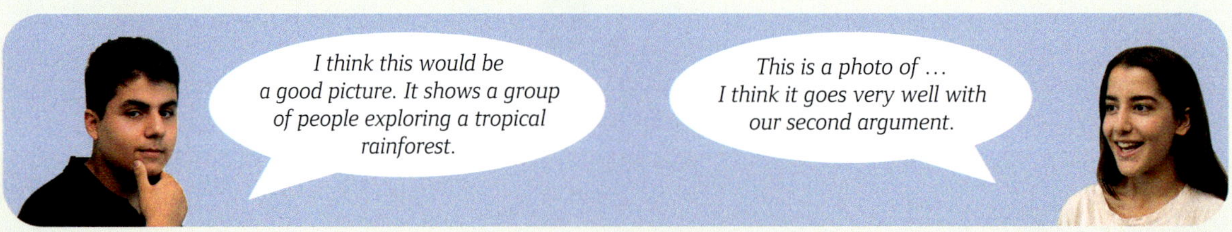

➔ **Workbook** *Wordbank 1 (p. 100)*

A 1 What can you do in Sydney?

a) Identify the activities that you can do in Sydney.
Make a sentence with each of the activities you can do there. Use participle clauses.

- come across a wild camel
- go kitesurfing
- see a kangaroo
- be surprised by an amethyst python
- dive to see the Great Barrier Reef
- walk along the wharf
- take a walk in the outback
- meet a cassowary
- spend the day at the beach
- visit *The Rocks*
- enjoy shrimps on the barbie
- go to the opera
- hike through the rainforest

b) Name the state or territory where the other activities might take place.

2 Paraphrases

a) Find the words that match these paraphrases.
Using four or more of the words, write a short paragraph about Australia.

1 The seven main parts of the earth
2 A political association of sovereign states
3 A person who has been proven guilty of a crime
4 A course of action done by a government
5 The negative treatment of a person or a group based on their nationality, religion, class, etc.
6 To push or make somebody angry enough that they react
7 A faraway place where prisoners are sent to separate them from the rest of the population

b) Paraphrase these words: *Aboriginal people, bully, confident, apologize.*

3 WORDS

a) Turn the nouns into adjectives.
e.g.: region – regional

agriculture • catastrophe • coast • colony • constitution • history • industry • suburb • tradition

b) Use some of the adjectives you made to complete the sentences about Australian facts.

1 Wool, minerals, and ... products were the main exports of the Australian ... economy in the 1800s.
2 Most of Australia's population lives in the ... region.
3 1 January, 1901 is the date that Australia's six colonies became a ... federation of states.
4 Woolloomooloo is a ... area outside of the city of Sydney.
5 Songlines were the ... way Aboriginal Australians found their way through the outback.
6 The landing of the first convict ship in Sydney is celebrated as a ... event.
7 Climate change is having a ... effect on the Great Barrier Reef.

4 A postcard from Australia

Complete the following email that Abby gets with the correct words. All the missing words are words that are made up of two words, like *postcard, website, kitesurfer* ...

Hey, Abby! I've only been in Australia for nine days, but I've already seen so much. First, I was in Sydney. The market at *The Rocks* was cool but [1].... My neck hurt from looking up at all the [2].... I watched a [3]... from the Manly scenic [4]..., a long nature hike right in the city that follows the [5]... for ten kilometres. Another day, my parents drove us to Perth, where we took a ferry to Tasmania. We saw amazing [6]... there, like little penguins and a wombat! My aunt's [7]... is way up north, so we had to drive through the [8]... to get there. We learned about Aboriginal [9]... and the [10].... Aunt Charlotte lives near the [11]..., and our hiking guide pointed out a plant that smells like almonds. I'll tell you all about it when I get back, OK?

5 MIXED BAG Boomerangs

Complete the text about boomerangs with the correct words.

What [1]... a boomerang? You [2]... ... it as something shaped like a wide 'V' that, when [3]... in the right way, [4]... return to the owner. There are many types and sizes [5]... boomerangs and they [6]... found in Ancient Egypt and in Native American communities [7]... North America. The [8]... image of a boomerang appears in a 50,000 year old rock carving in the Kimberley region in Western Australia, while the [9]... Aboriginal boomerang – dating from 10,000 B.C.! – [10]... ... in the Wyrie Swamp in South Australia. Boomerangs [11]... originally [12]... by Aboriginal Australians as hunting weapons, music instruments, battle clubs, digging tools and [13]... fire starters. When used [14]... an experienced person, a boomerang [15]... ... a kangaroo, long-necked emu [16]... ... parrot. It [17]... also [18]... two or more animals at a time when thrown into a flock. [19]... boomerangs [20]... often carved or [21]... with decorative designs, becoming meaningful, prized objects to [22]... makers.

6 MIXED BAG The quest for a national anthem

Complete the text about Australia's search for a national anthem with the correct words.

Australia became [1]... independent state [2]... 1901, but until 1974 still [3]... 'God Save the Queen', the British national anthem, as its own. In 1973 the Australian government, [4]... by Prime Minister Whitlam, decided the country [5]... a new and unique national anthem, this [6]... be, in his words, a "symbolic expression of our own pride and dignity." A nationwide competition [7]... the 'Australian National Anthem Quest" [8]... organized. [9]... writers and composers [10]... ... in the competition, but the judges believed none of the entries [11]... good enough! The Australian Council of the Arts [12]... another idea: one of three well-known songs, 'Waltzing Matilda', 'The Song of Australia', and 'Advance Australia Fair', [13]... ... the new anthem. In 1974, the government [14]... a nationwide survey: 60,000 people were asked to choose [15]... favourite song, and the winner [16]... 'Advance Australia Fair'. But before the song became the National Anthem, a new government was [17]... and the quest for a national anthem [18]... all again. In 1976, instead of a 'survey', the new government [19]... the question to a nationwide vote. The results? 'Advance Australia Fair' [20]... the clear winner [21]... 43.29% of the votes. 'Waltzing Matilda' [22]... second with 28.28%, 'God save [23]... Queen' was third with 18.78%, while 'Song of Australia' [24]... ... than 10%. In 1984, 'Advance Australia Fair', a song [25]... by Scottish composer Peter Dodds McCormick and [26]... at the inauguration of the Constitution of Australia on January 1, 1901, became the [27]... National Anthem.

B 7 Welcome to the First Fleet Monument

a) Listen to the guide and write in one sentence what the story is about.

b) Listen again and complete the statements.
1 The eleven ships that left Britain in 1787 were called …
2 The ships carried …
3 If the convicts made trouble …
4 The trip to Australia took …
5 The convicts ate …

b) Answer the following questions with key words or numbers.
1 Where did the passengers of the First Fleet settle? Explain why.
2 What did the crew do at Cape Town?
3 What is a mutiny?
4 Why was the meat they ate salted?
5 How many of the passengers made it to Australia?
6 How were the convicts separated from other passengers?

C 8 The Sydney Opera House

The Sydney Opera House has become a cultural symbol in Australia and is considered one of the greatest buildings in the world. The Opera House was designed by the Danish architect Jørn Utzon, who won an international competition organized by the Australian government in 1957. People describe the building, which was built on a concrete platform in Sydney Harbour, as giant, glistening white shells or sails billowing in the wind when viewed from a distance. Although the Sydney Opera House has been celebrated all over the world, the history of its construction included many struggles. Instead of being completed within four years as planned, it took 14 years to finish and cost 14 times the original budget. Queen Elizabeth officially opened the Sydney Opera House in 1973, and since then, more than seven million people have visited each year. Inside the huge shells are five theatres, as well as rehearsal spaces, restaurants and a souvenir shop. Visitors enjoy famous operas, of course, and all kinds of other music and theatre performances, like rock concerts and circuses. Visual artists show their work, too – even on the outer 'sails'! In 2016, the Sydney Opera House featured the works of six Aboriginal artists who represented their songlines in animated lights across the outside walls of the building. The show, called 'Songlines', also included contemporary Aboriginal music. Vivid Sydney Creative Director Ignatius Jones says: "By putting Songlines on our most significant cultural icon, we put Indigenous art at the heart of Australian culture and showcase this amazing story to visitors across the world."

a) Complete the sentences in your own words:
- Jørn Utzon is …
- The Sydney Opera House has been compared to …
- Queen Elizabeth …
- Aboriginal artists …

b) Write sentences that explain:
- what goes on inside and outside the Opera House
- the challenges in building the Opera House
- why the Opera House is a cultural symbol (icon).

c) Write a text (about 200 words) about a building that you consider to be a cultural symbol in Germany or somewhere else you've been.

The Commonwealth and New Zealand

The **Commonwealth of Nations**, established in 1949, is an association of 54 countries, most of which were former colonies of the British Empire. Although all member states must recognize the British monarch as the head of the Commonwealth, each member nation has its own independent government and constitution. The Commonwealth is a huge organization which includes nations from every continent. The citizens of the Commonwealth make up 30% of the world's population, with India as its most populous member.

Although membership in the Commonwealth used to require a past relationship to the British Empire, this is no longer necessary. The British monarch is the head of state of sixteen member nations which are known as Commonwealth Realm countries. They include Jamaica, Canada, Australia, Papua New Guinea and New Zealand. The English language and a shared history connect the Commonwealth nations, but they have no legal obligations.

New Zealand is one of the Commonwealth's founding member nations and is made up of two larger islands – the North and South Islands – and several smaller islands. It has a mountainous landscape with a complex system of fast-moving rivers and lakes as well as 360 glaciers. New Zealand, part of the "Pacific ring of fire", has active volcanoes, and earthquakes are common. The most recent significant earthquake occurred in 2016. It had a magnitude of 7.8 and caused major damage.
New Zealand is also known for its rich, diverse and often unique species of plants and animals. Some species, such as the kiwi, a flightless bird, exist nowhere else in the world.
The first inhabitants of New Zealand were the Maori: Polynesian settlers who arrived in the first millennium between 500 and 1300 CE.
The Dutch were the first Europeans to arrive in 1642. The British followed. New Zealand was claimed as a British colony in 1840 after Maori leaders signed a treaty with the British government. The Maori fought against the British occupation of their land in what came to be known as the Maori Wars. Despite strong resistance, the Maori lost most of their land and many were killed.
Despite these conflicts, the Maori people fared better than the indigenous people of Australia. Today, Maori and English are New Zealand's two official languages. Maori culture is a celebrated part of New Zealand identity and many Maori words have become part of New Zealand English.

Pacific Coast, Coromandel Peninsula

Kiwi are an endangered species

New Zealand Parliament buildings, Wellington

New Zealanders have a reputation for being a very easy-going, friendly and open-minded people who don't get angry easily. BUT there are a few common mistakes which you would do better to AVOID!

1. *Don't ask a Kiwi (not the bird, but what New Zealanders call themselves) if they live near Sydney, or if they've ever been to the 'outback'. New Zealand is over 4000 km from the nearest point in Australia and it takes about four and a half hours to travel there by plane!*
2. *Don't ask if there are any kangaroos in their backyard. Before Europeans introduced sheep and other livestock, there were NO MAMMALS in New Zealand.*
3. *Avoid saying something negative about rugby and especially about the National NZ rugby team, the All Blacks. Kiwis tend to be very proud fans!*
4. *When you visit,* be 'a clean, green Kiwi', and respect *the environment. Don't litter.' New Zealand has some of the most beautiful, protected beaches and natural landscapes in the world. Keeping these landscapes clean is something Kiwis take very seriously.*

New Zealand English includes many words from the Maori language. Many of New Zealand's place names are Maori as well. Before you visit, it's helpful to learn how to pronounce some Maori words and phrases, as well as some New Zealand slang, so you won't be scratching your head wondering what your Kiwi friends are talking about … Let's start with the first meeting:

All Blacks rugby team performing a 'haka'

Your New Zealand friends might say '**Kia ora**'. That means 'hello' in Maori. It also means 'I accept you and accept where you come from.'

You might be invited to a '**hangi**', which is a Maori word for a traditional BBQ feast in which meat and vegetables are cooked over heated volcanic rocks in a pit in the ground.

'**Waka**' is the Maori word for boat or canoe and a '**land waka**' is a bus! You might take a **land waka** to visit your Kiwi friend, who you can call your '**cuz**', your '**bro**' or your '**cuzzy bro**'.

You and your '**cuz**' might take a walk to a nearby '**dairy**' (a corner store) to pick up some '**tomato sauce**' (ketchup) to serve at the '**hangi**'. But the '**dairy**' might be all out of '**tomato sauce**'.

"'**No worries**' (it will be fine)", says your Kiwi friend. After the '**hangi**', everyone gathers around the screen to watch the All Blacks rugby team play against New Zealand U-20. Before the game starts, the team performs a '**haka**' or traditional Maori war dance. The All Blacks win the game. "The last try was '**mint**'! (awesome!)", shouts your friend.

a) About the text:
- What is 'the Commonwealth of Nations'?
- Describe the landscape and name some unique animal species in New Zealand.
- Who were the first inhabitants of New Zealand?

b) Work in groups of five. Each member should choose one of these Commonwealth countries: *Pakistan, Zimbabwe, Cyprus, Belize, Rwanda.* Find the answers to these questions:
- What was this country's relationship to Great Britain before it joined the Commonwealth?
- When did it join the Commonwealth?
- Is it still part of the Commonwealth? If not, why not?

Present your answers to your group.

c) **EXTRA** Imagine you are an exchange student in New Zealand, living with a local family. Write a dialogue that you have with your Kiwi friend. Use as many of the New Zealand words and phrases you have learned on these two pages as you can.

→ **Workbook** *6-7 (pp. 88-89)*

Stepping out

1 What are your opportunities

a) Describe photos D and E and speculate about the situations pictured in these photos. Have you ever been in a similar situation?

b) Look at the wordle at the bottom of this page. Make sure you know the meaning of all the words. Look up unknown words in a dictionary.

c) Describe the jobs and internships shown in the other photos as well as other jobs/internships you would like to do or have done. The words in the wordle might be useful to you.

2 What are the challenges?

a) THINK: Choose one of the three options: participating in an exchange programme, having a job or doing an internship while you are in high school. Make a list of pros and cons.

b) PAIR: Find someone in class with the same option and compare your arguments. Agree on one pro and on one con that you consider to be most important.

c) SHARE: Discuss your findings with the class.

service opportunity apprenticeship
responsibility job participate dog walker
soup kitchen search internship
intern supervisor abroad training
workplace train application
qualify exchange apply
profession solar panel volunteer
community service workshop
customer mentor interview
competitive requirements

A

C

E

B

D

F

G

Your task **EXTRA**

At the end of this unit: You will prepare an application and do an interview for a volunteer summer job abroad.

1 Going to school in the US

The kindergarten through twelfth grade (K–12) education system in the United States is shown in the chart below.
Each US state is divided into school districts. School districts follow one of the five systems (A–E) shown here.

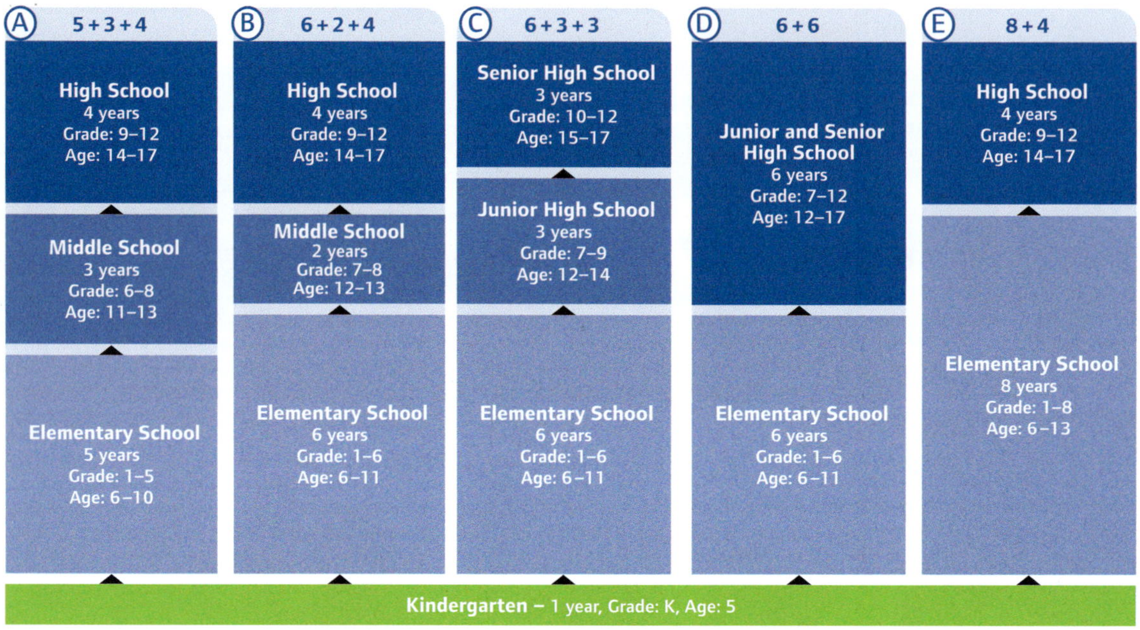

MORE INFORMATION ON THE US SCHOOL SYSTEM

School system
- chosen by each state
- fixes the number of years students must attend school

School calendar
- Two or three terms – called 'semesters'
- School year begins: August or September; Ends: May or June

Private vs. Public
- Public schools are state-run schools
- 90% students (50.8 million): public schools
- 10% students (5.8 million): private schools

Assessment
- Exams are issued by state
- GPA – 'Grade Point Average' – average of grades received for student work during four years in high school
- High School Diploma – confirms graduation

2 At school in the US

Study the diagram of the US school system, then answer these questions.
- John is attending his first year of middle school. If he attends high school in 2 years, which district system (A–E) is he in now?
- Jade is in her last year of elementary school in district A. If she transfers to district E next year, how many more years of elementary school will she have to complete?
- Ingrid is in the *Neunte Klasse* and will be participating in an exchange programme in the US this year. In which districts would she be attending Junior High School?

Early finisher Write two questions like the ones above. Swap questions and answer your partner's questions.

→ Text File 1 *(pp. 138–139)* · Text File 2 *(pp. 140–141)*

3 Going to school in the UK

Read the text about the UK education system below. There are differences across the UK. The text focuses mainly on the English education system. Using information from the text, make a chart for the English school system similar to the chart on p. 80 that represents the US system.

Compare your chart with your partner.

Imagine you are a kid in England. This is what is waiting for you:
Your years of fun and play at nursery school won't last long. In most parts of the UK you'll start primary school in the September after your fourth birthday. There are three school terms in England: from September to Christmas, from January to Easter, after Easter to July. Some parents send their children to primary school a little later, so you might be five when you start school.
After six years of primary school, when most of the students in your class are 11 years old, you'll move to secondary school, which starts in Year 7. Your parents might send you to an independent school. These are private schools which you have to pay to attend. Nearly seven per cent of school students in the UK go to independent schools. Some independent schools are also boarding schools, so you might have to live and sleep there during term.
Most kids go to state comprehensive schools, which are free. They offer a general education to students of all abilities. What will you learn there? Well, all students have to do the subjects on the National Curriculum. Many subjects are similar to those in Germany, but there is Citizenship in Years 7–11, Design and Technology in Years 7–9, and Work-related Learning in Years 10–11.

How will you find out how you are doing? Your teachers will assess you, and there are exams in Year 9 and national GCSE (General Certificate of Secondary Education) exams in Year 11 (you might do GCSEs in some subjects in Year 10).
At the end of Year 11 you have several options. You have the choice to leave school to look for a job or to go to a College of Further Education. If you stay at school for Years 12 and 13, known as the Sixth Form, you'll study four or five subjects and take A-level (advanced level) exams in three subjects at the end of each year. Depending on your A-level results, you might be eligible for a place at a university.

4 Two different systems

Compare the US and English education systems. Take notes on the differences in:

- the age you start primary/elementary school
- the academic calendar
- the names of the different divisions in each system
- the way a student's performance is assessed.

5 Your school

a) Work with a partner.

Partner A: Compare the US system to the education system at your school.

Partner B: Compare the English system to the education system at your school.

b) **Both:** Explain the differences to your partner.

6 Two weeks in Bristol

A German ninth-grade class on a class trip to Bristol in the UK visits a British school. They attend classes and have the chance to exchange experiences with the British students. Have you ever been to the UK? Tell the class about your experience.

At twenty past noon the lunch bell rang. Mr Gordon's Year 9 class led their German partners into the bright new lunch room at Huntington Secondary School in Bristol.

"Mmm, pastries. I might try one of those", said Lina. "What's inside?"

Molly made a face. "That's a pot pie. It's made with meat – not my favourite. You probably won't like it either. I'm going to take the pasta with tomato sauce. It's a much safer choice."

Although Lina was still curious about the pot pie, she followed the advice of her British host.

Steven chose a curry chicken sandwich while Asil, his German partner, chose a tuna fish sandwich with chocolate milk.

The other German students and their British partners were sitting together at one of the long white tables, but it was full. Steven pointed to an empty table by the window overlooking the sports fields.

"Let's go over there … that has one of the best views – but let's hurry – it won't be empty long!"

They sat down and started eating. Steven swallowed half of his sandwich in one bite. "So," he said, "how did you like our Technology Class? Do you have a class like that in Germany?"

"I think it's really cool that you are going to design your own website", Asil replied.

"Well, some of us will. We each do different projects. I'm going to write a programme that solves geometry problems", said Molly proudly.

"Wow! That sounds amazing. Will you send it to me when you're done?" asked Lina. "It might help me get a better grade in Maths!"

"Sure, I will", said Molly smiling.

"Do you want to be a computer programmer?" asked Asil.

"I don't know yet. I might apply to a computer science camp for the summer holidays though."

"What are you doing this summer, Asil?" asked Steven.

"My family might spend a few weeks at my grandparents' house in Turkey … That's what we usually do. What about you, Molly?"

"I need to work. I'm going to apply for a bike delivery job at three different takeaway shops. I'm going to try to save as much money as I can so I can buy a new bike. What about you, Lina?"

Lina shrugged. "I'm not sure – no plans yet."

"What was that?" asked Asil.

"That's the bell", said Molly. "Time for English. We have to hurry or we're going to be late!"

7 Being a teenager in the UK

a) Identify the nationalities of each student.

b) Compare the British students' plans for the summer with the German students' plans.

Do the differences surprise you? Comment on the result.

8 Being polite

a) Exchange your first impressions of all four students. The adjectives in the box can help you.

> curious · polite · +ambitious · shy · +cautious · proud · +adventurous · +bossy · self-confident · +humble

b) Evaluate each student's politeness and level of courtesy. Which student is the most courteous to the others? Find evidence from the text to support your opinion.

→ **Workbook** *2 (p. 47)*

1 REVISION Your plans for the summer (*going to*-future)

a) What are you going to do during the summer holidays?
Walk around the room and ask three classmates. For each interview, ask more questions to find out more. e.g.: if your classmate is planning a trip, you can ask:
- How are you going to get there?
- Where are you going to stay?
- …

b) Meet with a partner and tell them what you have found out.
Asil is going to visit his grandparents in Turkey. He is going to fly there. …
Note: If you haven't made any plans for the summer holidays yet, just make something up!

c) Work in groups of three and choose a celebrity you know a lot about. Imagine an event that he/she is going to take part in. It can be:
- a sports match
- a concert
- a film in which you play a leading role
- an election, etc.

Prepare for an interview by making notes about the event: where is it going to be, how are you going to get there, who is going to attend …

d) **Role play:** Work in groups of three.
The celebrity: Using the going to-future, tell the two reporters about the event.
Reporters: Take turns asking questions to find out more.

e) **Reflection:** Did you notice what verb forms you used to speak about the future? Were they always the same?

2 Saying goodbye (*will*-future)

a) Read the text about Mr Kuhn and his students. On a copy, underline every phrase that uses the *will*-future. Note down the function of the *will*-form in the sentence. Is it a *prediction, a promise, a request, an offer, a refusal* or *a conditional I sentence?*

Mr Kuhn raised his arms to get his students' attention. "OK, everyone," he said, "if it's not late, our plane will take off at 12:14, so you have about twenty minutes to say goodbye to your Huntington friends."
Asil turned to Steven. "Hey, it's been great to meet you. Will you text me sometimes to tell me what you've been up to?"
Steven shook Asil's hand. "Of course I'll stay in touch. I also hope you'll come back soon for a longer visit!"
"I promise I'll send you my computer programme as soon as it's ready", offered Molly.
"Thanks", said Lina. "When do you think your class will come to visit us in Germany?"
"Well, If we're able to raise the money for the trip, we'll be there early in October."
"Great! We'll take you to the best places and treat you to Weißwurst at the Oktoberfest!"
"OK, everyone … time to go!"
Lina had a heavy bag and a big suitcase.
"I'll help you with that …," offered Steven.
Molly didn't want to be left out. "And I'll carry your rucksack, Asil!"

b) Compare your answers with a partner.

More help → p. 149

→ Workbook 3 (p. 48)

Language help

Making predictions

a) You already know that the *will*-future is used to make predictions. You've also learned verbs like *may* and *might*.

- You'll probably start primary school after your fifth birthday.
- Some parents send their children to primary school earlier, so you might be only four.

b) We use the *going to*-future for predictions when we can see from a situation that something is about to happen:
Look at those clouds. It's going to rain.

We often use *going to* in warnings:
Be careful! You're going to fall.

➜ *GF 1.5: Talking about the future (pp. 184-186)*

3 REVISION Summer camp (Predictions with *will* and *might*)

a) Look at the camp application form. What do you think your partner will/will not choose, and why? Make notes.

Choose one activity from each category.

Category 1	*Canoeing*	*Tennis*	*Riding*
Category 2	*Photography*	*Cooking*	*Gardening*
Category 3	*Dance*	*Singing*	*Juggling*
Category 4	*Chess*	*Crosswords*	*Poetry*

Choose your diet

Regular	*Vegetarian*	*Vegan*	*Other**

* *Please give details*

b) Say what you think your partner will do and react to their predictions about you. Try to use each of these phrases once.

1 I think you'll ...
2 I don't think you'll ...
3 You'll probably ...
4 You probably won't ...
5 I'm sure you'll ...
6 Maybe you'll ...
7 You might ...
8 You might not ...

I don't think you'll choose riding, but you might ...

Why don't you think I'll choose riding?

Well, you ...

4 It looks like there's going to be a storm (Predictions with the *going to*-future)

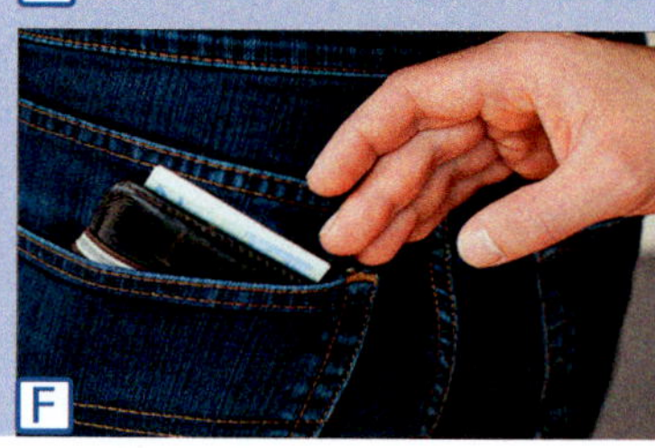

a) Say what's going to happen in each picture.

A I'm sure it's going to rain.
It looks like there's going to be a storm.

b) Choose one picture and write a short dialogue to warn others about what's about to happen.

➜ **Workbook** *4 (p. 48)*

5 At Huntington Secondary School (Predictions with *will* and *might* and *going to*)

You are going to listen to four short dialogues between the German and British students you read about on p. 82.

a) Describe the situation in each dialogue. Say whether the speakers are making a prediction about the future or if they are talking/giving a warning about what is (probably) going to happen.

b) Listen to the dialogues again and take notes about:
- the phrases that are used for warnings.
- what form of the future the speakers are using to make predictions.

c) Write two short dialogues. Include a prediction about the future in one and a warning about what is going to happen in the other.

d) Practise reading your dialogues with a partner.

More help → *p. 149*

THINKING ABOUT LANGUAGE Expressing the future

Learning how to express the future in English can be confusing.
This short dialogue talks about the future in a variety of ways:

Julie: *I'm going to meet a friend at the mall in about an hour.*
Mom: *Will you call when you get there, please?*
Julie: *Yes, Mom - I'll text you when I arrive.*
Mom: *How will you get there?*
Julie: *I'm going by bike.*
Mom: *I don't think that's a good idea. Look out the window. It's going to pour any moment now!*

- planned actions
- requests
- offers and promises
- prediction that something is about to happen

Key words and tone may also give you clues about time, possibility, intention, danger and predictions.

Listen to the dialogue. Say whether certain words or tone helped you understand what the speaker meant.
In German, the *will*-form exists, but not the *going to*-form. What about in other languages that you can speak?

Look at these sentences. Translate them into German or another language that you speak. Say what you notice about the verb forms and context.
- *Hurry! Close the window ... it's going to rain!*
- *I think he'll be home soon!*

6 Uncle John's farm (Predictions with *will* and *might* and *going to*)

Complete Ella's letter to her sister with the correct future form: may/might, will/won't or going to.

Hi, Sis! It's my last day at Uncle John's farm. Tomorrow, you ...[1] find this note on the bed when you unpack. Things are old school here, but I'm sure you ...[2] enjoy the experience. Here's what you ...[3] expect: work and more work. You ...[4] get up at 6 am to feed the sheep, cats and dogs. You ...[5] get hungry! ...[6] you eat breakfast then? No, not until 8 am! After feeding the animals, you ...[7] dig up potatoes under the hot sun. After lunch, Uncle John ...[8] probably walk to town and I'm sure you ...[9] want to go with him. There's a country store where you ...[10] find everything you need. You ...[11] even want to buy a present for me! You ...[12] always hang out at home. Some evenings, you ...[13] go to a disco in town. If you meet Patrick, ...[14] you say hello for me? Gotta go! They ...[15] leave without me!!!

→ **Workbook** 5 *(p. 49)*

On this page you will work with words that help you to describe a person's character.

1 Word field: Character and emotion (Structuring vocabulary)

a) Copy the table. Then read the tip and add these adjectives: brave · loyal · thrilled

Character	Character/Emotion	Emotion
easy-going	nervous	annoyed
…	…	…

TIP
Character adjectives tell us about someone's qualities. He's an easy-going guy.
Emotion adjectives describe people's feelings at a particular time: She felt really annoyed.
Some adjectives refer to character or emotion. He's a nervous kind of guy. / He felt nervous.

b) Think about the meaning of these adjectives and add them to your table.
Then compare and discuss your results. Try to add other words you know.

calm · cautious · excited · +generous · +hard-working · +jealous · kind · lazy · +mean · natural · negative · old-fashioned · optimistic · patient · practical · relaxed · rude · self-confident · shy · surprised · +tolerant · +tough · weird · proud · curious · bossy · ambitious

2 Prefixes and suffixes (Understanding new words)

Prefixes like *dis-*, *un-*, *im-*, *in-*, *ir-* give a word the opposite meaning, e.g. *polite – impolite*.
Suffixes like *-ness*, *-ance*, *-ence*, *-y* are used to make nouns out of adjectives.
Recognizing prefixes and suffixes can help you to understand a lot of words you haven't met before.

a) Choose five words from the box and write a sentence with a relative clause for each word that shows its meaning.

+dishonest · +disrespectful · impatient · impolite · +impractical · +intolerant · irresponsible · +unkind

A dishonest person is someone who …

b) Compare your sentences in class.

c) Group the nouns in the box by their suffixes. Write down the adjective in a second column.

kindness - noun	kind - adjective
laziness	…

+honesty · +impatience · +jealousy · +kindness · laziness · +liveliness · +meanness · +patience · +politeness · +rudeness · self-confidence · tolerance

Together think of one figure from a book or film. Then write separate character descriptions. Refer to personal qualities you like or dislike. Use eight words from this page. Read your partner's text. Comment on what is similar or different.

 Workbook 6 (p. 50) · Wordbank 6 (p. 106)

7 Ein Praktikum in Bayern

Fachbegriffe in Texten sind oft schwierig zu verstehen, besonders für Menschen, die nicht so gut Deutsch sprechen. Manche Begriffe lassen sich nur schwer direkt übersetzen.

a) Lies Yvonnes Anfrage auf der 'Global Student: Ask Anything' Plattform.

b) Lies den Text und suche die wichtigsten Informationen für Yvonnes Fragen heraus. Wenn du Wörter nicht verstehst, kannst du sie im Wörterbuch nachschlagen. Schreibe Yvonne eine Mail (ca. 180 Wörter), in der du ihr auf Englisch das Wichtigste über die Vorbereitung für das Praktikum und die Zeit während des Praktikums erklärst. Paraphrasiere schwierige Schlüsselwörter, wenn du kein geeignetes englisches Wort findest.

Hi, mein Name ist Yvonne und ich bin eine Austauschschülerin aus Texas. Ab September gehe ich für ein Jahr auf ein Gymnasium in München. Ich habe gehört, dass jeder in der 9. Klasse ein Betriebspraktikum machen muss. Ich habe online dazu diese Informationen gefunden, aber obwohl mein Deutsch ziemlich gut ist, habe ich nur wenig verstanden. Könnte mir bitte jemand erklären, wie ich mich auf das Praktikum vorbereite und worauf ich während des Praktikums achten muss?
Danke! Yvonne

c) Vergleicht eure Mails und einigt euch hinsichtlich der Schlüsselbegriffe und Paraphrasen.

➔ *SF 11: Mediating written or spoken information (p. 165) • SF 13: Paraphrasing (p. 166)*

Betriebspraktikum in der 9. Klasse

In einem Betriebspraktikum sollen die Schülerinnen und Schüler einen direkten Einblick in die Arbeitswelt gewinnen. Sie erfahren im Rahmen des Betriebspraktikums, ob ihre Erwartungen und Vorstellungen von einem bestimmten Beruf zutreffen und ob dieser ihren Neigungen, Interessen und Fähigkeiten entspricht. Für die berufliche Orientierung am Gymnasium ist Wirtschaft und Recht Leitfach. Es empfiehlt sich deshalb, das Betriebspraktikum im Rahmen des Faches Wirtschaft und Recht in der Jahrgangsstufe 9 durchzuführen. Der Lehrplan für das Fach Deutsch enthält zudem das Verfassen standardisierter Texte, wie z. B. Lebenslauf oder Bewerbungsschreiben. Dies trifft ebenfalls auf das Fach Englisch zu.

Das Betriebspraktikum hat drei Phasen:

1 Vorbereitungsphase:
Die Schülerinnen und Schüler schreiben ihren Lebenslauf und sind mit der individuellen Praktikumsplatzsuche im Internet sowie der Bewerbung auf diesen Platz beschäftigt. Sie werden dabei von ihren Lehrkräften unterstützt. Um den Blick auf das Berufsfeld im Praktikumsbetrieb zu schärfen und ihre Erfahrungen im Praktikum zu ordnen, werden vorab im Unterricht Leitfragen erarbeitet, z.B. Was ist das Besondere an dem Berufsfeld? Welche Qualifikation ist für den Beruf erforderlich? Passt das Berufsfeld zu meinen Stärken, Interessen und Neigungen? Ist das Berufsfeld mit meinen Vorstellungen von Arbeitszeiten, Reisetätigkeit, Einkommen usw. zu vereinbaren?

2 Durchführungsphase:
Während des Betriebspraktikums sind die Schülerinnen und Schüler aktive Teilnehmer/innen des Betriebes und Beobachter des Geschehens im Betrieb. Es wird den Schülerinnen und Schülern empfohlen, während oder nach ihrem Arbeitstag Notizen über ihre Beobachtungen zu machen, da sie einen Praktikumsbericht erstellen müssen. Außerdem werden die Schülerinnen und Schüler während ihres Praktikums von einer Lehrkraft besucht. Die Lehrkraft wird sich ein Meinungsbild der Schülerin bzw. des Schülers sowie des Betriebes einholen. Die Schülerinnen und Schüler sind während des Betriebspraktikums vom Schulunterricht befreit.

3 Nachbereitungsphase:
In dieser Phase wird der Praktikumsbericht geschrieben, der die vorab aufgestellten Leitfragen beantworten sollte. Insbesondere soll der Bericht Auskunft darüber geben, ob die Erwartungen der Schülerinnen und Schüler erfüllt worden sind und ob sie sich vorstellen können, nach Beendigung der Schul- und Ausbildungszeit in diesem Berufsfeld tätig zu sein. Die Erfahrungen und Berichte der Schülerinnen und Schüler werden im Klassenverband diskutiert.

➔ Workbook 7 (p. 51)

1 Summer science programme

Summer vacation in the US usually lasts 10–11 weeks – much longer than the six-week summer holiday in Germany. What do students do during this long break? Some work, and for those who don't, there are many summer programmes available. Some of these programmes are designed to attract students with special interests and hobbies. Here is an example which might attract students interested in science.

ABOUT | BLOG | UNDERGRADUATE STUDY | SUMMER PROGRAMS | GAP YEAR | GALLERY | APPLICATIONS | FAQs | CONTACT

2-WEEK PROGRAM | MARINE BIOLOGY PROGRAM

The Edisto Island Ocean Excursion is a two-week marine science program for high school students. After orientation, participants in this unique academic adventure will be spending the entire two weeks aboard the sailboat HMS Edisto.

Research: The North Carolina coast is home to many rare and endangered marine animals. Students will design experiments to collect data on changes that might affect the biodiversity and species survival in this delicate ecosystem.
Students will also take classes taught by professional scientists to better understand the environment they are experiencing first-hand. Here they will learn data-collecting and analysis skills. At the end of the two week program students will present their results to their classmates and guests from the Edisto Island Environmental Protection Agency.

Teamwork: This is a very challenging programme as sailing and research activities can sometimes continue round the clock. Students do not need sailing experience to participate in the program, but they should have a desire to learn and work together. In this exciting environment, students will develop teamwork and leadership skills that are valuable in all areas of their lives.

Requirements / Applications: Admission to our program is competitive. Please complete the online application and send it in before the March deadline. Successful applicants will be notified mid-April. The program is offered to sophomores and juniors who have successfully completed at least one year of both high-school level science and math.
This year we will offer five full scholarships to students with the highest academic achievements who would otherwise not be able to attend the program.

2 A challenging programme

a) You would like to apply to this programme. Read the text again and make notes on:
- where the programme takes place
- what activities you will take part in
- what skills you will learn
- the requirements/skills you need to be accepted into the programme.

b) Review your notes with your partner. Are there other useful qualifications for taking part in the programme that aren't mentioned in the text?

3 Your application

Answer the application form question:

In one paragraph explain why you have chosen to apply to the summer programme, what you expect to gain from your experience and what you expect to contribute to the programme.

More help → p. 149

→ Workbook 8 (p. 52)

4 Summer camp for the performing arts

Karen, who loves doing theater, is spending her summer holiday at Camp Sakinaw for the Performing Arts. Trying to convince her friend Mike to attend the camp, she sends this email about her experiences.

Subject: Re: You'll have a blast!

Dear Mike,

How's it going with your summer job? I miss you even though I'm having a great time at camp. I think Camp Sakinaw would be an incredible place for you too. The campus is on a mountain – you can go hiking and there is lots of wildlife here (especially the other campers!). 😄 My new friend Stacey and I share a cabin with 4 other girls. We all jump in the pool together at the end of a long day of rehearsals: SPLASH! After breakfast, I'll be hanging out with Stacey because we have to rehearse our scene in Little Shop of Horrors ... you know the musical, right?

You've been telling me that you don't have enough time to play the saxophone. Well, here you'll be able to practise with a jazz band for hours every day and study with really cool teachers. In fact, I'm going to a jazz concert tonight after dinner and I'll be thinking of you. If you come next summer, a CIT (counselor-in-training) will show you around; the camp has tennis courts, a sports field and a big lake for boating, and I know you love water sports.

If we're together here next summer, we'll get a chance to prepare our own meals in the kitchen, and you can even go horseback riding. Every afternoon, we all get together for a super-short performance by a camper. We might hear you play your sax on the big lawn if you come.

Oh! I just realized that I'm 5 minutes late for rehearsal, but I'll text you when I get back, OK?

Big hug,

Karen (that's me in the pic with some of my friends!)

Mike Hey, Karen. Does the camp offer scholarships? My parents asked me to find out. 3:25 pm

Hi, Mike. I'm not sure, but I'll ask a counselor and I'll get back to you. 3:27 pm

Guess what, Mike! There's a visiting day next week! 4:45 pm

Mike Really? Then I'll come visit you and I'll check out the camp! 4:46 pm

5 Questions and intentions

a) Say why you think Karen is writing to Mike. Support your answer with lines from her email.

b) ✎ Imagine you are Mike. Write an email to Karen, including any questions you may have and why you want to go or not go to Camp Sakinaw next summer.

More help → p. 150

6 Have a go

Look at how Karen answers Mike.

Mike: Does the camp offer scholarships?

Karen: I'm not sure, but I'll ask a counselor.

Decide what to do in these situations:

You don't know an English word. – I'll ...

Somebody knocks on the door. – I'll ...

Something falls to the floor. – I'll ...

You lose your friend's book. – I'll ...

Looking at language

If you announce a decision as you make it (spontaneous decision), you use the *will*-future.
Look at these two sentences from p. 55. Say which one is a spontaneous decision.

- If you come next summer, a CIT (counselor-in-training) *will* show you around …
- Karen: There's a visiting day next week! Mike: Really? Then *I'll come* visit you …

➜ *GF 1.5: Talking about the future (pp. 184-186)*

1 I'll help you (Spontaneous decisions: *will*-future)

a) Brian and Aaron are doing their homework. Complete Brian's reactions to Aaron.
Use I'll … or I won't … in each sentence.

	A	B
1	I can't do this exercise. I don't understand it.	Just a moment. I'll help you if I can.
2	Would you like something hot to drink?	Yes, please. I'll have …
3	Don't forget it's your grandma's birthday tomorrow.	Don't worry, …
4	The dog's barking. He wants to come back inside.	OK, …
5	I can't have lost my phone! I had it a minute ago.	What's your number? …
6	No, you can't use my bike. You always give it back dirty.	Please, I promise …

b) Check each other's sentences. Suggest improvements if necessary.

2 Maybe I'll go as a ghost (Spontaneous *will* or *going to*)

Brian and Aaron are talking during the lunch break.
Choose the correct future form to complete their sentences: will or going to.

A: Are you going to Jan's Halloween party?
B: Yes, I [1]… (dress) up as a pirate. And you? What [2]… you … (dress) up as?
A: I'm not sure. Maybe I [3]… (go) as a ghost. Do you have plans for the weekend?
B: Yes. I [4]… (play) my new computer game. Do you want to play too?
A: Uh, I'm not sure. I [5]… (let) you know later.

A: It's much too hot in here.
B: Is it? OK, I [6]… (open) a window.
A: But it's so loud outside.
B: OK, if you prefer, I [7]… (not open) it.
A: Can I borrow your good camera?
B: Sure, I [8]… (give) it to you tomorrow. What do you need it for?
A: I have to take photos for a project I [9]… (do).

3 Text messages (Spontaneous *will* or present progressive)

Read the text messages and use the notes below to write a reply to each one.
Use the *will*-future or the present progressive for the coloured verbs.

1 Hey! What's up? Can we meet this evening?
Sorry • play football • phone you • weekend
Sorry mate, but I'm playing …

2 How's it going? What are you doing in the holidays?
OK • visit uncle New York • send card when there

3 Hi. We need someone to feed the cat this weekend. Do you think Jack could do it?
not sure • I ask • but think he go • London

4 My computer isn't working – again! Can you help me please?
OK I have a look • not do anything else this evening

More help ➜ p. 150

➜ Workbook 9-11 (p. 53)

Language help

a) Use the future progressive tense when describing an action that will continue over a period of time in the future.
Participants *will be spending* the entire two weeks aboard the HMS Edisto.

b) Use the future progressive to talk about what you will be doing at a definite time in the future.
After breakfast, *I'll be hanging out* with Stacey.

➜ *GF 1.5: Talking about the future (pp. 184-186)*

4 A new summer job (Future progressive)

Complete Maria and Sarah's dialogue using the correct verb in the future progressive.

babysit • deliver • do (2x) • look for • organize • visit • work (2x)

Maria: Hey, Sarah. I finally found a summer job! This time next week, I [1]... at the Spotty Dog Bookstore.
Sarah: Wow, Maria, that's great! So, tell me, what [2]... at the bookstore?
Maria: The owners haven't told me yet. They [3]... the store all week. On Monday, they'll let me know.
Sarah: Do you already know your schedule?
Maria: Yeah, I [4]... from 9 am to 2 pm on Tuesdays and Wednesdays.
Sarah: Those are good hours. I'm jealous! My usually lazy brother Tom just got a job, too, but he has to work every Saturday.
Maria: What [5]... ?
Sarah: He [6]... groceries for Wiggly Piggly supermarket. By the way, I think he likes you. He wants to know if you will come to his birthday party on June 9th.
Maria: No, I can't, I [7]... my cousins in London that weekend.
Sarah: Oh, that's too bad.
Maria: Do you really think he likes me?
Sarah: Yes! He's my brother!
Maria: [8]... a job too?
Sarah: I don't need to. I already have a job. I [9]... my neighbor's kids for three hours a day.
Maria: Oh, that sounds good, too. Please come visit me at the bookstore, OK? And tell Tom that I'm really sorry I can't come.

5 What will the campers be doing? (Future progressive)

a) Make sentences about the different people at Camp Sakinaw.

The rock/jazz band The theatre group The tech crew The cooks The camp counselors The campers' parents	be	build practise cook train rehearse visit	during the entire summer all morning next week during the open days every afternoon

The rock band will be practising all morning for their next concert.

b) Tell your partner what you will be doing at these times in the future. Use the future progressive.

- ... at 5 pm tomorrow.
- ... after dinner tonight.
- ... on Friday, after school.
- ... on Sunday at 1 pm.
- ... at 8 pm on Saturday evening.

6 STUDY SKILLS Finding the right English word in a dictionary

A bilingual (German-English) dictionary helps you to find English words you need. You can find good dictionaries online. You can also use a print dictionary.

a) Use the dictionary extracts on the right to do the tasks for each of the following tips.

Words often have more than one meaning.

1 You need the English word for *Note* to say how you did in your class test. Find it on the right. What helped you to choose the right word?

2 Find another example of a 'school word' which also has other meanings.

British and American English may use different words for the same thing.

3 Find two examples.

Nouns can take a different verb in English.

4 Find how to say *eine Prüfung machen*. What verb(s) can you use in English?

The use of prepositions can be different, e.g. im Internet = *on* the internet.

5 Find the English expression for *sich vorbereiten auf ... , einen Aufsatz über ... schreiben*

What are the prepositions in the German examples? What are they in the English ones?

6 Find a verb which takes a preposition in English, but not in German.

Deutsch-Englisch

Aufsatz der
1 *(Schularbeit) BE* essay ['eseɪ], *AE* paper ['peɪpə];
einen Aufsatz über Goethe schreiben
write an essay on Goethe
2 *(Abhandlung)* paper
3 *(Möbel)* top section ['tɒp sekʃn]

behandeln transitives Verb
1 treat [triːt];
jn. mit Antibiotika behandeln
treat sb. with antibiotics
2 *(Thema, Fall)* deal with [diːl];
Das Buch behandelt die Geschichte der Kelten.
The book deals with the history of the Celts.

Note die
1 *(Musik)* note; *(gedruckte Noten)* sheet music;
Kannst du Noten lesen? Can you read music?
2 *(Schule) BE* mark [mɑːk], *AE* grade [greɪd]
3 eine persönliche Note a personal touch [tʌtʃ]

Prüfung die
1 exam [ɪg'zæm], examination [ɪgˌzæmɪ'neɪʃn]; test;
eine Prüfung machen do/sit/take an exam;
eine Prüfung bestehen/nicht bestehen
pass/fail an exam
2 *(technische Überprüfung)* inspection [ɪn'spekʃn]
3 *(von Dokumenten)* check [tʃek]

vorbereiten transitives Verb
1 *(Mahlzeit; Reise)* prepare [prɪ'peə];
Wir sind dabei, unseren Urlaub vorzubereiten.
We're making preparations for our holiday.
2 sich auf etwas vorbereiten prepare for sth.;
Ich bereite mich auf die mündliche Prüfung vor.
I'm preparing for my oral exam.

b) Look at the dictionary entries again. What kind of information do they give you? Make a list.
- different meanings of a word
- ...

c) Look at some online dictionaries. Check if they give you the kind of information you have put in your list. Decide which online dictionary you find most helpful.

EXTRA Write a short text using the words that you have looked up.

Study skills

Using a bilingual dictionary

Ein deutsch-englisches Wörterbuch hilft mir, wenn ich ...
Wenn ich ein Wörterbuch benutze, sollte ich
- überprüfen, ob ich die richtige Bedeutung eines Wortes gefunden habe
- ...

Überprüfe deine Ideen.

→ *SF 30: Using a dictionary (pp.178–179)*

 → **Workbook** *13 (p. 54)*

1 Bruce Lee played badminton too

a) Form a buzz group. In two minutes, describe the poster in the still on the right and say what you think its message is. Refer to
- the man's appearance
- the expression on his face
- the different sports that are shown.

Now say what you think the film might be about.

I think the film is probably about …

I'm not sure if I agree. In my view, …

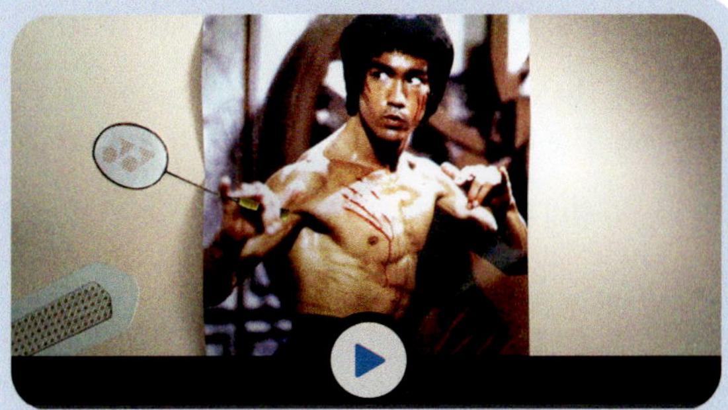

b) Watch the first 60 seconds of the film (Part 1). Describe the characters and say what happens. Then compare the still on the right with the poster in a). What do they have in common?

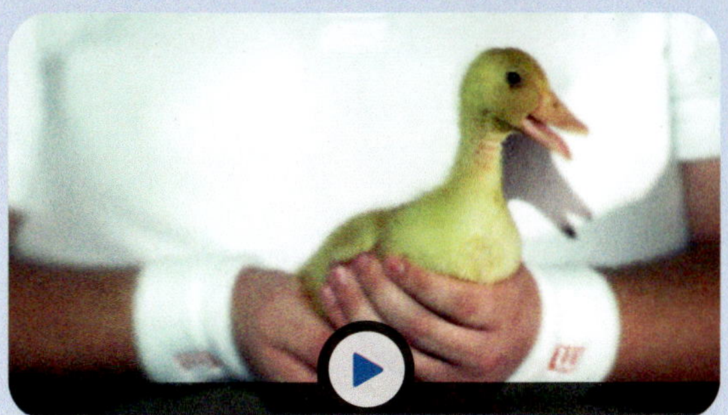

c) Watch the rest of the film (Part 2). Explain what Nic's goals are and if he achieves them.

d) Which of Nic's parents gave this advice?
- *Sometimes you're just not good enough.*
- *Being a champion – it's not about being the best in the game.*

Say which piece of advice you think was more helpful to Nic. Give reasons.

2 Making the film: Setting and effects

a) Watch the two different scenes again and describe what happens.

b) Say what the film-maker does differently. Refer to
- the setting
- the use of light
- the use of sound and music.

Explain what effect these differences have.

EXTRA Watch Nic's two matches again. Each student concentrates on one aspect:
- editing and cuts
- close-ups
- body language and gestures.

Describe the effect of the aspect you focused on.

➜ *SF 15: Viewing (p. 167)*

1 Your CV in English for a summer job abroad

Imagine that you want to apply for a summer job in the UK or the US. You'll need to prepare your CV in English. The format and expected information for a CV in the UK and the US is different than in Germany.

a) Read the guidelines in the TIP box and look at Daniel Koch's CV.
Say what you think the purpose of a personal statement can be.

TIP If you apply for a job in the UK or the US, follow these guidelines:

- Include **a personal statement** that describes your relevant strengths and interests.
- List the dates of your education and work experience starting with the most recent.
- Do not include a photo!
- Explain any German terms like *Abitur.*
- Check your CV carefully and have it proofread by a good English speaker.

CURRICULUM VITAE
Daniel Koch

Muellerstrasse 56, 80337 Munich, Germany · Email: danko55@gmx.de

Personal statement
I have always loved working with other people, in team projects at school or volunteer projects in my neighbourhood. I like to give 100 per cent of my energy to the project.
My favourite subjects are English and sports, and I have always looked for ways to increase my skills in these two areas.

Education

2013 to date	Karlsgymnasium, München (secondary school)
2009–2013	Römerschule München (primary school)

Qualifications/Skills

Lifeguard certification	Successful completion of lifeguard training DRSA Silber, Wasserwacht, German Red Cross, Munich
IT Skills	Good knowledge of MS Word, PowerPoint, Excel and Adobe Photoshop
Languages	German native speaker; good spoken and written English; some Latin

Work experience

2019 to date	Photographer for school yearbook
May 2018	Two weeks working at St. Peter Kindergarten

Hobbies and interests
Swimming; member of school photography club; I play volleyball in an after-school club; I make short videos of sport events.

b) Read these two personal statements. Tell your partner which you think is better. Give reasons.

Personal statement
I am enthusiastic about all outdoor sports. I have supervised younger children in our school's afternoon programme with patience and good humour. I am a quick learner and my teachers have appreciated my strong sense of responsibility.

Personal statement
My family usually spends the summer holidays by the sea, so I am a great swimmer. I have a younger brother and often have to take care of him when my parents are away. I would love to have a summer job abroad. I'm a hard worker!

 ➜ **Workbook** *14 (p. 55)*

2 Cool summer jobs

a) Read the two job adverts and say which interests you more. Give reasons.

Lifeguard at Silver Lake

The Parks and Recreation Department of the Town of Spofford is looking for a lifeguard for the summer season at Silver Lake. The successful candidate will have completed a certified Red Cross Lifeguard training programme by the end of the school semester. Duties will include supervising the lake, preventing accidents and assisting in swim lesson programmes for middle school students. Applicants, who must be 15 and over, will need to have strong communication skills, enjoy working with young children, and be able to work well in a team. If you want a fun-filled summer working outside, apply in person at the Silver Lake Clubhouse and bring copies of your certifications. Interviews, which will be held at the end of May, are necessary for all applicants.

Amusement Park - food service

Are you looking for an awesome summer job? Do you have what it takes to join our food and beverage team at the Bedford Great Days Amusement Park? Do you enjoy working as part of a team? Then we have the job for you! Even if you don't have experience, our training programme, which is offered the first week of the summer, will prepare you for the fun and fast-paced positions making summer drinks, pizzas, wraps and salads for our hungry visitors.

We're looking for enthusiastic, hard-working, reliable young people to work at the Bedford Theme Park from June 1 to August 30. Employees must be flexible with their time since hours can vary from week to week. If you are outgoing, friendly, and willing to work on weekends, apply online today!

b) Read through the adverts again. Make notes about what skills and qualifications you need for each job, what your duties will be and which character traits the employer prefers.

c) Choose one of the jobs. Using your notes from b), write your own personal statement in a digital format.

More help → *p. 150*

d) Read your partner's personal statement and give feedback. Make any necessary revisions.

e) Go to p. 94. Study the model CV and copy these headings on your digital document.
- Education
- Qualifications/Skills
- Work/Volunteer Experience
- Hobbies/Interests

Fill in each category for yourself. Using your results from c)–e), put together your CV in English in a digital format.

f) Swap your completed CVs and give each other feedback. Make revisions wherever necessary.

→ **Workbook** *15-16 (pp. 55-56)*

Language help

Non-defining relative clauses

A non-defining relative clause gives extra information about someone or something, but the sentence will still be complete and make sense if you remove it.

Read the sentences below without the relative clause.

- *Applicants,* ***who must be 15 and over****, will need to have strong communication skills ...*
- *Interviews,* ***which will be held at the end of May****, are necessary for all applicants.*
  ... our training programme, ***which is offered the first week of the summer****, will prepare you ...*

Use a relative pronoun (*who, whom, whose,* or *which*) to introduce the clause, and use commas before and after it. Never use *that* in non-defining relative clauses.

➜ *GF 9.3: Non-defining relative clauses (p. 202)*

1 All about volunteering ... (Non-defining relative clauses)

Use the information in brackets to add a non-defining relative clause to the sentences about Robert. Use *whose, who* or *which.*

1 Robert (...) decided to volunteer at a local soup kitchen. (He just moved to Bristol from London.)
2 His mother (...) explained that it's one of the best ways to make friends in a new community. (She wanted him to volunteer.)
3 Volunteers (...) tend to work hard without complaining. (They are given clear instructions.)
4 The term 'skills-based volunteering' (...) means that someone uses their own training in a different environment. (It is now used in many organizations.)
5 Robert (...) was given the task of preparing vegetables for the lunchtime meal. (His skills include cooking.)
6 One old man (...) told Robert that the food was better than usual. (He was a regular visitor.)
7 At the end of the lunch period, Robert told his manager (...) "I'm coming back next week for sure!" (He was cleaning the floor.)
8 The manager (...) told Robert that he was looking forward to seeing him then. (He was happy with Robert's work.)

2 Letter home from an exchange student (Non-defining relative clauses)

Add a non-defining relative clause to each sentence in Mina's letter home to her parents using the clues.

Dear Mama and Papa,

I am writing to you in English since my host family, (kind), want me to do it. I hope you can read it! Yesterday, (holiday), they took me to a birthday party in the countryside. I ate lots of cake, (too sweet), and had a stomach ache soon after. Sylvia, (worried), told me to lie down on the couch. Some kids, (host family's neighbors), came over to play cards. The game, (difficult), lasted for an hour and I won! One of the kids, (parents are from Germany), wanted to speak German with me. But Sylvia, (heard him ask), told him that I had to practice my English. During the ride home, (took two hours), I slept the whole way! Please write back soon.

Love, Mina

➜ **Workbook** *17 (p. 56)*

3 A great opportunity! (Non-defining and defining relative clauses)

Here is some good advice from Lisa about summer internships. Identify each relative clause, say if it is defining or non-defining and put commas where needed. Your teacher will give you a copy of Kim's internship text to work with.

This is for all my classmates who thought I was crazy to do a summer internship at an architecture office. I learned more in eight weeks than during the entire school term. My boss who is a great architect told me I have a good eye for design. But I would also like to talk about those people's skills that are important in any workplace. For example, I was part of a team which included other interns and my job was to keep track of each member's deadlines. I learned to speak respectfully to everyone which has to do with good office behaviour and to make sure I had all the information that I needed. This was a lesson which I learned from the office assistant who has to help every person in the office. Most importantly, because of my internship, I now know for sure that I want to be an architect.
For all those classmates who still have no clue what they want to major in, I recommend that you consider a summer internship!

Language help

Future perfect
The future perfect (*will* + *have* + the past participle of the verb) is used to describe a completed action in the future. It is often used with a time expression and/or the word *by*.
- *By May of this year, I* ***will have earned*** *my Lifeguard Certification.*
- *The successful candidate* ***will have completed*** *a certified Red Cross Lifeguard training programme by the end of the school semester.*

→ *GF 1.5: Talking about the future (pp. 184-186)*

4 New jobs and internships (Future perfect)

Complete the sentences about Susan and her friends with the correct form of the verb in the future perfect.
By the time the last customers leave, we will have served twenty meals!

1. At this time tomorrow, I (hear) if I got the job at the café around the corner.
2. I'm hoping that by the end of the school year, I (receive) my Lifeguard Certification.
3. Susan doesn't know much about New York, but she (read) a lot of books about it by the time she gets there.
4. We (attend) the training programme before we start our internship at the hospital.
5. Sean and I (completed) our science projects before the competition deadline.
6. My cousin (not finish) setting up the website before his internship ends.
7. ... Yannick (learn) enough English by the time he arrives in Scotland for his internship?

5 A 'to-do list' ... (Future perfect)

a) Make a "to do list" with actions you want to complete by a certain time or day.

b) Swap your table/list with a partner.
Make sentences using the future perfect with your partner's list about what they want to get done.

By the end of next week, I'll have searched the internet for summer jobs.

What to do?	By/before	When?
search the internet for summer jobs	end of	next week
write my CV	10 o'clock	tomorrow

→ *SF 6: Wriiting a formal letter or email (p. 160)*

6 Writing a letter of application

a) Daniel is applying for the job as a lifeguard.
Look at the letter layout (1–8) and choose the best modules (a–y) for each point.

Letter layout

1 Your address
2 Name and address of the person/organization you're writing to
3 Heading: what the letter is about
4 Date
5 Start
Dear …
6 Main body of letter
Paragraph 1: Say why you are writing.
Paragraph 2: Describe your qualifications.
7 Conclusion
8 Finish

1
(a) Muellerstrasse 56
(b) Müllerstraße 56
(c) 80337 München
BRD
(d) 80337 Munich
Germany

2
(e) Hathaway Health Charity,
25 Wise Street,
Morecambe,
UK
(f) Ms Sue Hancock
Hathaway Health Charity
25 Wise Street
Morecambe LA4 5HX
United Kingdom

3
(g) **Your advert**
(h) **Lifeguard Silver Lake**

4
(i) 20 February 2021
(j) Feb 20, 2016

5
(k) *Hi Sue,*
(l) *Dear Ms Hancock*
(m) *Dear Sir or Madam*

6
(n) *Hey great, I found this ad on the internet, and I love swimming. That's why I want to work for you this summer.*
(o) *I am writing about your advert of 13th January on the internet. I would love to work as a lifeguard this summer.*
(p) *I'm writing about the lifeguard position at Silver Lake. I'll be spending the summer in the States and am very interested in this exciting job.*
(q) *As you can see from my CV, I have a 'Silver' lifeguard certification from the German Red Cross. I am currently in the more advanced level course and will have earned the 'gold' certification by the summer holidays.*
(r) *I am 16 years old and am an excellent swimmer. My school internship was at a local kindergarten, where my responsibilities included teaching the children some basic English. I got along well with the kids, so feel I have the right skills to be a good swimming instructor.*
(s) *I've included my CV so you'll be able to see everything I can do. I'm one of the best in my class at English, so language really won't be a problem. I love working outside and with kids so I'm sure I think this job is perfect for me.*

7
(t) *It would be great if you chose me for the job. Please let me know.*
(u) *Please let me know as soon as possible if I get the job.*
(v) *Thank you for considering my application. I am looking forward to hearing from you.*

8
(w) *Yours sincerely, Daniel Koch*
(x) *Bye, see you this summer. Yours, Daniel*
(y) *Yours Daniel Koch*

b) Compare and explain your answers.
Refer to both content and style.
Using a placemat, make a list of tips on how to write a good letter of application.

c) Choose a summer job.
Then write your own letter of application.

→ *SF 6: Writing a formal letter or email (p. 160)*

→ **Workbook** *20 (p. 59) · Wordbank 5 (p. 105)*

On this page, you will practise getting ready for, and taking part in, a job interview.

STEP 1 Evaluate an interview

a) Watch a job interview and take notes on
- the applicant's clothes
- his body language
- the way he answers questions
- his interaction with the interviewer.

b) Say what impression you think the student made, and what you think he could do better.

STEP 2 Think of tips

You'll give a better interview if you remember the 4 Ps: Prepare – Practise – Present – Participate.
Think of more tips for each of the 4 Ps and make lists.

Before the interview	PREPARE	1: Find out what you can about the job and employer. 2: ...
	PRACTISE	1: Think of possible questions and answer them aloud.
At the interview	PRESENT	1: Think about the right clothes for the occasion.
	PARTICIPATE	1: Introduce yourself at the beginning.

More help → p. 151

STEP 3 Prepare

Think of a job you'd like to apply for. Then read the questions below. Decide:
- what information you might need about the job you're applying for
- what answers you will give.

Personal questions	Questions about you and the job
• Tell me about yourself.	• Why should we hire you?
• What are your strengths/weaknesses?	• What can you do that other candidates can't?
• What are your goals?	• Why do you want this job?
• Where do you see yourself in five years from now?	• Do you have any questions about the job?

STEP 4 Practise

a) Partner A: You are the interviewer. Decide what questions you are going to ask.
Partner B: You are the applicant. Read your tips from Step 2 and think about what you'll say.

b) Now practise. You may need language to …
- start your answers: *Well, I'm 16 years old and ...* • *Actually, one of my main strengths is ...*
- explain what you mean: *What I mean is ...* • *What I'm really trying to say is ...*
- move to another point: *Another point I should mention is ...* • *There's something else I'd like to say.*
- show you are following the other person: *I see.* • *Right.* • *Uh-huh.*
- show you don't understand something: *Sorry, I don't quite understand.* • *Sorry, but do you mean ...*

c) Swap roles.

→ *SF 19: Taking part in an interview (p. 170)*

→ **Workbook** *21-23 (pp. 60-61)*

Good behaviour in the workplace

IMAGE-BASED TEXTS

In the *Oberstufe*, you will be asked to interpret image-based texts that combine words and images. There are three important steps:

- *comprehension* You describe the content of the image-based text: What is it about?

This is a skill you have often used, for example when describing images like photos or posters.

- *analysis* You study how the content is presented and what effect that has on the viewer.
- *comment* You react with a critical or personal comment in written or spoken form.

a) Comprehension: Describe one of the posters to your partner.

b) Analysis: Analyse how the two posters convey their message about good conduct in the workplace.

➔ SF 25: Describing and interpreting images (p. 175)

Refer to the kind of image used, e.g.photo, drawing, icons, etc. Also mention qualities such as colour or size, how realistic or unrealistic the image is, etc.
- The use of a photo/illustration/ ... makes the message clearer/ more effective/ ...
- The dark/bright/different/ ... colours make it easier to understand/reinforce/ .... the message.

Refer to the kind of information the text contains, e.g. emotional, humorous, etc. You can also mention the amount of text, the colour, size of the letters used, the use of capital letters, etc.
- The use of only a few words/list of words/capital letters/larger and smaller letters/ ... makes the message ...
- By including references to social media ... the poster ....

Explain how the image and text fit together.
- The image of the interlocking wheels/ ... reinforces/ complements ... the text
- The poster focuses on/highlights/ ... the message of the text ...

c) Comment: Compare the two posters and comment on how effective they are.

Compare the message and goal of the posters.
- In my view, the message of the two posters is similar/different/ ...
- Although ... focuses on ... is seems to me that they both want to ...

You may also wish to give your opinion on the issue
- I feel that the issue of behaviour in the workplace is very important because ...

Refer to points you covered in your analysis.
- In general I think a photo/illustration/reference to social media ... influence/reach ... people more than ...
- In this case, I feel/don't feel that the illustration/photo/colours/ ... work very well.
- In my opinion a shorter/longer/more detailed/ ... text is/would be/ ... more effective.

THINKING ABOUT LANGUAGE Polite language in the workplace

Using polite phrases in different situations is one way to make a good impression at a new job.
When you arrive: *Good morning. How are you today?*
When you leave: *Goodbye, have a great evening!*
Making requests: *Would you mind helping me with this? / Would it be OK if ...*
Offering help: *I can help you with that ... / Can I offer you some help?*
And just in case you need to **correct someone**, you can say: *I think you might be mistaken ...*

Make short dialogues using at least two of these phrases.

EXTRA You choose a) or b).

a) In a short article, comment on the relevance of following a behaviour code in the workplace.

b) Write a story showing how following or not following a workplace behaviour code can affect a person's experience.

EXTRA In a discussion of the two posters, assess how effective campaigns of this kind can be.

➔ **Workbook** 24 (p. 61)

Workbook Checkpoint 3 (pp. 62–65)

Role-play: Applying for a volunteer job

Work in groups of six. Three students will play an applicant. Three will play an interviewer.

Applicants	Interviewers
STEP 1: The application	
a) Read the advert. Invent a character who is suitable for the job. Think of their name, address, school etc., and about their interests, skills and experience.	a) Read the advert. Brainstorm the qualities, skills and experience that the successful applicant will need.

Park and aquarium volunteers
Aquariums accept volunteers as office helpers or to clean the park. We also encourage volunteers to do more unusual jobs. For example, volunteers work at the aquarium to feed the fish and clean the tanks and habitats. We also allow older volunteers with dive training to swim with the fish, examine them for injuries, or just to play with them from time to time.

Applicants	Interviewers
b) Together, write <u>one</u> CV for your character. Make a copy for each member of the group. ➜ p. 94	b) Agree on criteria for choosing the right candidate. Make a checklist.
c) Alone, each member of the group should write their own letter of application for your character. Give a letter and CV to each interviewer. ➜ p. 98	c) Alone, each member of the group should think of their own questions to ask the candidates and write them down.
STEP 2: The interview	
d) Prepare for the interview. Imagine questions the interviewers might ask and practise answering them.	d) Discuss the CV and letters of application. Make notes on what you think is interesting, well done or less well done.
e) Take turns to go to the three interviewers for your interview.	e) Interview the applicants. All three interviewers should ask each applicant questions and take notes.
STEP 3: Evaluation	
f) Note down what you did well. Discuss how you could improve your performance.	f) Discuss the interviews. Use your checklists and notes to decide who should get the job.
g) Join up with the interviewers. Together, say what you have learned from the task.	g) Join up with the applicants. Together, say what you have learned from the task.

➜ *SF 19: Taking part in an interview (p. 170)*

A

1 Paraphrases

a) When you talk to someone and you don't know a word, you can describe what you want to say. Find the words to match these paraphrases and write them down.
1 Work done by someone who is not paid and it helps the local area.
2 The American name for school for six- to ten- or eleven-year-olds.
3 The training or preparation at the beginning of an event like a summer camp or a new job.
4 A British secondary school that you have to pay to attend.
5 Money given to pay for the studies of a good student whose family can't pay for it themselves.

b) Write English paraphrases for these words. Use relative clauses.
1 volunteer 2 supervisor 3 semester 4 nursery school 5 A level exams

c) Write a short text using at least six of the words from parts a) and b).

2 Collocations

a) Make collocations with the words in the boxes.

apply · be · do · complete · gain · have · participate · write	a personal statement · an internship · eligible for a college/university place · experience of/in · for a course/job · in an exchange programme · an (online) application/a form · responsibility (for) · to a college/company

b) Use correct collocations to complete the sentences about Robert in your exercise book.
Robert is [1]... for an internship on a company's website. He would like to [2]... where he will [3]... some designing advertising and this one seems perfect. He is now [4]... explaining something about himself and why he wants the internship. He writes that he got interested in this area last year when he [5]... with a secondary school in France. During that year he did an internship at a French company where he [6]... using computers for graphic design. He has already [7]... for a course in that subject and he only needs to pass his A levels next spring to [8]... . He attaches examples of his own designs and that's it – application completed!

c) Write eight sentences of your own using the collocations in a).

3 Big decisions (Future forms)

John meets Trevor on the street, while Miriam and Becca are at a careers exhibition.
Choose the correct future form to complete the dialogues.

John: Wow Trevor! You're all dressed up. What's the special occasion?
Trevor: There isn't one. I'm on my way to the photo studio. I [1]... (have) my photo taken.
John: OK, and what [2]... (do) with it?
Trevor: I [3]... (put) it on my CV and on my profile on Candidate.com.
John: Brilliant! I [4]... (come) with you. If you don't mind, that is.
Trevor: OK, but only if you promise you [5]... (make) me laugh.

Miriam: This exhibition is great, isn't it? So many stands, so many interesting companies.
Becca: So many people! I [6]... (go) back to the Bristol Uni stand when there aren't so many people around it. They have an interesting degree in animal medicine that maybe I [7]... (apply for).
Miriam: I gave my details to a German scientific company. You can work and study with them. They [8]... (hold) interviews next month. But they had a long list of names already, so I'm not sure they [9]... (invite) me.
Becca: What?! Not interview Miriam? Miriam who got second prize in the UK Young Scientist of the Year? I'm sure you [10]... (be) top of their list.

4 The Duke of Edinburgh Award (Non-defining relative clauses)

The following sentences are about the Duke of Edinburgh Award. Write the two sentences as a single sentence by adding the second sentence as a non-defining relative clause.
Use *whose, who,* or *which*, and add commas.

1 In 1956, the Duke of Edinburgh started the Duke of Edinburgh Award with the help of a German expert on education, Kurt Hahn. The Duke was married to Queen Elizabeth. He died in 2021.
2 The DoEA organization recognizes the work of young people in volunteering, becoming healthy and gaining work-related skills. Its goal is to help young people improve their life and career chances.
3 The Award is normally done in your free time and can take between six and twelve months. The award exists in gold, silver, and bronze.
4 The international version of the organization currently has over a million participants in 130 countries. It is also active in Germany.
5 Sixteen-year-old Anja is doing the Bronze Award. She lives in Augsburg.
6 She volunteers at a local charity every Saturday afternoon.
The charity makes and delivers meals to older people living alone.
7 As part of the 'Bronze', Anja and some other DoEA participants are going on a camping trip for two nights in August. The participants are around her age.
8 Then later this year, she is going to do work experience in a hospital. This will complete her Bronze Award.

5 MIXED BAG Hello from Munich!

Jennie is a British exchange student in Munich. She emails her friends.
Complete her email with the right words.

F K U T

Hi everyone,

I can't believe that I [1]… *here in Munich* [2]… *a month already. Times flies when you're* [3]… *fun! My host family – the Brauns - are wonderful and my host sister,* [4]… *I share a room with, is really cool. But the Bavarian accent! I* [5]… *never* [6]… *German spoken in such a sing-song sort of way before I* [7]… *here. Our German books in school* [8]… *have a better range of accents in the listening tasks. The Brauns live in a two-bedroom apartment* [9]… *is quite smaller than what we have at home. Plus, I* [10]… *remember that we* [11]… *wear our street shoes inside,* [12]… *is a good idea actually. The Brauns watch a lot less TV than we do (I miss English TV!) and* [13]… *family things together is really important. Sunday is the big family day. Back home, we* [14]… *shopping on Sundays, but here the shops* [15]… *to open. If the weather* [16]… *nice on Sundays, the Brauns always* [17]… *on an Ausflug (a trip) to the countryside. My host dad,* [18]… *doesn't speak much English, works in a company* [19]… *makes products for hospitals. That's where this time next month I* [20]… *my two-week work experience. I'm really* [21]… *to doing that. I'm enjoying school a lot* [22]… *the fact that we* [23]… *wear uniforms. The school itself is much bigger than ours back in Nuneaton and there's even a girl in my class* [24]… *dad comes from London.* [25]… *all the school subjects in German is much more tiring* [26]… *I expected, but while the rest of my class are in their English lesson, I attend an extra German lesson,* [27] … *is for kids who moved to Germany, and that's a big help. OK, I have to finish now. Will you write to me when you* [28]… *time? It* [29]… *great to hear from you.*

Love, Jennie.

B 6 Learning from experience

Read the text about work experience all the way through. Then do the exercises.

a It's a problem many young people face when they enter the job market for the first time: it's difficult to get a job without having experience, but how can you get that experience without having a job? That's why the chance to do an internship while still at school is such a good opportunity. Hopefully your work experience is a rewarding experience, but nothing is perfect, and we have some tips for you if it isn't going as well as you'd hoped.

b You might find yourself given boring tasks – making coffee or photocopying for example. But remember! Somebody has to do these tasks and it's an easy way to make a good impression. Watch and listen. Get to know the names of the employees – you can learn a lot by watching how they work together, how they talk to each other, and how they handle disagreements. If you still feel bored, then think of ideas and talk to your supervisor. Your chances of making your internship more interesting will be better if you suggest something positive, instead of complaining.

c Sometimes work experience participants feel they are being asked to work as an unpaid full-time employee. While it is positive to have some real responsibility in your work experience, it is important that it is not too much. Being enthusiastic doesn't mean saying 'yes' to every request. Learning to say 'no' when you need to is an important life and work skill. But do not wait until the end of your internship – try to talk to your supervisor at an earlier stage and have positive suggestions ready.

d Do you regret your school's or your own choice of internship? Well, it's not forever and you can still try and get the most out of it. Think about why you don't like it. Maybe you don't find the work as interesting as you expected. It's better to find that out now rather than later – after a degree in the subject, for example. Completing a successful work experience, even if you dislike it, shows a future employer that you are reliable and willing to stay with something until the end. And learning what you do not want to do with your life is a valuable lesson in itself.

a) Read the text and then match the headings (1–4) with the paragraphs (a–d)

1 Feeling under-challenged? Keep your eyes and ears open
2 No experience – no job
3 Not the place for you? Make the most of it!
4 Overworked? You are not a slave

b) Choose the best answer based on your reading of the text.

1 Why is doing work experience while still at school a good opportunity?
   a) It means spending less time at school.
   b) It can help you get your first job.
   c) Because it is always a positive experience.

2 What should someone do if they have to do boring tasks in their work experience?
   a) They should make a list of the problems and complain to their supervisor.
   b) They should get to know the employees and ask them to help.
   c) They should make positive suggestions to the supervisor.

3 Why can doing an internship you didn't like be a positive experience?
   a) It can help you decide which career you really want to do.
   b) It teaches you how to accept that nobody has the perfect job.
   c) It shows you that you should be more careful about what choices you make.

c) Write a comment (about 200 words) explaining whether you agree or disagree with this statement.
"Young people doing work experience should be paid."
Use ideas from the text and your own ideas.

C 7 A holiday job

Imagine you want a new phone, but your parents don't want to give you the money for it.
They also don't want you to spend your summer working a holiday job.
Prepare a four-minute talk to convince your parents that a holiday job is the right thing for you.
Consider arguments for and against holiday jobs.

Next steps: Going to university in the UK and US

Young people all around the globe wonder about who they will become and how they will get there. The opportunities and paths after they finish school can be very different.

In the UK:

- Over 300 universities and colleges.
- 2.3 million students attend college or university including over 430,000 international students.
- Around 40% of all 18-year-olds apply to university and college.

In the US:

- Over 2,600 colleges and universities.
- About 20 million students attend college or university.
- Around 65% of high school graduates enrol in college or university after graduating.

What steps do students take to study at a university or college?

In the UK:

- Universities often require that students do their A levels (or Highers / Advanced Highers in Scotland) in the subject area they plan to study, so they need to have a good idea of their course interest by the beginning of Sixth Form (or S5 in Scotland).
- All students apply to university through the online platform UCAS – Universities and Colleges Admissions Service.

  To complete the UCAS application students:
  - Select the subject that most interests them.
  - Select five universities or colleges to apply to.
  - Write a personal statement.
  - Ask a teacher or coach who knows them and their work well to write a recommendation letter.

In the US:

- Students do not need to have a clear idea of what they want to study when they apply to university in their last year of high school.
- Most students take standardized tests (SAT or ACT), which cover general knowledge and academic skills learned over the four years of high school, including multiple-choice questions in math, English, and science.
- Most colleges evaluate a student's entire high school performance, as well as considering after-school activities in sports, the arts and community service in their decision whether to accept a student or not.
- Students can use the online platform 'Common App' to apply to as many colleges and universities as they wish. As in the UK, students must write a personal statement and include a letter of recommendation in their application.

a) **Role play:** Read the text on p. 68 carefully.
Partner A: You are a student in the UK in the Sixth form.
Partner B: You work at the university admissions office in the UK. Explain to the Sixth Form student what steps they must take to earn a place at your university.

b) **Role play:** Swap roles.
Partner B: You are a senior at a high school in the US.
Partner A: You work at the university admissions office in the US. Explain to the student what steps they must take to earn a place at your university.

UK school system reconsidered!

(blog excerpt by Adam McNulty)

Before my mum opened the envelope with my A-level results, I felt like I was about to fall into a hole in the earth. I had been worried sick for days, weeks.
After all, my whole future life depended on those letters and numbers.
It was happening to all my friends too – the terrible pressure! That's the reality in the UK's education system.
If you want to go to a good uni, you've got to have the numbers! Is that how I really wanted to be defined?

After all, from what I hear, top colleges in the US look at all the students' strengths, not just the academic ones: in the arts, as a volunteer, in summer enrichment programmes, clubs, and sports. They even say that there are no minimum grade requirements.

If I could present my experiences like that, I wouldn't be so stressed out about my results. I'm not just a set of numbers!

Stressed Samantha

(blog excerpt by Teen Voices USA)

I'm a high school senior and I want to be a research biologist. But these days, I barely have time to finish my lab reports.

I'm applying to some of the most competitive colleges in the country that, in addition to top scores on the SATs and the highest GPAs, are looking for 'all-around' high achievers. This means that I'm spending my school hours doing all sorts of after-school activities: I'm an editor of the student newspaper, a member of the robotics club and I sing in the school choir.

After school, I have basketball practice, do many hours of community service, and next month, I'm doing a two-week internship at a biology lab.

When I finally get home, I still have to do homework, study for the SATs and work on my college applications. The personal statement is the hardest! How can I know what I should write about when I'm involved in so many different things! I know the colleges are looking for students who are good at everything, but that's just not me!

c) Read the excerpts from two articles above. In groups, discuss the challenges that students applying to college and university in the UK and US face.
Make notes about the similarities and the differences.

Report your results to the class.

EXTRA Imagine you are applying to study at college or university in the UK or US. Research the programmes at one or more universities in the UK or the US.

Write a paragraph explaining which country and which course of study you would choose and why.

➜ **Workbook** *8 (p. 90)*

Next steps: Degree programmes

Degree programmes in the US and UK

What are the possible paths for students that have completed four years of high school in the US or their A levels in the UK? Although there are some differences, higher-education programmes in both countries are quite similar and mostly are identified by the same terminology.

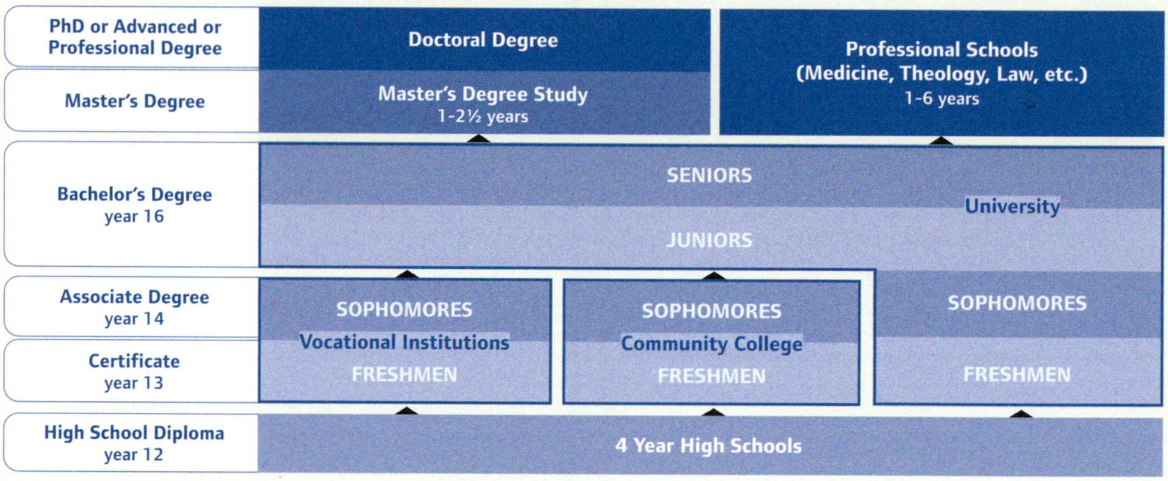

Higher education in the USA

The path of higher education

As you progress through the system of degree programmes at a university – from the bachelor's degree to the master's and finally the doctorate, your studies and research become more specialized and independent. When you are in a doctorate programme, your research is usually mostly independent and you are also often guiding undergraduate students as an assistant teacher.

Associate's degree In the US, associate degrees are offered by community colleges and take about two years to complete. These programmes cost much less than the programmes listed below and are often attended by students who have part-time or full-time jobs.

Bachelor's degree (BA, BS) programmes are usually completed in four years in the US and 3–4 years in the UK. While students in the US can study a variety of subjects in their first two years and choose their subject of study at the end of their second year, students in the UK must decide on their course of study from the outset.

A Master's Degree (MA) can be completed in one or two years following the bachelor's degree in the US and UK. Doing a major research paper or project is usually a requirement for graduation.

Professional degrees in the UK and US: Medicine, dentistry and veterinary studies are four-year programmes for students with a BS or BA degree.
Law school requires three years of full-time study after a BA or BS, while engineering, pharmacy or architecture can be earned through a five to six year program after high school or an MA program for students with a BA or BS.

Doctoral programmes (PhD) require an additional three to five years of study beyond the master's degree. They are the highest degrees awarded and often involve writing a book-length research project.

Princeton University Campus, Princeton. NJ, USA

What is the cost of attending a university or college in the UK or the US?

The cost of attending college or university in the US can range from $4,000 a year for two-year community colleges to $26,000 for public universities. Private colleges and universities are extremely expensive, with yearly tuition often costing over $35,000 a year.

In the UK, tuition fees were first introduced in 1998 and are now £9,000 (or over $12,000) per year at many universities.

A ticket to success?

Where you attend university in the US and the UK can have a big impact both on your learning experience and your future success.

Princeton, Harvard, Yale and Columbia Universities – all on the east coast of the US – are well-known throughout the world. Earning a degree from one of these universities is considered a high achievement. They are also among the oldest universities in the nation; all were established before the signing of the Declaration of Independence in 1776! Eighteen US presidents, 300 Nobel laureates, many politicians, Supreme Court judges and billionaires attended these institutions.

Oxford and Cambridge are the most famous and oldest universities in the UK. Like the American universities mentioned above, top politicians – including 28 Prime Ministers and 72 Nobel laureates – studied and graduated from Oxford.

Admission to all of these universities is competitive and yearly tuition is very costly.

Although it has often been said that a degree from one of these institutions is a ticket to success, many influential and successful people have studied at community colleges as well, including the actors Morgan Freeman and Tom Hanks, US Senator Elizabeth Warren, Star Wars director George Lucas and the creator of Apple computers, Steve Jobs.

a) Review the chart and the texts. Make notes about the differences between the degree programmes in the US and UK.

b) Do you remember being asked as a child: 'What do you want to be when you grow up?' What did you answer then? What about now? Working in groups, discuss these points:
- Your answer to that question then and now.
- How that question made you feel then and now.
- Whether you would consider attending one of the degree programmes described on this page.

Use adjectives from p. 86 to describe your response.

c) Research a university in the UK or the US. Find out:
- the location: city, suburban, small town,
- the degree programmes they offer,
- the yearly tuition,
- other features or special facilities they offer.

Report your results to the class.

www Follow the link for more information.

→ **Workbook** *9 (p. 91)*

A sustainable world – online and off

1 Our world

a) Imagine you are in one of the scenes depicted in the photos. Describe the situation.

b) Write a provocative or catchy caption for each photo.

c) Compare your captions and agree on the best one for each photo. Then present your group's best captions in class.

2 A clear perspective

a) Read the six quotes on the right and choose the one which is most meaningful to you.

b) Connect the meaning of your quote to one of the four images A–D. Make notes about:
- what connects the image to the quote
- why you chose it
- how you would explain the quote's meaning to your classmates.

c) Form groups with classmates who have chosen a different quote.
Explain your quote to the other group members using your notes from b).

EXTRA Read the quote below and discuss how this definition helps you interpret photos A and C.

In 1987, the United Nations Brundtland Commission defined sustainable development as "development that meets the needs of the present without compromising the ability of future generations to meet their own needs."

A

1 *"Waste isn't waste until we waste it."*
Will.I.Am, American rapper

2 *"We, as youth, must now be the change that we seek. If you don't stand for something, you'll fall for anything."*
D'Angelo McDade, 18, Leader of Chicago's Peace Warriors at March for Our Lives, March 24, 2018

C

 → Workbook 1 (p. 66)

B

3 *"Humankind has not woven the web of life. We are but one thread within it. Whatever we do to the web, we do to ourselves. All things are bound together. All things connect."*
Chief Seattle, Native American Suquamish and Duwamish Chieftain, 1854

4 *"We don't have to engage in grand, heroic actions to participate in change. Small acts, when multiplied by millions of people, can transform the world."*
Howard Zinn, American historian

5 *"The greatest threat to our planet is the belief that someone else will save it."*
Robert Swan, British renewable energy advocate

6 *"Social media has taken over in America to such an extreme that to get my own kids to look back a week in their history is a miracle, let alone 100 years."*
Steven Spielberg, film director (E.T., Indiana Jones, etc.)

D

Your task **EXTRA**

At the end of this Unit: You will give a four-minute speech that expresses your opinion on fast fashion, a specific type of food diet or long-distance air travel. Your speech should also explain how your position can help lead to a more sustainable future.

1 Shireen's clean teen challenge

Shireen is about to graduate from the Bayside Prep School in Tampa, Florida, USA and enjoys public speaking. Here is a transcript of a talk that Shireen gave to an audience of students from her school. Her talk is similar to the kind of presentations you can see on the internet where a speaker has a short time to share an idea, usually with nothing on the stage but a microphone headset and some visuals.

Hi everyone! I want you to raise your hand if you've gone for more than an hour today without looking at your phone. I'm Shireen and I used to be addicted to my cell phone. Look around you. How many hands do you see? From this little experiment it's clear we're addicted to our phones.

At exam time we would normally be studying, right? Didn't you use to worry about end of semester grades coming up? All of that stress ... you know how it is. I used to spend my days texting, tweeting and scrolling. I wouldn't eat, let alone study. And then, at night, my friends would ping me right and left, all of them worried that they were going to fail. So I decided to do something about it.

I cleaned my room. No, not my bedroom. That stayed as messy as ever! But I did clean a room – my digital room. And you know what I found out? That it is **definitely** possible to control *it* instead of *it* controlling *me*.

I also challenged myself to get off social media for a week. It changed my life. No joke. The first couple of days, it did feel strange. I only communicated in person, so in the evenings I spent much more time doing homework and watching movies, and I was more focused and alert. And then I got used to it. My friends started putting down their phones when they hung out with me. I started looking around at my environment, noticing things, feeling things. It really did change my life!

Under no circumstances do I expect you to stop using social media forever, so I came up with NEW RULES for using our devices wisely, and here they are:

- Allow yourself only three apps and delete the apps that you use the most (I know ... it's hard!).
- Go grayscale!
- Don't take your phone to the school cafeteria or restroom.
- Remove notifications and turn off your phone's sound during times you know you shouldn't be on social media or shouldn't be disturbed.
- Charge your phone and laptop anywhere but in your bedroom.
- Make sure you are seeing your friends instead of texting them.
- Go on dates instead of flirting online.

Now, I challenge you to stay off social media for one week, just like I did! I'll call it SHIREEN'S CLEAN TEEN CHALLENGE. At the end of the week, share your experiences (the highs and lows) at our next assembly. Our principal agreed to give a prize to whoever can show no social media use for a week. All the details are on our school website.
Happy unplugging!

2 Shireen's message

a) Identify the main idea that Shireen presented in her Clean Teen Challenge talk.

b) Make a table and compare Shireen's life before and after she completed the social media challenge. More help → *p. 151*

c) In a paragraph, explain why you would be interested in staying off social media for one week or not.

d) Discuss Hofmann's quote above with reference to an example from your own life.

3 Using visuals well

a) Match each of the slides 1–8 above to a statement from Shireen's talk.

b) Imagine that you are Shireen and write an additional (personal and/or funny) statement for two of the slides.

c) Read your statements to your group and evaluate how effective they are.

4 Being persuasive

The statements below are guidelines for a strong presentation from Chris Anderson, a curator at TED Talks.

- *Limit your talk to one major idea.*
- *Give your listeners a reason to care and make it worth sharing.*
- *Build your idea, piece by piece, using concepts that your audience already understands.*
- *Use media to make ideas accessible.*

a) Evaluate Shireen's presentation according to the points on the left. Where is she effective and where could she improve?

b) Present your ideas to the class.

EXTRA Say if Shireen's Teen Talk is informal or formal and what effect that might have on the audience. Give examples from the text.

→ **Workbook** *2–3 (pp. 66–67)*

Language help

Used to* and *would

Both *would* and *used to* can be used to describe repeated actions in the past:
Before I turned 10, I used to sleep with the light on.

Would is sometimes used to give the idea of remembering in a sentimental way:
When I was a child, my grandma would always give me the biggest piece of cake.

Used to can also be used to describe past situations, with verbs such as *be, have, live, love*:
This building used to be a hotel.

Would cannot be used with that kind of verb.

➜ *GF 1.3: Talking about the past (p. 182)*

1 My sister used to be nice (*used to* and *would*)

Complete this text about looking back at a relationship in the past with *would* or *used to*. Point out the sentences where only *used to* is possible. Explain why you chose *used to* or *would* for the other gaps.

I remember that my little sister ...[1] always sit next to me when I played my favourite video game. She ...[2] look over my shoulder, but she never really understood how it worked. She ...[3] love hearing the sounds and watching the images. She ...[4] even imitate the sounds. I ...[5] have a big screen cell phone and whenever I picked it up, her face ...[6] light up with excitement. I remember how she ...[7] try to grab my phone to play. She ...[8] be so cute, but now that she's older, she tends to ignore me and my video games!

2 Simon used to be my best friend (*used to* and *would*)

Read what different people say about people they know.
Then complete the sentences with *used to, didn't use to, would, or wouldn't.*

Joe: I ...[1] love visiting my aunt on the farm because she ...[2] prepare fresh eggs for breakfast every morning.
Ann: Last year, Simon ...[3] text me every 10 minutes, but I ...[4] answer back until after class was over.
Pete: My baby brother ...[5] like broccoli, but now he loves it!
Sam: I think I recognize that girl from last year; ...[6] she ...[7] attend our dance class?
Kay: ...[8] Miriam ...[9] work hard? Now, she seems so lazy!
Chris: My best friend ...[10] live in Hamburg, but that was 10 years ago.

3 How they used to do it (*used to* and *would*)

Look at the pictures of old devices. Make notes about how technology was different in the past.

Write at least four sentences with *used to* and *would* describing how people used technology back then.

4 I used to play with dolls, but now I wear jeans ... (*used to*)

a) Write three *I used to + verb-* and three *but now I + verb*-clauses on six separate index cards.

b) Make two piles: one with the *'I used to ...'* cards and one with the *'but now I ...'* cards.

c) Take turns choosing a card from the *'I used to ...'* pile and one from the *'but now I ...'* pile to form new and 'funny' sentences. Read them aloud.

Language help

Adding emphasis

The auxiliaries *do*, *does* and *did* can be used to give additional emphasis to verbs or to contradict what someone else has claimed.

It really did change my life.

Other ways to give emphasis are using adverbs such as: *really, fairly, pretty, totally, definitely, somewhat, so, such, never, ever.*

Some expressions with a negative or restrictive meaning can go at the beginning of the sentence for special emphasis. Examples are: *never, rarely, only later, under no circumstances, no sooner,* etc. Note the change in word order (inversion) in this example:

Under no circumstances do I expect you to stop using social media forever.

➔ *GF 11: Emphatic structures (pp. 209-210)*

5 Even the principal uses social media (Expressing emphasis)

The principal of Shireen's school gave a short speech on the dangers of social media. Here is an excerpt. Identify which underlined verbs use the emphatic *do* or and which do not. Then find the three adverbs that add emphasis.

Do you find yourselves getting headaches from your phone beeping constantly? Do you like being reachable whenever and wherever you are? I must say, I do find social media really stressful. Don't get me wrong! I do appreciate being able to stay in contact with my friends and family who live far away. But I wonder ... Does social media totally control my life? It definitely does seem impossible to get away from it. While you do your homework, do you resist checking your phone when it flashes? I know that I do tend to check my phone at meetings. I do urge you to consider Shireen's new rules for using your phones. In the future, more social networks will appear. Do pay attention to what role they play in your lives, ok?

6 I followed Shireen's advice but ... (Expressing emphasis)

Use the emphatic *do* + *find, manage, use, think* to fill in the gaps. Then identify the inversions.

After listening to Shireen's talk the other day, I ...[1] myself inspired. It was really hard to delete most of the apps on my phone. I ...[2] to get rid of four of them, but I kept two. It was strange to find my phone charging in the kitchen instead of in my bedroom, but I ...[3] it less often at night. I ...[4] my friends appreciate how we are talking together more, but I should ask them myself. It's been only a day that I haven't used my phone at all except for calls, and already I'm missing being on social media. No way will I be able to keep this up for a week!

7 Stephanie's date with a cell phone (Expressing emphasis)

Find sentences in the text about Stephanie and Mark that you can change to emphasize contrasts and remember to invert the subject and verb.

Stephanie had rarely been asked out on a date. Then Mark asked her out. Of course, she said yes! She realized only later that Mark was addicted to video games. They had no sooner ordered their pizza than Mark took out his cell phone. While she ate, he played. She had never felt so uncomfortable. There was no way she was going to get through the evening! Stephanie decided only later that she would tell all her friends about her date with a cell phone.

More help ➔ *p. 151*

On this page you will work with words that help you talk about relationships and feelings. Then you will write a short text about the relationship between two people.

1 Word field: Relationships (Structuring vocabulary)

a) Order the phrases in the box in a sequence in which they might occur.
1 be attracted to sb. 2 ...

+be attracted to sb. · +be seeing sb. · +fall in love · +date sb. · get back together · give sb. a second chance · go out with sb. · +break up (with sb.) · +get to know sb.

b) Compare your sequences.

2 Adjectives (Feelings)

a) Group these words in two lists.

afraid · angry · annoyed · confused · +cross · disappointed · frightened · glad · glum · happy · hopeful · nervous · optimistic · pessimistic · +pleased · sad · scared · shocked · unhappy · upset · worried

negative feelings	positive feelings
afraid	...

b) Make a table like this:

afraid	angry	happy	sad
...	...	...	

Then find words in a) with a similar meaning and add them to your table.

c) Adjectives can be normal or strong. Match a strong adjective to each normal adjective.
normal: afraid · angry · happy · sad
strong: +furious · +heartbroken · +terrified · thrilled

d) Using at least two of the new adjectives for each sentence, write about how you felt when:
- you were lost in a dark forest · your cat died
- you won a race · your bike was stolen.

TIP Words like very, +absolutely or really make adjectives stronger. Use
- very only with normal adjectives:
  I was very happy to see him again.
- absolutely only with strong adjectives:
  I was absolutely thrilled to see him again.
- really with normal or strong adjectives.
  I was really happy/thrilled to see him again.

3 Collocations (Relationships)

Choose one word from each box to make a collocation for each underlined name. Then rewrite the sentences using the collocation you've made.

1 Jake has just started going out with Sarah.
Sarah is Jake's latest girlfriend/new girlfriend.
2 My family knows Mr Green, but not very well.
Mr Green is ...
3 Dad knew Sally well years ago at school.
4 Jane isn't seeing Max any more.
5 Helen is one of the few girls Mike is friendly with.
6 Pete is almost the only person I can talk to about this.

family · school · +ex- · old · new · latest · +male · +female · close · good · great · best · special · true

+acquaintance
friend
mate
boyfriend
girlfriend

Write a short text about the relationship between two characters (from a book, film, TV series ...) Use eight words from 1, 2 and 3.

More help → p. 152

Read each other's text and check the correct use of the new words/phrases. Did the new words/phrases make the text more interesting to read?

1 Noah

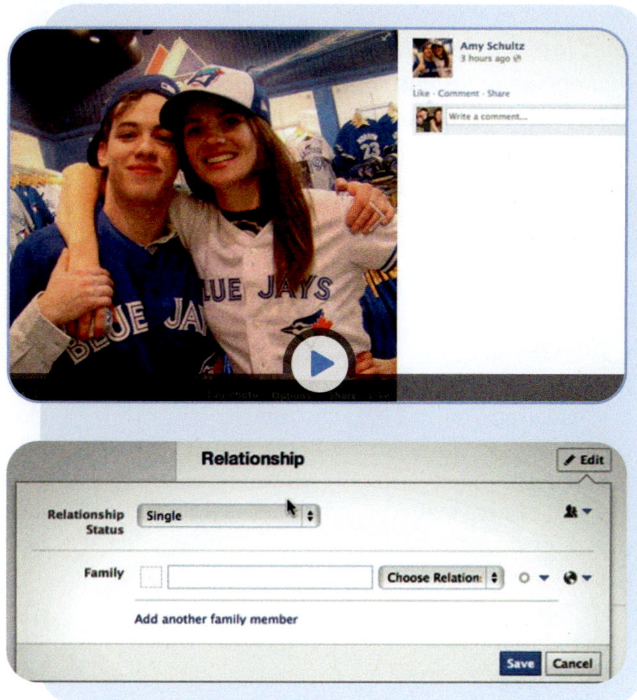

a) Say what the film still shows you.

b) Watch the film and say what happens.
These phrases may help you:
· visit a website · open a window
· log in/out · enter a password
· post sth. · send a message
· update your status/profile
· hack sb's account/texts
· end a call

c) Write a summary of the film in about five sentences.
Comment on each other's summaries and revise yours if necessary.

d) Say if you think Noah listens to what Amy says while they're chatting.
Give reasons for your opinion.

e) Look at the still on the right.
Say how you think Noah feels at this moment in the film.
How might Amy feel when she finds out what has happened?

EXTRA How might the situation at the end of the film have been different if Noah and Amy had spoken face to face?

2 Making the film: Sounds

a) Say what kind of sounds you can hear in films.
Think of voices, music and other sounds, including background noise.

b) Listen as Noah chats to three girls on webcam later in the film (sound only).
Make a table like this and take notes to describe the sounds you hear.

	Voices	Music	Other sounds
I can hear	girls: excited voices ...	...	...

c) Now watch the scene and say what it is about.
Then use your notes to link the sounds to the scene.
• You hear the excited voices when three girls ...
• ...

Say what effect all the different sounds have on the viewer.
• The voices/music/... give you the impression that / make you think that ...

➜ *SF 15: Viewing (p. 167)*

1 Fast fashion – clothing and sustainability

'Fast fashion' describes a trend in the fashion industry of producing cheap versions of designer clothes that appear in fashion shows and magazines. The low prices and rapid change in styles encourage people to buy more clothes to keep up with new trends. They throw out barely worn clothes either because they are no longer 'in' or to make room in their closets! When people buy so much cheap clothing, there is also a dramatic rise in waste: clothes essentially become a single-use product like plastic forks.

What's it made of?
The material of the clothes we wear matters. Synthetic fibres, like polyester, are made from oil and coal, which are both fossil fuels.
Polyester fibres take over 200 years to decompose.
Microplastics are released into waste water each time clothes made from synthetics are washed.

What about natural fibres?
Cotton clothing can also be environmentally destructive: more land, large volumes of fresh water, polluting chemicals and pesticides are needed for the production of new cotton textiles.
The need for water causes problems for water supplies in places like China, India and Central Asia where much of our clothing is produced.

Who makes our clothes?
Garment workers are exploited across the globe in order to produce cheap clothing. Exploitation takes place at every level of production, from the picking of cotton to the manufacture of clothing.
There are 40 million garment workers in the world today. Nine out of ten garment workers interviewed in Bangladesh said they were paid such a low wage that they were not able to buy enough food for their families.

Is fast fashion sustainable?
Textile production contributes more to climate change than aviation and shipping combined.
If the fast fashion trend continues, the UN says that by 2050 the equivalent of almost three planets could be required to provide the natural resources for clothing production.

Environmental impact produced by clothing made of synthetic fibres

2 Environmental effects of synthetics

a) Match statements from the text to the illustration.

b) Partner A: Explain the environmental impact shown in phases 1 and 2 of the diagram to your partner.
Partner B: Explain the environmental impact shown in phases 3 and 4 of the diagram to your partner.

3 Made in ...: A class survey

a) Check the labels on your partner's shirt or dress.
Note down the material and country where it was manufactured. Add your findings to the class survey.

b) Discuss the survey's results with the entire class.

4 A passion for fashion ... but at what cost?

Every week, my fashion blog, ***THE JAZZY PRINCESS****, will give you ideas of how to look trendy with clothes that don't cost a lot. Please post your comments ... I really like to hear from my followers! Your favourite fashionista, Jennifer*

This is my new look for the summer. What do you think? I bought a bunch of these white T-shirts for almost nothing. The Young Value Shop has tons of these T-shirts in lots of colours. I'm decorating them with rhinestones. Have you got other ideas for decorating them? Let me know. By the way, they're so cheap, you can own a dozen!

Samantha Brilliant idea, Jennifer. I have colourful fabric markers, so I'm going to get a few of the same T-shirts to decorate. *30 minutes ago*

Tom I don't know, Samantha. By buying new, cheap fashion, you're contributing to global pollution. Try being a fashionista activist and buy the T-shirts at a charity shop. *20 minutes ago*

Samantha Yuck! Who wants to wear someone else's thrown-out clothes? Jennifer, you're my favorite fashion influencer and I love your creativity. Anyway, we recycle at home, so I don't feel guilty buying a few T-shirts … *15 minutes ago*

Kaya @Tom: lots of us who like to follow the latest trends only have what we make from babysitting or granny gifts. We have no choice but to shop at the stores Jennifer is recommending if we want to look good. *6 minutes ago*

Katie @Kaya: I'm with Tom. I bought black jeans and a button-down shirt at a charity shop for less than the cost of one T-shirt! We're going to be responsible for making sure the planet can sustain life in a healthy way. We owe it to ourselves to shop responsibly! *2 minutes ago*

www Follow the link for more information.

5 Words in the fashion industry

Find the phrases from the box in the texts on pp. 118–119. Write a sentence explaining the relationship between the phrase and the topic of fast fashion.

ex.: Synthetic fibres: Many inexpensive clothes are made from synthetic fibres. Synthetics are produced from coal and oil.

charity shop • environmental impact • fashion trends • garment worker • pesticides • synthetic fibres • textiles

6 Reversing the trend

After carefully reading both texts, discuss what you think of second-hand shopping and its relationship to sustainability.

Think about your own shopping habits and write a comment in response to both Samantha and Tom.

EXTRA Choose one action and write a statement that presents the action, the challenge and how to overcome the challenge.

Action: Organize a clothing swap with friends. • **Challenge:** Not wanting to look like someone else.

Statement: Invite all your friends to your house to swap clothes. Personalize your tops and bottoms with iron-on patches, embroidery or mixing and matching, so your own style shines through!

More help → p. 152

→ Workbook 10 (p. 71)

1 REVISION Do you know what you are eating? (Simple present and present progressive)

In addition to clothing, our eating habits can contribute to CO_2 emissions. Complete the text with the correct form of the verb.

melt • enjoy • consider • know • eat / not eat • become • produce • enjoy • come from • bring • go • dream • be

A science teacher takes her students out for lunch and explains: "You might be surprised to know that right now, you ...[1] a vegan meal. Sarah, you ...[2] a meatless soyburger. And the cheese that ...[3] on Tom's pizza? It's not made from milk! In general, people ...[4] about vegetarianism, but they ...[5] confused about veganism. ...[6] they the same? Not at all! Vegans ...[7] no animal products, while vegetarians ...[8] animals, but ...[9] products that ...[10] from them (such as dairy and eggs). ...[11] you all ...[12] now about sausages, fried chicken and roast beef? Or ...[13] you ...[14] veganism to help the planet? After all, cows, pigs, sheep and other animals ...[15] 14.5% of global greenhouse gas emissions!! Look! The waitress ...[16] dessert to our table! Black bean brownies! Hey! Kids? Where ...[17] you ...[18] ?"

➜ *GF 1.2: Talking about the present (p. 181)*

2 REVISION A trip to the second-hand shop (Simple past and past progressive)

Tom and Melanie went shopping at a second-hand shop. Here is Melanie's text to her friends about the experience. Complete her text with the correct form of the verb in brackets.

First, Tom ...[1] (fall) on the stairs as we ...[2] (board) the bus to go downtown. As we ...[3] (enter) the shop, he ...[4] (bump) into an old lady. He ...[5] (hold) a vase to show me when he suddenly ...[6] (drop) it! He even ...[7] (damage) a T-shirt while he ...[8] (try) it on! We ...[9] (leave) the shop in a hurry and ...[10] (go) to a pizza place. I suppose you already ...[11] (guess) what ...[12] (happen). As he...[13] (take) his pizza, all the toppings ...[14] (fall) off onto his lap!

➜ *GF 1.3: Talking about the past (p. 182)*

More help ➜ *p. 152*

3 REVISION The future game (*going to-* and *will-*future)

Play the future game. Work in groups of three. Take turns in throwing the dice and moving your piece on a copy of the game board. Use complete sentences to answer the question or to give your ideas about the topic in the box.

➜ *GF 1.5: Talking about the future (pp. 184–186)*

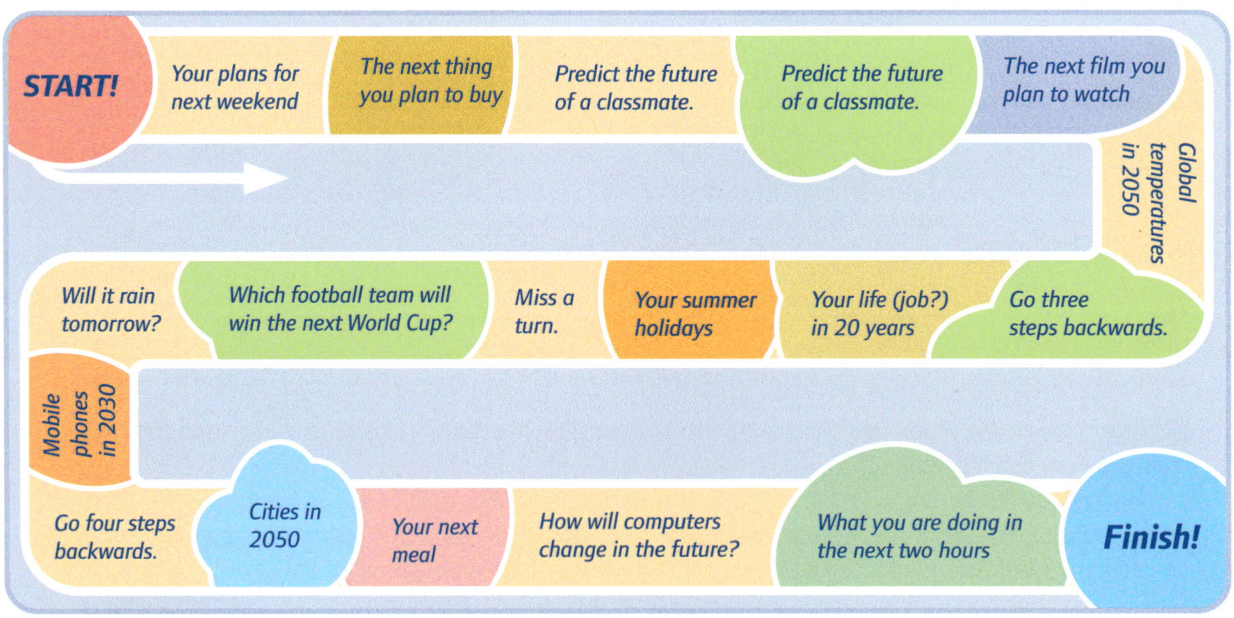

4 REVISION Problems with polyester (Present perfect and present perfect progressive)

Put the verbs in brackets into either the present perfect or present perfect progressive. Match the clauses (half sentences) 1–8, with the clauses a–h.

1 My friend Sarah ... (wear) a polyester shirt every day
2 Spots ... (appear) on her skin
3 Her boss says he ... (think) of ordering cotton shirts
4 He ... (read) the articles
5 I ... already ... (think) about refusing to eat there
6 I ... (enjoy) fish and chips there for ages
7 My mom ... (prepare) fish and chips at home
8 Still, I ... (hope) for weeks that he would switch to cotton

a since his wife mentioned her dislike of polyester.
b and I'm going to warn the boss.
c since she was hired at the fish and chip shop.
d so maybe I won't have to!
e so I've been telling her to wear cotton.
f and then I may even apply to work there too!
g so it would be hard to give that up!
h Sarah has given him recently.

➜ *GF 1.4 Talking about the past and the present (pp. 182–183)*

5 REVISION The Earth Guardian (Past perfect and past perfect progressive)

Complete the text about Xiuhtezcatl Martinez with the correct form of one of the verbs from the box. Use either the past perfect or the past perfect progressive.

speak up • teach • believe • ask • learn • speak

Xiuhtezcatl (pronounced 'Shoe-Tez-Caht') Martinez ...[1] people to open their eyes to the Earth's destruction for years before receiving the 2013 United States Volunteer Service Award from President Obama. He was only 13 at the time! By the age of 15, he ...[2] already ... to the General Assembly at the United Nations in New York. Before becoming the director of an international youth activist organization called Earth Guardians, Xiuhtezcatl ...[3] about ecology and sustainability from his mother, who started Earth Guardians high school in Hawaii. Throughout his childhood, his father Siri ...[4] Xiuhtezcatl about his Aztec roots, which influenced his outlook on the environment. After he ...[5] for most of his childhood, Xiuhtezcatl turned to rap music, using his own songs to communicate the message of his ancestors. The Aztecs ...[6] always ... that there was a single sacred force that sustains nature, which is now one of Xiuhtezcatl's main messages to young people.

➜ *GF 1.3: Talking about the past (pp. 183–184)*

More help ➜ *p. 152*

6 REVISION The Bavarian forest

For an assignment in her English class, Ingrid gave a talk about saving forests in Bavaria. Fill in the correct tense of the verb in brackets.

Good morning, class. I ...[1] always ... (love) trees, ever since I ...[2] (be) little. I remember one time – I must have been about five – I ...[3] (climb) my favourite tree when I ...[4] (fall) from a tall branch. While I ...[5] (heal) from a broken leg, my father ...[6] (teach) me about the amazing variety of trees in our state. Bavaria ...[7] (be) the woodland champion of Germany with a forest area of 2.6 million hectares. But Germany's forests ...[8] (suffer) lately. This past year, heat, drought, storms, forest fires and insects ...[9] (destroy) a great deal of German forests. For many months now, I ...[10] (work) with a youth organization to teach very young children about the importance of saving our forests. I ...[11] (give) a talk to elementary school students next week. [12]... you all ... (come)? I [13]... also ... (plan) to visit the Zwiesel Forest Museum next month to learn more about forests. I ...[14] (tell) you all more when I return! ...[15] (not forget): the Bavarian forest ...[16] (be) our heritage!

➜ **Workbook** *13–15 (pp. 73–74)*

7 STUDY SKILLS Talking about statistics

On this page you'll learn to identify different kinds of statistics and talk about what they tell you.

a) Choose the right word for each way of presenting statistics.

bar chart · pie chart · table

1 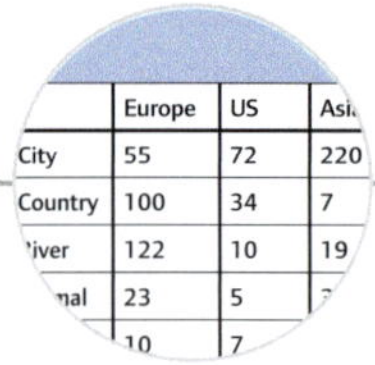

2 

3 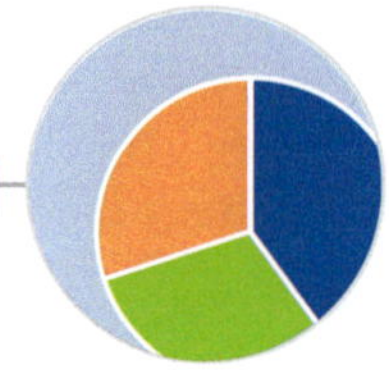

b) In groups of three, each student chooses one chart or table below. Use phrases from the box to tell your partners what information it gives.

1 *Where does the impact on the climate come from?*

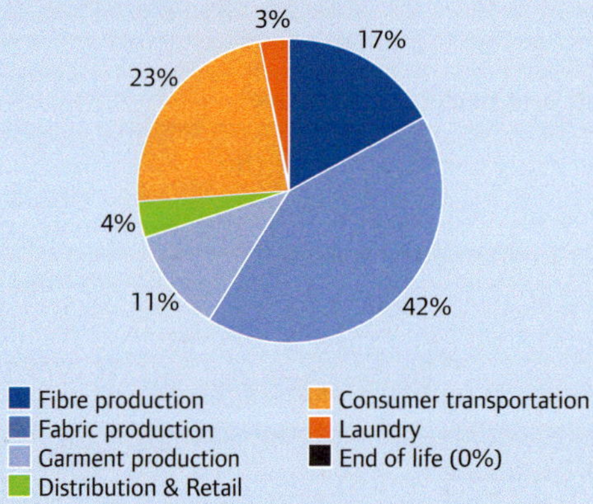

TIP Useful language

The table / bar chart / pie chart is about …

It gives us information about …
- *the percentage of / the number of …*
- *who / what / how many / what percentage of …*

The chart/table shows that …
- *most/more/fewer …*
- *a high percentage of / 25 per cent of …*
- *twice as many / three times as many …*

If you compare …
- *the percentage of / the number of …*

… you can see …

2 *CO_2 emissions by fibre type*

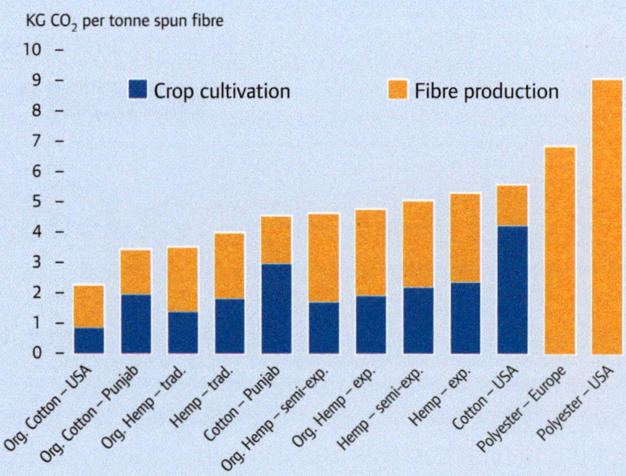

3 *Global share of market by types of fibre*

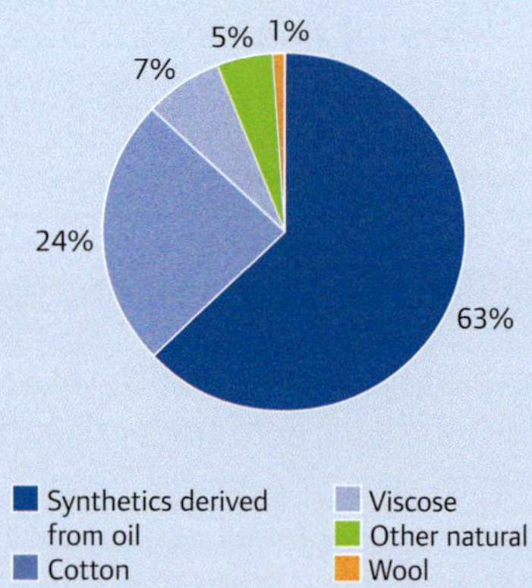

Source: SEI/ Schroders.com

c) Finish with a conclusion about what you have found out.

My main conclusion is that …

The most important thing I've learned is that …

One thing that I hadn't realized is …

➔ *SF 26: Talking about statistics (p. 176)*

 ➔ **Workbook** *16 (pp. 74–75)*

A balloon debate: Lifestyle choices and sustainability

a) Form groups of 5. Each group member should choose one lifestyle change from the list below. Imagine you represent that particular lifestyle choice and that, without your influence, people would not consider it.

- No air travel
- No meat-eating
- No using plastic
- No buying new clothes
- No having more than one child

b) Research your lifestyle change, take notes and collect statistics that support your arguments. Make sure you cover its impact on the environment, some of its 'leaders' and its effect on a sustainable future.
Use TED Talk curator Chris Anderson's guidelines for a strong presentation on p. 113 to help you organize your arguments.

c) Have a balloon debate:
Imagine your group will be participating in a hot air balloon trip to raise money for an Earth Day event. You are floating over a mountain range and the weather is perfect.
The captain (your teacher) suddenly tells you that, because of a small leak in the balloon, you must greatly reduce the weight in the basket. Everyone is wearing a parachute.
It may be that one, two or even three of you will have to be thrown overboard!

Taking turns, you:

- Make a one-minute speech to convince the others that you must not be thrown overboard.
  I should not …
- Then, make a two-minute speech, this time arguing against their specific claims.
  The others …
- During each balloon debate the rest of the class should fill out the checklist that your teacher will hand out. Use it to vote for the order of participants that have to jump out of the basket with their parachutes on their backs.

TIP – PRACTISE GIVING A SPEECH

Study and practice these tips on how to be effective when you present your arguments.

1 **Body language:** *the way you stand, gestures, eye contact*
Practice in front of a mirror. You need to be standing up straight, looking at people to catch their eyes (catch your own in the mirror!) and using your hands to make gestures, but not too many or too wild.

2 **Pronunciation:** *the way you say words and how clearly you say them*
Make sure you are pronouncing words with the correct English sounds and stressing the right syllables.

3 **Flow:** *what kind of language you use and how smoothly you speak*
Avoid slang and words/phrases such as: *like, uh, you know,* etc.

4 **Pitch:** *how you vary your voice so that emphasis is added*
Ask your partner to stand about six metres away from you and practise saying a few sentences to make sure they can hear you.
Use your deeper, louder voice when you want to signal importance.
Avoid monotone.

→ **Workbook** *17 (p. 75)*

1 Social media and youth movements

Have you ever been on a protest march? Describe your experience.
Look at the three pictures on p. 125. Speculate how they might be connected.

THE SENTINEL WE PRINT WHAT MATTERS ...

A MOVEMENT BORN OUT OF SOCIAL MEDIA: MARCH FOR OUR LIVES

On February 14, 2018, Nikolas Cruz, a former student from the Marjory Stoneman Douglas High School in Parkland, Florida, killed 17 people in the school with a semi-automatic rifle. On March 24, one of the largest protest marches in United States history took place in Washington, DC. It all started with high school students who wanted immediate action to be taken on tightening gun control laws. How did a small group of young people succeed in creating this huge event? Social media had a lot to do with it. Our newspaper's editor-in-chief, Jenna McDonald (class of 2019), explains ...

"I am in a school shooting right now ..."
"My school is being shot up and I am locked inside. I'm fing scared right now."***
Aidan Minoff, freshman at Marjory Stoneman Douglas High School at 2:59 pm, February 14, 2018

"People believe that the youth have no voice. I say that we were the only people who could have made this movement possible."
Alex Wind, from his speech at March for Our Lives, March 24, 2018

#guncontrolnow

"What if leading politicians valued children's lives over dollars?"
Jaclyn Corin, #whatif video

March 28, 2018 Right from the start, social media played an important role in the events leading up to March for Our Lives. First, of course, was the shooting itself. Students used their cell phones to post messages to their loved ones as Nikolas Cruz opened fire. As it was happening, Aidan Minoff, a freshman, tweeted that he was in a school shooting and that he was locked in and scared. It's one of the reasons that the police were able to rush to the school and arrest Cruz.

Twitter, rather than Facebook, seems to be the main choice of social media among youth. In fact, Emma Gonzalez, who helped organize March for Our Lives, explained that Facebook was not really used by the people in her community. Students primarily used Twitter to tell the world that #enough was enough. That was the beginning of March for Our Lives.

Young activists from the Parkland school used social media to rally people together, including youth from around the world, as well as celebrities and politicians. Suddenly, the organizers were in the news. Many quotes from their speeches went viral. Paul McCartney showed up to the March and said that one of his best friends (John Lennon) had been killed by gun violence. Jaclyn Corin, one of the movement's leaders, posted a video asking what would happen if leading politicians valued children's lives over dollars. The video has well over three million views. Ms. Corin said she believed that social media was an effective tool and that without it, the movement wouldn't have spread this fast. Alex Wind, a Parkland student, said that people believed that youth had no voice but for him they were the only ones who could have made the movement possible.

Now, March for Our Lives has a website that shows ways to fight for gun control. It also shares Tweets from youth organizers. One Tweeter maintained that young people were innovators in making change in challenging times.

#neveragain

#marchforourlives

"Facebook is not really used by the people in my community."
Emma Gonzalez, student at Marjory Stoneman Douglas High School

"One of my best friends was killed by gun violence right around here."
Paul McCartney on his Beatles' bandmate John Lennon, March 24, 2018.

"People always say, 'Get off your phones', but social media is our weapon. Without it, the movement wouldn't have spread this fast."
Jaclyn Corin, one of the organizers of March for Our Lives

#enoughisenough

2 The role of social media

a) Identify the different parts of the newspaper article and explain what their functions are.

b) Summarize the main idea of the article. List at least three claims the article makes and write the evidence the author gives to support each claim. More help → p. 153

3 Reaching an audience

Choose one quote or hashtag and write 2–3 sentences explaining why you think it's effective.

4 Have a go

Imagine the following tweets appeared on your news feed:
There are over 20,000 students here ready to march! • *There are some amazing posters!*
We are now on the steps of the parliament building.
Report what the tweets said on a social media post.
They tweeted that there were over ...

Looking at language

a) Look at how the verb in the first quote changed when it was reported in the newspaper article on p. 124. Read the other quotes and write them as indirect speech (reported speech). Check your completed sentences against those in the article.

Direct speech	Indirect speech
"I am in a school shooting right now ..."	• Aidan Minoff tweeted that he was in a school shooting …
"People believe that the youth have no voice"	• Alex Wind said …
"Facebook is not really used by the people in my community"	• Emma Gonzalez explained …

b) Say how the verb changes.

➜ *GF 7: Indirect speech / Reported speech (pp. 198–199)*

1 School newspaper interviews protesters (Reported speech)

A reporter for the school newspaper asked some students why they were protesting. Report the students' answers using the verbs *say, claim, complain* and *stress*.

Example: Jerry said that they wanted the principal to let them go out for lunch once a week.

Jerry: Well, we want the principal to let us go out for lunch once a week. We need some time to hang out with our friends and have lunch nearby.
Deborah: Our school cafeteria is noisy and the food isn't good.
James: I feel excited to be part of a protest.
Sarah: I am angry because the school on the other side of town allows students to go out for lunch, but we don't have that right.
Matthew: Teachers get an hour every day to enjoy their lunch. We demand the same respect!

Language help

Don't forget that **time, place and personal pronouns** can change in reported speech.
"I'll meet you here tomorrow." → *Frank said he would meet me there the next day.*

Language help

Verbs 'backshift' when you report what someone has said in direct speech. Backshifting happens when the reporting verb is in the past. The verb tense is shifted back.

- **Simple present → Simple past**
  "I'm happy." → *She **said** that she was happy.*
- **Present progressive → Past progressive**
  "I'm spending my holiday at the beach." → *She **said** she was spending her holiday at the beach.*

To report **questions** we also use backshifting. The word order in reported questions is the same as in statements: *S – V –…* If there is no question word, we can use *if* or *whether*.
"Do you eat lunch at school?" → *She asked him if he ate lunch at school.*
"When are you going to the beach?" → *He asked me when I was going to the beach.*

→ *GF 7: Indirect speech / Reported speech (pp. 198–199)*

2 Concert for the planet (Reported speech: present tenses)

Paul promised his parents that he would text them regularly while he was at a concert against climate change in Hyde Park. Report what Paul texted, using the verbs ***text, write, tell*** and ***ask***.

7:19 pm — I'm sitting here on our picnic blanket with Marcy and Dave. The sun's going down.
7:42 pm — Most people here have banners. They say "No nature / no future" and "There is no Planet B".
8:13 pm — The concert is starting! Are you watching it on TV?
9:20 pm — I'm at the snack bar. Most of the music here is great but I don't like the band that's playing now.
10:15 pm — The concert is ending. We're feeling exhausted. When are you picking us up?

More help → *p. 125*

Language help

Backshifting:

- **Simple past / present perfect → Past perfect**
  "I've been to a lot of concerts." → *She **said** she had been to a lot of concerts.*
  "We enjoyed the concert at Hyde Park." → *He **told** me they had enjoyed the concert at Hyde Park.*

3 After the concert (Reported speech: present perfect and simple past)

Paul told his friend Maria about the concert in Hyde Park. Write what Marie later told her parents about Paul's experience. Use verbs like ***say, tell, explain, mention***, etc.

"I've been to a lot of events related to climate change and the concert at Hyde Park was the best. We went there to protest about something incredibly important but we all also really enjoyed ourselves. I haven't heard yet how many people took part but it was a huge crowd, which made us feel quite powerful. I've never felt powerful before!"

4 A more ecological supermarket (Reported speech)

You've received a call from your friend Justine and you are now telling your friend Robert about the conversation. Write what you tell Robert, using *she/I said, told me/her, claimed, asked,* etc.

Justine: You won't believe where I've just been: I went shopping in the new supermarket in town.
You: But you're against shopping in supermarkets! You won't help the environment by supporting new ones.
Justine: Well, actually I may help a lot by shopping in this one. It sells all its products without packaging.
You: But how does that work?
Justine: Customers have to bring their own bags, jars and bottles. You must come with me!
You: OK, I will. When can we go?
Justine: I can go with you tomorrow.

Language help

Backshifting:
Modal verbs: *will* → *would, can* → *could, may* → *might, must* → *had to*
"The protest will make people think." → *She **said** that the protest would make people think.*
"Can I go with you?" → *He **asked** if he could go with them.*

→ *GF 7: Indirect speech / Reported speech (pp. 198–199)*

5 How to shop at the packaging-free supermarket
(Reported commands, requests and advice)

You went to the packaging-free shop to buy pasta but you didn't know how it worked, so you asked a shop assistant to show you. Report what she said using *told, asked* and *advised.*

"Follow me to the pasta shelf, please. Decide which type of pasta you want. You should try our green pasta – it's great! Weigh your empty jar. Now fill it with pasta and weigh it again. Don't use too many glass jars as it will make your shopping too heavy."

She asked me to ...

→ *GF 7: Indirect speech / Reported speech (pp. 198–199)*

Language help

When we report commands, requests or advice, we usually use infinitive constructions:
"Come with me!" → *She told him to go with her.*
"Can you help me with my shopping?" → *She asked me to help her with her shopping.*
"Don't buy things that you don't need." → *He advised them not to buy things they didn't need.*

6 Fast fashion in my life (Reported speech)

a) Ask each other three questions about fast fashion from the box. Take turns.
Note down your partner's questions to you and your answers.

b) Find a new partner and tell them about your interview.

- Do you like to follow fashion trends?
- Have you ever shopped in a second-hand store?
- How much did you spend on clothes last spring?
- What's your opinion of fast fashion?
- Would you ever swap clothes with a classmate?
- What are you doing to help save the planet?
- Can you predict next season's colours?

→ **Workbook** *18–20 (pp. 76–77)*

7 THINKING ABOUT LANGUAGE Translation

English has always dominated the internet. About 55.5% of all web content is in English. However, only around 20% of the world's population speaks English at all, and just 5% of the world speaks English as a native language. That's why, with globalization, the demand for high-quality and high-speed translations has been increasing worldwide. Until recently, online dictionaries have been useful tools for translators. Now,TMs (or translation machines) like Google Translate, are going much further, and even replacing human translators.

TMs are different from online dictionaries. The more text TMs translate, the better at translation they become. Also, unlike an online dictionary, which usually gives results for single words or short phrases, TMs can translate large chunks of text, whole documents or entire web pages almost instantly. This means that internet users across the globe can access almost any web page without a human translator.

What does this mean for students learning English in school? Michael Haugh, Professor of Linguistics at the University of Queensland, Australia, explains that while TMs are a useful tool, they cannot replace "the deep cross-cultural knowledge that comes with learning languages ...," especially since what we don't say is as important as what we say. Translation machines can't translate the complex ways we communicate.

Nikolaos Sitsanis is a professional translator who also gives reasons that TMs aren't always the best solution for translating. In an article he offers these reasons:

- ***Machines cannot understand culture.***
  He explains that a word can mean one thing in one culture and an entirely different thing in another culture. For example, the English word *'handy'* means cell phone to a German speaker while Americans use the word as an adjective meaning *'easily accessible'*.
  Plus TMs can't always understand slang or idioms.
- ***Machines can't relate words to context.***
  Think of the word *tears*. It could mean damages in fabric or what comes out of our eyes when we cry.
- ***Machines cannot copy style and tone.***
  Writers have different styles and tones (funny, poetic, angry, etc.) but machines can't recognize them.

a) Write down some ways you might use TMs in your daily life. Now, think about Michael Haugh's quote and discuss the ways using TMs is different from learning a language in school.

b) Look at the list of text types below. Say if you'd use a TM or your own language knowledge plus a dictionary.
- An email to a friend
- A grocery shopping list
- A poem
- An essay on the habits of squirrels
- A short story
- A school talk (like Shireen's)
- A joke

More help → p. 153

→ Workbook 21 (p. 77)

In the *Oberstufe*, you will often have to analyse English non-fictional texts, including reports or news articles written to inform you about the world around us or comments or reviews that try to influence you. When analysing a text you will need to:

- describe, outline and explain its content or summarize certain aspects of the text (comprehension)
- study how it is written and what effect that has on the reader (analysis)
- give an opinion (comment).

Now read this newspaper article, making sure that you understand it. Use a dictionary to look up words you don't understand.

Experience: I am 16 and live alone in the wilderness

I have an open fire and spend my evenings tanning animal and fish skins, and carving wood

Zeki Basan: 'I've had a few hairy moments."
Photograph: Murdo Macleod for the Guardian

I live alone on the Isle of Skye in a tipi almost impossible to find without detailed directions. It might seem unusual for someone of 16, but I love my own company and I'm passionate about preserving wild spaces. I grew up with my mum, Ghillie, and older sister, Yazzie, in the wilds of the Cairngorms, in a remote and sometimes inaccessible home, using cross-country skis to haul food and supplies to the house. Mum, a cookbook writer, taught us about possible dangers and how to cope with them, then let us run wild from an early age. We also travelled abroad regularly, visiting remote tribes and cultures, where we lived for weeks as Mum studied food and recipes to write about. I spent so much time with tribes who rely on the land that this became second nature to me.
When I gained a place at the School of Adventure Studies on Skye last year, I decided to live in a tipi, practising what I preach.
I sleep on an ancient canvas camp bed my grandfather gave me, with two old army blankets and some skins I tanned myself from roadkill for warmth. I have an open fire and spend my evenings tanning animal and fish skins, and carving wood. I store clothes and books in an old metal trunk of my mum's – it's covered in stickers from her travels. I wash my clothes in the river and dry them in the wind or in the heat from the fire. I have a bush shower using water from the river.

I wake at 6 am and get the fire on straight away using flints and steel. There's usually a good bed of embers from the previous day, so the fire is soon blazing while I have cereal or bannock, which I bake myself, for breakfast. I collect kindling for later in the day, then I wash at the river. Sometimes I just jump in, especially when there's frost on the ground. When I rush back to the tipi, it's like a sauna.
I get my backpack organised, including any food and kit I need for the day, bank the fire (by covering it, which keeps it low, but alive) and walk 30 minutes to the school. There are 12 of us on the course, of all ages, and we've just finished mountaineering, focusing on practical navigation in the Red Cuillin. We're about to start white-water kayaking.
My friends used to love coming to our home and running wild with me, so they are used to the way I live. I hope some of them will visit me soon.

wilderness ['wɪldənəs] *Wildnis* · (to) **tan** [tæn] *(Fell) gerben* · **isle** [aɪl] *Insel* · (to) **haul** [hɔːl] *schleppen* · (to) **cope** (with) [kəʊp] *klarkommen (mit)* · (to) **preach** [priːtʃ] *predigen* · **canvas** ['kænvəs] *Segeltuch* · **roadkill** ['rəʊdkɪl] *totgefahrene Tiere* · **trunk** [trʌŋk] *Kiste, Truhe* · **hairy** *haarig, brenzlig* · **straight away** [ˌstreɪtə'weɪ] *sofort* · **flint** *Feuerstein* · **embers** ['embəz] *Glut* · **previous** ['priːviəs] *vorherige/r/s* · (to) **blaze** [bleɪz] *brennen, lodern* · **cereal(s)** ['sɪəriəlz] *Frühstücksflocken* · **bannock** ['bænək] *schottisches Fladenbrot* · **kindling** ['kɪndlɪŋ] *Anfeuerholz* · (to) **bank (up) a fire** *Kohlen/Brennstoff auf ein Feuer schichten, sodass es nicht mehr lodert, aber auch nicht ausgeht* · **mountaineering** [ˌmaʊntə'nɪərɪŋ] *Bergsteigen*

People ask if I miss the internet, but I never used to use it much, or watch television. I am sociable, but I have always enjoyed my own company.
I use my mobile every few weeks to catch up with friends and my mum, who I usually see once a month when I go back to the Cairngorms. I work with a bushcraft expert, Willow Lohr, teaching wild skills to others. I also visit a small tribe of bushmen in Namibia. We show each other our ancestral skills to keep them alive.
What I'm doing isn't for everyone, but it makes me happy. I'd like to see more people look after the land and not be scared of getting outside, getting wet, learning how to survive. I'd like to learn western riding (horse riding like a cowboy), because my ambition is to run my own wilderness school, travelling on horseback. When my studies are over, I'll move the tent back to Mum's house and use it to tan skins. Until then, I'm happiest sitting by the flickering fire, carving a spoon in perfect silence and watching the northern lights through the open tipi door.

As told to Joan McFadden. The Guardian, 29 April 2016; downloaded 30.04.2016

STEP 1 Comprehension

Task: Describe how Zeki lives now.

- Read the task carefully. The word 'now' shows that you needn't cover the past or future.
- Scan the text to identify the relevant content.
- Only summarize the main points.
  Zeki lives by himself in a lonely spot .... He leads a ... life ...
  On a typical day he .... In addition to this, ...

STEP 2 Analysis

Task: Explain how the text expresses Zeki's feelings about his way of life.

- Refer to the text's structure and how it affects our understanding of the writer's choices.
  At the beginning, Zeki describes how he experienced outdoor life .... This shows ...
- Look at the language the writer uses.
  He uses simple/descriptive/... sentences such as ... • He uses everyday language, which ...
- Look at the way he presents himself.
  Zeki describes himself as passionate /... • He refers to how he feels about ...
- Support your analysis with quotes or with a line number reference.
  It seems clear that he really enjoys ... /is very relaxed about/... when he says "... ... ...".

STEP 3 Comment

Task: *"... practising what I preach"* (l.18) Comment on Zeki's choices from his perspective and yours.

- Explain what the quote says about Zeki.
  By "practising what I preach" Zeki means that ... / wants to express how ... /...
- State your view of Zeki's choices, giving reasons.
  To me, such a life seems quite attractive/hard/... because .../although .../.... Another reason is ...
- Say if you could imagine living in a similar way and explain why/why not.
  Personally, I would choose a different/similar/... path. This is because ... / The reason for this is ...

sociable ['səʊʃəbl] *gesellig* · (to) **catch up (with sb.)** *Neuigkeiten austauschen (mit jm.)* · **bushcraft** ['bʊʃkrɑːft] *Überlebenstraining* · (to) **flicker** ['flɪkə] *flackern*

➜ **Workbook** *22–23 (pp. 78–79)*

Workbook Checkpoint 4 (pp. 80–83)

A speech: Convince others about what you believe in

Give a 4-minute speech that expresses your opinion on fast fashion, a specific type of food diet or long-distance air travel. Your speech should also explain how your position can help lead to a more sustainable future.

STEP 1 Clarify and state your position

Write down your position/opinion in a few sentences.
Note: if you don't already have a specific position about either topic, do the research first. Often, by learning more about a topic, you will find it easier to establish your own opinion.

STEP 2 Research your topic

Research your topic on the Internet and look for:
- relevant statistics
- convincing and surprising facts
- interesting/shocking/funny quotes.

➔ *SF 27: Internet research (p. 177)*

STEP 3 Structure your speech

Find a way to introduce your topic and your position:
- with a surprising/shocking fact or statistic
- with an anecdote from your own life like Shireen did in her 'Clean Teen Challenge' presentation.

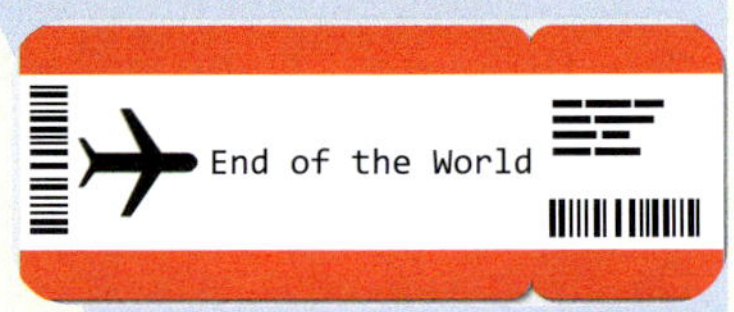

Organize your arguments in a strong, logical sequence:
- present arguments/quotes that support your position
- present arguments against opposing positions
- present arguments on why others should follow your lead.
- use the guidelines for a strong presentation on p. 113 to help you organize your arguments.

Find a way to conclude:
- with a challenge to your audience
- with an invitation for them to follow the lifestyle approach you've suggested
- with a warning about what might happen if your suggestion is not followed.

STEP 4 Practise and give your speech

Follow the tips on the speaking course on p. 123 for making a persuasive/effective speech.
Go to p. 174 of the skills file for more tips.
Give your speech!

➔ *SF 24: Giving a good presentation (p. 174)*

STEP 5 Give feedback

Give constructive feedback to your classmates on how or why their speech was or wasn't effective.

➔ *Giving feedback to your classmates (pp. 343–344)*

A 1 Describing words

a) Sometimes you have to describe words when you speak to somebody. Find the words to match these paraphrases and write them in your exercise book.

1 It describes somebody who feels the strong need to do something and is not able to stop doing it even if it is bad for them.
2 When you move down through a screen, e.g. on a mobile phone, to see or read more.
3 To type something in a box on a screen, e.g. your username.
4 When you send someone a written message from your phone, but without the internet.
5 When someone illegally breaks into a person's computer, their online accounts or a website, for example.
6 When something spreads quickly all over the internet through e.g. social media and email.

b) Write English paraphrases for these words.
1 notifications 2 greyscale 3 acquaintance 4 to post sth. 5 hashtag

c) Write a short text about something you have read or written on the internet. Use six words from parts a) and b).

2 Rebecca and Rob

ask • be • break • engage • fall • get • give • go • keep • show

for • in • off • out • touch • up • with

Make collocations with the words in the boxes and use the correct ones to complete the text about Rebecca and Rob. You can use some words more than once. Be careful with the verb tenses and forms.

Rebecca [1]... Rob as soon as he [2]... in her class on the first day of tenth form. It was the passion he had for the environment and the planet – and his deep brown eyes – that attracted her. She [3]... him ... after two weeks and he said yes. It was exciting. Rob [4]... any and every green issue. Rebecca [5]... him on most topics, except being vegetarian - she couldn't [6]... meat. Rob, it seemed, had the same problem with his phone – he couldn't [7]... it. He was in so many Facebook groups and he needed to [8]... them all, he said. The worst time was before school exams – Rebecca couldn't study as much as she needed, and Rob didn't seem to think the exams were important. That made Rebecca's parents think Rob was becoming a problem. Rebecca decided that she couldn't [9]... seeing Rob. After [10]... for eight months, Rebecca and Rob agreed to [11]... and just be friends.

3 Shireen does have a point, but ... (Adding emphasis)

Some Bayside Prep School students are discussing Shireen's 'clean teen challenge' in a group chat. Change the word order or add auxiliary verbs to add emphasis to what the kids say.

Shireen must be crazy! [1]I would delete my TikTok under no circumstances!

I agree. [2]I have never been so insulted! **Clean** teen challenge? [3]So, you are not only addicted to your phone, but also dirty if you don't follow Shireen's rules?

Relax, guys. [4]Shireen has good intentions. [5]But she sounds like my parents.

[6]I would like to try Shireen's challenge, definitely. But my family, friends and basketball club all use different apps. And if I delete one or two apps? [7]I will in no way be able to keep track of everyone in my life. Chaos!

[8]I heard only later that Principal Richardson gave a speech about 'the dangers of social media'.

4 The Student Council (Reported speech)

The Student Council are meeting, and it is your job to make notes on what everyone says. Report what the students say. Use six different verbs to introduce the reported speech. Use 'to say' only once. Pay attention to verb tense and pronoun changes.

Larry: OK, everyone. You all promised to think of ideas for this semester's youth action event. Can we decide what kind of event we are going to organize? Anne?

Anne: Thanks, Larry. The idea I have had is a school concert with student bands.

Paul: I thought of that idea too!

Larry: OK. Thanks guys. Let's hear from the younger students. Mae – what do the guys in seventh form want our action day to be?

Mae: Well, some of my classmates want to have a no-uniform day.

Paul: That is boring. We have done that lots of times before.

Mae: Don't call our idea boring. Maybe you have done it before, but this is our first year in the school.

Paul: Yeah, sorry, you're right. What if we had a school concert and a no-uniform day together?

Anne: Hey, I know! We can all wear green clothes and call the day 'Green Day' – like the rock band.

Paul/Mae: Yeah!

Larry: But what will the theme of our 'Green Day' be?

Mae: Wildlife! Everyone can pay £5 to take part and the money we raise can go to a wildlife charity.

Larry: That sounds good. OK. Anne and Mae should write out a clear plan of the idea. The parent/teacher council are going to meet on Thursday evening. They may have some things to say about our idea.

5 MIXED BAG I'm starting with the guy in the mirror!

Paul wants to live in a more sustainable way. Complete his blog with the right words.

Hi guys! If you [1]... my blog since last month, you [2]... that I've been thinking about [3]... some changes to how I live my life. So I've decided now, and here's what I [4]... do:

MY DIGITAL LIFE There's too [5]... digital noise in my life – Snapchat, TikTok, WhatsApp – you know what I mean. I'm going to try [6]... on my Wi-Fi/data for only one hour per day.

SHOPPING [7]... things online is super practical, yes. But when you think of all the packaging on the stuff [8]... and all those delivery vans [9]... around: it all means more trees cut down, more pollution in the streets where we [10]... and in the air we [11]... . So I've talked with my mum and dad and we've agreed [12]... what we need in real-world, local shops, and they promised we [13]... only ... the car to go shopping once a week.

FOOD Our local grocery store claims that it gets most of its food from farmers in our region. That means [14]... pollution from big trucks, ships and planes [15]... food from foreign countries. We are also going to eat food that is in season, [16]... means not [17]... strawberries from the store in December because they [18]... far away.

CLOTHES Before, I [19]... buy a lot of my clothes in a store that [20]... trendy but cheap clothes. I did some research online and [21]... that their clothes [22]... in Bangladesh, [23]... workers are exploited. What to do? I can't trust my parents, [24]... taste in fashion is terrible, to help and the most popular brands that everyone loves cost [25]... ... I can pay. Well, I talked with some of the guys at school and we've decided [26]... a clothes exchange. Once a month, we'll bring clothes [27]... us or we [28]... any longer, and we'll exchange them with each other. If we do this, we [29]... money and clothes manufacturers [30]... treat their workers so badly [31]... more money from us.

OK. I [32]... finish now because my dad needs the computer. Check at this time tomorrow (5:30 pm) when I [33]... about my plan for recycling electronic waste.

B 6 Pod save us

Jennie talks with Chris on her podcast. Read a)–c) first. Then listen twice.

a) Find the correct ending.

1 Chris feels that some people think teenagers
   a) are lazy and think negative things. b) are always online and don't like reading.
   c) go on too many demonstrations.

2 Chris thinks there is pressure on young people to
   a) all think and act the same. b) concentrate on their studies. c) be individuals.

b) Jennie and Chris disagree quite often. Complete what they say.

1 Jennie: I … … … …, but some older people never understand young people, do they?
2 Jennie: Hang on, Chris, I … … … … there.
3 Chris: I'm sorry, Jennie, but you're … … … .
4 Jennie: OK, Chris, I think we'll … … … … disagree on some issues.

c) Write short answers in your exercise book.

1 How has the number of American young people suffering from stress changed in the last decade?
2 From what age can people in Scotland vote?
3 Why does Chris think under-eighteens should not have the right to vote?
4 What do Jennie and Chris agree about?

C 7 A 'Zero Waste' life

Dein amerikanischer Freund Caleb muss einen Bericht für die Schule über das folgende Thema schreiben:
Wie können die Menschen in Amerika und in anderen Ländern ihren Müll reduzieren? Er hat einen interessanten Artikel auf einer deutschen Website gefunden, aber er versteht nicht alles.
Beantworte seine Fragen in einer E-Mail (ca. 150 Wörter):

Hi! It's great that you can help me with my report. Here are the parts I need help with:

- How did Mathilda get interested in 'Zero Waste'?
- What is the most important step, according to Mathilda?
- Can you save money when you reduce waste? How?

Thanks, Caleb

„Zero Waste": Gut leben und gleichzeitig Abfall vermeiden

Anhänger der „Zero Waste"-Bewegung versuchen, keinen Müll zu produzieren, der auf der Deponie landet. Wie dies in der Großstadt geschehen kann, erzählt die 17-jährige Mathilda aus Berlin.

Meine Eltern waren schon immer umweltbewusst. Plastiktüten, Einwegstrohhalme und unnötige Werbeartikel wie Kugelschreiber haben wir immer vermieden. Vor fünf Jahren ist meine Mutter über einen Blog gestolpert, der unser Leben verändert hat. Er wurde von einer Frau in den USA geführt, die zu Hause überhaupt keinen Abfall produzierte, der nicht recycelt oder kompostiert werden kann. Meine Eltern fanden die Idee toll und fingen an zu recherchieren.

Der wichtigste Schritt war, in „Unverpackt-Läden" einzukaufen, um Verpackungsmüll zu vermeiden. Wir kaufen regelmäßig bei Bauernhöfen, beim Bäcker, im Bioladen und auf dem Wochenmarkt ein, weil dort lose Waren angeboten werden. Es ist toll, weil wir nur so viel einkaufen, wie wir wirklich brauchen, das spart auch Geld. Man kann auch viele Produkte selber machen, um Plastikmüll zu vermeiden. Meine Mutter macht zum Beispiel Shampoo aus Avocadokernen und wir mischen uns Zahnpulver aus Birkenzucker (in der Apotheke erhältlich) und Natron. Wir verwenden Kaffeesatz in der Dusche als Körperpflege. Ich habe auch vor Kurzem gelernt, wie man Makeup selbst erstellt. Ich mache auch gern Kerzen aus Kerzenresten.

Obwohl wir in einer Wohnung im dritten Stock wohnen, kompostieren wir viele Reste im Gemeinschaftsgarten. Wer Gemüse selbst anbaut, spart Geld und viel Müll. Auf den Fensterbrettern in unserer Wohnung stehen kleine Töpfe mit Kräutern. Wichtig ist, dass wir kaum Lebensmittel verschwenden. Jeden Sonntag planen meine Eltern, was sie in der kommenden Woche kochen wollen. Natürlich kann es trotzdem Speisereste geben. In dem Fall bereiten wir daraus andere Mahlzeiten, wie z.B. eine Suppe, zu. Aus Obstresten kann man ein leckeres Müsli kreieren. (Mein Lieblingstipp? Bananenschalen zum Schuheputzen. Meine Freunde fanden das total abgefahren – bis sie es ausprobierten.) Eine gute Vorbereitung ist ebenfalls unerlässlich, wenn man draußen isst. Wir haben immer Stoffservietten, Trinkflaschen und Reisebesteck dabei.

Handys sind ein tolles Mittel, um Papier zu vermeiden. Wenn ich unterwegs bin, fotografiere ich Flyer oder Flugblätter, damit ich sie nicht mitnehmen muss. Wir benutzen Elektrogeräte so lange wie möglich und lassen sie reparieren, bis sie nicht mehr zu retten sind. Ich bin es mittlerweile gewohnt, „abfallfrei" zu leben. Das möchte ich gern fortsetzen, weil es einfach schön ist, zu wissen, dass man etwas für die Umwelt tut.

English as a *lingua franca*

Facts about English

Before doing the quiz, describe the globe and say what you think its message is.

Quiz – Who speaks English?

1 Rank these languages 1 to 4, based on how many people speak them as a native language (1=highest number)
a) Spanish b) Chinese c) English d) Hindi

2 What percentage of the world's people speak English as a native language?
a) 2 b) 4 c) 10 d) 16

3 What percentage of the world's people speak English (native and non-native)?
a) 5 b) 10 c) 15 d) 20

4 In how many countries is English an official language?
a) 24 b) 49 c) 75 d) 81

5 Rank these countries 1 to 4 based on the percentage of the population that can speak English (1=highest percentage).
a) Denmark b) Germany c) Spain d) Sweden

6 Which of these countries show English films in the original language with subtitles? In which are English films dubbed?
a) Denmark b) Germany c) Spain d) Sweden

7 Rank these languages 1 to 4, based on how many students learn them at German schools. (1=highest number of learners)
a) Spanish b) English c) French d) Latin

8 What percentage of internet content is in English?
a) 25 b) 55 c) 85 d) 95

9 What percentage of the world's technical and scientific magazines are in English?
a) 20 b) 50 c) 75 d) 90

10 Which language has the most words in the dictionary?
a) Spanish b) German c) English d) Italian

a) Check your answers (p. 154). Then say what surprised you.

b) Look at the photo of the signs. Say what you notice.

c) Say which language(s) you have used to speak to someone who speaks a different native language and describe the experience.

TIP
You may look at the map on the inside back cover of this book when answering questions 2-4.

English is going global

Have you ever wondered how many languages are spoken throughout the world? Over 6,000! Once people began to travel across land and sea, they needed to communicate. During the early Renaissance, a mixed language made up of Italian with bits of Turkish, Spanish, Greek, and Arabic, was used in the region around the Mediterranean Sea, especially for trade. This language was called lingua franca (lingua means language in Italian, and franca meant European back then). It was used when people spoke different languages but had to communicate. Today, any language that serves the same purpose is called a lingua franca.

Although Latin, French and German were all lingua francas at different times in history, today English is the lingua franca in much of the world. It is used in international business, science, technology, air travel and diplomacy, and unofficially, just to chat.

When people are speaking English as a lingua franca (ELF), the rules are not as strict as when they study it in school. That's because getting the message across is more important than correctness. And because ELF is a language that depends on the speaker and not on strict grammar rules, people's culture and native language have an effect on its usage. For example, because the Japanese are quite formal, they might say: "Allow the bill to be paid by me" instead of "I'll pay."

English became a popular lingua franca starting in the 1600s when the British Empire began to colonize many areas of the world. The influence of American culture and the widespread use of English on the internet have also contributed to its usage. But English is not the only lingua franca. On the continent of Africa, for example, which was mostly colonized by the French, the French language is often used to communicate among people who speak different native languages.

Scholars disagree as to the effects on global communication of English as a lingua franca. Some say that ELF discourages multilingualism (speaking more than one language) and allows American culture to dominate the globe. Others see it as a way for important discoveries in different countries to be shared by everyone.

But is ELF really English? That's up to you to decide.

d) Read the following ELF dialogues. Say which parts (if any) are confusing/incorrect and rewrite using standard English.

A: Aye! I lost my handy on train. It is a black colour.
B: You want that we call to the station to see if it is there?

A: Have you ever been in the zoo?
B: Yes, my mother take me every year.

A: I've been learning English since two years.
B: Me too. Can you explain me the difference with 'Mrs' and 'Ms'?

e) Check your revisions with your partner.

→ **Workbook** *10-13 (pp. 92-93) · Wordbank 7 (p. 107)*

Text 1 The Poet X by Elizabeth Acevedo *(excerpt from the novel)*

Wednesday, September 5

Night before First Day of School

As I lie in bed,
thinking of this new school year,

I feel myself
stretching[1] my skin apart.

Even with my Amazon[2] frame[3],
I feel too small for all that's inside me.

I want to break myself open
like an egg smacked[4] hard against an edge.

Teachers always say
that each school year is a new start:

but even before this day
I think I've been beginning.

Thursday, September 6

H.S.

My high school is one of those old-school structures
from the Great Depression[5] days, or something.

Kids come from all five boroughs, and most of us bus or train,
although since it's my zone school, I can walk to it on a nice day.

Chisholm H.S. sits wide and squat[6], taking up half a block,
redbrick[7] and fenced-in[8] courtyard with ball hoops[9] and benches.

It's not like Twin's fancy[10] genius[11] school: glass, and futuristic.
This is the typical hood[12] school, and not too long ago

it was considered one of the worst in the city:
gang fights in the morning and drug deals[13] in the classroom.

It's not like that anymore, but one thing I know for sure
is that reputations last longer than the time it takes to make them.

So I walk through metal detectors[14], and turn my pockets out[15],
and greet[16] security guards[17] by name, and am one of hundreds

who every day are sifted[18] like flour[19] through the doors.
And I keep my head down, and I cause no waves.

I guess what I'm trying to say is, this place is a place,
neither safe nor unsafe[20], just a means[21], just a way to get closer

to escape.

a) Read the excerpt and quickly write down two or three words that describe your reaction to the text. Share them with a partner or with the class.

b) Read the excerpt again and make notes: What do you learn about the narrator?

c) Compare your notes with a partner.

d) Explain the following lines:
- Night before the first day of school, ll. 5–8
- H.S., ll. 13–16
- Ms. Galiano, ll. 12–15

1 **(to) stretch** dehnen, (aus)strecken 2 **Amazon** Amazone 3 **frame** Rahmen, hier: Statur 4 **(to) smack** schlagen, knallen 5 **the Great Depression** Weltwirtschaftskrise (ab 1929) 6 **squat** gedrungen 7 **redbrick** aus rotem Backstein 8 **fenced-in** eingezäunt 9 **ball hoops** Basketballkörbe 10 **fancy** schick, nobel 11 **genius** Genie 12 **hood** (= neighborhood) 13 **drug deals** Drogengeschäfte 14 **detector** Detektor 15 **(to) turn pockets out** (Hosen-)Taschen auf links drehen 16 **(to) greet** (be-)grüßen 17 **security guards** Sicherheitsleute 18 **(to) sift** sieben 19 **flour** Mehl 20 **neither safe nor unsafe** weder sicher noch unsicher 21 **means** Mittel, Weg

Ms. Galiano

Is not what I expected.
Everyone talks about her
like she's super strict
and always assigning
the toughest homework.

So I expected someone older,
a buttoned-up[22], floppy[23]-haired,
suit-wearing[24] teacher,
with glasses sliding down her nose.

Ms. Galiano is young, has on bright colors,
and wears her hair naturally curly[25].
She's also little—like, for real[26] petite[27]—
but carries herself big, know what I mean?
Like she's used to shouldering her way[28]
through any assumptions[29] made about her.

Today, I have her first-period[30] English,
and after an hour and fifteen minutes of icebreakers[31],
where we learn one another's names
(Ms. Galiano pronounces mine right on the first try),
she gives us our first assignment:

"Write about the most impactfu[32] day of your life."

And although it's the first week of school,
and teachers always fake the funk[33] the first week,
I have a feeling Ms. Galiano
actually wants to know my answer.

INFO BOX

Elizabeth Acevedo is a Dominican-American author who was born in New York, NY. She grew up in Morningside Heights, a mostly Dominican and Puerto Rican neighborhood. She joined the poetry club of her high school and took part in her first poetry slam at the age of 14. *The Poet X*, her debut novel that was published in 2018 won many awards and describes the struggle of growing up as an Afro-Latina girl and dealing with her sexuality and religion as well as her dream to write and perform poetry.

e) **You choose** Do Ms. Galiano's assignment. Choose one of the following.
1 Write a text (about 150 words).
2 Write a poem.

EXTRA In the text (H.S., ll. 17–19) the narrator says:
"… this place is a place, neither safe nor unsafe, just a means, just a way to get closer to escape."
What do you think the Poet X needs to escape from? Discuss.

22 buttoned-up zugeknöpft **23 floppy** schlaff, strähnig (Haare) **24 suit-wearing** Anzug/(Damen-)Kostüm tragend **25 curly** lockig **26 for real** *infml.* echt *(Adv.)* **27 petite** zierlich **28 (to) shoulder your way somewhere** sich (mit der Schulter) den Weg bahnen **29 assumption** Annahme, Vermutung **30 period** *(AE)* Unterrichtsstunde **31 icebreaker** Kennenlern-Aktivitäten (= um das Eis zu brechen) **32 impactful** einschneidend (z.B. Erlebnis) **33 (to) fake the funk** etwas vortäuschen, unecht sein

Text 2

7 Years by Lukas Forchhammer and others

*Once I was seven years old, my mama told me,
"Go make yourself some friends or you'll be lonely."
Once I was seven years old*

*It was a big big world, but we thought we were bigger
Pushing each other to the limits, we were learning quicker
By eleven smoking herb and drinking burning liquor*[1]
Never rich so we were out to make that steady figure[2]

*Once I was eleven years old, my daddy told me,
"Go get yourself a wife or you'll be lonely."
Once I was eleven years old*

*I always had that dream, like my daddy before me
So I started writing songs, I started writing stories
Something about that glory*[3] *just always seemed to bore*[4] *me
'Cause only those I really love will ever really know me*

*Once I was twenty years old, my story got told
Before the morning sun, when life was lonely
Once I was twenty years old*

I only see my goals, I don't believe in failure[5]
'Cause I know the smallest voices, they can make it major[6]
I got my boys with me, at least those in favor[7]
And if we don't meet before I leave, I hope I'll see you later

*Once I was twenty years old, my story got told
I was writing about everything I saw before me
Once I was twenty years old*

a) Listen to the song, then describe your first impression.

b) Read the lyrics of the song.
Say what advice the narrator's parents give him and whether he follows it.

c) Explain the narrator's dream and whether or not he realizes it.

---

1 liquor ['lɪkə] Spirituosen, Alkohol **2 make a steady figure** ['stedi] ein regelmäßiges Einkommen erzielen **3 glory** Ruhm, Ehre **4 bore sb.** jn. langweilen **5 failure** ['feɪljə] Versagen, Scheitern **6 make it major** ['meɪdʒə] groß rauskommen **7 those in favor** die, die für mich sind/die mich unterstützen

Soon we'll be thirty years old, our songs have been sold
We've traveled around the world and we're still roaming[8]
Soon we'll be thirty years old

I'm still learning about life
My woman brought children for me
So I can sing them all my songs
And I can tell them stories
Most of my boys are with me
Some are still out seeking[9] *glory*
And some I had to leave behind[10]
My brother, I'm still sorry

Soon I'll be sixty years old, my daddy got sixty-one
Remember life, and then your life becomes a better one
I made a man so happy when I wrote a letter once
I hope my children come and visit once or twice a month

Soon I'll be sixty years old, will I think the world is cold
Or will I have a lot of children who can warm[11] *me?*
Soon I'll be sixty years old

Soon I'll be sixty years old, will I think the world is cold
Or will I have a lot of children who can warm me?
Soon I'll be sixty years old

Once I was seven years old, my mama told me,
"Go make yourself some friends or you'll be lonely."
Once I was seven years old

Once I was seven years old

d) Listen to the song again. Use these lines to write your own lyrics about your life:

- Once I was seven years old, my mama told me …
- Once I was … years old …
- Soon we'll be … years old …
- Soon I'll be … years old …

8 roam [rəʊm] umherziehen, durch die Gegend ziehen **9 seek** *(fml)* suchen, streben nach **102 leave sb./sth. behind** jn./etwas zurücklassen **11 warm** wärmen

Text 3

Titus and Sym (from the novel *The White Darkness* by Geraldine McCaughrean)

a) Read these quotations and put them into your own words. Say which one you like better and why.

- "Your mind can be either your prison or[1] your palace. What you make it is yours to decide." *Bernard Kelvin Clive*
- "When reality is a prison, your mind can set you free." *Zack Snyder*

b) Now look at these quotations from the excerpt below. Speculate on what the story might be about.

- "It's true that none of my teachers knows much about Antarctica."
- "The day I came to school and said my dad had died, I heard Maxine say to Nats, "Don't worry. I expect she just *imagined* it."
- "I was powerless to rewrite the past – to change the outcome[2] of the story; …"

Chapter One "Titus"

I have been in love with Titus Oates for quite a while now—which is ridiculous, since he's been dead for ninety years. But look at it this way. In ninety years I'll be dead, too, and then the age difference won't matter.

Besides, he isn't dead inside my head. We talk about all kinds of things. From whether hair colour can change spontaneously to whether friends are better than family, and the best age for marrying: 14 or 125. Generally speaking, he knows more than I do, but on that particular subject we are even[3]. He wasn't married—at least, he wasn't when he died, which must have substantially cut down his chances.

Uncle Victor says I shouldn't marry at all. Uncle Victor knows about these things and he says that "marriage is a bourgeois relic of Victorian sentimentality"[4]. That suits[5] me. No one would match up to Titus. And we have a kind of understanding, Titus and I.

Uncle Victor is marvellous: he's done so much for us—for Mum and me, I mean. And anyway, he's just so clever. Uncle Victor knows a fantastic amount. He knows at what temperature glass turns to liquid, and where Communism went wrong and how the Clifton Suspension Bridge was built and just what the Government ought to be doing: you can't fault[6] him. He's read books about

1 either … or … entweder … oder … **2 outcome** Ausgang **3 even** gleich(auf), ausgeglichen **4 a bourgeois relic of Victorian sentimentality** ein bürgerliches Relikt viktorianischer Sentimentalität **5 suit sb.** jm. recht sein, jm. passen **6 fault sb.** etwas an jm. auszusetzen haben; Fehler an jm. finden

everything: history, geography, politics, astrology, animals … The Fount[7] of All Knowledge, Dad used to call him.

I would get stuck doing my homework, and Dad would say, "Ask the Fount of All Knowledge." And I'd telephone Victor and he would tell me. Quite often he knew more than the teachers, so they'd think I'd got my homework wrong, but as Victor says, "What teachers don't understand is that the body of learning is still growing. They reckon it stopped the day they came out of college. That, or they're bog ignorant. Lot of ignorance in yon schools."

It's true that none of my teachers knows much about Antarctica. When Dad and Victor and I went to Iceland, one of the teachers had been, too, and knew all about Dettifoss and the hot springs and people having stinking saunas in their back gardens. But none of the teachers at school has been to Antarctica. Some of them know about Scott of the Antarctic going to the South Pole and not coming back. But they mostly mean John Mills in the movie. I don't.

In the general way of things, I don't know much about anything. Uncle Victor says I'm "the victim[8] of a shoddy[9] education system". But I do know about the Polar Regions. The bookshelves over my bed are full of books about the North and South Poles. Ice-bound[10] almost. A glacial cliff-face[11] teetering[12] over my bed. I remember: the night after Dad had been rushed into hospital, one of the shelves sheared off and crashed down on me. I woke up thinking the house was collapsing—books gouging at my head, bouncing off the bed-frame, slapping flat on the floor. I looked at the hole in the wall and the rawlplugs[13] on the pillow[14] and I didn't know what to do.

About the shelf. About anything.

So I went back to sleep, and dreamt I was sailing towards the Ross Ice Barrier, and that crags[15] were splitting off its face, plunging down, massive as sea-going liners[16] foundering[17].

…

If we ever did a project at school on Antarctica, I could shine. Like Mount Erebus in midsummer, I could, I could shine!

Except that I don't think I would choose to. It's all bound up with Titus, and I know better than to mention[18] Titus at school. I do now, anyway. I made that mistake once. I won't do it again.

"Symone has a pretend friend! Symone has a pretend friend!"

7 fount Quelle **8 victim** Opfer **9 shoddy** schäbig, lausig **10 ice-bound** im Eis gefangen **11 a glacial cliff-face** eine eisige Klippenwand **12 teeter** schwanken, wanken **13 rawlplug** Dübel **14 pillow** (Kopf-)Kissen **15 crag** Fels **16 liner** Schiff, Dampfer **17 founder** *(fml)* sinken **18 mention** erwähnen

It was the conversation about snogging[19]. Like the ant nest in the larder[20]: you think you've done everything to be rid of[21] it—that it can't possibly come back again—but there it is: "How many boys have you snogged?" There is no right answer. You say "None" and you're sad and frigid or they know someone whose brother would be willing to snog you for a quid[22]. You refuse to answer and you are sadder still—or hiding something, or prefer girls, or ... It's not that they care; they only want to tell you how many they've snogged—chiefly because they like saying the word. It makes them feel as if they are wearing red underwear[23]. But on and on they go: "How many boys, Sym? How many boys have you snogged?"

Why is it that all the words to do with sex are ugly[24]? Words to do with love aren't. No wonder Titus thought women were a nuisance[25]. No wonder he died without ever ... getting mixed up with all that.

Anyway, I said that I could do without it. (At least that's what I tried to say. I don't explain things very well out loud.) I tried to say that I was happy to stick with imagining for the time being, thanks all the same. Later, maybe. If I ever met anyone who could compare with Titus ...

And after that I was the mad girl—sad, frigid, and mad; all three—the retard[26] who had an imaginary friend: "Like little kids do, oo-hoo. Like little kids do!"

The day I came into school and said my dad had died, I heard Maxine say to Nats, "Don't worry. I expect she just *imagined* it."

So that's when I sealed[27] myself inside. Laced up[28] the tent, so to speak. Filled the locks[29] with water so that they would freeze. That's when Titus and I looked at one another and decided we could do without them, so long as we had each other.

"You and me now, Sym."

"You and me now, Titus."

...

Chapter Two Freeze Frame[30]

I remember the day Titus arrived in my head—not when I first heard of him, I don't mean, but the day he arrived, like some distant cousin you've heard tell of but who suddenly comes to visit. I remember. Uncle Victor had given me the box-set DVDs for my birthday: The Last Place on Earth—an old TV series made before I was born.

I had the house to myself, because Dad was bad in hospital and Mum had gone to see him. So I plugged the DVD player into the TV, turned the sound right up and I sat down and I watched all the episodes straight off, one after another—six hours—the cellophane wrapping[31] still scrunched up in my hand, my breakfast bowl on the table.

I knew this story—thought it held no surprises for me. But I was seeing people that I'd read about, so already I felt I knew them. I was like one of those relatives[32] on the dockside[33] waving the men goodbye, minding about whether or not they came home again.

And then it came real.

I watched so intently—concentrated so hard that there was no sofa, and no screen, no chime from the clock, no traffic outside, no whine from the fridge or thump from the central heating. And it came real. So real. So real. So real. So real. So real.

When one disc came to an end, I suppose I must have put in another, but I don't remember doing it. I knew this story: it shouldn't have held any surprises for me. Five men trekked to the South Pole. A Norwegian expedition made it ahead of[34] them, so they didn't even have the joy[35] of being first. And then they didn't quite get home.

If he had been there, Dad would have said, "What do we want to watch this for? We know how it turns out[36]."

Mum would have said, "I wonder where they filmed it? Wasn't he in something else?"

Even Uncle Victor would have spotted an

19 snog knutschen, schmusen **20 larder** Speisekammer, Vorratsschrank **21 be rid of sth.** etwas los sein **22 quid** *(infml)* Pfund (£) **23 underwear** Unterwäsche **24 ugly** hässlich **25 nuisance** Ärgernis **26 retard** Vollidiot/in **27 seal** versiegeln, verriegeln **28 lace up** zuschnüren **29 lock** Schloss **30 freeze frame** Standbild **31 wrapping** Verpackung **32 relative** Angehörige(r) **33 dockside** Kai **34 make it ahead of sb.** es vor jm. schaffen **35 joy** Freude **36 how it turns out** wie es ausgeht inaccuracy[37] in somebody's cap badge[38] or the rigging[39] on the *Terra Nova*.

But me, I didn't think anything. I let it soak into me like water into salt, until I was invisible[40], absorbed. It blew me away. That's what people say, isn't it? It blew me away—like wind ripping a tent loose of its guy-ropes[41], or the blizzard[42] submerging[43] a man in powdery, edgeless Death.

And there, at the heart of it, was Captain Oates: so sublimely[44] beautiful that his image passed clean through my retina[45] and scorched itself on my brain. And his voice flowed into me, so sensuous[46] that I was wading across the River Jordan, up to my ears and deeper in milk and honey, towards Paradise on the other side. He was perfect—as I've always known he would be if ever the blurred photographs, the expedition portraits, were to come to life. Like everything perfect, he set up a ferocious pain[47] inside me—a flickering, griping sort of pain, because nothing so marvellous[48] is ever within reach[49], is it? Nothing so beautiful can ever last[50]. I was powerless to rewrite the past—to change the outcome of the story; to save Oates from dying—in the film—in real life ... The DVD-player grew hotter and hotter in my lap[51], so that after Oates got up, and went outside into the blizzard, and crawled away into the snow to die, his body warmth was still there in my lap, slow to cool. He lingered[52] in my lap.

And then the phone rang.

And it was Mum to say that Dad had died.

I thought there was really bad static[53] on the line[54], but it was only the cellophane clenched in my hand, crackling by the receiver[55]. And all I could say was "Oh", because it had been on the cards[56] for weeks. I had been half-expecting the call all day. The news held no surprise for me.

And besides[57], Dad never liked me.

a) Make groups of 4. Each partner should choose one task.

Partner A:
Make notes on what the excerpt you've read tells you about Titus Oates and Symone's relationship with him. Prepare to share your ideas with your group.

Partner B:
Make notes on what the excerpt you've read tells you about Symone's relationship with her uncle and his role in the story. Prepare to share your ideas with your group.

Partner C:
Imagine you are Symone. Write a diary entry in which you speak about your relationship with your classmates. Prepare to read it to your group.

Partner D:
Relate one of the quotations from a) on p. 98 to the excerpt you've just read.
Make notes about your ideas and prepare to share them with your group.

b) Share your ideas with your group or read out the text you wrote.

37 inaccuracy Ungenauigkeit **38 badge** Abzeichen **39 rigging** Takelage **40 invisible** unsichtbar **41 guy-rope** Zeltschnur, Abspannseil **42 blizzard** Schneesturm **43 submerge** bedecken, versenken **44 sublimely** außergewöhnlich **45 retina** Netzhaut **46 sensuous** sinnlich **47 a ferocious pain** ein heftiger Schmerz **48 marvellous** wundervoll **49 within reach** erreichbar **50 last** (an)dauern **51 lap** Schoß **52 linger** (ver)weilen; nachklingen **53 static** Rauschen **54 line** Leitung **55 receiver** (Telefon-)Hörer **56 be on the cards** zu erwarten sein **57 besides** außerdem

1 More help

3 Time traveller

p. 9 Lead-in

You could write about:

- what/who you have come to see
- what you see, hear, feel
- who you meet and what you do
- the advantages and disadvantages of life in the city
- why you would/wouldn't like to stay longer
- ...

2 It wasn't founded by Britons

p. 20 Part B Practice

Correct the wrong information about London in each sentence. You can check the facts on pages 18/19.

1 London was founded by Britons.
   – No, it wasn't founded by Britons. It was founded by ...
2 The city was first named London.
   – No, it ... first ... London. It ... Londinium.
3 The food in the Brixton café is cooked the night before.
   – No, it ... in the mornings. It ... there fresh every day.
4 The Huguenots were driven to London from Spain.
   – No, they ... to London from Spain. They ... to London from France.
5 London was burned by a Great Fire in 1665.
   – No, it ... by a Great Fire in 1665. It ... by a Great Fire in 1666.
6 After World War II, Europeans were brought to London to help rebuild the country.
   – No, after World War II Europeans ... to London to help rebuild the country. Commonwealth people ... to London to help rebuild the country.

2 More help

3 A road trip

p. 44 Lead-in

Here are some nouns and adjectives which may help you to describe how the film made you feel.

anticipation • fear • freedom • happiness • peace • surprise

confused • disappointed • excited • grateful • inspired • shocked

5 I heard the wind blowing

p. 49 Part A Practice

b) You might see/hear/smell/feel ...

- street performers / play / didgeridoo
- street artists / draw / pavement
- seagulls / cry
- ferries / cross / harbour
- children / play / beach
- restaurants / preparing meals
- people / eat / street food market
- a warm wind / blow

6 The Sydney Harbour Bridge

p. 49 Part A Practice

Complete the text with the correct forms or clauses, or leave a gap if it is possible.

My little sister Cathy and I decided to climb a bridge [1]... (that/–) we had seen many times in photos and films: the Sydney Harbour Bridge. Dr JJC Bradfield, [2]... (design) the bridge, based it on the Hell Gate Bridge in New York City, our hometown! [3]... (walk) on the catwalk [4]... ... (lead) to the lower arch, I noticed Cathy [5]... (look) scared. Luckily our guide, [6]... (see) Cathy hesitating, whispered something in her ear. Within seconds, I saw her [7]... (relax). Together we climbed to the top of the upper arch, [8]... (have) a staircase to the summit. Later, she told me the guide had helped her overcome the worst fear [9]... (that/–) she had ever felt. [10]... (wonder) what he had whispered in Cathy's ear, I asked her to tell me. [11]... (smile), she said "Everyone [12]... (reach) the summit is a hero!"

2 Tropical life

p. 53 Part B

a) Your comment needs a structure. Use these ideas to help you.

Introduction	Why are you writing this comment? Tell Emily that you liked her post.
Main body	What is unique about your environment? Describe two interesting things. Think about the countryside / animals / culture / famous buildings …
Conclusion	Would Australians be interested in your environment? Suggest that they visit!

1 Everyone was outside, ...

p. 54 Part B Practice

Match the sentence beginnings to the pictures.
Then finish each sentence using the words below or your own ideas.

1 Everyone was outside, / queue / buy ice cream
2 Fluff is walking along the piano, / make / funny music
3 Jake was standing in the greenhouse, / show / tomatoes / people
4 Mum was in the car, / relax / and / listen / her favourite music
5 Have you seen the photo of Rover, / catch / frisbee
6 This is Ella on her way to a party, / wear / Father Christmas costume

3 Paul and Jake

p. 55 Part B Practice

Complete the text with the correct verb form, relative clause or participle.

It was a January morning in Cairns, Far North Queensland, and Paul, who always [1]... (get up) early, woke up to the radio [2]... (give) news of a big rainstorm. [3]... (look) through the window while [4]... (dress), he noticed the trees [5]... (bend) in the strong wind. But Paul decided [6]... (go) to school anyway, [7]... (not want) to miss his band practice. While [8]... (put on) his raincoat and rubber boots, he heard his phone [9]... (ring) in his back pocket. It was his best friend Jake. "[10]... (do) you hear the good news?" "No, what is it?"
"All the roads [11]... (flood) so, no school today, mate!" While [12]... (listen) to his friend talk about all the things he was planning to do that day, Paul watched the rain [13]... (hit) the window.
"But there's bad news too", said Jake, "when [14]... ...(remove) some fallen trees from the road, a workman got hurt."
"That is bad."
"Yeah, anyway, I'll call you later", Said Jake.
[15]... (feel) disappointed, Paul took out his guitar. He always liked to play when [16]... (feel) frustrated.
He called his song 'Rain Rebecca', [17]... ... (make) him smile.

4 A trip that went wrong

p. 55 Part B Practice

You could write about:

- forgetting to pack something important
- not getting to the station/airport on time
- a bus/train/flight that didn't leave
- a terrible hotel/holiday apartment/campsite
- meeting some people that you didn't like
- not understanding because of not speaking a language
- things that went wrong because of bad weather
- a lost bag

5 Being new in Australia, ...

p. 55 Part B Practice

Use participle clauses to explain the reasons.

1 I'm new in Australia. That's why I don't understand Aussie English very well.
Being new in Australia, I don't understand Aussie English very well.
2 We know all about floods because we live in the tropics.
3 I saw a python in the garden. I pulled out my camera to take a photo.
4 I knew that pythons are dangerous. That's why I was careful not to get too close.
5 I felt really tired, which is why I fell asleep in the middle of the movie.

2 More Aussie facts

p. 62 Part C Practice

Use the present or past participle to join two sentences or shorten the single sentences.
First look at the underlined verbs. Are they in the active or passive form?
Active forms will become present participles and passive forms will become past participles.

1 Aboriginal people who sang songlines were able to navigate their way around the huge continent.
2 Uluru is one of the most famous landmarks in Australia. It was called Ayers Rock by European immigrants in the past.
3 Banjo Paterson didn't expect 'Waltzing Matilda' to become so popular. He sold it for only five pounds.
4 'Neighbours' is a TV programme which is watched by millions of young people in Australia, the UK and Ireland.
5 National Sorry Day, which has been celebrated since 1998, is a day to remember the suffering of the Stolen Generations.
6 The fact that you know where a waterhole is can save your life.
7 When they are asked to name the Australian national anthem, most people say 'Waltzing Matilda'.

1 Goodes continued to stand up against racism

p. 66 Part D Practice

Complete the sentences. Combine a verb from the box with the verb already given.

be · build · fall off · hunt · point out · sign up · sing · stand up · surf · visit

1 The film *The Final Quarter* shows how Adam Goodes continued to stand up for what he believed in.
2 In some parts of the outback, Aboriginal Australians continue ... animals the way their ancestors did.
3 "Can I try ... today?" Thomas asked his mum, after he saw the surfers ride the waves on the coast of New South Wales.
4 Thomas tried (not) ... the surfboard when the waves broke at the shore.
5 Australians prefer ... 'Waltzing Matilda' rather than the official anthem at sports events.
6 German tourists plan (not) ... Australia in the summer when the weather is cooler.

7 The teen tour guide at Sydney's Museum of Contemporary art remembered ... the café for hungry visitors.
8 She also told the visitors, "Please remember ... for membership. You'll get lots of discounts!"
9 In the 1800s, British colonists planned ... a large number of railway lines across the continent of Australia.
10 When he grows up, Thomas ... ... a professional surfer.

More help 3

2 Saying goodbye

p. 83 Part A

Here are some examples of the different functions of *will* sentences. Before you do exercise 2 in your Student's Book, match the sentences with the functions here.

1 Will you phone me soon?
2 If I go to England next year, I'll visit my friends in Bristol.
3 I think you'll enjoy school in England.
4 Stop phoning me. I won't talk to you!
5 I'll take you to all the best places in my town.
6 I'll open the door for you.

A future prediction •
A promise •
A request •
An offer •
A refusal •
Conditional 1

5 At Huntington Secondary School

p. 85 Part A Practice

Here are some ideas which might help you with your dialogues.

PREDICTIONS:
- You are taking a friend to a favourite place and you know she'll love it.
- You and a friend are going to a party, and a person that your friend really likes will be there.
- You and your family are going camping but you don't think your father will enjoy it much.

WARNINGS:
- You are out in the park with a friend when you see that a dog is going to bite him.
- Your mother is going to sit down at a café and you see that her chair is broken.
- You and your brother are riding your bikes together when your brother hears his friend call him. He looks to the side and does not see that he is riding towards a tree.

3 Your application

p. 88 Part B

Here are some reasons to apply to the summer programme, some expectations and some ways to contribute. Decide which ones are most important, and write your paragraph.

- It's a chance to do work that makes a difference to species survival.
- You are ready for a real challenge.
- It's a chance to meet people who work in marine science and to find out about possible careers.
- You love being at sea.
- You will be able to develop data-collecting skills.
- You will learn about analysis techniques.
- You expect to make friends who are interested in the same things as you.
- You are good at finding creative solutions to problems.
- You can work well with all kinds of people.
- Science and math are your best subjects.

5 Questions and intentions

p. 89 Part B

Here are some ideas for questions. You can use some of them in your email to Karen.

- Are there scholarships?
- How do people get there? Is there any public transport near the camp?
- What are the cabins like?
- Do you stay in the camp all the time or is there a town you can visit?
- Do students decide what they want to do or is there a fixed timetable?
- Do we have to prepare our own meals? Do we have to go shopping for food?
- How good are the other musicians? Am I good enough?

3 Text messages

p. 90 Part B Practice

Remember, we can use the present progressive as a future form when we talk about fixed plans.
Example:
I'm meeting Julie and Lou in the park tomorrow afternoon. Would you like to come? – I'd love to but I can't.
Why not? What are you doing? – I'm not doing anything special but my uncle is coming to visit us so I have to stay at home.

Complete the sentences with the *will*-future and the present progressive.

1 Hey! What's up? Can we meet this evening?

Sorry mate, but I ... (play) football. I ... (phone) you at the weekend.

2 How's it going? What are you doing in the holidays?

I'm OK. I ... (visit) my uncle in New York. I ... (send) you a card when I'm there.

3 Hi. We need someone to feed the cat this weekend. Do you think Jack could do it?

I'm not sure. I ... (ask) but I think he ... (go) to London.

4 My computer isn't working – again! Can you help me please?

OK, I ... (have) a look. I ... (not do) anything else this evening.

2 Cool summer jobs

p. 95 Part C

c) All this information could be important for your CV but not all of it should be part of a personal statement. Choose sentences you could include in a personal statement.

- I finished primary school in 2015.
- I enjoy team sports and have won several sports awards.
- My teachers appreciate my ability to communicate clearly.
- In 2020, I had a two-week internship at Electronics World.
- I am outgoing and willing to lead groups and speak in public.
- I'm a German native speaker with good spoken and written English, and some French.
- My favourite subjects are languages, and I enjoy developing my language skills through travel and real-life communication.
- I have shown that I am reliable and responsible in my volunteer work.

A job interview

p. 99 Part C Practice

STEP 2) Here are some ideas for the 4 Ps. Which P is each sentence?

- If possible, find out who will interview you. Remember their names.
- Think of questions that you could ask and practise asking them.
- Look at your interviewer(s) while they talk to you.
- Make sure your clothes are clean and fit you well.
- Thank the interviewer(s) for seeing you and tell them you're happy to be here.
- Make sure you have any documents you might need to show the interviewers.
- If you need to go to the hairdresser's, do it before the interview.
- Practise talking about real examples that show your strengths.
  For example: "I am good at leading a team. I showed this is a school project …"
- Make sure your hands are very clean.
- Look at the company's website.
- Ask and answer typical interview questions with a friend.
- Smile and try to relax!

2 Shireen's message

p. 112 Part A

b) Make a table like this and complete it with notes.

	before	after
Time spent studying for exams	not enough	…
Time spent texting, tweeting and scrolling	…	…
Feeling in control of her digital life	…	
Time spent doing homework	…	
Feeling focussed and alert		
Time her friends spent looking at their phones		
Noticing things around her		

7 Stephanie's date with a cell phone

p. 115 Part A Practice

Change the underlined sentences to add emphasis to the text. Put the highlighted words and phrases at the beginning of the sentences.

Stephanie had rarely been asked out on a date. Then Mark asked her out. Of course, she said yes! She realized only later that Mark was addicted to video games. They had no sooner ordered their pizza than Mark took out his cell phone. While she ate, he played. She had never felt so uncomfortable. There was no way she was going to get through the evening! Stephanie decided only later that she would tell all her friends about her date with a cell phone.

1–3 Word field: Relationships, Adjectives, Collocations

p. 116 Part A Practice

Think of two characters from a book, film, TV series …
Use these questions to help you write about their relationship.

- Who are the two characters?
- How do they get to know each other?
- Are they attracted to each other when they first meet?
- How does their relationship develop?
- Do they break up and then get back together? Why?
- How do they feel in different parts of the story?
- What part do other friends or acquaintances play in their relationship?
- What happens to their relationship at the end of the story?

6 Reversing the trend

p. 119 Part B

You can use these ideas for your discussion.

Some advantages of second-hand shopping:

- less pollution from production if fewer clothes are made
- less exploitation in factories
- less waste if fewer clothes are thrown away
- clothes are cheap but could be good quality
- find things that not everyone is wearing
- profits from second-hand shops often go to charity

Some disadvantages of second-hand shopping:

- clothes may not be in perfect condition
- may not find what you want

2 A trip to the second-hand shop

p. 120 Part B Practice

Remember: the past progressive is used for an activity in progress.
It is often signalled by *as* and *while*.
Find these two signal words in the text to help you decide which tense is correct.
Then find the one example in the text of present progressive <u>not</u> signalled by *as* or *while*.

5 The Earth Guardian

p. 121 Part B Practice

Complete the text with the correct form of the verbs in brackets.
Use either the past perfect or the past perfect progressive.

Xiuhtezcatl (pronounced 'Shoe-Tez-Caht') Martinez [1]… (ask) people to open their eyes to the Earth's destruction for years before receiving the 2013 United States Volunteer Service Award from President Obama. He was only 13 at the time! By the age of 15, he [2]… already … (speak) to the General Assembly at the United Nations in New York. Before becoming the director of an international youth activist organization called Earth Guardians, Xiuhtezcatl [3]… (learn) about ecology and sustainability from his mother, who started Earth Guardians high school in Hawaii. Throughout his childhood, his father Siri [4]… (teach) Xiuhtezcatl about his Aztec roots, which influenced his outlook on the environment.
After he [5]… (speak up) for most of his childhood, Xiuhtezcatl turned to rap music, using his own songs to communicate the message of his ancestors. The Aztecs [6]… always … (believe) that there was a single sacred force that sustains nature, which is now one of Xiuhtezcatl's main messages to young people.

2 The role of social media

p. 125 Part C

These are the functions of the different paragraphs in the article.
Give the paragraph number for each function.

- Explaining which social media are popular or less popular with young people.
- A conclusion suggesting that young people are making real change through communication technology.
- An introduction to the idea that social media can be used to create a huge movement.
- Examples of how social media helped the March for Our Lives movement to grow very quickly.
- Showing how social media immediately helped students in the school shooting.

2 Concert for the planet

p. 127 Part C Practice

Complete this report of what Paul texted to his parents.
Think about 'backshifting' and about changes in place and pronouns.

At 7:19 Paul texted that he [1]... sitting ... on their picnic blanket with Marcy and Dave. The sun [2]... ... down. At 7:42 he said that most people [3]... ... banners. They said that there [4]... No nature / no future and there [5]... no Planet B. At 8:13 he texted that the concert [6]... ... . He asked them [7]... they ... ... it on TV. At 9:20 he wrote that [8]... ... at the snack bar. He said that most of the music [9]... great but ... ... like the band that [10]... ... . At 10:15 he texted that the concert [11]... ... and said [12]... ... ... exhausted. He asked his parents if [13]... ... ... him and his friends up.

7 THINKING ABOUT LANGUAGE

p. 129 Part C Practice

b) Think about these questions when you decide whether or not a TM is better for the text types.

- An email to a friend – will a TM recognize your personal style?
- A grocery shopping list – will a TM know all the words for the things you need?
- A poem – how much does a TM understand about which words sound good together?
- An essay on the habits of squirrels – can a TM manage the vocabulary and grammar you need for an essay?
- A short story – how important are a writer's style and a writer's culture in a story?
- A school talk (like Shireen's) – does a TM know the difference between spoken language and written language?
- A joke – how do jokes work? What if a joke depends on two different meanings of one word?

4 Which is the oldest?

p. 21

b) Partner A: Ask the questions about 1, 3 and 5.

When was Liverpool Cathedral started?

Liverpool Cathedral

start
finish

Mona Lisa

paint
1503–1507

Berlin Underground

open

Treasure Island

write
1881–1883

Lift

invent

1

Cologne Cathedral

start
finish

2

Portrait of Ludwig van Beethoven

paint
1820

3

London Underground

open

4

Oliver Twist

write
1837–1839

5

Escalator

invent

Answers

Quiz – Who speaks English?

p. 136

1 1. Mandarin Chinese (918 million) · 2. Spanish (480 million) · 3. English (380 million) · 4. Hindi (340 million)

2 b) 4 per cent

3 d) 20 per cent

4 c) 75 countries
(English is the de facto official language (or mother language) in the United Kingdom, the United States, Australia and New Zealand; it's the official language in 54 countries and one of the official languages in 17 countries.)

5 1. Sweden (86%) · 2. Denmark (80%) · 3. Germany (56%) · 4. Spain (28%)

6 original language with subtitles:
a) Denmark · d) Sweden

dubbed:
b) Germany · c) Spain

7 1. English · 2. French · 3. Latin · 4. Spanish

8 b) 55%

9 b) 50%

10 d) Italian

Skills File

In diesem **Skills File** findest du **Lernhilfen und Methoden,** die dir z.B. den Umgang mit Texten erleichtern, beim Schreiben von eigenen Texten und bei der Sprachmittlung helfen oder Tipps zum Vorbereiten von Präsentationen geben.

READING SKILLS

SF 1 Skimming and scanning (Media skills)

Skimming *(reading for gist)* und Scanning *(reading for specific information)* sind Lesetechniken, die viel Zeit sparen, v. a. beim Lesen von langen Texten.

SKIMMING

Skimming hilft, schnell zu sehen, ob ein Text für deinen Zweck geeignet ist.

Step 1: Sieh dir diese Textteile an, um zu sehen, worum es im Text geht:
- Überschrift und Unterüberschriften
- Bilder und Bildunterschriften
- den ersten Satz jedes Absatzes – dieser Satz ist meist der *topic sentence*, der die Hauptidee des Absatzes nennt
- den letzten Absatz des Textes, der oft eine Zusammenfassung des Textes enthält

Step 2: Fasse für dich selbst den Text in ein paar Worten zusammen. Wenn dir das ohne Probleme gelingt, dann weißt du, um was es in dem Text geht – und dass dein Skimming erfolgreich war.

TIPP
Mache dir um unbekannten Wortschatz erstmal keine Gedanken – dafür ist Zeit, wenn du feststellst, dass der Text für dich geeignet ist.

SCANNING

Scanning hilft, in einem Text schnell nach bestimmten Informationen zu suchen.

Step 1: Überlege dir *keywords*. Suchst du z. B. die Öffnungszeiten eines Museums, könnten das Wörter sein wie *open, hours* oder *days*.

Step 2: Überfliege den Text und suche nach den *keywords*. Du kannst dabei mit dem Finger in einer "S-Form" durch den Text gehen.

Step 3: Lies die Textstelle, die dein *keyword* enthält, um zu sehen, ob sie die gewünschten Informationen enthält. Wenn nicht, scanne weiter.

TIPP
Wenn du mit Texten im Internet arbeitest, kann dein Browser dir viel Arbeit abnehmen.
Mit Strg+F (Cmd+F am Mac) kannst du nach deinen *keywords* suchen und nur die Textstellen lesen, in denen ein *keyword* markiert ist.

SF 2 Marking up a text

Auf Kopien von Texten kannst du Informationen markieren, um sie einfacher wiederzufinden, z. B. wenn du eine Zusammenfassung schreiben sollst.

Step 1: Lies die Aufgabe genau und überlege, welche Informationen du zur Beantwortung brauchst. Behalte dies beim Lesen des Textes im Kopf.

Step 2: Markiere nur Informationen, die wichtig sind (z. B. durch Unterstreichen, Einkreisen oder Markieren mit einem Textmarker). Oft reicht es, nur ein oder zwei Wörter in einem Satz zu markieren.

Step 3: Mach dir kurze Notizen am Rand – z. B. kurze Überschriften oder Stichwörter –, die den Inhalt kurz zusammenfassen. (➜ *SF 31*)

TIPP
1. Verwende unterschiedliche Farben für unterschiedliche Aufgaben/Fragestellungen.
2. Markiere wirklich nur Stichwörter, sonst wird es unübersichtlich.

An exhibition at the *Black Cultural Archives* recently took me back to my childhood in Brixton. As I wandered the colourful South London streets where I grew up, my senses were treated to the sounds of many different languages

For centuries, foreigners have arrived here through the Port of London. Some came from not so far away: Irish, Welsh, Scots. At the time of the Great Fire in 1666 a majority of Londoners had been born abroad, like protestant Huguenot. Th

WRITING SKILLS

SF 3 The stages of writing

Wenn deine Texte präzise und gut lesbar sind, machst du es deinen Lesern leichter, deinen Gedanken zu folgen, egal ob du eine Geschichte, einen Kommentar oder eine Zusammenfassung schreibst.

Du solltest deine Texte stets gut planen und zuerst einen Entwurf erstellen, den du dann überarbeitest, bis das Ergebnis so ist, wie du es haben willst – gut lesbar, leicht zu verstehen und ohne Fehler. Dieses Vorgehen braucht Zeit, aber es macht deine Texte besser.

PLANUNGSPHASE

Step 1: Plane für diese Phase ausreichend Zeit ein und denke über folgende Fragen nach:

- über welches Thema willst du schreiben?
- was genau sollst du tun (beschreiben, erläutern, zusammenfassen …)?
- welche Dinge musst du für den geforderten Text beachten?

Step 2: Dann solltest du

- alle nötigen Informationen für dein Thema recherchieren (➡ *SF 27*),
- Ideen/Argumente sammeln und sortieren
- Notizen anfertigen zu dem, was du schreiben willst (➡ *SF 31*)

ENTWURFSPHASE

Jetzt schreibe deinen ersten Entwurf:

- Füge deinen Notizen *linking words* (➡ *SF 5*) und *topic sentences* hinzu (➡ *SF 4*).
- Beginne für jede neue Idee einen neuen Absatz.
- Führe deine Ideen aus und gib Beispiele (wenn das die Textsorte erfordert).
- Denke über das Ende deines Textes nach. Wenn du weißt, wie dein Text endet, ist es leichter, eine gute Einleitung zu schreiben, die darauf hinführt. (➡ *SF 4*)

ÜBERARBEITUNGSPHASE

Wenn dein Entwurf fertig ist, heißt das leider noch nicht, dass dein Text auch schon so weit ist. Jetzt ist es an der Zeit, dass du oder jemand anderes deinen Text noch einmal kritisch durchliest. Am besten ist es, wenn du den Text mehrmals liest, jedes Mal mit einem anderen Schwerpunkt:

- Liest sich der Text gut? Ist er logisch aufgebaut und hat eine gute Struktur? (➡ *SF 4*)
- Sieh dir die verschiedenen sprachlichen Aspekte deines Textes an: Grammatik, Rechtschreibung, Zeichensetzung, Ausdruck, *linking words, time markers* etc. (➡ *SF 5, SF 10*)
- Schreibe deinen Text noch einmal. Verbessere alles, was im ersten Entwurf noch nicht ganz gepasst hat. Wenn du Feedback von jemand anderem bekommen hast, sieh es dir genau an und entscheide dann, was davon du für deinen Text übernehmen möchtest.

TIPP

Wenn du mehr Informationen zum Verfassen guter Texte haben möchtest, sieh dir auch die folgenden Skills files an:

- SF 4: Structuring texts
- SF 5: Writing good sentences
- SF 6: Writing a formal letter or email
- SF 7: Writing a comment / opinion piece
- SF 8: Argumentative writing
- SF 9: Writing a summary
- SF 10: Revising texts
- SF 27: Internet research

SF 4 Structuring texts

STRUCTURE

Ein guter Text besteht in der Regel aus den folgenden drei Teilen:

- Einleitung *(introduction)*:
  Hier steht, worum es in dem gesamten Text geht. An dieser Stelle kann auch ein Problem genannt werden, das in dem Text erörtert werden soll.
- Hauptteil *(main body)*:
  Dieser Teil ist in mehrere Absätze gegliedert und präsentiert die Details (Fakten, Beispiele etc.) zu deinem Thema.
- Schluss *(conclusion)*:
  Hier gibst du deinem Text ein passendes, interessantes Ende.

My Trip to Wales

Last summer I wanted to go to Wales because I like the mountains.

First I had to find some information on Wales. So I went to the library and looked for books about Wales. I found a book with some interesting information on hiking tours and I also found a camping guide for Wales. I went home with three books under my arm.

At home I started to plan for my trip. I read all the books and took notes on hiking trails, the weather and the equipment I would need for camping and hiking. After a few days I knew where I wanted to go and what I wanted to do there.

I did not want to go to Wales alone, so I had to find someone to go with me. I called most of my friends and told them about my plan. Some of them did not want to go hiking and others had no money for the trip. But my friend Judith agreed to go with me. We decided to go in late August.

Judith and I spent two lovely weeks in Wales. We went to Snowdonia and enjoyed the fantastic mountains. We stayed in a lovely bed and breakfast and met lots of really nice people. Before we went home we spent two very interesting days in Cardiff.

This was one of the best summer holidays I ever had. Go to Wales – it's fantastic!

PARAGRAPHS

Längere Texte sind einfacher zu lesen und schneller zu verstehen, wenn sie in Absätze eingeteilt sind. Dabei solltest du folgende Dinge beachten:

- Fange für jeden neuen Aspekt einen neuen Absatz an.
- Beginne mit einem interessanten *topic sentence*.
- Beende deinen Text im letzten Absatz mit einer Zusammenfassung oder etwas Persönlichem.

TOPIC SENTENCES

Jeder Absatz sollte mit einem Einleitungssatz beginnen.

Dieser *topic sentence* beschreibt, worum es in dem Absatz geht. Wichtige Dinge, die du in einem *topic sentence* ansprechen kannst, sind z. B.

- ***Orte:*** *My trip to Berlin was exciting.*
- ***Personen:*** *The Beatles are one of the most famous bands in the world.*
- ***Aktivitäten:*** *Lots of people ride their bike every day.*

SF 5 Writing good sentences

Gute Texte bestehen aus gut formulierten, abwechslungsreichen Sätzen. Die folgenden Techniken helfen dir, dich gut auszudrücken und damit den Stil deiner Texte zu verbessern.

ADJEKTIVE

Verwende Adjektive, wenn du Dinge, Orte und Menschen näher beschreiben möchtest:

- *a bright face*
- *a fantastic trip*

Stelle aber sicher, dass du die Adjektive *good, bad* und *nice* nicht zu häufig einsetzt. Ersetze sie durch andere Adjektive mit einer ähnlichen bzw. genaueren Bedeutung:

- *a nice teacher: a friendly teacher, a helpful teacher, ...*
- *a good book: an interesting book, a funny book, ...*

ADVERBIEN

Verwende Adverbien, um Handlungen näher zu beschreiben:

- *They walked home slowly.*
- *She talked quietly.*

Verwende Ausdrücke wie *really, very, a bit* etc., um Aussagen zu verdeutlichen oder zu verstärken:

- *It was a really sad story.*
- *The houses are very high.*

KONJUNKTIONEN

Konjunktionen wie *and, but* oder *because* geben deinen Sätzen eine klare, gut nachvollziehbare Struktur:

- *We went to the London Eye, but it was very expensive.*
- *We're going out tonight because I want to try that new restaurant.*

RELATIVSÄTZE

Relativsätze verbinden Sätze oder geben mehr Informationen zu einer Sache oder einer Person:

- *This is the shop which sells the best ice cream in Berlin.*
- *This is the woman who sent you the flowers.*

ZEITANGABEN

Time markers / adverbiale Bestimmungen der Zeit helfen dem Leser, sich in einem Text oder einer Geschichte zeitlich zurechtzufinden. Verwende *time markers*, um ...

- die Reihenfolge von Ereignissen zu verdeutlichen:
  at first, next, finally, ...
- zu zeigen, wie viel Zeit zwischen einzelnen Ereignissen vergeht:
  for half an hour, just two minutes later, ...
- zu verdeutlichen, wie langsam oder schnell etwas passiert:
  immediately, it took hours, faster than I could look, ...
- zu sagen, wenn etwas zeitgleich passiert:
  while I was waiting, during the lesson, as we came round the corner, ...
- die Ereignisse eines Textes/einer Geschichte zeitlich einzuordnen:
  two summers ago, last Halloween, on my way home from school yesterday, ...

SF 6 Writing a formal letter or email

➜ p. 23

Wenn du einen Brief oder eine Mail an eine Organisation, einen potenziellen Arbeitgeber oder Ähnliches schreibst, sollte dein Schreiben gewissen formalen Regeln folgen.

Schreibe deine Adresse (ohne Namen) oben rechts. Verwende keine typisch deutschen Buchstaben wie ä, ö, ü oder ß.

Schreibe die volle Anschrift (mit Namen, wenn du ihn weißt) des Adressaten auf die linke Seite.

Schreibe das Datum auf die rechte Seite.

Sage kurz im Betreff, worum es geht.

Beginne deinen Brief/deine Mail mit *Dear Sir or Madam,* wenn du keinen genauen Ansprechparntner hast.
Ansonsten schreibe *Dear Mr/Mrs/Ms …* (ohne Komma danach!). Fange danach immer groß an.

Nenne den Grund des Schreibens im ersten Absatz.
- Ergänze weitere Informationen in den folgenden Absätzen.
- Verwende Langformen *(I am/We are/I would)* statt Kurzformen *(I'm/We're/I'd)* und Abkürzungen.

Wenn du den Adressaten um etwas bittest (z.B. Informationen), bedanke dich im Voraus.

Beende das Schreiben mit *Yours sincerely* wenn du den Namen des Ansprechpartners kennst; ansonsten schreibe *Yours faithfully* (wenn du an einen amerikanischen Kontakt schreibst, kannst du in diesem Fall auch *Yours truly* schreiben). Tippe deinen Namen am Ende des Briefes, aber lasse ausreichend Platz für deine Unterschrift.

Kruemelstrasse 12
12345 Berlin
Germany

John Keats
Donne House
Ipswich IP3 4BA
United Kingdom

3 March 2021

Enquiry about exchange programme

Dear Mr Keats

I am writing to enquire about the exchange programme which I saw advertised in The English Magazine.

I have been studying English at school for six years now and I would like to take part in an exchange programme to improve my English.

Could you please tell me if you offer any exchange programmes for one month in the summer? It would be helpful to know about dates, application procedures and the cost of such an exchange. Any additional information would be very welcome.

Thank you for your help. I look forward to hearing from you soon.

Yours sincerely,

Paul Panther

Paul Panther

TIPP
Bei einer formellen E-Mail brauchst du Datum und Adressaten nicht zu nennen. Ansonsten gelten dieselben Regeln wie bei einem formellen Brief. Liste am Ende der Mail deine Kontaktdaten auf (Name, Adresse, ggf. Telefonnummer). Ganz wichtig: verwende auf keinen Fall Emoticons oder Smileys.

SF 7 Writing a comment / opinion piece

→ p. 29

In einem Meinungsartikel oder Kommentar (*opinion piece/comment)* geht es darum, deine persönliche Meinung zu präsentieren und mit Argumenten zu stützen.

PLANUNGSPHASE

Step 1: Sammle Ideen und mache erste Notizen. Was willst du sagen? Was willst du erreichen? Welche Fakten oder Zitate unterstützen deine Meinung? Hast du schon eine Lösungsidee, von der du andere überzeugen möchtest?

Step 2: Überlege dir eine gute Überschrift. Sie sollte die Aufmerksamkeit der Leser wecken und sie neugierig machen.

Step 3: Erstelle Notizen/eine Outline. Überlege, wie du deine Argumentation/Meinung unterstützen kannst (Fakten, Statistiken, Zitate etc.).

Step 4: Recherchiere passendes Material. (→ *SF 27*)

SCHREIBPHASE

Step 1: Beginne deinen *comment* mit einem kurzen Absatz zu dem Thema und deiner Meinung dazu.

Step 2: Präsentiere Argumente für deine Meinung in den folgenden Absätzen und ergänze sie mit weiteren Fakten, Beispielen oder Zitaten.

- Benutze das simple present für generelle Aussagen und das simple present oder simple past für die Beispiele, Anekdoten etc., die deine Meinung stützen.
- Verwende Überzeugungstechniken. Das sind z.B
  – Personalpronomen, um den Text persönlicher zu machen: mit you sprichst du Leser direkt an, mit we stellst du eine Gemeinsamkeit her und mit I unterstreichst du, dass es sich um deine Meinung handelt.
  – Zitate, Anekdoten, Statistiken stützen deine Meinung: Zitate zeigen, dass andere Menschen deine Meinung teilen, Anekdoten bringen deine Punkte den Lesern näher und Statistiken belegen, dass deine Meinung auf Fakten beruht.
  – Ausdrucksstarke Sprache: schreibe abwechlungsreich (→ *SF 5*) und verwende Wörter, die emotional ansprechen, wie z. B. Adjektive und Adverbien, die den Leser wütend oder glücklich, traurig oder fröhlich machen
  – Rhetorische Fragen: mit Fragen, auf die eigentlich keine Antwort erwartet wird, kannst du deine Aussage nochmal unterstreichen: Is climate change real? Is killing wrong? Who can deny this?

Step 3: Im letzten Absatz, der *conclusion*, wiederholst du noch einmal deine Meinung und schlägst entweder eine Lösung vor (wenn es sich z. B. um ein Problem handelt) oder forderst deine Leser auf, etwas zu tun.

Outline / Notes

1. Headline
   - catch your readers' attention (clear statement, provocative question etc.)
2. First paragraph
   - state your topic AND your opinion clearly (keep it short!)
   - keep your readers interested
3. Supporting paragraphs
   use statistics, facts, quotes etc. to back up your main statement
4. Final paragraph / Conclusion
   - restate your opinion
   - suggest a solution or call for action

TIPP
Übertreibe es nicht mit den Statistiken, Anekdoten und Zitaten, sondern konzentriere dich auf besonders interessante oder spannende Punkte wie z. B. Zahlen, die dich in einer Statistik selber überrascht haben.

SF 8 Argumentative writing

→ p. 50

Wenn du eine Erörterung schreibst – also schriftlich für oder gegen etwas argumentierst – solltest du deinen Text gut strukturieren und deine Argumente klar und schlüssig präsentieren, um deine Leser zu überzeugen.

PLANUNGSPHASE

Step 1: Lies die Aufgabe sorgfältig durch.

Step 2: Sammle Ideen und mache erste Notizen. Schreibe alle Argumente pro *und* contra auf, die dir einfallen.

Step 3: Ordne deine Argumente, z.B. in Form einer Outline. Hebe das Argument hervor, das deine Position am besten unterstreicht – damit solltest du deinen Hauptteil beenden, denn das merken sich die Leser am ehesten.

Outline / Notes

1. Introduction
introduce the topic

2. Main body
1. paragraph: arguments contra
- argument 1
- argument 2 etc
2./3. paragraph: arguments pro
- argument 1
- argument 2 etc
end with strongest argument!

4. Conclusion
sum up your arguments
give your opinion

SCHREIBPHASE

Step 1: Schreibe deine Einleitung: sage kurz, um welches Thema es geht, ohne deine eigene Meinung dazu zu äußern.

Step 2: Im Hauptteil präsentierst du die Argumente, die du dir überlegt hast. Dabei helfen folgende Redemittel:

- Presenting arguments:
  One of the main reasons why … • *It is often said that …* • *Some people think …* • *In addition to these points …*
- Ordering arguments:
  To start with, … • *Firstly,/Secondly,/Thirdly, …* • *Finally, …* • *First of all …*
- Contrasting arguments:
  On the one hand – on the other hand • *Contrary to what most people believe, …* • *While / Although …* • …
- Giving examples:
  For example, … • *This is clear because …*

Step 3: Am Schluss fasst du deine Argumente nochmal kurz zusammen und erklärst deine Schlussfolgerung:

- Summing up arguments:
  To sum up, … • *In conclusion, …* • *All in all, …* • *I would like to finish by pointing out again that …*
- Explaining your conclusion:
  After looking at both sides of the argument … • *Although I understand the other side of the argument, I still think …* • *Personally, I believe that …*

TIPP
Deine Argumente wirken überzeugender, wenn du:
- dich wo möglich auf deine eigenen Erfahrungen berufst,
- Fakten (Quellen, Experten, Statistiken usw.) präsentierst: *It can't be denied that …, It's a fact that …, It goes without saying that … .*

SF 9 Writing a summary

Wenn du eine Zusammenfassung schreiben sollst, ist es wichtig, den Text gut zu verstehen. Erst dann kannst du entscheiden, welche Aspekte so wichtig sind, dass sie in deiner Zusammenfassung erwähnt werden sollten – und welche nicht. Die folgenden Schritte können beim Schreiben einer Zusammenfassung helfen:

PLANUNGSPHASE

Step 1: Lies den Text genau. Mache dir Notizen (➡ *SF 31*) oder markiere wichtige Stellen im Text (➡ *SF 2*).

Step 2: Beantworte die *wh*-Fragen *Who? What? Where? When? Why?* zum Text. Du kannst dir dazu Stichworte am Rand machen.

Who? Who does something? Who is the text about?
What? What happens? What does person X do?
Where? Where does it take place?
When? When does it take place?
Why? Why does person X act this way? Why does something happen?

Step 3: Entscheide, welche Textteile wichtige Informationen enthalten. Beispiele, Vergleiche, direkte Rede oder Zahlen und Ähnliches gehören nicht in eine Zusammenfassung.

LANGUAGE HELP
Folgende *phrases* können dir bei der Einleitung helfen:
- The story/text is about …
- The text deals with …
- The topic of the text is …
- The article/text shows …

TIPP
Du kannst Teile, die für deine Zusammenfassung überflüssig sind, im Text einklammern.

SCHREIBPHASE

Step 1: Schreibe einen ersten Entwurf.

- Beginne mit der Einleitung, in der wichtige Informationen wie Titel, Autor/in, Thema und Hauptaussage des Textes stehen. Wenn du einen Artikel zusammenfasst, solltest du hier die Quelle nennen.
- Verwende immer das *simple present*.
- Kopiere nicht den Text, sondern benutze deine eigenen Worte.
- Wichtig: gib nie deine eigene Meinung oder Wertung.

Step 2: Überarbeite deine Zusammenfassung.

- Hast du alle wichtigen Aspekte genannt und unwichtige Details weggelassen?
- Ist der Text durchgängig im *simple present*?
- Vergiss nicht, Rechtschreibung/Grammatik zu prüfen. (➡ *SF 10*)

LANGUAGE HELP
Folgende *phrases* können dir bei der Einleitung helfen:
- *The story/text is about …*
- *The text deals with …*
- *The topic of the text is …*
- *The article/text shows …*

SF 10 Revising texts

Egal, ob du eine Rückmeldung von einem Partner/einer Partnerin bekommen hast oder nicht – einen Text solltest du auf jeden Fall noch einmal gut prüfen, bevor du ihn deinem Lehrer/deiner Lehrerin übergibst.

TEXTÜBERARBEITUNG

1. **Stimmt die Struktur?**
   Jeder Text braucht
   - eine Einleitung, die in das Thema einführt,
   - einen Hauptteil, der das Thema ausführt,
   - einen Schluss, der alles auf den Punkt bringt.

   (➡ *SF 4*)

2. **Stimmt der Aufbau der Absätze?**
   Jeder Absatz
   - befasst sich mit einem zusammenhängenden Gedanken,
   - beginnt mit einem ***topic sentence***, der diesen Gedanken einführt.

   (➡ *SF 4*)

3. **Stimmen die Verknüpfungen?**
   Gute *linking words*
   - schaffen Verbindungen zwischen Sätzen oder Satzteilen,
   - helfen, Zusammenhänge besser darzustellen und verständlich zu machen.

   (➡ *SF 5*)

4. **Sind die Zeitangaben richtig gesetzt?**
   Time markers
   - helfen, sich z. B. in einer Geschichte zurechtzufinden,
   - machen das Geschehen anschaulicher.

   (➡ *SF 5*)

5. **Enthält der Text Adjektive und Adverbien?**
   Adjektive und Adverbien
   - erlauben nähere Beschreibungen von Personen und Dingen,
   - machen Texte anschaulicher.

   (➡ *SF 5*)

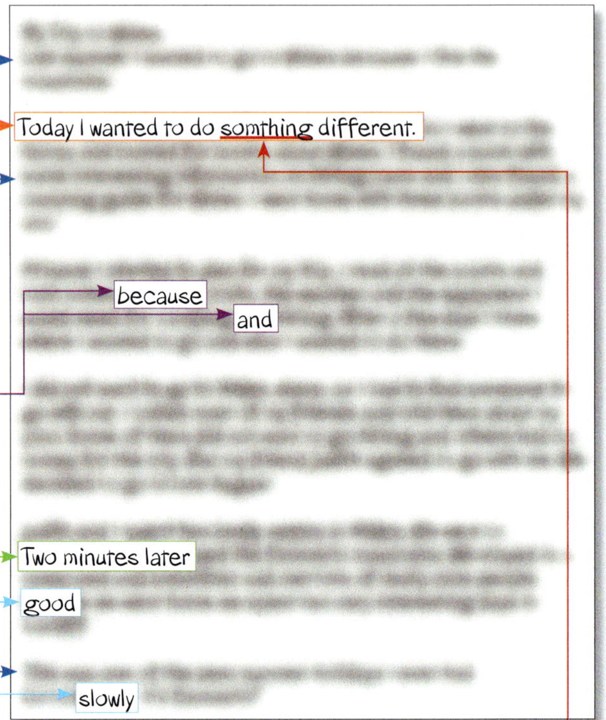

6. **Hat der Text sprachliche/grammatikalische Fehler?**
   Überprüfe deinen Text
   - auf Rechtschreibung,
   - auf grammatische Formen, z. B. Verbformen, Satzbau *(word order)* usw.

FEHLERPROTOKOLL

Die Fehler in einem Text zu finden und zu korrigieren ist eine Sache, aber es wäre natürlich noch viel besser, dieselben Fehler nicht wieder zu machen.

Dabei hilft ein Fehlerprotokoll, in dem du dir die wichtigsten Fehler – diejenigen, die du immer wieder machst – notierst und dir immer wieder veranschaulichst. Dieses Fehlerprotokoll kann ein kleines Extra-Heft sein oder auch eine Sammlung von Klebezetteln, die du dir über deinen Schreibtisch hängst.

Hauptsache, es ist etwas, worauf du immer wieder schnell zurückgreifen kannst, wenn du einen Text schreiben sollst.

TIPP

Häufige Fehlerquellen sind z. B.
- Groß-/Kleinschreibung
- Wörter, die gleich klingen, aber unterschiedlich geschrieben werden: *their/there/they're*
- Verwendung des Apostrophs
- Bildung der Zeitformen der Verben: *stop* → *stopping*, *try* → *tries*
- Wörter mit „stummen" Buchstaben: *walk, talk, know*

MEDIATION SKILLS

SF 11 Mediating written or spoken information

Nicht jeder spricht und versteht sowohl Deutsch als auch Englisch; daher kann es vorkommen, dass du in bestimmten Situationen für Andere zwischen den Sprachen mitteln musst – das nennt man dann Mediation.

Wie und was genau du mitteln musst, hängt von der Situation ab und auch davon, ob du den Inhalt eines geschriebenen Textes wiedergeben oder zwischen zwei Sprechern mitteln sollst.

Sprachmittlung bedeutet nicht Übersetzen (von Texten) oder Dolmetschen (bei Unterhaltungen), sondern das sinngemäße Übertragen von Inhalten in die andere Sprache.

MEDIATION VON SCHRIFTLICHEN ODER MÜNDLICHEN INFORMATIONEN

Wenn du Informationen in einer anderen Sprache wiedergeben sollst, geht es nicht darum, alles zu übersetzen, sondern es kommt darauf an, die wichtigsten Informationen herauszusuchen. Oft stellt dir die Person, für die du die Informationen wiedergibst, gezielte Fragen – so weißt du, worauf du achten musst.

Schriftliche Informationen

- Scanne den Text gezielt nach den geforderten Informationen. (➜ *SF 1*)
- Mach dir keine Sorgen, wenn du nicht jedes Wort verstehst. Das ist oft nicht nötig, um die wichtigen Punkte zu verstehen und wiederzugeben.
- Wenn der Text länger ist und du viele Informationen im Blick behalten musst, markiere die wichtigsten Textstellen. (➜ *SF 2*)
- Mach dir Notizen in deinen eigenen Worten. (➜ *SF 31*)

Mündliche Informationen

- Achte beim Hören gezielt auf die gesuchten Informationen. (➜ *SF 20*)
- Mach dir Notizen. (➜ *SF 31*)
- Überlege, wie du deine Notizen am besten in der anderen Sprache wiedergeben kannst.

TIPP
Bei Mediation im Unterricht hast du in der Regel eine Aufgabenstellung, die dir sagt, worauf du beim Lesen oder Hören achten musst bzw. welche Stellen du wiedergeben sollst. Konzentriere dich beim Lesen des Textes auf diese Stellen *(scanning)* bzw. mache dir gezielt zu diesen Stellen Notizen.

TIPP
Wenn du den Inhalt eines Texts schriftlich in einer anderen Sprache wiedergeben sollst, achte darauf, dass deine Mediation nicht länger ist als ca. 35-40% des Originaltextes, ähnlich wie bei einer *summary*. (➜ *SF 9*)

SF 12 Finding key information

Manchmal gibt es keine gezielten Fragen oder Aufgabenstellungen, die dir sagen, welche Informationen du aus einem Text heraussuchen und wiedergeben sollst. In der Regel hast du aber trotzdem Anhaltspunkte, die sich aus der Situation ergeben oder aus dem, was dir dein Gegenüber erzählt hat.

Wenn du in einer solchen Situation bist, helfen folgende Hinweise:

- Analysiere die Situation, um abzuschätzen, um welche Informationen es gehen könnte (Restaurant, Bahnhof, Flughafen usw.).
- Wenn du unsicher bist, frage nach.
- Übersetze wichtige Stichworte direkt, wenn du die Wörter kennst.
- Umschreibe Begriffe, die du nicht kennst.

TIPP
Wenn du Informationen wiedergibst, kannst du oft Details zu einem Begriff zusammenfassen. Wenn z. B. in einem Text *Twitter, Facebook, Tumblr* und *Pinterest* vorkommen, kannst du *social media* sagen anstatt alle aufzuzählen.

SF 13 Paraphrasing

Es fällt dir eventuell manchmal schwer, mündliche Aussagen oder Texte in Englisch wiederzugeben, z. B. weil

- dein Wortschatz nicht ausreicht
- dir bekannte Wörter in der Aufregung nicht einfallen
- oder spezielle Fachbegriffe auftauchen.

Wenn dir das passiert, dann solltest du versuchen, diese Wörter zu umschreiben, z. B. mithilfe von Relativsätzen wie:

It's somebody/a person who …
It's something that you use to …
It's an animal that …
It's a place that/where …

TIPP
Oft helfen beim Umschreiben auch Synonyme (gleiche Bedeutung) oder Antonyme (gegenteilige Bedeutung). Wenn du die weißt, kannst du z. B. sagen:
- *It's the same as …*
- *It's the opposite of …*

SF 14 Cultural differences

➔ p. 31

Wenn du anderen Menschen hilfst, Texte oder Gehörtes zu verstehen, kann es neben Wortschatzproblemen auch noch andere Schwierigkeiten geben. Diese sind häufig in kulturellen Unterschieden begründet. Um hier helfen zu können, musst du dir beim Sprachmitteln bewusst machen, dass dein Gegenüber evtl. bestimmte Dinge nicht weiß, die für dich selbstverständlich sind, oder dass er/sie dich nicht sofort versteht, obwohl du den Inhalt korrekt übertragen hast.

Dinge, die häufig zu Missverständnissen führen, sind z. B.
- Temperaturen: 30 Grad bei uns sind heiß, in den USA eher kalt, weil in den USA Temperaturen in Fahrenheit angegeben werden, nicht in Celsius.
- Längenangaben/Geschwindigkeit: Bei uns wird das metrische System verwendet (Meter, Kilometer usw.), in den USA das *imperial system* mit *inch*, *yard* und *mile*. Das kann auch bei Geschwindigkeitsangaben zu Verwirrung führen, denn 75 *mph* (Meilen pro Stunde) sind z. B. ca. 120 km/h.

Am besten ist es, wenn du immer noch mal höflich nachfragst, ob dein Gegenüber alles verstanden hat. Wenn du dann feststellst, dass es zu einem Missverständnis gekommen ist, dann kannst du folgende Dinge probieren:
- Frage höflich nach, wo das Missverständnis ist.
- Versuche, das Missverständnis durch eine neue Erklärung zu beseitigen.
- Ergänze deine Erläuterung evtl. mit Hintergrundinformationen: Es kann sein, dass du bestimmte Dinge, die für dich völlig normal sind, erklären musst (wie z. B. Mülltrennung oder das Benutzen des Nahverkehrs).
- Sei auch offen für die Erklärungen, die du evtl. im Gegenzug bekommst – hier kannst du Dinge über das Land deines Gegenübers lernen.

VIEWING SKILLS

SF 15 Viewing (Media skills)

Wenn du verstehst, wie Filmtechniken eingesetzt werden, um beim Zuschauer z.B. Angst, Freude, Spannung oder Lachen auszulösen, bekommst du ein besseres Verständnis dafür, wie Filme funktionieren.

Es gibt viele verschiedene Elemente, die die Atmosphäre und die Wirkung eines Filmes beeinflussen:

- *Genre:* Handelt es sich um einen Dokumentarfilm *(documentary)*, einen Spielfilm *(feature film)* wie z. B. *thriller, science-fiction/sci-fi movie, comedy* oder ein *drama*? Oder ist es ein Videoclip oder ein Werbefilm?
- *Story:* Wo und wann spielt der Film *(setting)*? Besetzung der Rollen *(cast)*, Schauplatz *(location)*, Handlung *(plot)*.
- *Camera:* Erst durch die Bilder der **Kamera** ist der Zuschauer in der Lage, einen Film wahrzunehmen. Die Kamera stellt das Blickfeld her und begrenzt es gleichzeitig, z. B. hinsichtlich der Beziehung der Charaktere zueinander. Auch die Stimmung oder Spannung in einer Szene wird von der Kameraführung beeinflusst. Dafür gibt es z. B. folgende Mittel:
  - *Shots:* Die **Kameraeinstellung** beeinflusst, wie man Szenen wahrnimmt, ob z. B. Personen oder Objekte als Nahaufnahme *(close-up)*, aus der mittleren Distanz *(medium shot)* oder als Totale *(long shot)* gefilmt sind.
  - *Editing:* Filme werden in der Regel nicht chronologisch gedreht und auch nicht nur mit einer einzigen Kamera, d. h. am Ende der Dreharbeiten müssen viele einzelne Shots zu einem Film zusammengefügt werden. Dieser **Filmschnitt** bestimmt, wie eine Szene wirkt. Er bestimmt den Rhythmus – lange Einstellungen mit wenigen Schnitten wirken eher ruhig, können aber auch große Spannung erzeugen, während schnelle, harte Schnitte eher actiongeladen wirken. Wie genau eine Szene wirkt, hängt oft auch vom Zusammenspiel von Schnitt und Musik ab.
- *Soundtrack:* Die **Musik**, die für eine Szene gewählt wird, hat großen Einfluss darauf, wie man die Szene wahrnimmt. Eine Actionszene wird meist mit schneller, lauter Musik unterlegt, eine romantische Szene eher mit ruhiger, leiser Musik. Dies geschieht, um die Wirkung des Gesehenen zu verstärken.

long shot

medium shot

close-up

VIEWING LOG

Wenn du eine Szene oder einen ganzen Film sehr intensiv analysieren möchtest, hilft es, ein Filmtagebuch *(viewing log)* anzulegen, in dem du die Handlung oder einzelne wichtige Szenen sowie deine Reaktion darauf festhältst.

Das Filmtagebuch kann z. B. eine simple, zweispaltige Tabelle sein:
Spalte 1: *What you noticed* – images, sounds, dialogue, lighting, costumes, mood, characterization, plot, etc.
Spalte 2: *Your reaction* – What did you think? How did the scene make you feel?

TIPP

Wenn du über Filme sprechen möchtest, können dir folgende Redewendungen helfen:

- *The film is about … / shows … / tells the story of …*
- *The music creates/builds/supports tension/ suspense/joy …*
- *The actor's body language helps to create a feeling of happiness/joy/anger/suspense …*
- *In this scene the music/effects/camera angle … supports the plot /mood of the scene / …*
- *The camera movement creates a feeling of …*
- *The camera work/soundtrack helps to …*
- *The close-ups show his/her feelings.*

SPEAKING SKILLS

SF 16 Communicating in everyday situations

Es ist nicht immer einfach, sich mit Menschen aus anderen Ländern zu unterhalten. Neben der Sprachbarriere gibt es oft auch kulturelle Unterschiede, wie das folgende Beispiel zeigt.

Lies dieses Gespräch zwischen Paul, einem deutschen Schüler, und seinem Austauschpartner Jack in den USA:

Jack: How's your school at home?
Paul: It's okay.
Jack: Oh … good. What are your favorite subjects?
Paul: Er, I don't know.
Jack: Oh, well. Maybe you'll enjoy our school too.
Paul: Maybe.
Jack: Er … want to play a game?

Das Gespräch kommt nicht so richtig in Gang, und Jack gibt irgendwann auf. Wenn man aber einige Regeln beachtet, werden Unterhaltungen einfacher und für beide Parteien erfreulicher. Vergleiche das folgende Gespräch mit dem obigen:

Jack: How's your school at home?
Paul: I like it … but of course I don't like all my teachers.
Jack: Yeah, I think that's normal. What are your favorite subjects?
Paul: I'm not sure. I like history and maths, but art and German are okay too.
Jack: Ah, my favorite subject is English. Anyway, I'm sure you'll enjoy our school too. Our history teacher is pretty cool. Have you met any of the teachers yet?
Paul: No, not yet, but I think …

Die folgenden Schritte helfen dir, wenn du dich freundlich und flüssig unterhalten willst:

Step 1: Beginne freundlich, z. B. mit etwas, was beide Gesprächspartner verbindet (der Ort, die Situation usw.).

Step 2: Halte die Unterhaltung am Laufen:
- zeige dein Interesse, indem du Fragen stellst
- vermeide einsilbige Antworten, um nicht desinteressiert oder unfreundlich zu wirken
- wenn du etwas nicht verstehst, frage nach
- wenn du etwas nicht sagen kannst, versuche es zu umschreiben oder bitte deinen Gesprächspartner um Hilfe

Step 3: Beende das Gespräch so freundlich, wie du es angefangen hast:
- bedanke dich, wenn du um Hilfe gebeten hast
- verabschiede dich freundlich

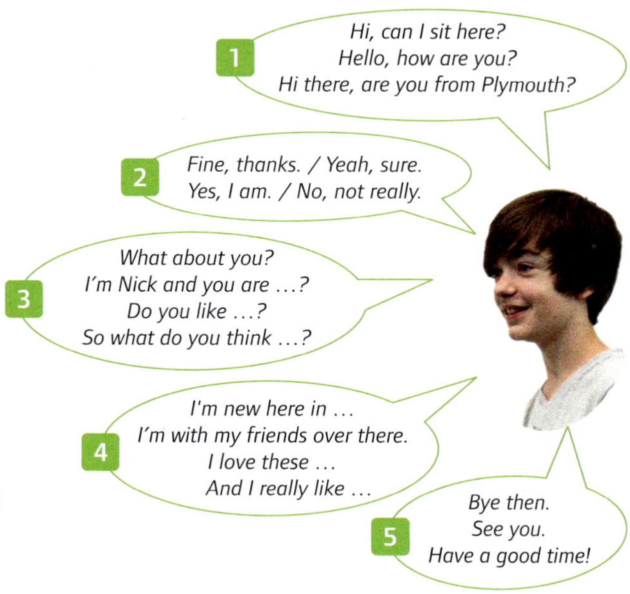

TIPP
Mache dir vor dem Gespräch klar, mit wem du redest. Wenn du mit einem gleichaltrigen Jugendlichen sprichst, kannst du viel informeller sprechen als wenn du mit jemand Älterem sprichst. Überlege auch, ob es kulturelle Unterschiede gibt und passe deine Sprache entsprechend an (➔ *SF 14*).

SF 17 Having a discussion

➔ p. 57

In einer Diskussion tauscht man Meinungen und Ideen zu einem bestimmten Thema aus.

VORBEREITUNGSPHASE

Step 1: Bereite dich auf das Thema vor: Recherchiere Fakten und Beispiele und überlege, was deine Meinung zu dem Thema ist. Mache dir Notizen.

Step 2: Halte deine Notizen für die Diskussion bereit – z.B. auf kleinen Zetteln – damit du darauf zugreifen kannst, falls du sie brauchst.

Step 3: Überlege dir vorher ein Statement, das deine Meinung zum Thema gut ausdrückt; das erleichtert den Einstieg in die Diskussion.

DISKUSSION

Step 1: *Starting the discussion:* Sage deine Meinung (z.B. mithilfe der Eröffnung, die du dir überlegt hast).

Step 2: *Continuing the discussion:* Tausche deine Meinung mit anderen aus. Bleibe höflich und sachlich. Hör den anderen zu und lass sie ausreden.

- Wenn du sprichst, beziehe dich auf die Anderen und sage, weshalb du ihren Argumenten zustimmst (oder nicht).
- Stütze deine Meinung mit Fakten und Beispielen.

Step 3: *Ending the discussion:*

- Fasse deinen Standpunkt noch einmal knapp zusammen.
- Versuche, Gemeinsamkeiten festzustellen (v.a. wenn es darum geht, sich auf etwas zu einigen) oder einigt euch darüber, dass es nicht *eine* gemeinsame Lösung gibt *(agree to disagree)*.
- Wenn gefordert, einigt euch auf eine Lösung oder einen Kompromiss.

TIPP

Bei Rollenspielen musst du manchmal eine Meinung vertreten, die anders ist als deine eigene. Dann kannst du in deinen Notizen z.B. versuchen, Argumente und Gegenargumente einander gegenüberzustellen, um dann in der Diskussion schnell und gut reagieren zu können.

TIPP

Im Englischen ist man häufig weit weniger direkt als im Deutschen. Das bedeutet, dass du bei Diskussionen
- besonders gut zuhören musst, weil du sonst evtl. nicht genau mitbekommst, ob man dir zustimmt oder widerspricht;
- kurze, zu direkte Antworten wie *"No."* vermeiden solltest, weil sie unhöflich wirken.

SF 18 Agreeing and disagreeing with people's opinions

➔ p. 57

Wenn du mit anderen diskutierst, wirst du anderen Gesprächsteilnehmern zustimmen oder widersprechen. Wie im Deutschen, gibt es dafür auch im Englischen bestimmte Redewendungen, die du dafür gut verwenden kannst.

LANGUAGE HELP

Es ist bei Diskussionen hilfreich, einige Standard-Redewendungen parat zu haben. Wenn du die beherrscht, kannst du dich mehr auf deine Argumente konzentrieren. Folgende Phrasen solltest du dir aufschreiben und sie lernen:

Stating your opinion
- *In my opinion ...*
- *Well, I'd say ...*
- *It's a fact that ...*
- *Personally, I think...*
- *If you ask me ...*
- *I think/feel/believe ...*
- *First of all, I'd like to point out...*
- *I'm certain that ...*

Agreeing
- *I agree ...*
- *Exactly./Absolutely./...*
- *You're quite right.*
- *I think so too.*
- *You've got a good point there.*
- *That's exactly how I see it.*
- *That's true/right.*
- *I couldn't agree with you more.*

Disagreeing
- *I'm afraid I don't quite agree ...*
- *I'm not sure about that.*
- *Do you really think so?*
- *I'm not convinced that ...*
- *I doubt that (very much).*
- *I don't agree with you at all.*
- *I disagree (completely).*
- *It's not as simple as that.*

SF 19 Taking part in an interview

➔ p. 99

Interviews sind häufig Bestandteil von Prüfungen oder Bewerbungen. Es ist wichtig, gerade wenn es um Bewerbungsgespräche oder Prüfungen geht, dass du dich gut darauf vorbereitest.

Bei Bewerbungsgesprächen helfen die folgenden 4 Ps:

PREPARE

- Finde so viel wie möglich über den Job und den Arbeitgeber heraus.
- Notiere mögliche Fragen, die du dem Arbeitgeber stellen kannst.
- Überlege dir aber auch, welche Fragen man dir stellen könnte und bereite Antworten darauf vor.

PRACTISE

- Übe das Bewerbungsgespräch mit einem Partner/einer Partnerin.
- Gib deinem Übungspartner die Fragen, die du von deinem Arbeitgeber erwartest und beantworte sie. Sage deinem Übungspartner auch, dass er/sie dir ruhig unerwartete Fragen stellen soll. So übst du, auf unvorbereitete Fragen zu antworten.

PRESENT

- Überlege dir im Vorfeld, was du zu dem Bewerbungsgespräch anziehen möchtest. Besprich das ruhig auch mit einem Freund/einer Freundin oder deinen Eltern. Die Auswahl der Kleidung hängt vom Arbeitgeber ab.
- Stelle sicher, dass du pünktlich bist. Suche dir vorher heraus, wie du zum Ort des Gespräches kommst. Plane Zeit für Unvorhergesehenes ein. Es ist immer besser, zehn Minuten zu früh als zu spät zu sein.

PARTICIPATE

- Stelle dich am Anfang vor, am besten mit einem freundlichen Lächeln.
- Lass dir Zeit, Fragen zu beantworten, besonders wenn es unerwartete Fragen sind. Antworte nicht mit "Yes." oder "No.", sondern versuche, Fragen ausführlich und höflich zu beantworten.
- Wenn du eine Frage nicht verstehst, frag nach.
- Am Ende des Gespräches, verabschiede dich mit einem freundlichen Lächeln und bedanke dich für das Gespräch.

TIPP

Achte auch auf deine non-verbale Kommunikation – wie du stehst, gehst, sitzt – und siehe deinem Gegenüber in die Augen.

LANGUAGE HELP

Folgender Wortschatz hilft dir ...

- bei der Begrüßung: *Nice to meet you too. • Thank you for inviting me today. • I'm fine, thank you.*
- über dich selbst zu sprechen: *Well, I'm 16 years old and ... • Actually, one of my main strengths is ...*
- zu erklären, was du meinst: *What I mean is ... • What I'm really trying to say is ... • I'm glad you asked that question because ... • ... is very important to me, as is ...*
- weitere Punkte anzubringen: *Another point I should mention is ... • There's something else I'd like to say. • Let me explain that in some more detail.*
- aufmerksam zu wirken: *I see. • Right. • Uhuh.*
- bei Unklarheiten nachzufragen: *Sorry, I don't quite understand. • Sorry, but do you mean ... • I am not sure I have understood your question correctly. • Sorry, could you rephrase that?*
- bei der Verabschiedung: *Thank you for the chance to speak to you.*

SF 20 Listening strategies

Wenn du Englisch hörst, kann es sein, dass du entweder Details heraushören musst *(listening for detail)*, z. B. bei Ansagen am Bahnhof, oder generell verstehen musst, um was es geht *(listening for gist)* wie z. B. bei einem Film. Dazu kannst du verschiedene Hörverstehenstechniken anwenden.

LISTENING FOR DETAIL

- Überleg dir vorher, auf welche Informationen du achten musst.
  - Bei einem Wetterbericht sind das z. B. Beschreibungen wie *sunny, cloudy, chance of rain* etc., bei Bahnhofsansagen z. B. Wörter wie *platform* oder Orte und Zeiten.
  - Höre dann gezielt auf solche Wörter und notiere sie. (➔ *SF 31*)
- Manchmal können dir Signalwörter helfen, dem Inhalt zu folgen und dich auf die Details zu konzentrieren:
  - Gründe, Folgen: *because, so, so that, …*
  - Vergleiche: *larger/older/… than, as … as, more, most, …*
  - Reihenfolge: *before, after, then, next, later, …*

TIPP
Im Unterricht kannst du Texte oft zweimal hören und hast weitere Hilfen:
- Sieh dir die Aufgabenstellung an: Was sollst du heraushören?
- Sieh dir Titel und Bilder an.
- Vergleiche nach dem Hören mit einem Partner, was ihr verstanden habt.
- Vervollständige deine Notizen sofort.

LISTENING FOR GIST

- Mache dir keine Sorgen, wenn du nicht jedes Wort verstehst – das brauchst du nicht, um dem Inhalt oberflächlich folgen zu können. Überlege dir anhand der Aufgabe, um was es gehen könnte und konzentriere dich darauf.
- Versuche, von den Sachen, die du verstehst, auf Inhalte zu schließen, die noch kommen könnten.

HÖRVERSTEHENSTECHNIKEN

Es gibt zwei verschiedene Techniken beim Hörverstehen:
- Bei der *bottom-up-Technik* gehst du vom Gesprochenen an das Hören heran: Konzentriere dich darauf, *was* gerade gesagt wird und beachte dabei z. B die Besonderheiten verschiedener Akzente. Wie gut du das verstehst, was du in der Fremdsprache hörst, ist eine Frage der Übung.

  Du solltest beim Hören folgende Dinge beachten:
  - *Chunks/connected speech:* Im Englischen spricht man oft mehrere Wörter als Einheit aus, bei der Wortgrenzen verschwinden. Das findet man verstärkt bei
    - Ausdrücken mit Modalverben: *she'd've told me* • *you shouldn't've bought it* • *you mustabin asleep*
    - häufigen Alltagsphrasen: *Whatcha think o'that?* • *Howdju feel?* • *Dincha see it?* • *Whatchadoin'?*
  - Wörter, die gesprochen gleich klingen, sich in der Bedeutung aber unterscheiden:
    We'd like ice in our drinks. – *We like ice in our drinks.*
    I can't see them now. – *I can see them now.* (besonders im AE)
    Hier schafft im Gespräch gezieltes Nachfragen Sicherheit: *Sorry, was that can or can't?*
- Bei der *top-down-Technik* gehst du von der Gesprächssituation aus an das Hören heran und versuchst, mögliche Inhalte vorherzusagen:
  - Du kannst Gesprächsinhalte erschließen und das Verstehen erleichtern, wenn du dir Gedanken über die Situation machst:
    - Wer redet in dieser Situation?
    - Über was wird in dieser Situation eventuell gesprochen?
    - Wie sprechen die Personen in dieser Situation miteinander?
    - Werden die Personen eher freundlich, höflich oder verärgert sein?

TIPP
Beim Hörverstehen hilft vor allem Übung, v.a. wenn es um *Chunks/connected speech* oder verschiedene Dialekte und Akzente geht.
Höre dir deshalb so oft du kannst Originaltexte an, z. B Audiobooks oder in Videos online, um ein Gefühl dafür zu entwickeln.

Um dich in unterschiedliche Akzente reinzuhören und sich an sie zu "gewöhnen", kannst du z. B Filme und Serien im Original ansehen, bei denen du zur Hilfe englische Untertitel einblenden kannst.

- Sprechen sie in der gegeben Situation eher schnell oder langsam, eher formell oder informell?

– Diese Vorüberlegungen helfen dir vorherzusagen, was im Gespräch gesagt wird *(prediction)*, selbst wenn du nicht jedes Wort verstehst oder durch äußere Umstände wie z. B laute Nebengeräusche nicht hören kannst: *It's very warm in here, isn't it? Should I open …? • It's my brother's birthday next week. I don't know what to …*

– Häufig kannst du das Thema eines Gespräches erkennen, auch wenn du nicht hörst, worum es genau geht *(inference)*. Du hörst dabei die Situation sozusagen „zwischen den Zeilen" heraus. Im folgenden Kurzdialog geht es z. B um Essen und sehr wahrscheinlich um Pizza, ohne dass davon direkt gesprochen wird: *Hey, do you want one slice or two? – I'll have two. Ham and extra cheese.*

PROJECT AND PRESENTATION SKILLS

SF 21 Teamwork

Bei Projekten arbeitet ihr oft im Team. Dabei solltet ihr eure unterschiedlichen Fähigkeiten und Talente einbringen und bestimmte Regeln beachten. Folgende Schritte können helfen, die Arbeit zu organisieren:

Step 1: Legt Regeln für die Arbeit in der Gruppe fest, z. B. gegenseitige Unterstützung, pünktliches und zügiges Arbeiten, einander zuhören oder verschiedene Lösungen diskutieren usw.

Step 2: Sammelt Ideen für die Bearbeitung eures Themas (z. B. in einer Mindmap). Wählt gemeinsam Unterthemen aus und legt die Arbeitsschritte fest, die für die Bearbeitung nötig sind.

Step 3: Verteilt Rollen und Aufgaben nach euren Interessen und Fähigkeiten. Wenn ihr euch nicht einigen könnt, hilft Auslosen oder Würfeln. Folgende Rollen solltet ihr auf jeden Fall verteilen:
- *coordinator*
- *writer*
- *researcher*

Step 4: Macht einen Zeitplan für eure Arbeiten, an den sich alle halten.

Step 5: Am Ende der Arbeit sollte ein Rückblick stehen: Besprecht, was gut war und wo ihr Verbesserungsmöglichkeiten seht.

SF 22 Putting a page together (Media skills)

Wenn du einen Text gestalten möchtest, z. B. für einen Vortrag, einen Blog oder als Poster für eine Präsentation, können dir folgende Hinweise helfen:

- Sortiere die Informationen, die du vermitteln willst: Was ist wichtig? Was ist ein Unterpunkt? Hast du Beispiele für Thesen/Argumente?
- Gib deinem Produkt eine klare Struktur: Texte haben meist drei Teile (Einleitung, Hauptteil, Schluss), während Poster häufig aus Aufzählungen wichtiger Punkte bestehen. Beginne für jeden neuen Gedanken einen neuen Absatz bzw. einen neuen Stichpunkt.

- Eine Überschrift verdeutlicht, worum es in deinem Text geht. Sie soll Leser neugierig machen auf das, was kommt. Wenn es in deinem Produkt um mehrere Themengeht, dann kannst Du für einzelne Abschnitte auch Zwischenüberschriften verwenden. Das hilft dem Leser, sich zu orientieren.
- Ergänze dein Produkt mit passenden Fotos, Videos, Audios, Statistiken etc. Vergiss nicht anzugeben, woher die Medien stammen (➔ *SF 23*).
- Wenn nicht auf den ersten Blick erkennbar ist, was z.B. ein Bild zeigt, füge Bildunterschriften ein.
- Formatiere dein Produkt so, dass es gut lesbar ist. Dabei ist das Medium wichtig – für einen ausgedruckten Handzettel kannst du andere Schriftarten wählen als für einen Text, der am Bildschirm gelesen wird. (➔ *SF 23*) Für ein Poster (z.B. für einen *gallery walk)* muss die Schriftgröße größer sein als für einen Ausdruck. Eine große Schriftgröße hilft dir auch, nicht zu viele Punkte auf dem Poster unterzubringen – hier ist weniger mehr.

SF 23 Making slides for an electronic presentation

Media skills

➔ *p. 16*

Vieles, was für das Layout von Texten/Postern gilt, kannst du auch auf Folien für Präsentation anwenden. Es gibt aber einige Besonderheiten zu beachten. Generell gilt: gut ist, was deine Folien übersichtlich und leicht zu lesen macht.

TEXT

- Verwende möglichst wenige Folien.
- Nutze Aufzählungen mit *keywords*, keine ganzen Sätze und schreibe nicht mehr als sechs Zeilen auf eine Folie.
- Wähle eine ausreichende Schriftgröße (mindestens 30pt, gerne mehr) und eine gut lesbare Schrift und gehe sparsam mit Texthervorhebungen wie fett, kursiv, Unterstreichung um; lass einen ausreichend großen Abstand zwischen den Zeilen.
- Richte den Text linksbündig aus, außer du verfolgst ein ganz besonderes Ziel damit (z.B. zentriert zum Herausheben eines Zitats), aber mische die Ausrichtung nicht auf einer Folie. Zitate z.B. wirken oft am besten, wenn sie zentriert alleine auf einer Folie stehen.

FARBE UND KONTRAST

- Du kannst einzelne Wörter in einer anderen Farbe setzen, um sie hervorzuheben. Aber auch hier gilt: weniger ist mehr – mehrere Wörter in unterschiedlichen Farben zu setzen, kann beim Lesen eher hinderlich sein.
- Wenn du mit farbigem Untergrund oder Fotos als Hintergrund arbeitest, solltest du darauf achten, dass dein Text in einer Farbe ist, die ausreichend Kontrast zum Hintergrund bietet – je stärker der Kontrast, desto besser die Lesbarkeit.

ABBILDUNGEN

- Ein Bild sagt mehr als tausend Worte – das gilt auch für Folien: manche Inhalte kannst du ebenso mit einem passenden Bild oder einer Grafik ausdrücken.
- Suche ein Bild, dass die Aussage deines Vortrages unterstreicht: z.B. ein Foto, das eine Fragestellung gut illustriert oder eines, das das Problem gut darstellt. Es muss auch kein Foto sein – manchmal ist eine passende Grafik genauso gut, um z.B. statistische Aussagen auf den Punkt zu bringen.
- Wichtig: bei allen Bildern, die verwendest, musst du die Quelle angeben, d.h. der Fotograf/die Fotografin, Illustrator/Illustratorin etc. sowie der Ort, wo du das Bild gefunden hast (eine Suchmaschine im Internet ist keine Quellenangabe!).

TIPP

- Eine gute Faustregel lautet 6 x 6: pro Folie maximal 6 Zeilen mit je maximal 6 Wörtern
- Bedenke: Folien sind eine visuelle Unterstützung für eine Präsentation, keine Zusammenfassung. Die Zuhörer sollen hören, nicht lesen – die Texte sollten daher auf das Wichtigste reduziert sein.
- Vermeide Spezialeffekte wie verspielte Übergänge, tanzende Buchstaben etc. Sie kosten viel Zeit und helfen den Zuhörern nicht.

TIPP

Wenn du deine Folien/Poster nur vor der Klasse zeigst, darfst du Bilder verwenden, ohne die Urheber um Erlaubnis zu fragen, weil es sich um eine begrenzte Öffentlichkeit handelt. Wenn die Folien aber öffentlich zugänglich sind (z.B. auf einer Webseite oder der Schulzeitung), musst du die Urheber unbedingt um Erlaubnis fragen.
Als Faustregel gilt: veröffentliche kein Bild ohne Erlaubnis, das du nicht selbst gemacht hast.

SF 24 Giving a good presentation

Ob in der Schule oder später im Beruf, es ist wichtig, eine gute Präsentation halten zu können, z.B. um andere über ein Thema zu informieren oder um sie von einer Idee oder einem Projekt zu überzeugen. Dabei ist die Vorbereitung genauso wichtig wie der eigentliche Vortrag, denn eine gut vorbereitete Präsentation ist eine gut strukturierte und überzeugende Präsentation.

Die folgenden Schritte helfen dir bei beiden Schritten:

VORBEREITUNG DER PRÄSENTATION

Step 1: Recherchiere dein Thema (➡ *SF 27*) und mach dir Notizen, am besten gleich auf Englisch (➡ *SF 31*).

Step 2: Strukturiere die Informationen, z. B. mit einer Gliederung.

Step 3: Wähle eine Form der Präsentation aus, die das Thema gut veranschaulicht (Poster, Folie, ...). Gestalte dein Poster/deine Folie und beachte dabei die Grundsätze für ein gutes Poster.

Step 4: Bereite deine Notizen für die Präsentation vor, z. B. auf nummerierten Karteikarten. Verwende keine ganzen Sätze, sondern Stichworte, Symbole oder Halbsätze. Notiere dir z.B. auch schwierige Wörter und ihre Aussprache.

TIPP
Um ein gutes Poster zu gestalten, solltest du folgendes beachten:
- Wähle eine passende Überschrift.
- Schreibe groß und für alle gut lesbar.
- Ergänze passende Bilder, um den Text/die Inhalte zu veranschaulichen.

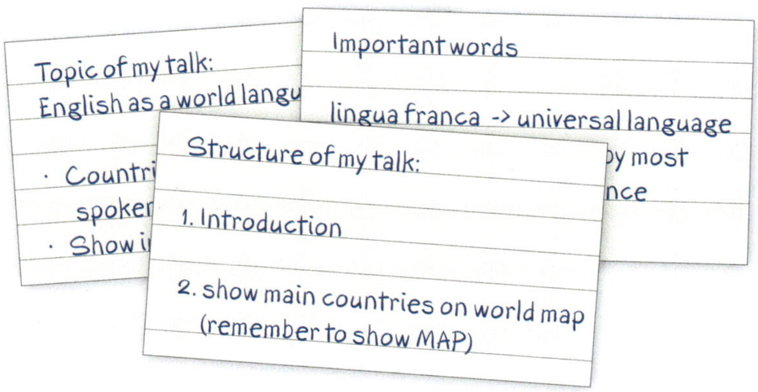

Step 5: Wenn du in einem Team arbeitest, entscheidet gemeinsam, wer welchen Teil der Präsentation übernimmt. (➡ *SF 21*)

Step 5: Übe deine Präsentation zu Hause vor einem Spiegel oder vor einem kleinen Publikum (Eltern, Großeltern, Freunde).

HALTEN DER PRÄSENTATION

Step 1: Warte, bis es ruhig ist. Schau die Zuhörer/innen an. Erkläre, worüber du sprechen wirst und wie deine Präsentation aufgebaut ist.

Step 2: Sprich langsam und deutlich und möglichst frei. Lies nicht von deinen Notizen ab.

Step 3: Beende deine Präsentation mit einer kleinen Zusammenfassung der wichtigsten Punkte. Bedanke dich fürs Zuhören und beantworte Fragen zu deinem Vortrag.

SF 25 Describing, presenting and interpreting pictures

➜ p. 101

Manchmal sollst du im Unterricht ein Bild (Fotos, Cartoons etc.) beschreiben und interpretieren. Hier sind ein paar Hilfen dazu:

BESCHREIBUNG

Step 1: Stelle das Bild vor und sage, woher es kommt.

Step 2: Beschreibe das Bild:

- Sage, was wo zu sehen ist: *at the top/bottom* · *in the foreground/background* · *in the middle* · *on the left/right*
- Geh bei der Beschreibung in einer bestimmten Reihenfolge vor, z. B. von links nach rechts oder von oben nach unten.
- Diese Präpositionen sind auch hilfreich: *behind* · *between* · *in front of* · *next to* · *under* · *above*
- Beziehe dich – v.a. bei Cartoons – auch auf Bildunterschriften, Sprechblasen etc.:
  The caption reads …
  One of the characters says/thinks …

INTERPRETATION

Step 1: Sage, was deiner Meinung nach die Botschaft des Bildes/Cartoons ist:
This is a political/environmental/educational/… photo/cartoon.
I think the message is …
It's about …
… shows that …
The fact that there is … means …
The picture/cartoon may be meant to show …

Step 2: Sage, weshalb du das Bild/den Cartoon wirksam/witzig findest (oder nicht):
The picture/cartoon clearly shows …
The message is made clear by showing/saying …
I really laughed at the cartoon because it …
I don't find the cartoon funny because …
The picture/cartoon speaks to us directly by …

Wenn du das Bild/den Cartoon in einer Präsentation vorstellst, musst du evtl. genauer erklären, weshalb du es ausgewählt hast oder was daran witzig ist:
I chose this picture because …
The joke is that …
It's funny because …
The picture/cartoon is criticizing / making fun of …

"Now don't forget to go on social media and rate today's lesson plan."

SF 26 Talking about statistics

➔ p. 122

Statistiken können auf unterschiedliche Weise dargestellt werden: Tortendiagramm *(pie chart)*, Säulendiagramm *(bar chart)*, Kurvendiagramm *(line graph)* oder in einer Tabelle *(table)*. Wenn du Statistiken analysieren und vorstellen sollst, gehst du am besten wie folgt vor:

Step 1: Identifiziere, welche Art von Diagramm du vor dir hast – *pie chart, bar chart, line graph* oder Tabelle – und sieh dir die Quelle an:

- Ist die Quelle verlässlich?
  Ist der Herausgeber z.B. ein Ministerium/eine Behörde oder eine Organisation wie *amnesty international*?
- Sind die Angaben/Zahlen im Diagramm aktuell?
  Wenn du z.B. eine Statistik zu Kinderarmut in Großbritannien vor dir hast, ist es ein wichtiger Unterschied, ob die Zahlen von 1973 oder 2013 sind.

Step 2: Beschreibe das Diagramm/die Tabelle:

- Worum geht es? Welche Informationen gibt das Diagramm?
  The bar chart / pie chart / line graph / table … shows the different … / compares the size/number of … / is about … / contrasts … with …
- Zeigen die Daten eine Entwicklung oder werden verschiedene Zeitpunkte miteinander verglichen?
  It shows … in contrast to …
  The chart gives us information about who/what/how many/…
- Werden absolute Zahlen oder Prozentangaben verwendet?
  The chart/table shows us the number of/percentage of …
  It shows which percentage of …

Step 3: Ziehe deine Schlussfolgerungen aus dem Diagramm/der Tabelle:
My main conclusion is that …
The most imporant thing I've learned is that …
One thing that I hadn't realized before is …

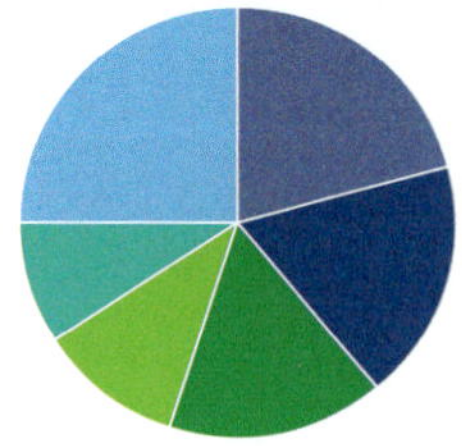
pie chart

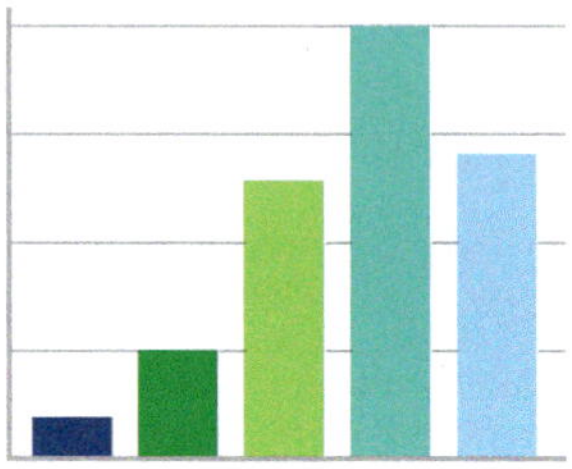
bar chart

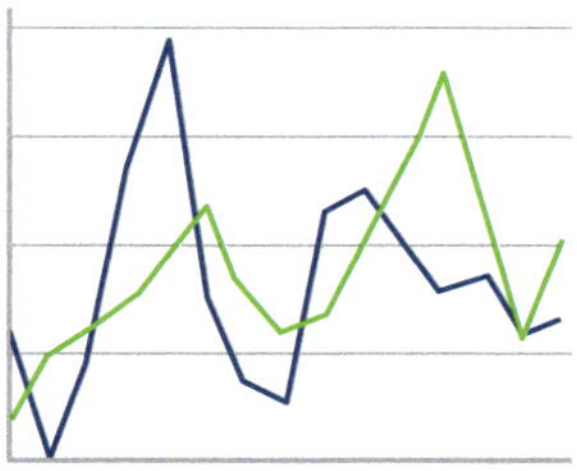
line graph

LANGUAGE HELP

Wenn du über Diagramme sprichst, können dir folgende Redewendungen helfen:

Pie chart
- *The pie chart is divided into … segments, which show/represent …*
- *The smallest/biggest segment …*
- *The segments representing … and … constitute the majority …*
- *A huge majority/minority is …*

Bar chart
- *The bars are arranged horizontally/vertically.*
- *There are big/vast/surprising differences between …*
- *At the top/bottom of the ranking comes …*
- *… is first/last in rank*
- *… has the largest / second largest …*

Line graph
- *The graph shows the relationship between … and …*
- *… is twice/three times as high as …*
- *There are more than / nearly twice as many … as there are …*
- *… increase/decrease / reach a high point / rise/fall/drop/ grow steadily*

SF 27 Internet research (Finding information online)

Das Internet ist voller Informationen, und es ist nicht einfach, genau das zu finden, was du benötigst.

Step 1: Überlege dir gute Stichwörter für dein Thema und gib sie in eine Suchmaschine ein. Je besser die Suchbegriffe sind, desto genauer sind die Ergebnisse. Die Infografik rechts hilft dir, wenn du ganz spezielle Informationen suchst.

Step 2: Nutze die Erweiterte Suche. Dort kannst du nicht nur festlegen, in welcher Sprache deine Ergebnisse sein sollen, sondern auch das Land eingrenzen (z.B. nur Ergebnisse aus den USA) oder die Domäne (z.B. .edu, .gov, .org).

Step 3: Sieh dir mehrere Suchergebnisse an, um zu sehen, ob sie passen (➡ *SF 1*).

Step 4: Achte darauf, wer die Webseite erstellt hat, um die Qualität der Suchergebnisse einzuschätzen.

Step 5: Speichere die besten Ergebnisse als Lesezeichen ab, damit du schnell darauf zugreifen kannst. Ordne deine Lesezeichen thematisch zur besseren Übersichtlichkeit.

Step 6: Setz dir ein Zeitlimit für deine Recherche und ordne dann dein Material. Prüfe, ob etwas fehlt, und suche dann ggf. gezielt nach diesen Informationen.

Step 7: Wenn du einen Text oder eine Präsentation vorbereitest, kopiere nicht einfach Inhalte von Webseiten. Mach dir Notizen und verwende deine eigenen Worte, um die Inhalte wiederzugeben. (➡ *SF 31*)

Internet research
Tipps und Tricks

Wenn du ganz spezifische Informationen suchst, helfen diese Tricks:

Was du suchst: Artikel aus der *Wikipedia*, in denen du Informationen über die Zeit der Beatles in Hamburg findest.

Wie du danach suchst:

site:wikipedia.com "the beatles" "hamburg"

site: sucht nur auf der genannten Seite

" " sucht den exakten Begriff und erzwingt das Vorkommen im Suchergebnis

Was du suchst: Einen englischsprachigen Bericht, am liebsten als PDF, über den Lebensraum von Füchsen.

Wie du danach suchst:

filetype:pdf intitle:habitat of *fox

filetype: sucht nur diesen Dateityp (pdf, doc, jpg usw.)

intitle: zeigt nur Ergebnisse, in denen dieses Wort im Titel auftaucht

***** sucht auch Worte wie Red Fox, Black Fox, Desert Fox usw.

SF 28 Giving feedback

Gegenseitige Rückmeldungen sind für dich und deine Partner wichtig, damit du siehst, was dir gut gelungen ist und woran du noch arbeiten musst. Wenn du eine Rückmeldung gibst, solltest du grundsätzliche Regeln beachten, die für einen geschriebenen Text genauso gelten wie für eine mündliche Präsentation.

Diese Dinge solltest du beachten:

- Lies den Text sorgfältig durch oder höre der Präsentation gut zu.
- Bei Feedback zu einer Präsentation mach dir Notizen zu den Punkten, auf die du achten sollst, z. B. Inhalt, Struktur, Sprache, Verständlichkeit des Vortrags. Wenn du einen Feedbackbogen hast, kannst du deine Notizen gleich darauf festhalten.
- Bei Feedback zu einem Text lies den Text noch einmal genau und achte dabei besonders auf Inhalt, Struktur, Wortwahl, Grammatik und Rechtschreibung. Wenn du einen Feedbackbogen hast, mach dir darauf Notizen (siehe rechts).
- Begründe deine Einschätzungen.
- Gib dein Feedback mit Respekt – niemand soll sich angegriffen fühlen. Nenne erst Gelungenes und mache dann Verbesserungsvorschläge zu Punkten, die aus deiner Sicht noch nicht so gelungen sind.
- Wenn du Feedback bekommst, überdenke die Vorschläge gut. Korrigiere die Fehler, die andere gefunden haben, und arbeite an den Stellen nach, wo du eventuell Probleme hattest.

PEER FEEDBACK CHECKLIST

	☺☺	☺	😐	☹
Content				
Lena's text is:				
· interesting			✓	
· exciting				✓
· funny				✓
· ______				
· easy to understand.		✓		
Language				
You connected short sentences with linking words.		✓		
You connected short sentences with relative clauses.		✓		
You used different adjectives in your description of places, people and things.			✓	
You used time phrases to show the order of events.		✓		
You chose interesting words.				✓
You used adverbs.			✓	

STUDY SKILLS

SF 29 Dealing with unknown words

Nachschlagen kostet Zeit und ist nicht immer nötig. Diese Tipps können dir helfen, unbekannte Wörter auch ohne ein Wörterbuch zu erschließen:

- Sieh dir die Überschrift, die Zwischenüberschriften und Bilder sowie den Kontext an. Beispiel: *Let's hurry. The train departs in ten minutes.*
- Wenn du einen Teil des Wortes kennst, kannst du oft die Bedeutung erschließen, z. B.
  knowledge = things someone knows
  bottle opener = something you use to open bottles
- Viele englische Wörter haben eine Ähnlichkeit zu deutschen Wörtern (z. B. *brochure, statue, insect)* oder Wörtern aus anderen Sprachen, z. B. *voice (French: voix; Latin: vox).*

TIPP
Nicht alle Wörter, die im Deutschen und Englischen ähnlich sind, haben auch dieselbe Bedeutung.
Achte daher auf false friends:
handy = praktisch, *nicht* Handy

SF 30 Using a dictionary

➜ *p. 92*

Es gibt unterschiedliche Wörterbücher, in denen du nachschlagen kannst. Wenn du die Bedeutung eines unbekannten Wortes nachschlagen willst, dann benutzt du am besten ein zweisprachiges Wörterbuch (Englisch-Deutsch bzw. Deutsch-Englisch). Wenn du mehr Informationen zu englischen Wörtern haben möchtest, etwa Beispielsätze, Definitionen oder Alternativen, dann bietet sich ein einsprachiges Wörterbuch an.

ZWEISPRACHIGE WÖRTERBÜCHER

Die Leitwörter *(running heads)* oben auf der Seite helfen dir, schnell zu finden, was du suchst. Auf der linken Seite steht das erste Stichwort, auf der rechten Seite das letzte Stichwort der Doppelseite.

- *resign* ist das Stichwort *(headword)*. Stichwörter sind alphabetisch geordnet: *r* vor *s*, *ra* vor *re*, *rhe* vor *rhi* usw.
- Die kursiv gedruckten Hinweise helfen dir, die für deinen Text passende Bedeutung zu finden.
- Die Ziffern 1, 2 usw. zeigen, dass ein Stichwort unterschiedliche Bedeutungen haben oder unterschiedlichen Wortarten angehören kann (z. B. Adjektiv, Nomen, Verb).
- Beispielsätze und Redewendungen sind dem Stichwort zugeordnet.
- Unregelmäßige Verbformen, besondere Pluralformen, die Steigerungsformen der Adjektive und ähnliche Hinweise stehen oft in Klammern oder sind kursiv gedruckt.
- Die Lautschrift gibt Auskunft darüber, wie das Wort ausgesprochen und betont wird.

resort

resign /rɪˈzaɪn/
1 BERUF • *als Vorsitzender usw* zurücktreten: ***He resigned from the company.*** Er verließ das Unternehmen.
2 (*job, post*) aufgeben (*Stelle, Posten*)
3 **resign oneself to something** sich mit etwas abfinden
resignation /ˌrezɪɡˈneɪʃn/
1 BERUF • *bei Unternehmen* Kündigung; *von Minister usw* Rücktritt
2 **hand in one's resignation** *von Angestelltem* kündigen; *von Minister usw* sein Amt niederlegen
3 *Gemütszustand* Resignation
resigned /rɪˈzaɪnd/ (*look, sigh*) resigniert

resit[1] /ˌriːˈsɪt/ *Verb* (→ *sit*) *BE* (*exam*) wiederholen (*Prüfung*)
resit[2] /ˈriːsɪt/ *Substantiv* • *BE* Wiederholungsprüfung
resolution /ˌrezəˈluːʃn/
1 POLITIK Beschluss, Resolution
2 *bei Problem, Streit* Lösung
3 ≈ *Entschiedenheit* Entschlossenheit

TIPP
Wenn du ein Online-Wörterbuch verwenden möchtest, erkundige dich vorher bei deinem Lehrer/deiner Lehrerin, welche zu empfehlen sind, denn nicht alle sind gleich gut. Fast alle funktionieren aber nach den gleichen Prinzipien wie gedruckte Wörterbücher.

EINSPRACHIGE WÖRTERBÜCHER

Wenn du selbst einen englischen Text schreibst, kannst du ein einsprachiges englisches Wörterbuch zu Hilfe nehmen. Hier findest du mehr über ein englisches Wort heraus als in einem zweisprachigen Wörterbuch:

- Ein einsprachiges Wörterbuch erklärt die Bedeutung eines englischen Wortes auf Englisch. Da manche Wörter mehrere Bedeutungen haben, ist es wichtig, alle Einträge und Beispielsätze zu einem Wort zu lesen und mit deinem englischen Text zu vergleichen, um die korrekte Bedeutung herauszufinden.
- Das Wörterbuch hilft dir, die passende Verbindung mit anderen Wörtern zu finden, z. B. zu Verben, Präpositionen oder in bestimmten feststehenden Wendungen. Das ist nützlich, wenn du selbst einen englischen Text schreiben willst und nach den richtigen Wörtern suchst.

deadly ['dedli] *adj*
1 *able or likely to kill people* {= lethal}: This is no longer a deadly disease.
deadly to The HSN virus is deadly to chickens.
a deadly weapon The new generation of biological weapons is more deadly than ever.
2 *(only before noun)* {= complete}: ***deadly silence*** There was deadly silence after his speech.
a deadly secret Don't tell anyone – this is a deadly secret.
deadly serious *completely serious:* Don't laugh – I am deadly serious!
3 *(informal) very boring*: Many TV programmes are pretty deadly!

SF 31 Making and taking notes

Wenn du Informationen oder eigene Gedanken kurz für dich notierst – z.B. als Vorbereitung auf einen eigenen Vortrag oder eine Präsentation –, heißt das im Englischen making notes. Wenn du dir Notizen beim Lesen oder Zuhören machst, heißt das taking notes. Für beide Varianten gelten aber die gleichen Grundsätze.

Step 1: Achte auf keywords, die die wichtigsten Informationen enthalten, um deine Frage/Aufgabe zu beantworten oder den Inhalt eines Textes grob zu verstehen.

Step 2: Notiere nur die wichtigsten Informationen. Verwende Abkürzungen und Symbole, aber achte darauf, dass du ein System hast und immer dieselben verwendest, damit du deine Notizen auch später noch verstehst. Markiere offene Fragen.

Step 3: Geh im Anschluss an das Lesen oder Hören nochmal durch deine Notizen und ergänze evtl. noch fehlende Informationen.

TIPP

Wenn du kein eigenes System von Abkürzungen hast, kannst du diese verwenden:

the same as	=	*for example*	*e.g.*
not the same as	≠	*important*	*!*
about the same as	≈	*not*	*x*
and	+	*with*	*w/*
becomes/will be	->	*without*	*w/o*
between	*b/w*	*open question*	*??*

Grammar File

Inhalt Seite

GF 1 The tenses Die Zeitformen

1.1 Tense and time

1a *Leon* ***is enjoying*** *his stay in Australia.*
1b *Next month, Leon* ***is flying*** *home.*

2a *Leon's host family* ***taught*** *him to surf.*
2b *Leon would be so happy if his parents* ***bought*** *him some surf equipment back home in Germany.*

He ***has been*** *in Australia for almost six months now.*	**present perfect**
Er **ist** jetzt seit fast sechs Monaten in Australien.	**Präsens**
*I'****ll take*** *the fish, please.*	***will*-future**
Ich **nehme** den Fisch, bitte.	**Präsens**

➔ *The simple and the progressive form: GF 2, pp. 186–187*

There is a difference between a **grammatical tense** (a form of the verb) and **real time**.

◂ A **grammatical tense** can refer to **different times**:
The *present progressive tense* in **1a** refers to the present; in **1b** it refers to the future.
The *simple past tense* in **2a** refers to the past; in **2b** it refers to the future.

! Note that the use of tenses in English is often different from their use in German. Compare the examples on the left.

1.2 Talking about the present

The simple present

At home, Leon ***usually gets*** *the bus to school.*
On Fridays *his mother* ***takes*** *him in the car.*
He ***never cycles*** *to school because it's too far.*

Olivia Wilson and her family ***live*** *in Nottingham.*
Her mum is Italian, so she ***speaks*** *two languages.*
She ***plays*** *hockey and* ***collects*** *old computer games.*
Her parents ***work*** *for a computer company.*

➔ *Unit 4: p. 120, exercise 1*

We use the ***simple present*** …

◂ to say that something happens **repeatedly**, **regularly**, **normally**, **often**, **always** or **never**.
Signal words for the *simple present* are *always, usually, often, every week, on Fridays, never, every summer* etc.

◂ to talk about **hobbies**, **jobs** and **abilities** and about things that are **permanent**, i.e. not limited to a particular time.

The present progressive

*What****'s*** *Mr Bennett* ***doing****?*
*– He****'s making*** *a salad.*

Mr Bennett (on the phone): *"I'm busy, Jack.*
*I****'m making*** *a salad."*

*Olivia has got a holiday job: she****'s working*** *as a waitress in a small café in Devon. She****'s sharing*** *a room with another waitress while she's there.*

➔ *Unit 4: p. 120, exercise 1*

We use the ***present progressive*** …

◂ when we want to say that **someone is doing something now** or that **something is happening as we speak**.
The action or event is **in progress** and **not yet complete**.
Signal words for the *present progressive* are *at the moment, now, just* and *still*.

! The action we are talking about can be **interrupted**:
Mr Bennett is on the phone, so he is not making a salad at the moment of speaking. But the action is not yet complete, so he uses the *present progressive*.

◂ to express the idea that something is happening for a **limited period of time** (… *while she's there*).

In German

Über die Gegenwart sprechen

Simple present	wenn etwas wiederholt, regelmäßig, oft, immer oder nie geschieht wenn man über Hobbys, Berufe, Fähigkeiten und Dauerzustände spricht
Present progressive	wenn eine Handlung oder ein Ereignis im Verlauf und noch nicht abgeschlossen ist

1.3 Talking about the past

The simple past

***Twenty years ago**, Olivia's mother **moved** to England.*
Vor zwanzig Jahren ist Olivias Mutter nach England gezogen / zog Olivias Mutter nach England.

***Last Friday** Olivia's family **flew** to Italy.*

*Yesterday Olivia **went** into town with a friend. First they **looked** round the shops, and Katie **bought** a CD. Then they **tried** on shoes in four shops, but they **didn't buy** any. After that they **had** an ice cream.*

➜ *Unit 1: p. 20, exercise 1 • Unit 4: p. 120, exercise 2*

We use the ***simple past*** …

◄ to say that **something happened at a particular point of time in the past** or **in a particular period of time in the past** (which is now over).
Signal words for the *simple past* are *twenty years ago, last Friday, yesterday, in 2012, an hour ago* etc.

◄ in **reports about past events** and in **stories** (often with *first …, then …, after that …*).

! In German, past events can be reported in the *Perfekt* or in the *Imperfekt*. In English, there are special rules for the use of the *simple past* and the *present perfect*.

NEW

German "Früher …" – *used to* + infinitive / *would* + infinitive

*We **used to live** in Manchester.*
Wir wohnten früher in Manchester.
*Manchester United **used to be** my favourite team.*
Früher war Manchester United meine Lieblingsmannschaft.
*I **used to spend** lots of money on sports magazines.*
Ich habe früher immer viel Geld für Sportzeitschriften ausgegeben.

*Grandpa **would visit** us every Sunday after church.*
Opa besuchte uns jeden Sonntag nach der Kirche. /
Opa pflegte uns jeden Sonntag nach der Kirche zu besuchen.
*We **would** often **go** for long walks in the woods.*
Wir haben oft lange Spaziergänge im Wald gemacht. /
Wir pflegten lange Spaziergänge im Wald zu machen.

➜ *Unit 4: p. 114, exercises 1-4*

◄ With ***used to* + infinitive**, we can describe **states**, **habits** and **regular actions** in the past (German "Früher …").

◄ For **regularly repeated <u>actions</u>** in the past, we can also use ***would* + infinitive**. Compare the examples in the box on the left.

The past progressive

*Yesterday at 3.30 Olivia **was walking** home from school. It **was raining**, so lots of people **were hurrying** to the bus stop.*

*Sally **was cycling** home when a dog **ran** out in front of her bike.*
Sally radelte (gerade) nach Haus, als ihr ein Hund vors Fahrrad lief.

➜ *Unit 4: p. 120, exercise 2*

We use the ***past progressive*** …

◄ to talk about actions or events that **were in progress and not yet complete at a particular time in the past**.

◄ to describe **what was going on** *(she was cycling home)* when something else happened; the second action is in the *simple past (a dog ran out in front of her bike)*.

The past perfect (simple)

*When Emily arrived at the diner, her parents **had** already **eaten**.*
Als Emily im Restaurant ankam, hatten ihre Eltern schon gegessen.

*Grandpa **had** already **been** in hospital for a week when we returned from Spain.*
Opa lag schon eine Woche im Krankenhaus, als wir aus Spanien zurückkehrten.

➜ *Unit 4: p. 121, exercise 5*

We use the ***past perfect*** …

◄ to say that **one past action happened before another past action**; the action that happened first is in the *past perfect*.

◄ to express the idea that **a <u>state</u> began before a point of time in the past** and continued up to that time.

NEW

The past perfect progressive

CHECK 1: p. 210

Olivia was very tired when she arrived home. She ***had been studying*** *for a test all day.*
... Sie hatte den ganzen Tag für einen Test gelernt.

We ***had been playing*** *tennis for half an hour when it started to rain.*
Wir hatten eine halbe Stunde Tennis gespielt, ...

Unit 4: p. 121, exercise 5

We use the ***past perfect progressive*** to talk about **actions or events that had begun before a point of time in the past** and continued up to (or almost up to) that time.

In German

Über die Vergangenheit sprechen

Simple past	wenn wir sagen oder fragen wollen, wann etwas geschah wenn wir über vergangene Ereignisse berichten oder Geschichten erzählen
Past progressive	wenn etwas zu einer bestimmten Zeit in der Vergangenheit im Gange war
Past perfect	wenn etwas noch vor etwas anderem in der Vergangenheit stattgefunden hatte
Past perfect progressive	wenn eine Handlung vor einem Zeitpunkt in der Vergangenheit begonnen hatte und bis (oder fast bis) zu jenem Zeitpunkt andauerte

1.4 Talking about the past and the present

Present perfect and ***present perfect progressive*** relate to the past and the present.

The present perfect (simple)

1 *Kristen Stewart is great. I've seen all her films.*
2 *My sister loves books about horses. She's read hundreds of them.*
3 *Mel has lost her mobile. Now she can't phone her friends and her mum is angry.*
4 *I've bought some new jeans, look. They'll go well with my red top.*
5 *Luke has* ***already*** *done his Maths homework, but he hasn****'t*** *started his French* ***yet****.*
6 *I've* ***never*** *been to Paris. Have you* ***ever*** *been there?*
– *No, I haven't. But I've* ***always*** *wanted to go.*

We use the ***present perfect*** ...

◀ to talk about **actions and events that happened at some time in the past**.

The action or event often has **direct consequences for the present or the future** (compare examples **3** and **4**).

The **exact time is not important** (or not known) and is **not mentioned**. Often you find adverbs like *already, always, before, ever, just, not ... yet, often, never* with the *present perfect* (compare examples **5** and **6**).

Leon has been a member of his football club ***for*** *ten years now /* ***since*** *his sixth birthday.*
Leon ist jetzt seit zehn Jahren / seit seinem sechsten Geburtstag Mitglied in seinem Fußballverein.

◀ to say that **a state began in the past and is still continuing** – often with *since* or *for* (German "seit").

! In German we often use the *Präsens* to express this idea, but in English the *present perfect* is used:
Ich kenne ihn seit ... — *I've known him since/for ...*

German "seit ..." – *since / for*

since **+ point of time** (when it began)

We've had our dog ***since April****.*
... seit April

for **+ period of time** (how long it lasted)

We've had our dog ***for three months****.*
... seit drei Monaten

Unit 4: p. 121, exercise 4

State verbs are *be, have, know, like, hate*, for example.

State verbs: GF 2.3, p. 187

The present perfect progressive

1 *She's **been writing** letters all afternoon.*
Sie schreibt (schon) den ganzen Nachmittag Briefe.

2 *My brother **has been playing** the piano since 2013.*
Mein Bruder spielt seit 2013 Klavier.
3 *I've **been learning** French for three years now.*
Ich lerne jetzt seit drei Jahren Französisch.

➜ *Unit 4: p. 121, exercise 4*

We use the ***present perfect progressive*** to say that an **action or event began in the past and has continued up to** (or almost up to) **the present**.
(Examples **2** and **3** show that the action or event can be **interrupted**.)

! Note the German equivalent of the *present perfect progressive*:
Sie schreibt (schon) … *She's been writing …*
Er spielt seit … *He's been playing … since/for …*

In German

Über die Vergangenheit und die Gegenwart sprechen

Present perfect	wenn wir sagen wollen, dass etwas geschehen ist (nicht wann) wenn wir sagen wollen, seit wann oder wie lange ein Zustand schon andauert
Present perfect progressive	wenn eine Handlung / ein Ereignis in der Vergangenheit begonnen hat und bis (oder fast bis) in die Gegenwart andauert

Wir verwenden ***since*** mit **Zeitpunkten** (wann etwas begann).
Wir verwenden ***for*** mit **Zeiträumen** (wie lange etwas schon andauert).

1.5 Talking about the future

The *will*-future

➜ *CHECK 2: p. 211*

*I'**ll be** 15 next October.*
*It **will be** cold and windy, and we **will get** some rain in the afternoon.*

*I suppose Ella **will be** late again as usual.*
Ich nehme an, Ella kommt wie üblich wieder zu spät.

➜ *Unit 3: pp. 83-84, exercises 2-3 • p. 85, exercises 5-6*

We use the ***will-future*** …

◂ to make a **prediction** or **assumption** about the future (often when we are talking about things that we cannot control, e.g. the weather).
You often find expressions like *I think, I'm sure, I expect, I suppose, probably, maybe* with the *will-future*.

NEW

*Just a moment. I'**ll open** the door for you.*
Moment. Ich mache Ihnen die Tür auf.

*I **won't tell** anyone what's happened. I promise.*
Ich sage niemandem, was passiert ist. …

➜ *Unit 3: p. 90, exercises 1–3*

◂ when we make a **spontaneous decision**, especially an **offer** or a **promise**.

The *going to*-future

➜ *CHECK 2: p. 211*

*After school I'**m going to study** architecture.*
Nach der Schule werde ich Architektur studieren / habe ich vor, Architektur zu studieren.

*The Millers **are going to move** to New Zealand.*
Die Millers werden/wollen nach Neuseeland ziehen.

➜ *Unit 3: p. 83, exercises 1–2 • p. 90, exercise 2*

We use the ***going to-future*** …

◂ to talk about **intentions** or **plans** for the future.

NEW

*Look at those clouds. There'**s going to be** a storm.*
… Es wird ein Gewitter geben.

*Oh dear! Your mother'**s going to be** very angry with us.*
… Deine Mutter wird sehr wütend auf uns sein.

➜ *Unit 3: pp. 84-85, exercises 4-6*

◂ to say that **something will very probably happen** (usually there are already signs of it happening).

The present progressive (with future meaning)

*We**'re driving** to Scotland next weekend to visit my grandparents.*
*I**'m meeting** a friend in town tomorrow at 12.*
*All my friends **are coming** to my birthday party on Friday.*

➜ *Unit 3: p. 90, exercise 3*

When something is **definitely planned** or **arranged** for the future, we can also use the ***present progressive***. It must be clear that we are talking about the future, either from the context or from the use of a phrase of future time (e.g. *next weekend, tomorrow*).

(This use of the *present progressive* is sometimes called the ***diary future***: when we use it, we are talking about appointments or arrangements that have already been noted down in a diary.)

The simple present (with future meaning)

*Our cookery classes **start** on 2 September.*
*The film **starts** at 8 o'clock.*
*When **does** the next train to Liverpool **leave**?*
*The club **meets** in an hour, so we'll have to hurry.*

We can use the ***simple present*** to say that a future event is a fixed part of a **timetable**, a **schedule** or a **programme** of events. (Verbs like ***arrive, leave, go, open, close, start, stop*** are often used in this way).

(This use of the *simple present* is sometimes called the ***timetable future***.)

When you want to talk about the future, the terms ***decision, prediction*** and ***arrangement*** can help you to decide which tense to use.
Look at the following table:

	will- future	*going to-* future	present progressive	simple present
DECISION (Entscheidung)	spontaneous decision	planned in advance		
PREDICTION (Vorhersage)	assumptions and predictions	strong probability (signs are there)		
ARRANGEMENT (Vereinbarung)		(not used very often – but not wrong)	definitely planned ("diary future")	timetable, programme ("timetable future")

The future progressive

➜ *CHECK 3: p. 211*

NEW

*This time next week my sister will be on her way to Spain – and I**'ll be doing** my maths exam.*
Nächste Woche um diese Zeit wird meine Schwester auf dem Weg nach Spanien sein – und ich werde dabei sein, meine Mathe-Prüfung zu machen.

We use the ***future progressive*** for actions or events which will be **in progress at a point of time in the future**. The action or event has begun before the future point of time and may possibly continue after it.
You often find time phrases like *a week today* ("heute in einer Woche"), *this time next week* and the like.

*What **will** you **be doing** over the next couple of days?*

*How long **will** you **be staying** in Washington?*

***Will** you **be staying** for dinner?*

◄ The ***future progressive*** is often used to politely inquire about somebody else's plans.

➜ *Unit 3: p. 91, exercises 4–5*

NEW

The future perfect CHECK 4: p. 211

***Next Friday** we **will have finished** all our exams.*
Nächsten Freitag werden wir alle unsere Prüfungen geschafft haben.

*And **by the end of next week** we**'ll have received** our results.*
Und bis Ende nächster Woche werden wir unsere Ergebnisse erhalten haben.

Unit 3: p. 97, exercises 4–5

We use the ***future perfect*** for actions or events which will be **complete at a point of time in the future**. The point of time is often mentioned (here: *next Friday; by the end of next week*.)

In German

Über die Zukunft sprechen

***will*-future**	für Vorhersagen und Vermutungen über die Zukunft für spontane Entscheidungen (z.B. Angebote und Versprechen)
***going to*-future**	für Vorhaben und Pläne für die Zukunft wenn man sicher ist, dass etwas gleich geschehen wird (Anzeichen sind vorhanden)
Present progressive	wenn etwas für die Zukunft fest verabredet ist („diary future")
Simple present	für zukünftige Ereignisse, die durch einen Fahrplan, ein Programm o.Ä. festgelegt sind („timetable future")
Future progressive	wenn eine Handlung oder ein Ereignis in der Zukunft im Gange sein wird
Future perfect	wenn etwas in der Zukunft geschehen oder getan sein wird

GF 2 Aspect: the simple form and the progressive form
Aspekt: die einfache Form und die Verlaufsform

2.1 Simple and progressive form in contrast

Tense	Simple form	Progressive form
Present tense	**sing(s)**	**am/are/is singing**
Past tense	**sang**	**was/were singing**
Present perfect	**have/has sung**	**have/has been singing**
Past perfect	**had sung**	**had been singing**
***will*-future**	**will sing**	**will be singing**

In contrast to German, English verbs have **simple forms** and **progressive forms**.

We use these forms to say
- if something is done **regularly** or **repeatedly** **or** if the action is **in progress** at the moment of speaking
- if the action is **complete** **or** if the action is **not yet complete**.

1 *Tom **works** at a garage.* (always; it's his job)
2 *Mr Clark **goes** to work by bike.* (regularly)
3 *Sue **has written** three letters today.* (she has finished)

◄ We use the ***simple form*** to express the idea that
- an action is long-lasting or permanent (**1**)
- someone does something regularly/repeatedly (**2**)
- an action is complete (**3**).

4 *Tom isn't in. He**'s working**.* (right now)
5 *This week Mr Clark **is going** by bus.* (just this week – his bike is broken)
6 *Sue **has been writing** letters all day.* (she hasn't finished yet)

◄ We use the ***progressive form*** to express the idea that
- an action is in progress at the moment of speaking (**4**)
- an action is going on for a temporary period only (**5**)
- an action is not yet complete (**6**).

Activity verbs and state verbs: GF 2.2–2.3, p. 187

2.2 Activity verbs

CHECK 5: p. 211

(in a shop window) *We **make** the best pizza in town!*
(on the phone) *Carol **is making** a pizza. Can she call you back?*

*It **gets** dark very early here in winter.*
*At 5 o'clock it **was** already **getting** dark.*

Activity verbs *(Tätigkeitsverben)* describe **activities** *(do, go, make, read, sing, write, …)* or **events** *(become, get, rain, …)*.

They can be used in the ***simple form*** and in the ***progressive form***.

2.3 State verbs

CHECK 5: p. 211

State verbs *(Zustandsverben)* describe **states**.
We generally use them only in the ***simple form***.

The most important **state verbs** are …

*The price **doesn't include** breakfast.*
*Emily **seems** really happy at her new school.*
*Jake's uncle **owns** a nice house in the country.*

◄ verbs which express **characteristics** or **possession**, e.g. *be, exist, seem, sound, mean* ("bedeuten"), *cost, need, own, belong, …*

***Do** you **believe** their story?*
*I **don't know** the answer to question 5.*
*Anna **didn't understand** what Julie **meant**.*

◄ verbs of **thinking** and **knowing**, e.g. *believe, know, mean* ("meinen"), *remember, imagine, realize, recognize, understand, …*

*Lucy **doesn't like** people who talk a lot.*
*I **don't mind** waiting for you here.*
*We **prefer** brown bread to white bread. It's healthier.*

◄ verbs of **liking, disliking** and **wishing**, e.g. *like, love, dislike, hate, mind, prefer, want, …*

States and activities

*Sue **has** dark hair.*	**state:**	"haben"
*Sue **is having** a shower.*	**activity:**	"duschen"
*Sue **had a shower** and went to school.*		
***Do** I **look** silly with my hair like this?*	**state:**	"aussehen"
*I didn't see him. I **wasn't looking**.*	**activity:**	"(hin)schauen, gucken"
*They **looked** at me and smiled.*		
*The flowers **smell** wonderful.*	**state:**	"riechen"
*Sophie **is smelling** the roses.*	**activity:**	"*an etwas* riechen"
*Sophie **smelled** the roses and sighed.*		
*The pizza **tastes** good.*	**state:**	"schmecken"
***I'm tasting** the soup now.*	**activity:**	"kosten, probieren"
*I **tasted** the soup and added some salt.*		
*I **think** that's a great idea.*	**state:**	"denken, meinen"
*He **was thinking** of moving to Paris.*	**activity:**	"überlegen, nachdenken"
*We **thought** hard but couldn't find the answer.*		

Some English verbs are used as **activity verbs and as state verbs** (with different meanings).

As a **state verb**, they are used in the ***simple form***.

As an **activity verb**, they can be used in both forms, depending on what we want to express.

Look at the examples in the box on the left.

In German

Tätigkeitsverben und Zustandsverben

- **Tätigkeitsverben** wie *do, make, cook, read, work* werden in der *simple form* und der *progressive form* verwendet:
  *Tom **cooks** lunch every Sunday.* (Tom kocht jeden Sonntag das Mittagessen.)
  *Tom is busy. He**'s cooking** lunch now.* (… Tom kocht gerade das Mittagessen.)
- **Zustandsverben** wie *seem, belong, believe, know, like, need, …* werden nicht in der *progressive form* verwendet:
  *I **don't believe** you.* (**nicht:** *~~I'm not believing~~ you.*)
- Einige Verben werden als Zustands- **und** als Tätigkeitsverben verwendet – mit verschiedenen Bedeutungen:
  *The soup **tastes** good.* (Die Suppe schmeckt gut.)
  *Quiet now. Grandpa **is tasting** the soup.* (… Opa probiert gerade die Suppe.)

GF 3 The passive Das Passiv

3.1 Active and passive

Active ***John Lennon*** ***wrote*** *"Imagine" in 1971.*
John Lennon schrieb „Imagine" im Jahr 1971.

Passive ***"Imagine"*** ***was written*** *in 1971.*
„Imagine" wurde im Jahr 1971 geschrieben.

◄ The choice of active or passive depends on our point of view:

The **active** sentence is about John Lennon; it tells us that John Lennon wrote "Imagine" in 1971.

The **passive** sentence is about the song "Imagine"; it tells us when the song was written.

Active *The manager* ***asked*** ***Ms Jones*** *to work late.*

Passive ***Ms Jones*** ***was asked*** *to work late.*
Ms Jones wurde gebeten, länger zu arbeiten.

◄ We can form the passive **with almost all verbs which in the active are followed by an object.**

The **subject of the passive sentence** corresponds to the **object of the active sentence** (here: *Ms Jones*).

Active *The manager* ***paid*** ***her*** *£12 an hour.*

Passive ***She*** ***was paid*** *£12 an hour.*
Ihr wurden £12 die Stunde bezahlt. /
Sie erhielt £12 die Stunde.

◄ As you can see on the left, the **subject of the English passive sentence** (here: *She*) can correspond to a German **dative object** (here: *Ihr*).

(See also GF 3.4: The passive of verbs with two objects, p. 189)

3.2 The passive: use

1 *The first goal* ***was scored*** *in the seventh minute.*
… wurde erzielt …

2 *A new sports centre* ***has been opened*** *in Paddington.*
… ist eröffnet worden …

3 *Breakfast* ***is served*** *from 7 to 10.30 am.*
… wird serviert …

4 *The bank robbers* ***have been sentenced*** *to ten years.*
… sind verurteilt worden …

We use the **passive** to say what is done or what happens to someone or something.

Who does the action is often
- **unknown** or **unimportant** (sentences **1** and **2**)
- **obvious** and thus not worth mentioning (sentences **3** and **4**).

Yesterday a drunk driver hit a 15-year-old boy in Lichfield Road. The boy was taken to hospital, where he was treated for shock. He is now recovering. The driver was taken to Horton Road police station. He is answering police questions.

The passive is often found
- in the news,
- in reports about accidents, crimes or natural disasters,
- in official texts,
- in technical or scientific writing,
- on signs.

Yesterday a drunk driver ***hit*** *a 15-year-old boy … The boy* ***was taken*** *… where he* ***was treated*** *… He* ***is*** *now* ***recovering****. …*

◄ Note that we often switch between **active** and **passive** sentences.

The driver ***was questioned*** ***by*** *the police.*
Der Fahrer wurde von der Polizei verhört/befragt.

The preposition ***by*** is used to add information about the "doer" (who or what does the action).

➜ *Unit 1: pp. 20–21, exercises 2-6*

3.3 The passive: form

The passive	
Simple present	*English **is spoken** in lots of countries.*
Simple past	*The bridge **was completed** in 1998.*
Present perfect	*All the biscuits **have been eaten**.*
Past perfect	*I didn't go to the party because I **hadn't been invited**.*
***going to*-future**	*Look, the lions **are going to be fed** soon.*
***will*-future and modal auxiliaries**	*The last match of the season **will be played** next Friday.* *Mobile phones **should be turned off** during lessons.* *Concert tickets **can be bought** online.*
Future perfect	*I'm sure lots of new planets **will have been discovered** by 2050.*
Present progressive	*Three new blocks of flats **are being built** in King Street.*
Past progressive	*The museum was closed. The rooms **were being painted**.*

We form the **passive** with a **form of *be* + past participle** (Partizip Perfekt).

➔ *Irregular verbs: pp. 338-340*

We form the **passive progressive** with *being*: *are being built; were being painted*.

*A boy **got hurt** yesterday when he was hit by a car.*

*John's parents **got killed** in a fire when he was 12.*

◄ In informal English we sometimes use **a form of *get* instead of a form of *be***, especially when something happens suddenly and unexpectedly (e.g. in an accident).

3.4 The passive of verbs with two objects

➔ *CHECK 6: p. 212*

NEW

	subject	object	object
Active	*The manager promised*	***her***	***a job***.
Passive	***She** (subject) was promised **a job**.* **Ihr** *(Dativobjekt)* wurde **eine Stelle** *(Subjekt)* versprochen.		

Some verbs can have **two objects**, an **indirect object** (usually a person) and a **direct object** (usually a thing): *give/promise/send/show **somebody something** (**jemandem etwas** geben/versprechen/schicken/zeigen).*

! **English passive sentences** with verbs like these usually begin with the **person**. This structure is called ***personal passive*** ("persönliches Passiv").

In **German**, only the **direct object** (the thing) can become the subject of the passive sentence (here: "eine Stelle"). The indirect dative object of the active sentence (here: "ihr") does not change in the passive: „**Ihr** wurde **eine Stelle** versprochen".

***She was paid** a lot of money for her book.*
Ihr wurde eine Menge Geld gezahlt für ihr Buch. / Sie bekam eine Menge Geld für ihr Buch.

***He was given** the key and went up to his room.*
Ihm wurde der Schlüssel gegeben, ... / Er bekam den Schlüssel ...

***I've been told** she has lost her job.*
Mir wurde erzählt, dass sie ihre Stelle verloren hat.

◄ On the left you will find some more examples of the **personal passive**.
Passive sentences like these are quite common in English. In German, other structures are used.

➔ *Unit 1: p. 26, exercises 1-3*

In German

Das Passiv

• Ein **Aktivsatz** beschreibt, was jemand (oder etwas) tut.	***My uncle** designed lots of museums all over England.* (Es geht um den Onkel.)
• Ein **Passivsatz** beschreibt, was mit Menschen oder Dingen geschieht; oft wird nicht gesagt, wer die Handlung ausführt. Passivsätze werden mit einer Form von ***be*** + **past participle** gebildet.	***Our local museum** was designed by a world-famous architect.* (Es geht um das Museum.)
• Das Passiv findet man oft in Nachrichten, in Zeitungsartikeln (z.B. über Unfälle, Verbrechen, Katastrophen), in offiziellen Texten, in technischen Beschreibungen und auf Schildern.	*The boy **was taken** to hospital, where he **was treated** for shock.*
• Mit ***by*** kann man den „Täter" oder „Verursacher" nennen.	*We were interrupted **by a German couple**.*
• In informellem Englisch wird manchmal eine Form von ***get*** zur Passivbildung verwendet, vor allem bei kurzen Vorgängen, die plötzlich und unerwartet eintreten (wie etwa Unfälle).	*Three people **got killed** in the fire.*
• Im Englischen kann das indirekte Objekt des Aktivsatzes (die Person) zum Subjekt des Passivsatzes werden (***personal passive***). Im Deutschen kann nur das direkte Objekt (Sachobjekt) zum Subjekt des Passivsatzes werden; die Dativform des Personenobjekts bleibt im Passivsatz erhalten.	*Two Swedes joined **us**.* ***We** were joined by two Swedes.* (Zwei Schweden schlossen sich **uns** an.) *They offered **her** a job in Bristol.* ***She** was offered a job in Bristol.* (**Ihr** wurde ein Job in Bristol angeboten.)

GF 4 Modals and their substitutes Modale Hilfsverben und ihre Ersatzverben

4.1 Modal auxiliaries

can, may, must, should, … are **modal auxiliaries** (also called **modal verbs** or just **modals**). After a modal auxiliary we use an **infinitive without *to*** (**1**).
Modals can only be used on their own – i.e. without a full verb – in short answers (**2**).

1 ***Can** you **play** the piano?*
2 *– Yes, I **can**. / No, I **can't**.*

Other characteristics:

3 *She's so good at drawing. She **should** study art.*

– Modal auxiliaries only have **one form**, there are no endings (no *-s*, no *-ing*, no *-ed*) (**3**).

4 ***Could** you **do** the exercise? – No, I **couldn't**.*

– Questions and negative statements are formed without *do/does/did* (**4**).

5 ***Can** we help you in the kitchen, Mum?*
6 *We **can** play tennis on Saturday if you like.*

– Modal auxiliaries usually refer to the present or the future (**5**, **6**).

4.2 Substitutes

1 *I'd love **to be able to** play the piano.*
Ich würde liebend gern Klavier spielen können.

2 ***Being able to** play the piano must be great.*
Es muss großartig sein, Klavier spielen zu können.

3 *We **weren't allowed to** use dictionaries in the test.*
Wir durften im Test keine Wörterbücher benutzen.

Modal auxiliaries cannot be used in all the verb tenses. That is why **some modals have substitute forms** with a similar meaning. With these substitutes, we can form
– the infinitive (**1**),
– the *-ing* form (**2**),
– all the tenses (**3**, here: *simple past*).

Study the example sentences for German **"können"**, **"dürfen"** and **"müssen"** on the next page.

"können" – can / (to) be able to

My little brother ***can / is able to*** *swim.*	*present:* *can* and *am/is/are able to*
Tim ***could / was able to*** *read when he was four.* *I* ***could*** *smell fire, but I* ***couldn't*** *see any smoke.*	*past:* *could* and *was/were able to* (*could* is used mainly in negative statements and questions and with verbs of perception like *smell, see, hear.*)
I ***haven't been able to*** *contact him yet.*	*present perfect:* *have/has been able to*
*I'm taking driving lessons, so next year I'****ll be able to*** *drive.*	*will-future:* *will be able to*

"dürfen" – can, may / (to) be allowed to

Can / May *I have a sleepover on Friday, Mum?* *We* ***aren't allowed to*** *stay up late in the week.*	*present:* *can*, *may* und *am/is/are allowed to*
Under-12s ***couldn't / weren't allowed to*** *see the film without an adult.*	*past:* *could* und *was/were allowed to*
*I'****ve*** *always* ***been allowed to*** *have pets.*	*present perfect:* *have/has been allowed to*
Will *you* ***be allowed to*** *go to the party on Friday?*	*will-future:* *will be allowed to*
Jeans ***must not*** *be worn at this school.* *At my school we'****re not allowed to*** *wear jeans.*	! We use *must not (mustn't)* or *be not allowed to* to say that something is forbidden.

"müssen" – must / (to) have to

Teacher: *You* ***must*** *work harder, Noah.* *His teacher says Noah* ***has to*** *work harder.* *I* ***needn't*** *get up at 6 on Sundays. /* *I* ***don't have to*** *get up at 6 on Sundays.*	*present:* *must* und *have/has to* – **Negation:** *needn't* or *don't/doesn't have to*
I ***had to*** *rewrite my essay.* *We* ***didn't have to*** *wait long.*	*past:* *had to* – **Negation:** *didn't have to*
Lauren ***has had to*** *go to the dentist's.*	*present perfect:* *have/has had to*
You ***will have to*** *go to the dentist's too if you eat so many sweets.*	*will-future:* *will have to*
Everyone ***needs to*** *take a break now and again.* *You* ***don't need to*** *wait for us.* *I* ***didn't need to*** *tell her. She already knew it.* ***Do*** *we* ***need*** *to book a table?*	◄ We can also use *(to) need to* to express the idea that someone has to do something (or doesn't have to do something).

4.3 Modal auxiliaries – what do they express?

A modal auxiliary adds something extra to the meaning of a sentence. We use ***can***, for example, to express **ability** or **permission**, to make a **request** or an **offer**, or to **ask for permission**. The following boxes give you an overview.

Ability (Fähigkeit)

*I **can** speak French and a little German.*	Ich **kann** Französisch und ein bisschen Deutsch.
*They **could** hear someone in the next room.*	Sie **konnten** jemanden im Nebenzimmer hören.

Request (Bitte / Aufforderung)

***Would** you help me to wash the dishes?*	**Würdest** du mir helfen abzuwaschen?
***Could** you be quiet, please?*	**Kannst/Könntest** du bitte leise sein?

Permission, prohibition (Erlaubnis, Verbot)

***Can**/**May** I use your phone, please?*	**Kann/Darf** ich mal dein Telefon benutzen, bitte?
*You **can't** take photos in the museum.*	Du **darfst** im Museum nicht fotografieren.
*In 1968, children **could** leave school at 15.*	… **konnten/durften** Kinder mit 15 die Schule verlassen.
*You **mustn't** tell Julie about the concert. It's a surprise.*	Du **darfst** Julie nichts von dem Konzert erzählen. …

Suggestion (Vorschlag)

***Couldn't** you ask your grandma?*	**Könntest** du nicht deine Oma fragen?
*You **could** talk to your teacher.*	Du **könntest** (doch) mit deiner Lehrerin sprechen.
***Shall** we eat first and go shopping later?*	**Sollen/Wollen** wir erst essen …?

Offer (Angebot)

***Can**/**Could** I get you a drink?*	**Kann** ich Ihnen (vielleicht) etwas zu trinken holen?
***Would** you like to stay for dinner?*	**Möchten** Sie (nicht) zum Essen bleiben?
***Shall** I help you with the dishes?*	**Soll** ich dir beim Abwasch helfen?

Refusal, rejection (Weigerung, Ablehnung)

*My father **won't** let me stay out after ten.*	Mein Vater **will nicht**, dass ich nach zehn noch draußen bin.
*I can't get in. The gate **won't** open.*	… Das Tor **will nicht** aufgehen / geht nicht auf.
*He knew the answer, but he **wouldn't** tell me.*	…, aber er **wollte** sie mir **nicht** sagen / …, aber er weigerte sich, sie mir zu sagen.

Necessity (Notwendigkeit)

*You **needn't** tell Mel about the concert. She already knows.*	Du **brauchst** Mel **nicht** von dem Konzert zu erzählen. …
*I've got a temperature. I **must** stay in bed.*	Ich habe Fieber. Ich **muss** im Bett bleiben.

Obligation, advice (Verpflichtung, Ratschlag)

*Dogs **should** be left outside.*	Hunde **sollten** draußen gelassen werden / draußen bleiben.
*You **should** tell him the truth.*	Du **solltest** ihm die Wahrheit sagen.

Possibility, probability, deduction (Möglichkeit, Wahrscheinlichkeit, Schlussfolgerung)

*That **must** be Luke.*	Das **muss** Luke sein.
*– No, it **can't** be Luke. Luke is in Spain.*	– Nein, das **kann nicht** Luke sein. Luke ist in Spanien.
*Where's Dad? – He **could** be at Grandma's.*	… – Er **könnte** bei Oma sein.
*They **may**/**might** still be alive.*	Sie sind **vielleicht** noch am Leben/**könnten** noch am Leben sein.
*Kathy **should** be here by now.*	Kathy **sollte** jetzt (eigentlich) hier sein.
*There's somebody at the door. – That **will** be Sue.*	Es ist jemand an der Tür. – Das **wird** Sue sein.
*That **can't** have been easy.*	Das **kann nicht** einfach gewesen sein.
*They **must** have fallen asleep.*	Sie **müssen** eingeschlafen sein.

➔ *would* for repeated actions in the past: GF 1.3, p. 182

In German

Modale Hilfsverben und ihre Ersatzverben

- **Modale Hilfsverben** (kurz auch: **Modalverben**) wie *can, could, may, might, must,* usw.
  - haben nur eine Form — *He may be a bit late.*
  - bilden Verneinungen und Fragen ohne *do/does/did* — *I can't hear them. Can you hear them?*
  - stehen vor einem Infinitiv ohne *to* — *You should ask your teacher.*
  - beziehen sich in der Regel auf Gegenwart oder Zukunft — *Can I go now? / Can I call you back tomorrow?*
  - können verschiedene Dinge zum Ausdruck bringen.

can	*I can play tennis.*	(Fähigkeit)
	Can I borrow your ruler?	(Bitte)
	You can take my bike.	(Erlaubnis)
	That can't be Joe. Joe's in Italy.	(Möglichkeit)

  - können nicht alle Zeitformen bilden.

- **Ersatzverben** werden verwendet, um andere Zeitformen zu bilden:
  - *can* („können") – *(to) be able to* — *After six months, he was able to understand French.*
  - *can, may* („dürfen") – *(to) be allowed to* — *We were not allowed to use a dictionary in the test.*
  - *must* („müssen") – *(to) have to; (to) need to* — *We had to do extra homework yesterday.* / *I need to get a new pair of trainers.*

GF 5 The gerund Das Gerundium

You already know the **-ing form** of a verb.

As a **present participle**, it is used

1 *Emily isn't in. She**'s working**.*
*Tom was tired. He **had been working** in the garden.*

1 in the **progressive forms** of the verb (➔ *GF 2.1, p. 186*)

2 *Luckily, everyone got out of the **burning** house alive.*

2 like an **adjective**

3 *The park was full of young men **playing** football.*
***Walking** down the street, I saw a beautiful horse.*

3 in certain **participle constructions**. (➔ *GF 10.2–10.7, pp. 203–205*)

4 ***Hiking** is fun.*
*All my friends enjoy **playing** football.*

4 If an **-ing form** is used like a **noun**, we call it a **gerund**. On pages 194–196, you will find more information about the use of **-ing forms** as **gerunds**.

5.1 The gerund as subject and object

Subject	Object
Travelling is fun. Reisen macht Spaß.	*I love **travelling**.* Ich liebe das Reisen. / Ich reise sehr gern.

An ***-ing* form** that is used like a **noun** is called a **gerund**.

Compare: *I love **pop music**.* (*I love* + noun)
*I love **travelling**.* (*I love* + gerund)

The gerund can be the **subject** or the **object** of a sentence.

*I love **playing board games**.*
Ich spiele sehr gern Brettspiele.

***Cycling in the rain** can be fun too.*
Radfahren im Regen kann auch Spaß machen. / Im Regen Rad zu fahren kann auch Spaß machen.

◄ Like a verb, the gerund can be followed by an object (here: *board games*) or an adverbial phrase (here: *in the rain*).

! Note:

1 *Nobody **enjoys going** to the dentist's.*
Niemand geht gern zum Zahnarzt.

*I can't **imagine living** in the country.*
Ich kann mir nicht vorstellen, auf dem Land zu leben.

*Tom **suggested going** for an ice cream.*
Tom schlug vor, ein Eis essen zu gehen.

1 The gerund comes after certain verbs, e.g.

admit, consider, deny, discuss, dislike fancy, finish, give up, keep, mind miss, practise, regret, risk – *doing sth.*

These verbs **cannot be followed by an infinitive** – unlike their German equivalents:

~~*I enjoy to go*~~ … / ~~*I can't imagine to live*~~ …

2 *When it **started** **raining** / **to rain** we all went home.*

*I **hate** / I **don't like** **getting up** / **to get up** when it's still dark.*

2 The verbs ***begin/start, continue, hate, like, love, prefer*** can be used with either a gerund or a *to*-infinitive (with little or no change in meaning).

3 *My mother **would prefer to move** to a small village, but I **would hate to live** in the country.*

3 After ***would like, would love, would hate, would prefer*** we can only use the *to*-infinitive.

4 *I'll never **forget meeting** the Queen.*
Ich werde nie vergessen, wie ich … getroffen habe.
*I **forgot to phone** Grandpa. I'm sorry.*
Ich habe vergessen, Opa anzurufen. Es tut mir leid.

*I **remember meeting** her.*
Ich erinnere mich daran, dass ich sie getroffen habe.
*I must **remember to phone** Grandpa.*
Ich muss daran denken (= ich darf nicht vergessen), Opa anzurufen.

*I've **stopped eating** hamburgers.*
Ich habe aufgehört, Hamburger zu essen.
*I **stopped to buy** a hamburger.*
Ich hielt an, um einen Hamburger zu kaufen.

*It's very sour. – **Try using** more sugar.*
… Probier's mal mit mehr Zucker.
*I **tried to kick** the door open and hurt myself.*
Ich versuchte/bemühte mich, die Tür aufzutreten …

4 The verbs ***forget, remember, stop, try*** can be followed by a **gerund** or a ***to*-infinitive**, but the meaning is different. Compare:

– ***forget doing sth.***	vergessen, dass/wie man etwas getan hat
forget to do sth.	vergessen, etwas zu tun
– ***remember doing sth.***	sich daran erinnern, dass/wie man etwas getan hat
remember to do sth.	daran denken *(nicht vergessen)*, etwas zu tun
– ***stop doing sth.***	aufhören, etwas zu tun
stop to do sth.	anhalten, um etwas zu tun
– ***try doing sth.***	etwas (aus)probieren
try to do sth.	versuchen, etwas zu tun

➔ *Unit 2: p. 66, exercises 1–3*

5.2 The gerund after prepositions

1 *The man left the shop* ***without paying****.*
… ohne zu bezahlen.

2 *You can save petrol* ***by driving*** *more slowly.*
… indem man langsamer fährt.

3 *My little brother is* ***afraid of sleeping*** *in the dark.*
… hat Angst davor, im Dunkeln zu schlafen.

4 *What were his* ***reasons for leaving*** *school?*
… seine Gründe dafür, die Schule zu verlassen?

5 *They* ***decided against moving*** *to Italy.*
Sie entschieden sich dagegen, nach Italien zu ziehen.

When a **preposition** *(about, at, for, in, instead of, of, without, …)* is followed by a **verb**, this verb takes the form of a gerund.

◄ The preposition

– can be used on its own (**1 and 2**) or

– can be linked to another word (an adjective, a noun, or a verb) (**3 to 5**).

Here are a couple of useful phrases with **adjective/noun/verb + preposition + gerund**:

Adjective + preposition + gerund:

(to) be	***afraid of***	***doing*** *sth.*	Angst haben vor
	excited about		gespannt sein auf; aufgeregt sein wegen
	good/bad at		gut/schlecht sein in; etwas gut/schlecht können
	interested in		interessiert sein an, sich interessieren für
	keen on		begeistert sein von; interessiert sein an
	tired of		genug haben von; etwas über/satt haben

Noun + preposition + gerund:

the	***chance of***	***doing*** *sth.*	Chance, (günstige) Gelegenheit (zu)
	danger of		Gefahr (zu)
	hope of		Hoffnung (zu/auf)
	idea of		Idee, Gedanke (zu)
	reason for		Grund (für)
	way of		Art und Weise, Weg (zu)

Verb + preposition + gerund:

(to)	***believe in***	***doing*** *sth.*	glauben an
	decide against		sich entscheiden gegen
	dream of/about		träumen von
	look forward to		sich freuen auf
	talk about/of		reden von
	think of		denken an; in Betracht ziehen
	worry about		sich Sorgen machen wegen/um

5.3 The gerund with "its own subject"

1a *Ava can't* ***imagine moving*** *to Wales.*
Ava kann sich nicht vorstellen, nach Wales zu ziehen.
1b *Ava can't* ***imagine her family moving*** *to Wales.*
Ava kann sich nicht vorstellen, dass ihre Familie nach Wales zieht.

2a *Do you* ***mind me leaving*** *early today?*
2b *Do you* ***mind my leaving*** *early today?*
Macht es Ihnen etwas aus, wenn ich heute früher gehe?

◄ In **1b** the gerund has its own subject: *moving* refers to *her family* (and not to *Ava*, the subject of the sentence).

◄ If the subject of the gerund is a **personal pronoun** as in **2a**, we normally use the object form:
… mind ***me*** *leaving …* (not: *… mind ~~I l~~eaving …*).

Sometimes we use a **possessive pronoun** instead of a personal pronoun (**2b**):
… mind ***my*** *leaving …*

5.4 The gerund in certain phrases

*Leo **is busy** preparing dinner.*
Leo ist damit beschäftigt, das Abendessen vorzubereiten.

*The band **had a great time** performing at the festival.*
Die Band genoss es sehr, auf dem Festival aufzutreten.

*I **had a hard time** finding my way in London.*
Ich fand es schwierig, mich in London zurechtzufinden.

***It wasn't much fun** waiting for the bus in the rain.*
Es war nicht gerade ein Vergnügen, … zu warten.

***It's not worth** watching the film. It's boring.*
Es lohnt sich nicht, den Film anzuschauen. …

***It's no use** having a good canoe if you can't paddle.*
Es nützt nichts, ein gutes Kanu zu haben, …

The gerund is used in certain phrases, e.g.

- ***be busy doing sth.***
  (beschäftigt sein mit …)
- ***have a great time doing sth.***
  (eine großartige Zeit haben …; es genießen …)
- ***have a hard time / have a problem doing sth.***
  (Schwierigkeiten / ein Problem haben …)
- ***it is fun / no fun doing sth.***
  (es ist ein / kein Vergnügen …)
- ***it is (not) worth doing sth.***
  (es ist es (nicht) wert …; es lohnt sich (nicht) …)
- ***it is no use doing sth. / it is no good doing sth.***
  (es hat keinen Zweck …; es nützt nichts …)

In German

Die *-ing*-Form

- Als **Partizip Präsens** wird die ***-ing*-Form** zur **Bildung der Verlaufsformen** des Verbs verwendet. Außerdem kann das Partizip Präsens **wie ein Adjektiv** und in einer Reihe von **Partizipialkonstruktionen** verwendet werden.
- Eine ***-ing*-Form**, die **wie ein Nomen** verwendet wird, nennt man **Gerundium**.
- **Gerundien** können – **Subjekt** des Satzes sein: *Surfing / Playing tennis is fun.*
  – **Objekt** des Satzes sein: *I love surfing / playing tennis.*
- Nach einigen Verben steht nicht ein *to*-Infinitiv, sondern ein Gerundium.
  Beispiele: ***admit, consider, deny, discuss, dislike, enjoy, fancy, finish, give up, imagine, keep, mind, miss, practise, regret, risk, suggest** doing sth.*
- Folgt ein Verb auf eine **Präposition**, steht es als Gerundium: *Dad gave me some money **for cleaning** his bike.*
- **Gerundien** können ihr eigenes Subjekt haben: *They're very happy about **their son passing** the test.*

GF 6 The *to*-infinitive Der Infinitiv mit *to*

6.1 Verb/adjective/noun + *to*-infinitive

1 *They **decided** to take part in the race.*
Sie beschlossen, am Rennen teilzunehmen.

2 *It is **easy** to make new friends at our youth camp.*
Es ist einfach, … neue Freunde zu finden.

3 *There are lots of good **reasons** to learn a language.*
Es gibt viele gute Gründe, eine Sprache zu lernen.

4 *It's **important** for us to keep quiet.*
Es ist wichtig, dass wir leise sind.

*There's no **reason** for you to stay here.*
Es gibt keinen Grund für dich, hierzubleiben. /
Es gibt keinen Grund, dass du hierbleibst.

5 *My brother **asked** me not to wear his T-shirts.*
Mein Bruder bat mich, nicht seine T-Shirts zu tragen.

*His parents **expect/want** him to be home by ten.*
… erwarten/wollen, **dass** er um zehn zu Hause ist.

***I'd like** you to sit down in a circle now.*
Ich möchte, **dass** ihr euch jetzt im Kreis hinsetzt.

Certain verbs, adjectives and nouns can be followed by the ***to*-infinitive**. These structures usually correspond to the German infinitive with **"zu"**.

1 **Verb + *to*-infinitive:** *decide/offer/plan/… to do sth.*

2 **Adjective + *to*-infinitive:** *difficult/easy/… to do sth.*

3 **Noun + *to*-infinitive:** *plan/reason/way/… to do sth.*

4 **Adjective/noun + for sb. + *to*-infinitive:**
difficult/easy/… for sb. to do sth.
time/reason/ … for sb. to do sth.

5 **Verb + object + *to*-infinitive**:
allow/ask/help/invite/teach sb. to do sth.

! Note that the verbs ***cause, expect, tell, want, would like, would love*** can also be followed by an **object + *to*-infinitive**.
In German, we use a **"dass"**-clause in these cases.
But in English, we **cannot use a *that*-clause** with these verbs.

6.2 Question word + *to*-infinitive

*Can you tell me **how to get** to the station?*
Können Sie mir sagen, wie ich zum Bahnhof komme/ kommen kann?

*I don't know **what to do**.*
Ich weiß nicht, was ich tun soll.

*I need help, but I don't know **who to ask**.*
…, aber ich weiß nicht, wen ich fragen kann/soll.

*We had no idea **where to go**.*
Wir hatten keine Ahnung, wohin wir gehen sollten.

Question words (*what, who, how, when, where* etc.) can be followed by a ***to*-infinitive**.
This construction is often used instead of a subordinate clause with a modal auxiliary (*can, could, should* usw.).

Compare: *I don't know who to ask.*
I don't know who I can ask/who I should ask.

We often use this construction after *ask, explain, find out, know, show, tell, wonder*.

6.3 The *to*-infinitive instead of a relative clause

→ *CHECK 7: p. 212*

The *to*-infinitive can correspond to a **relative clause**:

◄ after ***the first, the last, the next, the only***

*The **first/last (person) to arrive** was Jonathan.*
(The first/last person who arrived …)

*We're **the only shop to offer** this service.*
(… the only shop that offers this service)

*Ava was **the only person/the only one to tell** the truth.*
(… the only person/the only one who told …)

! After *the only*, we always use a noun or *one/ones*.

◄ after a **superlative**

*Sophie was **the youngest (girl) to take** part.*
(… the youngest girl who took part)

◄ after a **noun** (often after ***person, place, way***) and after **compounds with *some-*, *any-* and *no-*** (*someone, something, anybody, nowhere, …*).

Here, the *to*-infinitive corresponds to a **relative clause with a modal auxiliary**.

*Philip is **the person to ask** about computers.*
*(… the person who you **should** ask …)*

*Luigi's is **the place to go** for a good pizza.*
*(… the place that you **must/should** go to …)*

*I'm looking for **someone to share** a flat with.*
*(… someone who I **can** share a flat with)*

*There's **nothing to do** and **nowhere to go**.*
*(… nothing that I **can** do and nowhere that I **can** go)*

In German

Der *to*-Infinitiv

Der *to*-Infinitiv wird verwendet …

- nach **Verben**, **Adjektiven** und **Nomen** — *They **decided to leave**. / It's **easy (for you) to say** that. / It's **time (for you) to go** to bed.*

  ! Nach *cause, expect, tell, want, would like, would love* darf kein Nebensatz mit *that* stehen. — *Dad **wants you to help** him.* (nicht: ~~*Dad wants that you help him*~~.)

  ! Beachte, dass nach einigen Verben nicht ein *to*-Infinitiv, sondern ein Gerundium stehen muss. Vergleiche dazu die Anmerkungen und Beispiele zu den Ziffern 1 bis 4 auf S. 194.
- nach einem Fragewort (anstelle eines Nebensatzes) — *I don't know **what to do**.*
- nach *the first (person), the last (one), the only one* (anstelle eines Relativsatzes) — *Sue is always **the first to arrive**. He was **the only one to tell** the truth.*
- nach einem Superlativ (anstelle eines Relativsatzes) — *Tom was **the oldest to join** us.*
- nach Nomen und nach *someone, anything, nowhere*, usw. (anstelle eines Relativsatzes). — *That's **the way to do** it! Grandpa needs **someone to talk** to.*

NEW

GF 7 Indirect speech / Reported Speech Indirekte Rede

7.1 Direct and indirect speech

CHECK 8: p. 212

Norah: *I **love** music. I **go** dancing every Saturday.*

Direct speech *Norah says, "I **love** music. I **go** dancing every Saturday."*

◀ In **direct speech** we repeat **word for word** what someone has said, written or thought.

Indirect speech (reporting verb: simple present) *Norah **says that** she **loves** music, and **that** she **goes** dancing every Saturday.*

◀ In **indirect speech** (also called **reported speech**) we **report** what someone has said, written or thought. (Reporting verbs: *say, tell sb., answer, write, think, …*)

Indirect speech (reporting verb: simple past) *Norah **said that** she **loved** music, and **that** she **went** dancing every Saturday.*

◀ When the **reporting verb** is in the **simple past** (e.g. *said, told me, added, wrote* etc.), we usually "backshift" the verb forms of direct speech a step into the past. This is known as the **backshift of tenses**.
Compare: *"I **love** music." – She said she **loved** music.*

Backshift of tenses after a reporting verb in the past

	Direct speech	Indirect speech
present → past	"I **don't like** musicals." "We**'re** just **having** dinner."	She **told** us she **didn't like** musicals. He **said** they **were** just **having** dinner.
past → past perfect[1]	"I **arrived** on Friday evening." "Alex **was waiting** for Olivia."	She **said** she **had arrived** on Friday evening. Bobby **said** Alex **had been waiting** for Olivia.
present perfect → past perfect	"I**'ve seen** that film before."	I **told her** that I **had seen** the film before.
***will*-future → *would* + infinitive**	"I**'m** sure you**'ll qualify**."	Mr Jones **said** he **was** sure I **would qualify**.
***going to*-future → *was/were going to* + infinitive**	"We**'re going to fly** to Italy in July."	They **said** they **were going to fly** to Italy in July.
can* → *could	"You **can use** my laptop."	Her dad **said** she **could use** his laptop.

[1]Past tense forms in direct speech often stay the same in indirect speech (i.e. are not backshifted to the past perfect): *I **arrived** on Friday evening. → She told us she **arrived** on Friday evening.*

*Norah **said** she loved music.*
Norah sagte, dass sie Musik liebt.

! In English we do **not use a comma** before indirect speech, and the conjunction ***that*** ("dass") **is often left out**, especially after *say, tell sb.* and *think*.

Direct speech Norah *"**I** can lend **you my** bike, Ava."*
(Norah reports) *I told Ava **I** could lend **her my** bike.*
(Ava reports) *Norah said **she** could lend **me her** bike.*

◀ As in German, **pronouns** und **possessive determiners** sometimes have to be changed, depending on the point of view of the person who is reporting.

(On a postcard from Alex) *I like it a lot **here** in France. I'm flying to Paris **tomorrow** and …*

His mother (to a friend, a week later) *He wrote that he liked it a lot **there**, and that he was flying to Paris **the next day**.*

◀ As in German, **phrases of place and time** sometimes have to be changed, depending on the point of view of the person who is reporting.

Unit 4: pp. 126-127, exercises 1-4

NEW

7.2 Indirect speech: questions

CHECK 9: p. 212

with question word

1 *"**Why don't** you **like** musicals?"*
*I **asked** her **why** she **didn't like** musicals.*

2 *"**What's going** on here?"*
*Miss Cleveland **wanted to know what was going** on.*

◄ When the **reporting verb** is in the **simple past** (e.g. *asked, wanted to know, wondered*), backshifting takes place – just as in reported statements.

yes/no question

3 *"**Do** you **want to join** us?"*
*He **asked if** I **wanted to join** them.*

4 *"**Are** you **going to stay**?"*
*Jake **asked** me **whether** I **was going to stay**.*

◄ If there is **no question word** in the direct question (i.e. if it is a *yes/no* question), we use *if* or *whether* (= "ob") in the indirect question.

			S	V	
statement			"We	live	in Hamburg."
direct questions		"**Do**	you	live	in Hamburg?"
		"Where **do**	you	live?"	
indirect question	I asked	**if**	**they**	**lived**	in Hamburg.
	I asked	**where**	**they**	**lived**.	

! The word order in indirect questions is the same as in statements: **S – V – …**

We **do not use *do/does/did*** before the subject in indirect questions.

Direct question *"What **are** you **waiting for**?"*

Indirect question *He asked me what I **was waiting for**.*
…, worauf/auf was ich wartete.

◄ Note the position of **prepositions** in indirect questions.

➜ *Unit 4: p. 128, exercise 2*

NEW

7.3 Indirect speech: requests, commands, advice, suggestions

Direct speech
"Can you lend me your pen?"
"Don't touch the paintings."
"I'd get a holiday job if I were you."

Indirect speech
*A man **asked** me **to lend** him my pen.*
*The guide **told** us **not to touch** the paintings.*
*Mr Williams **advised** Norah **to get** a holiday job.*

◄ We usually use **infinitive constructions** to report **requests, commands** and **advice.**

- **requests**: ***ask* sb. *to do* sth.** (or ***ask* sb. *not to do* sth.**)
- **commands**: ***tell* sb. *to do* sth.** (or ***tell* sb. *not to do* sth.**)
- **advice: *advise* sb. *to do* sth.** (or ***advise* sb. *not to do* sth.**)

*Norah **was advised to get** a holiday job.*

◄ We often use **passive constructions**.

Direct speech *"Let's go for a pizza."*

Indirect speech *He **suggested going** for a pizza.*
*He **suggested that we go** for a pizza.*
*He **suggested we should go** for a pizza.*

◄ Never use an infinitive after *suggest* – you can use the structures on the left to report **suggestions.**

➜ *Unit 4: p. 128, exercise 5*

In German

Die indirekte Rede

- Wenn in der **indirekten Rede** das **einleitende Verb im *simple past*** steht (z. B. *said, told me*), werden die Zeitformen der direkten Rede meist um eine Zeitstufe in die Vergangenheit „zurückverschoben" a(*backshift of tenses*):

present ➝ **past**
past ➝ **past perfect**
present perfect ➝ **past perfect**
***going to*-future** ➝ ***was/were going to* + infinitive**
***will*-future** ➝ ***would* + infinitive**
can ➝ ***could***

- In **indirekten Fragen** ist die Wortstellung **S – V – …**, und *do/does/did* wird nicht verwendet:
I asked where they lived. | *She wanted to know if we needed anything else.*

- **Bitten, Aufforderungen, Ratschläge, Vorschläge**

– Bitten: ***ask*** *sb. (not) to do sth.*
– Aufforderungen: ***tell*** *sb. (not) to do sth.*
– Ratschläge: ***advise*** *sb. (not) to do sth.*
– Vorschläge: ***suggest*** *doing sth. …*

GF 8 Conditional sentences Bedingungssätze

Subordinate clause	Main clause
If *you give me your number,*	*I'll call you.*
Wenn du mir deine Nummer gibst,	rufe ich dich an.

Conditional sentences consist of a **main clause** and a **subordinate clause** with ***if*** (= "wenn/falls").
The *if*-clause expresses a **condition**.
The main clause expresses **consequences**.

if + present	*will*-future

*If I **miss** the bus, I**'ll take** a taxi.*
Wenn ich den Bus **verpasse**, **nehme** ich ein Taxi.

*If Dan **misses** the bus, he **can/should/must take** a taxi.*
*If you **miss** the bus, **take** a taxi.*

◄ **Typ 1** ("What will be if …")

These conditional sentences refer to the **future** or the **present**. They tell us what will or will not happen if the condition stated in the *if*-clause is fullfilled.

In the ***if*-clause**, we usually use the **simple present**.
In the **main clause**, we use the ***will*-future** or a **modal auxiliary + infinitive** or an **imperative**.

if + past	*would* + infinitive

*If I **missed** the bus, I**'d** (= I **would**) **take** a taxi.*
Wenn ich den Bus **verpasste/verpassen würde**, **würde** ich ein Taxi **nehmen**.

*If Dan **missed** the bus, he **could/might take** a taxi.*

◄ **Typ 2** ("What would be if …")

Although the **verb in the *if*-clause** is in the **simple past**, these conditional sentences also refer to the **future** or the **present**. They express what would or would not happen if the condition stated in the *if*-clause were fulfilled.

In the **main clause**, we use the ***would/could/might* + infinitive**.

if + past perfect	*would have* + past participle

*If I **had missed** the bus, I **would have taken** a taxi.*
Wenn ich den Bus **verpasst hätte**, **hätte** ich ein Taxi **genommen**.

*If Dan **had missed** the bus, he **could have taken**/ he **might have taken** a taxi.*

◄ **Typ 3** ("What would have been if …")

These conditional sentences refer to the **past**.
We imagine a past situation which in reality did not happen.
The **condition** stated in the *if*-clause was **not fulfilled**:
In reality, the speaker **did not miss the bus**.
We only imagine what would have happened (but in reality did not happen):
The speaker would have taken a taxi.

In the **main clause**, we use ***would have/could have/might have* + past participle**.

*If I **knew** her better, I **would have asked** her.*
Wenn ich sie besser kennen würde, hätte ich sie gefragt.

*If you**'ve been** here before, you**'ll know** the rules.*
Wenn du schon mal hier warst, dann kennst du (ja) die Regeln.

*If they **left** at seven, they **won't be** here until twelve.*
Wenn sie um sieben losgefahren sind, werden sie nicht vor zwölf hier sein.

◄ As in German, there can be **mixed types of conditional sentences**, depending on the context.

Study the examples and their translations on the left.

Wenn wir mit dem Auto gefahren wären, wären wir schon da.

In German

Bedingungssätze

- **Type 1** (bezogen auf Gegenwart oder Zukunft):
  simple present — ***will*-future** oder ***can/must/should/...*** **+ Infinitiv**
  *If they **score** another goal, they **will win**.*
  Der Sprecher hält es für gut möglich, dass sie noch ein Tor schießen. (Das Spiel hat gerade begonnen.)
- **Type 2** (bezogen auf Gegenwart oder Zukunft):
  simple past — ***would/could/might*** **+ Infinitiv**
  *If they **scored** another goal, they **would win**.*
  Der Sprecher hält es für wenig wahrscheinlich, dass sie noch ein Tor schießen. (Das Spiel ist fast vorbei.)
- **Type 3** (bezogen auf die Vergangenheit):
  past perfect — ***would/could/might*** **+ *have* + Partizip Perfekt**
  *If they **had scored** another goal, they **would have won**.*
  Das Spiel ist vorbei. Sie haben kein weiteres Tor erzielt und somit auch nicht gewonnen.
- Ähnlich wie im Deutschen werden – je nach Situation – auch andere Kombinationen von Zeitformen verwendet:
  *If they **had scored** another goal, they **would be** in the final round now.*
  *If they **have scored** six goals, they surely **must have won** the match.*

GF 9 Relative clauses Relativsätze

9.1 Defining relative clauses

1 *Do you know the girl **who/that works at the Oxfam shop**?*
… *das Mädchen, das im Oxfam-Shop arbeitet?*

2 *That's the shop **which/that sells second-hand clothes and books and stuff**.*
… *der Laden, der gebrauchte Kleidung und Bücher und so etwas verkauft.*

➜ *Unit 2: p. 49, exercise 4 • Unit 3: p. 97, exercise 3*

Defining relative clauses ("bestimmende Relativsätze") begin with a **relative pronoun**. We use ***who*** or ***that*** for people **(1)** and ***which*** or ***that*** for things **(2)**.

A defining relative clause defines a word – usually a noun – more closely. It gives us **information that we need to fully understand the sentence**. Without the relative clauses *(who works at the Oxfam shop / which sells second-hand clothes)* it would be unclear which girl or which shop is meant.

In English, defining relative clauses are **not separated** from the main clause **by commas**.

9.2 Contact clauses

1 *Mr Jones is the teacher **who I like the most**.*
or *Mr Jones is the teacher **I like the most**.*

2 *These are the photos **that Dad took in Wales**.*
or *These are the photos **Dad took in Wales**.*

3 *Who was the man **who was talking** to Jeremy at the bus stop?*

When the relative pronoun is the **object** of a defining relative clause, we often leave it out **(1, 2)**.
A relative clause without a relative pronoun is called a **contact clause**.

! When the **relative pronoun is followed directly by the verb,** it is the **subject** – you **must not** leave it out **(3)**.

Compare:
– … *the man **who was talking to** Jeremy*
("… der Mann, **der** mit Jeremy gesprochen hat")
– … *the man **who Jeremy was talking to*** or
… *the man **Jeremy was talking to***
("… der Mann, mit dem **Jeremy** gesprochen hat")

NEW

9.3 Non-defining relative clauses

➜ CHECK 10: p. 213

*Agatha Christie, **who died in 1976,** wrote about 70 detective novels and 17 plays.*

*John Lennon, **whose mother taught him to play the banjo in the 1950s,** later became world-famous as a member of the Beatles.*

*At 11.35 we landed at Atlanta International, **which is one of the world's busiest airports**.*

Non-defining relative clauses ("nicht bestimmende Relativsätze") are used mainly in written English. They give **additional information** about the word they relate to. If we left out the relative clause, the main clause on its own would still make sense: We would understand the sentence *Agatha Christie wrote about 70 detective novels* even if we left out *who died in 1976*.

In non-defining relative clauses,

- you **must not leave out the relative pronoun**;
- the pronoun ***that*** cannot be used;
- the relative clause is separated **by commas**.

*The president, **whom I had never seen before,** looked much younger than I had expected.*
..., den ich nie vorher gesehen hatte, ...

◀ In formal English, ***whom*** is often used instead of ***who*** when the relative pronoun is the **object** of the non-defining relative clause.

➜ *Unit 3: pp. 96-97, exercises 1–3*

NEW

9.4 Relative clauses with *which* to refer to a whole clause

➜ CHECK 11: p. 213

*In December 1980, John Lennon was murdered, **which shocked people all over the world**.*
..., was Menschen auf der ganzen Welt schockierte.

*Our neighbours helped us to tidy up after the party, **which I think was very good of them**.*
..., was ich sehr nett von ihnen fand.

*We're moving to Leeds in the summer, **which means I'll have to change school**.*
..., was bedeutet, dass ich die Schule wechseln muss.

Relative clauses with ***which*** relate to the whole of the main clause. They express a comment on the content of the main clause.

In German, we use relative clauses with "was" to comment on the content of the main clause.

This type of relative clause is separated from the main clause by a comma.

Little Stevie has made dinner for his dad, which is very nice of him.

In German

Relativsätze

• Ein **bestimmender Relativsatz** gibt Informationen, die zum Verständnis des Satzes notwendig sind. Es stehen keine Kommas.	*<u>The man</u> **who answered the phone** was very friendly.*
• Das **Relativpronomen kann nur weggelassen werden**, wenn es **Objekt** des Relativsatzes ist. Relativsätze ohne Relativpronomen werden ***contact clauses*** genannt.	*Don't forget the book **that you borrowed last week**.* ➜ *Don't forget the book **you borrowed last week**.*
• **Nicht bestimmende Relativsätze** geben **Zusatzinformationen** über das Nomen, auf das sie sich beziehen (der Hauptsatz ist auch ohne diese Zusatzinformationen verständlich). In nicht bestimmenden Relativsätzen kann *that* nicht verwendet werden, und es stehen Kommas.	*My friend Jane, **whose dad is English,** is bilingual.*
• Relativsätze mit ***which*** können sich auf einen ganzen Satz beziehen. Sie kommentieren die Aussage im vorausgehenden Hauptsatz und werden durch Kommas abgetrennt.	*Stevie has made dinner for his dad, **which is very nice of him**.*

GF 10 Participles Partizipien

10.1 Participle forms

Present participle: -ing

work →	***working***	*try* →	***trying***
dance →	***dancing***	*plan* →	***planning***

Like the infinitive, participles are **non-finite forms** of the verb, i.e. their form does not change.

◄ The **present participle** ("Partizip Präsens") ends in ***-ing***.

It is used in the **progressive forms** of the verb.

➜ *The tenses, GF 1, pp. 181–186*
➜ *Aspect, GF 2, pp. 186–187*

On pages 203–205, you will find more information about the use of **present participles in certain participle constructions**.

(Note that ***-ing* forms** that are **used as nouns** are called **gerunds**. ➜ *The gerund, GF 5, pp. 194–196*)

Past participle, regular verbs: -ed

work →	***worked***	*try* →	***tried***
dance →	***danced***	*plan* →	***planned***

Past participle, irregular verbs:

build →	***built***	*grow* →	***grown***
make →	***made***	*see* →	***seen***
teach →	***taught***	*write* →	***written***

◄ The **past participle** ("Partizip Perfekt") of **regular verbs** ends in ***-ed***.
Irregular verbs have special past participle forms.

➜ *Irregular verbs: pp. 338-340*

The past participle is used in the **perfect tenses** of active verbs and in all **passive forms**.

➜ *The tenses, GF 1, pp. 181–186*
➜ *The passive, GF 3, pp. 188–190*

On pages 203–205, you will find more information about the use of **past participles in certain participle constructions**.

10.2 Participle clauses instead of relative clauses

➜ *CHECK 12: p. 213*

NEW

Participle clauses are often used instead of a **relative clause**:

*The city is always full of people **who are looking for a parking space**.*
→ *The city is always full of people **looking for a parking space**.*
… voller Menschen, die nach einem Parkplatz suchen.

◄ The **present participle** is equivalent to a **relative pronoun + active verb**.
Compare:
… *people **looking** for a parking space*
… *people **who are looking** for a parking space*

*The Eurovision Song Contest is an international competition **which is watched by millions of people**.*
→ *The Eurovision Song Contest is an international competition **watched by millions of people**.*
… Wettbewerb, der … angeschaut wird.

➜ *Unit 2: p. 49, exercise 4 • p. 62, exercises 1–2*

◄ The **past participle** is equivalent to a **relative pronoun + passive verb**.
Compare:
… *competition **watched** by millions of people*
… *competition **which is watched** by millions of people*

NEW

10.3 Verb of perception + object + present participle

CHECK 13: p. 213

	Verb of perception	Object	Present participle	
1 *We*	***heard***	***a baby***	***crying***.	
2 *She*	***saw***	***someone***	***climbing***	*on the roof.*
3 *He*	***watched***	***the band***	***getting***	*ready for the show.*
4 *I*	***noticed***	***two women***	***arguing***	*outside the hotel.*

◄ After **verbs of perception** like ***feel, hear, listen to, notice, see, smell, spot, watch*** we can use an **object** + **present participle**.

We use this construction to express the idea that we perceive an action which is (or was) in progress and not yet complete.

1 Wir hörten ein Baby weinen.
2 Sie sah jemanden auf das Dach klettern. / …, wie/dass jemand auf das Dach kletterte.
3 Er beobachtete, wie sich die Band für die Show bereitmachte.
4 Ich bemerkte zwei Frauen, die sich vorm Hotel stritten. / …, dass sich zwei Frauen … stritten.

◄ In German, we use an infinitive, a subordinate clause with "wie" or "dass", or a relative clause.

(We can also use an **infinitive without *to*** after verbs of perception. This construction expresses the idea that the complete action is perceived from beginning to end:
*We **saw him grab** the money and **run** away.*
Wir sahen, wie er sich das Geld schnappte und davonlief.)

Unit 2: p. 49, exercises 5–6

NEW

10.4 Participle clauses giving additional information

CHECK 14: p. 214

*It rains a lot here, **sometimes flooding the roads**.*
Hier regnet es viel, und manchmal überschwemmt es (dabei) die Straßen.

*Last Sunday morning, we stayed in bed, **reading and listening to the radio**.*
Letzten Sonntagmorgen sind wir im Bett geblieben und haben gelesen und Radio gehört.

*Charlotte ran down the stairs, **losing a shoe**.*
…, wobei sie einen Schuh verlor.

***Using a knife**, she was able to open the door.*
Indem sie ein Messer benutzte, …

Unit 2: p. 54, exercise 1

We often use **present participle clauses** to give **additional information** or to describe the **accompanying circumstances** of an action.
(Usually the actions or events take place simultaneously or almost simultaneously.)

In German we normally use a main clause with "und" or a subordinate clause with "wobei" or "indem".

NEW

10.5 Participle clauses instead of adverbial clauses of time

CHECK 15: p. 214

***When planning a trip to a foreign country**, start early and ask people who have been there.*
Wenn du eine Reise in ein fremdes Land planst, …

***While walking down the street**, I saw a huge black dog.*
Als/Während ich die Straße hinunterging, …

***When asked why he left school so early**, he answered that he wanted to earn his own money.*
Als er gefragt wurde, …

*Always be polite **when asking for information**.*
…, wenn du um Informationen bittest.

Participle clauses beginning with ***when*** or ***while*** correspond to **subordinate clauses of time**.

The **present participle** is equivalent to an **active verb** *(while walking = while I was walking)*.

The **past participle** is equivalent to a **passive verb** *(when asked = when he was asked)*.

Often the sentence begins with the participle clause.

These participle constructions are typical of written English.

***Walking* down the street**, *I saw a huge black dog.*
Als/Während ich die Straße hinunterging, …

***Asked* why he left school so early**, *he answered that he wanted to earn his own money.*
Als er gefragt wurde, …

◄ Sometimes we leave out the conjunction.

1a *Joe met* *<u>an old friend</u>* ***while* looking for a job**.
(= Joe met an old friend while he – Joe – was looking for a job)
…, während er auf der Suche nach einer Stelle war.

1b *Joe met* *<u>an old friend</u>* ***looking for a job***.
(= Joe met an old friend who was looking for a job)
…, der auf der Suche nach einer Stelle war.

➜ *Unit 2: pp.54-55, exercises 2–4 · p. 62, exercises 1–2*

! Be careful when the participle clause comes after the main clause!
Compare **1a** and **1b**:

- In **1a**, Joe was looking for a job.
- In **1b**, his friend was looking for a job.

We saw three seals ***while walking*** *along the beach.*

We saw three seals ***walking*** *along the beach.*

NEW

10.6 Participle clauses instead of adverbial clauses of reason

➜ *CHECK 16: p. 214*

***Feeling* very tired**, *I decided to go to bed early.*
Weil/Da ich sehr müde war, …

***Being* a doctor**, *she knew exactly what to do.*
Weil/Da sie Ärztin ist, …

***Warned* by his wife**, *the man was able to escape.*
Weil er von seiner Frau gewarnt wurde, … /
Von seiner Frau gewarnt, …

➜ *Unit 2: p. 55, exercise 5*

Participle clauses can also correspond to **subordinate clauses of reason**.

! Note that the conjunction *because* cannot be used in participle clauses.
Never: ~~*Because feeling very tired*~~, …
~~*Because being a doctor*~~, …

10.7 Other participle clauses

***Although asked* to stop by the police**, *he drove on.*
Obwohl er von der Polizei aufgefordert wurde anzuhalten, fuhr er weiter.

You will have to wait outside ***until asked* to enter**.
Sie werden draußen warten müssen, bis Sie gebeten werden einzutreten.

***If posted* before 12 o'clock**, *the letter should arrive tomorrow.*
Wenn der Brief vor 12 Uhr eingeworfen wird, sollte er morgen ankommen.

***After winning* gold**, *she decided to resign.*
Nachdem sie Gold gewonnen hatte, beschloss sie zurückzutreten.

Participle clauses can also begin with other conjunctions, e.g. with ***although, until, if, after, before***.

In German

Partizipien

• ***Present participle:*** Infinitiv + ***-ing*** bei allen Verben ***Past participle:*** Infinitiv + ***-ed*** bei regelmäßigen Verben Unregelmäßigen Verben haben eigene ***Past participle***-Formen.	*(to)* ***dance*** → ***dancing*** *(to)* ***dance*** → ***danced*** *(to)* ***see*** → ***seen*** / *(to)* ***write*** → ***written***
• **Relativsätze** können zu **Partizipialsätzen** verkürzt werden.	*The man* ***who was driving*** *the red car …* → *The man* ***driving*** *the red car …* *A song* ***which was written*** *by …* → *A song* ***written*** *by …*
• Auf **Verben der Wahrnehmung** kann ein **Objekt + *present participle*** folgen.	***I felt my heart beating*** *faster.* *Can you* ***hear someone crying****?*
• Mit ***present participle clauses*** kann man **Zusatzinformationen** geben.	*We stayed in bed,* ***listening to music****.* *He ran out of the house,* ***forgetting his keys****.*
• **Partizipialsätze** mit *when* oder *while* können anstelle von **adverbialen Nebensätzen der Zeit** verwendet werden.	*Try to be friendly* ***when asking for help****.* ***(While) walking down the street****, I met Sue.*
• **Partizipialsätze** (ohne Konjunktion!) können anstelle von **adverbialen Nebensätzen der Grundes** verwendet werden.	***Feeling very tired****, I went to bed early.* ***Being new at his school****, he felt very lonely.*
• **Partizipialsätze** können auch anstelle anderer **adverbialer Nebensätze** verwendet werden. Sie werden dann bspw. mit den Konjunktionen *although, until, if, after, before* eingeleitet.	***Although badly hurt****, he tried to help us.* ***If asked for money****, do not send it!* *Please wait* ***until asked to enter****.*

NEW

GF 11 Adjectives used as nouns Das Adjektiv als Nomen

→ *CHECK 17: p. 214*

Our class collected money for ***the blind****.*
… die Blinden / Blinde / blinde Menschen …

The homeless *need our help.*
Die Obdachlosen / Obdachlose Menschen …

◂ Some English **adjectives** can be **used as nouns**. They refer to a **group of people with something in common**: ***the blind*** (i.e. blind people in general), ***the homeless, the poor, the rich, the Irish, …***

Amelia helped ***the blind woman*** *at the ticket office.*
… der Blinden / der blinden Frau …

A lot of rich people *live in this area.*

! When you talk about **one individual person** or about **a group of several individual people**, the adjective must be followed by a noun such as ***girl(s), boy(s), man/men, woman/women, people***.

It is a journey into ***the unknown****.* … ins Unbekannte …

Always expect ***the unexpected****.* … das Unerwartete …

◂ ***The*** **+ adjective** does not always refer to a group of people. It can also have a **general, abstract meaning**, e.g. ***the unknown, the unexpected, the impossible, the good, the evil, …***

The good thing *about school is that you meet your friends there.*

! When you talk about **something specific**, you have to use a noun like ***thing***.

→ *Unit 1: p. 30, exercise 2*

In German

Das Adjektiv als Nomen

Einige englische Adjektive können als Nomen verwendet werden, um über eine **Gruppe von Menschen** zu sprechen, die eine Eigenschaft gemeinsam haben. Beispiel: ***the blind*** („blinde Menschen im Allgemeinen", „alle Blinden")
Wenn man über eine oder mehrere **Einzelpersonen** spricht, muss im Englischen ein Nomen folgen: ***the blind man***.

The **+ Adjektiv** kann auch für **allgemeine, abstrakte Begriffe** verwendet werden: ***the unknown, the good***.
Wenn es um eine **bestimmte** Sache oder Situation geht, muss auf das Adjektiv ein Nomen folgen: ***the good thing***.

GF 12 Subject-verb agreement Subjekt-Verb-Kongruenz

CHECK 18: p. 214

NEW

12.1 Group nouns

*The **band** **has** / **have** finished playing.*

*His **family** **wants** / **want** to move to Bristol.*

*The **government** **has** / **have** introduced a new tax.*

*The **team** **was** / **were** sure **it** / **they** would win.*

More group nouns

audience	Publikum, Zuhörer/innen
choir	Chor
class	Klasse
club	Klub, Verein
crowd	(Menschen-)Menge
enemy	Feind
majority	Mehrheit
minority	Minderheit

Nouns like ***band, family, government, group, team*** refer to **a group of people**.

If we are thinking of the **group as a whole**, we use the **singular form of the verb** and following **pronoun** *(it; its)*.

If we are thinking of the **individual members**, we use the **plural form of the verb** and following **pronoun** *(they; their)*.

(In American English, the singular is normally used.)

*The **police** **are** on **their** way.*

Unit 1: p. 15, exercise 10

! Note that the noun ***police*** is always used with **plural verbs** and **pronouns**.

NEW

12.2 Singular nouns ending in -s

***Economics** **is** an interesting subject.*

***Maths** **was** my best subject at school.*

***Fake news** **has** become a big problem.*

***Politics** **plays** an important role in my life.*

A number of nouns **end in -s** but are still used with a **singular verb**, e.g. ***aerobics, economics, maths/ mathematics, news, physics, politics***.

***The United States** / **The USA** **consists** of 50 states.*
Die Vereinigten Staaten / Die USA bestehen aus 50 Staaten.

Unit 1: p. 15, exercise 10

! Note that you use a **singular verb** after ***the United States (the USA, the US)***.

In German

Subjekt-Verb-Kongruenz

- Nomen wie ***band, family, government, group, team*** bezeichnen Gruppen von Menschen.
  Wenn man bei diesen Nomen an die **Gruppe als Ganzes** denkt (die Band/Familie/... **als eine Einheit**), steht die **Singularform des Verbs**, und die zugehörigen Pronomen stehen ebenfalls im Singular: *it, its*.
  Wenn man an die **einzelnen Mitglieder** der Gruppe denkt, steht die **Pluralform des Verbs**, und die zugehörigen Pronomen stehen im Plural: *they, their*.
- Es gibt eine Reihe von Nomen, die zwar auf **-s** enden, aber dennoch mit **einem Verb im Singular** verwendet werden. Beispiele:
  aerobics, economics, maths/mathematics, news, physics, politics, the United States (the USA, the US)

NEW

GF 13 The definite article Der bestimmte Artikel

➜ CHECK 19: p. 215

1 ***Life*** *isn't always easy.*
Das Leben ist nicht immer einfach.

Pollution *is a big problem.*
Die Umweltverschmutzung …

2 *Most* ***people*** *are worried about climate change.*
Die meisten Menschen …

Rules *are important in competitive sports.*
Regeln sind wichtig …

3 *What will happen if we run out of* ***oil / water****?*
…, wenn uns das Öl / das Wasser ausgeht?

◄ In English, there is **no definite article** when a noun is used **in a very general sense**.
This is especially the case with

- **abstract nouns**, e.g. *culture, death, history, life, music, nature, noise, peace, pollution, research, sport(s), time*
- **nouns in the plural**
- **nouns for substances or materials**, e.g. *air, oil, gold, tea, glass, snow, water*.

! You do not use an article even if there is an adjective in front of the noun: *When did* ***human life*** *begin?*

4 ***The life of a film star*** *isn't always easy.*
Das Leben eines Filmstars …

What can we do to stop ***the pollution of our oceans****?*
… die Verschmutzung unserer Ozeane …

5 ***The people who live here*** *all help each other.*
Die Menschen, die hier leben, …

6 ***The oil that was found on his land*** *made him rich.*
Das Öl, das auf seinem Land gefunden wurde …

◄ Those nouns are used **with a definite article** when they are made **more concrete** or when we **specify** which we mean, for example with an *of*-phrase or a relative clause.

Compare sentences **1 – 3** with sentences **4 – 6**.
Sentences **1 – 3** are about life, pollution, people, oil etc. in general.
Sentences **4 – 6** are about the particular life of a film star, the particular pollution of our oceans, the people who live here, the particular oil on someone's land.

1 ***Breakfast*** *is at 8 o'clock today.*
We had pizza for ***lunch*** *yesterday.*
I'm going to call Grandma after ***dinner****.*

2 ***The breakfast*** *we had at the airport was very good.*
Can I have the recipe for ***the lunch*** *we had on Friday?*

! Note that words for **meals** *(breakfast, lunch, dinner, …)* are **usually used without the definite article** (1).

You only use the definite article if you are talking about a **particular meal**, most often specified with a relative clause (2).

1 *We go to* ***church*** *every Sunday.*
… in die Kirche *(zum Gottesdienst)*
He spent two years in ***prison****.*
… im Gefängnis *(um eine Strafe zu verbüßen)*
I know her from ***school****.*
… aus der Schule *(vom gemeinsamen Unterricht)*
Dad's ill. He's in ***hospital****. (AE: in* ***the hospital****)*
… *im Krankenhaus (zur Behandlung)*

2 *There's a concert in* ***the church*** *on Friday.*
He works in one of the shops behind ***the prison****.*
Go straight on till you get to ***the school****, then turn left.*
Let's meet in the park next to ***the hospital****.*

➜ *Unit 1: p. 13, exercises 4-6*

! Be careful with the nouns ***church, hospital, prison, school, college, university***:

1 They are used **without the definite article** when we are talking about **the purpose of the building**.

2 They are used **with the definite article** when we are talking about **the building (the place)**.

In German

Der bestimmte Artikel

- **Abstrakte Begriffe** *(death, history, life, …)*, **Nomen im Plural** und **Stoffbezeichnungen** *(air, oil, milk, …)* stehen **ohne bestimmten Artikel**, wenn sie **ganz allgemein** verwendet werden. Beispiel: ***Life*** *is sweet.* ***Milk*** *tastes great.*
- Sie stehen **mit bestimmtem Artikel**, wenn sie **näher bestimmt** sind: ***the life*** *of Shakespeare;* ***the milk*** *we bought.*
- Die **Gebäudebezeichnungen** *church, hospital, prison, school, college, university* stehen **ohne bestimmten Artikel**, wenn die **Funktion** / der **Zweck** des Gebäudes im Vordergrund steht: *We often go to* ***church****.*
Sie stehen **mit bestimmtem Artikel**, wenn es um den **Ort** / das **Bauwerk** geht: *Let's meet behind* ***the church****.*

GF 14 Emphatic structures Strukturen zur Hervorhebung

NEW

14.1 Word stress

__Mum__ thinks he'll help you.
Mum __thinks__ he'll help you.
Mum thinks __he__'ll help you.
Mum thinks he __will__ help you.
Mum thinks he'll __help__ you.
Mum thinks he'll help __you__.

◂ Any word in an English sentence can be **emphasized** if you **stress** it when speaking.

! We use the **long form of auxiliary verbs** (e.g. *is, have, will, would*) **if we stress them**:

I think he __will__ help you.

14.2 Emphatic *do/does/did*

➔ CHECK 20: p. 215

NEW

without emphasis	*I **think** you should talk to your dad.* *You **promised** to help me.* *She **said** she was sorry though.*
with emphasis	*I **do think** you should talk to your dad.* Ich finde wirklich, du solltest … *You **did promise** to help me.* Aber du hast doch versprochen … *She **did say** she was sorry though.* Aber sie hat sich immerhin entschuldigt.

➔ *Unit 4, p. 115, exercises 5-6*

In **simple present** and **simple past sentences** we can use **stressed *do*, *does*** or ***did*** + infinitive to add emphasis.

14.3 Emphasizing pronouns

➔ CHECK 20: p. 215

NEW

without emphasis	*The room was OK.* *He wants to do it.* *We were able to talk to the director.*
with emphasis	***The room itself** was OK but the food was awful.* Das Zimmer selbst war in Ordnung … ***He** wants to do it **himself**. He doesn't need us.* Er möchte es selbst machen. … *We were able to talk to **the director herself**.* Wir konnten mit der Regisseurin selbst sprechen.

The ***-self/-selves* pronouns** can be used to emphasize nouns or pronouns that come earlier in the sentence.

14.4 Adverbs

➔ CHECK 20: p. 215

NEW

*I couldn't answer the interviewer's questions – I felt **pretty/really/so/extremely** stupid.*

***Such** a stupid mistake – I won't **ever** make it again.*

We often use certain **adverbs** to add emphasis, e.g. ***really, fairly, pretty, completely, totally, absolutely, extremely, somewhat, so, such, never, ever***.

14.5 *It's … /It was … + who/that …*

➔ CHECK 20: p. 215

NEW

*It was **the Bartons who/that** were late again.*
Es waren die Bartons, die wieder zu spät kamen.

*It's **him that** I'm talking about, not you.*
Von ihm rede ich, nicht von dir.

*It was **only last month that** they met.*
Erst letzten Monat haben sie sich kennengelernt.

We can emphasize a **noun**, a **pronoun** or an **adverbial** using *It's … / It was …* + ***who/that …***

We mainly use this structure to express a **contrast**.

! Note that the verb after ***It*** is in the singular, even if the noun that follows is in the plural:
*It **was the Bartons** …*

NEW

14.6 'Negative' adverbials + inversion

→ CHECK 20: p. 215

***Never (before)* had we seen** *so many people.*
Nie (zuvor) hatten wir so viele Leute gesehen.

***Only much later* did they realize** *who the woman was.*
Erst viel später wurde ihnen klar, wer die Frau war.

***Hardly* had he left** *when the phone started ringing.*
Kaum war er gegangen, als das Telefon zu klingeln begann.

→ *Unit 4: p. 115, exercise 7*

Some expressions with a **negative** or **restrictive meaning** can go at the beginning of the sentence for special emphasis, e.g. ***never (before)***, ***rarely*** ("selten"), ***only later***, ***hardly*** ("kaum"), ***under no circumstances*** ("unter keinen Umständen"), ***at no time***.

! Note the **change in word order** (**inversion**):
***Never* had we** *seen …*
***Only much later* did they** *realize …*

In German

Strukturen zur Hervorhebung

- Man kann beim Sprechen einzelne Wörter oder Satzteile **besonders betonen**, um sie hervorzuheben.
- Im *simple present* und *simple past* kann man **betontes *do/does/did*** vor den Infinitiv des Vollverbs stellen, um der Aussage des Satzes Nachdruck zu verleihen.
- Mit den Pronomen auf ***-self/-selves*** kann man Nomen oder Pronomen besonders hervorheben.
- Mit **Adverbien** wie *really, pretty, absolutely, so, ever* u. Ä. kann man einzelne Wörter oder Satzteile hervorheben.
- Mit ***It's … / It was … + who/that …*** kann man Nomen, Pronomen und adverbiale Bestimmungen hervorheben.
- Einige Ausdrücke mit **verneinender** oder **einschränkender Bedeutung** (*never, hardly, only later, …*) können zu Betonungszwecken an den Satzanfang rücken. In diesem Fall ändert sich die Wortstellung (**Inversion**).

Check (Aufgaben zur Selbstüberprüfung)

CHECK 1

The past perfect (simple), the past perfect progressive

→ *Answers: p. 218*

a) Make sentences. Use the past perfect progressive. Example sentence 1 can help you.

1 *Mrs Jones was really tired. She (work) in the garden all afternoon.*
She had been working in the garden all afternoon.

2 *Jonathan felt disappointed. He (wait) for Emily for over an hour, but she still hadn't come.*
3 *We (watch) the show for only 20 minutes when it started to rain.*
4 *I didn't know what to say when our teacher asked me because I (not – listen). I (think) of my girlfriend the whole lesson.*

b) Past perfect (simple) oder past perfect progressive? Complete the sentences.

*Last night on the way to the cinema, I realized that I (**1** leave)* had left *my money at home. I (**2** look forward) to the film for weeks and I didn't want to miss it, so I got off the bus and ran home. When I arrived, I realized that I (**3** forget) my keys too, so I couldn't get in. I rang the doorbell, but everybody (**4** go) out. So I ran as fast as I could to my friend Jeremy's place. His mother opened the door, but Jeremy wasn't in. He (**5** not – come) home yet. His mother saw that I (**6** run), so she asked me to sit down and gave me a drink. I started playing a game on my phone. I (**7** play) for twenty minutes when Jeremy finally arrived. He lent me some money, and I ran back to the bus stop. When I finally got to the cinema, the film (**8** already – start).*

CHECK 2
The *will*-future, the *going to*-future

➜ *Answers: p. 218*

a) What is B's reaction? Complete the dialogues.

1 **A** *There's somebody at the door.* – **B** *(see)* I'll see who it is.
2 **A** *I can't do this exercise.* – **B** *(help)*
3 **A** *This glass was very expensive.* – **B** *(not drop)*
4 **A** *Olivia mustn't find out.* – **B** *(not tell)*

b) Spontaneous decision or planned in advance?
Complete the sentences with the correct tense (*will*-future or *going to*-future).

1 *Tea or coffee? – I think I (have) coffee.*
2 *Michael says he (study) art in Berlin.*
3 *Oh no, it's starting to rain. – Don't worry. I (drive) you home.*
4 *There are no buses into town on Sundays, but my father (drive) us.*
5 *The phone is ringing! – OK, I (answer) it.*
6 *Do you have plans for the summer holidays? – Yes, we do. We (spend) two weeks in France.*
7 *Would you like to join us? – Uh … I (think) about it. I (let) you know later, OK?*

CHECK 3
The future progressive

➜ *Answers: p. 218*

What will they be doing this time next week? Use the future progressive and complete the sentences.

1 **Jeremy** *Next week I … (lie) on a beach in Spain.* Next week I'll be lying on a beach in Spain.
2 **Filiz** *And I … (sightsee) in Munich. What about you, Paul? What … (you – do) this time next week?*
3 **Paul** *I … (sit) on a plane on my way to Rome.*
4 **Emily** *Ava and I … (rock climb) in the Alps.*
5 **Mike** *Lucky you! I … (work) at the supermarket while you're having fun.*
But in August, my brother and I … (cycle) along the Dordogne in France.

CHECK 4
The future perfect

➜ *Answers: p. 218*

Choose a verb from the box and complete the sentences. Use the future perfect.

calm down · come down · miss · repair · finish · not finish

1 *If you start your homework now, you … by the time the TV programme starts.*
…, you'll have finished by the time the TV programme starts.
2 *It's too late to go to the cinema now. By the time we get there, we … too much of the movie.*
3 *I can't present this report to the class tomorrow. I … it by then.*
4 *Don't call Linda yet – she's still angry with you. Wait until tomorrow – she … after a night's sleep.*
5 *You should wait until after Christmas to get a new phone. The prices … by then.*
6 *If I come back next Monday, … you … my bike by then? I can't ride my old bike in the race.*

CHECK 5
Simple form and progressive form

➜ *Answers: p. 218*

Simple form or progressive form? Complete the sentences with the correct tense.
Remember: State verbs are only used in the simple form.

1 *(**A** Do you like / **B** Are you liking) my new aftershave? I think it (**C** smells / **D** is smelling) great.*
2 *Caroline (**A** seems / **B** is seeming) to enjoy her training course in London.*
*She told me she (**C** had / **D** was having) a lot of fun.*
3 *It was a great preformance, but not many people (**A** watched / **B** were watching).*
4 *Does anyone know who this watch (**A** belongs to / **B** is belonging to)?*
5 *It says here that the price (**A** includes / **B** is including) a day trip to Brighton.*
6 *Nobody (**A** noticed / **B** was noticing) that he left early.*
*Everybody (**C** looked / **D** was looking) at the people on the stage.*

CHECK 6
The passive of verbs with two objects

➔ *Answers: p. 218*

Look at the example. Then complete sentences 2 to 6.

1 *(Someone **gave us** the key.)* — ***We** … key and went up to our room.*
We were given the key and went up to our room.
2 *(They **gave us** ten minutes)* — ***We** … ten minutes to read the questions.*
3 *(They **offered me** a job)* — ***I** … a job at the local radio station.*
4 *(Someone **told him** the news)* — *He was shocked when **he** …*
5 *(They **promised her** a TV role)* — ***She** … a TV role.*
6 *(Someone **sent them** a letter bomb)* — ***They** …*

CHECK 7
The *to*-infinitive instead of a relative clause

➔ *Answers: p. 218*

a) Look at the boxes and the example sentence. Think of your family – who is the first / the last / the only one to do these things? (You can add *always, usually, often* etc.)

I *My parents* *My mother* *My father* *My sister* *My brother*	*the first* *the last* *the only one(s)*	*get up* *have a shower* *have breakfast* *leave home* *come home* *go to bed*

1 My … is (usually) the first to get up.
2 I'm (always) …
3 …
4 …
5 …
6 …

b) Melinda is unhappy. But why?
Choose verbs from the box and complete her sentences. Example sentence 1 can help you.

ask · do · give · go · go with · listen to

1 *I'd like to go dancing tonight. The Funk House would be the perfect place* to go*, but it's a long way from where I live.*
2 *And there are no buses after 11, so I'd need someone … me a lift back home.*
3 *Jacob would be the person …, but he's away on holiday.*
4 *And I've got nobody … anyway.*
5 *I wish I had some new music …*
6 *I guess it'll be another evening at home with nothing … but watch a film.*

CHECK 8
Indirect speech: statements

➔ *Answers: p. 218*

What do they do at the weekend to help at home? Look at the table on the right. Write down what they said.

1 *Tyler said that* he often washed the dishes.
2 *Sarah told us …*
3 *Anna said …*
4 *David said …*
5 *Grace said …*
6 *James told us …*

Tyler	often – wash the dishes
Sarah	always – clear the table
Anna	always – do the shopping
David	usually – make breakfast
Grace	often – walk the dog
James	sometimes – do the cooking

CHECK 9
Indirect speech: questions

➔ *Answers: p. 218*

Look at the questions below and report what Jacob and Ella asked each other.

1 *How long have you had your motorbike, Ella?* — Jacob asked Ella how long she had had her motorbike.
2 *How much did you pay for it?* — He wondered how much …
3 *And how often do you ride it?* — He also wanted to know …
4 *When did you buy your motorbike, Jacob?* — Ella asked Jacob …
5 *Where do you usually park it at night?* — And she also wanted to know …

CHECK 10

Non-defining relative clauses

Answers: p. 218

Rewrite the sentences on the left including the correct extra information from the right. Don't forget to use commas.

Example: **1** E-readers, which I don't often use, can never replace real books.

1 *E-readers can never replace real books.*
2 The Little Hero *was the last book I read.*
3 *The main character is a young girl from Scotland.*
4 *I went to the library to take back the books.*
5 *My mother is writing her own detective story.*
6 *I was sad that Old Mr Bumblebore died in the end.*

who loves crime novels
who reminded me of my grandfather
which is around the corner from my house
who has the same first name as me
which I don't often use
which is the first part of a series.

CHECK 11

Relative clauses with *which* to refer to a whole clause

Answers: p. 218

Read sentences 1–5. Choose a comment from a) to e) and rewrite the sentences as in the example.

Example: **1** We're moving to Leeds in the summer, which means I'll have to change school.

1 *We're moving to Leeds in the summer.*
2 *Emily won the 100 metres.*
3 *Jonathan offered to help with the dishes.*
4 *In 1968, Martin Luther King was killed.*
5 *I'm going to get a pay rise next month.*

a) *It means I'll be able to buy a new computer soon.*
b) *It shocked people all over the world.*
c) *It means I'll have to change school.*
d) *That was very nice of him.*
e) *It surprised everybody.*

CHECK 12

Participle clauses instead of relative clauses

Answers: p. 218

Use participle clauses to shorten the relative clauses.

1 *The line of fans who are waiting to buy the latest book in the Harry Wolf series stretches for a mile.*
The line of fans waiting to buy the latest book in the Harry Wolf series stretches for a mile.

2 Wolf on the Moor *– the first in the series which was published in 2012 – was an unexpected success.*
3 *It is one of those books that are loved by people of different age groups.*
4 *One of the fans shouts out, "Who is that man who is standing at the door?!"*
5 *It's a man who is wearing a black coat and who is carrying a bag with the picture of a wolf on it.*
6 *Every fan would love to get a copy of the book which is signed by the author himself.*

CHECK 13

Verb of perception + object + present participle

Answers: p. 218

Choose a verb from the box and complete the sentences.

come · drop · look · play · tell · walk

1 *Do you know where Julia is going? I saw her … down the road.*
… I saw her walking down the road.

2 *John, I heard you … Suzy a joke – what was the last part? I missed it.*
3 *I saw you … football and wanted to ask if I can join in?*
4 *Quick, kids, hide your father's present, I can hear him …!*
5 *On the bus, I noticed a girl … at me. I asked her if she knew me – it was Molly, our ex-neighbour!*
6 *Mum didn't notice my little brother … stones behind him on our walk – like in the Hansel and Gretel story.*

CHECK 14

Participle clauses giving additional information → *Answers: p. 219*

Rewrite the sentences. Use participle clauses. Example sentence 1 can help you.

1 *George was walking down King Street. He was talking on his mobile.*
George was walking down King Street, talking on his mobile.
2 *We were standing at the bus stop. We were waiting for the Number 10 bus.*
3 *Amelia was on her way to the station. She was carrying a rucksack and two heavy bags.*
4 *We stood in the queue and waited to buy tickets.*
5 *He used a stone to break the window and climbed into the flat.*

CHECK 15

Participle clauses instead of adverbial clauses of time → *Answers: p. 219*

Rewrite the sentences. Use participle clauses with *while*. Example sentence 1 can help you.

1 *Jessica walked home from school on Friday afternoon and found a set of keys.*
While walking home from school on Friday afternoon, Jessica found a set of keys.
2 *Ava played tennis and hurt her shoulder.* Ava hurt ...
3 *We sat on the beach and watched the seals on the rocks.* While ..., we watched ...
4 *Noah rode the roller coaster and lost his glasses.* Noah lost ...
5 *Emily was washing the dishes when she cut her finger.* Emily cut ...
6 *He walked through the jungle and was bitten by a snake.* While ..., he ...

CHECK 16

Participle clauses instead of adverbial clauses of reason → *Answers: p. 219*

Rewrite the sentences. Use participle clauses. Example sentence 1 can help you.

1 *Oliver was new in London. That's why he found it very difficult to find his way around.*
Being new in London, Oliver found it very difficult to find his way around.
2 *He didn't know the way to the job centre and got lost.* Not ...
3 *I felt very nervous, so I drove much too slowly in my first driving lesson.*
4 *We didn't have much money, so we went to a cheap restaurant.*
5 *He saw that he had made a mistake, so he said he was sorry.*

CHECK 17

Adjectives used as nouns → *Answers: p. 219*

Read sentences 1–6 and the phrases given in brackets. Choose the correct alternative to complete the sentences.

1 *Every year, our church invites … to celebrate Christmas together. (the lonely / the lonely people)*
2 *It's difficult for … to imagine how … feel. (a rich / a rich person – the unemployed / the unemployed people)*
3 *Winter is a hard time for … . (the homeless / the homeless people).*
4 *In most films … wins over … in the end. (the good / the good thing – the bad / the bad thing)*
5 *… about this new design program is that it is very easy to handle. (The good / The good thing)*
6 *What's … about this new museum in your opinion? (the most exciting / the most exciting thing)*

CHECK 18

Subject-verb agreement → *Answers: p. 219*

Complete the sentences with the correct form of the verbs in brackets. Use the simple present.

1 *The USA … (play) an important role for the German manufacturing industry.*
2 *The news from the Middle East … (be) getting better.*
3 *The politics of a country … (have) an influence on the happiness of its population.*
4 *Of course, the economics of a country … (be) important, but money isn't everything.*
5 *Physics … (have) always been my brother's favourite subject.*

CHECK 19
The definite article

➜ *Answers: p. 219*

Write the sentences into your exercise book. Add *the* where necessary.

1 *We can learn a lot from … history.*
2 *What do you know about … history of Canada?*
3 *We take the bus to … church every Sunday morning.*
4 *What's the name of … school you go to?*
5 *She's always friendly and helpful. That's why … people love her.*
6 *… scientists agree that we have to do something against … pollution.*
7 *I'm reading a book about … history of … architecture.*
8 *I think … life in … prison can be worse than … death.*

CHECK 20
Emphatic structures

➜ *Answers: p. 219*

a) There is only one emphatic auxiliary in each sentence. Decide which verb the speaker wants to emphasize and write the sentences correctly. Example sentence 1 can help you.

1 *I promise, Mr Roberts, I did / did do the homework but I forgot / did forget to bring it.*
I promise, Mr Roberts, I did do the homework but I forgot to bring it.

2 *I can't understand why the plant died / did die. I remembered / did remember to water it.*
3 *You needn't worry, Mum – you packed / did pack the raincoats. I saw / did see you pack them.*
4 *I like / do like you, Jake, really – it's just that I think / do think we're too young for a serious relationship.*

b) Add the correct *-self/-selves* pronouns and write the sentences in your exercise book.

1 *She wants to do it … .* She wants to do it herself.
2 *You can do it … – it's not very difficult.*
3 *Mr Jones said we didn't have to do it … .*
4 *Their parents said they could do it … .*

c) Use **two** of the three adverbs and rewrite the sentences.

1 *The film was terrible. We were disappointed. (absolutely / really / such)*
2 *I forgot about your birthday. I am sorry. (so / absolutely / completely)*
3 *The charity concert was a success. It went well. (completely / such / so)*

d) Use ***It's … / It was …*** **+ relative clause** and rewrite the sentences. (Sometimes there is more than one solution.)

1 *She doesn't like pork, but she eats beef and chicken.* It's pork that she doesn't like, but she eats beef …
2 *I don't like his friends – I think he is OK.*
3 *They stole Brian's bike, not mine.*
4 *I didn't suggest it, Peter did.*
5 *I prefer the blue blouse, not the red one.*

e) Rewrite these sentences. Begin with the underlined words.
Be careful with the word order. Change the verb forms if necessary.

1 *In all my years as a teacher, I have never taught such good students.*
Never in all my years as a teacher have I taught such good students.

2 *We had hardly begun to eat dinner when the doorbell rang.*
3 *They understood only later how dangerous their behaviour had been.*
4 *You can find better prices nowhere than at MediaMagic!*

Grammatical terms (Grammatische Fachbegriffe)

active ['æktɪv]	Aktiv	*A heavy storm* ***destroyed*** *twelve houses.*
activity verb [æk'tɪvəti vɜːb]	Tätigkeitsverb	*do, go, make, read, repair, …*
adjective ['ædʒɪktɪv]	Adjektiv (Eigenschaftswort)	*good, new, green, interesting, …*
adverb ['ædvɜːb]	Adverb	*today, there, outside, very, …*
adverb of degree [dɪ'griː]	Gradadverb	*very, really, so, quite, almost, a bit, …*
adverb of frequency ['friːkwənsi]	Häufigkeitsadverb	*always, usually, often, sometimes, never*
adverb of indefinite time [ɪn'defɪnət]	Adverb der unbestimmten Zeit	*already, ever, just, never, before, yet, …*
adverb of manner ['mænə]	Adverb der Art und Weise	*nicely, happily, quietly, slowly, well, fast, …*
adverbial clause [æd,vɜːbiəl 'klɔːz]	adverbialer Nebensatz	*I went to bed* ***because I was tired****.*
article ['ɑːtɪkl]	Artikel	*the, a, an*
aspect ['æspekt]	Aspekt	
auxiliary [ɔːg'zɪliəri]	Hilfsverb	*be, have, do; will, can, must, …*
backshift of tenses ['bækʃɪft]	Rückverschiebung der Zeitformen	*"I'm tired."* → *She said (that) she* ***was*** *tired.*
command [kə'mɑːnd]	Befehl, Aufforderungssatz	*Open your books. Don't talk.*
comparative [kəm'pærətɪv]	Komparativ (1. Steigerungsform)	*older; more expensive*
comparison [kəm'pærɪsn]	Steigerung	*old – older – oldest;* *expensive – more expensive – most expensive*
compound ['kɒmpaʊnd]	Zusammensetzung	*somebody, anyone, something, …*
conditional sentence [kən'dɪʃənl]	Bedingungssatz	*If I see Sam, I'll tell him.*
conjunction [kən'dʒʌŋkʃn]	Konjunktion	*and, but, …; because, when, …*
contact clause ['kɒntækt klɔːz]	Relativsatz ohne Relativpronomen	*Here's the report* ***I've written****.*
countable noun ['kaʊntəbl]	zählbares Nomen	*girl – girls, car – cars, idea – ideas, …*
defining relative clause [dɪ'faɪnɪŋ]	bestimmender Relativsatz	*I like teachers* ***who laugh a lot****.*
definite article [,defɪnət‿'ɑːtɪkl]	bestimmter Artikel	*the*
direct speech [,daɪrekt 'spiːtʃ]	direkte Rede	***"I'm tired."***
emphasis ['emfəsɪs]	Hervorhebung, Betonung	
future perfect [,fjuːtʃə 'pɜːfɪkt]	vollendete Zukunft, Futur II	*On Friday I* ***will have finished*** *my exams.*
future progressive [,fjuːtʃə prə'gresɪv]	Verlaufsform des *will-future*	*How long* ***will*** *you* ***be staying****?*
gerund ['dʒerənd]	Gerundium	*I like* ***dancing****.* ***Dancing*** *is fun.*
***going to*-future** ['fjuːtʃə]	Futur mit *going to*	***I'm going to watch*** *TV tonight.*
***if*-clause** ['ɪf klɔːz]	*if*-Satz, Nebensatz mit *if*	***If I see Jack****, I'll tell him.*
imperative [ɪm'perətɪv]	Imperativ (Befehlsform)	*Open your books. Don't talk.*
indirect speech [,ɪndərekt 'spiːtʃ]	indirekte Rede	*She said (that)* ***she was tired****.*
infinitive [ɪn'fɪnətɪv]	Infinitiv (Grundform des Verbs)	*(to) open, (to) go, …*
irregular verb [ɪ'regjələ]	unregelmäßiges Verb	*(to) go – went – gone, (to) see – saw – seen*
main clause ['meɪn klɔːz]	Hauptsatz	*If I see Jack,* ***I'll tell him****.*
modal auxiliary [,məʊdl‿ɔːg'zɪliəri]	modales Hilfsverb, Modalverb	*can, may, might, needn't, should, must, …*
negative statement ['negətɪv]	verneinter Aussagesatz	*I don't like oranges.*
non-defining relative clause [dɪ'faɪnɪŋ]	nicht bestimmender Relativsatz	*Drew,* ***who goes to Mobridge-Pollock High School,*** *wants to qualify for the rodeo finals.*
noun [naʊn]	Nomen, Substantiv	*Justin, girl, man, time, name, …*
object ['ɒbdʒɪkt]	Objekt	*Justin has* ***a new camera****.*
object question	Objektfrage, Frage nach dem Objekt	***Who did*** *Mrs Pascoe* ***invite*** *to tea?*
participle ['pɑːtɪsɪpl]	Partizip	*planning, taking; planned, taken*
participle clause [,pɑːtɪsɪpl 'klɔːz]	Partizipialsatz	*The man* ***waiting at the bus stop*** *is my uncle.*
passive ['pæsɪv]	Passiv	*Twelve houses* ***were destroyed*** *by a storm.*
past participle [,pɑːst 'pɑːtɪsɪpl]	Partizip Perfekt	*checked, phoned, tried, gone, eaten, …*
past perfect [,pɑːst 'pɜːfɪkt]	*past perfect* (Vorvergangenheit, Plusquamperfekt)	*I* ***had*** *already* ***gone*** *to bed when they arrived.*

past perfect progressive [ˌpɑːstˌpɜːfɪkt prəˈgresɪv]	Verlaufsform des *past perfect*	*He was tired. He* ***had been working*** *in the garden for 3 hours.*
past progressive [ˌpɑːst prəˈgresɪv]	Verlaufsform der Vergangenheit	*Olivia* ***was playing*** *cards.*
personal passive [ˌpɜːsənl ˈpæsɪv]	persönliches Passiv	*I was offered a job.*
personal pronoun [ˌpɜːsənl ˈprəʊnaʊn]	Personalpronomen (persönliches Fürwort)	*I, you, he, she, it, we, they; me, you, him, her, it, us, them*
plural [ˈplʊərəl]	Plural, Mehrzahl	
positive statement [ˈpɒzətɪv]	bejahter Aussagesatz	*I like oranges.*
possessive determiner [pəˌzesɪv dɪˈtɜːmɪnə]	Possessivbegleiter (besitzanzeigender Begleiter)	*my, your, his, her, its, our, their*
possessive form [pəˌzesɪv ˈfɔːm]	s-Genitiv	*Sam's sister, the Blackwells' house, …*
possessive pronoun [pəˌzesɪv ˈprəʊnaʊn]	Possessivpronomen	*mine, yours, his, hers, ours, theirs*
preposition [ˌprepəˈzɪʃn]	Präposition	*after, at, in, into, near, next to, …*
present participle [ˌpreznt ˈpɑːtɪsɪpl]	Partizip Präsens	*checking, phoning, trying, planning, going, …*
present perfect [ˌpreznt ˈpɜːfɪkt]	*present perfect*	*We****'ve made*** *some scones for you.*
present perfect progressive [ˌpreznt ˌpɜːfɪkt prəˈgresɪv]	Verlaufsform des *present perfect*	*He****'s been watching*** *TV for hours.*
present progressive [ˌpreznt prəˈgresɪv]	Verlaufsform der Gegenwart	*Olivia* ***is playing*** *cards.*
pronoun [ˈprəʊnaʊn]	Pronomen (Fürwort)	
quantifier [ˈkwɒntɪfaɪə]	Mengenangabe	*some, a lot of, many, much, a few, …*
question tag [ˈkwestʃn tæg]	Frageanhängsel	*isn't he?, are you?, can't we?, …*
question word [ˈkwestʃn wɜːd]	Fragewort	*who?, what?, when?, where?, how?, …*
reflexive pronoun [rɪˌfleksɪv ˈprəʊnaʊn]	Reflexivpronomen	*myself, yourself, themselves, …*
regular verb [ˈregjələ]	regelmäßiges Verb	*(to) help – helped, (to) look – looked, …*
relative clause [ˌrelətɪv ˈklɔːz]	Relativsatz	*I like teachers* ***who laugh a lot****.*
relative pronoun [ˌrelətɪv ˈprəʊnaʊn]	Relativpronomen	*who – which – that*
reported speech [rɪˌpɔːtɪd ˈspiːtʃ]	indirekte Rede	*She said (that)* ***she was tired****.*
request [rɪˈkwest]	Bitte; Aufforderung	*Can you help me with this?*
short answer [ˌʃɔːt‿ˈɑːnsə]	Kurzantwort	*Yes, I am. / No, we don't. / …*
simple past [ˌsɪmpl ˈpɑːst]	einfache Form der Vergangenheit	*Olivia* ***played*** *cards last Friday.*
simple present [ˌsɪmpl ˈpreznt]	einfache Form der Gegenwart	*Olivia* ***plays*** *cards every Friday evening.*
singular [ˈsɪŋgjələ]	Singular, Einzahl	
state verb [ˈsteɪt vɜːb]	Zustandsverb	*be, know, like, own, sound, want*
statement [ˈsteɪtmənt]	Aussage(satz)	
subject [ˈsʌbdʒɪkt]	Subjekt	***Justin/He*** *has a new camera.*
subject question	Subjektfrage, Frage nach dem Subjekt	***Who invited*** *the Coopers to tea?*
subordinate clause [səˌbɔːdɪnət ˈklɔːz]	Nebensatz	*I like Plymouth* ***because I like the sea****.*
substitute [ˈsʌbstɪtjuːt]	Ersatzverb (eines Modalverbs)	*be able to, be allowed to, have to*
superlative [suˈpɜːlətɪv]	Superlativ (2. Steigerungsform)	*(the) oldest; (the) most expensive*
tense [tens]	Zeitform	
uncountable noun [ʌnˈkaʊntəbl]	nicht zählbares Nomen	*bread, milk, money, news, work, …*
verb [vɜːb]	**1.** Verb; **2.** Prädikat	*go, help, look, see, …* *Reading* ***can be*** *fun.*
verb of perception [pəˈsepʃn]	Verb der Wahrnehmung	*(to) hear, (to) see, (to) notice, (to) smell, …*
***will*-future** [ˈfjuːtʃə]	Futur mit *will*	*I'm sure you****'ll like*** *the new maths teacher.*
word order [ˈwɜːd‿ˌɔːdə]	Wortstellung	
yes/no question	Entscheidungsfrage	*Are you 14? Do you like oranges?*

Check – answers

1 a) (p.210) **1** *had been working* – **2** *had been waiting* **3** *had been watching* **4** *hadn't been listening … had been thinking*

1 b) (p.210) **1** *had left* – **2** *had been looking forward* – **3** *had forgotten* – **4** *had gone* – **5** *hadn't come* – **6** *had been running* – **7** *had been playing* – **8** *had already started*

2 a) (p.211) **1** *I'll see who it is.* – **2** *I'll help you.* **3** *I won't drop it.* – **4** *I won't tell her.*

2 b) (p.211)
1 *… – I think **I'll** have coffee.*
2 *Michael says he**'s going to** study art in Berlin.*
3 *… – Don't worry. **I'll** drive you home.*
4 *…, but my father **is going to** drive us.*
5 *… – OK, **I'll** answer it.*
6 *… – Yes, we do. We**'re going to** spend two weeks in France.*
7 *… – Uh … **I'll** think about it. **I'll** let you know later, OK?*

3 (p.211) **2** *I'll be sightseeing … What will you be doing* **3** *I'll be sitting* – **4** *Ava and I will be rock climbing* **5** *I'll be working … my brother and I will be cycling*

4 (p.211) **2** *we will have missed* – **3** *I won't have finished it* **4** *she'll have calmed down* **5** *the prices will have come down* **6** *will you have repaired*

5 (p.211) **1 A / C – 2 A / D – 3 B – 4 A – 5 A – 6 A / D**

6 (p.212)
2 ***We were given** ten minutes to read the questions.*
3 ***I was offered** a job at the local radio station.*
4 *He was shocked when **he was told the news**.*
5 ***She was promised** a TV role.*
6 ***They were sent a letter bomb.***

7 a) (p.212)
*… **is/are the first to** get/have/leave/come/go …*
*… **is/are the last to** get/have/leave/come/go …*
*… **is/are the only one/ones to** get/have/leave/come/go …*

7 b) (p.212)
1 *… the perfect place to go …*
2 *… someone to give me a lift …*
3 *… the person to ask …*
4 *… nobody to go with …*
5 *… some new music to listen to …*
6 *… nothing to do …*

8 (p.212)
2 *(that) she always cleared the table*
3 *(that) she always did the shopping*
4 *(that) he usually made breakfast*
5 *(that) she often walked the dog*
6 *(that) he sometimes did the cooking*

9 (p.212)
2 *how much she had paid for it*
3 *how often she rode it*
4 *when he had bought his motorbike*
5 *where he usually parked it at night*

10 (p.213)
2 The Little Hero*, **which is the first part of a series,** was the last book I read.*
3 *The main character**, who has the same first name as me,** is a young girl from Scotland.*
4 *I went to the library**, which is around the corner from my house,** to take back the books.*
5 *My mother**, who loves crime novels,** is writing her own detective story.*
6 *I was sad that Old Mr Bumblebore**, who reminded me of my grandfather,** died in the end.*

11 (p.213)
2 *Emily won the 100 metres**, which surprised everybody**.*
3 *Jonathan offered to help with the dishes**, which was very nice of him**.*
4 *In 1968, Martin Luther King was killed**, which shocked people all over the world**.*
5 *I'm going to get a pay rise next month**, which means I'll be able to buy a new computer soon**.*

12 (p.213)
2 Wolf on the Moor *– the first in the **series published** in 2012 – …*
3 *It is one of those **books loved** by people of different age groups.*
4 *… "Who is that **man standing** at the door?!"*
5 *It's a **man wearing** a black coat and **carrying** a bag …*
6 *Every fan would love to get a copy of the **book signed** by the author himself.*

13 (p.213)
2 *John, I heard you **telling** Suzy a joke – …*
3 *I saw you **playing** football …*
4 *… I can hear him **coming**.*
5 *… I noticed a girl **looking** at me …*
6 *Mum didn't notice my little brother **dropping** stones behind him …*

14 (p.214)
2 *We were standing at the bus stop,* ***waiting*** *for the Number 10 bus.*
3 *Amelia was on her way to the station,* ***carrying*** *a rucksack and two heavy bags.*
4 *We stood in the queue,* ***waiting*** *to buy tickets.*
5 ***Using*** *a stone, he broke the window and climbed into the flat.*

---

15 (p.214)
2 *Ava hurt her shoulder* ***while playing*** *tennis.*
3 ***While sitting*** *on the beach, we watched the seals on the rocks.*
4 *Noah lost his glasses* ***while riding*** *the roller coaster.*
5 *Emily cut her finger* ***while washing*** *the dishes.*
6 ***While walking*** *through the jungle, he was bitten by a snake.*

---

16 (p.214)
2 ***Not knowing the way to the job centre,*** *he got lost.*
3 ***Feeling very nervous,*** *I drove much too slowly in my first driving lesson.*
4 ***Not having much money,*** *we went to a cheap restaurant.*
5 ***Seeing that he had made a mistake,*** *he said he was sorry.*

---

17 (p.214)
1 *Every year, our church invites* ***the lonely*** *to celebrate Christmas together.*
2 *It's difficult for* ***a rich person*** *to imagine how* ***the unemployed*** *feel.*
3 *Winter is a hard time for* ***the homeless****.*
4 *In most films* ***the good*** *wins over* ***the bad*** *in the end.*
5 ***The good thing*** *about this new design program is that it is very easy to handle.*
6 *What's* ***the most exciting thing*** *about this new museum in your opinion?*

---

18 (p.214)
1 *The USA* ***play*** *an important role for the German manufacturing industry.*
2 *The news from the Middle East* ***is*** *getting better.*
3 *The politics of a country* ***has*** *an influence on the happiness of its population.*
4 *Of course, the economics of a country* ***is*** *important, but money isn't everything*
5 *Physics* ***has*** *always been my brother's favourite subject.*

---

19 (p.215)
1 *We can learn a lot from* ***history****.*
2 *What do you know about* ***the history*** *of Canada?*
3 *We take the bus to* ***church*** *every Sunday morning.*
4 *What's the name of* ***the school*** *you go to?*
5 *… That's why* ***people*** *love her.*
6 ***Scientists*** *agree that we have to do something against* ***pollution****.*
7 *I'm reading a book about* ***the history*** *of architecture.*
8 *I think* ***life*** *in prison can be worse than* ***death****.*

---

20 a) (p.215)
2 *I can't understand why the plant* ***died****. I* ***did remember*** *to water it.*
3 *You needn't worry, Mum – you* ***did pack*** *the raincoats. I* ***saw*** *you pack them.*
4 *I* ***do like*** *you, Jake, really – it's just that I* ***think*** *we're too young for a serious relationship.*

20 b) (p.215)
2 *You can do it* ***yourself*** *– it's not very difficult.*
3 *Mr Jones said we didn't have to do it* ***ourselves****.*
4 *Their parents said they could do it* ***themselves****.*

20 c) (p.215)
1 *The film was* ***absolutely*** *terrible. We were* ***really*** *disappointed.*
2 *I* ***completely*** *forgot about your birthday. I am* ***so*** *sorry.*
3 *The charity concert was* ***such*** *a success. It went* ***so*** *well.*

20 d) (p.215)
2 ***It's his friends who I don't like*** *– I think he's OK.*
3 ***It was Brian's bike that they stole****, not mine. /* ***It wasn't my bike that they stole****, it was Brian's.*
4 ***It wasn't me who suggested it****, it was Peter. /* ***It was Peter who suggested it****, not me.*
5 ***It's the blue blouse that I prefer,*** *not the red one. /* ***It's not the red blouse that I prefer****, it's the blue one.*

20 e) (p.215)
2 ***Hardly had we begun*** *to eat dinner when the doorbell rang.*
3 ***Only later did they understand*** *how dangerous their behaviour had been.*
4 ***Nowhere can you find*** *better prices than at MediaMagic!*

Das **Vocabulary** (S.220 – 286) enthält alle Wörter und Wendungen deines Englischbuches, die du lernen musst. Sie stehen in der Reihenfolge, in der sie im Buch zum ersten Mal vorkommen.

Hier siehst du, wie das **Vocabulary** aufgebaut ist:

Diese Zahl gibt die **Seite** an, auf der die Wörter zum ersten Mal vorkommen.
p. 10 = Seite 10

Die **Lautschrift** zeigt dir, wie ein Wort ausgesprochen wird.
Eine Übersicht über alle **Lautschriftzeichen** findest du auf S. 286.
Die Lautschriftzeichen stehen auch unten auf den **Vocabulary**-Seiten.

p. 10	**magnificent** [mæɡ'nɪfɪsnt]	prächtig	St Paul's Cathedral is a ~ building.
	inside the dome [ˌɪn'saɪd]	in der Kuppel, innerhalb der Kuppel	**inside** a building ◄► **outside** a building ! **inside** = 1. drinnen; nach drinnen 2. in, innerhalb (von)
	cultural ['kʌltʃərəl]	kulturell	noun: cul
	acoustics *(pl)* [ə'kuːstɪks]	Akustik	! spelling:
	(to) **overlook** [ˌəʊvə'lʊk]	überblicken; übersehen	! (to) **overlook** = 1. übe 2. übe
	headphones *(pl)* ['hedfəʊnz]	Kopfhörer	I always use ~ if I want to listen to loud music.
	wireless ['waɪələs]	drahtlos, Funk-	
p. 11	**everyone else** [els]	alle anderen; sonst jeder	Oh Mum! Why can't I go to Tim's party? **Everyone** ~ is allowed to go.

Dies ist das „Gegenteil"-Zeichen: **inside** ist das Gegenteil von **outside**.

Das **rote Ausrufezeichen** bedeutet: Vorsicht, hier macht man leicht Fehler!

... else

I'm so tired. **Someone else** will have to wash the dishes.	**jemand anders**
No one else has to help at home as much as I do.	**niemand anders; niemand sonst**
Do you need **anything else** from the shops?	**sonst noch etwas**

Diese **Kästen** solltest du dir immer besonders gut ansehen:
Hier sind Vokabeln zu einem bestimmten Thema zusammengestellt.
Oder du erfährst mehr über ein Wort und wie es verwendet wird.

= *BE* **tourist (information) office**

There's a "no junk food"-~ at my school.
free-movement ~ = Politik der Freizügigkeit (= der offenen Grenzen) *(in der EU)*

German "Politik"

1. *(politisches Leben, Geschehen)*	**politics** *(no pl)*	Are you interested in **politics**? – No, I think **politics** is boring.
2. *(politische Linie, Richtlinien)*	**policy**	What is the prime minister's **policy** on education? What is the company **policy** on working from home?

Im **Vocabulary** werden folgende **Abkürzungen** verwendet:

p. = page • pp. = pages

adj = adjective • adv = adverb

conj = conjunction • prep = preposition

sth. = something (etwas) • sb. = somebody (jemand)

jn. = jemanden • jm. = jemandem

pl = *plural* (Mehrzahl)

infml = *informal* (umgangssprachlich) • *fml* = *formal* (formell, förmlich)

BE = *British English* • *AE* = *American English*

Ⓕ = *verwandtes Wort im Französischen* • Ⓛ = *verwandtes Wort im Lateinischen*

Wenn du **nachschlagen** möchtest, was ein bestimmtes englisches Wort bedeutet oder wie man es ausspricht, dann verwende das **English – German Dictionary** auf den Seiten 287 – 333.

Unit 1 London changing

pp. 8/9	**Victorian** [vɪk'tɔːriən]	viktorianisch; Viktorianer/in	
	circa (c.) ['sɜːkə]	zirka (ca.)	I'm not sure of the exact year, but it was ~ 1350. ! **circa/c.** is only used with dates. (L) circa
	era ['ɪərə]	Ära, Epoche	the post-war ~; an ~ of peace (F) l'ère (L) aera
	advantage [əd'vɑːntɪdʒ]	Vorteil	(F) l'avantage *(m)*
	disadvantage [ˌdɪsəd'vɑːntɪdʒ]	Nachteil	**advantage** ◄► **disadvantage** Not being able to drive can be a ~ when you're looking for a job. (F) le désavantage

Part A

p. 10	**magnificent** [mæg'nɪfɪsnt]	prächtig	St Paul's Cathedral is a ~ building. (F) magnifique (L) magnificus, a, um
	inside the dome [ˌɪn'saɪd]	in der Kuppel, innerhalb der Kuppel	**inside** a building ◄► **outside** a building ! **inside** = **1.** drinnen; nach drinnen **2.** in, innerhalb (von)
	opposite ['ɒpəzɪt]	gegenüberliegende(r, s); entgegengesetzte(r, s)	You'll find the answers to our quiz on the ~ page. ! **opposite** = **1.** *(n)* Gegenteil; **2.** *(prep)* gegenüber (von); **3.** *(adj)* gegenüberliegende(r, s); entgegengesetzte(r, s) (L) oppositus, a, um
	acoustics *(pl)* [ə'kuːstɪks]	Akustik	! spelling: **acoustics** (F) l'acoustique *(f)*
	How's that for acoustics?	Ist das nicht eine tolle Akustik? / Das nennt man tolle Akustik!	Three bedrooms, a large garden and a swimming pool on the roof – **how's that for** a holiday home for you and your family?
	cultural ['kʌltʃərəl]	kulturell	noun: **culture** – adj: **cultural** (F) culturel, le (L) cultura *(Pflege, Kultur)*
	archive ['ɑːkaɪv]	Archiv	! stress and pronunciation: **archive** ['ɑːkaɪv] (F) l'archive *(f)*
	in the 1940s	in den 40er-Jahren (des 20. Jahrhunderts)	
	origin ['ɒrɪdʒɪn]	Ursprung, Herkunft	*English:* **... of African origin** *German:* **... afrikanischer Herkunft** (F) l'origine *(f)* (L) origo, inis *f*
	destination [ˌdestɪ'neɪʃn]	Reiseziel, Fahrtziel; Bestimmungsort	We offer cheap hotel rooms at popular holiday ~**s**. (F) la destination
	audio ['ɔːdiəʊ]	Audio-, Ton-	(F) audio (L) audire *(hören)*
	(to) **overlook** [ˌəʊvə'lʊk]	überblicken; übersehen	! (to) **overlook** = **1.** überblicken – a room **overlooking** the Thames (ein Raum mit Blick auf die Themse) **2.** übersehen – (to) **overlook** a question / a mistake
	headphones *(pl)* ['hedfəʊnz]	Kopfhörer	I always use ~ if I want to listen to loud music.
	wireless ['waɪələs]	drahtlos, Funk-	

[eɪ] name · [aɪ] time · [ɔɪ] boy · [əʊ] old ·
[aʊ] town · [ɪə] here · [eə] where · [ʊə] tour

	channel ['tʃænl]	Kanal; Sender	In the evenings, we watch the news on **Channel** 5.
p. 11	**chat** [tʃæt]	Chat; Unterhaltung *(Gespräch)*	
	pretty old/expensive/… ['prɪti]	ziemlich alt/teuer/…	! **pretty** = **1.** *(adj)* hübsch; **2.** *(adv)* ziemlich £ 220? That's ~ expensive for a pair of jeans, isn't it?
	mom [mɒm], [mɑːm] *(AE)*	Mutti, Mama	
	round … [raʊnd]	um (… herum); in (… umher)	= **around** … Let's walk ~ the lake / ~ the West End. (um … herum / in … umher)
	tourist (information) bureau ['tʊərɪst ˌbjʊərəʊ] *(AE)*	Touristeninformation, Fremdenverkehrsbüro	= *BE* **tourist (information) office**
	No idea. *(infml)*	Keine Ahnung.	Do you know where the tourist office is? – **No** ~, sorry.
	high commission [ˌhaɪ kə'mɪʃn]	*Diplomatische Vertretung eines Commonwealth-Landes in einem anderen Commonwealth-Land*	
	embassy ['embəsi]	Botschaft *(diplomatische Vertretung)*	(F) l'ambassade *(f)*
	because of [bɪ'kɒz‿əv]	wegen	! • **because of** *(prep)* = wegen We stayed at home **because of** the rain. • **because** *(conj)* = weil We stayed at home **because** it rained.
	Commonwealth ['kɒmənwelθ]	*Gemeinschaft der Länder des ehemaligen britischen Weltreichs*	
	member ['membə]	Mitglied	**Nur für Mitglieder!**  (F) le membre
	organization [ˌɔːɡənaɪ'zeɪʃn]	Organisation	noun: **organization** – verb: (to) **organize** (organisieren; ordnen) (F) l'organisation *(f)*
	diplomatic [ˌdɪplə'mætɪk]	diplomatisch, Diplomaten-	(F) diplomatique
	everyone else [els]	alle anderen; sonst jeder	Oh Mum! Why can't I go to Tim's party? **Everyone** ~ is allowed to go.

… else

I'm so tired. **Someone else** will have to wash the dishes.	**jemand anders**
No one else has to help at home as much as I do.	**niemand anders; niemand sonst**
Do you need **anything else** from the shops?	**sonst noch etwas**

	Catch you later. *(infml)*	Bis später dann!	= See you later.
p. 12	**success** [sək'ses]	Erfolg	noun: **success** – adj: **successful** (F) le succès (L) successus
	forgetful [fə'ɡetfl]	vergesslich	
	level ['levl]	Grad, Stufe; Niveau, Ebene	Here in the factory the ~ of noise is very high. You should protect your ears! What ~ is this course, beginners'?

[b] **boat** · [p] **pool** · [d] **dad** · [t] **ten** · [ɡ] **good** · [k] **cat** ·
[m] **mum** · [n] **no** · [ŋ] **song** · [l] **hello** · [r] **red** · [w] **we** · [j] **you**

	bitter ['bɪtə]	bitter; erbittert; verbittert	I don't like coffee. I think it tastes ~. When I see happy couples I feel ~. adj: **bitter** – noun: **bitterness** (Bitterkeit, Verbitterung)
p. 13	**certain** ['sɜːtn]	sichere(r, s); gewisse(r, s), bestimmte(r, s)	That would mean ~ disaster / ~ death. Try to learn a ~ number of new words each week. A ~ Mr Davidson called this morning. (F) certain (L) certus
	(to) **serve** [sɜːv]	servieren *(Essen, Getränke)*; bedienen *(Kundschaft)*; dienen	Who can ~ the drinks at our party? I want to work at a pub. It must be fun to ~ people. I think it's a mayor's job to ~ those who elected him. verb: (to) **serve** – noun: **service** (Dienst(leistung), Service) (F) servir (L) servire
	diverse [daɪ'vɜːs]	unterschiedlich, vielfältig	London's population has become more ~ than ever.
	pollution [pə'luːʃn]	(Umwelt-)Verschmutzung	Diesel cars cause a lot of air ~. noun: **pollution** – (F) la pollution verb: (to) **pollute** [pə'luːt] (*(die Umwelt)* verschmutzen) (L) polluere *(beschmutzen)*
p. 14	**greeting** ['griːtɪŋ]	Gruß(formel), Begrüßung	
	act [ækt]	Tat, Akt, Handlung	(F) l'acte *(m)* (L) acta *n pl*
	contact ['kɒntækt]	Kontakt	**!** stress: **<u>contact</u>** ['kɒntækt] noun: **contact** – verb: (to) **contact sb.** (Kontakt mit jm. aufnehmen, sich mit jm. in Verbindung setzen) (F) le contact (L) contingere *(berühren)*
	Goodnight. [ˌgʊd'naɪt]	Gute Nacht!	
	(to) **share** sth. [ʃeə]	(sich) etwas teilen	My sister and I ~ a room. = I ~ a room with my sister.
	(to) **subscribe to** sth. [səb'skraɪb]	etwas abonnieren	(to) **subscribe to** ◄► (to) **unsubscribe from** [ˌʌnsəb'skraɪb] (abbestellen, kündigen; sich aus einer Mailingliste austragen lassen) (L) subscribere *(unterschreiben)*
	(to) **email** (sb. sth.) ['iːmeɪl]	(jm. etwas) mailen	noun: **email** – verb: (to) **email**
	How's things? *(infml)*	Wie geht's?	
	messenger service ['mesɪndʒə sɜːvɪs]	Messenger *(Dienst zur Nachrichtenübermittlung im Internet)*	**messenger** = Kurier/in, Bote/Botin
	(to) **consult with** sb. [kən'sʌlt] *(AE)*	sich mit jm. beraten	(to) **consult** sb. = jn. fragen, jn. konsultieren (F) consulter (L) consulere
	(to) **trend** [trend]	im Trend liegen, angesagt sein	Last week, the news story about Prince William was **~ing** on Twitter. This week no one is talking about it. verb: (to) **trend** – noun: **trend**
	(to) **message** (sb.) ['mesɪdʒ]	(jm.) eine *(elektronische)* Nachricht schicken/übermitteln	verb: (to) **message** – noun: **message** (Nachricht; Botschaft, Aussage)
	face to face	von Angesicht zu Angesicht	I would like to meet her **~ to ~**.
p. 15	**separate** ['seprət]	getrennt, separat	The library has a ~ room for children's books. They didn't drive there together (= in the same car) – they drove there **~ly** (= in different cars). (L) separatus, a, um

[f] **f**ather · [v] **r**iver · [s] **s**ister · [z] plea**s**e · [ʃ] **sh**op · [ʒ] televi**s**ion · [tʃ] **t**eacher · [dʒ] **G**ermany · [θ] **th**anks · [ð] **th**is · [h] **h**ere

	positive ['pɒzətɪv]	positiv	**positive** ◄► **negative** ['negətɪv] (F) positif / positive (L) positivus, a, um
	MP [ˌem 'piː] **(= Member of Parliament)**	Parlamentsangehörige(r), Abgeordnete(r)	*in Britain:* **MP** (= Member of Parliament) *in Germany:* **MdB** (= Mitglied des Bundestags)
p. 16	**slide** [slaɪd]	Dia; Folie *(Präsentationssoftware)*	
	damage (to) *(no pl)* ['dæmɪdʒ]	Schaden, Schäden (an)	noun: **damage (to)** – verb: (to) **damage** ((be)schädigen; schaden) The fire **~d** the garage, but there was no ~ to the house.
p. 17	**absurd** [əb'sɜːd]	absurd	(F) absurde (L) absurdus, a, um *(widersinnig)*
	humorous ['hjuːmərəs]	humorvoll, witzig	! spelling: **humour** *(noun)* – **humorous** *(adj)* (F) humoristique
	realistic [ˌriːə'lɪstɪk]	realistisch	I want to see all the sights! – Come on, be ~. We only have two days in London. adj: **realistic** – adv: **realistically** [ˌriːə'lɪstɪkli] (F) réaliste
	feature ['fiːtʃə]	Merkmal, Eigenschaft	This car has an interesting ~: it can park itself automatically.
	titanium [tɪ'teɪniəm]	Titan *(Metall)*	
	frame [freɪm]	Rahmen; Gestell, Fahrgestell	This bike is cheaper, but its ~ is much heavier.
	(to) **fire** ['faɪə]	(ab)schießen, (ab)feuern	The two men shot at each other, but nobody knows who ~d first.
	horn [hɔːn]	Horn; Hupe	 **horn**  **She's blowing the horn.**
	reaction (to) [ri'ækʃn]	Reaktion (auf)	! stress: **reaction** [ri'ækʃn] verb: (to) **react (to)** – noun: **reaction (to)** (F) la réaction (à)
	unicorn ['juːnɪkɔːn]	Einhorn	(L) unus *(ein)* + cornus *(Horn)*
	long shot ['lɒŋ ʃɒt]	Totale *(Film)*	
	close-up ['kləʊs‿ʌp]	Nahaufnahme *(Film)*	

Part B

p. 18	**exhibition** [ˌeksɪ'bɪʃn]	Ausstellung; Messe	I want to see the Chagall ~ at the museum. This new machine was presented at last month's technology ~. (L) exhibere *(vorführen)*
	anniversary [ˌænɪ'vɜːsəri]	Jahrestag	Last weekend, my parents celebrated their 25th wedding ~. (F) l'anniversaire *(m)* (L) anniversaria *n pl*
	mural ['mjʊərəl]	Wandgemälde	a large painting on a wall (L) murus *(Mauer)*
	(to) **protect** sb./sth. **(from** sb./sth.**)** [prə'tekt]	jn./etwas (be)schützen (vor jm./etwas)	Wear a hat to ~ your head **from** the sun. Animals might get dangerous if they're trying to ~ their young. (F) protéger (L) protegere

[iː] green · [i] happy · [ɪ] big · [e] red · [æ] cat · [ɑː] class · [ɒ] song ·
[ɔː] door · [uː] blue · [ʊ] book · [ʌ] mum · [ɜː] girl · [ə] a partner

cover ['kʌvə]	Abdeckung, Deckel	verb: (to) **cover** – noun: **cover** (F) couvrir (L) cooperire
windmill ['wɪndmɪl]	Windmühle	a **windmill** 
wheat [wiːt]	Weizen	**wheat** 
(to) **grind** [graɪnd], **ground, ground** [graʊnd]	(zer)mahlen	**He's grinding coffee beans.** 
p. 19 **opinion piece** [ə'pɪnjən piːs]	Stellungnahme	an article in which the writer gives his personal opinion (F) l'opinion *(f)* (L) opinio, onis *f (Meinung)*
recently ['riːsntli]	in letzter Zeit; vor Kurzem	There have been a lot of accidents in our street ~. (F) récemment (L) recens
childhood ['tʃaɪldhʊd]	Kindheit	the time in your life when you are a child
(to) **treat** sb. **to** sth. ['triːt]	jn. zu etwas einladen; jm. etwas spendieren	The special guests were **~ed to** a magnificent show. verb: (to) **treat sb. to sth.** – noun: **treat** (Hochgenuss, besonderes Vergnügen; (besondere) Leckerei)
dialect ['daɪəlekt]	Dialekt	! stress: **dialect** ['daɪəlekt] (F) le dialecte (L) dialectus
aroma [ə'rəʊmə]	Duft, Aroma	(F) l'arôme *(m)* (L) aroma *n*
multicultural [ˌmʌlti'kʌltʃərəl]	multikulturell	adj: **multicultural** – noun: **multiculturalism** [ˌmʌlti'kʌltʃərəlɪzm] (Multikulturismus, kulturelle Vielfalt) (F) multiculturel (L) multi *(viele)* + cultura *(Kultur)*
vibe [vaɪb] *(infml)*	Ausstrahlung, Atmosphäre	I love that club. It has such a cool ~.
(to) **claim** [kleɪm]	angeben, behaupten	He looks about 15, but **~s** he's 18. verb: (to) **claim** – noun: **claim** (Behauptung)
failure ['feɪljə]	Misserfolg, Fehlschlag	It was a ~. = It wasn't successful. noun: **failure** – verb: (to) **fail** [feɪl] (scheitern; (es) nicht schaffen)
inhabitant [ɪn'hæbɪtənt]	Einwohner/in, Bewohner/in	In 1750, Munich had about 32,000 **~s**. (F) l'habitant/e (L) inhabitantes *m pl*
CE [ˌsiː‿'iː] (= **Common Era** [ˌkɒmən‿'ɪərə])	Christliche Zeitrechnung	**43 CE ◄► 43 BCE (= before the Common Era)**
province ['prɒvɪns]	Provinz	! stress: **province** ['prɒvɪns] (F) la province (L) provincia

[eɪ] name · [aɪ] time · [ɔɪ] boy · [əʊ] old ·
[aʊ] town · [ɪə] here · [eə] where · [ʊə] tour

(ever) since [ˌevə ˈsɪns]	seitdem, seither; seit	! **since** = 1. *(prep)* seit – **since** 10 o'clock 2. *(adv)* seitdem, seither – We saw Jill last May, but haven't seen her **(ever) since**.
foreigner [ˈfɒrənə]	Ausländer/in; Fremde(r)	noun: **foreigner** – adj: **foreign** [ˈfɒrən] (ausländisch, fremd) **foreign language** = Fremdsprache
abroad [əˈbrɔːd]	im/ins Ausland	= in or to another country
(to) **drive** [draɪv], **drove** [drəʊv], **driven** [ˈdrɪvn]	treiben; antreiben	The farmer **drove** the cows into another field. Famine **drove** millions of people to leave the country. ! (to) **drive, drove, driven** = 1. fahren *(mit dem Auto)*; 2. treiben; antreiben
persecution [ˌpɜːsɪˈkjuːʃn]	Verfolgung	The ~ of Native Americans led to the deaths of millions. (F) la persécution (L) persequi *(verfolgen)*
Jew [dʒuː]	Jude/Jüdin	noun: **Jew** – adj: **Jewish** [ˈdʒuːɪʃ] (jüdisch) (F) le juif / la juive
(to) **flee (from)** [fliː], **fled, fled** [fled]	flüchten (aus), fliehen (vor)	Thousands of people **fled** their country. They tried to ~ from the war.
the more ..., the more ...	je mehr ..., desto mehr ...	**The** ~ you work here, **the** ~ money you can make.
people [ˈpiːpl], *pl* **peoples**	Volk	! **people** = 1. Menschen – A lot of **people** are afraid of dogs. 2. Volk – the Zulu **people** (das Volk der Zulu) the native **peoples** of Africa (die Urvölker Afrikas) (L) populus
(to) **attract** [əˈtrækt]	anziehen, anlocken	London ~**s** millions of tourists every summer.
policy [ˈpɒləsi]	Politik *(politische Linie)*, Richtlinie(n), Bestimmung(en)	There's a "no junk food"-~ at my school. **free-movement** ~ = Politik der Freizügigkeit (= der offenen Grenzen) *(in der EU)*

German "Politik"

1. *(politisches Leben, Geschehen)*	**politics** *(no pl)*	Are you interested in **politics**? – No, I think **politics** is boring.
2. *(politische Linie, Richtlinien)*	**policy**	What is the prime minister's **policy** on education? What is the company **policy** on working from home?

mixture [ˈmɪkstʃə]	Mischung	= mix (L) mixtura
unique [juˈniːk]	einmalig, einzigartig	Our ketchup has a ~ and special taste. (F) unique (L) unicus, a, um
diversity [daɪˈvɜːsəti]	Vielfalt	In London, you'll experience a unique ~ of people and cultures. noun: **diversity** – adj: **diverse** (F) la diversité (L) diversitas *f (Verschiedenheit)*
mythical [ˈmɪθɪkl]	mythisch; fiktiv	(F) mythique
(to) **exist** [ɪgˈzɪst]	existieren	Do you believe that life ~**s** on Mars? (F) exister (L) exsistere

[b] **boat** · [p] **pool** · [d] **dad** · [t] **ten** · [g] **good** · [k] **cat** · [m] **mum** · [n] **no** · [ŋ] **song** · [l] **hello** · [r] **red** · [w] **we** · [j] **you**

	tolerance (of/for) ['tɒlərəns]	Toleranz (für/gegenüber)	noun: **tolerance** – adj: **tolerant (of/towards)** ['tɒlərənt] (tolerant (gegenüber)) ! stress: **tolerance** ['tɒlərəns], **tolerant** ['tɒlərənt] Ⓕ la tolérance Ⓛ tolerare *(ertragen, aushalten)*
	(to) **transform** [træns'fɔːm]	(sich) verwandeln; umwandeln	They're planning to ~ the station into an art gallery. Ⓕ transformer Ⓛ transformare
	brand [brænd]	Marke, Markenname *(bei Produkten)*	My bike is from *RACERS*. What ~ is yours?
	byline ['baɪlaɪn]	*Zeile mit Angabe des Verfassers/der Verfasserin eines Zeitungsartikels*	
	headline ['hedlaɪn]	Überschrift; Schlagzeile	
	illustration [ˌɪlə'streɪʃn]	Abbildung, Illustration	Ⓕ l'illustration *(f)*
	immigration [ˌɪmɪ'greɪʃn]	Einwanderung	Ⓕ F l'immigration *(f)*

Auswanderung – Einwanderung

(to) **emigrate**	['emɪgreɪt]	auswandern	(to) **immigrate**	['ɪmɪgreɪt]	einwandern
emigration	[ˌemɪ'greɪʃn]	Auswanderung	**immigration**	[ˌɪmɪ'greɪʃn]	Einwanderung
emigrant	['emɪgrənt]	Auswanderer/Auswanderin	**immigrant**	['ɪmɪgrənt]	Einwanderer/Einwanderin

p. 20	(to) **hold** [həʊld], **held, held** [held]	abhalten *(Veranstaltung)*	Our next meeting will be **held** on the first Saturday in July.
	(to) **name** [neɪm]	(be)nennen	We ~**d** our cat Blueberry. (= Her name is Blueberry.) noun: **name** – verb: (to) **name**
p. 21	(to) **invent** [ɪn'vent]	erfinden	verb: (to) **invent** – noun: **invention** (Erfindung) Ⓕ inventer Ⓛ invenire
	escalator ['eskəleɪtə]	Rolltreppe	Ⓕ l'escalier (mécanique) *(m)*
	(to) **design** [dɪ'zaɪn]	entwerfen, konstruieren, entwickeln	What's your aunt's job? – She ~**s** cars. verb: (to) **design** – noun: **design**
	aka [ˌeɪ keɪ‿'eɪ] **(= also known as)**	alias, auch bekannt als	Jan Phillip Eißfeldt, **aka** Jan Delay, is a German singer and songwriter.
p. 22	**fabulous** ['fæbjələs]	sagenhaft, fabelhaft	
	site [saɪt]	Ort, Platz, Stelle, Stätte	the ~ of the accident (Unfallstelle) a tourist ~ (touristischer Ort)
	anywhere ['eniweə]	überall(hin)	Accidents can happen ~.
	discovery [dɪ'skʌvəri]	Entdeckung	noun: **discovery** – verb: (to) **discover** [dɪ'skʌvə] (entdecken)
	district ['dɪstrɪkt]	Bezirk, Gebiet, (Stadt-)Viertel	! stress: **district** ['dɪstrɪkt]
	bakery ['beɪkəri]	Bäckerei	= baker's shop **baker** ['beɪkə] = Bäcker/in
	loads of … [ləʊdz] *(infml)*	eine Menge (von) …	= lots of
	neighbourhood *(AE:* **neighborhood**) ['neɪbəhʊd]	Viertel, Gegend, Umgebung; Nachbarschaft	Do you live in a poor or rich ~?
	lively ['laɪvli]	lebendig, lebhaft	My grandma is still very ~ at 75. She goes dancing twice a week.
	case [keɪs]	Fall	In ~ of fire do not use the elevator! Take an umbrella **in** ~ it rains. (… falls es regnet.)

[f] **f**ather · [v] ri**v**er · [s] **s**ister · [z] plea**s**e · [ʃ] **sh**op · [ʒ] televi**s**ion · [tʃ] **t**eacher · [dʒ] **G**ermany · [θ] **th**anks · [ð] **th**is · [h] **h**ere

p. 23	**volunteer** [ˌvɒlən'tɪə]	Freiwillige(r), Ehrenamtliche(r)	! • **volunteer** *(noun)* – I work as a **volunteer** for a charity. • (to) **volunteer** *(verb)* – I **volunteer** for a charity. (freiwillig/ehrenamtlich arbeiten *(unbezahlt)*) • **volunteer** *(adj)* – I do **volunteer** work for a charity. Ⓕ le/la volontaire Ⓛ voluntarius
	subject ['sʌbdʒɪkt]	Thema; *(in E-Mails)* Betreff	I'm reading a book on the ~ of terrorism. Ⓕ le sujet ! **subject** = **1.** Schulfach **2.** Thema; *(in E-Mails)* Betreff
	contact details *(pl)* ['kɒntækt ˌdi:teɪlz]	Kontaktdaten	
	grateful ['greɪtfl]	dankbar	We are ~ for the help they offered. Ⓛ gratus, a, um
	in advance [əd'vɑ:ns]	im Voraus	I've already made tomorrow's lunch **in** ~.
	Yours sincerely [ˌjɔ:z sɪn'sɪəli]	Mit freundlichen Grüßen *(Briefschluss)*	
	All the best [ˌɔ:l ðə 'best]	Mit besten Grüßen / Alles Gute *(Briefschluss)*	
	Yours, Finn [jɔ:z]	Dein/Euer Finn *(Briefschluss)*	

Part C

p. 24	**monument (to)** ['mɒnjumənt]	Monument, Denkmal (für/zum Gedenken an)	! stress: **monument** ['mɒnjumənt] Ⓕ le monument Ⓛ monumentum
	spiral ['spaɪrəl]	spiralförmig	! stress: **spiral** ['spaɪrəl] Ⓕ en spirale Ⓛ spira *(Spirale)*
	staircase ['steəkeɪs]	Treppe; Treppenhaus	a **spiral staircase** (eine Wendeltreppe)
	(to) **regret** [rɪ'gret]	bedauern, bereuen	I'm so sorry! I really ~ what I did to you. verb: (to) **regret** – noun: **regret** (Bedauern) Ⓕ regretter
	(to) **emerge (from …)** [ɪ'mɜ:dʒ]	herauskommen, hervortreten, auftauchen (aus …)	Suddenly three men **~d from** the forest. She came up the dark staircase and **~d** into the light. Give me a call if problems ~. Ⓛ emergere
	daylight ['deɪlaɪt]	Tageslicht	
	(to) **be all ears** [ˌɔ:l‿'ɪəz] *(infml)*	ganz Ohr sein *(gespannt zuhören)*	We **were all** ~ as Grandpa told his story.
	(to) **commemorate** sb./sth. [kə'meməreɪt]	jemandes/einer Sache gedenken	The monument **~s** the Battle of Trafalgar and all the people that died there. Ⓛ commemorare

[i:] green · [i] happy · [ɪ] big · [e] red · [æ] cat · [ɑ:] class · [ɒ] song · [ɔ:] door · [u:] blue · [ʊ] book · [ʌ] mum · [ɜ:] girl · [ə] a partner

	(to) **last (for)** [lɑːst]	(an)dauern; halten *(von Bestand sein)*	The concert will ~ **(for)** about an hour. Cheap toys often don't ~ very long.
	nickname ['nɪkneɪm]	Spitzname	

p. 25 **so**

- In Antworten auf Entscheidungsfragen wird nach Verben wie ***think, hope, guess, expect*** oft **so** verwendet:

  Is Evie home? – I **think so**. / I **don't think so**. / I **guess so**. / I **expect so**. Will she get the job? – I **hope so**.

- Um die Wiederholung von Informationen aus der vorhergehenden Äußerung zu vermeiden, steht **so** …
  - nach ***say*** und ***tell sb.***:

    They're going to win the match. Everybody **says so**. Emily is getting married. Her mother **told me so**.
    That's a stupid idea. – Who **says so**? If you don't want to join us, just **say so**.
  - nach ***if***:

    Would you like to visit London? **If so**, what would you do there?

	role-play ['rəʊl pleɪ]	Rollenspiel	
p. 26	**bill** [bɪl]	Rechnung	**the bill** 
	staff [stɑːf]	Personal, Mitarbeiter/innen	the people who work at a company/school/shop … How many ~ are there at your school?
p. 27	**brick** [brɪk]	Ziegelstein; Ziegel-	
	upwards ['ʌpwədz]	nach oben	A spiral staircase leads ~ to the top of the tower.
	idiom ['ɪdiəm]	Redewendung	a phrase whose meaning you can't guess from the meanings of the words that make up the phrase (F) l'idiome *(m)* (L) idioma *n*
	(to) **pull** sb.'s **leg** *(infml)*	jn. auf den Arm nehmen *(veräppeln)*	He's not serious – he's just **pulling your ~**.
	(to) **mind** [maɪnd]	aufpassen auf, achten auf	**Mind the doors.** *(im Bahnhof:* Vorsicht an den Türen!) **Mind your head.** (Pass auf deinen Kopf auf! / Kopf weg!)
	(to) **joke** [dʒəʊk]	Witze machen, scherzen	*English:* You're **joking**! / You must be **joking**! *German:* Du machst wohl Witze! / Das kann doch nicht dein Ernst sein! (to) **joke around** = herumscherzen
	Congratulations (on sth.**)!** [kənˌɡrætʃʊ'leɪʃnz]	Herzlichen Glückwunsch (zu etwas)!	~ **on** finding a new job! (L) congratulari *(beglückwünschen)*

Part D

p. 28	**constant** ['kɒnstənt]	ständig, andauernd	! stress: **<u>con</u>stant** ['kɒnstənt]
	gap [ɡæp]	Lücke	The horses escaped through a ~ in the fence. Fill in the **~s** with the right verb from the box. ! **a gap year** = ein Jahr Auszeit *(oft zwischen Schulabschluss und Beginn des Studiums)*
	equality [i'kwɒləti]	Gleichheit, Gleichberechtigung	**equality** ◄► **inequality** (Ungleichheit)

[eɪ] **name** · [aɪ] **time** · [ɔɪ] **boy** · [əʊ] **old** ·
[aʊ] **town** · [ɪə] **here** · [eə] **where** · [ʊə] **tour**

low [ləʊ]	niedrig	**low ◄► high**
income ['ɪnkʌm]	Einkommen	**low-income** *(adj)* = einkommensschwach
poverty ['pɒvəti]	Armut	adj: **poor** – noun: **poverty**
(to) **rise** [raɪz], **rose** [rəʊz], **risen** ['rɪzən]	(an)steigen, aufsteigen; (sich) erhöhen	It is getting warmer. = Temperatures are **rising**. Food prices have **risen** again. Clouds of smoke **rose** from the building. verb: (to) **rise, rose, risen** – noun: **rise** (Erhöhung, Anstieg)
living ['lɪvɪŋ]	Lebensunterhalt	**cost of living** = Lebenshaltungskosten
offer ['ɒfə]	Angebot	**on offer** = im Angebot, angeboten verb: (to) **offer** – noun: **offer**
(to) **increase (by)** [ɪn'kriːs]	steigern, (sich) erhöhen; steigen, zunehmen (um)	Our profits **~d** by 10% last year. = We were able to ~ our profits by 10%. House prices in London have **~d** again. verb: (to) **increase** [ɪn'kriːs] – noun: **increase** ['ɪŋkriːs] (Anstieg, Wachstum, Zunahme)
violence ['vaɪələns]	Gewalt, Gewalttätigkeit	noun: **violence** – adj: **violent** ['vaɪələnt] (gewalttätig; gewaltsam)
perspective [pə'spektɪv]	Perspektive	(to) **put sth. in perspective** = etw. ins rechte Licht rücken ! stress: **perspective** [pə'spektɪv]
distant ['dɪstənt]	(weit) entfernt, fern	It will take you a long time to get to such a ~ place. The Romans ruled Britain in the ~ past. adj: **distant** – noun: **distance**
complaint [kəm'pleɪnt]	Beschwerde	The shop assistant listened to my ~ and said sorry. (to) **make a complaint (about sth.)** = eine Beschwerde vorbringen (über etwas), etwas beanstanden noun: **complaint** – verb: (to) **complain**
(to) **fail** sb. [feɪl]	jn. enttäuschen; jn. im Stich lassen	She felt she had **~ed** her parents when she didn't pass her exam.
optimistic [ˌɒptɪ'mɪstɪk]	optimistisch	**optimistic ◄► pessimistic** [ˌpesɪ'mɪstɪk] (pessimistisch) adj: **optimistic** – adv: **optimistically** adj: **pessimistic** – adv: **pessimistically**
quality ['kwɒləti]	Qualität, Qualitäts-; Eigenschaft	What is the most important ~ in people for you? I always try to buy high-~ clothes. (von hoher Qualität, hochwertig) What **qualities** does a good teacher need? ! stress: **quality** ['kwɒləti]
economic [ˌiːkə'nɒmɪk]	wirtschaftlich, Wirtschafts-	The ~ situation was a lot worse after the war. adj: **economic** – adv: **economically**
hub [hʌb]	Mittelpunkt, (Verkehrs-) Knotenpunkt	
opportunity [ˌɒpə'tjuːnəti]	Gelegenheit, Möglichkeit, Chance	I think you'll have better job **opportunities** if you speak more than one language.
(to) **express** sth. [ɪk'spres]	etwas ausdrücken, zum Ausdruck bringen	"In my view" is a useful phrase to ~ your opinion. verb: (to) **express** – noun: **expression** (L) exprimere

[b] **boat** · [p] **pool** · [d] **dad** · [t] **ten** · [g] **good** · [k] **cat** ·
[m] **mum** · [n] **no** · [ŋ] **song** · [l] **hello** · [r] **red** · [w] **we** · [j] **you**

	colloquial [kə'ləʊkwiəl]	umgangssprachlich	
	emotional [ɪ'məʊʃənl]	emotional	adj: **emotional** [ɪ'məʊʃənl] – noun: **emotion** [ɪ'məʊʃn] (Emotion, Gefühl) (F) émotionnel, le
	informational [ˌɪnfə'meɪʃənl]	Informations-	adj: **informational** – noun: **information**
	personal ['pɜːsənl]	persönlich	Could we meet? I need to talk about a ~ problem.
p. 29	(to) **provide** [prə'vaɪd]	(an)bieten, zur Verfügung stellen	We can't ~ equipment for so many people. = We can't ~ so many people with equipment. (to) **provide sb. with sth.** = jn. mit etwas versorgen, jm. etwas zur Verfügung stellen
	evidence *(no pl)* ['evɪdəns]	Nachweis(e), Beweis(e)	There is no ~ to suggest that it was Mr Carter who stole your money. ! *German* **Beweis** = 1. **proof** *(sth. that shows you that sth. is true)* 2. **evidence** *(sth. that suggests that sth. is true)*
	statistics *(pl)* [stə'tɪstɪks]	Statistik(en)	! The **statistics show** that … = die Statistik zeigt / die Statistiken zeigen, dass … noun: **statistics** – adj: **statistical** [stə'tɪstɪkl] (statistisch)
	(to) **back** sth. **up** [ˌbæk‿'ʌp]	etwas belegen; etwas untermauern, etwas bekräftigen	Do you have any evidence to ~ **up** your opinion?
	statement ['steɪtmənt]	Aussage(satz); Feststellung, Behauptung	
	solution (to) [sə'luːʃn]	Lösung (für) *(Problem, Aufgabe)*	The ~**s** to your tasks are at the back of the book. noun: **solution (to a problem)** – verb: (to) **solve (a problem)** [sɒlv] (lösen *(Rätsel, Problem)*, lüften *(Geheimnis)*)
	(to) **issue** ['ɪʃuː]	ausgeben, (offiziell) bekannt geben; ausstellen *(z.B. Dokument)*	verb: (to) **issue** – noun: **issue** (Ausstellung, Ausgabe) **issue date** / **date of issue** = Ausstellungsdatum, Ausgabedatum
	reality [ri'ælɪti]	Realität, Wirklichkeit	! stress: **re<u>a</u>lity** [ri'ælɪti] noun: **reality** – adj: **real**
	(to) **support** [sə'pɔːt]	unterstützen	verb: (to) **support** – My parents always ~ my dreams and plans. noun: **support** – My parents are a great ~. (Unterstützung)
	comparison [kəm'pærɪsn]	Vergleich	On this website you can make ~**s** between different schools. noun: **comparison** – verb: (to) **compare** *English*: (to) **make comparisons** *German*: Vergleiche anstellen
	in the first place	erstens, in erster Linie; überhaupt	**In the first** ~, you need to get your facts right. But why did she marry him **in the first** ~?
	Firstly ['fɜːstli], **…** **Secondly** ['sekəndli], **…** **Thirdly, …** ['θɜːdli]	Erstens … Zweitens … Drittens …	There's a lot of shopping to do: **firstly**, we need something to eat. **Secondly**, we have to get some cola. And **thirdly**, …
	On the one hand … **On the other hand …**	Einerseits … Andererseits …	**On the one** ~, Australia is close to Asia. **On the other** ~, it has a strong British tradition.
p. 30	**nationality** [ˌnæʃə'næləti]	Staatsangehörigkeit, Nationalität	adj: **national** – noun: **nationality**

educated ['edʒukeɪtɪd]	gebildet	verb: (to) **educate sb.** (jn. ausbilden, unterrichten, erziehen) noun: **education** [ˌedʒu'keɪʃn] (Schulbildung, Ausbildung; Erziehung)
homeless ['həʊmləs]	obdachlos	adj: **homeless** – noun: **homelessness** (Obdachlosigkeit)
exit ['eksɪt]	Ausgang; Ausfahrt	**entrance ◀▶ exit**

Text: Escape from Uncle Jack

p. 32	**Latin** ['lætɪn]	lateinisch; Latein	
	(to) **strike** [straɪk], **struck, struck** [strʌk]	jn. heimsuchen *(Krankheit)*; schlagen; treffen	Kimmich **struck** the ball into the goal. You must never ~ a child. A flash of lightning **struck** the farm. Terrorists have **struck** again, this time in Paris.
	(to) **abandon** [ə'bændən]	zurücklassen, verlassen, im Stich lassen	I think it's terrible how people ~ dogs on busy roads. (F) abandonner
	(to) **separate** ['sepəreɪt]	trennen	It's not right to ~ children from their parents. (F) séparer (L) separare
	(to) **search for** sth. [sɜːtʃ]	(nach) etwas suchen	The police **~ed for** clues, but they couldn't find any. verb: (to) **search** – noun: **search** (Suche)
	forward(s) ['fɔːwəd], ['fɔːwədz] **backwards** ['bækwədz]	vorwärts, nach vorn rückwärts, nach hinten	It's easier to count **forwards** from 1 to 100 than to count **backwards** from 100 to 1. Dad still finds it difficult to drive **backwards**. He stumbled **backwards** and fell down the stairs.
	pain [peɪn]	Schmerz(en)	The doctor asked me where the ~ was exactly.
	(to) **stumble** ['stʌmbl]	stolpern; torkeln	As I was coming in, I **~d** over the dog. That man is **stumbling** terribly. – Maybe he's ill?
	direction [də'rekʃn]	Richtung	That's the wrong way. We must go in the opposite ~. (F) la direction
	frequent ['friːkwənt]	häufig	Mum **~ly** flies to the USA, about 10 times a year. (F) fréquent
	(to) **keep up (with** sb.**)** [ˌkiːp‿'ʌp]	(mit jm.) Schritt halten	I've stopped going jogging with my older brother. He's too fast for me, and I can't ~ **up with** him.
	(to) **lift** sth. **up** [ˌlɪft‿'ʌp]	etwas hochheben	Can you ~ this rock **up**? It's very heavy.
p. 33	(to) **be trapped** [træpt]	gefangen sein, in der Falle sitzen	The dog **was** ~ in the attic for five hours.
	(to) **fear** [fɪə]	fürchten, befürchten	verb: (to) **fear** – The workers **~ed** their boss. noun: **fear (of)** – I have a ~ **of** rats. (= I'm afraid of / scared of rats.) (Angst (vor))
	heat [hiːt]	Hitze, Wärme	noun: **heat** verb: (to) **heat** (erwärmen, erhitzen) adj: **hot**
	(to) **trust** [trʌst]	trauen, vertrauen	She's a friend of the family. You can ~ her. verb: (to) **trust** – noun: **trust** (Vertrauen)
	repeatedly [rɪ'piːtɪdli]	wiederholt	We have ~ pointed out that problems might emerge.
	(to) **make it**	es schaffen, Erfolg haben	Don't give up! You'll ~ **it**! I'm sure our team will ~ **the finals**. I'm sorry I couldn't ~ **your party**.

[iː] green · [i] happy · [ɪ] big · [e] red · [æ] cat · [ɑː] class · [ɒ] song · [ɔː] door · [uː] blue · [ʊ] book · [ʌ] mum · [ɜː] girl · [ə] a partner

	(to) **creep** [kriːp], **crept, crept** [krept]	schleichen; kriechen	A man **was ~ing** quietly along the wall outside our house.
	protective [prə'tektɪv]	schützend, beschützend, Schutz-	verb: (to) **protect** – Animals usually try to **protect** their young. adj: **protective** – We had to wear a **protective** jacket. adv: **protectively** – She stepped **protectively** in front of her children. (L) protegere *(schützen)*
p. 34	(to) **reach out a hand (to** sb.**)** [ˌriːtʃ‿'aʊt]	die Hand ausstrecken (nach jm.)	Dad **~ed out a hand to** Mum to help her to the top of the mountain.
	(to) **bend over** [ˌbend‿'əʊvə], **bent, bent** [bent]	sich bücken, sich vorbeugen	The door was so small that I had to ~ **over** to get in.
	sweat [swet]	Schweiß	noun: **sweat** – verb: (to) **sweat** (schwitzen) **!** pronunciation: **sweat** [swet]
	(to) **be frightened of** sth. ['fraɪtnd]	Angst haben vor etwas	Don't **be** ~ **of** the thunder. It sounds scary but isn't dangerous. **frightened** *(adj)* = verängstigt
	(to) **swallow** ['swɒləʊ]	(ver)schlucken	He thought he was going to be sick when he realized that he had **~ed** an ant.
	(to) **slap** [slæp]	schlagen (auf)	We could hear the heavy rain **~ping** on the ground. (to) **slap sb.'s face** = jm. eine Ohrfeige verpassen *(jm. ins Gesicht schlagen)* verb: (to) **slap** – noun: **slap** (Schlag)
p. 35	(to) **float** [fləʊt]	schwimmen, *(auf der Wasseroberfläche)* treiben	Wood **~s** on water; stones don't.
	by the time [ˌbaɪ ðə 'taɪm]	als; wenn	**!** **by the time** = **1.** als – **By the time** we arrived, the concert had already started. **2.** wenn – I'll have dinner ready **by the time** you get back.
	(to) **stink** [stɪŋk], **stank** [stæŋk], **stunk** [stʌŋk]	stinken	The water looked dirty and **stank**. His breath **stank** of onions.
	(to) **hesitate** ['hezɪteɪt]	zögern	Don't ~ to get in touch if there is anything I can do. (F) hésiter (L) haesitare
	quote [kwəʊt]	Zitat	I find **~s** from famous people interesting.

Access to cultures: Guy Fawkes

p. 40	**gunpowder** ['ɡʌnpaʊdə]	Schießpulver	
	plot [plɒt]	Verschwörung	noun: **plot** – verb: (to) **plot** (sich verschwören)
	conspirator [kən'spɪrətə]	Verschwörer/in	Over 20 **~s** took part in the plot. (L) conspiratus
	bonfire ['bɒnfaɪə]	*(großes Freuden-)*Feuer	 a **bonfire**
	guy [ɡaɪ]	Guy-Fawkes-Puppe	**!** **guy** = **1.** Typ, Kerl; **2. guys** *(pl)* Leute; **3.** Guy-Fawkes-Puppe

	(to) **part with** sth. ['pɑːt wɪð]	sich von etwas trennen	I love my dog so much. I could never ~ **with** him.
	vendetta [ven'detə]	Blutrache; Hetzkampagne	The two families hate each other and have had a ~ for 20 years.
	graphic ['græfɪk]	grafisch; anschaulich	The news reported about the plane crash in ~ detail. **graphic novel** = Bildroman, Comicroman
	nuclear ['njuːkliə]	Kern-, Atom-, Nuklear-	~ **power** = Atomenergie, Kernenergie (F) nucléaire (L) nucleus *(Kern)*
	fascist ['fæʃɪst]	faschistisch	adj: **fascist** – noun: **fascist** (Faschist/in)
	rebel ['rebəl]	Rebell/in	! stress: **rebel** ['rebəl]
	explosive [ɪk'spləʊsɪv]	Sprengstoff; Sprengsatz	noun: **explosive** – adj: **explosive** (explosiv)
p. 41	**anonymous** [ə'nɒnɪməs]	anonym	! stress: **anonymous** [ə'nɒnɪməs]
	(to) **admire** [əd'maɪə]	bewundern	She's a great artist. I ~ her paintings and sculptures. (F) admirer (L) admirari
	identity [aɪ'dentəti]	Identität	! stress: **identity** [aɪ'dentəti]
	resistance [rɪ'zɪstəns]	Widerstand	This is an unusual plan. Do you expect ~? (F) la résistance (L) resistere *(Widerstand leisten)*
	cellar ['selə]	Keller	(L) cella *(Kammer, Zelle)*
	barrel ['bærəl]	Fass	a **barrel** 
	(to) **blow** sth. **up** [ˌbləʊ_'ʌp]	etwas in die Luft sprengen	Terrorists tried to ~ **up** the local police station this morning.
	(to) **torture** ['tɔːtʃə]	foltern, quälen	verb: (to) **torture** – noun: **torture** (Folter) (F) torturer (L) torquere
	rebellion [rɪ'beljən]	Rebellion, Aufstand	! stress: **rebellion** [rɪ'beljən] (F) la rébellion
	(to) **execute** ['eksɪkjuːt]	hinrichten	verb: (to) **execute** – noun: **execution** [ˌeksɪ'kjuːʃn] (Hinrichtung) (F) exécuter (L) exsequi, exesecutus sum *(strafen)*
	pike [paɪk]	Spieß	a **pike** 

Access to cultures: Elections in the US and the UK

p. 42	**election** [ɪ'lekʃn]	Wahl *(Abstimmung)*	**Elections** for President of the United States are held every four years. (F) les élections *(f)* (L) eligere
	electoral [ɪ'lektərəl]	Wahl-	**electoral system** = Wahlsystem
	(to) **vote** [vəʊt]	wählen, zur Wahl gehen; (ab)stimmen	You have to be 18 before you can ~. Who did you ~ for as band of the year? verb: (to) **vote** – noun: **vote** – There were 16 ~**s** for the idea and 11 against. (Stimme) In what year did women get the ~ in this country? (Stimmrecht) **voter** = Wähler(in)
	(to) **receive** [rɪ'siːv]	erhalten, empfangen	a more formal word for "(to) get" **receive a letter** ◄► **send a letter**

[b] **b**oat · [p] **p**ool · [d] **d**a**d** · [t] **t**en · [g] **g**ood · [k] **c**at ·
[m] **m**u**m** · [n] **n**o · [ŋ] so**ng** · [l] **h**e**ll**o · [r] **r**ed · [w] **w**e · [j] **y**ou

	congress ['kɒŋgres]	Kongress	! stress: **congress** ['kɒŋgres]
	(to) **consist of** [kən'sɪst‿əv]	bestehen aus	My family **~s of** my parents, my two sisters and me. (F) consister (en/dans) (L) consistere
	representative [ˌreprɪ'zentətɪv]	Repräsentant/in, Abgeordnete(r)	**Representatives** from all of the age groups made the decision.
	senate ['senət]	Senat	
	(to) **divide (up) (into)** [dɪ'vaɪd]	auf-/einteilen (in)	The teacher **~d** the class **(up) into** 6 groups.
	highly ['haɪli]	sehr, höchst, äußerst	= very **highly** interesting/dangerous/effective/… a **highly**-respected sportsperson (hoch angesehen)
	(to) **populate** ['pɒpjuleɪt]	bevölkern, besiedeln	English people moved there and began to ~ the area.
	therefore ['ðeəfɔː]	deshalb, deswegen	We live in a village high up in the mountains and are ~ difficult to reach.
	senator ['senətə]	Senator/in	! stress: **senator** ['senətə]
	no matter what/how/who ['mætə]	(ganz) egal, was/wie/wer	I want to do this, **no ~ how** long it takes and **no ~ what** it costs.
	presidential election [ˌprezɪˌdenʃl‿ɪ'lekʃn]	Präsidentschaftswahl	
	limited (to) ['lɪmɪtɪd]	beschränkt, begrenzt (auf)	The price is ~ for one month only.
	(to) **represent** [ˌreprɪ'zent]	vertreten, repräsentieren	It's an honour to ~ your country in the Olympic Games.
	even though [ˌiːvn 'ðəʊ]	selbst wenn, obwohl *(betont)*	It was still dark outside **even ~** it was already 9 am.
	(to) **indicate** ['ɪndɪkeɪt]	anzeigen	Pointing to the left, the police officer **~d** the direction we should take. With a small movement of his hand, he **~d** that we should sit down. (F) indiquer (L) indicare
p. 43	**constitutional monarchy** [ˌkɒnstɪˌtjuːʃənl 'mɒnəki]	konstitutionelle Monarchie	
	head of state [ˌhed‿əv 'steɪt]	Staatsoberhaupt	= the official leader of a country, e.g. the Queen of the UK or the US president
	democracy [dɪ'mɒkrəsi]	Demokratie	
	House of Lords [lɔːdz]	Oberhaus *(des britischen Parlaments)*	
	House of Commons ['kɒmənz]	Unterhaus *(des britischen Parlaments)*	
	cabinet ['kæbɪnət]	Kabinett, Regierung	
	political [pə'lɪtɪkl]	politisch	adj: **political** – noun: **politics**
	regional ['riːdʒənl]	regional	local – **regional** – national – international adj: **regional** – noun: **region**
	(to) **publish** ['pʌblɪʃ]	veröffentlichen	The first Harry Potter book was ~ **ed** in 1997. (F) publier (L) publicus
	coalition [ˌkəʊə'lɪʃn]	Bündnis, Zusammenschluss; Koalition	! stress: **coalition** [ˌkəʊə'lɪʃn]
	so-called [ˌsəʊ 'kɔːld]	sogenannt	Nobody of his **so-~** friends offered to help him.

[f] **f**ather · [v] **r**iver · [s] **s**ister · [z] plea**s**e · [ʃ] **sh**op · [ʒ] televi**s**ion · [tʃ] **t**ea**ch**er · [dʒ] **G**ermany · [θ] **th**anks · [ð] **th**is · [h] **h**ere

Unit 2 Australia, country and continent

pp. 44/45	**continent** ['kɒntɪnənt]	Kontinent	Europe and Asia are ~**s**. Ⓕ le continent ! stress: **continent** ['kɒntɪnənt] Ⓛ continens, ntis *f*
	territory ['terətri]	Gebiet, Territorium	
	coastal ['kəʊstl]	Küsten-	Plymouth is a ~ town in England. noun: **coast** – adj: **coastal**
	coral ['kɒrəl]	Koralle; Korallen-	! stress: **coral** ['kɒrəl] **coral reef** [ˌkɒrəl 'riːf] = Korallenriff • **reef** = Riff
	desert ['dezət]	Wüste	 Ⓕ le désert Ⓛ deserere *(verlassen)*
	kangaroo [ˌkæŋgə'ruː] *(AusE infml:* **roo**)	Känguru	! stress: **kangaroo** [ˌkæŋgə'ruː]
	the outback ['aʊtbæk]	das Hinterland Australiens	Australia's **outback** is far away from the coast and the towns.
	spider ['spaɪdə]	Spinne	**spiders** 
	wildlife ['waɪldlaɪf]	Tiere *(in freier Wildbahn)*, Tierwelt	The ~ of Africa is very different from the ~ in Europe. You can find all kinds of ~ in our national parks.
	exotic [ɪg'zɒtɪk]	exotisch	We saw lots of ~ animals at the zoo. Ⓕ exotique Ⓛ exoticus, -a, -um *(ausländisch)*
	humid ['hjuːmɪd]	feucht, feuchtwarm	We get a lot of rain here in the summer, so it's often very ~. Ⓕ humide Ⓛ umidus, -a, -um **humid** ◄► **dry**
	marine [mə'riːn]	Meeres-	**marine** life, **marine** animals, **marine** scientists Ⓛ mare *n (Meer)*
	remote [rɪ'məʊt]	entlegen, abgelegen	We stayed in a ~ village 60 miles from the nearest town. Ⓛ remotus, -a, -um
	sandy ['sændi]	Sand-, sandig	noun: **sand** – adj: **sandy**
	stunning ['stʌnɪŋ]	phantastisch, umwerfend	extremely beautiful, wonderful, amazing, fantastic Don't they look ~ in their wedding clothes? 
	urban ['ɜːbən]	städtisch, urban	**Urban** planners think about the future of towns and cities. Ⓕ urbain, e Ⓛ urbanus
	Aboriginal [ˌæbə'rɪdʒənl]	Aborigine- *(die Ureinwohner/-innen Australiens betreffend)*	**Aboriginal** artists/culture; the **Aboriginal** population **Aboriginal** Australian = australische/r Ureinwohner/in the **Aboriginal** flag 
	camel ['kæml]	Kamel	! stress: **camel** ['kæml]
	convict ['kɒnvɪkt]	Sträfling, Strafgefangene(r)	somebody who has been sent to prison
	poisonous ['pɔɪzənəs]	giftig	adj: **poisonous** – noun: **poison** ['pɔɪzn] (Gift) – verb: (to) **poison** (vergiften)

[b] boat · [p] pool · [d] dad · [t] ten · [g] good · [k] cat ·
[m] mum · [n] no · [ŋ] song · [l] hello · [r] red · [w] we · [j] you

Part A

p. 46 **in-flight** ['ɪn flaɪt]	während des Fluges, Bord-	an **in-flight** magazine/meal (ein Bordmagazin / eine Bordmahlzeit)
suburb ['sʌbɜːb]	Vorstadt, Vorort	It's so noisy in the town centre that we have moved to a ~. (L) sub *(unter)*, urbs *f (Stadt)*
wharf [wɔːf], *pl* **wharfs** *or* **wharves**	Kai	
business ['bɪznəs]	Geschäft, Geschäfts-; Unternehmen, Betrieb	**Business** was good. (Die Geschäfte liefen gut.) a ~ trip/lunch (Geschäftsreise/-essen) Mike started his own ~ when he was 17.
flying fox [ˌflaɪɪŋ 'fɒks]	Flughund	 a **flying fox**
fox [fɒks]	Fuchs	 a **fox**
opera ['ɒprə]	Oper	**opera house** = Opernhaus (F) l'opéra *(m)*
waterfront ['wɔːtəfrʌnt]	Hafenviertel *(oft modernisiert und zum Wohnviertel umgebaut)*	
honest ['ɒnɪst]	ehrlich	Be ~ with me! Say what you really think. adj: **honest** – noun: **honesty** ['ɒnəsti] (Ehrlichkeit) ! silent "**h**": **honest** ['ɒnɪst], **honesty** ['ɒnəsti] (F) honnête (L) honestus, -a, -um
take (on sth.**)**	Einstellung (zu etwas), Sicht(weise) (auf etwas)	What's your ~ **on** the new band?
(to) **catch** a bus/ferry/...	einen Bus/eine Fähre nehmen; einen Bus/eine Fähre (noch) erwischen	Walk to the waterfront and ~ a bus to the city centre. If we run we might still be able to ~ the ferry.
scenic ['siːnɪk]	(landschaftlich) schön	Let's take the ~ coastal route, not the main road.
walkway ['wɔːkweɪ]	Fußweg; Laufgang	a path for walking along, often outside and above the ground, e.g. between buildings
landmark ['lændmɑːk]	Wahrzeichen	St Paul's Cathedral is one of London's ~**s**.
anybody ['enibɒdi] / **anyone** ['eniwʌn]	jede/r (beliebige)	**Anybody/Anyone** can learn to ride a bike.

any – anybody/anyone – anything – anywhere

- The words **any**, **anybody** (or **anyone**), **anything** and **anywhere** are used **in questions** and **negative statements**:

Are there **any** buses after midnight?	I don't need **any** help with this.
Do you know **anybody/anyone** here?	I did**n't** know **anybody/anyone** at the party.
Do you need **anything** from the shops?	She did**n't** say **anything**.
Have you seen my keys **anywhere**?	I **can't** find my shoes **anywhere**.

- They can also be used **in positive statements**, but then the meaning is different:

You'll get that book in **any** bookshop.	*in jedem (beliebigen) Buchladen*
Anybody/Anyone looking for cheap CDs should try this shop.	*jeder; alle*
I guess **anything** is better than having to sit at home.	*alles*
Accidents can happen **anywhere**.	*überall*

paradise ['pærədaɪs]	Paradies	! stress: **paradise** ['pærədaɪs] (F) le paradis (L) paradisus

[f] father · [v] river · [s] sister · [z] please · [ʃ] shop · [ʒ] television · [tʃ] teacher · [dʒ] Germany · [θ] thanks · [ð] this · [h] here

p. 47 (to) **apply (to** sb. **for** sth.) [ə'plaɪ]	sich (bei jm. um etwas) bewerben	He **applied for** the job, but he didn't get it. I'd love to go to university in Berlin, but I think it's better to ~ **to** more than one university.

Group nouns

Nomen wie **audience, band, class, family, government, group, team** bezeichnen eine **Gruppe von Menschen**. Sie werden daher **group nouns** (oder **collective nouns**) genannt.

Auch wenn solche **group nouns** im **Singular** verwendet werden, stehen **Verben und Pronomen** danach oft im **Plural**:

Leon's host **family were** great. **They** quickly made him feel at home.
The **audience are** still cheering although the **band have** already started to put away **their** instruments.
Class 8PW are difficult to teach.

though [ðəʊ] (*kurz für:* **although**)	obwohl	I really liked my host family, ~ (= **although**) it was hard to understand them at first. **even though** = selbst wenn, obwohl *(betont)* **Even** ~ it was already 9 am, it was still dark outside.
sausage ['sɒsɪdʒ]	(Brat-, Bock-)Würstchen, Wurst	 **sausages**
tons of ... ['tʌnz_əv] *(infml)*	jede Menge ...	It was so hot! We could have sold ~ **of** ice cream.
private ['praɪvət]	privat; persönlich	! pronunciation and stress: **private** ['praɪvət] **private** ◄► **public** Ⓕ privé, e Ⓛ privatus, -a, -um
(to) **accept** [ək'sept]	akzeptieren, annehmen	I've asked eight people to our barbecue, and most of them have already **~ed** the invitation. As a child I found it hard to get **~ed** into a group. Ⓕ accepter Ⓛ accipere
talkative ['tɔːkətɪv]	gesprächig	He seemed shy at first, but by the end of the evening he was really ~.
photography [fə'tɒgrəfi]	Fotografie *(Hobby)*	• **photo(graph)** ['fəʊtəʊ, 'fəʊtəgrɑːf] Foto • (to) **photograph** ['fəʊtəgrɑːf] fotografieren • **photography** [fə'tɒgrəfi] Fotografie *(Hobby)* • **photographer** [fə'tɒgrəfə] Fotograf/in
(to) **be/get homesick** ['həʊmsɪk]	Heimweh haben/bekommen	*English:* (to) **be**/**feel homesick** *German:* **Heimweh haben**
confident ['kɒnfɪdənt]	(selbst)sicher; zuversichtlich	He's very shy. He'd like to become more ~. The interview went very well. I'm ~ I'll get the job. **self-confident** = selbstbewusst
easy-going [,iːzi'gəʊɪŋ]	gelassen, locker	Our teachers are **easy-~**. Only Mr Sand is very strict.
way of life [,weɪ_əv 'laɪf]	Lebensweise	I love the relaxed **way of** ~ in Ireland.
p. 48 **mate** [meɪt] *(infml)*	Kumpel, Freund/in	Weekends are a good time to hang out with your **~s**.
mosquito [məs'kiːtəʊ], *pl* **mosquitos** *or* **mosquitoes**	(Stech-)Mücke	I love the summer, but I hate **~es**.  An informal word for **mosquito** is **mozzie**.
(to) **pronounce** [prə'naʊns]	aussprechen	verb: (to) **pronounce** – noun: **pronunciation** Ⓕ prononcer Ⓛ pronuntiatio *f (Aussprache)*

[iː] green · [i] happy · [ɪ] big · [e] red · [æ] cat · [ɑː] class · [ɒ] song · [ɔː] door · [uː] blue · [ʊ] book · [ʌ] mum · [ɜː] girl · [ə] a partner

(to) **lower** ['ləʊə]	senken, herabsetzen; sinken lassen	adj: **low** – verb: (to) **lower**
jaw [dʒɔː]	*(der)* Kiefer	each of the two parts of your face where your teeth are; they move when you talk or eat
pitch [pɪtʃ]	Tonhöhe, Stimmlage	**"Pitch"** describes how high or low a sound is, e.g. in music or spoken language.
(to) **signal** ['sɪgnəl]	signalisieren	(to) show, (to) make clear verb: (to) **signal** – noun: **signal**
(to) **tend to be/do** sth. [tend]	dazu neigen etwas zu sein/tun, meistens etwas sein/tun	When I like a place very much, I **tend to** spend every holiday there. (= I usually spend …)
among [ə'mʌŋ]	zwischen, unter *(mehreren Personen, Tieren, Dingen)*	 **among** the boys  **between** the boys
since [sɪns]	da, weil	! **since** = **1.** seit – I've lived here **since** I was born. **2.** seitdem, inzwischen – John and I met in May, but I haven't seen him **since**. **3.** da, weil – I don't eat meat **since** I'm a vegetarian.
sb. **lacks** sth. [læks]	jm. fehlt es an etwas	verb: (to) **lack** – Why didn't you help? Was it because you **~ed** courage? (… weil dir/euch der Mut fehlte) noun: **lack** – Why didn't you help? Was it for ~ of courage? (… aus Mangel an Mut)
confidence ['kɒnfɪdəns]	(Selbst-)Vertrauen, Zuversicht	adj: **confident** – noun: **confidence** (L) confidentia
(to) **pay attention (to)** [ə'tenʃn]	achten (auf), aufpassen (auf)	Stop talking now and **pay** ~, please. "Ladies and gentlemen, may I have your ~, please." **attention** = Aufmerksamkeit (F) l'attention *(f)*
(to) **distract** [dɪ'strækt]	ablenken	verb: (to) **distract** – noun: **distraction** [dɪ'strækʃn] (Ablenkung)
p. 49 **lifestyle** ['laɪfstaɪl]	Lebensstil	
(to) **base** sth. **on** sth. [beɪs]	etwas auf etwas gründen, etwas als Grundlage benutzen für etwas	I wrote a new piece of music, but I **~d** it **on** a well-known pop song. (= it's **~d on** a well-known pop song)
within [wɪ'ðɪn]	innerhalb (von)	Do you think you can finish your project ~ a week? We respect all cultures ~ our school.
arch [ɑːtʃ]	Bogen *(Torbogen, Triumphbogen)*	 (F) l'arc, l'arche (L) arcus
upper ['ʌpə]	obere(r, s)	**the upper arch ◄► the lower arch**

p. 50	**argumentative** [ˌɑːgju'mentətɪv]	argumentativ; streitsüchtig	(L) argumentum *(Beweis, Grund)*

(to) argue – argument – argumentative

• (to) **argue**	1. argumentieren; behaupten 2. (sich) streiten, (sich) zanken	He tried to **argue** that Shakespeare was German! My brothers **argue** all the time.
• **argument**	1. Argument 2. Streit, Auseinandersetzung	Try to present **arguments** for and against the statement. Sorry about the noise. Our neighbours are having another **argument**.
• **argumentative**	1. argumentativ 2. streitsüchtig	**argumentative writing** (Erörterung, Argumentation) He's a bit **argumentative**. That's why he didn't agree with us.

	(to) **structure** ['strʌktʃə]	strukturieren, aufbauen	verb: (to) **structure** – noun: **structure**
	(to) **oppose** sth. [ə'pəʊz]	etwas ablehnen, gegen etwas sein; sich einer Sache widersetzen	Most people **~d** the plan to build a new road. (to) **support** ◄► (to) **oppose** verb: (to) **oppose** – noun: **opposition (to)** [ˌɒpə'zɪʃn] (Widerstand (gegen), Opposition) (L) opponere *(entgegenstellen)*
	however [haʊ'evə]	aber; allerdings; jedoch	Sophie wanted to stay up late. **However,** she fell asleep at 8 pm. She was born in France. She isn't French, ~.
	in addition [ə'dɪʃn]	außerdem	• This mobile is very expensive. **In ~**, it's made of cheap plastic and will break easily. • **in addition to …** = zusätzlich zu …; neben … – **In ~ to** the guitar and the piano, he also plays the drums. (L) addere *(hinzufügen)*
	briefly ['briːfli]	in Kürze, in wenigen Worten	Don't go into detail. Just explain ~. (F) brièvement (L) brevis, -e *(kurz)*
	furthermore [ˌfɜːðə'mɔː]	außerdem; des Weiteren	The government want to improve our hospitals. **Furthermore**, they have promised to spend more money on education.

Part B

p. 52	**season** ['siːzn]	Jahreszeit; Saison	Spring, summer, autumn and winter are the four **~s**.
	(to) **flood** [flʌd]	überfluten, überschwemmen	The rain **~ed** our garden. It looked like a swimming pool. ! pronunciation: **flood** [flʌd] verb: (to) **flood** – noun: **flood** (Flut; Überschwemmung, Hochwasser)
	(to) **be determined to do** sth. [dɪ'tɜːmɪnd]	(fest) entschlossen sein, etwas zu tun	Nothing will stop me: **I'm ~ to** win the race. (F) déterminer (L) determinare
	cyclone ['saɪkləʊn]	Wirbelsturm, Zyklon	! stress: **cyclone** ['saɪkləʊn]
	insect ['ɪnsekt]	Insekt	! stress: **insect** ['ɪnsekt] (F) l'insecte *(m)* (L) insectum
p. 53	**backyard** [bæk'jɑːd] *(AE)*	(Hinter-)Hof; Garten hinter dem Haus	! *AE* **yard** = *BE* **garden** *AE* **backyard** = the area behind the house

[b] **boat** · [p] **pool** · [d] **dad** · [t] **ten** · [g] **good** · [k] **cat** · [m] **mum** · [n] **no** · [ŋ] **song** · [l] **hello** · [r] **red** · [w] **we** · [j] **you**

	python ['paɪθən]	Python	❗ pronunciation: **python** ['paɪθən] 
	(to) **feed on** sth. [fiːd]	sich von etwas ernähren	These animals aren't dangerous. They ~ **on** plants.
	(to) **provoke** [prə'vəʊk]	provozieren	He's an easy-going guy – it's difficult to ~ him. Ⓕ provoquer Ⓛ provocare
	(to) **injure** ['ɪndʒə]	verletzen	verb: (to) **injure** – noun: **injury** ['ɪndʒəri] (Verletzung)
	moth [mɒθ]	Nachtfalter; Motte	a **moth** 
	crocodile ['krɒkədaɪl]	Krokodil	❗ pronunciation and stress: **crocodile** ['krɒkədaɪl] An informal word for **crocodile** is **croc**.
	(to) **bump into** sb. [bʌmp] *(infml)*	jn. zufällig treffen, jm. zufällig begegnen; mit jm. zusammenstoßen	In a small town you often ~ **into** people you know. A man ~**ed into** me and I fell down.
	(to) **look out for** sb./sth.	nach jm./etwas Ausschau halten; auf jn./etwas achten	We need some bread. Can you **look** ~ **for** a bakery? **Look** ~ **for** snakes during your camping trip. (= make sure you see them, they could be dangerous)
	(to) **snorkel** ['snɔːkl]	schnorcheln	**snorkelling**  verb: (to) **snorkel** – noun: **snorkel** (Schnorchel)
p. 54	**greenhouse** ['griːnhaʊs]	Gewächshaus, Treibhaus	a **greenhouse** 
	flight [flaɪt]	Flug	noun: **flight** – verb: (to) **fly, flew, flown**
	(to) **attend** [ə'tend]	(hin)gehen zu, teilnehmen (an); besuchen	(to) **attend a school** = (to) go to a school
p. 55	**anyway** ['eniweɪ]	trotzdem	

anyway

1. Jedenfalls …	Is her mother American? – I don't really know. But **anyway**, she lives in California now. We'll arrive at 7:35 or 7:45, I'm not sure. **Anyway**, we'll be there before 8.
2. Und überhaupt, …	I don't have the time to go on holiday. **And anyway**, it's too expensive.
3. sowieso	I can give you a lift. I'm going there **anyway**.
4. trotzdem	It was freezing cold, but we went out **anyway**.

	(to) **frustrate** [frʌ'streɪt]	frustrieren	❗ • **frustrating** – We weren't successful. It was very **frustrating**. (frustrierend) • **frustrated** – We were very **frustrated**. (frustriert) Ⓛ frustra *(vergeblich)*
p. 56	**climate** ['klaɪmət]	Klima	❗ pronunciation: **climate** ['klaɪmət] Ⓕ le climat
	coastline ['kəʊstlaɪn]	Küste, Küstenlinie	From the boat we could see the rocky Irish ~.

[f] **f**ather · [v] **r**iver · [s] **s**ister · [z] plea**s**e · [ʃ] **sh**op · [ʒ] televi**s**ion ·
[tʃ] tea**ch**er · [dʒ] **G**ermany · [θ] **th**anks · [ð] **th**is · [h] **h**ere

dramatic [drə'mætɪk]	dramatisch	I saw a ~ film about a man who escaped from prison. adj: **dramatic** – adv: **dramatically** [drə'mætɪkli] (F) dramatique
entertainment [ˌentə'teɪnmənt]	Unterhaltung *(Zeitvertreib)*	There's lots of ~ at our summer camps, so you won't get bored.
facilities *(pl)* [fə'sɪlətiz]	Einrichtungen, Geräte	The ~ at the first hotel were much better than the ones in this place!
overcrowded [ˌəʊvə'kraʊdɪd]	überfüllt, übervölkert	~ streets/beaches/classrooms/cities/prisons
rural ['rʊərəl]	ländlich, Land-	**rural ◄► urban** (F) rural, e ◄► urbain, e (L) rus, ruris *n (Land)*
suburban [sə'bɜːbən]	Vorort-, Vorstadt-; vorstädtisch	He walked around the ~ streets taking photos. noun: **suburb** ['sʌbɜːb] – adj: **suburban** [sə'bɜːbən]
vast [vɑːst]	riesig, sehr groß	Africa is a ~ continent. It's over 5,000 miles from north to south. (L) vastus, -a, -um **vast ◄► tiny**
inland ['ɪnlænd]	im Landesinneren, landeinwärts; Binnen-	Duisburg has the world's largest ~ harbour. **coastal ◄► inland**
mild [maɪld]	mild; sanft; leicht *(Schmerzen; Medikamentendosierung)*	a **mild climate** ◄► a **tropical climate** a **mild cheese** ◄► a **strong cheese** **!** pronunciation: **mild** [maɪld]
mountainous ['maʊntənəs]	bergig, gebirgig	noun: **mountain** – adj: **mountainous** (L) montanus, -a, -um
old-fashioned [ˌəʊld'fæʃənd]	altmodisch	**old-fashioned ◄► modern, trendy**
collocation [ˌkɒlə'keɪʃn]	Kollokation *(Wörter, die oft zusammen vorkommen)*	words that are often used together, for example: strong wind, heavy rain (L) collocatio *f (Stellung, Anordnung)*
descriptive [dɪ'skrɪptɪv]	beschreibend	verb: (to) **describe** – adj: **descriptive** (F) descriptif/-ive (L) describere *(beschreiben)*
p. 57 (to) **disagree (with)** [ˌdɪsə'griː]	anderer Meinung sein (als); nicht übereinstimmen (mit); nicht zustimmen	I'm sorry, but I completely ~ **with** you/**with** that statement. (to) **agree ◄►** (to) **disagree**

English "so" – German "auch"

Nick **loves** surfing, and **so does** Leon. (... und Leon **auch**.)

Mit **so** + **Hilfsverb** + **(Pro-)Nomen** kann man zum Ausdruck bringen, dass etwas **auch** für jemand anders gilt. Weitere Beispiele:

John **is** really clever.	**So is** Joanna.
He**'s got** a great voice.	**So has** Joanna.
He **can** speak several languages.	**So can** Joanna.
He **owns** a house in France.	**So does** Joanna.
He **has been** to Australia.	**So has** Joanna.
He **got** married last year.	**So did** Joanna.
He **would like** to move to Spain.	**So would** Joanna.

nonsense ['nɒnsns]	Unsinn, dummes Zeug	What are you talking about? It's all ~, none of it is true!
rubbish ['rʌbɪʃ]	Unsinn, dummes Zeug	an informal word for **nonsense** **! rubbish** = **1.** Müll, Abfall; **2.** Unsinn, dummes Zeug
hurtful ['hɜːtfl]	verletzend	a ~ comment = a comment that hurts/might hurt

[iː] green · [i] happy · [ɪ] big · [e] red · [æ] cat · [ɑː] class · [ɒ] song · [ɔː] door · [uː] blue · [ʊ] book · [ʌ] mum · [ɜː] girl · [ə] a partner

I'm afraid … [ə'freɪd]	Leider …; Ich fürchte, …	 ! **afraid: 1. I'm afraid** of spiders. (Ich habe Angst …) **2. I'm afraid** I can't help you. (Leider …)
point	Argument; Standpunkt	

point ("Argument"; "Standpunkt")

That's a good point.
Das ist ein (gutes) Argument.

You have a point there, but …
Da hast du nicht ganz Unrecht, aber …

I take your point, but …
Ich sehe/verstehe Ihren Standpunkt, aber …

What's your point?
Worauf willst du hinaus?

! (to) **miss the point** = nicht verstehen, worum es geht; an der Sache/am Thema vorbeireden/vorbeigehen:
I'm sorry, Sophie, but **you're missing the point** here. — …, aber darum geht es nicht.
His statement completely **misses the point** of the discussion. — Seine Aussage geht völlig an der Diskussion vorbei.

(to) **borrow** ['bɒrəʊ]	(aus)leihen, sich borgen	Can I ~ your bike tomorrow? Mine is broken.
gift [gɪft]	Geschenk; Gabe; Talent	She has a ~ for understanding things very quickly. **gift voucher** ['gɪft vaʊtʃə] = Geschenkgutschein

Part C

p. 58	**industrial** [ɪn'dʌstriəl]	industriell, Industrie-	! stress: **in<u>dus</u>trial** [ɪn'dʌstriəl]
	revolution [ˌrevə'luːʃn]	Revolution	! stress: **revo<u>lu</u>tion** [ˌrevə'luːʃn] (F) la révolution
	crime [kraɪm]	Kriminalität; Verbrechen	The worst ~ is to kill another person. In most cities, ~ is a big problem. **crime fiction** = Kriminalromane (F) le crime (L) crimen *n*
	(to) **face** sth. [feɪs]	vor etwas stehen; mit etwas konfrontiert werden *(Problem)*	Jamie, ~ the facts. You'll never be a rock star. As a single parent, you'll have to ~ problems other parents don't have. (L) facies *f*
	authority [ɔː'θɒrəti]	Behörde	**local authority** = Gemeinde(behörde), Kommune/Kommunalbehörde
	explorer [ɪk'splɔːrə]	Forschungsreisende(r), Entdecker/in	noun: *(person)* **explorer** – verb: (to) **explore** (L) explorare *(erforschen)*
	the first European to land …	der erste Europäer, der … an Land ging / die erste Europäerin, die … an Land ging	Neil Armstrong was **the first person to** walk on the moon. (= … the first person who walked on the moon)
	(to) **chart** sth. [tʃɑːt]	etwas kartografieren; etwas aufzeichnen, darstellen	**uncharted** = unerforscht, unbekannt, auf keiner Landkarte verzeichnet
	(to) **establish** [ɪ'stæblɪʃ]	etablieren, gründen, aufbauen, einrichten	Munich was ~**ed** in 1158. The film ~**ed** her as a famous actor.
	(to) **transport** [træn'spɔːt]	transportieren, befördern	! verb: (to) **trans<u>port</u>** [træn'spɔːt] – noun: **<u>trans</u>port** ['trænspɔːt] (F) transporter (L) transportare

[eɪ] name · [aɪ] time · [ɔɪ] boy · [əʊ] old ·
[aʊ] town · [ɪə] here · [eə] where · [ʊə] tour

eight **out of** ten ['aʊt‿əv]	acht von zehn	Eight ~ **of** ten people in the world have never been on a plane.
theft [θeft]	Diebstahl	! **theft** = the crime – **thief** = the person
bar [bɑː]	Stange, Balken, (Gitter-)Stab	**behind bars** *(pl)* = hinter Gittern ! **bar** = **1.** Stange, Balken, (Gitter-)Stab **2.** Riegel *(Schokolade, Müsli)*; Tafel *(Schokolade)*
(to) **chain** [tʃeɪn]	anketten, fesseln *(mit Ketten)*	During the protests people ~**ed** themselves to the factory gates. I always ~ my bike to our fence. noun: **chain** – verb: (to) **chain**
conditions *(pl)* [kən'dɪʃnz]	Bedingungen, Verhältnisse	It's too cold and too noisy in this office. I can't work in these ~. (F) les conditions *(f)* (L) condicio, -onis *f*
arduous ['ɑːdjuəs]	beschwerlich	very hard or difficult
(to) **raise** [reɪz]	(er)heben	(to) **raise a flag** = eine Flagge hissen (to) **raise one's head** = den Kopf heben (to) **raise one's voice** = die Stimme erheben
public holiday [ˌpʌblɪk 'hɒlədeɪ]	öffentlicher/gesetzlicher Feiertag	Next Monday we're not going to school: it's a ~ **holiday**.
(to) **estimate** ['estɪmeɪt]	schätzen	verb: (to) **estimate** ['estɪmeɪt] It is **estimated** that … (es wird geschätzt, dass …) noun: **estimate** ['estɪmət] (Schätzung) **Estimates** say that … (Schätzungen besagen, dass …)
(to) **disturb** [dɪ'stɜːb]	stören	I'm sorry to **disturb** you, but I have a question. **undisturbed** = ungestört; unberührt (L) disturbare *(zerstören)*
(to) **prove** [pruːv]	sich erweisen als	Our new business has ~**d** successful / has ~**d** a success. *English:* Later, it **would prove** a mistake. *German:* Es **sollte sich** später als Fehler **herausstellen/erweisen**. ! (to) **prove** = **1.** beweisen, nachweisen **2.** sich erweisen als
catastrophic [ˌkætə'strɒfɪk]	katastrophal, verhängnisvoll	adj: **catastrophic** [ˌkætə'strɒfɪk] – noun: **catastrophe** [kə'tæstrəfi] (Katastrophe)
sorrow ['sɒrəʊ]	Kummer, Leid	the feeling of being very sad
mourning ['mɔːnɪŋ]	Trauer	noun: **mourning** – verb: (to) **mourn for sb./sth.** (trauern um jn./etwas) (to) **mourn sb./sth.** (jn/etwas betrauern/beklagen)
penal ['piːnl]	Straf-, strafrechtlich	connected with or used for the punishment of convicts (L) poenalis, -e
settlement ['setlmənt]	(Be-)Siedlung	verb: (to) **settle** – nouns: **1. settlement; 2.** *(person)* **settler**

colonial [kə'ləʊniəl]	kolonial, Kolonial-	(F) colonial (L) colonia *(Kolonie)*
economy [ɪ'kɒnəmi]	(Volks-)Wirtschaft	noun: **economy** – adj: **economic**
wool [wʊl]	Wolle	noun: **wool** – Scottish kilts are often made of **wool**. adj: **woollen** (*AE:* **woolen**) ['wʊlən] (Woll-) Scottish men often wear **woollen** kilts.
mineral ['mɪnərəl]	Mineral(stoff)	**mineral water** = Mineralwasser
agricultural [ˌægrɪ'kʌltʃərəl]	landwirtschaftlich, Agrar-	adj: **agricultural** – noun: **agriculture** ['ægrɪkʌltʃə] (Landwirtschaft) (L) agricultura *(Landwirtschaft)*
product ['prɒdʌkt]	Produkt	verb: (to) **produce** [prə'djuːs] (produzieren, herstellen) nouns: 1. **product** ['prɒdʌkt] (Produkt) 2. **production** [prə'dʌkʃn] (Produktion) 3. *(person)* **producer** [prə'djuːsə] (Produzent/in) (F) produire; le produit; la production (L) producere *(herstellen)*
attempt [ə'tempt]	Versuch	noun: **attempt** – verb: (to) **attempt** (versuchen) (L) attemptare *(versuchen)*
(to) **unify** ['juːnɪfaɪ]	(ver)einen, vereinigen	In 1871 most of the German states were **unified** to become the German empire.
federation [ˌfedə'reɪʃn]	Föderation, Bund; Verband	Individual states form a ~. It is one country, but each state still has its own state government. (L) foederare *(verbünden)*
anything but …	alles andere als …	Houses in this area are **anything but** cheap. (= they are expensive)
period ['pɪəriəd]	Zeit(raum), Zeitspanne	the ~ from 1800 to 1900; a ~ of growth
community [kə'mjuːnəti]	Gemeinschaft, Gemeinde	Bayern Munich have a big ~ of fans all over Germany. (F) la communauté (L) communis, -e *(gemeinsam)*
smallpox ['smɔːlpɒks]	Pocken *(Erkrankung)*	
measles *(pl)* ['miːzlz]	Masern	a disease that gives you a high temperature and small red spots that cover the whole body
constitution [ˌkɒnstɪ'tjuːʃn]	Verfassung	(F) la constitution (L) constitutio *f*
(to) **control** [kən'trəʊl]	kontrollieren, regulieren	verb: (to) **control** – Should parents ~ how much TV their kids watch? noun: **control** – The driver **lost ~ of** his car in the snow. (verlor die Kontrolle über)
various ['veəriəs]	(mehrere) verschiedene	several, many different (L) varius, -a, -um
p. 59 (to) **manage** ['mænɪdʒ]	verwalten; regeln; zurechtkommen mit, fertigwerden mit, kontrollieren *(z.B. Brand)*	My brother is too young to ~ his own money. I've just read an article about how to ~ bushfires. **!** (to) **manage sth.** = **1.** etwas verwalten; etwas regeln; mit etwas zurechtkommen, fertigwerden, etwas kontrollieren **2.** etwas schaffen; etwas zustande bringen

[f] **f**ather · [v] ri**v**er · [s] **s**ister · [z] plea**s**e · [ʃ] **sh**op · [ʒ] televi**s**ion · [tʃ] **t**ea**ch**er · [dʒ] **G**ermany · [θ] **th**anks · [ð] **th**is · [h] **h**ere

aspect ['æspekt]	Aspekt	There are many **~s** to think about before you go on a student exchange programme. ❗ stress: **aspect** ['æspekt]
institution [ˌɪnstɪ'tjuːʃn]	Anstalt, Heim; Einrichtung, Institution	He said he would kill himself and was taken to an ~. Universities and colleges are **~s** of higher education.
physical ['fɪzɪkl]	körperlich, physisch	I try to keep **~ly** fit.
sexual ['sekʃuəl]	sexuell	❗ stress: **sexual** ['sekʃuəl]
(to) **abuse** [ə'bjuːz]	missbrauchen	verb: (to) **abuse** [ə'bjuːz] He **~d** his friend's trust. noun: **abuse** [ə'bjuːs] (Missbrauch) This car has taken a lot of ~. (L) abuti, abusus sum
(to) **stamp** [stæmp]	stempeln; (auf)prägen	verb: (to) **stamp** – noun: **stamp** (Stempel)
labour ['leɪbə]	Arbeit; Arbeitskräfte	**child labour** = Kinderarbeit (L) labor *m*
shortage (of sth.**)** ['ʃɔːtɪdʒ]	Mangel (an etwas), Knappheit	a **shortage of** bread/water/petrol/labour/…
racial ['reɪʃl]	ethnisch, rassisch; Rassen-	adj: **racial** – noun: **race** [reɪs] (Rasse) (F) la race
discrimination (against) [dɪˌskrɪmɪ'neɪʃn]	Diskriminierung (von)	*English:* **discrimination against** women/black people (F) la discrimination *German:* **Diskriminierung von** Frauen/Schwarzen noun: **discrimination (against)** – verb: (to) **discriminate against sb.** [dɪ'skrɪmɪneɪt] (jn. diskriminieren)
(to) **shift** [ʃɪft]	(sich) verlagern; (sich) verändern	The company wants to ~ production to a country where labour is cheaper. Has people's attitude towards democracy **~ed**?
(to) **reclaim** sth. [rɪ'kleɪm]	etwas zurückfordern; etwas zurückerobern	(to) get something back or ask to have it back (L) reclamare *(widersprechen)*
citizen ['sɪtɪzn]	Staatsbürger/in	(L) civis *m/f (Bürger/in)*
suffering ['sʌfərɪŋ]	*(das)* Leid, Leiden	verb: (to) **suffer** – noun: **suffering** (L) sufferre *(ertragen)*
decade ['dekeɪd]	Jahrzehnt	a **decade** = ten years (L) decem *(zehn)*
(to) **apologize (to** sb. **for** sth.**)** [ə'pɒlədʒaɪz]	sich (bei jm. für etwas) entschuldigen	verb: (to) **apologize** – noun: **apology** [ə'pɒlədʒi] (Entschuldigung)
society [sə'saɪəti]	(die) Gesellschaft	❗ *No article:* **in (modern) society** **in der (modernen) Gesellschaft** (F) la société (L) societas *f*
chief executive (officer) (CEO) [ˌtʃiːf‿ɪg'zekjətɪv]	Hauptgeschäftsführer/in	the person who leads a company or an organization
reconciliation [ˌrekənsɪli'eɪʃn]	Versöhnung	We attempted ~ with our sister after we hadn't spoken to her for years. (L) reconciliatio *f*
p. 62 (to) **sentence** sb. **(to** sth.**)** ['sentəns]	jn. (zu etwas) verurteilen	He was **~d to** six years in prison for his crime.
minor ['maɪnə]	weniger bedeutend; gering(er), klein(er)	Everything went well. We only had ~ problems. (L) minor

[iː] green · [i] happy · [ɪ] big · [e] red · [æ] cat · [ɑː] class · [ɒ] song ·
[ɔː] door · [uː] blue · [ʊ] book · [ʌ] mum · [ɜː] girl · [ə] a partner

supply [sə'plaɪ]	Versorgung, Lieferung; Vorrat	Wars make the ~ of food to the population difficult. noun: **supply** – verb: (to) **supply** (liefern, bereitstellen, zur Verfügung stellen) (L) supplere *(nachfüllen)*
fleet [fliːt]	Flotte	a group of military ships
(to) **award** sb. sth. **/** (to) **award** sth. **to** sb. [ə'wɔːd]	jm. etwas zuerkennen, zusprechen, verleihen	verb: (to) **award sb. sth.** / (to) **award sth. to sb.** – noun: **award** (Preis *(Auszeichnung)*)
secret ['siːkrət]	geheim; Geheimnis	noun: **secret** – It's our **secret**. Don't tell anyone! adj: **secret** – This is a **secret** message. adv: **secretly** – She **secretly** put a present in his jacket pocket. (heimlich, insgeheim)
series ['sɪəriːz], *pl* **series**	Serie; (Sende-)Reihe	It's my favourite ~. I watch it every day. (L) series *f*
(to) **top** sth. [tɒp]	an der Spitze von etwas stehen; etwas übertreffen, übersteigen	(to) be at the top of sth.; (to) be better than sth. verb: (to) **top sth.** – noun: **top**
(to) **achieve** [ə'tʃiːv]	erreichen *(Ziel)*, erzielen *(Resultat)*; zustande bringen	Is this the result you wanted to ~? I've been working all day, but I haven't ~**d** much. verb: (to) **achieve** – noun: **achievement** [ə'tʃiːvmənt] (Errungenschaft, Leistung)
(to) **collaborate (on/in** sth.**)** [kə'læbəreɪt]	zusammenarbeiten (an/bei etwas); mitarbeiten (an/bei etwas)	verb: (to) **collaborate** – noun: **collaboration** [kəˌlæbə'reɪʃn] (Zusammenarbeit, Gemeinschaftsprodukt(ion)) (F) collaborer (L) collaborare
optimism ['ɒptɪmɪzəm]	Optimismus	**optimism** ◄► **pessimism** ['pesɪmɪzəm] (L) optimus, -a, -um *(beste, bester, bestes)*
role model ['rəʊl mɒdl]	Vorbild	a person you like very much; you try to be like them
(to) **navigate** ['nævɪgeɪt]	navigieren, steuern	How did you manage to ~ your way through London without a map?
p. 63 **hilly** ['hɪli]	hügelig	It's a ~ area. = There are a lot of **hills** in the area.
(to) **get married (to** sb.**)** ['mærɪd]	(jn.) heiraten	(to) **get married** ◄► (to) **get divorced** [dɪ'vɔːst] / (to) **get a divorce** [dɪ'vɔːs] (sich scheiden lassen)
exhibit [ɪg'zɪbɪt]	Ausstellungsstück	noun: **exhibit** – verb: (to) **exhibit** (ausstellen, zeigen)

Part D

p. 64 **professional** [prə'feʃənl]	professionell, Profi-	adj: **professional** – noun: *(what you do)* **profession** (Beruf); *(person)* **professional** (*infml auch:* **pro**) (Fachmann/Fachfrau, Profi) (F) professionnel, le (L) professio *f (Beruf)*
throughout ... [θruː'aʊt]	der/die/das ganze ... (hindurch); überall in ...	I didn't go away last summer. I stayed at home ~ the school holidays. How often people should fly is being discussed ~ all of Europe.
career [kə'rɪə]	Karriere; *(schulischer/beruflicher)* Werdegang	Choosing a ~ as a police officer is one way to help your community. (F) la carrière

[eɪ] name · [aɪ] time · [ɔɪ] boy · [əʊ] old ·
[aʊ] town · [ɪə] here · [eə] where · [ʊə] tour

(to) **stand up for/against**	eintreten für/gegen, sich einsetzen für/gegen	It's important to ~ **up for** your rights.
right [raɪt]	Recht	**civil rights** *(pl)* = Bürgerrechte
recognition [ˌrekəg'nɪʃn]	Anerkennung; (Wieder-)Erkennen	She got an award in ~ of her fight against discrimination. (L) recognoscere *(wiedererkennen)* noun: **recognition** – verb: (to) **recognize** ['rekəgnaɪz] (anerkennen; (wieder)erkennen)
stand [stænd]	Standpunkt, Haltung	(to) **take a stand (on/for/against sth.)** = Stellung beziehen (zu/für/gegen etwas) I think it's important to **take a strong** ~ **on/against** cyberbullying. (= to make it very clear that you are against cyberbullying)
racism ['reɪsɪzəm]	Rassismus	(F) le racisme nouns: **racism;** *(person)* **racist** (Rassist/in) – adj: **racist** (rassistisch) ! stress: **racism** ['reɪsɪzəm]
(to) **criticize** sb. **(for)** ['krɪtɪsaɪz]	jn. kritisieren (wegen)	She was **~d for** her article in the school magazine. ! stress: **criticize** ['krɪtɪsaɪz] (F) critiquer
(to) **speak out**	den Mund aufmachen; sich (kritisch) äußern	You can't change things if you don't ~ **out**.
ape [eɪp]	Menschenaffe	three **apes** 
(to) **be seated** ['siːtɪd]	*(auf einem Platz)* sitzen	*(Sign in a restaurant)* "Please wait to **be** ~." (= wait to be shown where your table is)
stadium ['steɪdiəm]	Stadion	(F) le stade (L) stadium *(Rennbahn)*
insult ['ɪnsʌlt]	Beleidigung	I take your comment as a personal ~ to me. ! noun: **insult** ['ɪnsʌlt] – verb: (to) **insult sb.** [ɪn'sʌlt] (jn. beleidigen) (F) insulter – l'insulte *(f)* (L) insultare
(to) **interview** ['ɪntəvjuː]	befragen, interviewen	verb: (to) **interview** – noun: **interview**
innocent ['ɪnəsnt]	unschuldig	I didn't take the money! I'm ~! adj: **innocent** – (F) innocent, e (L) innocens noun: **innocence** ['ɪnəsns] (Unschuld)
(to) **put the blame on** sb. **(for** sth.**)** [bleɪm]	jm. (an etwas) die Schuld geben	They **put the blame on** Joe **for** what happened. = They **blamed** Joe **for** what happened.
(to) **call** sb. **names**	jn. beschimpfen, jm. Schimpfwörter nachrufen	The kids **~ed him names** because of his big nose.
(to) **bully** sb. ['bʊli]	jn. tyrannisieren, mobben	verb: (to) **bully** – noun: **bully** (Mobber/in, Tyrann/in)
appearance [ə'pɪərəns]	Erscheinung(sbild), Aussehen	You should have a nice ~ at a job interview. I was shocked by his **~.** He looked much older than the last time we met. verb: (to) **appear** – noun: **appearance** (F) l'apparence *(f)* (L) apparere *(erscheinen)*

[b] **boat** · [p] **pool** · [d] **dad** · [t] **ten** · [g] **good** · [k] **cat** ·
[m] **mum** · [n] **no** · [ŋ] **song** · [l] **hello** · [r] **red** · [w] **we** · [j] **you**

	debate [dɪ'beɪt]	Debatte	Let's **hold/have a debate** about this. (eine Debatte führen) noun: **debate** – verb: (to) **debate** (debattieren)
	well over a year	weit über ein Jahr, weit länger als ein Jahr	The play has been performed at this theatre for ~ **over** 20 years.
	incident ['ɪnsɪdənt]	Vorfall, Zwischenfall	The police are still looking into the ~. (F) l'incident *(m)* (L) incidere *(geschehen)*
	(to) **boo** [buː]	buhen; ausbuhen	The fans **~ed** when their team had lost the match. The play was terrible. The audience **~ed** the actors off the stage.
	(to) **release** [rɪ'liːs]	veröffentlichen, herausbringen	verb: (to) **release** – noun: **release** (Veröffentlichung)
	behaviour *(BE)* / **behavior** *(AE)* [bɪ'heɪvjə]	Verhalten; Benehmen	noun: **behavio(u)r** – These whales show a strange ~. verb: (to) **behave** – They ~ strangely.
	subject ['sʌbdʒɪkt]	Ziel(person); Gegenstand	The poor kid doesn't have any friends and has become the ~ of bullying. ! **subject** = **1.** Schulfach; **2.** Subjekt; **3.** Thema; *(in E-Mails)* Betreff; **4.** Ziel(person); Gegenstand
	(to) **appreciate** [ə'priːʃieɪt]	(wert)schätzen, zu schätzen wissen	Thank you for your help. I really ~ what you did for me.
	(to) **call** sth. **out** / (to) **call** sb. **out on** sth.	etwas anprangern / jn. wegen etwas zur Rede stellen	You should ~ **out** sexist behaviour. You should ~ **people out on** sexist behaviour.
	(to) **let** sb. **down**	jn. im Stich lassen, enttäuschen	If you need any help, call us. We won't ~ you **down**.
	(to) **belong** [bɪ'lɒŋ]	dazugehören; (hin)gehören	! (to) **belong** = **1.** gehören – These trainers ~ **to** Mike. **2.** hingehören – This book **~s** on that shelf. **3.** dazugehören – I was very unhappy in that class. I had the feeling I didn't really ~. verb: (to) **belong** – noun: **belonging** (Zusammengehörigkeit(sgefühl); Zugehörigkeit)
p. 65	**environment** [ɪn'vaɪrənmənt]	Umwelt; Umfeld, Umgebung	Cycling isn't just good for you. It's good for the ~ too. (F) l'environnement *(m)* a good **working/learning environment** noun: **environment** – adj: **environmental** [ɪnˌvaɪrən'mentl] (Umwelt-)
	exceptional [ɪk'sepʃənl]	außergewöhnlich	adj: **exceptional** – noun: **exception** [ɪk'sepʃn] (Ausnahme)
	(to) **ignite** [ɪg'naɪt]	(sich) entzünden; zünden; entfachen	Petrol **~s** easily. This material is hard to ~. (= It doesn't burn easily.) The President's speech **~d** positive reactions. (L) ignis *m (Feuer)*
	respectful (to) [rɪ'spektfl]	respektvoll (gegenüber)	
	(to) **trigger** ['trɪgə]	auslösen, triggern	Smells can ~ strong emotions.
	(to) **oppress** [ə'pres]	unterdrücken; bedrücken	Women are still **~ed** in some countries.
	people of colour	Nichtweiße, Menschen nicht-weißer Hautfarbe	people who are not white
p. 66	**plus** [plʌs]	plus	Only three more hours till the party starts. We still have to do all the shopping ~ prepare all the food!

[f] **f**ather · [v] ri**v**er · [s] **s**ister · [z] plea**s**e · [ʃ] **sh**op · [ʒ] televi**s**ion · [tʃ] tea**ch**er · [dʒ] **G**ermany · [θ] **th**anks · [ð] **th**is · [h] **h**ere

	prejudice ['predʒudɪs]	Vorurteil, Voreingenommenheit	Is the old ~ against women who are company managers beginning to disappear?
	zookeeper ['zu:ki:pə] (*kurz auch:* **keeper**)	Tierpfleger(in)	A ~ looks after the animals in a zoo.
	species ['spi:ʃi:z], *pl* **species**	Art *(Biologie)*	You can't see these animals anywhere any more. This ~ died out some years ago. (L) species, ei *f*
	outdoors [ˌaʊt'dɔ:z]	im Freien, draußen	adj: **outdoor** – **outdoor** activities/sports adv: **outdoors** – I like to be **outdoors**.
	zebra ['zebrə]		 a **zebra**
	badge [bædʒ]	Anstecknadel, Button; Abzeichen	a red **badge** 
p. 67	**setting** ['setɪŋ]	Schauplatz *(z.B. Film/Geschichte)*	The ~ of the film is a small village in France.
p. 71	**narrative** ['nærətɪv]	Erzählung, Geschichte	**first-person narrative** = Ich-Erzählung (L) narrare *(erzählen)*

Access to cultures: The Commonwealth and New Zealand

p. 76	**association** [əˌsəʊsi'eɪʃn], [əˌsəʊʃi'eɪʃn]	Verband, Vereinigung	The English Football **Association** (FA) was formed in 1863.
	(to) **make** sth. **up**	etwas bilden, etwas ausmachen	• Girls ~ **up** 58 % of the students at our school. • (to) **be made up of** = bestehen aus: Air **is made up of** different gases.
	populous ['pɒpjələs]	bevölkerungsreich	a ~ region = a region where a large number of people live (L) populus *(Volk)*
	membership ['membəʃɪp]	Mitgliedschaft	**Membership of/in** this club costs £150 per year. (= It costs … to be a member.)
	(to) **require** [rɪ'kwaɪə]	erfordern, benötigen	This isn't an easy task. It **~s** a lot of thinking. verb: (to) **require** – noun: **requirement** [rɪ'kwaɪəmənt] (Voraussetzung, Anforderung, Erfordernis)
	(to) **connect (with/to)** [kə'nekt]	verbinden (mit); anschließen	! (to) **connect** = **1.** verbinden (mit); anschließen – Can you ~ these things? Now ~ the printer **to** the computer. **2.** verbunden sein (mit) – How do these things ~? **3.** sich verbinden (mit) – Can your phone ~ **to** our Wi-Fi? verb: (to) **connect (with/to)** – noun: **connection** [kə'nekʃn] (Verbindung; Anschluss)
	legal ['li:gl]	legal	**legal** ◄► **illegal** [ɪ'li:gl] (illegal) (F) légal, e – illégal, e (L) lex *f (Gesetz)*
	obligation [ˌɒblɪ'geɪʃn]	Pflicht, Verpflichtung	You have the ~ to do this. = You **are obliged** to do this. [ə'blaɪdʒd] (Du musst das tun. / Du hast die Pflicht, das zu tun.)

[i:] green · [i] happy · [ɪ] big · [e] red · [æ] cat · [ɑ:] class · [ɒ] song · [ɔ:] door · [u:] blue · [ʊ] book · [ʌ] mum · [ɜ:] girl · [ə] a partner

complex ['kɒmpleks]	komplex, kompliziert	! stress: **complex** ['kɒmpleks]
… as well as …	sowohl … als auch …	I have a motorbike **as well as** a car. = I have a motorbike, and I have a car **as well**. = I have a motorbike, and I have a car, **too**.
glacier ['glæsiə]	Gletscher	slow-moving ice, made up of snow on mountains
volcano [vɒl'keɪnəʊ], *pl* **volcanos** *or* **volcanoes**	Vulkan	noun: **volcano** – (L) Vulcanus *(der Gott des Feuers)* adj: **volcanic** [vɒl'kænɪk] (vulkanisch, Vulkan-)
earthquake ['ɜːθkweɪk]	Erdbeben	destroyed by an **earthquake** 
significant [sɪg'nɪfɪkənt]	bedeutend, wichtig; signifikant, erheblich	**significant** ◄► **insignificant** [ˌɪnsɪg'nɪfɪkənt] (unbedeutend, geringfügig)
(to) **occur** [ə'kɜː]	passieren, vorkommen	(to) take place, (to) happen ! *simple past* und *-ing*-form mit **-rr-**: **occurred, occurring** (L) occurrere
magnitude ['mægnɪtjuːd]	Stärke *(Erdbeben)*; Größe, Ausmaß	It was a challenge of great **magnitude**. (= a huge challenge) (L) magnitudo *f*
major ['meɪdʒə]	groß, bedeutend; Haupt-	Nothing worked. We had ~ problems. (L) maior **major** ◄► **minor**
millennium [mɪ'leniəm], *pl* **milleniums** *or* **millennia** [mɪ'leniə]	Jahrtausend, Millennium	1,000 years (L) mille *(tausend)*
(to) **claim** [kleɪm]	beanspruchen, fordern	! (to) **claim** = **1.** angeben, behaupten; **2.** beanspruchen, fordern; **claim** = **1.** Behauptung; **2.** Anspruch, Forderung
(to) **come to** be/do sth.	schließlich etwas sein/tun	It was only late in life that he **came to** realize how important good friends are.
despite [dɪ'spaɪt]	trotz	**despite** the dangers = although it is/was dangerous
conflict ['kɒnflɪkt]	Konflikt, Auseinandersetzung, Streit	! stress: **conflict** ['kɒnflɪkt] (F) le conflit (L) conflictus
peninsula [pə'nɪnsjələ]	Halbinsel	a **peninsula**  (L) paeninsula
p. 77 **reputation** [ˌrepju'teɪʃn]	Ansehen, Ruf, Reputation	! stress: **reputation** [ˌrepju'teɪʃn] (F) la réputation
open-minded (about) [ˌəʊpən 'maɪndɪd]	offen, aufgeschlossen (gegenüber)	**open-minded** ◄► **narrow-minded** [ˌnærəʊ 'maɪndɪd] (engstirnig)
the nearest … ['nɪərəst]	der/die/das nächstgelegene …	! • **nearest** = nächstgelegen *(räumlich)*: The **nearest** shop is just round the corner. • **next** = nächstfolgend *(Reihenfolge)*: We have to get off at the **next** stop.
livestock *(no pl)* ['laɪvstɒk]	Vieh	a word for the animals that are kept on a farm (e.g. cows, sheep, pigs, horses)

[eɪ] name · [aɪ] time · [ɔɪ] boy · [əʊ] old ·
[aʊ] town · [ɪə] here · [eə] where · [ʊə] tour

mammal ['mæml]	Säugetier	Whales are not fish, they are large marine **~s**. **marine mammal** [məˌriːn 'mæml] = Meeressäuger (L) mamma *(Brust)*
(to) **litter** ['lɪtə]	Abfälle zurücklassen	verb: (to) **litter** – noun: **litter** (Müll, Abfall)
(to) **scratch** [skrætʃ]	(sich) kratzen; zerkratzen	verb: (to) **scratch** – noun: **scratch** (Kratzer) (to) **scratch your head (over sth.)** = sich den Kopf zerbrechen (über etwas)
pit [pɪt]	Grube, Loch *(im Boden)*	a large deep hole in the ground
canoe [kə'nuː]	Kanu, Paddelboot	a **canoe**  She's about to go **canoeing**. nouns: *(boat)* **canoe**; *(sport)* **canoeing** – verb: (to) **canoe** (Kanu fahren, paddeln)
dairy ['deəri]	Milch-, Molkerei-	**dairy products** *(pl)* = Milch- ,produkte, Molkereiprodukte **dairy** *(infml, New Zealand)* = Laden an der Ecke
(to) **gather** ['gæðə]	sammeln; (sich) versammeln	We stopped and **~ed** some wild flowers. Many people had **~ed** to watch the parade. verb: (to) **gather** – nouns: *(person)* **gatherer** (Sammler/in); *(meeting)* **gathering** (Treffen, Versammlung)

Unit 3 Stepping out

pp. 78/79 (to) **step** (somewhere) [step]	(irgendwohin) treten *(einen Schritt tun)*	Please ~ closer and have a look!
responsibility [rɪˌspɒnsə'bɪləti]	Verantwortung; Zuständigkeit	adj: **responsible** – noun: **responsibility** (F) la responsabilité
application [ˌæplɪ'keɪʃn]	Antrag; Bewerbung	verb: (to) **apply (to sb. for sth.)** – nouns: *(what you send to a company)* **application**; *(person)* **applicant** (Bewerber/in)
supervisor ['suːpəvaɪzə]	Betreuer/in, Leiter/in; Aufsichtsperson	verb: (to) **supervise** (beaufsichtigen) – nouns: *(person)* **supervisor**; *(what you do)* **supervision** [ˌsuːpə'vɪʒn] (Aufsicht; Beaufsichtigung)
community service [kə'mjuːnəti sɜːvɪs]	gemeinnützige Arbeit	Sometimes people have to do ~ **service** as a punishment for minor crimes.
customer ['kʌstəmə]	Kunde, Kundin	"Can I help you?" the shop assistant asked the ~.
apprenticeship [ə'prentɪʃɪp]	Ausbildung, Lehre	My brother is doing an ~ as a hairdresser. = He works as an **apprentice** at a hairdresser's. (Lehrling, Auszubildende/r)
(to) **participate (in)** [pɑː'tɪsɪpeɪt]	teilnehmen (an), sich beteiligen (an)	= (to) take part (in) verb: (to) **participate (in)** – (F) participer noun: *(person)* **participant** (Teilnehmer/in)

[b] **boat** · [p] **pool** · [d] **dad** · [t] **ten** · [g] **good** · [k] **cat** ·
[m] **mum** · [n] **no** · [ŋ] **song** · [l] **hello** · [r] **red** · [w] **we** · [j] **you**

solar panel [ˌsəʊlə 'pænl]	Sonnenkollektor	**solar panels** 
(to) **qualify** ['kwɒlɪfaɪ]	(sich) qualifizieren	If we win this match, we'll ~ for the finals. Ⓕ se qualifier
internship ['ɪntɜːnʃɪp]	Praktikum	Someone who does an ~ is an **intern**. (Praktikant/in)
mentor ['mentɔː]	Mentor/in, Berater/in, Vertrauenslehrer/in	
(job) interview ['dʒɒb‿ɪntəvjuː]	Vorstellungsgespräch	noun: **interview** (Interview; Vorstellungsgespräch) verb: (to) **interview** (befragen, interviewen; ein Vorstellungsgespräch führen)
competitive [kəm'petətɪv]	leistungsorientiert, ehrgeizig; wettbewerbsorientiert	Olivia is very ~ and always wants to win. This isn't a ~ race – it's just for fun. noun: **competition** – adj: **competitive** – verb: (to) **compete with** [kəm'piːt] ((*in Wettbewerben)* antreten gegen; konkurrieren mit))

Part A

p. 46

Schools in the US

elementary school [ˌelɪ'mentri skuːl] (= *BE* **primary school**)	Grundschule
middle school ['mɪdl skuːl]	Mittelschule
junior high (school) [ˌdʒuːniə 'haɪ skuːl]	*Schule für Kinder zwischen 12 und 14*
senior high (school) [ˌsiːniə 'haɪ skuːl]	*Schule für Kinder zwischen 15 und 17*

grade [greɪd] *(AE)*	Klasse, Jahrgang(sstufe); (Schul-)Note, Zensur	= *BE* **1. (school) year;** **2. mark** [mɑːk] (Schulnote, Zensur) I'm in third **grade** *(AE)* / in the third **year** *(BE)*. This year I'll get good **grades** *(AE)* / **marks** *(BE)* in maths and science.
kindergarten ['kɪndəgɑːtn]	*BE:* Kindergarten; *AE:* Vorschule	
(to) **fix** sth. [fɪks]	festlegen; feststellen; befestigen; reparieren, in Ordnung bringen	Have you **~ed** a price for the car yet? We should ~ the board to the wall first. The printer didn't work, but Emily managed to ~ it.
semester [sɪ'mestə] *(bes. AE)*	Semester	
versus ['vɜːsəs] (**v.** *or* **vs.**)	gegenüber; gegen *(bei Wettkämpfen)*	It's England **vs.** Scotland this evening. I hope Scotland wins! Ⓛ versus, -a, -um *(zugewandt)*
(to) **run** sth.	etwas leiten, führen, betreiben *(Firma, Schule)*	My uncle **~s** a hostel near New Orleans. **state-run schools** = schools run by the state
assessment [ə'sesmənt]	Beurteilung, Bewertung	noun: **assessment** – verb: (to) **assess** (beurteilen, bewerten)
examination [ɪgˌzæmɪ'neɪʃn] (*infml auch* **exam** [ɪg'zæm])	Prüfung	*English:* (to) **take/do an exam** *German:* **eine Prüfung machen** noun: **examination** (Überprüfung, Untersuchung) – verb: (to) **examine sb./sth. (for sth.)** (jn./etwas (auf etwas) untersuchen)
diploma [dɪ'pləʊmə]	Diplom, Abschlusszeugnis	a document which shows that you have completed a part of your education Ⓕ le diplôme Ⓛ diploma *n*

[f] **f**ather · [v] ri**v**er · [s] **s**ister · [z] plea**s**e · [ʃ] **sh**op · [ʒ] televi**s**ion ·
[tʃ] tea**ch**er · [dʒ] **G**ermany · [θ] **th**anks · [ð] **th**is · [h] **h**ere

(to) **confirm** [kən'fɜːm]	bestätigen	verb: (to) **confirm** – Ⓛ confirmare noun: **confirmation** [ˌkɒnfə'meɪʃn] (Bestätigung)
graduation [ˌgrædʒu'eɪʃn]	(Schul-/Universitäts-)Abschluss	Sean found a good job soon after his **graduation**. • nouns: *(finishing school/university)* **graduation**; *(person)* **graduate** ['grædʒuət] (Hochschulabsolvent/in) Sean is an Oxford **graduate**. • verb: (to) **graduate (from)** ['grædʒueɪt] Sean **graduated** from Oxford University last year.
(to) **transfer** ['trænsfɜː]	umziehen, (über)wechseln; überweisen *(Geld)*	She's going to ~ to the Bath office. I didn't pay cash. I **~red** the money from my bank account to theirs. Ⓛ transferre *(hinübertragen)* **!** *simple past* und *-ing*-form mit **-rr-**: **transfe<u>rr</u>ed, transfe<u>rr</u>ing**
p. 81 **nursery school** ['nɜːsəri skuːl]	Kindergarten	another word for *BE* kindergarten
secondary school ['sekəndri skuːl]	weiterführende Schule	• **primary school** = a school for children between the ages of 4 or 5 and 11 • **secondary school** = a school for young people between the ages of 11 and 16 or 18
general ['dʒenrəl]	allgemein	**in general** = im Allgemeinen, generell Ⓕ général, e Ⓛ generalis, e
comprehensive school [ˌkɒmprɪ'hensɪv skuːl]	Gesamtschule	
ability [ə'bɪləti]	Fähigkeit, Können	(to) have the ~ to do sth. = (to) be able to do sth. Ⓛ habilitas *f*
curriculum [kə'rɪkjələm], *pl* **curriculums** *or* **curricula** [kə'rɪkjələ]	Lehrplan	the subjects which are taught at each type of school; the content which is taught in each subject Ⓛ curriculum *(Verlauf)*
citizenship ['sɪtɪzənʃɪp]	Staatsbürgerschaft; Staatsbürgerkunde *(Schulfach)*	Ⓛ civis *m/f (Bürger/in)*
related to [rɪ'leɪtɪd]	verbunden mit	**work-related** = arbeitsbezogen; arbeitsbedingt
GCSE [ˌdʒiː siː‿es 'iː] (= **General Certificate of Secondary Education** [ˌdʒenrəl sətɪfɪkət‿əv ˌsekəndri‿edʒu'keɪʃn])	*Prüfung für Schüler/innen ab 15, mittlerer Schulabschluss*	a set of exams which British students take at school when they're around 16
option ['ɒpʃn]	Wahl(möglichkeit), Option	noun: **option** ['ɒpʃn] – adj: **optional** (wahlweise, freiwillig)
choice [tʃɔɪs]	(Aus-)Wahl	verb: (to) **choose** – noun: **choice**
college of further education [ˌkɒlɪdʒ‿əv ˌfɜːðər‿ edʒu'keɪʃn]	Berufsfachschule, Fachoberschule; Volkshochschule	
sixth form ['sɪksθ fɔːm]	*(BE, etwa:) 12. und 13. Klasse eines Gymnasiums*	**form** *(BE)* = Klasse
A level ['eɪ levl] (= **advanced level** [əd'vɑːnst])	*Prüfungen z. Hochschulzulassungs-berechtigung (etwa wie Abitur)*	
(to) **be eligible (for** sth. / **to do** sth.**)** ['elɪdʒəbl]	berechtigt sein (zu etwas / etwas zu tun)	Complete this form if you think you're ~ **for** money from the state / ~ **to** receive money from the state.

[iː] green · [i] happy · [ɪ] big · [e] red · [æ] cat · [ɑː] class · [ɒ] song · [ɔː] door · [uː] blue · [ʊ] book · [ʌ] mum · [ɜː] girl · [ə] a partner

academic [ˌækə'demɪk]	Schul-, akademisch	adj: **academic** – adv: **academically** – noun: *(person)* **academic** (Akademiker/in) Ⓛ Academicus, -a, -um
division [dɪ'vɪʒn]	(Ein-)Teilung, Aufteilung	noun: **division** – Ⓛ divisio *f* verb: (to) **divide (up)** [dɪ'vaɪd] (auf-/einteilen)
p. 82 **noon** [nuːn]	Mittag	12 o'clock? Do you mean ~ or midnight?
pastry ['peɪstri]	Pastete; Gebäck	 
tuna (fish) ['tjuːnə], *pl* **tuna** *or* **tunas**	Thunfisch	 
geometry [dʒi'ɒmətri]	Geometrie	❗ stress: **ge<u>o</u>metry** [dʒi'ɒmətri]
… though. [ðəʊ]	… aber …, … trotzdem …	She was born in France. She isn't French ~. (= … She isn't French, however.) ❗ Das Adverb **though** steht am Satzende.
delivery [dɪ'lɪvəri]	Lieferung	noun: **delivery** – verb: (to) **deliver** [dɪ'lɪvə] (liefern, ausliefern)
(to) **shrug (your shoulders)** [ʃrʌg]	mit den Achseln/Schultern zucken	"I don't know", he said and **~ged his shoulders**. verb: (to) **shrug (your shoulders)** – noun: **shrug** (das/ein Achselzucken)
ambitious [æm'bɪʃəs]	ehrgeizig	adj: **ambitious** – noun: **ambition** (Ehrgeiz, Bestreben) Ⓛ ambitiosus, -a, -um
cautious ['kɔːʃəs]	vorsichtig	= careful adj: **cautious** – noun: **caution** (Vorsicht) Ⓛ cautus, -a, -um
adventurous [əd'ventʃərəs]	abenteuerlustig; abenteuerlich	adj: **adventurous** – noun: **adventure**
bossy ['bɒsi]	herrisch, rechthaberisch	adj: bossy – noun: **boss**
humble ['hʌmbl]	demütig, bescheiden	People who are ~ think they are not as important as other people. Ⓛ humilis, -e
p. 83 **request** [rɪ'kwest]	Wunsch, Bitte; Anfrage	Nobody reacted to their ~ for help. Ⓛ requirere *(fragen)*
refusal [rɪ'fjuːzl]	Ablehnung, (Ver-)Weigerung	noun: **refusal** – verb: (to) **refuse** [rɪ'fjuːz] (sich weigern, ablehnen)
suitcase ['suːtkeɪs]	Koffer	**suitcases** 

[eɪ] name · [aɪ] time · [ɔɪ] boy · [əʊ] old ·
[aʊ] town · [ɪə] here · [eə] where · [ʊə] tour

p. 84	(to) **be about to do** sth.	im Begriff sein, etwas zu tun	I **was ~ to go** to bed when the doorbell rang.
	crossword ['krɒswɜːd]	Kreuzworträtsel	a **crossword** 
	poetry ['pəʊətri]	Poesie, Lyrik	poems
	diet ['daɪət]	Ernährung, Kost; Diät	Chips, chocolate and cola? What a ~! He thought he was too fat, so he went on a ~. *English:* (to) **go on a diet** *German:* **eine Diät machen** ! stress: **diet** ['daɪət]
	vegan ['viːgən]	Veganer/in; vegan	**Vegans** don't eat anything that comes from animals.
p. 85	(to) **confuse** [kən'fjuːz]	verwirren; verwechseln	I was **~d** when I got the strange message. I always ~ right with left. / I always ~ right and left. (L) confundere
	variety [və'raɪəti]	Variante, Sorte, Art	Germany is known for the ~ of its bread. (F) la variété (L) varietas, atis *f* *(Verschiedenheit)*
	tone [təʊn]	Ton(höhe)	Her ~ suggested that she wasn't happy with the situation.
	possibility [ˌpɒsə'bɪləti]	Möglichkeit	adj: **possible** – noun: **possibility** (F) la possibilité (L) possibilitas *f*

German "Möglichkeit"

Das deutsche Wort **Möglichkeit** hat mehrere englische Entsprechungen.
Achte darauf, dass du nicht automatisch **possibility** verwendest. Oft sind **opportunity/chance** oder **way** passender:

• **opportunity** oder **chance** entsprechen „Möglichkeit" im Sinne von „Gelegenheit, Chance". (**opportunity** ist etwas förmlicher als **chance**.)	After school, I had the **chance/opportunity** to go to Australia for a year. Dad says he has a better **chance/opportunity** of getting a job if we move to Bristol.
• Wenn „Möglichkeit" im Sinne von „Art und Weise" gemeint ist, kann man **way** verwenden.	We'll have to swim – there's no other **way** to get/of getting to the island.
• Wenn man sagen will, dass etwas möglicherweise der Fall sein könnte (aber es ist nicht sicher, vielleicht sogar unwahrscheinlich!), dann verwendet man **possibility**.	There is a **possibility** of snow in May, but it's not very likely.

	intention [ɪn'tenʃn]	Absicht, Vorsatz	noun: **intention** – (F) l'intention *(f)* adj: **intentional** [ɪn'tenʃənl] (absichtlich, vorsätzlich) verb: (to) **intend (to do sth.)** [ɪn'tend] (beabsichtigen, vorhaben (etwas zu tun))
	(to) **dig** [dɪg], **dug, dug** [dʌg]	graben	The dog is **digging** a hole in the sand. (to) **dig up potatoes** (Kartoffeln ausgraben *(ernten)*) 
p. 86	**brave** [breɪv]	mutig, tapfer	She was very ~: she jumped into the river and saved the little dog's life. ! • ein **mutiges** Kind = a **brave** child • ein **braves** Kind = a **well-behaved** child / a **good** child
	loyal ['lɔɪəl]	loyal	! stress: **loyal** ['lɔɪəl] adj: **loyal** – noun: **loyalty** ['lɔɪəlti] (Loyalität)

[b] **boat** · [p] **pool** · [d] **dad** · [t] **ten** · [g] **good** · [k] **cat** ·
[m] **mum** · [n] **no** · [ŋ] **song** · [l] **hello** · [r] **red** · [w] **we** · [j] **you**

thrilled [θrɪld]	fasziniert, begeistert	They were ~ to be invited to Paris for the weekend.
(to) **annoy** sb. [ə'nɔɪ]	jn. ärgern	It **~s** me that the trains are always late. = I find it very **~ing** that … (ärgerlich, nervig) / I'm **~ed** that … (verärgert)
particular [pə'tɪkjələ]	bestimmte(r, s), spezielle(r, s)	Are you looking for a ~ kind of bike? adj: **particular** – adv: **particularly** *or* **in particular** (F) particulier, particulière
generous ['dʒenərəs]	großzügig	adj: **generous** – (L) generosus, -a, -um noun: **generosity** [ˌdʒenə'rɒsəti] (Großzügigkeit)
hard-working [ˌhɑːd 'wɜːkɪŋ]	fleißig	**hard-working** people = people who work hard
jealous (of) ['dʒeləs]	neidisch (auf); eifersüchtig	You get so much pocket money! I'm really ~. She was ~ **of** her baby brother. She thought her parents loved him more. adj: **jealous** – noun: **jealousy** (Eifersucht) (L) zelus *(Eifersucht)*
mean [miːn]	gemein, fies; geizig	I hate my brother. He's often really ~ to me. Joe won't buy you a drink. He's very ~ with money. adj: **mean** – noun: **meanness**
tough [tʌf]	(knall)hart; zäh, robust	Rugby is a ~ game, and rugby players are ~ people.

Prefixes expressing the opposite

dis-
advantage – **dis**advantage
(to) appear – (to) **dis**appear
honest – **dis**honest
honesty – **dis**honesty
(to) like – (to) **dis**like
respectful – **dis**respectful
satisfied – **dis**satisfied

in-
correct – **in**correct
formal – **in**formal
tolerant – **in**tolerant

im- *(before* **p** *and* **b***)*
patience – **im**patience
patient – **im**patient
polite – **im**polite
possible – **im**possible
practical – **im**practical

ir- *(before* **r***)*
regular – **ir**regular
responsible – **ir**responsible

un-
friendly – **un**friendly
happy – **un**happy
healthy – **un**healthy
kind – **un**kind
kindness – **un**kindness
like – **un**like
(to) lock – (to) **un**lock
(to) pack – (to) **un**pack
usual – **un**usual

liveliness ['laɪvlinəs]	Lebhaftigkeit	adj: **lively** – noun: **liveliness**
politeness [pə'laɪtnəs]	Höflichkeit	**polite ◄► impolite / politeness ◄► impoliteness**
rudeness ['ruːdnəs]	Unhöflichkeit; Unverschämtheit	adj: **rude** – noun: **rudeness** (L) rudis, e *(roh, ungebildet)*

Part B

p. 88	**undergraduate** [ˌʌndə'grædʒuət]	Student/in *(vor dem ersten Hochschulabschluss)*	**undergraduate** = someone who studies at university **graduate** = someone who has finished university
	study ['stʌdi]	*(das)* Lernen; Untersuchung, Studie	noun: **study** – verb: (to) **study** (L) studium
	FAQ [ˌef‿eɪ 'kju] (= **frequently asked questions**)	häufig gestellte Fragen	If you don't find the information you need in our **FAQ** section, send us an email.
	excursion [ɪk'skɜːʃn]	Exkursion, Ausflug	a short trip, especially of a group of people, for entertainment or for education (F) l'excursion *(f)* (L) exercursio *f*

[f] **f**ather · [v] ri**v**er · [s] **s**ister · [z] plea**s**e · [ʃ] **sh**op · [ʒ] televi**s**ion ·
[tʃ] **t**ea**ch**er · [dʒ] **G**ermany · [θ] **th**anks · [ð] **th**is · [h] **h**ere

biology [baɪ'ɒlədʒi]	Biologie	**biology** = the science **biologist** = the scientist (Biologe/-in) ! stress: **biology** [baɪ'ɒlədʒi], **biologist** [baɪ'ɒlədʒɪst]
orientation [ˌɔːriən'teɪʃn]	Orientierung	training or information that you are given before starting a new job, starting to study at university, etc.
entire [ɪn'taɪə]	gesamte(r, s), ganze(r, s)	adj: **entire** – the **entire** time (= the whole time) adv: **entirely** (völlig) – Interesting! This is **entirely** new to me.
aboard [ə'bɔːd]	an Bord	! **aboard** = **1.** *(prep)* We went ~ **the ship / the plane**. **2.** *(adv)* Several passengers were already ~.
sailboat ['seɪlbəʊt] *(AE)*	Segelboot	= *BE* **sailing boat**
rare [reə]	selten	adj: **rare** – Wow! That's a **rare** old bike. Where did you get it? (L) rarus, -a, -um adv: **rarely** – Jill moved away, and I **rarely** see her any more. (= not very often)
(to) **endanger** [ɪn'deɪndʒə]	bedrohen, gefährden	an **endangered** species = a species that is in danger of dying out
experiment [ɪk'sperɪmənt]	Experiment	*English:* (to) **do** / (to) **carry out experiments** *German:* **Experimente machen / durchführen** noun: **experiment** – (L) experimentum verb: (to) **experiment (on/with)** (experimentieren (an/mit))
data ['deɪtə]	Daten	! **data** + singular verb: The **data shows** that ... (Die Daten zeigen, dass ...) The **data was** collected in ... (Die Daten wurden in ... gesammelt)
(to) **affect** [ə'fekt]	beeinflussen, betreffen, sich auswirken auf	Climate change will ~ all of us. (F) affecter (L) afficere
biodiversity [ˌbaɪəʊdaɪ'vɜːsəti]	Artenvielfalt	a large number of different kinds of animals and plants in a natural environment
survival [sə'vaɪvl]	Überleben	noun: **survival** – verb: (to) **survive** (L) supervivere *(überleben)*
delicate ['delɪkət]	empfindlich, zerbrechlich; heikel	That's a very ~ old glass. (= you can easily break it) That's a ~ topic. Be careful when you discuss it with Jeremy.
ecosystem ['iːkəʊsɪstəm]	Ökosystem	This is a unique ~ – these plants and animals exist only in this particular environment.
first-hand [ˌfɜːst 'hænd]	aus erster Hand	**first-hand experience** = experience you've had yourself
analysis [ə'næləsɪs], *pl* **analyses** [ə'næləsiːz]	Analyse	noun: **analysis** – verb: (to) **analyse** ['ænəlaɪz] (analysieren)
protection [prə'tekʃn]	Schutz	A hat is good ~ against the sun. (F) la protection (L) protegere *(schützen)*
agency ['eɪdʒənsi]	Agentur, Organisation	a business / an organization that offers a particular service: an advertising ~, a travel ~, a news ~
desire [dɪ'zaɪə]	Wunsch, Sehnsucht	noun: **desire** – verb: (to) **desire sth.** (sich etwas wünschen, etwas begehren)
(to) **develop** [dɪ'veləp]	(sich) entwickeln	verb: (to) **develop** – noun: **development** [dɪ'veləpmənt] (Entwicklung)

leadership ['li:dəʃɪp]	Führung	**leadership skills** *(pl)* = Führungseigenschaften, Führungsqualitäten
valuable ['væljuəbl]	wertvoll	adj: **valuable** – nouns: **value** ['vælju:] (Wert); **valuables** *(pl)* (Wertsachen)
admission (to) [əd'mɪʃn]	Zulassung (zu); Einlass, Zutritt (zu), Eintritt	How can I apply for ~ **to** this programme? The concert starts at 7:30, ~ is free.
(to) **notify** ['nəʊtɪfaɪ]	benachrichtigen, mitteilen	verb: (to) **notify** – (L) notificare noun: **notification** [,nəʊtɪfɪ'keɪʃn] (Benachrichtigung, Mitteilung)
sophomore ['sɒfəmɔ:]	*Schüler/in im 2. Jahr der amerikanischen High School*	
junior ['dʒu:niə]	Junior/in; *(AE) Schüler/in im vorletzten Schuljahr*	
senior ['si:niə]	Fortgeschrittene(r); Erwachsene(r) *(bei Sport-Teams);* *Schüler/in im letzten Schuljahr*	(L) senior *(älter)*
scholarship ['skɒləʃɪp]	Stipendium *(finanzielle Hilfe für Schüler/innen, Studierende o.Ä.)*	She would like to study biology in Germany and has applied for a ~.
otherwise ['ʌðəwaɪz]	anderenfalls, ansonsten, sonst; anders	We offer scholarships to students who would ~ not be able to attend the program. You really have to hurry up, ~ we'll miss the train! All guided tours finish at 9.30 pm, if not stated ~.
(to) **gain** [geɪn]	bekommen; gewinnen	= (to) get; (to) win (to) **gain** confidence/experience/strength/...
(to) **contribute (to/towards)** [kən'trɪbju:t]	beitragen, beisteuern (zu); spenden (für)	verb: (to) **contribute** – (L) contribuere noun: **contribution (to/towards)** (Beitrag; Spende (für))
p. 89 (to) **have a blast** [blɑ:st] *(infml)*	einen Mordsspaß haben	You'll **have a** ~. = You'll have great/huge fun.
campus ['kæmpəs], *pl* **campuses**	Campus, Unigelände	the area where university or college buildings are (L) campus *(Feld, Gelände)*
rehearsal [rɪ'hɜ:sl]	Probe *(Theater, Chor, Orchester usw.)*	noun: **rehearsal** – verb: (to) **rehearse (for)** (proben (für))
saxophone ['sæksəfəʊn] *(infml auch:* **sax**)	Saxofon	a **saxophone**  ! stress: **saxophone** ['sæksəfəʊn]
court [kɔ:t]	Platz, Court *(Tennis, Basketball)*	 a basketball **court**  a tennis **court**
horseback riding ['hɔ:sbæk raɪdɪŋ] *(AE)*	Reiten	= *BE* **horse riding**
(to) **get back to** sb.	sich bei jm. (wieder) melden	"Please leave your contact details, and I'll **get** ~ **to** you as soon as possible."
(to) **knock (at/on** sth.**)** [nɒk]	(an)klopfen (an etwas)	verb: (to) **knock** – noun: **knock** (Klopfen; Stoß, Schlag)

[eɪ] name · [aɪ] time · [ɔɪ] boy · [əʊ] old ·
[aʊ] town · [ɪə] here · [eə] where · [ʊə] tour

p. 90	(to) **announce** [ə'naʊns]	verkünden, bekanntgeben; durchsagen	The winner will be **~d** tomorrow. verb: (to) **announce** – noun: **announcement** (F) annoncer (L) annuntiare
	spontaneous [spɒn'teɪniəs]	spontan	He hadn't planned to go; it was a ~ decision.
p. 91	**definite** ['defɪnət]	bestimmte(r, s); definitiv, endgültig, eindeutig	adj: **definite** – Have you got any ~ plans for Friday? I need a ~ answer by tomorrow. adv: **definitely** – We'll ~ be home by ten. (auf jeden Fall; ganz bestimmt)
	schedule ['ʃedjuːl, 'skedʒuːl]	(Zeit-)Plan, Programm; *(AE auch:)* Stundenplan; Fahrplan	The starting time could change, so check the ~ before you come.
	groceries *(pl)* ['ɡrəʊsəriz]	Lebensmittel	**grocery store** *(AE)* = Lebensmittelgeschäft
	tech [tek] *(infml)*	Technik; Technologie	= **technology** [tek'nɒlədʒi]
p. 92	**print** [prɪnt]	Druck; Schrift(art)	noun: **print** – verb: (to) **print (out)** ((aus)drucken)
	use [juːs]	Gebrauch, Verwendung	! verb: (to) **use** [juːz] – noun: **use** [juːs] (L) usus *m*
p. 93	**cut** [kʌt]	Schnitt; Schnittwunde	verb: (to) **cut** – noun: **cut**
	gesture ['dʒestʃə]	Geste; Handbewegung	**gestures** *(pl)* = Gestik

Part C

p. 94	**CV** (= **curriculum vitae** [kəˌrɪkjələm 'viːtaɪ])	Lebenslauf	At the age of 15, your ~ is probably not very long. (L) curriculum vitae
	personal statement [ˌpɜːsənl 'steɪtmənt]	persönliche Beschreibung, Selbstbeschreibung	In the **personal ~** you describe what kind of person you are, e.g. your achievements or hobbies.
	relevant (to sb.**)** ['reləvənt]	relevant, wichtig (für jn.)	! stress: **relevant** ['reləvənt] / **irrelevant** [ɪ'reləvənt]
	interest (in) ['ɪntrəst]	Interesse (an)	noun: **interest (in)** – verb: (to) **interest sb.** (jn. interessieren) – adj: **interesting** (interessant); **interested in** (interessiert an)
	recent ['riːsnt]	aktuell, jüngst; kürzlich geschehen/erfolgt	(F) récent (L) recens

recent *(adj)* – recently *(adv)*

Recent research shows that …	**Jüngste** Forschungen zeigen, dass …
In the light of **recent** events …	Im Licht der **aktuellen** Ereignisse, …
I've done a lot of sport in **recent** weeks.	In den **letzten** Wochen habe ich viel Sport gemacht.
I talked to them just **recently**.	Ich habe erst **vor Kurzem** mit ihnen gesprochen.
There've been a lot of accidents in our street **recently**.	Es hat **in letzter Zeit** viele Unfälle … gegeben.

(to) **have** sth. **done (by** sb.**)**	etwas (von jm.) machen lassen *(erledigen lassen)*	Your hair looks nice. Did you cut it yourself or did you **~ it cut**? There's something wrong with our car. We need to **~ it checked**.
(to) **proofread** ['pruːfriːd], **-read, -read** ['pruːfred]	Korrektur lesen; korrigieren	There are so many mistakes in your text! Didn't you ~ it?
qualification [ˌkwɒlɪfɪ'keɪʃn]	Qualifikation; (Schul-)Abschluss	noun: **qualification** – verb: (to) **qualify**
lifeguard ['laɪfɡɑːd]	Rettungsschwimmer/in; Bademeister/in	The **~s** at a beach watch people who are swimming in the sea and help them if they are in danger.
certification [ˌsɜːtɪfɪ'keɪʃn]	Anerkennung; Zulassung, Bestätigung	noun: **certification** – verb: (to) **certify** ['sɜːtɪfaɪ] (anerkennen; bescheinigen, bestätigen)

[b] **boat** · [p] **pool** · [d] **dad** · [t] **ten** · [ɡ] **good** · [k] **cat** ·
[m] **mum** · [n] **no** · [ŋ] **song** · [l] **hello** · [r] **red** · [w] **we** · [j] **you**

completion [kəm'pliːʃn]	Vervollständigung; Abschluss, Fertigstellung	noun: **completion** – verb: (to) **complete** – adj: **complete** Ⓛ complere *(anfüllen)*
knowledge (of/about) ['nɒlɪdʒ]	Wissen (von/über), Kenntnis(se) (von/in)	**knowledge of art** (Wissen auf dem Gebiet der Kunst), **knowledge of geography** (Kenntnisse der Geographie, geografische Kenntnisse), **knowledge about nature** (Wissen über die Natur) noun: **knowledge** – verb: (to) **know, knew, known**
work experience *(no pl)* ['wɜːk‿ ɪkˌspɪəriəns]	Arbeitserfahrung(en), Praxis-erfahrung(en); Praktikum	She has a strong computer background and a lot of **work** ~. Last year I did some **work** ~ at our local supermarket.
to date [deɪt]	bis heute, bisher	I think his latest book is his best **to** ~. (= up to now)
yearbook ['jɪəbʊk]	Jahrbuch	This year's school ~ is great. There are lots of very funny photos in it.
enthusiastic (about) [ɪnˌθjuːzi'æstɪk]	begeistert (von)	Jack is ~ **about** cooking. His meals are delicious. adj: **enthusiastic** – adv: **enthusiastically** [ɪnˌθjuːzi'æstɪkli]
(to) **take care of** sb./sth. [keə]	sich (gut) um jn./etwas kümmern; auf jn. aufpassen	= (to) look after sb./sth. We **take** ~ **of** our neighbours' cat when they're on holiday.
p. 95 **recreation** [ˌriːkri'eɪʃn]	Freizeit(beschäftigung); Erholung	What do you do **for** ~? (= in your free time)
department [dɪ'pɑːtmənt]	Amt, Ministerium; Abteilung	A ~ **store** is a huge shop with many different ~**s**. (Kaufhaus)
duty ['djuːti]	Aufgabe, Pflicht	(to) **be on duty** = im Dienst sein, Dienst haben (to) **be off duty** = außer Dienst sein, keinen Dienst haben
(to) **assist (with)** [ə'sɪst]	assistieren, helfen (bei)	Could you ~ me **with** this English form? How may we ~? (*im Geschäft:* Wie können wir Ihnen helfen/behilflich sein?) Ⓛ assistere *(beistehen)*
in person	persönlich	I've written emails to Mrs Jones and spoken to her on the phone, but I've never met her **in** ~.
amusement [ə'mjuːzmənt]	Vergnügung, Unterhaltung	**amusement park** = Vergnügungspark Ⓕ l'amusement *(m)*
(to) **have what it takes to do** sth. *(infml)*	das Zeug dazu haben, etwas zu tun	**Do you have what it ~s / Have you got what it ~s** to do this job?
beverage ['bevərɪdʒ]	Getränk	 **No food or beverages in this shop.**
fast-paced [ˌfɑːst 'peɪst]	flott, rasant, tempogeladen	The film is a **fast-**~ comedy about the world of radio chat shows.
position [pə'zɪʃn]	Position, Standort, Platz; (Arbeits-)Stelle	From this ~, you can see the whole city. He called me to offer me the ~. **!** stress: **po<u>si</u>tion** [pə'zɪʃn] Ⓕ la position Ⓛ positio *f*

[f] **f**ather · [v] ri**v**er · [s] **s**i**s**ter · [z] plea**s**e · [ʃ] **sh**op · [ʒ] televi**s**ion · [tʃ] tea**ch**er · [dʒ] **G**ermany · [θ] **th**anks · [ð] **th**is · [h] **h**ere

reliable [rɪ'laɪəbl]	verlässlich, zuverlässig	adj: **reliable** – She's a very **reliable** person. If she says she'll do it, then she'll do it. verb: (to) **rely on** – I can **rely on** my best friend: she's always there for me when I need her. (sich verlassen auf)

(to) employ – employer – employee – …

• (to) **employ sb.**	jn. anstellen, beschäftigen	In the holiday season we **employ** lots of students. The company **employs** over 1,000 people.
• **employer**	Arbeitgeber/in	The company is the biggest **employer** in this area.
• **employee**	Arbeitnehmer/in	The company has over 1,000 **employees**.
• **employment**	Anstellung, Arbeit	Lots of people are looking for **employment**.
• **unemployment**	Arbeitslosigkeit	**Unemployment** is a huge problem where we live.
• **unemployed**	arbeitslos	Dad was **unemployed** for a year or so, but now he has a new job.
• **self-employed**	selbstständig	My aunt is a **self-employed** architect.

	flexible ['fleksəbl]	flexibel	! stress: **flexible** ['fleksəbl] (L) flexibilis, -e
	outgoing ['aʊtgəʊɪŋ]	kontaktfreudig	He's very ~. He's friendly, he likes to meet other people and enjoys being in their company.
	(to) **be willing to do** sth. ['wɪlɪŋ]	bereit sein, etwas zu tun; gewillt sein, etwas zu tun	**Are** you really ~ **to** help me? I don't want to make you do something that you don't want to do.
	(to) **communicate (with** sb.**)** [kə'mjuːnɪkeɪt]	(mit jm.) kommunizieren; sich (mit jm.) verständigen	(to) **communicate** – noun: **communication**
p. 96	(to) **remove** [rɪ'muːv]	entfernen, beseitigen; ausziehen *(Kleidung)*	(to) take sth. away; (to) take off (clothes)
	instruction [ɪn'strʌkʃn]	Anweisung	Read the **~s** carefully before you use this machine. verb: (to) **instruct sb. to do sth.** (jn. anweisen, etwas zu tun) – nouns: *(person)* **instructor** (Lehrer/in, Ausbilder/in); *(what you tell others)* **instruction** (L) instruere *(unterrichten, ausbilden)*
	term [tɜːm]	Ausdruck, Begriff	
	ache [eɪk]	Schmerz(en)	= pain *English:* (to) **have a stomach ache** *German:* **Bauch-/Magenschmerzen haben** noun: **ache** – verb: (to) **ache** (= (to) hurt) (schmerzen, wehtun)
p. 97	**architecture** ['ɑːkɪtektʃə]	Architektur	! stress: **architecture** ['ɑːkɪtektʃə] (F) l'architecture *(f)*
	(to) **keep track of** sth.	den Überblick behalten bei etwas, etwas im Auge behalten	Do you find it easy to **keep ~ of** the money you spend?
	(to) **recommend** sth. **(to** sb.**)** [ˌrekə'mend]	(jm.) etwas empfehlen	I can ~ the store on 3rd Street. They have great stuff! verb: (to) **recommend** – noun: **recommendation** [ˌrekəmən'deɪʃn] (Empfehlung) (F) recommander (L) commendare

[iː] green · [i] happy · [ɪ] big · [e] red · [æ] cat · [ɑː] class · [ɒ] song · [ɔː] door · [uː] blue · [ʊ] book · [ʌ] mum · [ɜː] girl · [ə] a partner

	(to) **consider** [kən'sɪdə]	nachdenken über; (sich) überlegen	(L) considerare *(überlegen)*

(to) consider

1. betrachten als, halten für	The Rolling Stones **are considered (to be)** one of the greatest rock bands in the world. Agree on three points that you **consider (to be)** important.
2. berücksichtigen; in Erwägung ziehen, in Betracht ziehen	Thank you for your letter. We will **consider** your ideas and suggestions for improvement. Are you **considering** attending one of our courses? Send us an email.
3. nachdenken über; (sich) überlegen	We didn't have much time to **consider** our options. The answer to that request should **be considered** very carefully. Before you start, **consider** the following questions: … I think unemployment is a big problem, especially **considering** how many young people are currently out of work. (… besonders, wenn man bedenkt/berücksichtigt, …)

	(to) **earn** [ɜːn]	verdienen *(Geld; Anerkennung)*	! German "Geld verdienen": **1.** *(Gehalt bekommen)* (to) **earn money** **2.** *(Profit machen)* (to) **make money**
p. 98	**Ms** Hancock [mɪz], [məz]	Frau Hancock	! Viele Frauen möchten lieber mit **Ms …** angesprochen werden, weil am Wort **Ms** nicht zu erkennen ist, ob sie verheiratet sind oder nicht.
	current ['kʌrənt]	aktuelle(r, s), gegenwärtige(r, s)	adj: **current** – The song is the **current** number 1 in the UK. adv: **currently** – The song is **currently** no. 1 in the UK. (zurzeit, aktuell) (L) currere *(laufen)*
	(to) **advance** [əd'vɑːns]	verbessern, voranbringen; voranschreiten, Fortschritte machen	**advanced** = fortgeschritten; für Fortgeschrittene Are you attending the beginners' or the **advanced** course? (F) avancé, e
	basic ['beɪsɪk]	einfach, elementar, Grund-	• adj: **basic** – The **basic** idea is quite simple really. • adv: **basically** (im Prinzip, grundsätzlich) – The verbs "ache" and "hurt" **basically** mean the same thing. • noun: **the basics** *(pl)* (Grundzüge, Grundlagen) – I'd like to know the **basics** of computer programming.
	(to) **get along (with** sb.**)**	(gut) zurechtkommen (mit jm.), sich (gut) verstehen (mit jm.)	I **get** ~ well **with** my dad. = My dad and I **get** ~ well. My father and his brother don't **get** ~.
p. 99	(to) **evaluate** [ɪ'væljueɪt]	bewerten, einschätzen; auswerten	verb: (to) **evaluate** – noun: **evaluation** [ɪˌvælju'eɪʃn] (Beurteilung, Bewertung, Einschätzung)
	interaction [ˌɪntər'ækʃn]	Interaktion, Umgang	noun: **interaction** – adj: **interactive** – verb: (to) **interact** [ˌɪntər'ækt] ((miteinander) interagieren, kommunizieren)
	occasion [ə'keɪʒn]	Gelegenheit; Ereignis, Anlass	• noun: **occasion** (F) l'occasion *(f)* (L) occasio We only go to the zoo on certain **occasions**. • adj: **occasional** [ə'keɪʒənl] (gelegentliche(r, s)) We only make **occasional** visits to the zoo. • adv: **occasionally** (gelegentlich, ab und zu) We only go to the zoo **occasionally**.
	weakness ['wiːknəs]	Schwäche	adj: **weak** ◄► **strong** – noun: **weakness** ◄► **strength**

[eɪ] name · [aɪ] time · [ɔɪ] boy · [əʊ] old · [aʊ] town · [ɪə] here · [eə] where · [ʊə] tour

	(to) **mention** ['menʃn]	erwähnen	She has never **~ed** that she has a horse. Now that you ~ it – yes, it was a bit strange! **Don't mention it.** = Gern geschehen. (L) mentionem facere

Text: Good behaviour in the workplace

p. 100	(to) **inspire** [ɪn'spaɪə]	inspirieren	It was the pope who **~d** her to work in Africa. (F) inspirer (L) inspirare
	(to) **deserve** [dɪ'zɜːv]	verdienen *(zu Recht bekommen)*	He's such a nice boy. He doesn't ~ to be treated so badly.
	healthy ['helθi]	gesund	**healthy ◄► sick, ill**
	courteous ['kɜːtiəs]	höflich	adj: **courteous** – noun: **courtesy** ['kɜːtəsi] (Höflichkeit; Höflichkeitsfloskel)
	gossip ['gɒsɪp]	Klatsch, Tratsch	noun: **gossip** – verb: (to) **gossip**
	appropriate [ə'prəʊpriət]	angemessen, passend, geeignet	**appropriate ◄► inappropriate** (unangemessen, unpassend, ungeeignet)
	clothing *(no pl)* ['kləʊðɪŋ]	Kleidung	*English:* **a piece of clothing** *German:* **ein Kleidungsstück** ! The word **clothing** is more formal than **clothes**.
	(to) **interpret** [ɪn'tɜːprɪt]	interpretieren; dolmetschen *(gesprochenen Text mündlich wiedergeben)*	verb: (to) **interpret** – nouns: **interpretation** [ɪnˌtɜːprɪ'teɪʃn] (Interpretation; (das) Dolmetschen); *(person)* **interpreter** [ɪn'tɜːprɪtə] (Dolmetscher/in)
	(to) **combine** [kəm'baɪn]	verbinden, kombinieren	verb: (to) **combine** – (F) combiner noun: **combination** [ˌkɒmbɪ'neɪʃn] (Kombination, Verbindung)
	comprehension [ˌkɒmprɪ'henʃn]	Verständnis	noun: **comprehension** – To check your ~ you can answer these questions. verb: (to) **comprehend** [ˌkɒmprɪ'hend] *(fml)* – We couldn't ~ what was happening. (verstehen) (F) la compréhension (L) comprehendere *(verstehen)*
	effect [ɪ'fekt]	(Aus-)Wirkung, Einfluss, Effekt	Cars, lorries, factories – they all have negative **~s** on the environment. verb: (to) **affect** (beeinflussen, betreffen, sich auswirken auf) – noun: **effect** – adj: **effective** [ɪ'fektɪv] (effektiv, wirksam)
	viewer ['vjuːə]	Zuschauer/in	noun: **viewer** – verb: (to) **view sth.** (etwas betrachten, etwas anschauen *(auch Film, TV)*)
	critical (of) ['krɪtɪkl]	kritisch (gegenüber)	adjective: **critical** – verb: (to) **criticize** – nouns: *(person)* **critic**; *(what you express when criticizing)* **criticism** ! *English:* **critic** = *German:* **Kritiker/in** *English:* **criticism** = *German:* **Kritik**
p. 101	**unrealistic** [ˌʌnrɪə'lɪstɪk]	unrealistisch	**realistic ◄► unrealistic**
	(to) **reinforce** [ˌriːɪn'fɔːs]	(ver)stärken, verfestigen	(to) make stronger (ideas, feelings, impressions, ...)
	(to) **contain** [kən'teɪn]	enthalten	I don't want this. It **~s** meat, and I'm a vegetarian. (L) continere verb: (to) **contain** – noun: **content**

[b] **boat** · [p] **pool** · [d] **dad** · [t] **ten** · [g] **good** · [k] **cat** ·
[m] **mum** · [n] **no** · [ŋ] **song** · [l] **hello** · [r] **red** · [w] **we** · [j] **you**

amount [ə'maʊnt]	Menge; Betrag *(Geld)*	! • Mit dem Plural von zählbaren Nomen: **number** a large **number** of cars/students/dogs/... • Mit nicht zählbaren Nomen: **amount** a large **amount** of money/water/snow/...
reference ['refrəns]	Bezug (zu)	**in/with reference to** = in/mit Bezug auf
(to) **fit** [fɪt]	passen (zu)	How do these things ~ together? verb: (to) **fit** – noun: **fit** (Übereinstimmung; Passform, Sitz)
(to) **interlock** [ˌɪntə'lɒk]	ineinandergreifen	(to) **interlock sth. (with sth.)** = etwas (mit etwas) verbinden, zusammenfügen
(to) **complement** sth. ['kɒmplɪment]	etwas ergänzen, vervollkommnen	They're a great couple. They ~ each other perfectly.
detailed ['di:teɪld]	ausführlich, detailliert	Can you give a ~ description of the person who attacked you?
(to) **be mistaken (about)** [mɪ'steɪkən]	sich irren, sich täuschen (in)	Bob and Joan are cousins, if **I'm** not ~. (= if I'm not wrong; if I have understood correctly)

Access to cultures: Next steps: Going to university in the UK and US

p. 106	**globe** [gləʊb]	Globus; Kugel	**all (a)round the globe** = all over the world (F) le globe (L) globus
	college ['kɒlɪdʒ]	Hochschule	
	course [kɔ:s]	Studium, Studiengang	! **course** = **1.** Studium, Studiengang; **2.** Kurs, Lehrgang (L) cursus
	(to) **select** [sɪ'lekt]	(aus)wählen	verb: (to) **select** – (L) seligere noun: **selection (of)** (Auswahl (an))
	coach [kəʊtʃ]	Trainer/in	verb: (to) **coach sb.** (jn. trainieren, jm. Unterricht geben) – noun: **coach**
	(to) **enrol (for/in/on** sth.**)** [ɪn'rəʊl]	sich (für etwas) anmelden, sich einschreiben	! *BE:* (to) **enrol on a course** *AE:* (to) **enroll in a course** verb: (to) **enrol/enroll** – noun: **enrolment** *(BE)* / **enrollment** *(AE)* (Anmeldung, Einschreibung)
	(to) **standardize** ['stændədaɪz]	standardisieren, normen	verb: (to) **standardize** – noun: **standard**
p. 107	(to) **reconsider** [ˌri:kən'sɪdə]	(noch einmal) überdenken	Do you really think this is a good idea? Don't you want to ~ your decision?
	excerpt (from) ['eksɜ:pt]	Auszug, Ausschnitt (aus)	We're going to read a short ~ from a novel.
	envelope ['envələʊp]	(Brief-)Umschlag	an **envelope**  (F) l'enveloppe *(f)*
	(to) **be worried sick** ['wʌrid]	krank vor Sorge sein	I think I left the kitchen window open. **I'm ~ sick** that someone might break into my flat.
	after all [ˌɑ:ftər‿'ɔ:l]	schließlich (doch)	Of course I want to help him. He's my brother ~ **all**!

[f] **f**ather · [v] ri**v**er · [s] **s**ister · [z] plea**s**e · [ʃ] **sh**op · [ʒ] televi**s**ion ·
[tʃ] **t**ea**ch**er · [dʒ] **G**ermany · [θ] **th**anks · [ð] **th**is · [h] **h**ere

uni ['ju:ni] *(infml, kurz für:* **university**)	Uni(versität)	I really love ~. I've made great friends since I started studying there.
(to) **define** [dɪ'faɪn]	definieren	verb: (to) **define** – noun: **definition** [ˌdefɪ'nɪʃn] (Definition)
enrichment [ɪn'rɪtʃmənt]	Bereicherung	noun: **enrichment** – verb: (to) **enrich** (bereichern) **summer enrichment programs** = *Sommerkurse von Universitäten für besonders begabte Schüler/innen*
minimum ['mɪnɪməm]	Mindest-, minimal; Minimum	What's the ~ age for driving in your country? I need a ~ of £500 for a good new bike. **minimum ◄► maximum (max)** ['mæksɪməm], [mæks] (Höchst-, maximal; Maximum) **minimum grade requirement** = Mindestanforderung beim Notendurchschnitt *(vergleichbar unserem Numerus Clausus)* Ⓛ minimus,-a,-um – maximus, -a, -um
(to) **stress** sb. **(out)** [ˌstres‿'aʊt]	jn. stressen, (über)belasten	verb: (to) **stress sb. (out)** – noun: **stress** (Stress, Belastung)
these days ['ði:z deɪz]	heutzutage	I don't believe things used to be so much better, but ~ **days** everyone seems to be complaining all the time.
barely ['beəli]	kaum	= **hardly**
lab [læb] *(infml, kurz für:* **laboratory** [lə'bɒrətri])	Labor	 **working in a science lab**
sort (of) [sɔ:t]	Art (von)	What ~ **of** music do you like? (= What kind of …) They had some ~ **of** problem. (… irgendwie ein Problem)
robotics [rəʊ'bɒtɪks]	Robotertechnik, Robotik	the science of designing and running robots
(to) **be involved in** [ɪn'vɒlvd]	beteiligt sein an; etwas zu tun haben mit	

involvement

involvement (in) [ɪn'vɒlvmənt]	Her **involvement** in the peace movement made her famous.	**Engagement (für); Beteiligung (an)**
(to) **involve** [ɪn'vɒlv]	Charity projects often **involve** a lot of work. It's important to **involve** everybody in the decision.	**mit sich bringen; beinhalten** **einbeziehen**
(to) **be involved (in)**	We **have been involved in** our local church for ten years.	**beteiligt sein (an); etwas zu tun haben (mit)**
(to) **get involved (in)**	At university, she **got involved in** a theatre group. Try not to **get involved.**	**sich engagieren (für, bei); sich beteiligen (an)** **Versuche, dich da rauszuhalten.**

[i:] green · [i] happy · [ɪ] big · [e] red · [æ] cat · [ɑ:] class · [ɒ] song · [ɔ:] door · [u:] blue · [ʊ] book · [ʌ] mum · [ɜ:] girl · [ə] a partner

	progress *(no pl)* ['prəʊgres]	Fortschritt(e)	❗ noun: **progress** ['prəʊgres] – verb: (to) **progress** [prə'gres] (vorankommen, Fortschritte machen; sich (vorwärts) bewegen; fortschreiten) (to) **make progress** = Fortschritte erzielen/machen; vorankommen (to) **be in progress** = im Gange sein Ⓛ progressio

Access to cultures: Next steps: Degree programmes

p. 108	**degree** [dɪ'gri:]	Universitätsabschluss, Diplom; Grad *(auch bei Temperatur)*	It'll be 14 **~s** (14°) and very cloudy. She finished university and now has a ~ as a biologist.
	higher education [ˌhaɪər‿edʒu'keɪʃn]	Hochschulbildung; Hochschulwesen	= education at universities
	mostly ['məʊstli]	größtenteils, hauptsächlich; meistens	We ~ grow potatoes in our garden. The milk we drink is ~ from cows.
	(to) **identify** [aɪ'dentɪfaɪ]	erkennen, identifizieren; sich identifizieren	Do you think you'll be able to ~ the man who attacked you? (to) **identify oneself (as)** = sich zu erkennen geben (als)
	terminology [ˌtɜ:mɪ'nɒlədʒi]	Terminologie, Fachwortschatz	the special words and phrases used in a particular subject
	PhD [ˌpi:‿eɪtʃ 'di:]	Doktor(grad)	
	certificate [sə'tɪfɪkət]	Urkunde, Bescheinigung	❗ stress: **cer<u>ti</u>ficate** [sə'tɪfɪkət] **birth certificate** = Geburtsurkunde
	vocational [vəʊ'keɪʃənl]	beruflich, Berufs-	**vocational college** = Berufsschule
	freshman ['freʃmən], *pl* **freshmen**	Studienanfänger/in; *Anfänger/in in der High School*	a first-year student at a university or college
	theology [θi'ɒlədʒi]	Theologie	the study of religion(s)

University degrees

bachelor's degree ['bætʃələz dɪgri:]	Bachelor(-Abschluss)
master's degree ['mɑ:stəz dɪgri:]	Master(-Abschluss)
Associate's degree [ə'səʊsiəts dɪgri:], [ə'səʊʃiəts dɪgri:]	Associate Degree *(Abschluss eines US-amerikanischen oder kanadischen College nach 2 Jahren)*
doctorate ['dɒktərət]	Doktorwürde; Promotion

(to) **specialize (in)** ['speʃəlaɪz]	sich spezialisieren (auf)	She's a microbiologist and has **~d in** the study of viruses.
part-time	Teilzeit-, Halbtags-	**part-time** ◄► **full-time** ❗ stress: **a part-time job** [ˌpɑ:t taɪm 'dʒɒb] – **a full-time job** [ˌfʊl taɪm 'dʒɒb] (to) **work part-time** [ˌpɑ:t 'taɪm] – (to) **work full-time** [ˌfʊl 'taɪm]
at the outset (of sth.**)** ['aʊtset]	am Anfang (einer Sache)	at the start of sth., at the beginning of sth.

	paper ['peɪpə]	(wissenschaftlicher) Aufsatz	an academic essay ! **paper** = **1.** Papier; **2.** Zeitung; **3.** (wissenschaftlicher) Aufsatz
	dentistry ['dentɪstri]	Zahnheilkunde, Zahnmedizin	If you want to become a dentist, you'll have to study ~ at university.
	veterinary ['vetnri], ['vetrənəri]	tierärztlich, Tier-	**veterinary medicine** = Tiermedizin **veterinary surgeon** ['sɜːdʒən] (*kurz auch:* **vet**) = Tierarzt/-ärztin
	engineering [ˌendʒɪ'nɪərɪŋ]	Ingenieurwesen, Maschinenbau	She studied **engineering** and became an **engineer**. **engineer** [ˌendʒɪ'nɪə] = Ingenieur/in; Techniker/in
	pharmacy ['fɑːməsi]	Pharmazie; Apotheke	Sam studied ~ and now runs a chemist's shop.
	doctoral ['dɒktərəl]	Doktor- *(zur Erlangung des Doktorgrads)*	I'd like to enrol in a **doctoral** program and do a PhD.
	additional [ə'dɪʃənl]	zusätzliche(r, s)	"I read your job advertisement, but I'd like some ~ information (= some more information) about the company before I apply." (L) addere *(hinzufügen)*
p. 109	**cost** [kɒst]	Kosten; Preis	noun: **cost** – verb: (to) **cost, cost, cost** – adj: **costly** (kostspielig, teuer)
	(to) **range (from ... to ...)** [reɪndʒ]	sich erstrecken, reichen (von ... bis ...)	verb: (to) **range (from ... to ...)** – noun: **range** (Bereich, Bandbreite, Palette)
	tuition [tju'ɪʃn]	Unterricht, Anleitung; Studiengebühren	**tuition** *or* **tuition fees** *(pl)* [tju'ɪʃn fiːz] = Studiengebühren **fee** = Gebühr; Honorar; (Mitglieds-)Beitrag
	impact ['ɪmpækt]	Einfluss, Auswirkung	What ~ does people's behaviour have on the environment? (= What effect ...) (L) impingere *(einwirken, aufprallen)*
	laureate ['lɒriət]	Preisträger/in	someone who has been awarded a prize for something they have achieved (L) laureatus,-a, -um *(mit Lorbeer bekränzt)*
	politician [ˌpɒlə'tɪʃn]	Politiker/in	Why are ~**s** all over the world so slow at making decisions that protect the environment? adj: **political** – nouns: *(person)* **politician**; *(what politicians do)* **politics** (L) politicus, -a, -um *(den Staat betreffend)*
	Supreme Court [suː'priːm kɔːt] *(AE)*	Oberster Gerichtshof	the highest law court in a country or state **court** = (Gerichts-)Hof (L) cors, cortis *f (Hof)* (L) supremus,-a, -um *(höchste, -r, -s)*
	judge [dʒʌdʒ]	Richter/in	• noun: **judge** – The ~**s** sentenced him to three years in prison. • verb: (to) **judge (sb. by ...)** – You shouldn't ~ people **by** their clothes or **by** their religion. (urteilen; jn. beurteilen (nach))
	billionaire [ˌbɪljə'neə]	Milliardär/in	someone who owns billions of dollars/euros/... **billion** ['bɪljən] = Milliarde
	influential [ˌɪnflu'enʃl]	einflussreich	An ~ person is someone with a lot of **influence**. adj: **influential** – noun: **influence** ['ɪnfluəns] (Einfluss) – verb: (to) **influence** ['ɪnfluəns] (beeinflussen)

[b] **boat** · [p] **pool** · [d] **dad** · [t] **ten** · [g] **good** · [k] **cat** · [m] **mum** · [n] **no** · [ŋ] **song** · [l] **hello** · [r] **red** · [w] **we** · [j] **you**

creator [kri'eɪtə]	Schöpfer/in	verb: (to) **create** – adj: **creative** [kri'eɪtɪv] (kreativ) – nouns: **creation** [kri'eɪʃn] (Schaffung; Schöpfung; Kreation, Werk)); *(person)* **creator** Ⓕ le créateur / la créatrice Ⓛ creator *m*
apple ['æpl]	Apfel	**apples** 

Unit 4 A sustainable world online and off

pp. 110/111 **sustainable** [sə'steɪnəbl]	nachhaltig, umweltverträglich; zukunftsfähig	using a small amount of energy, water, wood, etc., so that there is no damage to the environment adj: **sustainable** – noun: **sustainability** [səˌsteɪnə'bɪləti] (Nachhaltigkeit) verb: (to) **sustain** [sə'steɪn] ((aufrecht)erhalten) **Sustainable** living can help to **sustain** our planet.
(to) **waste** sth. **(on** sth.**)** [weɪst]	etwas (für etwas) verschwenden	I don't ~ money **on** cheap clothes. I always buy high-quality clothes. verb: (to) **waste** – noun: **waste**
(to) **seek (for)** [siːk], **sought, sought** [sɔːt]	suchen (nach); anstreben	If you were in trouble, where would you ~ advice? We're still **~ing for** better solutions to this problem.
(to) **fall for** sb. / (to) **fall for** sth.	sich in jn. verlieben / auf etwas hereinfallen	They **fell for** each other immediately. This is a well-known trick, I'm not **falling for** it.
warrior ['wɒriə]	Krieger/in	= a person who fights in a war
humankind [ˌhjuːmən'kaɪnd]	Menschheit	= all people, people in general Ⓛ humanus, -a, -um *(menschlich)*
(to) **weave** [wiːv], **wove** [wəʊv], **woven** ['wəʊvn]	weben	The material for these kilts is hand-**woven** in Scotland.
web [web]	Netz	Some spiders make **~s** to catch insects.
we are **but** …	wir sind nur …, wir sind nichts (anderes) als …	We are **but** dust in the wind.
thread [θred]	Faden	a **thread** 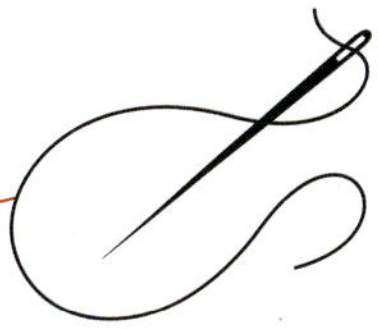
(to) **bind** [baɪnd], **bound, bound** [baʊnd]	(ver)binden	I love you so much – our hearts will be **bound** together forever.
chief [tʃiːf]	Häuptling	= the leader of a community or a Native American tribe, for example
chieftain ['tʃiːftən]	Oberhaupt *(Clan, Volksstamm)*	= the chief of a people, a tribe or a clan
threat [θret]	(Be-)Drohung	noun: **threat** – verb: (to) **threaten** ['θretn] (drohen, bedrohen)

[f] **f**ather · [v] ri**v**er · [s] **s**i**s**ter · [z] plea**s**e · [ʃ] **sh**op · [ʒ] televi**s**ion · [tʃ] **t**ea**ch**er · [dʒ] **G**ermany · [θ] **th**anks · [ð] **th**is · [h] **h**ere

(to) **engage in** sth. [ɪn'geɪdʒ]	sich beteiligen an etwas, aktiv werden für etwas, sich engagieren für etwas	verb: (to) **engage** – You should ~ **in** local politics. noun: **engagement (in)** [ɪn'geɪdʒmənt] (Engagement (bei)) I enjoy my **engagement** in local politics.
grand [grænd]	groß(artig), eindrucksvoll	= very large or important (L) grandis, -e
heroic [hə'rəʊɪk]	heroisch, heldenhaft	adj: **heroic** – adv: **heroically** – noun: **hero** (L) heroicus, -a, -um
(to) **multiply (by)** ['mʌltɪplaɪ]	multiplizieren (mit); (sich) vervielfachen, (sich) vermehren	3 **multiplied by** 4 is 12. These viruses ~ fast. These problems won't just go away. In fact, they'll ~. (L) multiplicare
historian [hɪ'stɔːriən]	Historiker/in	somebody who studies and is an expert in history (L) historicus
renewable [rɪ'njuːəbl]	erneuerbar; verlängerbar	This ticket isn't ~. You have to apply for a new one every year.
advocate ['ædvəkət]	Befürworter/in, Fürsprecher/in	noun: **advocate** ['ædvəkət] – verb: (to) **advocate sth.** ['ædvəkeɪt] (etwas befürworten, verfechten) (L) advocatus
to such an extreme that …	in so extremer Form, dass … / in so extremem Ausmaß, dass …	Don't take sport and fitness **to such an** ~ **that** you damage your body.
miracle ['mɪrəkl]	Wunder	It's a ~ that grandma's old motorbike is still working! (F) le miracle (L) miraculum
let alone …	ganz zu schweigen von …, geschweige denn …	There wasn't enough water for all of us, **let alone** for the horses. I've never driven a car, **let alone** owned one!
commission [kə'mɪʃn]	Kommission	! stress: **commission** [kə'mɪʃn] (F) la commission
(to) **compromise** sth. / (to) **compromise (with** sb. **on** sth.**)** ['kɒmprəmaɪz]	etwas beeinträchtigen / einen Kompromiss/Kompromisse schließen (mit jm. zu/über etwas), sich (mit jm. auf etwas) einigen	verb: (to) **compromise** – noun: **compromise** (Kompromiss) (F) le compromis (L) compromittere *(einen Kompromiss schließen)*
specific [spə'sɪfɪk]	bestimmte(r, s), spezielle(r, s); genau, präzise	! **specific** = **1.** bestimmte(r, s), spezielle(r, s) Any ~ time when you need the car back? **2.** genau, präzise She gave us very ~ instructions. adj: **specific** – adv: **specifically** (F) spécifique (L) specialis, -e

Part A

p. 112 **preparatory school** [prɪ'pærətri skuːl] (*kurz auch:* **prep school** ['prep skuːl])	*BE: Privatschule für Kinder zwischen 7 und 13 Jahren; AE: (meist private) Schule, die Schüler/innen auf die Universität vorbereitet*	
transcript ['trænskrɪpt]	Niederschrift, Protokoll	noun: **transcript** ['trænskrɪpt] – verb: (to) **transcribe** [træn'skraɪb] (niederschreiben, aufschreiben; transkribieren) (L) transcribere *(abschreiben)*

[iː] green · [i] happy · [ɪ] big · [e] red · [æ] cat · [ɑː] class · [ɒ] song · [ɔː] door · [uː] blue · [ʊ] book · [ʌ] mum · [ɜː] girl · [ə] a partner

nothing but …	nichts außer …, nichts als …; nur	There was **nothing** on the stage **but** a desk and a chair. My brother and sister do **nothing but** argue all day.

but

1. I didn't like coffee when I was younger, **but** now I love it.	aber
2. No, not the dress on the right **but** the one next to it.	sondern
3. That will bring you **nothing but** trouble. She trusts **nobody but** herself. It was unknown to **all but** his sister. He wished he was **anywhere but** at school.	nichts als …; nichts außer …; nur … niemand(em) außer …; nur … alle außer … (sonst) irgendwo, nur nicht …; irgendwo anders, außer …
4. Human life is **but** a tiny moment in time.	nur …; nichts (anderes) als …

microphone ['maɪkrəfəʊn]	Mikrofon	! stress: **<u>mi</u>crophone** ['maɪkrəfəʊn]
visuals *(pl)* ['vɪʒuəlz] (*kurz für:* **visual materials**)	visuelle Materialien/Hilfsmittel	noun: **visuals** – adj: **visual** (visuell; optisch) (L) videre *(sehen)*
addicted (to) [ə'dɪktɪd]	süchtig (nach), abhängig (von)	They're **addicted to** drugs. [ə'dɪktɪd] = They're drug **addicts**. ['ædɪkt] (Abhängige/r, Süchtige/r) Their **addiction** to drugs is terrible. [ə'dɪkʃn] (Sucht nach, Abhängigkeit von)

German "Früher …" – *used to* + infinitive / *would* + infinitive

- Remember: with ***used to* + infinitive** you can talk about things that were true in the past but are not true any more:

We **used to live** in London.	Wir wohnten früher in London.
I **used to spend** lots of money on sweets.	Ich habe früher immer viel Geld für Süßigkeiten ausgegeben.

Negative statements are made with ***didn't use to …***, questions with ***Did … use to …***:

He **didn't use to be** so shy.	**Did you use to cry** a lot when you were little?

- We use ***would* + infinitive (without *to*)** to talk about regular <u>actions</u> in the past:

Grandma **would take** us to the zoo every Sunday.	Oma ging (früher) jeden Sonntag mit uns in den Zoo. / Oma pflegte jeden Sonntag mit uns in den Zoo zu gehen.

(to) **come up** [ˌkʌm‿'ʌp]	auftauchen; vorkommen, erwähnt werden	She **came** ~ behind me and slapped me on the back. The question **came** ~ when we were talking about education.
I wouldn't eat ...	Ich wollte nichts essen.	! You can use the phrase **wouldn't + infinitive** to say that someone refused to do something or that something didn't work: He knew about the plan, but he **wouldn't tell** us. Sorry we're late – the car **wouldn't start**.
right and left *(infml)* (*oft auch:* **right, left and centre**)	überall; aus allen Richtungen; an allen Ecken und Enden	These hooligans are causing trouble **right and left** / **right, left and centre**.
messy ['mesi]	unordentlich	adj: **messy** – noun: **mess** [mes] (Chaos, Unordnung)
alert [ə'lɜːt]	aufmerksam, *(geistig)* hellwach	• adj: **alert** – He had been driving all night and found it difficult to stay **alert**. • verb: (to) **alert sb. (to sth.)** – We heard a noise and **alerted** the police. (alarmieren; warnen) • noun: **alert** – There was a bomb **alert** in the city centre this morning. (Warnung, Alarm)

[eɪ] name · [aɪ] time · [ɔɪ] boy · [əʊ] old ·
[aʊ] town · [ɪə] here · [eə] where · [ʊə] tour

circumstances *(pl)* ['sɜːkəmstənsɪz]	Umstände, Verhältnisse	Normally there's a football match here every week-end, but under these ~ there won't be any matches till autumn. (F) la circonstance
device [dɪ'vaɪs]	Gerät, Apparat; Mittel	A thermometer is a ~ that tells you the temperature.
greyscale ['greɪskeɪl] (*AE:* **grayscale**)	graustufig, in Graustufen	(to) **go greyscale/grayscale** = das Handy auf schwarz-weiß umstellen *(in den Einstellungen)*
cafeteria [ˌkæfə'tɪəriə] *(AE)*	Kantine; Cafeteria	= *BE* canteen
restroom ['restruːm] *(AE)*	Toilette *(in öffentlichen Gebäuden)*	! *(AE)* **Toilette**: in privaten Häusern/Wohnungen = **bathroom**; in öffentlichen Gebäuden = **restroom**
highs and lows *(pl)* [ˌhaɪz‿ən 'ləʊz]	Höhen und Tiefen	We all have our **highs and** ~. (= good times and bad times)
assembly [ə'sembli]	Schulversammlung	
principal ['prɪnsəpl] *(AE)*	Schulleiter/in	= *BE* **head teacher**
(to) **agree to do** sth. [ə'griː]	einwilligen, etwas zu tun; sich bereit erklären, etwas zu tun	We can only finish this project if everyone **~s to** work on Saturday.
whoever [huː'evə]	wer/wen/wem auch immer	= no matter who

whenever, wherever, whatever, whoever

We're allowed to use dictionaries **whenever** we want.	... wann immer wir wollen
I'll find you, **wherever** you are.	... wo immer du (auch) bist / egal, wo du bist
We will help you, **whatever** happens.	... was immer auch geschieht / egal, was geschieht
Whoever told you that was wrong.	Wer immer dir das auch erzählt hat, ...

(to) **unplug** sth. [ʌn'plʌg]	den Stecker von etwas heraus-ziehen, etwas ausstöpseln	= to pull out the plug of sth. 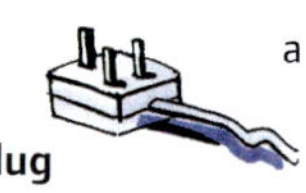 a British **plug** 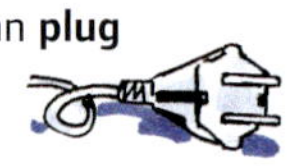 a German **plug** (to) **unplug sth.** ◄► (to) **plug sth. in** (etwas einstecken, anschließen)
(to) **simplify** ['sɪmplɪfaɪ]	vereinfachen	= (to) make sth. simpler (F) simplifier (L) simplex *(einfach)*
(to) **eliminate** [ɪ'lɪmɪneɪt]	eliminieren, beseitigen	Do you think we will ever be able to ~ disease? (L) eliminare *(hinausjagen)*
p. 113 **persuasive** [pə'sweɪsɪv]	überzeugend	adj: **persuasive** – verb: (to) **persuade** [pə'sweɪd] (überreden, überzeugen) – noun: **persuasion** [pə'sweɪʒn] (Überzeugung(skunst), Überredung(skunst)) (F) persuasif/-ive (L) persuadere *(überzeugen)*
curator [kjʊə'reɪtə]	Kurator/in; Museumsdirektor/in	That's a great exhibition at our museum. I wonder who the ~ is. (L) curator *(Verwalter)*
(to) **limit** sth. **(to)** ['lɪmɪt]	etwas beschränken, begrenzen (auf); etwas einschränken	verb: (to) **limit** – (L) limitare noun: **limit** (Grenze, Begrenzung, Beschränkung)
concept ['kɒnsept]	Konzept, Vorstellung, Begriff	! stress: **concept** ['kɒnsept] (F) le concept (L) concipere *(begreifen)*

[b] **boat** · [p] **pool** · [d] **dad** · [t] **ten** · [g] **good** · [k] **cat** ·
[m] **mum** · [n] **no** · [ŋ] **song** · [l] **hello** · [r] **red** · [w] **we** · [j] **you**

	accessible (to) [ək'sesəbl]	erreichbar (für), zugänglich (für)	**accessible** ◄► **inaccessible** (unzugänglich, schwer/nicht erreichbar) verb: (to) **access sth.** (auf etwas zugreifen; Zugang haben zu etwas) noun: **access (to)** Ⓛ accedere *(herankommen)*
p. 114	**sentimental** [ˌsentɪ'mentl]	sentimental	! stress: **sentimental** [ˌsentɪ'mentl] **sentimental value** = ideeller Wert **for sentimental reasons** = aus Gefühlsgründen Ⓕ sentimental/e
	(to) **imitate** ['ɪmɪteɪt]	imitieren	verb: (to) **imitate** – noun: **imitation** (Imitation) Ⓕ imiter Ⓛ imitari
	(to) **ignore** [ɪg'nɔː]	nicht beachten, ignorieren	verb: (to) **ignore** – They **~d** all the warning signs. noun: **ignorance (of/about sth.)** ['ɪgnərəns] – They showed complete ~ of the dangers. (Unwissenheit, Unkenntnis, Ignoranz) Ⓕ ignorer Ⓛ ignorare *(nicht wissen)*
p. 115	(to) **contradict** [ˌkɒntrə'dɪkt]	widersprechen	I can't confirm what's in this report. It **~s** my own personal experience. verb: (to) **contradict** – noun: **contradiction** (Widerspruch) Ⓕ contredire Ⓛ contradicere
	somewhat ['sʌmwɒt]	ein bisschen, einigermaßen	**somewhat** surprising = a bit surprising
	restrictive [rɪ'strɪktɪv]	einschränkend	adj: **restrictive** – noun: **restriction** (Beschränkung, Einschränkung) – verb: (to) **restrict** [rɪ'strɪkt] (einschränken, beschränken) Ⓕ restrictif/-ive Ⓛ restringere *(einschränken)*
	(to) **note** [nəʊt]	beachten; (sich etwas) notieren	Please ~ that this museum is closed on Mondays. verb: (to) **note** – noun: **note**
	inversion [ɪn'vɜːʃn]	Umkehrung, Inversion	noun: **inversion** – verb: (to) **invert** (umstellen, umkehren) Ⓛ invertere *(umkehren)*
	stressful ['stresfl]	anstrengend, aufreibend, stressig	The past couple of months have been very ~ for everyone.
	(to) **keep** / (to) **stay in contact (with)** ['kɒntækt]	in Kontakt bleiben (mit)	We really wanted to **keep/stay in** ~ **(with** each other), but I've never heard from them again.
	(to) **urge** sb. **to do** sth. [ɜːdʒ]	jn. drängen, etwas zu tun	• verb: (to) **urge** – My parents **urged** me **to** apply. • adj: **urgent** ['ɜːdʒənt] – Call me! It's **urgent**. (dringend, eilig) • nouns: **urge** – He felt the **urge** to write it all down. (Drang, Bedürfnis); **urgency** – This problem needs to be solved with some **urgency**. ['ɜːdʒənsi] (Dringlichkeit) Ⓛ urgere
	the other day	neulich	I met my old class teacher **the** ~ **day**. (= a short while ago)
	(to) **get rid of** sth. [rɪd]	etwas loswerden	We hardly drive our car. We could **get** ~ **of** it.

[f] **f**ather · [v] ri**v**er · [s] **s**ister · [z] plea**s**e · [ʃ] **sh**op · [ʒ] televi**s**ion · [tʃ] tea**ch**er · [dʒ] **G**ermany · [θ] **th**anks · [ð] **th**is · [h] **h**ere

(not) at all	überhaupt (nicht)	Have you seen Jack **at all** this week? – No, I have**n't** seen him **at all**.

not (...) at all

She did**n't** say anything **at all**.	Sie hat überhaupt nichts / gar nichts gesagt.
I do**n't** like cats **at all**.	Ich mag Katzen überhaupt nicht.
He has**n't** got any money **at all**.	Er hat überhaupt kein / gar kein Geld.
Do you mind if I open the window? – **Not at all**.	... – Überhaupt nicht. / Ganz und gar nicht.

	(to) **ask** sb. **out**	sich mit jm. verabreden	I really like him, but I think he's in a relationship. Should I ~ him **out** anyway?
	no sooner ... than ... *(fml)*	kaum ..., da ...	**No sooner** had he said it aloud **than** he knew it was a mistake and he would have to apologize.
	uncomfortable [ʌn'kʌmftəbl]	unbequem, ungemütlich; unangenehm, peinlich	This chair is very ~. I think I'll just stand. What she said about me in the group made me really feel ~. (= I found it very embarrassing.) **uncomfortable ◄► comfortable**
p. 116	(to) **attract** sb. **to** sb./sth. [ə'trækt]	jn. zu jm./etwas hinziehen	What **~ed** me **to** her was her sense of humour. (Was mich zu ihr hinzog / an ihr anzog, ...) (to) **be attracted to sb.** = sich zu jm. hingezogen fühlen, sich von jm. angezogen fühlen verb: (to) **attract** – noun: **attraction** – adj: **attractive** [ə'træktɪv] (attraktiv) (L) attrahere
	(to) **be seeing** sb.	mit jm. gehen, mit jm. eine Beziehung haben	They**'ve been** ~ each other for quite a while now. Next month he's going to meet her parents.
	in love (with) [lʌv]	verliebt (in)	Jo is **in love with** Sam. Jo fell **in love with** Sam last year. (= They fell in love last year.) (to) **fall in love (with sb.)** = sich verlieben (in jn.)
	(to) **date** sb.	jn. daten, mit jm. gehen, mit jm. eine Beziehung haben	Jill **~d** Julie for years before they got married. nouns: **date** = **1.** Datum; **2.** Verabredung, Date verbs: (to) **date sb.** = jn. daten, mit jm. gehen/eine Beziehung haben; (to) **date from** = stammen aus *(zeitlich)*
	(to) **go out with** sb. [ˌgəʊ_'aʊt wɪð]	mit jm. (aus)gehen *(eine Beziehung haben)*	Nick is Ray's new boyfriend. They**'ve been going** ~ (together) since last month. (= Nick **has been going ~ with** Ray since last month.)
	(to) **break up (with** sb.**)** [ˌbreɪk_'ʌp]	Schluss machen (mit jm.), sich trennen (von jm.)	Jonathan's parents were having lots of arguments and now they**'ve broken** ~.
	(to) **get to know** sb.	jn. kennenlernen	My parents **got to** ~ each other in high school. (= they met in high school)
	cross (with sb.**)** [krɒs]	verärgert, böse	= annoyed or angry (with sb.) Mum was ~ with me because I was late.
	disappointed [ˌdɪsə'pɔɪntɪd]	enttäuscht	He didn't get the job and was really ~. verb: (to) **disappoint** [ˌdɪsə'pɔɪnt] (enttäuschen)
	glum [glʌm]	niedergeschlagen, bedrückt, mürrisch	adj: **glum** – Don't be ~. Try to be more optimistic. adv: **glumly** – "We lost again," he said **~ly**.
	hopeful ['həʊpfl]	zuversichtlich, hoffnungsvoll	verb: (to) **hope** – noun: **hope** (Hoffnung) – adj: **hopeful**

[iː] green · [i] happy · [ɪ] big · [e] red · [æ] cat · [ɑː] class · [ɒ] song · [ɔː] door · [uː] blue · [ʊ] book · [ʌ] mum · [ɜː] girl · [ə] a partner

pleased [pli:zd]	froh, erfreut, zufrieden	I'm really ~ with my new phone. It's great! **Pleased to meet you.** = Freut mich, Sie kennenzulernen.
furious (with/at sb.**)** ['fjʊəriəs]	wütend	He was really ~ when I told him. I've never seen anyone so angry. adjective: **furious** – noun: **fury** ['fjʊəri] (Wut) (L) furiosus, -a, -um
heartbroken ['hɑ:tbrəʊkən]	todunglücklich, untröstlich	= very sad Nick was ~ when Ray broke up with him.
(to) **terrify** sb. ['terɪfaɪ]	jm. schreckliche Angst einjagen	It **terrified** me to see how dangerous the situation was. (= I was really terrified. (entsetzt)) (to) **be terrified (of sth.)** = schreckliche Angst (vor etwas) haben (L) terrificare
friendly with sb. ['frendli]	mit jm. befreundet	I'm ~ **with** a couple of self-employed artists, and their situation is really difficult.
male [meɪl]	männlich; männliche Person; Männchen	**man** – **male** ◄► **woman** – **female** ['fi:meɪl] (weiblich; Frau) Most of the workers here are **male**. (= are men) Police are looking for a 40-year-old **male**. Is it true that most teachers are **female**? **Females** often earn less than **males**. (L) masculus
acquaintance [ə'kweɪntəns]	Bekannte(r)	I wouldn't say he's a good friend. He's just an ~.
p. 117 **status** ['steɪtəs]	Status	(F) le statut (L) status *m (Stellung, Rang)*
(to) **make** sb. **do** sth.	jn. dazu bringen, etwas zu tun	You can't **make** people **do** what you want. = People can't **be made to do** what you want. (to) **be made to do sth.** = gezwungen werden, etwas zu tun; etwas tun müssen

Part B

p. 118 **version** ['vɜ:ʃn]	Version	**!** stress: **<u>ver</u>sion** ['vɜ:ʃn] (F) la version
rapid ['ræpɪd]	rapide, rasch, schnell	= very quick/fast (F) rapide (L) rapidus, -a, -um Wow, that was a ~ development!
(to) **encourage** [ɪn'kʌrɪdʒ]	ermutigen, ermuntern	My friends **~d** me to look for a new job. verb: (to) **encourage** – noun: **courage** (F) encourager
(to) **throw** sth. **away/out** [θrəʊ]	etwas wegwerfen	Don't ~ these clothes **away/out**. You can give them to a charity!
no longer (*auch:* **not any longer**)	nicht mehr, nicht länger	I have to go now. I can stay **no longer**. / I **can't** stay **any longer**.
essential [ɪ'senʃl]	(absolut) notwendig, wesentlich	= very important (L) essentialis, -e **essentially** *(adv)* = im Grunde genommen, grundsätzlich, prinzipiell
(to) **matter** ['mætə]	von Bedeutung sein, wichtig sein	Does it really ~ which team wins? – No, **it doesn't matter**. (Es/Das ist egal.)
synthetic [sɪn'θetɪk]	synthetisch, Kunst-	adj: **synthetic** – noun: **synthetic** (Gewebe aus Kunstfasern, synthetisches Gewebe, Kunststoff)

[eɪ] name · [aɪ] time · [ɔɪ] **boy** · [əʊ] **old** ·
[aʊ] **town** · [ɪə] **here** · [eə] **where** · [ʊə] **tour**

fibre (*AE:* **fiber**) ['faɪbə]	Faser; Ballaststoffe	Is this a cotton shirt or is it made of synthetic **~s**? A healthy diet includes fruit, vegetables and ~. (L) fibra *(Pflanzenfaser)*
fossil fuel ['fɒsl fjuːəl]	fossiler Brennstoff	**fossil** = fossil (L) fossilis, -e *(ausgegraben)* **fuel** = Treibstoff, Kraftstoff, Brennstoff
(to) **decompose** [ˌdiːkəm'pəʊz]	sich zersetzen, zerfallen	Don't just throw your plastic bags on the ground – they take centuries to ~.
microplastics *(pl)* ['maɪkrəʊplæstɪks]	Mikroplastik	
(to) **release** [rɪ'liːs]	abgeben, freisetzen	• verb: (to) **release** – 1 000 balloons were **~d** in Hyde Park this morning to celebrate the anniversary. We should stop **releasing** greenhouse gases into the atmosphere. (to) **release a prisoner** (eine/n Gefangene/n freilassen) • noun: **release** (Austritt, Freisetzung; Freilassung)
destructive [dɪ'strʌktɪv]	zerstörerisch, destruktiv	**destructive** ◄► (L) destruere *(zerstören)* **constructive** [kən'strʌktɪv] (konstruktiv)
volume ['vɒljuːm]	Volumen, Menge; Lautstärke	This old bridge wasn't made for today's ~ of traffic. Your music is too loud. Please turn the ~ down. ! stress: **<u>vo</u>lume** ['vɒljuːm]
fresh water [ˌfreʃ 'wɔːtə]	Süßwasser	• noun: **fresh water** – We can't drink water from the sea, we can only drink ~ **water**. • adj: **freshwater** ['freʃwɔːtə] (Süßwasser-) These are ~ fish – they live in lakes, not in the sea.
chemical ['kemɪkl]	Chemikalie; chemisch	! **chemical** = **1.** *(n)* Chemikalie – This is a dangerous **chemical** that harms the environment. **2.** *(adj)* chemisch – Please describe this **chemical** experiment.
pesticide ['pestɪsaɪd]	Schädlingsbekämpfungsmittel, Pestizid	You should wash those vegetables. They might have been treated with **~s**.
textiles *(pl)* ['tekstaɪlz]	Textilien	• noun: **textiles** – I don't like to wear **textiles** made of synthetic fibres. • adj: **textile** – Lots of workers in India who work for the **textile** industry are badly-paid. (Textil-) (L) texere *(weben)*
need (for) [niːd]	Bedarf (an), Bedürfnis (nach), Notwendigkeit	There's a great ~ **for** maths teachers at our school. No ~ to worry! Everything will be fine. noun: **need** – verb: (to) **need**
garment ['gɑːmənt]	Kleidungsstück	= a piece of clothing
(to) **exploit** [ɪk'splɔɪt]	*(Menschen)* ausnutzen; *(Bodenschätze)* ausbeuten; *(Gelegenheit)* ausnutzen	verb: (to) **exploit** – (F) exploiter noun: **exploitation** [ˌeksplɔɪ'teɪʃn] (Ausbeutung; Abbau *(von Rohstoffen)*)

[b] **boat** · [p] **pool** · [d] **dad** · [t] **ten** · [g] **good** · [k] **cat** ·
[m] **mum** · [n] **no** · [ŋ] **song** · [l] **hello** · [r] **red** · [w] **we** · [j] **you**

	in order to do sth. ['ɔːdə]	um etwas zu tun	We left early **in ~ to** arrive before dark.
	(to) **pick** [pɪk]	pflücken	If we don't ~ our strawberries now, the birds will eat them all!
	manufacture [ˌmænju'fæktʃə]	Herstellung, Produktion, Fertigung	= the production of large numbers/amounts of goods noun: **manufacture** – verb: (to) **manufacture** (herstellen, produzieren, fertigen)
	wage [weɪdʒ], *oft auch:* **wages** *(pl)*	Lohn, Gehalt	Many years ago my dad had a **wage** of £180 per week. Now his **wages** are much higher. **minimum wage** = Mindestlohn
	climate change ['klaɪmət tʃeɪndʒ]	Klimawandel	
	aviation [ˌeɪvi'eɪʃn]	Luftfahrt	= air traffic; the designing and building of planes
	shipping ['ʃɪpɪŋ]	Schiffstransport, Schifffahrt	= ships in general; transport or travel by ship
	equivalent [ɪ'kwɪvələnt]	Äquivalent, Gegenwert, Entsprechung	This is **the equivalent** of xxx. = This is **equivalent** to xxx. (= Dies entspricht …)
	resources *(pl)* [rɪ'sɔːsɪz]	Ressourcen; *(finanzielle)* Mittel	We should stop using non-renewable ~ like coal or oil.
p. 119	**passion** ['pæʃn]	Leidenschaft	noun: **passion** – adj: **passionate** ['pæʃənət] (leidenschaftlich) (to) **be passionate about sth.** = eine Leidenschaft haben für etwas, etwas leidenschaftlich gern tun
	jazzy ['dʒæzi] *(infml)*	auffallend, knallig, poppig	**jazzy** clothes = clothes that are brightly coloured and attract attention
	fashionista [ˌfæʃn'iːstə]	Modefreak	= a person who is interested in the latest fashions; a fashion designer
	a bunch of … [bʌntʃ] *(infml)*	eine Menge …; *(Menschen)* eine Gruppe …	I learned **a** whole **~ of** interesting new things on the course. Don't listen to them. They're **a ~ of** losers.
	(to) **decorate** ['dekəreɪt]	dekorieren, schmücken	verb: (to) **decorate** ['dekəreɪt] – adj: **decorative** ['dekərətɪv] – noun: **decoration** [ˌdekə'reɪʃn] (Dekoration, Schmuck, Verzierung) (F) décorer (L) decorare
	dozen ['dʌzn], *pl* **dozen**	Dutzend	**!** two **dozen** eggs = zwei Dutzend Eier *but:* **dozens** of people = dutzende Leute
	fabric marker ['fæbrɪk mɑːkə]	Stoffmarker *(Stift, mit dem man auf Stoff schreiben/malen kann)*	**fabric** = Stoff *(zum Nähen)* **marker** = Marker *(Stift)*
	global ['gləʊbl]	global, weltweit	**global warming** = Erderwärmung
	activist ['æktɪvɪst]	Aktivist/in	**!** stress: **activist** ['æktɪvɪst]
	charity shop ['tʃærəti ʃɒp]	*Geschäft, das gespendete Waren für wohltätige Zwecke verkauft*	Nice pair of jeans! – Thank you. They're from the local **~ shop** and cost only £4!
	creativity [ˌkriːeɪ'tɪvəti]	Kreativität, Ideenreichtum	nouns: *(abilitiy to create)* **creativity**; *(person)* **creator**; *(what you create)* **creation** verb: (to) **create** – adj: **creative** (F) la créativité
	(to) **recycle** [riː'saɪkl]	recyceln, wiederverwerten	verb: (to) **recycle** – noun: **recycling**

[f] **f**ather · [v] ri**v**er · [s] **s**ister · [z] plea**s**e · [ʃ] **sh**op · [ʒ] televi**s**ion ·
[tʃ] **t**ea**ch**er · [dʒ] **G**ermany · [θ] **th**anks · [ð] **th**is · [h] **h**ere

guilty ['gɪlti]	schuldig; schuldbewusst	What I did to you was unfair. I really feel ~ about it. (… fühle mich schuldig deswegen) **guilty of a crime** = eines Verbrechens schuldig adj: **guilty** – noun: **guilt** [gɪlt] (Schuld)
granny ['græni] *(infml)*	Oma	a **granny gift** = ein Geschenk von der Oma
(to) **be with** sb. **(on** sth.**)**	jn. unterstützen, jm. zustimmen (bei etwas)	= (to) support sb. in sth.; (to) agree with sb., to share their opinion
button ['bʌtn]	Knopf; Button; Schaltfläche	**buttons**  **a button-down shirt** = ein Button-down-Hemd *(dessen Kragenspitzen mit Knöpfen befestigt werden)*
(to) **owe** sb. sth. / (to) **owe** sth. **to** sb. [əʊ]	jm. etwas schulden, schuldig sein	I still ~ you some money. *(or:* I still ~ some money **to** you.) – No no, you don't ~ me anything.
inexpensive [ˌɪnɪk'spensɪv]	preiswert	= **good value for money**; not (too) expensive
(to) **reverse** [rɪ'vɜːs]	umkehren, rückgängig machen	I think it's important to ~ the trend towards big cars that use a lot of fuel. Ⓛ reverti *(umkehren)*
profit ['prɒfɪt]	Gewinn *(Profit)*	(to) **make a profit** = Gewinn/Profit machen **!** stress: **profit** ['prɒfɪt] noun: **profit** – verb: (to) **profit (from)** (profitieren (von)) Ⓛ proficere *(Gewinn bringen)*
condition [kən'dɪʃn]	Zustand; Bedingung	Our house is fifty years old, but still in an excellent ~. It's too cold and too noisy in this office. I can't work **in/under these ~s**. (bei/unter diesen Bedingungen) Ⓕ la condition Ⓛ condicio *f*
wardrobe ['wɔːdrəʊb]	Kleiderschrank	a **wardrobe** 
item ['aɪtəm]	Artikel, Gegenstand, Punkt *(auf einer Liste)*	I took my **~s** to the cash desk. Ⓛ item *(ebenfalls)*
p. 120 **soya** ['sɔɪə], *AE:* **soy** [sɔɪ]	Soja	a **soyburger** = a meatless burger made from soy(a) **soya bean** *(BE)* / **soybean** *(AE)* = Sojabohne
emission [ɪ'mɪʃn]	Emission; Ausstoß	noun: **emission** – verb: (to) **emit** [ɪ'mɪt] (emittieren, ausstoßen) Ⓛ emittere *(von sich geben, ausstoßen)*
(to) **fry** [fraɪ]	braten *(in der Pfanne)*	**fried eggs** 

[iː] green · [i] happy · [ɪ] big · [e] red · [æ] cat · [ɑː] class · [ɒ] song · [ɔː] door · [uː] blue · [ʊ] book · [ʌ] mum · [ɜː] girl · [ə] a partner

greenhouse gas [ˌgriːnhaʊs ˈgæs]	Treibhausgas	**gas** = **1.** Gas; **2.** *(AE)* Benzin
waiter [ˈweɪtə], **waitress** [ˈweɪtrəs]	Kellner, Kellnerin	a **waitress** and two customers 
lemon [ˈlemən]	Zitrone	**lemons** 
herbs *(pl)* [hɜːbz]	Kräuter	noun: **herbs** *(pl)* – adj: **herbal** [ˈhɜːbl] (Kräuter-) tea made from **herbs** = **herbal** tea (Kräutertee) (L) herba
hurry [ˈhʌri]	Eile	*English:* **in a hurry** – *German:* **in Eile**
I suppose [səˈpəʊz]	ich denke, ich glaube, ich nehme an	Getting tickets for that show will be hard, **I** ~. (to) **suppose** = glauben, denken, annehmen
topping [ˈtɒpɪŋ]	Überzug, Belag; Soße	with a cheese **topping** = mit Käse überbacken
lap [læp]	Schoß	The cat is sitting on his **lap**. 
(to) **predict** [prɪˈdɪkt]	vorhersagen, voraussagen	= (to) say that something will happen in the future verb: (to) **predict** – noun: **prediction** (L) praedicere
p. 121 **skin** [skɪn]	Haut; Fell	People shouldn't have disadvantages because of the colour of their ~.
(to) **warn** sb. **(about/against/ of** sth.**)** [wɔːn]	jn. warnen (vor etwas)	Nobody **~ed** us **of/about** the dangers. His father **~ed** him **against** (the dangers of) alcohol. **!** • (to) **warn sb. to do sth.** = jn. ermahnen, etwas zu tun; jm. dringend raten, etwas zu tun The teacher **~ed** Josie **to** work harder. • (to) **warn sb. not to do sth.** = jn. davor warnen, etwas zu tun They **~ed** me **not to** go there. verb: (to) **warn** – noun: **warning**
(to) **hire** [ˈhaɪə]	*(Person)* einsteldestroylen; mieten, leihen	We need to ~ three more people for the project. They **~d** a car and drove to the coast.
guardian [ˈgɑːdiən]	Beschützer/in, Hüter/in, Wächter/in	= someone who guards something
destruction [dɪˈstrʌkʃn]	Zerstörung	verb: (to) **destroy** – noun: **destruction**
ecology [iˈkɒlədʒi]	Ökologie	noun: **ecology** – adj: **ecological** [ˌiːkəˈlɒdʒɪkl] (ökologisch)
root [ruːt]	Wurzel	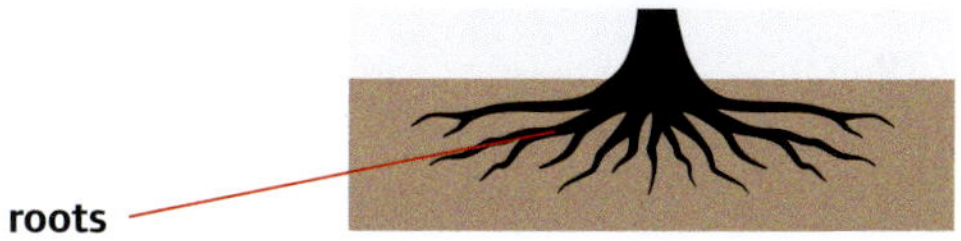

[eɪ] name · [aɪ] time · [ɔɪ] boy · [əʊ] old ·
[aʊ] town · [ɪə] here · [eə] where · [ʊə] tour

outlook (on sth.**)** ['aʊtlʊk]	Einstellung (zu etwas); (Zukunfts-)Aussicht(en); Aussicht, Blick	I have quite an optimistic ~ **on** life. (= attitude) The ~ for jobs is getting better. (= the chances of getting a job)
sacred (to) ['seɪkrɪd]	heilig (für)	Uluru is a famous rock in Australia. It is ~ **to** the indigenous Australian people. (… ist ihnen heilig) (F) sacré (L) sacer
nature ['neɪtʃə]	(die) Natur	*English:* (to) **protect nature** *German:* **die Natur beschützen** ! stress: **<u>na</u>ture** ['neɪtʃə] (F) la nature noun: **nature** – adj: **natural** (L) natura
branch [brɑːntʃ]	Ast, Zweig; (Neben-)Arm; Zweigstelle, Filiale	The road was covered with fallen ~**es** after the storm. More and more people bank online, so banks have closed ~**es** all over the country.
(to) **heal** [hiːl]	heilen	I need to give my foot time to ~.
lately ['leɪtli]	in letzter Zeit	Have you seen any good films ~? ! **late** = spät; zu spät – **lately** = in letzter Zeit
drought [draʊt]	Dürre, Trockenheit	= a long time without rain ! pronunciation: **drought** [draʊt]
a great deal (of) [ə ˌgreɪt 'diːl]	viel, eine Menge	= lots of
heritage ['herɪtɪdʒ]	(Kultur-, Natur-) Erbe	This church has been here for such a long time that it's now part of the city's ~. (L) hereditare *(erben, vererben)*
p. 122 **chart** [tʃɑːt]	Diagramm; Tabelle	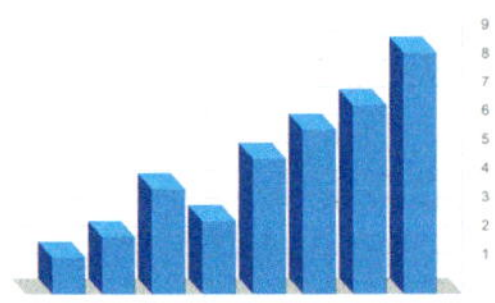 a **bar chart** (ein Balkendiagramm) 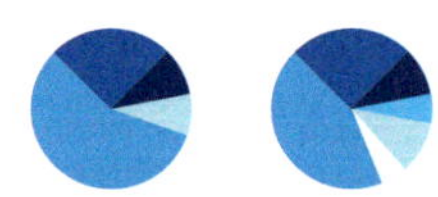 **pie charts** (Tortendiagramme)
useful ['juːsfl]	nützlich, hilfreich	Here are some ~ tips for your exam. (= tips you can use to get better results)
percentage [pə'sentɪdʒ]	Anteil, Prozentsatz	What ~ of your pocket money do you spend on clothes? (L) per centum *(pro hundert)*
few [fjuː]	wenige	

(a) little – (a) few

little / a little steht mit nicht zählbaren Nomen wie *cheese, milk, money, time, traffic*.
few / a few steht mit dem Plural von zählbaren Nomen.

! Beachte die Unterschiede zwischen **little** und **a little** und **few** und **a few**.

We had very **<u>little</u> money** (= *not much money*) when we were young.	**wenig/nicht viel Geld**
Dad gave me **<u>a little</u> money** (= *some money*) and sent me to the shops.	**etwas/ein bisschen Geld**
There were **<u>few</u> people** (= *not many people*) in the streets, so I felt a bit scared.	**wenige/nicht viele Leute**
There were **<u>a few</u> people** (= *some people*) at the ticket office, but I didn't have to wait long.	**einige/ein paar Leute**

! **Deutsch „weniger"**
„less" mit nicht zählbaren Nomen: My grandparents had even **<u>less</u> money**.
„fewer" mit dem Plural von zählbaren Nomen: There were **<u>fewer</u> people** than usual in the cinema.

[b] boat · [p] pool · [d] dad · [t] ten · [g] good · [k] cat ·
[m] mum · [n] no · [ŋ] song · [l] hello · [r] red · [w] we · [j] you

distribution [ˌdɪstrɪ'bjuːʃn]	(Aus-)Lieferung; Verteilung	noun: **distribution** [ˌdɪstrɪ'bjuːʃn] – verb: (to) **distribute** [dɪ'strɪbjuːt] (verteilen, vertreiben *(Handel)*) (L) distribuere *(verteilen)*
retail ['riːteɪl]	Einzelhandel; Einzelhandels-	= selling goods to people, e.g. in shops or on online platforms
consumer [kən'sjuːmə]	Konsument/in, Verbraucher/in	noun: **consumer** – verb: (to) **consume** [kən'sjuːm] (verbrauchen, konsumieren)
transportation [ˌtrænspɔː'teɪʃn] *(bes. AE)*	Beförderung, Transport(wesen), Verkehr	nouns: **transport** / **transportation** – verb: (to) **transport** (F) le transport (L) transportare *(hinüberbringen)*
laundry ['lɔːndri]	Wäsche; Wäscherei	 dirty **laundry**
carbon dioxide (CO_2) [ˌkɑːbən daɪ'ɒksaɪd]	Kohlendioxid	Motors which use fossil fuels produce ~ **dioxide** and other dangerous gases.
by type/size/…	geordnet nach Typ/Größe/…; abhängig von Typ/Größe/…	The books are arranged ~ author.
tonne [tʌn]	Tonne *(= 1.000 kg)*	! pronunciation: **tonne** [tʌn]
(to) **spin** [spɪn], **spun, spun** [spʌn]	spinnen *(Wolle, Garn)*	My great-grandma used to ~ thread from wool.
crop [krɒp]	Feldfrucht, Anbaupflanze; Ernte	What kinds of **~s** do you grow on your farm?
cultivation [ˌkʌltɪ'veɪʃn]	Kultivierung, Anbau; landwirtschaftliche Nutzung	noun: **cultivation** – verb: (to) **cultivate** ['kʌltɪveɪt] (kultivieren; *(Getreide, Gemüse)* anbauen) (L) colere *(anbauen)*
organic [ɔː'gænɪk]	biologisch (angebaut), Bio-	**Organic** products cost a bit more, but **organic** farming doesn't damage the environment so much. adjective: **organic** – adverb: **organically** [ɔː'gænɪkli]
hemp [hemp]	Hanf	 a **hemp** plant
(to) **derive** sth. **from** sth. [dɪ'raɪv]	etwas aus etwas gewinnen, erlangen; etwas aus etwas herleiten, ableiten	Petrol is **~d from** oil. "Happiness" is the noun **~d from** the adjective "happy". verb: (to) **derive** – (L) derivare noun: **derivation (from)** [ˌderɪ'veɪʃn] (Ableitung, Herleitung (von))
viscose ['vɪskəʊz]	Viskose	! stress: **viscose** ['vɪskəʊz]
p. 123 **leak** [liːk]	Leck *(undichte Stelle)*	noun: **leak** – verb: (to) **leak** (auslaufen, entweichen; sickern)
greatly ['greɪtli]	stark, erheblich	Speaking four languages has ~ helped him in his career.

[f] **f**ather · [v] ri**v**er · [s] **s**i**s**ter · [z] plea**s**e · [ʃ] **sh**op · [ʒ] televi**s**ion · [tʃ] tea**ch**er · [dʒ] **G**ermany · [θ] **th**anks · [ð] **th**is · [h] **h**ere

(to) **reduce (by)** [rɪ'dju:s]	reduzieren, verringern (um)	Oh look, they have **~d** the price (**by** £1). verb: (to) **reduce** – Ⓛ reducere noun: **reduction** [rɪ'dʌkʃn] (Reduzierung, Verringerung)
weight [weɪt]	Gewicht	noun: **weight** – I've lost some **weight**. verb: (to) **weigh** – Now I **weigh** less.
parachute ['pærəʃu:t]	Fallschirm	something you wear when you jump from a plane
overboard ['əʊvəbɔ:d]	über Bord	(to) **throw sb. overboard** = jn. über Bord werfen; *(übertragen)* jn. loswerden
(to) **take turns (in** sth.**/to do** sth.**)** [ˌteɪk 'tɜ:nz]	sich abwechseln (bei/mit etwas)	

My turn – your turn …

It's **my turn** / **your turn** / **his turn** / **Ava's turn** to ask a question.	dran sein, an der Reihe sein
Now **take turns in telling** / **to tell** a joke. *or* Now **take it in turns to tell** a joke.	sich abwechseln sich abwechseln
Please give little Jimmy his **turn**, too.	Lasst den kleinen Jimmy auch (mal) drankommen.
Haha! Go to prison and **miss two turns**.	zweimal aussetzen

flow [fləʊ]	Redefluss	Don't interrupt a speaker's ~. That's very impolite.
smooth [smu:ð]	glatt, eben, ruhig	Our trip was very ~.
monotone ['mɒnətəʊn]	monotone Stimme; Monotonie	noun: **monotone** – adj: **monotone** (monoton, ausdruckslos) ❗ stress: **mo**notone ['mɒnətəʊn]

Part C

p. 124	**sentinel** ['sentɪnl]	Wache	= a soldier who guards something
	automatic [ˌɔ:tə'mætɪk]	automatisch	**semi-automatic** = halbautomatisch adj: **automatic** – adv: **automatically** [ˌɔ:tə'mætɪkli] Ⓕ automatique
	rifle ['raɪfl]	Gewehr	 a **rifle**
	immediate [ɪ'mi:diət]	umgehend, sofortig	adj: **immediate** – adv: **immediately**
	gun [gʌn]	Schusswaffe	
	(to) **succeed** [sək'si:d]	Erfolg haben	(to) **succeed in doing sth.** = es schaffen, etwas zu tun verb: (to) **succeed** – noun: **success** – adj: **successful** Ⓛ succedere
	editor-in-chief [ˌedɪtər‿ɪn 'tʃi:f]	Chefredakteur/in	= the person who is responsible for the content of a newspaper
	(to) **lock** [lɒk]	abschließen *(z.B. Tür)*	(to) **lock** ◄► (to) **unlock** (aufschließen, entsperren) (to) **lock sb. in** = jn. einsperren verb: (to) **lock** – noun: **lock** ((Tür-)Schloss)
	(to) **value** ['vælju:]	wertschätzen, schätzen	verb: (to) **value** – noun: **value** (Wert)
	primarily [praɪ'merəli]	vor allem, hauptsächlich, vorrangig	= mainly, most importantly

[i:] green · [i] happy · [ɪ] big · [e] red · [æ] cat · [ɑ:] class · [ɒ] song ·
[ɔ:] door · [u:] blue · [ʊ] book · [ʌ] mum · [ɜ:] girl · [ə] a partner

	(to) **rally** ['ræli]	sich versammeln, sich zusammenscharen	verb: (to) **rally** – noun: **rally** (Versammlung, Kundgebung)
	(to) **go viral** ['vaɪrəl]	sich *(im Internet)* rasend schnell verbreiten *(viral = wie ein Virus)*	In just a few hours, the story of their divorce **has gone** ~. **viral** = Virus- viral
	(to) **show up** [ˌʃəʊ‿'ʌp]	erscheinen, auftauchen	He said he'd come and help us, but he didn't ~ **up**.
	view [vjuː]	Aufruf, Klick *(eines Videos im Internet)*	The video went viral – it had over 2 million ~**s**!
	this + *adv/adj*	so …	*English:* **this fast** – I didn't know that rabbits could move **this fast**. **this long** – The snake was about **this long**. *German:* … **so schnell** / … ungefähr **so lang**
	(to) **maintain** [meɪn'teɪn]	behaupten; beibehalten, aufrecht erhalten; instand halten, unterhalten	They ~**ed** that the other driver caused the accident. We always try everything to ~ our high standards. A castle is very expensive to ~. (L) manu tenere *(in der Hand halten)*
	innovator ['ɪnəveɪtə]	(Er-)Neuerer/(Er-)Neuerin, Wegbereiter/in	• nouns: *(person)* **innovator**; *(introducing sth. new)* **innovation** (Innovation, Neuerung) • adj: **innovative** ['ɪnəveɪtɪv] (innovativ) • verb: (to) **innovate** ['ɪnəveɪt] (Neuerungen einführen; (neu) einführen) (F) innovateur / innovatrice (L) innovare *(erneuern)*
p. 125	(to) **get off your phone**	ein Telefongespräch beenden; aufhören zu telefonieren	I really need your help. Could you please **get** ~ **your phone** just for a minute? I wish more people would **get** ~ **their phones** and start to protest.
p. 127	**exhausted** [ɪg'zɔːstɪd]	erschöpft	When I arrived, I was completely ~. (= very tired)
p. 128	**packaging** ['pækɪdʒɪŋ]	Verpackung	nouns: **packaging** (Verpackung *(generell)*); **package** (*(einzelne)* Verpackung, Schachtel; (Post-)Paket) verb: (to) **package sth. (up)** (etwas verpacken)
	jar [dʒɑː]	Glasgefäß	 three **jars**
	(to) **advise** sb. **to do** sth. [əd'vaɪz]	jm. raten, etwas zu tun	The doctor ~**d** him **to** eat more fruit. The doctor ~**d** him not **to** eat so much meat.
	(to) **swap** [swɒp]	(aus)tauschen	verb: (to) **swap** – noun: **swap** (Tausch)
p. 129	(to) **dominate** ['dɒmɪneɪt]	beherrschen, dominieren	verb: (to) **dominate** – adj: **dominant** (dominant) (L) dominari
	globalization [ˌgləʊbəlaɪ'zeɪʃn]	Globalisierung	noun: **globalization** – verb: (to) **globalize** ['gləʊbəlaɪz] (globalisieren)
	worldwide ['wɜːldwaɪd]	weltweit	= all over the world
	translator [træns'leɪtə]	Übersetzer/in	nouns: *(person)* **translator**; *(what you write out)* **translation** verb: (to) **translate**
	further ['fɜːðə]	weiter	

[eɪ] name · [aɪ] time · [ɔɪ] boy · [əʊ] old ·
[aʊ] town · [ɪə] here · [eə] where · [ʊə] tour

far – farther/further – farthest/furthest

Das Wort **far** hat zwei Steigerungsformen: **farther / further** – **farthest / furthest**.

- Für **räumliche Entfernungen** können beide Formen verwendet werden:
  The park is **farther/further** away than the swimming pool. And the forest is **farthest/furthest** from here.
- Für das deutsche **„weitere(r, s)"**, **„zusätzliche(r, s)"** wird nur der Komparativ **further** verwendet:
  Look at our website for **further** information/details. – Are there any **further** questions?

(to) **replace (with)** [rɪ'pleɪs]	ersetzen (durch), austauschen (gegen)	I sold my car and **~d** it **with** a special bike that can transport goods. verb: (to) **replace** – noun: **replacement** [rɪ'pleɪsmənt] ((das) Austauschen; Ersatz, Ersatz-)
unlike [ˌʌn'laɪk]	anders als, im Gegensatz zu	I'm not a good swimmer, ~ my sister. She swims like a fish. **like** my sister ◄► **unlike** my sister
chunk [tʃʌŋk]	große (Text-/Daten-)Menge; großes Stück, Batzen	I've already written a big ~ of my essay. I bought a big ~ of cheese.
document ['dɒkjumənt]	Dokument; Text(datei)	! stress: **<u>doc</u>ument** ['dɒkjumənt] Ⓕ le document
instant ['ɪnstənt]	sofortig, unmittelbar	adj: **instant** – adv: **instantly** Ⓛ instans
linguistics [lɪŋ'gwɪstɪks]	Linguistik (Sprachwissenschaft)	! Das Wort **linguistics** ist Singular, trotz des **-s**: **Linguistics <u>is</u>** a very interesting subject. nouns: *(science)* **linguistics**; *(person)* **linguist** ['lɪŋgwɪst] (Linguist/in, Sprachwissenschaftler/in) adj: **linguistic** [lɪŋ'gwɪstɪk] (linguistisch, sprachwissenschaftlich) Ⓛ lingua *(Sprache)*
cross-cultural [ˌkrɒs 'kʌltʃərəl]	kulturübergreifend, interkulturell	= representing ideas from two or more different cultures
handy ['hændi]	praktisch, nützlich; griffbereit, zur Hand, in der Nähe	! **handy** = **1.** praktisch, nützlich – With this ~ tool the job is much easier. **2.** griffbereit, zur Hand – Sorry, I don't have a pen ~ … do you have one? (to) **come in handy** = gelegen kommen, sich als nützlich erweisen
(to) **relate** sth. **to** sth. [rɪ'leɪt]	etwas mit etwas in Zusammenhang bringen; etwas zu etwas in Beziehung setzen	

(to) relate – related – relation – relationship

1. (to) **relate to sth.** (to) **relate <u>sth.</u> to sth.**	The text **relates to the situation** of school teachers. Translation machines can't **relate <u>words</u> to context**.	sich auf etwas beziehen in Zusammenhang bringen, in Beziehung setzen
2. related to	I'm sure his bad health is **related to** his lifestyle. Most of her problems are work-**related**.	bedingt durch, bezogen auf, verbunden mit
3. relation [rɪ'leɪʃn]	Speculate about the **relation** between the picture and the title. What are your ideas **in relation to** this problem? What's the number of immigrants **in relation to** the population?	Beziehung, Verhältnis in Bezug auf im Verhältnis zu
4. relationship	Describe the **relationship** between the two main characters.	Beziehung

[b] **boat** · [p] **pool** · [d] **dad** · [t] **ten** · [g] **good** · [k] **cat** ·
[m] **mum** · [n] **no** · [ŋ] **song** · [l] **hello** · [r] **red** · [w] **we** · [j] **you**

	tear [teə]	Riss	! 1. *(verb)* (to) **tear** [teə], **tore, torn** (reißen) 2. *(noun)* **tear** [teə] (Riss) 3. *(noun)* **tear** [tɪə] (Träne)
	poetic [pəʊ'etɪk]	poetisch	adj: **poetic** – nouns: *(person)* **poet** ['pəʊɪt] (Dichter/in); *(the work of a poet)* **poetry**; *(one piece of poetry)* **poem** (F) poétique (L) poeticus, -a, -um
	squirrel ['skwɪrəl]	Eichhörnchen	 a **squirrel**
	short story [ˌʃɔːt 'stɔːri]	Kurzgeschichte	

Access to cultures: English as a lingua franca

p. 136	**lingua franca** [ˌlɪŋgwə 'fræŋkə], *pl* **lingua francas**	Verkehrssprache	English is a **lingua franca** in many parts of the world.
	(to) **rank (by)** [ræŋk]	einstufen; anordnen (nach)	Angelique Kerber was **~ed** number 1 in the world for a while. These articles are **~ed by** price.
	non- [nɒn]	Nicht-	**non**-white; a **non**-stop flight; a **non**-smoking area
	(to) **dub** [dʌb]	synchronisieren	This film isn't **~bed**, but there are English subtitles.
	technical ['teknɪkl]	technisch	! pronunciation: **technical** ['teknɪkl]
	scientific [ˌsaɪən'tɪfɪk]	wissenschaftlich	adj: **scientific** – adv: **scientifically** [ˌsaɪən'tɪfɪkli] nouns: *(what you study)* **science**; *(person)* **scientist** (L) scientia *(Wissen)*
p. 137	(to) **be made up of**	sich zusammensetzen aus; gebildet sein/werden aus	The group **is ~ up of** students from different schools.
	Arabic ['ærəbɪk]	arabisch; Arabisch	! stress: **Arabic** ['ærəbɪk]
	Mediterranean Sea [ˌmedɪtə'reɪniən]	Mittelmeer	**Mediterranean** *(adj)* = Mittelmeer-, mediterran
	purpose ['pɜːpəs]	Absicht, Sinn, Zweck, Ziel	**on purpose** = intentionally I think Dad lost our last chess match **on purpose**. (mit Absicht, absichtlich)
	diplomacy [dɪ'pləʊməsi]	Diplomatie	noun: **diplomacy** [dɪ'pləʊməsi] – adj: **diplomatic** [ˌdɪplə'mætɪk]
	unofficial [ˌʌnə'fɪʃl]	inoffiziell	**official** ◄► **unofficial**
	correctness [kə'rektnəs]	Richtigkeit; Korrektheit	adj: **correct** – Have you checked whether these figures are ~? verb: (to) **correct** – Please ~ this sentence. There's a mistake. noun: **correctness** – Check the ~ of these figures. (L) corrigere *(verbessern)*

usage ['juːsɪdʒ]	(Sprach-)Gebrauch	This sentence shows you the typical ~ of the new phrase. (L) usus
(to) **colonize** ['kɒlənaɪz]	kolonisieren	verb: (to) **colonize** – nouns: *(person)* **colonist**; *(place)* **colony** – adj: **colonial** (L) colonus *(Siedler, Kolonist)*
widespread ['waɪdspred]	(weit) verbreitet	= affecting or existing in a large area or among lots of people
scholar ['skɒlə]	Gelehrte(r)	(L) scholasticus
as to … ['æz tə]	bezüglich …, hinsichtlich …, was … betrifft	**As to** Jill, I don't think she'll be helping you. She's on holiday.
(to) **discourage** [dɪs'kʌrɪdʒ]	unterbinden; entmutigen	(to) **discourage sb. from doing sth.** = jn. (davon) abhalten, etwas zu tun (to) **encourage** ◄► (to) **discourage**
multilingualism [ˌmʌlti'lɪŋgwəlɪzm]	Mehrsprachigkeit	noun: **multilingualism** – adj: **multilingual** [ˌmʌlti'lɪŋgwəl] (mehrsprachig) (L) multi *(viele)* + lingua *(Sprache)*
it is up to sb. **(to do** sth.**)**	es ist jemandes Sache / es liegt an jm. (etwas zu tun)	= it is sb.'s own decision (to do / not to do sth.)

English sounds

[iː] green, he, sea
[i] happy, monkey
[ɪ] big, in, expensive
[e] red, yes, again, breakfast
[æ] cat, animal, apple, black
[ɑː] class, ask, car, park
[ɒ] song, on, dog, what
[ɔː] door, or, ball, four, morning
[uː] blue, ruler, too, two, you
[ʊ] book, good, pullover
[ʌ] mum, bus, colour
[ɜː] girl, early, her, work, T-shirt
[ə] a partner, again, today

[eɪ] name, eight, play, great
[aɪ] time, right, my, I
[ɔɪ] boy, toilet, noise
[əʊ] old, no, road, yellow
[aʊ] town, now, house
[ɪə] here, year, idea
[eə] where, pair, share, their
[ʊə] tour
[b] boat, table, verb
[p] pool, paper, shop
[d] dad, window, good
[t] ten, letter, at

[g] good, again, bag
[k] cat, kitchen, back
[m] mum, man, remember
[n] no, one, ten
[ŋ] song, young, uncle, thanks
[l] hello, like, old, small
[r] red, ruler, friend, sorry
[w] we, where, one
[j] you, yes, uniform
[f] family, after, laugh
[v] river, very, seven, have
[s] sister, poster, yes
[z] please, zoo, quiz, his, music
[ʃ] shop, station, English
[ʒ] television, usually
[tʃ] teacher, child, watch
[dʒ] Germany, job, project, orange

[θ] thanks, three, bathroom
[ð] the, this, father, with
[h] here, who, behind
[x] loch

Am besten kannst du dir die Aussprache der einzelnen Lautzeichen einprägen, wenn du dir zu jedem Zeichen ein einfaches Wort merkst – das [iː] ist der **green**-Laut, das [eɪ] ist der **name**-Laut usw.

Im **Dictionary** kannst du nachschlagen, wenn du wissen möchtest, was ein englisches Wort bedeutet, wie man es ausspricht oder wie es geschrieben wird.

Im **Dictionary** werden folgende **Abkürzungen und Symbole** verwendet:
pl = plural • sb. = somebody • sth. = something • jd. = jemand • jm. = jemandem • jn. = jemanden • js. = jemand(e)s
infml = informal (umgangssprachlich) • *fml = formal* (formell, förmlich)
AE = American English • *BE = British English* • *AusE = Australian English*
° Mit diesem Kringel sind Wörter markiert, die nicht zum Lernwortschatz gehören.

Die **Fundstellenangaben** zeigen, wo ein Wort zum ersten Mal vorkommt:
I = erster Band (Jahrgangsstufe 6) • II = zweiter Band (Jahrgangsstufe 7)
III = dritter Band (Jahrgangsstufe 8) • IV 1 (22) = vierter Band (Jahrgangsstufe 9), Unit 1, Seite 22.

Tipps zur Arbeit mit einem Wörterbuch findest du im Skills File auf Seite 178/179.

A

a [ə] ein, eine I **a 1960s band** eine Band aus den 60er Jahren *(des 20. Jahrhunderts)* II **a bit** ein bisschen, etwas I **a few** ein paar, einige II **a lot** viel I **... a day/week/year** ... pro Tag/Woche/Jahr I
A level (= advanced level) ['eɪ levl] *Prüfungen zur Hochschulzulassungsberechtigung (etwa wie Abitur)* IV 3 (81)
abandon [ə'bændən] zurücklassen, verlassen, im Stich lassen IV 1 (32)
abbreviation [əˌbriːvi'eɪʃn] Abkürzung II
ability [ə'bɪləti] Fähigkeit, Können IV 3 (81)
able ['eɪbl]: **be able to do sth.** etwas tun können; fähig sein / in der Lage sein, etwas zu tun II
aboard [ə'bɔːd] an Bord IV 3 (88)
Aboriginal [ˌæbə'rɪdʒənl] Aborigine- *(die Ureinwohner/-innen Australiens betreffend)* IV 2 (45)
Aboriginal Australian australische/r Ureinwohner/in IV 2 (45)
about [ə'baʊt]:
1. about yourself über dich selbst I **It's about a seagull.** Es geht um eine Möwe. / Es handelt von einer Möwe. I **the best thing about ...** das Beste an ... III **What about ...?** Wie wäre es mit ...? II **What about you?** Und du? / Und was ist mit dir? Und ihr? / Und was ist mit euch? I **What is the story about?** Wovon handelt die Geschichte? / Worum geht es in der Geschichte? I
2. ungefähr I
about 300 people ungefähr 300 Leute I
3. be about to do sth. im Begriff sein, etwas zu tun IV 3 (84)
above [ə'bʌv] über, oberhalb (von); oben, darüber II
abroad [ə'brɔːd] im/ins Ausland IV 1 (19)
absolute ['æbsəluːt] absolut III **absolutely** vollkommen, total *(Adv.)* III
absurd [əb'sɜːd] absurd IV 1 (17)
abuse [ə'bjuːs] Missbrauch IV 2 (59)
abuse (sb./sth.) [ə'bjuːz] (jn./etwas) missbrauchen IV 2 (59)
academic [ˌækə'demɪk]:
1. Akademiker/in, Wissenschaftler/in IV 3 (81)
2. Schul-, akademisch IV 3 (81)
accent ['æksənt] Akzent III
accept [ək'sept] akzeptieren, annehmen IV 2 (47)
access ['ækses]:
1. access (to) Zugang, Zutritt (zu) I
2. access sth. auf etwas zugreifen; Zugang haben zu etwas IV 4 (113)
accessible (to) [ək'sesəbl] erreichbar (für), zugänglich (für) IV 4 (113)
accident ['æksɪdənt] Unfall; Zufall III
by accident zufällig III
according to ... [ə'kɔːdɪŋ] ... zufolge; laut ... III
account [ə'kaʊnt] Account, Konto III
ache [eɪk]:
1. Schmerz(en) IV 3 (96)
stomach ache Bauchschmerzen, Magenschmerzen IV 3 (96)
2. schmerzen, wehtun IV 3 (96)
achieve [ə'tʃiːv] erreichen *(Ziel)*, erzielen *(Resultat)*; zustande bringen IV 2 (62)
achievement [ə'tʃiːvmənt] Errungenschaft, Leistung IV 2 (62)
achiever [ə'tʃiːvə]: **high achiever** leistungsstarke Person, Spitzenkraft IV 3 (107)
acoustics *(pl)* [ə'kuːstɪks] Akustik IV 1 (10)
acquaintance [ə'kweɪntəns] Bekannte(r) IV 4 (116)
across [ə'krɒs]: **across the street** (quer) über die Straße II
act [ækt] schauspielern II **act sth. out** etwas vorspielen I
act [ækt]:
1. Tat, Akt, Handlung IV 1 (14)
2. Verordnung, Gesetz III
action ['ækʃn] Action; Handlung, Tat I
°course of action Vorgehen, Maßnahmen
active ['æktɪv] aktiv IV 1 (40)
activist ['æktɪvɪst] Aktivist/in IV 4 (119)
activity [æk'tɪvəti], *pl* **activities** Aktivität I **free-time activity** Freizeitaktivität I
actor ['æktə] Schauspieler/in I
actual ['æktʃuəl] tatsächliche(r, s), wirkliche(r, s) III
actually ['æktʃuəli] eigentlich; übrigens; tatsächlich III
ad [æd] **(***kurz für:* **advertisement)** Werbespot, Werbung; Anzeige, Inserat III
add (to) [æd] hinzufügen, ergänzen, addieren (zu) I
adder ['ædə] Kreuzotter II
addict ['ædɪkt] Abhängige/r, Süchtige/r IV 4 (112)
addicted (to) [ə'dɪktɪd] süchtig (nach), abhängig (von) IV 4 (112)
addiction (to) [ə'dɪkʃn] Sucht (nach), Abhängigkeit (von) IV 4 (112)
addition [ə'dɪʃn]: **in addition** außerdem IV 2 (50) **in addition to ...** zusätzlich zu ...; neben ... IV 2 (50)
additional [ə'dɪʃənl] zusätzliche(r, s) IV 3 (108)
address [ə'dres] Adresse, Anschrift I
adjective ['ædʒɪktɪv] Adjektiv II
admire [əd'maɪə] bewundern IV 1 (41)
admission (to) [əd'mɪʃn] Zulassung (zu); Einlass, Zutritt (zu), Eintritt IV 3 (88)
°adopt [ə'dɒpt] anwenden *(Maßnahme)*; übernehmen *(Brauch, Sprache)*; adoptieren
adopted [ə'dɒptɪd] adoptiert, Adoptiv- II
adult ['ædʌlt] Erwachsene(r) II
advance [əd'vɑːns] verbessern, voranbringen; voranschreiten, Fortschritte

machen IV 3 (98) **in advance** im Voraus IV 1 (23)
advanced [əd'vɑːnst] fortgeschritten; für Fortgeschrittene IV 3 (98)
advanced level (= A level) [əd'vɑːnst levl] *Prüfungen zur Hochschulzulassungsberechtigung (etwa wie Abitur)* IV 3 (81)
advantage [əd'vɑːntɪdʒ] Vorteil IV 1 (8/9)
adventure [əd'ventʃə] Abenteuer II
adventurous [əd'ventʃərəs] abenteuerlustig; abenteuerlich IV 3 (82)
adverb ['ædvɜːb] Adverb III
advert ['ædvɜːt] **(***kurz für:* **advertisement)** Werbespot, Werbung; Anzeige, Inserat III
advertise ['ædvətaɪz] Werbung machen (für); inserieren III
advertisement [əd'vɜːtɪsmənt] **(***kurz auch:* **ad** *or* **advert)** Werbespot, Werbung; Anzeige, Inserat III
advertising ['ædvətaɪzɪŋ] Werbung, Reklame III
advice [əd'vaɪs] *(no pl)* Rat, Ratschlag, Ratschläge III **Take my advice.** Hör auf meinen Rat. III
advise sb. to do sth. [əd'vaɪz] jm. raten, etwas zu tun IV 4 (128)
advocate ['ædvəkət]:
1. Befürworter/in, Fürsprecher/in IV 4 (110/111)
2. **advocate sth.** etwas befürworten, verfechten IV 4 (110/111)
aerobics [eə'rəʊbɪks] *(sg)* Aerobic IV 1 (15)
affect [ə'fekt] beeinflussen, betreffen, sich auswirken auf IV 3 (88)
afraid [ə'freɪd]: **be afraid (of sth./sb.)** Angst haben (vor etwas/jm.) III **I'm afraid ...** Leider ...; Ich fürchte, ... IV 2 (57)
°**Afro-Caribbean** [ˌæfrəʊ kærɪ'biːən] Afro-karibisch; Afrokaribe/Afrokaribin
after ['ɑːftə]:
1. nach I
after all schließlich (doch) IV 3 (107)
after that danach I **run after sb.** hinter jm. herrennen I
2. nachdem II
afternoon [ˌɑːftə'nuːn] Nachmittag I **in the afternoon** nachmittags, am Nachmittag I **on Monday afternoon** am Montagnachmittag I
again [ə'gen] wieder; noch einmal I **again and again** immer wieder II
against [ə'genst] gegen I
age [eɪdʒ]:
1. Alter I
... is your age ... ist so alt wie du II
It's been ages ... Es ist ewig her ... III
That was ages ago. Das ist ewig her. III
2. Zeitalter III
agency ['eɪdʒənsi] Agentur, Organisation IV 3 (88)
ago [ə'gəʊ]: **two days ago** vor zwei Tagen II
agree [ə'griː]: **agree on sth.** sich auf etwas einigen I **agree to do sth.** einwilligen, etwas zu tun; sich bereit erklären, etwas zu tun IV 4 (112) **agree with sb.** jm. zustimmen I
agricultural [ˌægrɪ'kʌltʃərəl] landwirtschaftlich, Agrar- IV 2 (58)
agriculture ['ægrɪkʌltʃə] Landwirtschaft IV 2 (58)
°**ahead** [ə'hed]: **go ahead with sth.** mit etw. beginnen; etw. durchführen
air [eə] Luft II
airport ['eəpɔːt] Flughafen II
aisle [aɪl] Gang II
aka (= also known as) [ˌeɪ keɪ 'eɪ] alias, auch bekannt als IV 1 (21)
album ['ælbəm] Album II
alert [ə'lɜːt]:
1. Warnung, Alarm IV 4 (112)
2. aufmerksam, *(geistig)* hellwach IV 4 (112)
3. **alert sb. (to sth.)** jn. alarmieren, jn. (vor etwas) warnen IV 4 (112)
°**algebra** ['ældʒɪbrə] Algebra
alive [ə'laɪv]: **be alive** leben, am Leben sein III
all [ɔːl] alles; alle I **all alone** ganz allein II **all around her** überall um sie herum III **all day** den ganzen Tag (lang) I **all in all** alles in allem III **all of Plymouth** ganz Plymouth, das ganze Plymouth I **all over the country / the city / the world** im ganzen Land / in der ganzen Stadt / auf der ganzen Welt II **All the best** Mit besten Grüßen, Alles Gute *(Briefschluss)* IV 1 (23) **all the time** die ganze Zeit II **(not) at all** überhaupt (nicht) IV 4 (115) **after all** schließlich (doch) IV 3 (107) **be all ears** *(infml)* ganz Ohr sein *(gespannt zuhören)* IV 1 (24) **of all time** aller Zeiten II
all right [ɔːl 'raɪt] okay; in Ordnung I
°**alley** ['æli] Gasse
°**alliance** [ə'laɪəns] Bündnis, Allianz
alligator ['ælɪgeɪtə] Alligator III
allow [ə'laʊ] erlauben, zulassen III **be allowed to do sth.** etwas tun dürfen II
°**almond** ['ɑːmənd] Mandel
almost ['ɔːlməʊst] fast, beinahe I
alone [ə'ləʊn] allein II **all alone** ganz allein II **let alone ...** ganz zu schweigen von ..., geschweige denn ... IV 4 (110/111)
along [ə'lɒŋ]:
1. **along the street** die Straße entlang I
2. **come along** mitkommen, herkommen I
aloud [ə'laʊd]: **read aloud** laut (vor) lesen II
already [ɔːl'redi] schon, bereits II
also ['ɔːlsəʊ] auch I
°**alternative** [ɔːl'tɜːnətɪv]:
1. alternativ
2. Alternative
although [ɔːl'ðəʊ] obwohl II
altitude ['æltɪtjuːd] Höhe III
altogether [ˌɔːltə'geðə] insgesamt, alles in allem III
always ['ɔːlweɪz] immer I
am [ˌeɪ‿'em]: **4 am** 4 Uhr morgens I
amazing [ə'meɪzɪŋ] erstaunlich, unglaublich III
ambition [æm'bɪʃn] Ehrgeiz, Bestreben IV 3 (82)
ambitious [æm'bɪʃəs] ehrgeizig IV 3 (82)
°**amethyst** ['æməθɪst] Amethyst *(Schmuckstein)*
among [ə'mʌŋ] unter, zwischen *(mehreren Personen oder Dingen)* IV 2 (48)
amount [ə'maʊnt] Menge; Betrag *(Geld)* IV 3 (101)
amusement [ə'mjuːzmənt] Vergnügung, Unterhaltung IV 3 (95)
amusement park [ə'mjuːzmənt pɑːk] Vergnügungspark IV 3 (95)
an [æn], [ən] ein, eine I **... an hour** ... pro Stunde III
analyse ['ænəlaɪz] analysieren, untersuchen IV 3 (88)
analyses [ə'næləsiːz] *plural of* **analysis**
analysis [ə'næləsɪs], *pl* **analyses** Analyse IV 3 (88)
ancestor ['ænsestə] Vorfahr/in III
°**ancestral** [æn'sestrəl] (...) der Vorfahren, Ahnen-
°**ancient** ['eɪnʃənt] (ur)alt, historisch
and [ænd], [ənd] und I **both ... and ...** sowohl ... als auch ... III
°**anecdote** ['ænɪkdəʊt] Anekdote, Geschichte, persönlicher Bericht
angel ['eɪndʒl] Engel III
°**anger** ['æŋgə] Zorn, Wut
angry ['æŋgri] wütend I **angry with sb.** böse/wütend auf jn. II
animal ['ænɪml] Tier I **state animal** Wappentier II
animal lover ['ænɪml lʌvə] Tierfreund/in IV 2 (66)
°**animate** ['ænɪmeɪt] animieren, beleben
anniversary [ˌænɪ'vɜːsəri] Jahrestag IV 1 (18)
announce [ə'naʊns] verkünden, bekanntgeben; durchsagen IV 3 (90)
announcement [ə'naʊnsmənt] Durchsage, Ansage III
annoy sb. [ə'nɔɪ] jn. ärgern IV 3 (86)
annoyed [ə'nɔɪd] verärgert IV 3 (86)
annoying [ə'nɔɪɪŋ] ärgerlich, nervig IV 3 (86)
anonymous [ə'nɒnɪməs] anonym IV 1 (41)
another [ə'nʌðə]:
1. ein(e) andere(r, s) I
one another sich (gegenseitig), einander III
2. noch ein(e) I

answer ['ɑːnsə]:
1. antworten; beantworten I
answer the phone ans Telefon gehen II
2. Antwort I
ant [ænt] Ameise I
anthem ['ænθəm] Hymne III
any ['eni] jegliche/r/s, jede/r beliebige IV 2 (46) **Are there any …?** Gibt es (irgendwelche) …? I **not … any more** nicht mehr II **There aren't any …** Es gibt/sind keine … I
anybody ['enibɒdi]:
1. (irgend)jemand I
2. jede/r (beliebige) IV 2 (46)
3. not … anybody niemand I
anyone ['eniwʌn]:
1. (irgend)jemand I
2. jede/r (beliebige) IV 2 (46)
3. not … anyone niemand I
anything ['eniθɪŋ]:
1. (irgend)etwas I
2. alles IV 2 (46)
anything but … alles andere als … IV 2 (58)
3. not … anything nichts I
anyway ['eniweɪ]:
1. sowieso IV 2 (55)
2. trotzdem IV 2 (55)
3. Anyway, … Jedenfalls … / Wie dem auch sei … / Aber egal … II
And anyway, … Und überhaupt, … III
anywhere ['eniweə]:
1. überall(hin) IV 1 (22)
2. irgendwo(hin) IV 2 (46)
3. not … anywhere nirgendwo(hin) IV 2 (46)
apart [ə'pɑːt] auseinander; getrennt III
apartment [ə'pɑːtmənt] Wohnung II
ape [eɪp] (Menschen-)Affe IV 2 (64)
apologize (to sb. for sth.) [ə'pɒlədʒaɪz] sich (bei jm. für etwas) entschuldigen IV 2 (59)
apology [ə'pɒlədʒi] Entschuldigung IV 2 (59)
apostrophe [ə'pɒstrəfi] Apostroph, Auslassungszeichen I
app [æp] App IV 1 (14)
appear [ə'pɪə] erscheinen, auftauchen II
appearance [ə'pɪərəns] Erscheinung(sbild), Aussehen IV 2 (64)
apple ['æpl] Apfel IV 3 (109)
applicant ['æplɪkənt] Antragsteller/in, Bewerber/in IV 3 (78/79)
application [ˌæplɪ'keɪʃn] Antrag; Bewerbung IV 3 (78/79)
°**application form** [æplɪ'keɪʃn fɔːm] Bewerbungsformular, Antragsformular
apply [ə'plaɪ]: **apply (to sb. for sth.)** sich (bei jm. um etwas) bewerben IV 2 (47)
appointment [ə'pɔɪntmənt] Verabredung, Termin II
appreciate [ə'priːʃieɪt] (wert)schätzen, zu schätzen wissen IV 2 (64)

apprentice [ə'prentɪs] Lehrling, Auszubildende/r IV 3 (78/79)
apprenticeship [ə'prentɪʃɪp] Ausbildung, Lehre IV 3 (78/79)
approach [ə'prəʊtʃ] sich nähern, herannahen III
appropriate [ə'prəʊpriət] angemessen, passend, geeignet IV 3 (100)
April ['eɪprəl] April I
aquarium [ə'kweəriəm] Aquarium; Aquarienhaus I
°**Arab Spring** [ˌærəb 'sprɪŋ] Arabischer Frühling
Arabic ['ærəbɪk] arabisch; Arabisch IV 4 (137)
arch [ɑːtʃ] Bogen *(Torbogen, Triumphbogen)* IV 2 (49)
architect ['ɑːkɪtekt] Architekt/in III
architecture ['ɑːkɪtektʃə] Architektur IV 3 (97)
archive ['ɑːkaɪv] Archiv IV 1 (10)
arduous ['ɑːdjuəs] beschwerlich IV 2 (58)
are [ɑː] bist; sind; seid I **The DVDs are …** Die DVDs kosten … I
area ['eəriə] Bereich; Gebiet, Gegend I
aren't [ɑːnt]: **you aren't … (= you are not)** du bist nicht …; du bist kein/e …; ihr seid nicht …; ihr seid kein/e … I
argue ['ɑːgjuː]:
1. streiten; sich streiten III
2. argumentieren; behaupten IV 2 (50)
argument ['ɑːgjumənt]:
1. Argument III
2. Streit, Auseinandersetzung III
argumentative [ˌɑːgju'mentətɪv] argumentativ; streitsüchtig IV 2 (50)
argumentative writing [ɑːgjuˌmentətɪv 'raɪtɪŋ] Erörterung, Argumentation IV 2 (50)
°**arid** ['ærɪd] trocken, dürr
arm [ɑːm] Arm II
armchair ['ɑːmtʃeə] Sessel I
army ['ɑːmi] Armee III
aroma [ə'rəʊmə] Duft, Aroma IV 1 (19)
around [ə'raʊnd]:
1. around … um … herum II
around the lake um den See (herum) II **all around her** überall um sie herum III
2. around the library in der Bücherei umher, durch die Bücherei I
3. walk/run/… around herum-, umherrennen/-gehen II
arrange [ə'reɪndʒ] anordnen I
arrest [ə'rest] verhaften, festnehmen III
arrival [ə'raɪvl] Ankunft II
arrive [ə'raɪv] ankommen, eintreffen I
art [ɑːt] Kunst I **work of art** Kunstwerk III
article ['ɑːtɪkl] Artikel II
artist ['ɑːtɪst] Künstler/in II
artwork ['ɑːtwɜːk] Kunstwerk III

°**arvo** ['ɑːvəʊ] *(AusE, infml)*, *pl* **arvos** Nachmittag *(kurz für „afternoon")*
as [æz]:
1. als, während II
2. da, weil III
3. wie II
(not) as big as (nicht) so groß wie II
as a child als Kind II **just as big** genauso groß III **as if** als ob III **as soon as** sobald, sowie III **as to …** bezüglich …, hinsichtlich …, was … betrifft IV 4 (137) **as well** auch, ebenso III **… as well as …** sowohl … als auch … IV 2 (76)
ash [æʃ] Asche III **ashes** *(pl)* Asche *(sterbliche Überreste)* III
ask [ɑːsk] fragen I **ask a question** eine Frage stellen I **ask for sth.** um etwas bitten II **ask sb. out** sich mit jm. verabreden IV 4 (115) **ask sb. the way** jn. nach dem Weg fragen II **ask sb. to do sth.** jemanden bitten, etwas zu tun I
asleep [ə'sliːp]: **be asleep** schlafen II
aspect ['æspekt] Aspekt IV 2 (59)
assembly [ə'sembli] Schulversammlung IV 4 (112)
assess [ə'ses] beurteilen, bewerten IV 3 (80)
assessment [ə'sesmənt] Beurteilung, Bewertung IV 3 (80)
°**assign sth. to sb.** [ə'saɪn] jm. etwas zuweisen, zuteilen
assignment [ə'saɪnmənt] *(AE)* Aufgabe, Arbeitsauftrag *(in der Schule oder daheim zu erledigen)* III
assist (with) [ə'sɪst] assistieren, helfen (bei) IV 3 (95) **How may we assist?** Wie können wir Ihnen helfen/behilflich sein? IV 3 (95)
assistant [ə'sɪstənt] Verkäufer/in II
Associate's degree [ə'səʊsiəts dɪgriː], [ə'səʊʃiəts dɪgriː] Associate Degree *(Abschluss eines US-amerikanischen oder kanadischen College nach 2 Jahren)* IV 3 (108)
association [əˌsəʊsi'eɪʃn], [əˌsəʊʃi'eɪʃn] Verband, Vereinigung IV 2 (76)
astronaut ['æstrənɔːt] Astronaut/in III
at [æt], [ət]:
1. *(in Ortsangaben)* an, bei, in I
at 14 Dean Street in der Dean Street 14 I **at Grandma's** bei Oma II **at home** zu Hause, daheim I **at school** in der Schule I **at the top (of)** oben, am oberen Ende (von) II
2. *(in Zeitangaben)* um, an I
at first zuerst, anfangs, am Anfang II
at lunchtime mittags I **at night** nachts, in der Nacht I **at one time** zur selben Zeit, gleichzeitig III **at the moment** gerade, im Moment I **at the weekend** am Wochenende I
3. at last endlich, schließlich I
at least zumindest, wenigstens II

ate [et], [eɪt] *siehe* **eat**
Atlantic [ət'læntɪk]: **the Atlantic (Ocean)** der Atlantik, der Atlantische Ozean II
atmosphere ['ætməsfɪə] Atmosphäre; Stimmung II
°**attach (to)** [ə'tætʃ] anfügen; anhängen (an) *(Brief, E-Mail)* **be attached to sth.** an etwas hängen (befestigt sein); an etwas angehängt/beigeheftet sein III
°**attachment** [ə'tætʃmənt] Anhang *(E-Mail)*
attack [ə'tæk]:
1. angreifen II
2. Angriff II
attempt [ə'tempt]:
1. Versuch IV 2 (58)
2. versuchen IV 2 (58)
attend [ə'tend] (hin)gehen zu, teilnehmen (an); besuchen IV 2 (54)
attention [ə'tenʃn] Aufmerksamkeit IV 2 (48) **pay attention (to)** achten (auf), aufpassen (auf) IV 2 (48)
attic ['ætɪk] Dachboden I **in the attic** auf dem Dachboden I
attitude (to/towards) ['ætɪtjuːd] Einstellung, (Geistes-)Haltung (zu/gegenüber) III
attract [ə'trækt] anziehen, anlocken IV 1 (19) **attract sb. to sb./sth.** jn. zu jm./etwas hinziehen IV 4 (116) **be attracted to sb.** sich zu jm. hingezogen fühlen, sich von jm. angezogen fühlen IV 4 (116)
attraction [ə'trækʃn] Attraktion; Anziehungspunkt III
attractive [ə'træktɪv] attraktiv IV 4 (116)
audience ['ɔːdiəns] Publikum, Zuschauer/innen, Zuhörer/innen II
audio ['ɔːdiəʊ] Audio-, Ton- IV 1 (10)
audition [ɔː'dɪʃn] Vorsprechen, Vorsingen, Vorspielen II
August ['ɔːgəst] August I
aunt [ɑːnt] Tante I
°**Aussie** ['ɒzi] *(infml)*:
1. Australier/in
2. australisch
°**Australian Rules football** [ɒstreɪliən ruːlz 'fʊtbɔːl] Australian Rules football *(australische Football-Variante)*
author ['ɔːθə] Autor/in I
authority [ɔː'θɒrəti] Behörde IV 2 (58) **local authority** Gemeinde(behörde), Kommune/Kommunalbehörde IV 2 (58)
automatic [ˌɔːtə'mætɪk] automatisch IV 4 (124)
automatically [ɔːtə'mætɪkli] automatisch *(Adv.)* IV 4 (124)
autumn ['ɔːtəm] Herbst I
available [ə'veɪləbl] erhältlich, verfügbar; erreichbar *(am Telefon)* III
avenue ['ævənjuː] Allee, Boulevard III
average ['ævərɪdʒ] durchschnittlich; Durchschnitt III **on average** im Durchschnitt, durchschnittlich III
aviation [ˌeɪvi'eɪʃn] Luftfahrt IV 4 (118)
avoid [ə'vɔɪd] (ver)meiden III
award [ə'wɔːd]:
1. Preis *(Auszeichnung)* IV 2 (62)
2. **award sb. sth.** *or* **sth. to sb.** jm. etwas zuerkennen, zusprechen, verleihen IV 2 (62)
away [ə'weɪ] weg, fort I
awesome ['ɔːsəm] *(bes. AE, infml)* klasse, großartig III
awful ['ɔːfl] schrecklich, fürchterlich II

B

baby ['beɪbi] Baby IV 2 (66)
baby seal ['beɪbi siːl] Robbenjunges; Heuler I
babysat ['beɪbisæt] *siehe* **babysit**
babysit ['beɪbisɪt], **babysat, babysat** babysitten IV 3 (91)
bachelor's degree ['bætʃələz dɪgriː] Bachelor(-Abschluss) IV 3 (108)
back [bæk]:
1. zurück I
back in Ottawa zu Hause in Ottawa IV 1 (11)
2. Rücken II
from the back of the bus aus dem hinteren Teil des Busses II
back sth. up [ˌbæk‿'ʌp] etwas belegen; etwas untermauern, etwas bekräftigen IV 1 (29)
background ['bækgraʊnd] Hintergrund I **background file** Hintergrundinformation(en) I
backpack ['bækpæk] Rucksack III
backwards ['bækwədz] rückwärts, nach hinten IV 1 (32)
backyard [bæk'jɑːd] *(AE)* (Hinter-)Hof; Garten hinter dem Haus IV 2 (53)
bacon ['beɪkən] Schinkenspeck II
bad [bæd] schlecht, schlimm I
badge [bædʒ] Anstecknadel, Button; Abzeichen IV 2 (66)
badminton ['bædmɪntən] Badminton, Federball IV 3 (93)
bag [bæg] Tasche, Beutel, Tüte I
school bag Schultasche I
bake [beɪk] backen III
baker ['beɪkə] Bäcker/in IV 1 (22)
baker's shop ['beɪkəz ʃɒp] Bäckerei IV 1 (22)
bakery ['beɪkəri] Bäckerei IV 1 (22)
balcony ['bælkəni] Balkon III
ball [bɔːl] Ball I
balloon [bə'luːn] (Luft-)Ballon II
band [bænd] Band, Musikgruppe I
bandmate ['bændmeɪt] Bandkollege/-kollegin IV 4 (125)
bang [bæŋ] Knall III
bank [bæŋk]:
1. Bank *(Geldinstitut)* III
2. Flussufer III
°**banner** ['bænə] Spruchband, Transparent
bar [bɑː]:
1. Riegel *(Schokolade, Müsli)*; Tafel *(Schokolade)* III
2. Stange, Balken, (Gitter-)Stab IV 2 (58)
behind bars hinter Gittern IV 2 (58)
bar chart ['bɑː tʃɑːt] Balkendiagramm IV 4 (122)
barbecue ['bɑːbɪkjuː] Grill; Grillfest/-party III
°**barbie** ['bɑːbi] *(AusE, infml)* Grillparty *(kurz für „barbecue")*
barely ['beəli] kaum IV 3 (107)
bark [bɑːk] bellen I
barman ['bɑːmən], *pl* **barmen** Barkeeper III
barn [bɑːn] Scheune, Stadel II
barrel ['bærəl] Fass IV 1 (41)
°**barrier** ['bæriə] Barriere
base sth. on sth. [beɪs] etwas auf etwas gründen, etwas als Grundlage benutzen für etwas IV 2 (49)
baseball ['beɪsbɔːl] Baseball II
basic ['beɪsɪk] einfach, elementar, Grund- IV 3 (98)
basically ['beɪsɪkli] im Prinzip, grundsätzlich IV 3 (98)
basics *(pl)* ['beɪsɪks] Grundlagen; *(das)* Wesentliche IV 3 (98)
basket ['bɑːskɪt] Korb I
basketball ['bɑːskɪtbɔːl] Basketball I
bath [bɑːθ] Bad II
bathroom ['bɑːθruːm]:
1. Badezimmer, Bad I
2. *(AE)* Toilette *(in privaten Häusern/Wohnungen)* IV 4 (112)
battery ['bætəri] Batterie, Akku III
battle ['bætl] Schlacht; Kampf II
Bavaria [bə'veəriə] Bayern I
°**Bavarian** [bə'veəriən] bayerisch; Bayer/in
bcc (= blind carbon copy (to)) [ˌblaɪnd kɑːbən 'kɒpi] Blindkopie (an) *(in E-Mails)* IV 1 (23)
BCE (= before the Common Era) [bɪˌfɔː ðə kɒmən‿'ɪərə] vor Christus (= vor der Christlichen Zeitrechnung) IV 1 (19)
be [bi], **was/were, been** sein I
beach [biːtʃ] Strand I
bean [biːn] Bohne III
bear [beə] Bär I
beard [bɪəd] Bart II
beat [biːt], **beat, beaten** schlagen; besiegen III
beaten ['biːtn] *siehe* **beat**
beautiful ['bjuːtɪfl] schön I
became [bɪ'keɪm] *siehe* **become**
because [bɪ'kɒz] weil I
because of [bɪ'kɒz‿əv] wegen IV 1 (11)

become [bɪˈkʌm], **became, become** werden I
bed [bed] Bett I
bed & breakfast [ˌbed‿ən ˈbrekfəst] Frühstückspension; Zimmer mit Frühstück III
bedroom [ˈbedruːm] Schlafzimmer I
beef [biːf] Rindfleisch II **roast beef** Rinderbraten I
been [biːn] *siehe* **be** **Have you ever been to …?** Bist du jemals in … gewesen? II
beep [biːp] piepen II
before [bɪˈfɔː]:
1. bevor I
2. vor I
before long schon bald III **before school/lessons** vor der Schule *(vor Schulbeginn)* / vorm Unterricht I
3. (vorher) schon mal II
not/never before (vorher) noch nie II
began [bɪˈgæn] *siehe* **begin**
begin [bɪˈgɪn], **began, begun** beginnen, anfangen II
beginner [bɪˈgɪnə] Anfänger/in III
beginning [bɪˈgɪnɪŋ] Anfang, Beginn III
begun [bɪˈgʌn] *siehe* **begin**
behave [bɪˈheɪv] sich verhalten, sich benehmen III
behaviour [bɪˈheɪvjə] *(AE* **behavior)** Verhalten; Benehmen IV 2 (64)
behind [bɪˈhaɪnd] hinter I **from behind** von hinten II
°**being** [ˈbiːɪŋ] (Lebe-)Wesen
belief (in) [bɪˈliːf] Glaube (an) III
believe (in) [bɪˈliːv] glauben (an) II
bell [bel] Klingel, Glocke I
belong [bɪˈlɒŋ] dazugehören; (hin)gehören IV 2 (64) **belong to sb.** jm. gehören; zu jm. gehören III
belonging [bɪˈlɒŋɪŋ] Zusammengehörigkeit(sgefühl); Zugehörigkeit IV 2 (64)
below [bɪˈləʊ] unter, unterhalb (von); unten, darunter III
°**bench** [bentʃ] Bank *(zum Sitzen)*
bend [bend], **bent, bent**: **bend down** sich hinunterbeugen, sich bücken III **bend over** sich bücken, sich vorbeugen IV 1 (34)
bent [bent] *siehe* **bend**
besides [bɪˈsaɪdz] außerdem III
best [best] beste(r, s) I **All the best** Mit besten Grüßen / Alles Gute *(Briefschluss)* IV 1 (23) **the best …** der/die/das beste …, die besten … I **the best thing about …** das Beste an … III
bet [bet], **bet, bet** wetten III
better [ˈbetə] besser I **better than ever** besser als je zuvor II **I'd better … (= I had better …)** Ich sollte lieber … III
between [bɪˈtwiːn] zwischen I
beverage [ˈbevərɪdʒ] Getränk IV 3 (95)

beyond … [bɪˈjɒnd] über … hinaus, jenseits von …, weiter als … III
big [bɪg] groß I **big wheel** Riesenrad I
bike [baɪk] Fahrrad I **ride a bike** Rad fahren I
bilingual [baɪˈlɪŋgwəl] zweisprachig III
bill [bɪl] Rechnung IV 1 (26)
billion [ˈbɪliən] Milliarde IV 3 (109)
billionaire [ˌbɪljəˈneə] Milliardär/in IV 3 (109)
°**billow** [ˈbɪləʊ] sich aufblähen, sich aufbauschen
bind [baɪnd], **bound, bound** (ver)binden IV 4 (110/111)
biodiversity [ˌbaɪəʊdaɪˈvɜːsəti] Artenvielfalt IV 3 (88)
biologist [baɪˈɒlədʒɪst] Biologe/Biologin IV 3 (88)
biology [baɪˈɒlədʒi] Biologie IV 3 (88)
bird [bɜːd] Vogel I
birth [bɜːθ] Geburt I
birth certificate [ˈbɜːθ sətɪfɪkət] Geburtsurkunde IV 3 (108)
birthday [ˈbɜːθdeɪ] Geburtstag I **My birthday is in May.** Ich habe im Mai Geburtstag. I **My birthday is on 5th May.** Ich habe am 5. Mai Geburtstag. I **When's your birthday?** Wann hast du Geburtstag? I
birthplace [ˈbɜːθpleɪs] Geburtsort II
biscuit [ˈbɪskɪt] Plätzchen, Keks I
bit [bɪt]:
1. *siehe* **bite**
2. Stück(chen), Teil III
a bit ein bisschen, etwas I
bite [baɪt]:
1. Biss, Bissen III
2. **bite, bit, bitten** beißen I
bitten [ˈbɪtn] *siehe* **bite**
bitter [ˈbɪtə] erbittert; verbittert; bitter IV 1 (12)
bitterness [ˈbɪtənəs] Bitterkeit, Verbitterung IV 1 (12)
black [blæk] schwarz I
blame [bleɪm]:
1. **blame sb.** jm. die Schuld geben, es jm. übelnehmen IV 2 (64)
2. **put the blame (for sth.)on sb.** jm. (an etwas) die Schuld geben IV 2 (64)
°**blank** [blæŋk] freie Stelle, Leerstelle *(in einem Text)*
blanket [ˈblæŋkɪt] Decke *(zum Zudecken)* III
blast [blɑːst] *(infml)*: **have a blast** einen Mordsspaß haben IV 3 (89)
blew [bluː] *siehe* **blow**
block [blɒk]:
1. (Häuser-, Wohn-)Block III
2. blockieren, sperren III
blog [blɒg] Blog II
blond [blɒnd] *(bei Frauen oft:* blonde*)* blond I
blood [blʌd] Blut III
bloom [bluːm] blühen III

blow [bləʊ], **blew, blown**: **blow sth. out** etwas auspusten, ausblasen II **blow sth. up** etwas in die Luft sprengen IV 1 (41) **blow the horn** hupen III **blow the whistle** pfeifen *(auf der Trillerpfeife)* III
blown [bləʊn] *siehe* **blow**
blue [bluː] blau I
blueberry [ˈbluːbəri] Blaubeere, Heidelbeere II
board [bɔːd]:
1. (Wand-)Tafel I
°2. **(game) board** (Spiel-)Brett
board game [ˈbɔːd geɪm] Brettspiel III
°**boarding call** [ˈbɔːdɪŋ kɔːl] Aufruf zum Einsteigen
boarding pass [ˈbɔːdɪŋ pɑːs] Bordkarte II
boarding school [ˈbɔːdɪŋ skuːl] Internat II
boat [bəʊt] Boot, Schiff I
boating [ˈbəʊtɪŋ] Bootfahren, Bootsfahrt IV 3 (89)
body [ˈbɒdi]:
1. Körper I
part of the body Körperteil II
2. Leiche III
3. Hauptteil *(eines Textes)* III
bonfire [ˈbɒnfaɪə] *(großes Freuden-)* Feuer IV 1 (40)
boo [buː] buhen; ausbuhen IV 2 (64)
book [bʊk] Buch I
bookshop [ˈbʊkʃɒp] Buchladen, Buchhandlung I
°**bookstore** [ˈbʊkstɔː] *(AE)* Buchladen, Buchhandlung
boom [buːm]:
1. Boom *(Hochkonjunktur)* IV 2 (59)
2. boomen *(Wirtschaft, Geschäft)* IV 2 (59)
°**boomerang** [ˈbuːməræŋ] Bumerang
boot [buːt] Stiefel II
border [ˈbɔːdə] Grenze III
bored [bɔːd]: **be/feel bored** gelangweilt sein, sich langweilen II
boring [ˈbɔːrɪŋ] langweilig I
born [bɔːn]: **be born** geboren sein/werden III
borough [ˈbʌrə], [ˈbɜːrəʊ] (Stadt-)Bezirk III
borrow [ˈbɒrəʊ] (aus)leihen, sich borgen IV 2 (57)
boss [bɒs] Boss, Chef/in IV 3 (82)
bossy [ˈbɒsi] herrisch, rechthaberisch IV 3 (82)
botanic garden [bəˌtænɪk ˈgɑːdn] botanischer Garten IV 2 (46)
both [bəʊθ] beide II **both … and …** sowohl … als auch … III
bottle [ˈbɒtl] Flasche I
bottom [ˈbɒtəm]:
1. **at the bottom (of)** unten, am unteren Ende (von) II
°2. Unterteil *(Kleidung; z.B. Hose, Rock)*
bought [bɔːt] *siehe* **buy**

bouldering ['bəʊldərɪŋ] Bouldern *(Klettern in Absprunghöhe, ohne Seil)* III
bound [baʊnd] *siehe* **bind**
bow [baʊ] sich verbeugen, sich verneigen II
bowl [bəʊl] Schüssel II
box [bɒks] Kasten, Kiste, Kästchen I
Boxing Day ['bɒksɪŋ deɪ] 2. Weihnachtstag (26. Dezember) I
boy [bɔɪ] Junge, Bub I
boyfriend ['bɔɪfrend] (fester) Freund III
°**bracket** ['brækɪt] Klammer
°**brain** [breɪn] Gehirn
°**brainstorm** ['breɪnstɔːm] Ideen (ungeordnet) sammeln
branch [brɑːntʃ] Ast, Zweig, (Neben-)Arm; Zweigstelle, Filiale IV 4 (121)
brand [brænd] Marke, Markenname *(bei Produkten)* IV 1 (19)
brass band [ˌbrɑːs 'bænd] (Blech-)Blaskapelle III
brave [breɪv] mutig, tapfer IV 3 (86)
bread [bred] Brot I
break [breɪk] Pause I
break [breɪk], **broke, broken:**
1. zerbrechen, kaputt machen I
break up (with sb.) Schluss machen (mit jm.), sich trennen (von jm.) IV 4 (116)
2. brechen, kaputt gehen I
breakfast ['brekfəst] Frühstück I **bed & breakfast** Frühstückspension; Zimmer mit Frühstück III **have breakfast** frühstücken I
breath [breθ] Atem, Atemzug II **..., he said under his breath.** ..., sagte er flüsternd / murmelte er. III
°**breathe (in/out)** [briːð] (ein-/aus-)atmen
breeze [briːz] Brise III
brick [brɪk] Ziegelstein; Ziegel- IV 1 (27)
bridge [brɪdʒ] Brücke II
briefly ['briːfli] in Kürze, in wenigen Worten IV 2 (50)
bright [braɪt] strahlend, leuchtend, hell I
brilliant ['brɪliənt] großartig, genial, glänzend II
bring [brɪŋ], **brought, brought** (mit-, her)bringen I **bring in** *(hay)* einbringen *(Heu)* II
British ['brɪtɪʃ] britisch I
°**bro** [brəʊ] *(infml für* **brother)** Bruder, Kumpel
°**broadcast** ['brɔːdkɑːst], **broadcast, broadcast** senden *(in Rundfunk und Fernsehen)*
broccoli ['brɒkəli] Brokkoli IV 4 (114)
brochure ['brəʊʃə] Broschüre, Prospekt III
broke [brəʊk] *siehe* **break**
broken ['brəʊkən]:
1. *siehe* **break**
2. zerbrochen, kaputt; gebrochen II
°**bronze** [brɒnz] Bronze; aus Bronze
brother ['brʌðə] Bruder I
brought [brɔːt] *siehe* **bring**

brown [braʊn] braun I
brownie ['braʊni] *Stück eines flachen Schokoladenkuchens, oft mit Nüssen* IV 4 (120)
buck [bʌk] *(infml für:* **dollar)** Dollar III
bucket ['bʌkɪt] Eimer II
buddy ['bʌdi] *(infml)* Freund/in, Kumpel III
°**budget** ['bʌdʒɪt] Etat, Budget
build [bɪld], **built, built** bauen II
building ['bɪldɪŋ] Gebäude II
built [bɪlt] *siehe* **build**
bully ['bʊli]:
1. Mobber/in, Tyrann/in IV 2 (64)
2. tyrannisieren, mobben IV 2 (64)
bump into sb. [bʌmp] *(infml)* jn. zufällig treffen, jm. zufällig begegnen; mit jm. zusammenstoßen IV 2 (53)
bunch [bʌntʃ] *(infml)*: **a bunch of ...** eine Menge ...; eine Gruppe ... *(von Menschen)* IV 4 (119)
buoy [bɔɪ], ['buːi] Boje III
burger ['bɜːgə] Hamburger II
burn [bɜːn]:
1. brennen; verbrennen III
°2. (Wald-)Brand, (Busch-)Feuer; Verbrennung
burst [bɜːst], **burst, burst** platzen III
bury ['beri] begraben, beerdigen III
bus [bʌs] Bus I **go by bus** mit dem Bus fahren I
bush [bʊʃ] Busch, Strauch *(auch: unerschlossenes, „wildes" Land in Australien u. Afrika)* III
bush fire ['bʊʃ faɪə] Buschfeuer, Buschbrand IV 2 (45)
business ['bɪznəs] Geschäft, Geschäfts-; Unternehmen, Betrieb IV 2 (46)
busy ['bɪzi] belebt, geschäftig, hektisch III **be busy** beschäftigt sein; viel zu tun haben I
but [bʌt], [bət]:
1. aber I
2. sondern IV 4 (112)
all but ... alle außer ...; nur ... IV 4 (112)
anything but ... alles andere als ... IV 2 (58) **anywhere but ...** überall außer ... / überall, nur nicht ... IV 4 (112)
nobody but ... niemand außer ...; nur ... IV 4 (112) **nothing but ...** nichts außer ..., nichts als ...; nur IV 4 (112)
we are but ... wir sind nur ..., wir sind nichts (anderes) als ... IV 4 (110/111)
butterfly ['bʌtəflaɪ] Schmetterling I
button ['bʌtn] Knopf; Button; Schaltfläche IV 4 (119)
button-down shirt [ˌbʌtn daʊn 'ʃɜːt] Button-down-Hemd *(dessen Kragenspitzen mit Knöpfen befestigt werden)* IV 4 (119)
buy [baɪ], **bought, bought** kaufen I
°**buzz group** ['bʌz gruːp] Murmelgruppe *(für kurze Zeit gebildete Kleingruppe zum Ideenaustausch/Lösen einer Aufgabe)*
by [baɪ]:
1. **by ...** von ... II

2. **by the sea** am Meer I
3. **go by car/bus/...** mit dem Auto/Bus/... fahren I
4. **by 8 am** bis (spätestens) 8 Uhr morgens III
by the time als; wenn IV 1 (35)
5. **by accident** zufällig III
by mistake aus Versehen III **by the way** übrigens III **by type/size/...** geordnet nach Typ/Größe/...; abhängig von Typ/Größe/... IV 4 (122) **call you by your name** dich beim Namen / bei deinem Namen nennen IV 2 (59) **one by one** einer nach dem anderen II
Bye. [baɪ] *(auch:* **Bye-bye.**) Servus. / Auf Wiedersehen. I
byline ['baɪlaɪn] *Zeile mit Angabe des Verfassers/der Verfasserin eines Zeitungsartikels* IV 1 (19)

C

cabin ['kæbɪn] Hütte; Kabine III
cabinet ['kæbɪnət] Kabinett, Regierung IV 1 (43)
café ['kæfeɪ] Café I
cafeteria [ˌkæfə'tɪəriə] *(AE)* Kantine; Cafeteria IV 4 (112)
cage [keɪdʒ] Käfig I
cake [keɪk] Kuchen I
calendar ['kælɪndə] Kalender III
call [kɔːl]:
1. anrufen; rufen; nennen I
call out the names die Namen aufrufen II **call sb. names** jn. beschimpfen, jm. Schimpfwörter nachrufen IV 2 (64)
call sb. out on sth. jn. wegen etwas zur Rede stellen IV 2 (64) **call sth. out** etwas anprangern IV 2 (64) °**boarding call** Aufruf zum Einsteigen
2. Anruf; Telefongespräch I
called [kɔːld]: **be called** heißen, genannt werden I
caller ['kɔːlə] Anrufer/in II
calm [kɑːm] ruhig III
came [keɪm] *siehe* **come**
camel ['kæml] Kamel IV 2 (45)
camera ['kæmərə] Fotoapparat, Kamera I **video camera** Videokamera I
cameraman ['kæmrəmæn], *pl* **cameramen** Kameramann I
camp [kæmp] (Zelt-)Lager IV 3 (82)
campaign [kæm'peɪn] Kampagne, Aktion IV 1 (42)
camper ['kæmpə] Camper/in IV 3 (91)
camping ['kæmpɪŋ] Camping, Zelten II **go camping** zelten/campen gehen II
campsite ['kæmpsaɪt] Zeltplatz II
campus ['kæmpəs], *pl* **campuses** Campus, Unigelände IV 3 (89)
can [kæn], [kən]:
1. können I
we can't ..., we cannot ... wir können nicht ... I

2. dürfen I
can [kæn] Dose III
°**cancel** ['kænsl] streichen, absagen
candidate ['kændɪdət] Bewerber/in, Kandidat/in IV 1 (42)
candle ['kændl] Kerze I
canoe [kə'nu:]:
1. Kanu, Paddelboot IV 2 (77)
2. Kanu fahren, paddeln IV 2 (77)
canoeing [kə'nu:ɪŋ] Paddeln, Kanusport IV 2 (77)
canteen [kæn'ti:n] Kantine, (Schul-) Mensa I
cap [kæp] Mütze, Kappe II
capable (of) ['keɪpəbl] fähig (zu), imstande (zu) III
°**cape** [keɪp] Kap
capital ['kæpɪtl] Hauptstadt I
capital letter [ˌkæpɪtl 'letə] Großbuchstabe I
captain ['kæptɪn] Kapitän/in I
caption ['kæpʃn] Bildunterschrift I
capture ['kæptʃə] einnehmen, in Besitz nehmen; gefangen nehmen III
car [kɑ:] Auto I **go by car** mit dem Auto fahren I
caravan ['kærəvæn] Wohnwagen II
carbon dioxide (CO_2) [ˌkɑ:bən daɪ'ɒksaɪd] Kohlendioxid IV 4 (122)
card (to) [kɑ:d] Karte (an) I
care [keə]:
1. **care about sth.** etwas wichtig nehmen III
I don't care about money. Geld ist mir egal. III **I really care about animals.** Tiere liegen mir sehr am Herzen. / Tiere sind mir sehr wichtig. III
People don't care. Es ist den Leuten egal. III **Who cares?** Na und? / Wen interessiert das? III °**care for** aufpassen auf, pflegen; sich kümmern um
2. **take care of sb./sth.** sich (gut) um jn./etwas kümmern; auf jn. aufpassen IV 3 (94)
career [kə'rɪə] Karriere; (schulischer/beruflicher) Werdegang IV 2 (64)
careful ['keəfl] vorsichtig I
carefully ['keəfəli] aufmerksam; sorgfältig III
carnival ['kɑ:nɪvl] Karneval, Fasching III
carpenter ['kɑ:pəntə] Tischler/in, Zimmerer/Zimmerin III
carrot ['kærət] Möhre, Karotte III
carry ['kæri] tragen III **carry out** durchführen IV 3 (88)
carry-on bag ['kæri‿ɒn] Handgepäckstück, (kleine) Reisetasche II
cart [kɑ:t] Karren I
°**cartoon** [kɑ:'tu:n] Comic
°**carve** [kɑ:v] meißeln, schnitzen; *(in Stein)* hauen
case [keɪs]:
1. Fall IV 1 (22)
2. **in (the) case of** im Falle von IV 1 (22)
in case ... falls ...; für den Fall, dass ... IV 1 (22)
cash desk ['kæʃ desk] Kasse *(in Geschäften)* II
°**cassowary** ['kæsəweəri] Kasuar *(Straußvogel)*
cast [kɑ:st] Besetzung; Mitwirkende *(Theaterstück, Film)* II
castle ['kɑ:sl] Burg, Schloss I
cat [kæt] Katze I
catastrophe [kə'tæstrəfi] Katastrophe IV 2 (58)
catastrophic [ˌkætə'strɒfɪk] katastrophal, verhängnisvoll IV 2 (58)
catch [kætʃ], **caught, caught**:
1. fangen I
Catch you later. *(infml)* Bis später dann! IV 1 (11)
2. **catch a bus/ferry/...** einen Bus/eine Fähre nehmen; einen Bus/eine Fähre (noch) erwischen IV 2 (46)
°**catchy** ['kætʃi] eingängig *(Lied, Slogan)*
category ['kætəgəri] Kategorie IV 2 (46)
cathedral [kə'θi:drəl] Kathedrale, Dom III
Catholic ['kæθlɪk] Katholik/in; katholisch III
°**catwalk** ['kætwɔ:k] Laufplanke, Steg; Laufsteg
caught [kɔ:t] *siehe* **catch**
cause [kɔ:z]:
1. Ursache IV 2 (76)
2. **cause sth.** etwas bewirken, verursachen III
caution ['kɔ:ʃn] Vorsicht IV 3 (82)
cautious ['kɔ:ʃəs] vorsichtig IV 3 (82)
cave [keɪv] Höhle II
cc (= carbon copy (to)) [ˌkɑ:bən 'kɒpi] Nachrichtlich:, Kopie (an) *(in E-Mails)* IV 1 (23)
CE (= Common Era) [ˌkɒmən‿'ɪərə] Christliche Zeitrechnung IV 1 (19)
celebrate ['selɪbreɪt] feiern II
celebration [ˌselɪ'breɪʃn] Feier II
°**celebratory** [ˌselə'breɪtəri] feierlich, Fest-
celebrity [sə'lebrəti] Prominente/r, Promi IV 1 (23)
cell phone ['sel fəʊn] *(AE)* Mobiltelefon, Handy II
cellar ['selə] Keller IV 1 (41)
Celtic ['keltɪk] keltisch III
cemetery ['semətri], ['seməteri] Friedhof III
cent [sent] Cent III
centimetre (cm) ['sentɪmi:tə] Zentimeter III
central ['sentrəl] zentral, Zentral-, Mittel- III
centre ['sentə] Zentrum; Mitte I **fitness centre** Fitnesszentrum IV 1 (15)
shopping centre Einkaufszentrum I
century ['sentʃəri] Jahrhundert I
ceremony ['serəməni] Feier, Zeremonie III
certain ['sɜ:tn] sichere(r, s); gewisse(r, s), bestimmte(r, s) IV 1 (13)
certainly ['sɜ:tnli] sicher(lich), auf jeden Fall, freilich III
certificate [sə'tɪfɪkət] Urkunde, Bescheinigung IV 3 (108)
certification [ˌsɜ:tɪfɪ'keɪʃn] Anerkennung; Zulassung, Bestätigung IV 3 (94)
certify ['sɜ:tɪfaɪ] anerkennen; bescheinigen, bestätigen IV 3 (94)
chain [tʃeɪn]:
1. Kette I
2. anketten, fesseln **(mit Ketten)** IV 2 (58)
chain sb./sth. to sth. jn./etwas an etwas (an)ketten IV 2 (58)
chair [tʃeə] Stuhl I
challenge ['tʃælɪndʒ]:
1. Herausforderung III
2. **challenge sb. (to sth.)** jn. herausfordern (zu etwas) III
champion ['tʃæmpiən] Meister/in, Champion II
chance [tʃɑ:ns] Gelegenheit, Möglichkeit, Chance III
change [tʃeɪndʒ]:
1. (ver)ändern; sich (ver)ändern II
2. umsteigen II
3. wechseln III
change money Geld wechseln, umtauschen III
change [tʃeɪndʒ]:
1. Veränderung, Wechsel IV 1 (35)
climate change Klimawandel IV 4 (118)
2. Wechselgeld II
channel ['tʃænl] Kanal; Sender IV 1 (10)
°**chant** [tʃɑ:nt] (liturgischer) Gesang, Sprechgesang, Sprechchor
chaos ['keɪɒs] Chaos I
character ['kærəktə]:
1. Figur, Person *(in Roman, Film, Theaterstück usw.)* I
°2. Charakter
charge ['tʃɑ:dʒ] (auf)laden III
charity ['tʃærəti] Wohlfahrtsorganisation; Wohltätigkeit, wohltätige Zwecke II
charity shop ['tʃærəti ʃɒp] *Geschäft, das gespendete Waren für wohltätige Zwecke verkauft* IV 4 (119)
chart [tʃɑ:t]:
1. Diagramm; Tabelle IV 4 (122)
2. **chart sth.** etwas kartografieren; etwas aufzeichnen, darstellen IV 2 (58)
chat [tʃæt]:
1. Chat; Unterhaltung *(Gespräch)* IV 1 (11)
2. chatten; plaudern III
cheap [tʃi:p] billig, preiswert I
check [tʃek]:
1. Überprüfung, Kontrolle I
2. (über)prüfen, kontrollieren I
check sth. in etwas einchecken, aufgeben *(Gepäck)* II **check sth. out** *(infml)* sich etwas anschauen, anhören; etwas ausprobieren III

check-in desk ['tʃek‿ɪn desk] Abflugschalter, Abfertigungsschalter II
checklist ['tʃeklɪst] Checkliste III
°**checkpoint** ['tʃekpɔɪnt] Kontrollpunkt
cheer [tʃɪə] jubeln II
cheese [tʃiːz] Käse I
chemical ['kemɪkl]:
1. Chemikalie IV 4 (118)
2. chemisch IV 4 (118)
chemist ['kemɪst] Apotheker/in II **at the chemist's** in der Apotheke, beim Apotheker II
chess [tʃes] Schach I
chest [tʃest] Brust, Brustkorb II
chicken ['tʃɪkɪn] Huhn; (Brat-)Hähnchen III
chief [tʃiːf] Häuptling IV 4 (110/111)
chief executive (officer) (CEO) [ˌtʃiːf‿ɪg'zekjətɪv] Hauptgeschäftsführer/in IV 2 (59)
chieftain ['tʃiːftən] Oberhaupt *(Clan, Volksstamm)* IV 4 (110/111)
child [tʃaɪld], *pl* **children** Kind I
child labour ['tʃaɪld leɪbə] Kinderarbeit IV 2 (59)
childhood ['tʃaɪldhʊd] Kindheit IV 1 (19)
children ['tʃɪldrən] *plural of* **child**
chips *(pl)* [tʃɪps] Pommes frites II
chocolate ['tʃɒklət]:
1. Schokolade I
2. Praline II
choice [tʃɔɪs] (Aus-)Wahl IV 3 (81)
have no choice but to do sth. keine andere Wahl haben, als etwas zu tun IV 3 (81) **It's a safe choice.** Damit liegst du auf der sicheren Seite. IV 3 (82)
choir ['kwaɪə] Chor II
°**chook** [tʃʊk] *(AusE, infml)* Huhn
choose [tʃuːz], **chose, chosen** aussuchen, (aus)wählen; sich aussuchen I
chorus ['kɔːrəs] Refrain II
chose [tʃəʊz] *siehe* **choose**
chosen [tʃəʊzn] *siehe* **choose**
Christmas ['krɪsməs] Weihnachten I
Merry Christmas! Frohe Weihnachten! I
Christmas Day [ˌkrɪsməs 'deɪ] 1. Weihnachtstag (25. Dezember) I
Christmas Eve [ˌkrɪsməs‿'iːv] Heiligabend I
Christmas pudding [ˌkrɪsməs 'pʊdɪŋ] *kein Pudding, sondern ein Nachtisch aus Butter, Zucker, Mehl, Rosinen, Nüssen, Eiern, Gewürzen, der traditionell zu Weihnachten gegessen wird* I
chubby ['tʃʌbi] pummelig, mollig III
chunk [tʃʌŋk] große (Text-/Daten-) Menge; großes Stück, Batzen IV 4 (129)
church [tʃɜːtʃ] Kirche I
cinema ['sɪnəmə] Kino I
circa (c.) ['sɜːkə] zirka (ca.) IV 1 (8/9)
circle ['sɜːkl] Kreis II
circumstances *(pl)* ['sɜːkəmstənsɪz] Umstände, Verhältnisse IV 4 (112)
°**circus** ['sɜːkəs] Zirkus

citizen ['sɪtɪzn] Staatsbürger/in IV 2 (59)
citizenship ['sɪtɪzənʃɪp] Staatsbürgerschaft; Staatsbürgerkunde *(Schulfach)* IV 3 (81)
city ['sɪti] Stadt, Großstadt I
civil rights *(pl)* [ˌsɪvl 'raɪts] Bürgerrechte IV 2 (64)
°**civilization** [ˌsɪvəlaɪ'zeɪʃn] Zivilisation
claim [kleɪm]:
1. angeben, behaupten IV 1 (19)
2. Behauptung IV 1 (19)
claim [kleɪm]:
1. **claim sth.** etwas beanspruchen, fordern IV 2 (76)
2. **claim (on/to)** Anspruch (auf), Forderung IV 2 (76)
clap [klæp] (Beifall) klatschen I **Clap your hands.** Klatscht in die Hände. I
°**clarify** ['klærəfaɪ] klären, klarstellen
class [klɑːs] (Schul-)Klasse I
class trip ['klɑːs trɪp] Klassenausflug IV 1 (8/9)
classmate ['klɑːsmeɪt] Mitschüler/in, Klassenkamerad/in I
classroom ['klɑːsruːm] Klassenzimmer I
clean [kliːn]:
1. sauber II
2. sauber machen, putzen I
clear [klɪə]:
1. klar, deutlich II
2. räumen; abräumen III
clever ['klevə] klug, schlau I
click [klɪk] klicken III
cliff [klɪf] Klippe II
climate ['klaɪmət] Klima IV 2 (56)
climate change ['klaɪmət tʃeɪndʒ] Klimawandel IV 4 (118)
climb [klaɪm]:
1. Aufstieg, Anstieg III
2. klettern; hinaufklettern (auf) I
climb a tree/a tower auf einen Baum / einen Turm klettern I
clock [klɒk] (Wand-, Stand-, Turm-)Uhr I
close [kləʊz] schließen, zumachen II
close (to) [kləʊs] nah, dicht (bei, an) I
close-up ['kləʊs‿ʌp] Nahaufnahme *(Film)* IV 1 (17)
closed [kləʊzd] geschlossen I
closet ['klɒzɪt] *(bes. AE)* Wandschrank *(oft begehbar)* III
clothes *(pl)* [kləʊðz] Kleidung, Kleidungsstücke I
clothing *(no pl)* ['kləʊðɪŋ] Kleidung IV 3 (100) **piece of clothing** Kleidungsstück IV 3 (100)
cloud [klaʊd] Wolke II
cloudless ['klaʊdləs] wolkenlos IV 1 (12)
cloudy ['klaʊdi] bewölkt II
clown [klaʊn] Clown II
club [klʌb]:
1. Klub, Verein I
join a club in einen Klub eintreten; sich einem Klub anschließen I
°2. Keule, Knüppel
clue [kluː] (Lösungs-)Hinweis; Anhaltspunkt III
coach [kəʊtʃ]:
1. Trainer/in IV 3 (106)
2. **coach sb.** jn. trainieren, jm. Unterricht geben IV 3 (106)
coal [kəʊl] Kohle III
coal mine ['kəʊl maɪn] Kohlebergwerk III
coalition [ˌkəʊə'lɪʃn] Bündnis, Zusammenschluss; Koalition IV 1 (43)
coast [kəʊst] Küste I
coastal ['kəʊstl] Küsten- IV 2 (45)
coastline ['kəʊstlaɪn] Küste, Küstenlinie IV 2 (56)
coat [kəʊt] Mantel II
cocoa ['kəʊkəʊ] Kakao II
°**code** [kəʊd] Code
coffee ['kɒfi] Kaffee III
coin [kɔɪn] Münze I
cola ['kəʊlə] Cola II
cold [kəʊld]:
1. kalt I
be cold frieren I
2. Erkältung II
have a cold eine Erkältung haben, erkältet sein II
collaborate (on/in sth.) [kə'læbəreɪt] zusammenarbeiten (an/bei etwas); mitarbeiten (an/bei etwas) IV 2 (62)
collaboration [kəˌlæbə'reɪʃn] Zusammenarbeit, Gemeinschaftsprodukt(ion) IV 2 (62)
collapse [kə'læps] einstürzen; zusammenbrechen III
collect [kə'lekt] sammeln I
college ['kɒlɪdʒ] Hochschule IV 3 (106)
college of further education [ˌkɒlɪdʒ‿əv ˌfɜːðər‿edʒu'keɪʃn] Berufsfachschule, Fachoberschule; Volkshochschule IV 3 (81)
collocation [ˌkɒlə'keɪʃn] Kollokation *(Wörter, die oft zusammen vorkommen)* IV 2 (56)
colloquial [kə'ləʊkwiəl] umgangssprachlich IV 1 (28)
colon ['kəʊlən] Doppelpunkt II
colonial [kə'ləʊniəl] kolonial, Kolonial- IV 2 (58)
colonist ['kɒlənɪst] Kolonist/in, Siedler/in III
colonize ['kɒlənaɪz] kolonisieren IV 4 (137)
colony ['kɒləni] Kolonie III
colour ['kʌlə] Farbe I **people of colour** Nichtweiße, Menschen nichtweißer Hautfarbe IV 2 (65) **What colour ...?** Welche Farbe ...? I
coloured ['kʌləd] farbig, bunt III
colourful ['kʌləfl] farbenfroh, farbenprächtig, bunt III
column ['kɒləm] Säule III
combination [ˌkɒmbɪ'neɪʃn] Kombination, Verbindung IV 3 (100)

combine [kəm'baɪn] verbinden, kombinieren IV 3 (100)
come [kʌm], **came, come** kommen I **come across sb./sth.** auf jn./etwas stoßen, jn./etwas (zufällig) treffen III **come along** mitkommen, herkommen I **come down with sth.** etwas bekommen *(Krankheit)*, an etwas erkranken III **come in** hereinkommen I **Come on, Dad.** Na los, Dad! / Komm, Dad! I **come over (to)** herüberkommen (zu/nach), vorbeikommen (bei) III **come to be/do sth.** schließlich etwas tun/sein IV 2 (76) **come up** auftauchen; vorkommen, erwähnt werden IV 4 (112) **come up with sth.** etwas haben, auf etwas kommen *(Idee, Vorschlag)* III
comedy ['kɒmədi] Komödie II
comfortable ['kʌmftəbl] bequem II
comma ['kɒmə] Komma II
commemorate sb./sth. [kə'meməreɪt] jemandes/einer Sache gedenken IV 1 (24)
comment ['kɒment]:
1. Bemerkung, Kommentar III
2. comment (on sth.) sich äußern (zu etwas), (etwas) kommentieren III
commission [kə'mɪʃn] Kommission IV 4 (110/111)
common ['kɒmən]:
1. häufig; weit verbreitet III
2. have sth. in common etwas gemeinsam haben, etwas miteinander gemein haben III
Commonwealth ['kɒmənwelθ] *Gemeinschaft der Länder des ehemaligen Britischen Weltreichs* IV 1 (11)
communicate (with sb.) [kə'mjuːnɪkeɪt] (mit jm.) kommunizieren; sich (mit jm.) verständigen IV 3 (95)
communication [kəˌmjuːnɪ'keɪʃn] Kommunikation, Verständigung III **Information and Communications Technology (ICT)** Informations- und Kommunikationstechnologie I
community [kə'mjuːnəti] Gemeinschaft, Gemeinde IV 2 (58)
community service [kə'mjuːnəti sɜːvɪs] gemeinnützige Arbeit IV 3 (78/79)
company ['kʌmpəni] Firma, Gesellschaft III
compare [kəm'peə] vergleichen III **compared to …** verglichen mit … III
comparison [kəm'pærɪsn] Vergleich IV 1 (29) **make comparisons** Vergleiche anstellen IV 1 (29)
compete (with) [kəm'piːt] *(in Wettbewerben)* antreten (gegen); konkurrieren (mit) IV 3 (78/79)
competition [ˌkɒmpə'tɪʃn] Wettbewerb II
competitive [kəm'petətɪv] leistungsorientiert, ehrgeizig; wettbewerbsorientiert IV 3 (78/79)

complain [kəm'pleɪn] sich beschweren, sich beklagen III
complaint [kəm'pleɪnt] Beschwerde IV 1 (28) **make a complaint (about sth.)** eine Beschwerde vorbringen (über etwas), etwas beanstanden IV 1 (28)
complement sth. ['kɒmplɪment] etwas ergänzen, vervollkommnen IV 3 (101)
complete [kəm'pliːt] vollständig, komplett III
complete sth. [kəm'pliːt]:
1. etwas abschließen, beenden IV 3 (80)
2. etwas ausfüllen *(z.B. Formular)* IV 3 (88)
completion [kəm'pliːʃn] Vervollständigung; Abschluss, Fertigstellung IV 3 (94)
complex ['kɒmpleks] komplex, kompliziert IV 2 (76)
°**compose** [kəm'pəʊz] komponieren
°**composer** [kəm'pəʊzə] Komponist/in
comprehend [ˌkɒmprɪ'hend] *(fml)* verstehen IV 3 (100)
comprehension [ˌkɒmprɪ'henʃn] Verständnis IV 3 (100)
comprehensive school [ˌkɒmprɪ'hensɪv skuːl] Gesamtschule IV 3 (81)
compromise ['kɒmprəmaɪz]:
1. Kompromiss IV 4 (110/111)
2. compromise sth. etwas beeinträchtigen IV 4 (110/111)
compromise (with sb. on sth.) (mit jm.) (zu/über etwas) einen Kompromiss/Kompromisse schließen, sich (mit jm.) (auf etwas) einigen IV 4 (110/111)
computer [kəm'pjuːtə] Computer I
concentrate (on sth.) ['kɒnsntreɪt] sich konzentrieren (auf etwas) III
concept ['kɒnsept] Konzept, Vorstellung, Begriff IV 4 (113)
concert ['kɒnsət] Konzert I
°**conclude** [kən'kluːd] (ab)schließen, beenden
conclusion [kən'kluːʒn] Schlussfolgerung III
°**concrete** ['kɒŋkriːt] Beton
condition [kən'dɪʃn] Zustand; Bedingung IV 4 (119)
conditions *(pl)* [kən'dɪʃnz] Bedingungen, Verhältnisse IV 2 (58)
°**conduct** ['kɒndʌkt] Verhalten, Benehmen
confidence ['kɒnfɪdəns] (Selbst-)Vertrauen, Zuversicht IV 2 (48)
confident ['kɒnfɪdənt] (selbst)sicher; zuversichtlich IV 2 (47)
confirm [kən'fɜːm] bestätigen IV 3 (80)
confirmation [ˌkɒnfə'meɪʃn] Bestätigung IV 3 (80)
conflict ['kɒnflɪkt] Konflikt, Auseinandersetzung, Streit IV 2 (76)
confuse [kən'fjuːz] verwirren; verwechseln IV 3 (85)

confusing [kən'fjuːzɪŋ] verwirrend IV 3 (85)
Congratulations (on sth.)! [kənˌgrætʃə'leɪʃnz] Herzlichen Glückwunsch (zu etwas)! IV 1 (27)
congress ['kɒŋgres] Kongress IV 1 (42)
connect (with/to) [kə'nekt]:
1. verbinden (mit); anschließen IV 2 (76) **be connected** verbunden sein III
2. sich verbinden (mit); verbunden sein (mit) IV 2 (76)
connection [kə'nekʃn] Verbindung; Anschluss IV 2 (76)
°**cons** *(pl)* [kɒnz]: **the pros and cons** *(pl)* das Für und Wider; die Vor- und Nachteile
consequence ['kɒnsɪkwəns] Folge, Konsequenz III
°**conservative** [kən'sɜːvətɪv]: **the Conservative Party** die konservative Partei
consider [kən'sɪdə]:
1. berücksichtigen; in Erwägung/in Betracht ziehen, erwägen IV 3 (98) **… considering how many …** wenn man bedenkt/berücksichtigt, wie viele … IV 3 (98)
2. nachdenken über; (sich) überlegen IV 3 (97)
°**3. consider sb./sth. (to be) sth.** jn./etwas halten für etwas, jn./etwas betrachten als etwas
consist of [kən'sɪst‿əv] bestehen aus IV 1 (42)
consonant ['kɒnsənənt] Konsonant, Mitlaut I
conspirator [kən'spɪrətə] Verschwörer/in IV 1 (40)
constant ['kɒnstənt] ständig, andauernd IV 1 (28)
constitution [ˌkɒnstɪ'tjuːʃn] Verfassung IV 2 (58)
constitutional monarchy [ˌkɒnstɪˌtjuːʃənl 'mɒnəki] konstitutionelle Monarchie IV 1 (43)
°**construction** [kən'strʌkʃn] Bau; Bauweise; Bauwerk, Konstruktion
constructive [kən'strʌktɪv] konstruktiv IV 4 (118)
consult [kən'sʌlt] *(AE)*: **consult with sb.** sich mit jm. beraten IV 1 (14)
consume [kən'sjuːm] verbrauchen, konsumieren IV 4 (122)
consumer [kən'sjuːmə] Konsument/in, Verbraucher/in IV 4 (122)
contact ['kɒntækt]:
1. Kontakt IV 1 (14) **contact details** *(pl)* Kontaktdaten IV 1 (23) **keep/stay in contact (with)** in Kontakt bleiben (mit) IV 4 (115) **make eye contact** Blickkontakt herstellen III
2. contact sb. Kontakt aufnehmen mit jm., sich in Verbindung setzen mit jm. IV 1 (14)
contain [kən'teɪn] enthalten IV 3 (101)

contemporary [kən'temprəri] modern, zeitgenössisch IV 2 (46)
content ['kɒntent] Inhalt III
context ['kɒntekst] (Text-, Satz-)Zusammenhang, Kontext II
continent ['kɒntɪnənt] Kontinent IV 2 (45)
continue [kən'tɪnjuː] sich fortsetzen, weitergehen III **continue sth.** etwas fortsetzen III **continue to do sth.** (mit) etwas weitermachen, fortfahren IV 2 (64)
contradict [ˌkɒntrə'dɪkt] widersprechen IV 4 (115)
contradiction [ˌkɒntrə'dɪkʃn] Widerspruch IV 4 (115)
°**contrast** ['kɒntrɑːst] Kontrast, Gegensatz
°**contrasting** [kən'trɑːstɪŋ] gegensätzlich
contribute (to/towards) [kən'trɪbjuːt] beitragen, beisteuern (zu); spenden (für) IV 3 (88)
contribution (to/towards) [kɒntrɪ'bjuːʃn] Beitrag; Spende (für) IV 3 (88)
control [kən'trəʊl]:
1. Kontrolle IV 2 (58)
2. kontrollieren, regulieren IV 2 (58)
conversation [ˌkɒnvə'seɪʃn] Gespräch, Unterhaltung II
°**convey** [kən'veɪ] vermitteln, übermitteln
convict ['kɒnvɪkt] Sträfling, Strafgefangene(r) IV 2 (45)
°**convince** [kən'vɪns] überzeugen
cook [kʊk] kochen; zubereiten III
cookie ['kʊki] *(AE)* Keks, Plätzchen II
cool [kuːl]:
1. cool I
2. kühl II
coordinator [kəʊ'ɔːdɪneɪtə] Koordinator/in III
copy ['kɒpi]:
1. kopieren, abschreiben I
2. Kopie; Exemplar II
°**copyright** ['kɒpiraɪt] Urheberrecht, Copyright
coral ['kɒrəl] Koralle/n IV 2 (45)
coral reef [ˌkɒrəl 'riːf] Korallenriff IV 2 (45)
corn *(no pl)* [kɔːn] *(AE)* Mais III
corner ['kɔːnə] Ecke I **on the corner of Church Road and London Road** Church Road, Ecke London Road II
corner shop ['kɔːnə ʃɒp] Laden an der Ecke; Tante-Emma-Laden I
cornflakes ['kɔːnfleɪks] Cornflakes I
°**corporation** [ˌkɔːpə'reɪʃn] (Handels-)Gesellschaft, Konzern; Körperschaft
correct [kə'rekt]:
1. richtig, korrekt II
2. korrigieren, verbessern II
°**correction** [kə'rekʃn] Berichtigung, Korrektur

correctness [kə'rektnəs] Richtigkeit; Korrektheit IV 4 (137)
corridor ['kɒrɪdɔː] Gang, Korridor III
°**cos** [kəz] *(infml)* weil *(= because)*
cost [kɒst]:
1. Kosten; Preis IV 3 (109)
at all cost(s) / at any cost um jeden Preis IV 3 (109) **At what cost ...?** Zu welchem Preis ...? IV 3 (109)
2. **cost, cost, cost** kosten II
cost of living [ˌkɒst_əv 'lɪvɪŋ] Lebenshaltungskosten IV 1 (28)
costly ['kɒstli] kostspielig, teuer IV 3 (109)
costume ['kɒstjuːm] Kostüm, Verkleidung II
cottage ['kɒtɪdʒ] Häuschen, Cottage II
cotton ['kɒtn] Baumwolle III
couch [kaʊtʃ] Couch IV 3 (96)
cough [kɒf] Husten II **have a cough** Husten haben II
could [kʊd]:
1. **he could ...** er konnte ... I
we couldn't ... wir konnten nicht ... I
2. **it could** es könnte II
council ['kaʊnsl] Ausschuss; Rat *(Stadtrat, Gemeinderat u.Ä.)* III
counsellor ['kaʊnsələ] *(AE* **counselor)** Berater/in III
count [kaʊnt] zählen I **count to ...** zählen bis ... I
counter ['kaʊntə] Theke; Ladentisch III
country ['kʌntri] Land I
countryside ['kʌntrisaɪd] Landschaft, ländliche Gegend II
county ['kaʊnti] Grafschaft *(in Großbritannien)* I
couple ['kʌpl]**: a couple** ein Paar; ein paar III
course [kɔːs]:
1. Kurs, Lehrgang I
2. Studium, Studiengang IV 3 (106)
°**course of action** [ˌkɔːs_əv 'ækʃn] Vorgehen, Maßnahmen
court [kɔːt]:
1. Platz, Court *(Tennis, Basketball)* IV 3 (89)
2. Gericht(shof) IV 3 (109)
courteous ['kɜːtiəs] höflich IV 3 (100)
courtesy ['kɜːtəsi] Höflichkeit; Höflichkeitsfloskel IV 3 (100)
courtyard ['kɔːtjɑːd] Hof, Innenhof; Vorplatz II
cousin ['kʌzn] Cousin, Cousine I
°**cove** [kəʊv] (kleine) Bucht
cover ['kʌvə]:
1. bedecken, zudecken III
2. behandeln, abdecken, ansprechen *(Thema; Fragen)* III
3. Schutz, Abdeckung IV 1 (18)
cow [kaʊ] Kuh II
crab [kræb] Krebs I
cracker ['krækə] Knallbonbon I
crash [kræʃ]:
1. crashen II
2. abstürzen *(Flugzeug; Computer)* III

crazy ['kreɪzi] verrückt III
cream [kriːm] Sahne I **ice cream** (Speise-)Eis I
create [kri'eɪt] schaffen, erschaffen, kreieren III
creation [kri'eɪʃn] Schaffung; Schöpfung; Kreation, Werk IV 3 (109)
°**creative** [kri'eɪtɪv] kreativ
creativity [ˌkriːeɪ'tɪvəti] Kreativität, Ideenreichtum IV 4 (119)
creator [kri'eɪtə] Schöpfer/in IV 3 (109)
credits *(pl)* ['kredɪts] Credits *(Vor- oder Nachspann, z.B. eines Films)* IV 1 (17)
creep [kriːp]**, crept, crept** schleichen; kriechen IV 1 (33)
crept [krept] *siehe* **creep**
crew [kruː] Mannschaft, Team; Clique IV 3 (91)
crib sheet ['krɪb ʃiːt] *(infml)* Spickzettel, Merkzettel II
cricket ['krɪkɪt] Kricket I
crime [kraɪm] Kriminalität; Verbrechen IV 2 (58)
crime fiction ['kraɪm fɪkʃn] Kriminalromane IV 2 (58)
°**crises** ['kraɪsiːz] *plural of* **crisis**
°**crisis** ['kraɪsɪs], *pl* **crises** Krise
°**criss-cross sth.** ['krɪs krɒs] etwas kreuz und quer durchziehen; kreuz und quer durch etwas ziehen/fahren
°**criteria** [kraɪ'tɪəriə] *plural of* **criterion**
°**criterion** [kraɪ'tɪəriən]**,** *pl* **criteria** Kriterium
critic ['krɪtɪk] Kritiker/in IV 3 (100)
critical (of) ['krɪtɪkl] kritisch (gegenüber) IV 3 (100)
criticism ['krɪtɪsɪzəm] Kritik IV 3 (100)
criticize sb. (for) ['krɪtɪsaɪz] jn. kritisieren (wegen) IV 2 (64)
croc [krɒk] *(infml)* Krokodil IV 2 (53)
crocodile ['krɒkədaɪl] Krokodil IV 2 (53)
crop [krɒp] Feldfrucht, Anbaupflanze; Ernte IV 4 (122)
cross [krɒs] überqueren, kreuzen; sich kreuzen II
cross (with sb.) [krɒs] verärgert (mit jm.), böse (auf jn.) IV 4 (116)
cross-cultural [ˌkrɒs 'kʌltʃərəl] kulturübergreifend, interkulturell IV 4 (129)
crossword ['krɒswɜːd] Kreuzworträtsel IV 3 (84)
crowd [kraʊd] (Menschen-)Menge II
crowded ['kraʊdɪd] voller Menschen; überfüllt III
crown [kraʊn] Krone II
cry [kraɪ] schreien; weinen II
cultivate ['kʌltɪveɪt] kultivieren; *(Getreide, Gemüse)* anbauen IV 4 (122)
cultivation [ˌkʌltɪ'veɪʃn] Kultivierung, Anbau; landwirtschaftliche Nutzung IV 4 (122)
cultural ['kʌltʃərəl] kulturell IV 1 (10)
°**cultural burning** [ˌkʌltʃərəl 'bɜːnɪŋ] kontrolliertes Feuerlegen
culture ['kʌltʃə] Kultur I

cup [kʌp] Tasse I **a cup of tea** eine Tasse Tee I
cupboard ['kʌbəd] Schrank I
curator [kjʊə'reɪtə] Kurator/in; Museumsdirektor/in IV 4 (113)
curious ['kjʊəriəs] wissbegierig, neugierig III
currency ['kʌrənsi] Währung III
current ['kʌrənt] aktuelle(r, s), gegenwärtige(r, s) IV 3 (98)
currently ['kʌrəntli] zurzeit, aktuell *(Adv.)* IV 3 (98)
curricula [kə'rɪkjələ] *plural of* **curriculum**
curriculum [kə'rɪkjələm], *pl* **curriculums** *or* **curricula** Lehrplan IV 3 (81)
curriculum vitae (= CV) [kəˌrɪkjələm 'viːtaɪ] Lebenslauf IV 3 (94)
curry ['kʌri] Curry(gericht) I
customer ['kʌstəmə] Kunde, Kundin IV 3 (78/79)
cut [kʌt]:
1. Schnitt; Schnittwunde IV 3 (93)
Cut! Schnitt! *(beim Filmen)* II
2. **cut, cut, cut** schneiden II
cute [kjuːt] niedlich, süß III
°**cuz** [kʌz] **(***infml für* **cousin)** Cousin/e
CV (= curriculum vitae) [ˌsiː 'vi] Lebenslauf IV 3 (94)
cyberbullying ['saɪbəbʊliɪŋ] Cyber-Mobbing *(Verleumdung/Diffamierung in sozialen Medien)* III
cyclone ['saɪkləʊn] Wirbelsturm, Zyklon IV 2 (52)

D

dad [dæd] Papa, Vati I
daily ['deɪli] täglich III
dairy ['deəri]:
1. Milch-, Molkerei- IV 2 (77)
2. *(infml, New Zealand)* Laden an der Ecke IV 2 (77)
dairy products *(pl)* ['deəri prɒdʌkts] Milchprodukte, Molkereiprodukte IV 2 (77)
damage ['dæmɪdʒ]:
1. (be)schädigen; schaden IV 1 (16)
2. **damage (to)** *(no pl)* Schaden, Schäden (an) IV 1 (16)
dance [dɑːns]:
1. tanzen I
2. Tanz II
dance floor ['dɑːns flɔː] Tanzfläche II
dancer ['dɑːnsə] Tänzer/in II
danger ['deɪndʒə] Gefahr II
dangerous ['deɪndʒərəs] gefährlich I
dark [dɑːk]:
1. dunkel I
2. Dunkelheit III
darkness ['dɑːknəs] Dunkelheit, Finsternis III
data ['deɪtə] Daten IV 3 (88)

date [deɪt]:
1. Datum III
to date bis heute, bisher IV 3 (94)
2. Verabredung, Date III
3. **date from** stammen aus *(zeitlich)* III
4. **date sb.** jn. daten, mit jm. gehen, mit jm. eine Beziehung haben IV 4 (116)
daughter ['dɔːtə] Tochter II
day [deɪ] Tag I **day of the week** Wochentag I **all day** den ganzen Tag (lang) I **the other day** neulich IV 4 (115) **these days** heutzutage IV 3 (107)
daylight ['deɪlaɪt] Tageslicht IV 1 (24)
dead [ded] tot I
°**deadline** ['dedlaɪn] Stichtag, Abgabetermin
deal [diːl]: **a great deal (of)** viel, eine Menge IV 4 (121)
dear [dɪə] liebe(r, s) II **Dear Sir or Madam** Sehr geehrte Damen und Herren II **Oh dear!** Oje! II
death [deθ] Tod III
°**Death Eaters** ['deθ iːtəz] „Todesser" *(Harry Potter, Gruppe von bösen Zauberern)*
°**Deathly Hallows** [ˌdeθli 'hæləʊz] „Heiligtümer des Todes" *(Harry Potter, Buchtitel)*
debate [dɪ'beɪt]:
1. debattieren IV 2 (64)
2. Debatte IV 2 (64)
hold/have a debate eine Debatte führen IV 2 (64)
decade ['dekeɪd] Jahrzehnt IV 2 (59)
December [dɪ'sembə] Dezember I
decide [dɪ'saɪd] beschließen, sich entscheiden I
decision [dɪ'sɪʒn] Entscheidung III
deck [dek] Deck *(eines Schiffes)* I
declaration [ˌdeklə'reɪʃn] Erklärung, Verkündung II **the Declaration of Independence** die Unabhängigkeitserklärung *(der Vereinigten Staaten im Jahr 1776)* II
declare sth sth. [dɪ'kleə] etwas zu etwas erklären IV 2 (58)
decompose [ˌdiːkəm'pəʊz] sich zersetzen, zerfallen IV 4 (118)
decorate ['dekəreɪt] dekorieren, schmücken IV 4 (119)
decoration [ˌdekə'reɪʃn] Dekoration, Schmuck, Verzierung IV 4 (119)
°**decorative** ['dekərətɪv] dekorativ
deep [diːp] tief II
deer [dɪə], *pl* **deer** Reh, Hirsch III
defeat [dɪ'fiːt] besiegen, schlagen III
defend sb./sth. (against sb./sth.) [dɪ'fend] jn./etwas verteidigen (gegen jn./etwas) II
define [dɪ'faɪn] definieren IV 3 (107)
definite ['defɪnət] bestimmte(r, s); definitiv, endgültig, eindeutig IV 3 (91)
definitely ['defɪnətli] auf jeden Fall; ganz bestimmt IV 3 (91)

definition [ˌdefɪ'nɪʃn] Definition IV 3 (107)
degree [dɪ'griː] Universitätsabschluss, Diplom; Grad *(auch bei Temperatur)* IV 3 (108) **bachelor's degree** Bachelor(-Abschluss) IV 3 (108)
master's degree Master(-Abschluss) IV 3 (108)
delete [dɪ'liːt] löschen; streichen III
delicate ['delɪkət] empfindlich, zerbrechlich; heikel IV 3 (88)
delicious [dɪ'lɪʃəs] köstlich, lecker II
°**delish** [dɪ'lɪʃ] **(***infml, kurz für:* **delicious)** köstlich, lecker
deliver [dɪ'lɪvə] (aus)liefern IV 3 (91)
delivery [dɪ'lɪvəri] Lieferung IV 3 (82)
demand: on demand auf Abruf, nach Bedarf III
democracy [dɪ'mɒkrəsi] Demokratie IV 1 (43)
°**democratic** [ˌdemə'krætɪk] demokratisch
°**demonstrate** ['demənstreɪt] zeigen, demonstrieren
demonstration [ˌdemən'streɪʃn] Demonstration, Vorführung II
dentist ['dentɪst] Zahnarzt/-ärztin II
dentistry ['dentɪstri] Zahnheilkunde, Zahnmedizin IV 3 (108)
department [dɪ'pɑːtmənt] Amt, Ministerium; Abteilung IV 3 (95)
department store [dɪ'pɑːtmənt stɔː] Kaufhaus IV 3 (95)
depend on sth. [dɪ'pend] von etwas abhängen; auf etwas angewiesen sein III
°**depending on** [dɪ'pendɪŋ ɒn] abhängig von, je nach(dem)
°**depict** [dɪ'pɪk] darstellen, abbilden
derivation (from) [ˌderɪ'veɪʃn] Ableitung, Herleitung (von) IV 4 (122)
derive sth. from sth. [dɪ'raɪv] etwas aus etwas gewinnen, erlangen; etwas aus etwas herleiten, ableiten IV 4 (122)
describe sth. (to sb.) [dɪ'skraɪb] (jm.) etwas beschreiben II
°**description** [dɪ'skrɪpʃn] Beschreibung
descriptive [dɪ'skrɪptɪv] beschreibend IV 2 (56)
desert ['dezət] Wüste IV 2 (45)
deserve [dɪ'zɜːv] verdienen *(zu Recht bekommen)* IV 3 (100)
design [dɪ'zaɪn]:
1. Design; Gestaltung III
2. entwerfen, konstruieren, entwickeln IV 1 (21)
design and technology [dɪˌzaɪn‿ənd tek'nɒlədʒi] Design und Technik I
designer [dɪ'zaɪnə] Designer/in IV 4 (118)
desire [dɪ'zaɪə]:
1. Wunsch, Sehnsucht IV 3 (88)
2. **desire sth.** sich etwas wünschen, etwas begehren IV 3 (88)
desk [desk] Schreibtisch I
despite [dɪ'spaɪt] trotz IV 2 (76)

dessert [dɪ'zɜːt] Nachtisch, Nachspeise I
destination [ˌdestɪ'neɪʃn] Reiseziel, Fahrtziel; Bestimmungsort IV 1 (10)
destroy [dɪ'strɔɪ] zerstören II
destruction [dɪ'strʌkʃn] Zerstörung IV 4 (121)
destructive [dɪ'strʌktɪv] zerstörerisch, destruktiv IV 4 (118)
detail ['diːteɪl] Detail, Einzelheit III **contact details** *(pl)* Kontaktdaten IV 1 (23)
detailed ['diːteɪld] ausführlich, detailliert IV 3 (101)
determined [dɪ'tɜːmɪnd]: **be determined to do sth.** (fest) entschlossen sein, etwas zu tun IV 2 (52)
°**detox** ['diːtɒks] *(infml)* Entzug, Entgiftung(sbehandlung)
develop [dɪ'veləp] (sich) entwickeln IV 3 (88)
development [dɪ'veləpmənt] Entwicklung IV 3 (88)
device [dɪ'vaɪs] Gerät, Apparat; Mittel IV 4 (112)
°**diagram** ['daɪəgræm] Diagramm
dialect ['daɪəlekt] Dialekt IV 1 (19)
dialogue ['daɪəlɒg] Dialog II
diary ['daɪəri] Tagebuch; Kalender I
°**dice** [daɪs], *pl* **dice** Würfel
dictionary ['dɪkʃənri] alphabetisches Wörterverzeichnis, Wörterbuch I
did [dɪd] *siehe* **do** **He didn't run.** Er rannte nicht. I **I did clean ….** Ich habe … wirklich/tatsächlich geputzt. IV 4 (112)
didgeridoo [ˌdɪdʒəri'duː] Didgeridoo IV 2 (46)
die [daɪ] sterben I **die out** aussterben III
diet ['daɪət]:
1. Ernährung, Kost IV 3 (84)
2. Diät IV 3 (84)
go on a diet eine Diät machen IV 3 (84)
difference ['dɪfrəns] Unterschied II
different ['dɪfrənt] verschieden; anders I
difficult ['dɪfɪkəlt] schwierig, schwer III
dig [dɪg], **dug, dug** graben IV 3 (85) **dig up potatoes** Kartoffeln ausgraben *(ernten)* IV 3 (85)
digital ['dɪdʒɪtl] digital III
°**dignity** ['dɪgnəti] Würde
dining room ['daɪnɪŋ ruːm] Esszimmer I
dinner ['dɪnə] Abendessen, Abendbrot I **have dinner** zu Abend essen I
dinosaur ['daɪnəsɔː] Dinosaurier I
diploma [dɪ'pləʊmə] Diplom, Abschlusszeugnis IV 3 (80)
diplomacy [dɪ'pləʊməsi] Diplomatie IV 4 (137)
diplomatic [ˌdɪplə'mætɪk] diplomatisch, Diplomaten- IV 1 (11)

direct [də'rekt] direkt II **direct train** durchgehender Zug II
direction [də'rekʃn] Richtung IV 1 (32)
director [də'rektə]:
1. Leiter/in III
2. Regisseur/in II
dirt [dɜːt] Dreck III
dirty ['dɜːti] schmutzig II
disadvantage [ˌdɪsəd'vɑːntɪdʒ] Nachteil IV 1 (8/9)
disadvantaged [ˌdɪsəd'vɑːntɪdʒd] benachteiligt IV 1 (30)
disagree (with) [ˌdɪsə'griː] anderer Meinung sein (als); nicht übereinstimmen (mit); nicht zustimmen IV 2 (57)
°**disagreement** [ˌdɪsə'griːmənt] Uneinigkeit; Streit
disappear [ˌdɪsə'pɪə] verschwinden II
disappoint sb. [ˌdɪsə'pɔɪnt] jn. enttäuschen IV 4 (116)
disappointed [ˌdɪsə'pɔɪntɪd] enttäuscht IV 4 (116)
disappointing [ˌdɪsə'pɔɪntɪŋ] enttäuschend IV 4 (116)
disco ['dɪskəʊ] Disko I
discourage [dɪs'kʌrɪdʒ] unterbinden; entmutigen IV 4 (137) **discourage sb. from doing sth.** jn. (davon) abhalten, etwas zu tun IV 4 (137)
discover [dɪ'skʌvə] entdecken IV 1 (22)
discovery [dɪ'skʌvəri] Entdeckung IV 1 (22)
discriminate against sb. [dɪ'skrɪmɪneɪt] jn. diskriminieren IV 2 (59)
discrimination against sb. [dɪˌskrɪmɪ'neɪʃn] Diskriminierung eines Menschen IV 2 (59)
discuss sth. [dɪ'skʌs] über etwas diskutieren; etwas besprechen III
discussion [dɪ'skʌʃn] Diskussion III
disease [dɪ'ziːz] *(ansteckende)* Krankheit III
disgusting [dɪs'gʌstɪŋ] ekelhaft, widerlich III
dishes *(pl)* ['dɪʃɪz]: **wash the dishes** das Geschirr abwaschen, spülen II
dishonest [dɪs'ɒnɪst] unehrlich IV 3 (86)
dishonesty [dɪs'ɒnɪsti] Unehrlichkeit IV 3 (86)
dislike [dɪs'laɪk] nicht mögen, nicht leiden können III
°**display** [dɪ'spleɪ] zeigen, zur Schau stellen
disrespectful (to) [ˌdɪsrɪ'spektfl] respektlos (gegenüber) IV 3 (86)
distance ['dɪstəns] Distanz, Entfernung; Strecke IV 1 (28) **keep your distance (from)** Abstand halten (zu/von) IV 1 (33)
distant ['dɪstənt] (weit) entfernt, fern IV 1 (28)
distract [dɪ'strækt] ablenken IV 2 (48)
distraction [dɪ'strækʃn] Ablenkung IV 2 (48)

distribute [dɪ'strɪbjuːt] verteilen, vertreiben *(Handel)* IV 4 (122)
distribution [ˌdɪstrɪ'bjuːʃn] (Aus-)Lieferung; Verteilung IV 4 (122)
district ['dɪstrɪkt] Bezirk, Gebiet, (Stadt-)Viertel IV 1 (22)
disturb [dɪ'stɜːb] stören IV 2 (58)
ditch [dɪtʃ] Graben III
°**dive** [daɪv]:
1. (ein)tauchen
2. einen Kopfsprung machen, *(ins Wasser)* springen
diverse [daɪ'vɜːs] unterschiedlich, vielfältig IV 1 (13)
diversity [daɪ'vɜːsəti] Vielfalt IV 1 (19)
divide (up) [dɪ'vaɪd] auf-/einteilen IV 3 (81)
divide (up) (into) [dɪ'vaɪd] auf-/einteilen (in) IV 1 (42)
division [dɪ'vɪʒn] (Ein-)Teilung, Aufteilung IV 3 (81)
divorce [dɪ'vɔːs] Scheidung III **get a divorce** sich scheiden lassen IV 2 (63)
divorced [dɪ'vɔːst] geschieden I **get divorced** sich scheiden lassen IV 2 (63)
dizzy ['dɪzi] schwindlig III
do [duː], **did, done** machen, tun I **do sport** Sport treiben I **Don't go.** Geh nicht. I **he doesn't have time** er hat keine Zeit I
dock [dɒk] Hafen, Dock III
doctor ['dɒktə] Arzt/Ärztin, Doktor II
doctoral ['dɒktərəl] Doktor- *(zur Erlangung des Doktorgrads)* IV 3 (108)
doctorate ['dɒktərət] Doktorwürde IV 3 (108)
document ['dɒkjumənt] Dokument; Text(datei) IV 4 (129)
documentary [ˌdɒkju'mentri] Dokumentarfilm III
dog [dɒg] Hund I **walk the dog** mit dem Hund rausgehen, den Hund ausführen III
°**dog walker** ['dɒg wɔːkə] Hundeausführer/in
°**dog walking** ['dɒg wɔːkɪŋ] Hunde ausführen
doll [dɒl] Puppe III
dollar ['dɒlə] Dollar ($) III
dome [dəʊm] Kuppel II
dominant ['dɒmɪnənt] dominant IV 4 (129)
dominate ['dɒmɪneɪt] beherrschen, dominieren IV 4 (129)
done [dʌn] *siehe* **do**
door [dɔː] Tür I
doorbell ['dɔːbel] Türklingel, Türglocke II
doorway ['dɔːweɪ] Eingang III
°**dot** [dɒt] Punkt, Pünktchen
°**dot painting** ['dɒt peɪntɪŋ] Punktmalerei; Punktgemälde
double ['dʌbl] Doppel- I
down [daʊn] hinunter, herunter; nach unten I **down there** da/dort unten;

nach da/dort unten II **up and down** auf und ab; rauf und runter I
downhill [ˌdaʊn'hɪl] bergab III
download sth. [ˌdaʊn'ləʊd] etwas herunterladen III
downstairs [ˌdaʊn'steəz] unten; nach unten *(im Haus)* I
downstream [ˌdaʊn'striːm] flussabwärts III
downtown ['daʊntaʊn] *(AE)*: **in downtown Albuquerque** im Zentrum von Albuquerque III
dozen ['dʌzn], *pl* **dozen** Dutzend IV 4 (119)
draft [drɑːft]:
1. Entwurf II
°2. entwerfen, aufsetzen
drag [dræg] zerren, schleifen *(mit Mühe ziehen)* IV 1 (41)
drama ['drɑːmə] Schauspiel; darstellende Kunst II
dramatic [drə'mætɪk] dramatisch IV 2 (56)
drank [dræŋk] *siehe* **drink**
draw [drɔː], **drew, drawn** zeichnen I
draw [drɔː] *(bes. BE)* Unentschieden III
drawing ['drɔːɪŋ] Zeichnung I
drawn [drɔːn] *siehe* **draw**
dream [driːm] Traum I
dress [dres]:
1. Kleid I
2. **dress up** sich verkleiden; sich schick anziehen II
drew [druː] *siehe* **draw**
drink [drɪŋk]:
1. Getränk I
2. **drink, drank, drunk** trinken I
drive [draɪv], **drove, driven**:
1. (mit dem Auto) fahren I
2. treiben; antreiben IV 1 (19)
driven ['drɪvn] *siehe* **drive**
driver ['draɪvə] Fahrer/in IV 1 (31)
drop [drɒp]:
1. fallen III
2. **drop sth.** etwas fallen lassen II
drought [draʊt] Dürre, Trockenheit IV 4 (121)
drove [drəʊv] *siehe* **drive**
drum [drʌm] Trommel I **drums** *(pl)* Schlagzeug I **play the drums** Schlagzeug spielen I
drummer ['drʌmə] Trommler/in; Schlagzeuger/in III
drunk [drʌŋk] *siehe* **drink**
dry [draɪ] trocken III
dub [dʌb] synchronisieren IV 4 (136)
dude [djuːd] *(bes. AE, Slang)* Typ, Kerl III
dug [dʌg] *siehe* **dig**
°**duke** [djuːk] Herzog
during ['djʊərɪŋ] während III
dust [dʌst] Staub III
duty ['djuːti] Aufgabe, Pflicht IV 3 (95) **be off duty** außer Dienst sein, keinen Dienst haben IV 3 (95) **be on duty** im Dienst sein, Dienst haben IV 3 (95)
DVD [ˌdiːviː'diː] DVD I

E

each [iːtʃ] jeder, jede, jedes (einzelne) II **each other** sich (gegenseitig), einander III **They're £ 2.75 each.** Sie kosten je 2 Pfund 75. *(2,75 pro Stück)* I
ear [ɪə] Ohr I **be all ears** *(infml)* ganz Ohr sein *(gespannt zuhören)* IV 1 (24)
early ['ɜːli] früh I
earn [ɜːn] verdienen *(Geld; Anerkennung)* IV 3 (97)
earphones *(pl)* ['ɪəfəʊnz] Ohrhörer, Kopfhörer II
earring ['ɪərɪŋ] Ohrring III
earth [ɜːθ]: **(the) earth** *(oft auch:* **Earth***)* (die) Erde *(der Planet)* II **on earth** auf der Erde II
earthquake ['ɜːθkweɪk] Erdbeben IV 2 (76)
east [iːst] Osten; nach Osten; östlich III
eastbound ['iːstbaʊnd] Richtung Osten III
Easter ['iːstə] Ostern I
eastern ['iːstən] östlich, Ost- III
easy ['iːzi] leicht, einfach I
easy-going [ˌiːzi 'gəʊɪŋ] gelassen, locker IV 2 (47)
eat [iːt], **ate, eaten** essen I
eaten ['iːtn] *siehe* **eat**
ecological [ˌiːkə'lɒdʒɪkl] ökologisch IV 4 (121)
ecology [i'kɒlədʒi] Ökologie IV 4 (121)
economic [ˌiːkə'nɒmɪk] wirtschaftlich, Wirtschafts- IV 1 (28)
economy [ɪ'kɒnəmi] (Volks-)Wirtschaft IV 2 (58)
ecosystem ['iːkəʊsɪstəm] Ökosystem IV 3 (88)
edge [edʒ] Rand, Kante III
edit ['edɪt] bearbeiten; schneiden *(Film, Video)* I
editor ['edɪtə] Redakteur/in; Herausgeber/in III
editor-in-chief [ˌedɪtər‿ɪn 'tʃiːf] Chefredakteur/in IV 4 (124)
educate ['edʒukeɪt] jn. ausbilden, unterrichten, erziehen IV 1 (30)
educated ['edʒukeɪtɪd] gebildet IV 1 (30)
education [ˌedʒu'keɪʃn] (Schul-, Aus-)Bildung; Erziehung III **higher education** Hochschulbildung; Hochschulwesen IV 3 (108)
°**educational** [ˌedʒu'keɪʃənl] Erziehungs-, Bildungs-
effect [ɪ'fekt] (Aus-)Wirkung, Einfluss, Effekt IV 3 (100)
effective [ɪ'fektɪv] effektiv, wirksam IV 3 (100)
e.g. [ˌiː 'dʒiː] *(from Latin:* exempli gratia) z.B. (zum Beispiel) II
egg [eg] Ei I
eight [eɪt] acht I
either ['aɪðə], ['iːðə]: **either … or …** entweder … oder … III **not … either** auch nicht I
°**elder** ['eldə] Älteste(r) *(z.B. eines Stammes)*
elect sb. (to be) sth. [ɪ'lekt] jn. zu etwas wählen III
election [ɪ'lekʃn] Wahl *(Abstimmung)* IV 1 (42)
electoral system [ɪˌlektərəl 'sɪstəm] Wahlsystem IV 1 (42)
°**electronic** [ɪˌlek'trɒnɪk] elektronisch
element ['elɪmənt] Element III
elementary school [ˌelɪ'mentri skuːl] *(AE)* Grundschule IV 3 (80)
elephant ['elɪfənt] Elefant I
elevator ['elɪveɪtə] *(bes. AE)* Fahrstuhl, Aufzug, Lift II
eleven [ɪ'levn] elf I
eligible ['elɪdʒəbl]: **be eligible (for sth. / to do sth.)** berechtigt sein (zu etwas / etwas zu tun) IV 3 (81)
eliminate [ɪ'lɪmɪneɪt] eliminieren, beseitigen IV 4 (112)
else [els]: **everyone else** alle anderen; sonst jeder IV 1 (11)
email ['iːmeɪl]:
1. E-Mail I
2. **email (sb. sth.)** (jm. etwas) mailen IV 1 (14)
embarrassing [ɪm'bærəsɪŋ] peinlich III
embassy ['embəsi] Botschaft *(diplomatische Vertretung)* IV 1 (11)
°**embroidery** [ɪm'brɔɪdəri] Stickerei
emerge (from …) [ɪ'mɜːdʒ] herauskommen, hervortreten, auftauchen (aus …) IV 1 (24)
emigrant ['emɪgrənt] Auswanderer, Auswanderin IV 1 (19)
emigrate ['emɪgreɪt] auswandern, emigrieren III
emigration [ˌemɪ'greɪʃn] Auswanderung IV 1 (19)
emission [ɪ'mɪʃn] Emission; Ausstoß IV 4 (120)
emit [ɪ'mɪt] emittieren, ausstoßen IV 4 (120)
emotion [ɪ'məʊʃn] Emotion, Gefühl IV 1 (28)
emotional [ɪ'məʊʃənl] emotional IV 1 (28)
emphasis ['emfəsɪs] Betonung, Hervorhebung III
°**emphasize** ['emfəsaɪz] betonen, hervorheben
°**emphatic** [ɪm'fætɪk] emphatisch, betont; betonend
empire ['empaɪə] Reich, Imperium III
employ sb. [ɪm'plɔɪ] jn. anstellen, beschäftigen IV 3 (95)

employee [ɪm'plɔiiː] Arbeitnehmer/in IV 3 (95)
employer [ɪm'plɔɪə] Arbeitgeber/in IV 3 (95)
employment [ɪm'plɔɪmənt] Arbeit, Anstellung IV 3 (95)
empty ['empti] leer III
°**emu** ['iːmju] Emu
encore ['ɒŋkɔː] Zugabe II
°**encounter** [ɪn'kaʊntə] Begegnung
encourage [ɪn'kʌrɪdʒ] ermutigen, ermuntern IV 4 (118)
end [end]:
1. Ende, Schluss I
put an end to sth. einer Sache ein Ende machen, einen Schlussstrich unter etwas ziehen IV 2 (59)
2. enden; beenden III
endanger [ɪn'deɪndʒə] bedrohen, gefährden IV 3 (88)
ending ['endɪŋ]:
1. Endung I
2. Ende, (Ab-)Schluss II
enemy ['enəmi] Feind/in II
energy ['enədʒi] Energie, Kraft III
engage in sth. [ɪn'geɪdʒ] sich beteiligen an etwas, aktiv werden für etwas, sich engagieren für etwas IV 4 (110/111)
engagement (in) [ɪn'geɪdʒmənt] Engagement (bei) IV 4 (110/111)
engineer [ˌendʒɪ'nɪə] Ingenieur/in; Techniker/in IV 3 (108)
engineering [ˌendʒɪ'nɪərɪŋ] Ingenieurwesen, Maschinenbau IV 3 (108)
English ['ɪŋglɪʃ] Englisch; englisch I
in English auf Englisch I
enjoy [ɪn'dʒɔɪ] genießen III **enjoy yourself** sich amüsieren, Spaß haben III
enough [ɪ'nʌf] genug I
enrich [ɪn'rɪtʃ] bereichern IV 3 (107)
enrichment [ɪn'rɪtʃmənt] Bereicherung IV 3 (107) **summer enrichment programs** *(pl)* Sommerkurse von Universitäten für besonders begabte Schüler/innen IV 3 (107)
enrol (for/in/on sth.) [ɪn'rəʊl] **(***AE* **enroll)** sich (für etwas) anmelden, sich einschreiben IV 3 (106)
enrolment [ɪn'rəʊlmənt] **(***AE* **enrollment)** Anmeldung, Einschreibung IV 3 (106)
enter ['entə]:
1. betreten, hineingehen in; eintreten II
2. **enter a password** ein Passwort eingeben III
entertainment [ˌentə'teɪnmənt] Unterhaltung *(Zeitvertreib)* IV 2 (56)
enthusiastic (about) [ɪnˌθjuːzi'æstɪk] begeistert (von) IV 3 (94)
entire [ɪn'taɪə] gesamte(r, s), ganze(r, s) IV 3 (88)
entirely [ɪn'taɪəli] völlig *(Adv.)* IV 3 (88)
entrance ['entrəns] Eingang III

entry ['entri]:
1. Eintrag, Eintragung *(im Tagebuch, Wörterbuch)* II
2. Eintritt, Zutritt III
°3. Beitrag, Einsendung *(z.B. zu einem Wettbewerb)*
envelope ['envələʊp] (Brief-)Umschlag IV 3 (107)
environment [ɪn'vaɪrənmənt] Umwelt; Umfeld, Umgebung IV 2 (65)
environmental [ɪnˌvaɪrən'mentl] Umwelt- IV 2 (65)
°**episode** ['epɪsəʊd] Episode; Folge *(z.B. einer TV-Serie)*
equal ['iːkwəl] gleich, gleichgestellt III
equality [i'kwɒləti] Gleichheit, Gleichberechtigung IV 1 (28)
equally [iːkwəli] gleichermaßen, genauso III
equipment *(no pl)* [ɪ'kwɪpmənt] Ausrüstung II
equivalent [ɪ'kwɪvələnt]:
1. Äquivalent, Gegenwert, Entsprechung IV 4 (118)
2. **be equivalent to sth.** einer Sache entsprechen IV 4 (118)
era ['ɪərə] Ära, Epoche IV 1 (8/9)
escalator ['eskəleɪtə] Rolltreppe IV 1 (21)
escape [ɪ'skeɪp]:
1. Flucht III
2. fliehen III
°**Esky** ['eski] *(AusE)* Kühlbox
especially [ɪ'speʃli] besonders, vor allem II
essay (on/about) ['eseɪ] Aufsatz (über) IV 4 (129)
essential [ɪ'senʃl] (absolut) notwendig, wesentlich IV 4 (118)
essentially [ɪ'senʃəli] im Grunde genommen, grundsätzlich, prinzipiell *(Adv.)* IV 4 (118)
establish [ɪ'stæblɪʃ] etablieren, gründen, aufbauen, einrichten IV 2 (58)
estimate ['estɪmeɪt] schätzen IV 2 (58)
estimate ['estɪmət] Schätzung IV 2 (58)
etc. (et cetera) [et'setərə] usw. (und so weiter) I
EU [ˌiː 'juː] EU (Europäische Union) III
euro (€) ['jʊərəʊ] Euro III
Europe ['jʊərəp] Europa III
European Union [ˌjʊərəpiːən 'juːniən] Europäische Union III
evaluate [ɪ'væljueɪt] bewerten, einschätzen; auswerten IV 3 (99)
evaluation [ɪˌvælju'eɪʃn] Beurteilung, Bewertung, Einschätzung IV 3 (99)
even ['iːvn] sogar II **not even** (noch) nicht einmal II
even if ['iːvn‿ɪf] selbst wenn II
even though [ˌiːvn 'ðəʊ] selbst wenn, obwohl *(betont)* IV 1 (42)
evening ['iːvnɪŋ] Abend I **in the evening** abends, am Abend I
event [ɪ'vent] Ereignis II

ever ['evə] jemals II **better than ever** besser als je zuvor II **Have you ever been to ...?** Bist du jemals in ... gewesen? II
every ['evri] jede(r, s) I
everybody ['evribɒdi] jeder; alle I
everyday ['evrideɪ] Alltags- I
everyone ['evribwʌn] jeder; alle I
everything ['evriθɪŋ] alles I
everywhere ['evriweə] überall II
evidence *(no pl)* ['evɪdəns] Nachweis(e), Beweis(e) IV 1 (29)
ex- [eks] Ex-; ehemalige(r, s) IV 4 (116)
exact [ɪg'zækt] genau III
exactly [ɪg'zæktli] genau III
exam [ɪg'zæm] Prüfung III
examination [ɪgˌzæmɪ'neɪʃn]:
1. Überprüfung, Untersuchung IV 3 (80)
2. **(***infml auch* **exam)** Prüfung IV 3 (80)
take/do an exam(ination) eine Prüfung machen IV 3 (80)
examine sb./sth. (for sth.) [ɪg'zæmɪn] jn./etwas (auf etwas) untersuchen IV 3 (80)
example [ɪg'zɑːmpl] Beispiel II **for example** zum Beispiel II
excellent ['eksələnt] ausgezeichnet, hervorragend I
except [ɪk'sept] außer, bis auf II
except for außer, bis auf IV 4 (115)
exception [ɪk'sepʃn] Ausnahme IV 2 (65)
exceptional [ɪk'sepʃənl] außergewöhnlich IV 2 (65)
excerpt (from) ['eksɜːpt] Auszug, Ausschnitt (aus) IV 3 (107)
exchange [ɪks'tʃeɪndʒ]:
1. Austausch; Austausch- III
°**clothes exchange** Kleider(tausch)börse
°2. austauschen
excited [ɪk'saɪtɪd] aufgeregt, gespannt I
exciting [ɪk'saɪtɪŋ] aufregend, spannend I
exclamation mark [ˌekskla'meɪʃn mɑːk] Ausrufezeichen II
excursion [ɪk'skɜːʃn] Exkursion, Ausflug IV 3 (88)
Excuse me, ... [ɪk'skjuːz miː] Entschuldigung, ... / Entschuldigen Sie, ... *(Darf ich mal stören?)* II
execute ['eksɪkjuːt] hinrichten IV 1 (41)
execution [ˌeksɪ'kjuːʃn] Hinrichtung IV 1 (41)
executive [ɪg'zekjətɪv] Exekutive IV 1 (43)
exercise ['eksəsaɪz] Aufgabe, Übung I
exercise book ['eksəsaɪz bʊk] Schulheft, Übungsheft I
exhausted [ɪg'zɔːstɪd] erschöpft IV 4 (127)
exhibit [ɪg'zɪbɪt]:
1. ausstellen, zeigen IV 2 (63)
2. Ausstellungsstück IV 2 (63)

exhibition [ˌeksɪˈbɪʃn] Ausstellung; Messe IV 1 (18)
exist [ɪgˈzɪst] existieren IV 1 (19)
exit [ˈeksɪt] Ausgang; Ausfahrt IV 1 (30)
exotic [ɪgˈzɒtɪk] exotisch IV 2 (45)
°**expand on sth.** [ɪkˈspænd ɒn] etwas weiter ausführen
expect sth. [ɪkˈspekt] etwas erwarten III
°**expectation** [ˌekspekˈteɪʃn] Erwartung
expensive [ɪkˈspensɪv] teuer I
experience [ɪkˈspɪəriəns]:
1. erfahren, erleben III
2. *(no pl)* Erfahrung(en) III
experiment [ɪkˈsperɪmənt]:
1. Experiment IV 3 (88)
2. **experiment (on/with)** experimentieren (an/mit) IV 3 (88)
expert [ˈekspɜːt] Experte/Expertin III
explain sth. to sb. [ɪkˈspleɪn] jm. etwas erklären, erläutern I
°**explanation** [ˌekspləˈneɪʃn] Erklärung
explode [ɪkˈspləʊd] explodieren III
exploit [ɪkˈsplɔɪt] *(Menschen)* ausnutzen; *(Bodenschätze)* ausbeuten; *(Gelegenheit)* ausnutzen IV 4 (118)
exploitation [ˌeksplɔɪˈteɪʃn] Ausbeutung; Abbau *(von Rohstoffen)* IV 4 (118)
explore [ɪkˈsplɔː] erkunden, erforschen III
explorer [ɪkˈsplɔːrə] Forschungsreisende(r), Entdecker/in IV 2 (58)
explosive [ɪkˈspləʊsɪv]:
1. explosiv IV 1 (40)
2. Sprengstoff; Sprengsatz IV 1 (40)
export [ˈekspɔːt] Export, Ausfuhr III
express [ɪkˈspres] ausdrücken, zum Ausdruck bringen IV 1 (28)
expression [ɪkˈspreʃn] Ausdruck IV 1 (28)
°**extract** [ˈekstrækt] Auszug *(aus einem Buch, Film)*
extreme [ɪkˈstriːm]:
1. extrem III
2. Extrem III
eye [aɪ] Auge I **make eye contact** Blickkontakt herstellen III

F

fabric [ˈfæbrɪk] Stoff *(zum Nähen)* IV 4 (119)
fabric marker [ˈfæbrɪk mɑːkə] Stoffmarker *(Stift, mit dem man auf Stoff schreiben/malen kann)* IV 4 (119)
fabulous [ˈfæbjələs] sagenhaft, fabelhaft IV 1 (22)
face [feɪs]:
1. Gesicht I
face to face von Angesicht zu Angesicht IV 1 (14)
2. **face sth.** vor etwas stehen; mit etwas konfrontiert werden *(Problem)* IV 2 (58)
be faced with konfrontiert werden mit IV 2 (58)
facilities *(pl)* [fəˈsɪlətiz] Einrichtungen, Geräte IV 2 (56)
fact [fækt] Tatsache, Fakt III **in fact** eigentlich, in Wirklichkeit III
factor [ˈfæktə] Faktor III
factory [ˈfæktri] Fabrik II
fail [feɪl] scheitern; (es) nicht schaffen IV 1 (19) **fail sb.** jdn. enttäuschen; jdn. im Stich lassen IV 1 (28)
failure [ˈfeɪljə] Misserfolg, Fehlschlag IV 1 (19)
fair [feə] fair, gerecht I
fairly [ˈfeəli] ziemlich, recht III
fall [fɔːl] *(AE)* Herbst II
fall [fɔːl], **fell, fallen** fallen, stürzen; hinfallen I **fall asleep** einschlafen I **fall for sb.** sich in jn. verlieben IV 4 (110/111) **fall for sth.** auf etwas hereinfallen IV 4 (110/111) **fall in love (with sb.)** sich verlieben (in jn.) IV 4 (116) **fall off a bike** vom Fahrrad (herunter)fallen III
fallen [ˈfɔːlən] *siehe* **fall**
false [fɔːls] falsch III
family [ˈfæməli] Familie I **a family of four** eine vierköpfige Familie III **the Blackwell family** (die) Familie Blackwell I
family tree [ˌfæməli ˈtriː] (Familien-) Stammbaum I
famine [ˈfæmɪn] Hungersnot III
famous (for) [ˈfeɪməs] berühmt (für, wegen) I **world-famous** weltberühmt IV 1 (16)
fan [fæn] Fan, Anhänger I
fantastic [fænˈtæstɪk] fantastisch I
FAQ (= frequently asked questions) [ˌef eɪ ˈkju] häufig gestellte Fragen IV 3 (88)
far [fɑː] weit (entfernt) I
so far bis jetzt; bis hierher II
go far weit reichen IV 1 (28)
°**fare** [feə]: **they fared better** es erging ihnen besser
farm [fɑːm] Bauernhof, Farm I
farmer [ˈfɑːmə] Bauer/Bäuerin, Landwirt/in I
farther [ˈfɑːðə] weiter IV 4 (129)
fascist [ˈfæʃɪst]:
1. Faschist/in IV 1 (40)
2. faschistisch IV 1 (40)
fashion [ˈfæʃn] Mode II
fashionista [ˌfæʃnˈiːstə] Modefreak IV 4 (119)
fast [fɑːst] schnell I **be fast** vorgehen *(Uhr)* III
fast-moving [ˌfɑːst ˈmuːvɪŋ] sich schnell bewegend IV 2 (76)
fast-paced [ˌfɑːst ˈpeɪst] flott, rasant, tempogeladen IV 3 (95)
fat [fæt] dick, fett I
father [ˈfɑːðə] Vater I
fault [fɔːlt] Schuld, Fehler III
favourite [ˈfeɪvərɪt]:
1. Lieblings- I
my favourite day mein Lieblingstag I
2. Liebling, Favorit/in IV 1 (22)
fear [fɪə]:
1. fürchten, befürchten IV 1 (33)
2. **fear (of)** Angst (vor) IV 1 (33)
feature [ˈfiːtʃə]:
1. Merkmal, Eigenschaft IV 1 (17)
°2. bieten, haben; vorkommen, eine Rolle spielen
February [ˈfebruəri] Februar I
fed [fed] *siehe* **feed**
federation [ˌfedəˈreɪʃn] Föderation, Bund; Verband IV 2 (58)
fee [fiː] Gebühr; Honorar; (Mitglieds-) Beitrag IV 3 (109)
feed [fiːd] Feed *(abonnierbare elektronische Nachricht im Internet)* IV 1 (14)
feed [fiːd], **fed, fed** füttern I **feed on sth.** sich von etwas ernähren IV 2 (53)
feedback *(no pl)* [ˈfiːdbæk] Rückmeldung, Feedback III
feeding time [ˈfiːdɪŋ taɪm] Fütterungszeit I
feel [fiːl], **felt, felt**:
1. fühlen; sich fühlen I
I don't feel well. Mir geht's nicht gut. / Ich fühle mich nicht gut. II **I feel sick.** Mir ist schlecht. II
2. sich anfühlen III
feeling [ˈfiːlɪŋ] Gefühl I
feet [fiːt] *plural of* **foot**
fell [fel] *siehe* **fall**
felt [felt] *siehe* **feel**
felt pen [ˌfelt ˈpen] Filzstift I
female [ˈfiːmeɪl] weiblich; Frau IV 4 (116)
fence [fens] Zaun II
ferry [ˈferi] Fähre I
festival [ˈfestɪvl] Fest, Festival II
few [fjuː] wenige IV 4 (122) **a few** ein paar, einige II
fibre [ˈfaɪbə] **(***AE* **fiber)** Faser; Ballaststoffe IV 4 (118)
°**fictional** [ˈfɪkʃənl] erfunden, fiktiv; fiktional
field [fiːld] Feld, Acker, Weide II
fierce [fɪəs] heftig, wild III
fight [faɪt]:
1. **fight, fought, fought** kämpfen I
2. **fight sb.** jn. bekämpfen II
fighter [ˈfaɪtə] Kämpfer/in II
figure [ˈfɪgə]:
1. Zahl, Ziffer III
2. Figur, Gestalt III
file [faɪl]: **background file** Hintergrundinformation(en) I **grammar file** *Zusammenfassung der Grammatik jeder Unit* I **skills file** Übersicht über Lern- und Arbeitstechniken I
fill [fɪl] füllen III °**fill out** ausfüllen
film [fɪlm]:
1. filmen I
2. Film I

°**film-maker** ['fɪlm meɪkə] Filmemacher/in
final ['faɪnl] Finale, Endspiel I
finally ['faɪnəli] endlich, schließlich III
°**finance** ['faɪnæns] finanzieren
°**financial** [faɪ'nænʃl] finanziell
find [faɪnd], **found, found** finden I
find sth. out etwas herausfinden II
°**findings** *(pl)* ['faɪndɪŋz] Ergebnisse
fine [faɪn] gut, in Ordnung, prima II
Fine, thanks. Gut, danke. I **That's fine.** Es ist gut so. II
finger ['fɪŋgə] Finger II
finish ['fɪnɪʃ] enden I **finish sth.** etwas beenden; mit etwas fertig werden/sein I **We're finished.** Wir sind fertig. I
fire ['faɪə]:
1. Feuer II
2. (ab)schießen, (ab)feuern IV 1 (17)
°**fire starter** ['faɪə stɑːtə] Anzünder *(etwas, womit man Feuer entfacht)*
fireplace ['faɪəpleɪs] Kamin II
°**firestick** ['faɪəstɪk] Feuerstock *(Werkzeug zum Entfachen eines Feuers)*
firework ['faɪəwɜːk] Feuerwerkskörper II **fireworks** *(pl)* Feuerwerk II
first [fɜːst] zuerst, als Erstes I **First, ...** Erstens, ... I **at first** zuerst, anfangs, am Anfang II **in the first place** erstens, in erster Linie; überhaupt IV 1 (29) **the first day** der erste Tag I
first-hand [ˌfɜːst 'hænd] aus erster Hand IV 3 (88)
first-person narrative [fɜːst ˌpɜːsn 'nærətɪv] Ich-Erzählung IV 2 (71)
Firstly, ... ['fɜːstli] Erstens ... IV 1 (29)
fish [fɪʃ]:
1. *pl* **fish** Fisch I
2. fish sth. out etwas herausfischen III
fishing village ['fɪʃɪŋ vɪlɪdʒ] Fischerdorf II
fit [fɪt] fit, in Form II
fit [fɪt] passen (zu) IV 3 (101)
fitness centre ['fɪtnəs sentə] Fitnesszentrum IV 1 (15)
five [faɪv] fünf I
fix sth. [fɪks] festlegen; feststellen; befestigen; reparieren, in Ordnung bringen IV 3 (80)
fixed [fɪkst] fest, festgelegt II
flag [flæg] Fahne, Flagge II
flash [flæʃ]:
1. Lichtblitz II
a flash of lightning ein Blitz II
°**2.** aufblitzen (lassen); blinken, leuchten
°**flashing lights** *(pl)* [flæʃɪŋ 'laɪts] Warnlicht; Blaulicht
flashlight ['flæʃlaɪt] *(AE)* Taschenlampe III
flat [flæt] Wohnung I
flat [flæt] flach; eben III

flavour ['fleɪvə] **(*AE* flavor)** Geschmack, Geschmacksrichtung II
fled [fled] *siehe* **flee**
flee (from) [fliː], **fled, fled** flüchten (aus), fliehen (vor) IV 1 (19)
fleet [fliːt] Flotte IV 2 (62)
flew [fluː] *siehe* **fly**
flexible ['fleksəbl] flexibel IV 3 (95)
flight [flaɪt] Flug IV 2 (54)
°**flightless** ['flaɪtləs] flugunfähig
flirt [flɜːt] flirten IV 4 (112)
float [fləʊt] schwimmen, *(auf der Wasseroberfläche)* treiben IV 1 (35)
°**flock** [flɒk] Herde
flood [flʌd]:
1. Flut; Überschwemmung, Hochwasser IV 2 (52)
2. überschwemmen, überfluten IV 2 (52)
be flooded unter Wasser stehen IV 2 (52)
floor [flɔː]:
1. Fußboden I
2. Stock(werk) I
flow [fləʊ] Redefluss IV 4 (123)
flower ['flaʊə] Blume; Blüte II
flown [fləʊn] *siehe* **fly**
fly [flaɪ], **flew, flown** fliegen II
flying fox [ˌflaɪɪŋ 'fɒks] Flughund IV 2 (46)
focus ['fəʊkəs]: **focus on sth.** sich auf etwas konzentrieren III
fold [fəʊld] falten III
folk [fəʊk] *(pl, infml)* Leute III
follow ['fɒləʊ] folgen I **Follow me.** Folge mir. / Folgt mir. I
follower ['fɒləʊə] Follower *(Anhänger/in, Fan)* IV 1 (14)
food [fuːd] Essen; Lebensmittel; Futter I
°**fool sb.** [fuːl] jm. etwas vormachen, jn. täuschen
foot [fʊt], *pl* **feet** Fuß *(auch Längenmaß: 30,5 cm)* II **go on foot** (zu Fuß) gehen III **on foot** zu Fuß III
football ['fʊtbɔːl] Fußball I
footprint ['fʊtprɪnt] Fußabdruck II
for [fɔː], [fə] für I **for a while** eine Weile, eine Zeit lang III **for example** zum Beispiel II **for free** kostenlos, umsonst III **for hours/weeks/...** seit Stunden/Wochen/... III **for miles** meilenweit I **for the first time** zum ersten Mal III **go for a walk** einen Spaziergang machen, spazieren gehen I **How's that for acoustics?** Ist das nicht eine tolle Akustik? / Das nennt man tolle Akustik! IV 1 (10) **What's for homework?** Was haben wir als Hausaufgabe auf? I **What's for lunch?** Was gibt es zum Mittagessen? I
forbade [fə'bæd] *siehe* **forbid**
forbid [fə'bɪd], **forbade, forbidden** verbieten, untersagen III
forbidden [fə'bɪdn] *siehe* **forbid**

force sb. to do sth. [fɔːs] jn. zwingen, etwas zu tun III
forearm ['fɔːrɑːm] Unterarm III
foreground ['fɔːgraʊnd] Vordergrund I
foreign ['fɒrən] ausländisch, fremd IV 1 (19)
foreign language [fɒrən 'læŋgwɪdʒ] Fremdsprache IV 1 (19)
foreigner ['fɒrənə] Ausländer/in; Fremde/r IV 1 (19)
forest ['fɒrɪst] Wald II
forever [fər'evə] **(*BE auch* for ever)** (für) immer; ewig II
forget [fə'get], **forgot, forgotten** vergessen I
forgetful [fə'getfl] vergesslich IV 1 (12)
forgot [fə'gɒt] *siehe* **forget**
forgotten [fə'gɒtn] *siehe* **forget**
fork [fɔːk] Gabel II
form [fɔːm]:
1. *(BE)* Klasse IV 3 (81)
2. form (of) Form (von) I
form sth. [fɔːm] etwas bilden, formen III
formal ['fɔːml] formell, förmlich III
°**format** ['fɔːmæt] Format
°**formation** [fɔː'meɪʃn] Bildung, Formierung
former ['fɔːmə] ehemalige(r, s), frühere(r, s) I
°**fort** [fɔːt] Fort *(Befestigungsanlage)*
fortunately ['fɔːtʃənətli] zum Glück, glücklicherweise IV 2 (64)
forward(s) ['fɔːwəd], ['fɔːwədz] nach vorne; vorwärts IV 1 (32) **look forward to sth.** sich auf etwas freuen II
fossil ['fɒsl] fossil IV 4 (118)
fossil fuel ['fɒsl fjuːəl] fossiler Brennstoff IV 4 (118)
fought [fɔːt] *siehe* **fight**
found [faʊnd]:
1. *siehe* **find**
2. gründen III
founding member [ˌfaʊndɪŋ 'membə] Gründungsmitglied IV 2 (76)
four [fɔː] vier I
fox [fɒks] Fuchs IV 2 (46) **flying fox** Flughund IV 2 (46)
frame [freɪm] Rahmen; Gestell, Fahrgestell IV 1 (17)
freak [friːk] Freak, Fan IV 1 (18)
free [friː]:
1. frei I
2. kostenlos II
for free kostenlos, umsonst III
free time [ˌfriː 'taɪm] Freizeit, freie Zeit I
free-time activity [ˌfriː taɪm‿æk'tɪvəti] Freizeitaktivität I
freeze [friːz], **froze, frozen** (ge)frieren; erstarren III
French [frentʃ] Französisch I
French fries *(pl)* [ˌfrentʃ 'fraɪz] *(AE)* Pommes frites II
frequent ['friːkwənt] häufig IV 1 (32)

frequently asked questions (FAQ) [ˌfriːkwəntli ɑːskt 'kwestʃənz] häufig gestellte Fragen IV 3 (88)
fresh [freʃ] frisch II
fresh water [ˌfreʃ 'wɔːtə] Süßwasser IV 4 (118)
freshman ['freʃmən], *pl* **freshmen** Studienanfänger/in; *Anfänger/in in der High School* IV 3 (108)
freshwater ['freʃwɔːtə] Süßwasser- IV 4 (118)
Friday ['fraɪdeɪ], ['fraɪdi] Freitag I
friend [frend] Freund/in I
friendly ['frendli] freundlich I **friendly with sb.** mit jm. befreundet IV 4 (116)
fries *(pl)* [fraɪz] *(AE)* (*kurz für:* French fries) Pommes frites II
fright [fraɪt]: **in fright** ängstlich, erschrocken III
frightened ['fraɪtnd] verängstigt IV 1 (34) **be frightened of sth.** Angst haben vor etwas IV 1 (34)
frisbee ['frɪzbi] Frisbee II
frog [frɒg] Frosch I
from [frɒm], [frəm] aus, von I **from … to …** von … bis … I **from behind** von hinten II **from the back of the bus** aus dem hinteren Teil des Busses II **I'm from Plymouth.** Ich bin aus Plymouth. / Ich komme aus Plymouth. I
front [frʌnt] Vorderseite I **in front of** vor *(räumlich)* I **to the front** nach vorn II
frown [fraʊn]:
1. die Stirn runzeln II
2. Stirnrunzeln IV 1 (24)
froze [frəʊz] *siehe* **freeze**
frozen ['frəʊzn] *siehe* **freeze** **frozen (food)** Tiefkühl-(Kost); gefroren(e Lebensmittel) III
fruit [fruːt] Obst, Früchte; Frucht I
fruit salad [ˌfruːt 'sæləd] Obstsalat I
frustrate [frʌ'streɪt] frustrieren IV 2 (55)
fry [fraɪ] braten *(in der Pfanne)* IV 4 (120)
fuel ['fjuːəl] Treibstoff, Kraftstoff, Brennstoff IV 4 (118)
full (of) [fʊl] voll (von, mit) I
full moon [ˌfʊl 'muːn] Vollmond II
full sentence [ˌfʊl 'sentəns] ganzer Satz II
full stop [ˌfʊl 'stɒp] Punkt *(Satzzeichen)* II
full-time [ˌfʊl 'taɪm] Vollzeit-, Ganztags- IV 3 (108)
fun [fʌn] Spaß I **have fun** Spaß haben, sich amüsieren I **make fun of sb./sth.** sich über jn./etwas lustig machen III **That sounds fun.** Das klingt nach Spaß. I **That's fun.** Das macht Spaß. I **Was it fun?** Hat es Spaß gemacht? I
fun park ['fʌn pɑːk] Vergnügungspark I
°**function** ['fʌŋkʃn] Funktion
funny ['fʌni] witzig, komisch I
furious (with/at sb.) ['fjʊəriəs] wütend IV 4 (116)
furniture *(no pl)* ['fɜːnɪtʃə] Möbel III
further ['fɜːðə]:
1. weiter II
2. weitere(r, s), zusätzliche(r, s) IV 4 (129)
furthermore [ˌfɜːðə'mɔː] außerdem, des Weiteren IV 2 (50)
furthest ['fɜːðɪst] am weitesten II
fury ['fjʊəri] Wut IV 4 (116)
future ['fjuːtʃə] Zukunft; zukünftige(r, s) II

G

gain [geɪn] bekommen; gewinnen IV 3 (88)
gallery ['gæləri] Galerie III
game [geɪm] Spiel I
gang [gæŋ] Gang *(Bande)* IV 1 (28)
gap [gæp] Lücke IV 1 (28)
gap year ['gæp jɪə] ein Jahr Auszeit *(das oft zwischen Schulabschluss und Beginn des Studiums genommen wird)* IV 1 (28)
garage ['gærɑːʒ], ['gærɪdʒ] Garage I
garbage ['gɑːbɪdʒ] *(AE)* Müll, Abfall III
garden ['gɑːdn] Garten I
gardener ['gɑːdnə] Gärtner/in III
gardening ['gɑːdnɪŋ] Gärtnern, Gartenarbeit I
garment ['gɑːmənt] Kleidungsstück IV 4 (118)
gas [gæs]:
1. Gas IV 4 (120)
2. *(AE)* Benzin III
gas station ['gæs steɪʃn] *(AE)* Tankstelle III
gate [geɪt] Tor, Pforte, Gatter II
gather ['gæðə] sammeln; (sich) versammeln IV 2 (77)
gatherer ['gæðərə] Sammler/in IV 2 (77)
gathering ['gæðərɪŋ] Treffen, Versammlung IV 2 (77)
gave [geɪv] *siehe* **give**
gaze [geɪz] blicken, starren III
GCSE (= General Certificate of Secondary Education) [ˌdʒiː siː‿es 'iː] *Prüfung für Schüler ab 15, mittlerer Schulabschluss* IV 3 (81)
°**g'day** [gə'deɪ] *(AusE, infml)* Hallo! / Guten Tag!
gel [dʒel] Gel II
general ['dʒenrəl] allgemein IV 3 (81) **in general** im Allgemeinen, generell IV 3 (81)
General Certificate of Secondary Education (= GCSE) [ˌdʒenrəl sətɪfɪkət‿əv ˌsekəndri‿edʒu'keɪʃn] *Prüfung für Schüler ab 15, mittlerer Schulabschluss* IV 3 (81)
generally ['dʒenrəli] generell, allgemein III
generation [ˌdʒenə'reɪʃn] Generation III
generosity [ˌdʒenə'rɒsəti] Großzügigkeit IV 3 (86)
generous ['dʒenərəs] großzügig IV 3 (86)
gentlemen ['dʒentlmən]: **Ladies and gentlemen** Meine Damen und Herren / Sehr geehrte Damen und Herren III
geography [dʒi'ɒgrəfi] Geografie I
geometry [dʒi'ɒmətri] Geometrie IV 3 (82)
German ['dʒɜːmən] Deutsch; deutsch I **in German** auf Deutsch I
gesture ['dʒestʃə] Geste; Handbewegung IV 3 (93) **gestures** *(pl)* Gestik IV 3 (93)
get [get], **got, got**:
1. bekommen I
get along (with sb.) (gut) zurechtkommen (mit jm.), sich (gut) verstehen (mit jm.) IV 3 (98) **get the hang of sth.** *(infml)* den Dreh raushaben/rausbekommen (bei etwas); etwas kapieren III **get the message across** die Botschaft rüberbringen IV 4 (137) **get the vote** das Stimmrecht erhalten IV 1 (42)
2. get sth. (sich) etwas besorgen, (sich) etwas holen II
3. gelangen, (hin)kommen I
get back to sb. sich bei jm. (wieder) melden IV 3 (89) **get in touch (with sb.)** (mit jm.) Kontakt aufnehmen; sich (mit jm.) in Verbindung setzen II **get in(to) a car/taxi** in ein Auto/Taxi einsteigen II **get into trouble** in Schwierigkeiten geraten, Ärger kriegen III **get lost** sich verlaufen, sich verirren III **get off (the bus/boat)** (aus dem Bus/Boot) aussteigen I **get off your phone** ein Telefongespräch beenden; aufhören zu telefonieren IV 4 (125) **get on** vorankommen, zurechtkommen II **get on (the bus/boat)** (in den Bus / das Boot) einsteigen I **get out of a car/taxi** aus einem Auto/Taxi aussteigen II **get up** aufstehen I
4. get angry/cold/… wütend/kalt/… werden I
get paid bezahlt werden III **get ready (for)** sich fertig machen (für); sich vorbereiten (auf) II
5. get sth. etwas verstehen, mitbekommen I
Did you get it? *(infml)* Hast du es verstanden? / Hast du es mitbekommen? I
ghost [gəʊst] Geist, Gespenst I
giant ['dʒaɪənt] Riese III

gift [gɪft] Geschenk; Gabe; Talent IV 2 (57)
giraffe [dʒəˈrɑːf] Giraffe I
girl [gɜːl] Mädchen I
girlfriend [ˈgɜːlfrend] (feste) Freundin III
°**gist** [dʒɪst]: **the gist (of sth.)** *(no pl)* das Wesentliche (an/von etwas)
give [gɪv], **gave, given** geben I **give a talk (about)** einen Vortrag / eine Rede halten (über) I **give sb. a hug** jn. umarmen II **give sb. a lift** jn. mitnehmen II **give up** aufgeben III
given [ˈgɪvn] *siehe* **give**
glacier [ˈglæsiə] Gletscher IV 2 (76)
glad [glæd] froh, dankbar III
glass [glɑːs] Glas II **a glass of ...** ein Glas ... II
glasses *(pl)* [ˈglɑːsɪz] (eine) Brille II
°**glisten** [ˈglɪsn] funkeln, glitzern
global [ˈgləʊbl] global, weltweit IV 4 (119)
global warming [ˌgləʊbl ˈwɔːmɪŋ] Erderwärmung IV 4 (119)
globalization [ˌgləʊbəlaɪˈzeɪʃn] Globalisierung IV 4 (129)
globalize [ˈgləʊbəlaɪz] globalisieren IV 4 (129)
globe [gləʊb] Globus; Kugel IV 3 (106) **all (a)round the globe** auf der ganzen Welt IV 3 (106)
glove [glʌv] Handschuh II **a pair of gloves** ein Paar Handschuhe II
glue [gluː] Klebstoff I
glue stick [ˈgluː stɪk] Klebestift I
glum [glʌm] niedergeschlagen, bedrückt, mürrisch IV 4 (116)
go [gəʊ], **went, gone**:
1. gehen; fahren I
go by vergehen, vorübergehen *(Zeit)* III **go by car/bus/...** mit dem Auto/Bus/... fahren I **go down** untergehen *(Sonne)* I **go down** (ab)sinken, fallen, nach unten gehen IV 2 (52) **go for a walk** einen Spaziergang machen, spazieren gehen I **go in** hineingehen II **go on** im Gang sein; andauern III **go on (with)** weiterreden, fortfahren (mit); weitermachen (mit) I **go out with sb.** mit jm. (aus)gehen *(eine Beziehung haben)* IV 4 (116) **go sailing** segeln; segeln gehen I **go shopping** einkaufen gehen I **go together** zusammenpassen, zueinander passen III **go with sth.** zu etwas passen; zu etwas gehören I **go wrong** schiefgehen III **Here we go.** Los geht's. / Jetzt geht's los. I
2. werden II
go bad/hard/mad schlecht/hart/verrückt werden II **go far** weit reichen IV 1 (28) **go red** rot werden, erröten II
3. Have a go. Versuch's mal. I

goal [gəʊl]:
1. Tor *(Sport)* II
2. Ziel *(Absicht, Lebensziel)* III
goat [gəʊt] Ziege II
god, God [gɒd] Gott III
going to [ˈgəʊɪŋ tʊ]: **He is going to visit his dad.** Er hat vor, seinen Vater zu besuchen. / Er wird seinen Vater besuchen. I
gold [gəʊld]:
1. Gold; Gold- I
2. golden, Gold- II
gone [gɒn] *siehe* **go** **be gone** weg sein, nicht (mehr) da sein III
good [gʊd]:
1. gut I
Good luck! Viel Glück! I **Good morning.** Guten Morgen. I **be good at kung fu** gut sein in Kung-Fu I **smell good** gut riechen II
2. brav II
good-looking [ˌgʊd ˈlʊkɪŋ] gutaussehend II
Goodbye. [ˌgʊdˈbaɪ] Auf Wiedersehen. I
Goodnight. [ˌgʊdˈnaɪt] Gute Nacht! IV 1 (14)
goods *(pl)* [gʊdz] Waren, Güter I
gossip [ˈgɒsɪp]:
1. Klatsch, Tratsch IV 3 (100)
2. klatschen, tratschen IV 3 (100)
got [gɒt] *siehe* **get** **have got** haben I
govern [ˈgʌvən] regieren III
government [ˈgʌvənmənt] Regierung II
governor [ˈgʌvənə] Gouverneur/in III
grab [græb] schnappen, packen III
grade [greɪd] *(AE)*:
1. Klasse, Jahrgang(sstufe) IV 3 (80)
2. (Schul-)Note, Zensur IV 3 (80)
passing grade Note/Zensur, mit der man bestanden hat III
graduate [ˈgrædʒuət] Hochschulabsolvent/in IV 3 (80)
graduate (from) [ˈgrædʒueɪt] den Abschluss machen (an) *(Schule, Hochschule)* IV 3 (80)
graduation [ˌgrædʒuˈeɪʃn] (Schul-/Universitäts-)Abschluss IV 3 (80)
gram [græm] Gramm II
grammar [ˈgræmə] Grammatik I
grammar file [ˈgræmə faɪl] *Zusammenfassung der Grammatik jeder Unit* I
grand [grænd] groß(artig), eindrucksvoll IV 4 (110/111)
grandfather [ˈgrænfɑːðə] Großvater I
grandma [ˈgrænmɑː] Oma I
grandmother [ˈgrænmʌðə] Großmutter I
grandpa [ˈgrænpɑː] Opa I
grandparents *(pl)* [ˈgrænpeərənts] Großeltern I
granny [ˈgræni] *(infml)* Oma IV 4 (119)
graphic [ˈgræfɪk] grafisch; anschaulich IV 1 (40)

graphic novel [ˌgræfɪk ˈnɒvl] Bildroman, Comicroman IV 1 (40)
graphics *(pl)* [ˈgræfɪks] Grafiken III
grass [grɑːs] Gras; Rasen I
grateful [ˈgreɪtfl] dankbar IV 1 (23)
grave [greɪv] Grab II
gravel [ˈgrævl] Kies, Schotter III
gravestone [ˈgreɪvstəʊn] Grabstein III
grayscale [ˈgreɪskeɪl] *(AE)* graustufig, in Graustufen IV 4 (112) **go grayscale** das Handy auf schwarz-weiß umstellen *(in den Einstellungen)* IV 4 (112)
great [greɪt] großartig I
Great Britain (GB) [ˌgreɪt ˈbrɪtn] Großbritannien I
great-grandfather [ˌgreɪt ˈgrænfɑːðə] Urgroßvater III
great-grandmother [ˌgreɪt ˈgrænmʌðə] Urgroßmutter III
greatly [ˈgreɪtli] stark, erheblich IV 4 (123)
green [griːn] grün I
greenhouse [ˈgriːnhaʊs] Gewächshaus, Treibhaus IV 2 (54)
greenhouse gas [ˌgriːnhaʊs ˈgæs] Treibhausgas IV 4 (120)
greeting [ˈgriːtɪŋ] Gruß(formel), Begrüßung IV 1 (14)
grew [gruː] *siehe* **grow**
grey [greɪ] grau I
greyscale [ˈgreɪskeɪl] graustufig, in Graustufen IV 4 (112) **go greyscale** das Handy auf schwarz-weiß umstellen *(in den Einstellungen)* IV 4 (112)
grid [grɪd] Gitter; Raster; Rechteckschema III
grin [grɪn] grinsen III
grind [graɪnd], **ground, ground** (zer)mahlen IV 1 (18)
groan [grəʊn]:
1. stöhnen II
2. *(ein/das)* Stöhnen II
groceries *(pl)* [ˈgrəʊsəriz] Lebensmittel IV 3 (91)
grocery store [ˈgrəʊsəri stɔː] *(AE)* Lebensmittelgeschäft IV 3 (91)
ground [graʊnd]:
1. *siehe* **grind**
2. ground sb. jm. Hausarrest/Ausgehverbot erteilen III
ground [graʊnd] (Erd-)Boden II
rugby ground Rugby-Platz/-Spielfeld III
group (of) [gruːp] Gruppe I
grow [grəʊ], **grew, grown**:
1. anbauen, anpflanzen I
2. wachsen I
grow up erwachsen werden; aufwachsen III
3. grow darker/old/..., grew, grown (allmählich) dunkler/alt/... werden III
growl [graʊl] knurren III
grown [grəʊn] *siehe* **grow**
growth [grəʊθ] Wachstum; Vegetation III

guard [gɑːd]:
1. bewachen III
2. Wachposten, Wache II
guardian ['gɑːdiən] Beschützer/in, Hüter/in, Wächter/in IV 4 (121)
guess [ges]:
1. raten, erraten I
Guess what, Dad ... Stell dir vor, Dad ... / Weißt du was, Dad ... I
2. I guess ... Ich nehme an, ... / Ich denke, ... III
°**3.** Vermutung
guest [gest] Gast III
guide [gaɪd]:
1. führen, begleiten III
2. Fremdenführer/in; Reiseleiter/in II
°**guidebook** ['gaɪdbʊk] Reiseführer *(Buch)*
°**guideline** ['gaɪdlaɪn] Richtlinie
guilt [gɪlt] Schuld IV 4 (119)
guilty ['gɪlti] schuldig; schuldbewusst IV 4 (119) **guilty of a crime** eines Verbrechens schuldig IV 4 (119)
guinea pig ['gɪni pɪg] Meerschweinchen I
guitar [gɪ'tɑː] Gitarre I **play the guitar** Gitarre spielen I
gun [gʌn] Schusswaffe IV 4 (124)
gunpowder ['gʌnpaʊdə] Schießpulver IV 1 (40)
guy [gaɪ]:
1. Typ, Kerl II
guys *(pl)* Leute II
2. Guy-Fawkes-Puppe IV 1 (40)
gym [dʒɪm] Turnhalle I
gymnastics [dʒɪm'næstɪks] Gymnastik, Turnen I

H

habit ['hæbɪt] (An-)Gewohnheit III
hack [hæk] hacken *(Computer)* IV 1 (40)
hacker ['hækə] Hacker/in *(Computer)* IV 1 (41)
hacktivist ['hæktɪvɪst] Hacktivist/in *(politisch engagierte/r Hacker/in)* IV 1 (41)
had [hæd] *siehe* **have** **I'd better ... (= I had better ...)** Ich sollte lieber ... III
hair [heə] Haar, Haare I
hairdresser ['heədresə] Friseur/in III
°**haka** ['hɑːkə] Haka *(ritueller Tanz der Maori)*
half [hɑːf]:
1. halbe(r, s) I
half an hour eine halbe Stunde III
half past ten halb elf (10.30 / 22.30) I
2. *pl* **halves** Hälfte; Halbzeit I
an hour and a half eineinhalb Stunden, anderthalb Stunden III
°**Half-Blood Prince** [ˌhɑːf blʌd 'prɪns] „Halbblutprinz" *(Harry Potter, Buch- und Filmtitel)*
halves [hɑːvz] *plural of* **half**
hamburger ['hæmbɜːgə] Hamburger II
hammer ['hæmə]:
1. Hammer III
2. hämmern III
hamster ['hæmstə] Hamster II
hand [hænd] Hand I **on the one hand** einerseits IV 1 (29) **on the other hand** andererseits IV 1 (29)
hand sb. sth. [hænd] jm. etwas geben, reichen III **hand sth. in** etwas abgeben; etwas einreichen II °**hand sth. out** etwas aushändigen, herausgeben
°**handle sth.** ['hændl] mit etwas umgehen, etwas handhaben
handout ['hændaʊt] Handout, Handzettel III
handshake ['hændʃeɪk] Handschlag, Händedruck III
handsome ['hænsəm] attraktiv, gut aussehend III
handy ['hændi] praktisch, nützlich; griffbereit, zur Hand, in der Nähe IV 4 (129) **come in handy** gelegen kommen, sich als nützlich erweisen IV 4 (129)
hang [hæŋ] *(infml)*:
1. get the hang of sth. den Dreh raushaben/rausbekommen (bei etwas); etwas kapieren III
2. hang, hung, hung hängen II
hang out *(infml)* abhängen, rumhängen III °**Hang on.** Moment mal. / Warte mal. °**hang sth. up** etwas aufhängen
°**hangi** ['hʌŋiː] traditionelle Art und Weise des Kochens bei den Maori *(aus der Sprache der Maori)*
happen (to) ['hæpən] geschehen, passieren (mit) I
happiness ['hæpinəs] Glück, Zufriedenheit III
happy ['hæpi] glücklich, froh I
harbour ['hɑːbə] Hafen I
hard [hɑːd]:
1. schwer, schwierig; hart I
2. try hard sich anstrengen; sich (große) Mühe geben III
hard-working [ˌhɑːd 'wɜːkɪŋ] fleißig IV 3 (86)
hardly ['hɑːdli] kaum III
harmless ['hɑːmləs] harmlos III
harmonica [hɑː'mɒnɪkə] Mundharmonika III
harvest ['hɑːvɪst] Ernte III
has [hæz]: **he/she has** er/sie hat I
°**hashtag** ['hæʃtæg] Hashtag; Rautezeichen
hat [hæt] Hut I **paper hat** Papierhut I
hate [heɪt] hassen III
have [hæv], [həv], **had, had** haben I **have a cold** eine Erkältung haben, erkältet sein II **Have a go.** Versuch's mal. I **have a look (at sth.)** nachschauen; einen Blick auf etwas werfen III **have a shower** (sich) duschen II **have breakfast** frühstücken I **have dinner** zu Abend essen I **have fun** Spaß haben, sich amüsieren I **have got** haben I **have lunch** zu Mittag essen I **have sth. done (by sb.)** etwas (von jm.) machen lassen *(erledigen lassen)* IV 3 (94) **have to do** tun müssen I **Have you ever been to ...?** Bist du jemals in ... gewesen? II **I'll have a tea/burger/...** Ich nehme einen Tee/Hamburger ... *(beim Essen, im Restaurant)* II
hay [heɪ] Heu II
he [hiː] er I
head [hed]:
1. Kopf I
2. Oberhaupt, Leiter/in III
head for sth. auf etwas zusteuern/zugehen/zufahren III
head of state [ˌhed‿əv 'steɪt] Staatsoberhaupt IV 1 (43)
head teacher [ˌhed 'tiːtʃə] Schulleiter/in III
headache ['hedeɪk]: **have a headache** Kopfschmerzen haben II
heading ['hedɪŋ] Überschrift III
headline ['hedlaɪn] Überschrift; Schlagzeile IV 1 (19)
headphones *(pl)* ['hedfəʊnz] Kopfhörer IV 1 (10)
headset ['hedset] Headset IV 4 (112)
headword ['hedwɜːd] Stichwort *(im Wörterbuch)* III
heal [hiːl] heilen IV 4 (121)
health [helθ] Gesundheit IV 3 (100)
health service ['helθ sɜːvɪs] Gesundheitswesen III
healthy ['helθi] gesund IV 3 (100)
hear [hɪə], **heard, heard** hören I
heard [hɜːd] *siehe* **hear**
heart [hɑːt] Herz II
heartbroken ['hɑːtbrəʊkən] todunglücklich, untröstlich IV 4 (116)
heartless ['hɑːtləs] herzlos IV 1 (12)
heat [hiːt]:
1. erwärmen, erhitzen IV 1 (33)
2. Hitze, Wärme IV 1 (33)
heaven ['hevn] Himmel *(im religiösen Sinn)* III
°**heavily populated** [ˌhevɪli 'pɒpjuleɪtɪd] bevölkerungsreich, dicht besiedelt
heavy ['hevi] schwer *(von Gewicht)* II
heavy rain starker Regen, heftiger Regen II
°**hectare** ['hekteə] Hektar (10.000 m²)
held [held] *siehe* **hold**
helicopter ['helɪkɒptə] Helikopter, Hubschrauber III
°**hell** [hel] Hölle

Hello. [hə'ləʊ] Hallo. / Grüß Gott. I **Say hello to … for me.** Grüß … von mir. II
help [help]:
1. helfen I
help yourself sich bedienen, zugreifen III
2. Hilfe I
helper ['helpə] Helfer/in II
helpful ['helpfl] hilfsbereit; hilfreich, nützlich IV 1 (12)
hemp [hemp] Hanf IV 4 (122)
her [hɜː], [hə]:
1. ihr, ihre I
her best friend ihr bester Freund / ihre beste Freundin I
2. sie; ihr I
herbal ['hɜːbl] Kräuter- IV 4 (120)
herbs *(pl)* [hɜːbz] Kräuter IV 4 (120)
here [hɪə] hier; hierher I **Here we go.** Los geht's. / Jetzt geht's los. I **Here you are.** Bitte sehr. / Hier bitte. II **near here** (hier) in der Nähe I **over here** hier herüber; hier drüben II **round here** hier in der Gegend III **up here** hier oben; nach hier oben II
heritage ['herɪtɪdʒ] (Kultur-, Natur-) Erbe IV 4 (121)
hero ['hɪərəʊ], *pl* **heroes** Held/in III
heroic [hə'rəʊɪk] heroisch, heldenhaft IV 4 (110/111)
hers [hɜːz] ihrer, ihre, ihrs *(zu „she")* II
herself [hɜː'self] sie/sich selbst/selber *(zu „she")* III
hesitate ['hezɪteɪt] zögern IV 1 (35)
Hi. [haɪ] Hallo. IV 1 (11)
hid [hɪd] *siehe* **hide**
hidden ['hɪdn] *siehe* **hide**
hide [haɪd], **hid, hidden** (sich) verstecken I
°**hide-and-seek** [ˌhaɪd‿ən 'siːk] Versteckspiel
high [haɪ] hoch I
high achiever [ˌhaɪ ə'tʃiːvə] leistungsstarke Person, Spitzenkraft IV 3 (107)
high commission [ˌhaɪ kə'mɪʃn] *Diplomatische Vertretung eines Commonwealth-Landes in einem anderen Commonwealth-Land* IV 1 (11)
high-quality [ˌhaɪ 'kwɒləti] von hoher Qualität, hochwertig IV 1 (28)
high school ['haɪ skuːl] *(USA) Schule für 14- bis 18-Jährige* III
higher education [ˌhaɪər‿edʒu'keɪʃn] Hochschulbildung; Hochschulwesen IV 3 (108)
highlight ['haɪlaɪt] hervorheben, markieren *(mit Textmarker)* II
highly ['haɪli] sehr, höchst, äußerst IV 1 (42)
highly respected [ˌhaɪli rɪ'spektɪd] hoch angesehen IV 1 (42)
highs and lows *(pl)* [ˌhaɪz‿ən 'ləʊz] Höhen und Tiefen IV 4 (112)

hike [haɪk]:
1. wandern III
°2. Wanderung
hill [hɪl] Hügel I
hilly ['hɪli] hügelig IV 2 (63)
him [hɪm] ihn; ihm I
himself [hɪm'self] er/ihn/ihm/sich selbst/selber III
°**Hindi** ['hɪndi] Hindi *(Amtssprache in Indien)*
hip [hɪp] Hüfte III
hire ['haɪə] *(Person)* einstellen; mieten, leihen IV 4 (121)
his [hɪz]:
1. **his friend** sein/e Freund/in I
2. seiner, seine, seins II
hiss [hɪs] zischen II
historian [hɪ'stɔːriən] Historiker/in IV 4 (110/111)
historic [hɪ'stɒrɪk] historisch *(geschichtlich bedeutsam)* II
historical [hɪ'stɒrɪkl] historisch, geschichtlich III
history ['hɪstri] Geschichte I **natural history** Naturkunde I
hit [hɪt], **hit, hit**:
1. schlagen II
2. prallen, stoßen gegen I
3. treffen II
°**HMS (= Her/His Majesty's Ship)** [ˌeɪtʃ em 'es] Königliches Schiff *(vor dem Namen eines Schiffs der britischen Marine)*
hobby ['hɒbi] Hobby I
hockey ['hɒki] Hockey II
hold [həʊld]:
1. Griff III
2. **hold, held, held** halten I
Hold on (a minute). Bleib / Bleiben Sie am Apparat. *(am Telefon)* II **hold onto sth.** sich an etwas festhalten III **hold sth.** etwas abhalten *(Veranstaltung)* IV 1 (20)
hole [həʊl] Loch II
holiday ['hɒlədeɪ]:
1. Urlaub I
holidays *(pl)* Ferien I **be on holiday** im Urlaub sein I **go on holiday** in Urlaub fahren I
2. Feiertag III
public holiday öffentlicher/gesetzlicher Feiertag IV 2 (58)
home [həʊm] Heim, Zuhause I **at home** zu Hause, daheim I **be home to sth.** Heimat sein für etwas; etwas beheimaten III **come home** nach Hause kommen I **go home** nach Hause gehen I
homeland ['həʊmlænd] Heimat(land) IV 2 (58)
homeless ['həʊmləs]:
1. obdachlos IV 1 (30)
2. Obdachlose/r IV 1 (30)
homelessness ['həʊmləsnəs] Obdachlosigkeit IV 1 (30)

homesick ['həʊmsɪk]: **be/feel homesick** Heimweh haben IV 2 (47) **get homesick** Heimweh bekommen IV 2 (47)
hometown [ˌhəʊm'taʊn] Heimatstadt I
homework ['həʊmwɜːk] Hausaufgabe(n) I **Do your homework.** Mach deine Hausaufgaben. I **What's for homework?** Was haben wir als Hausaufgabe auf? I
honest ['ɒnɪst] ehrlich IV 2 (46)
honesty ['ɒnəstɪ] Ehrlichkeit IV 2 (46)
honey ['hʌni] Honig; *(infml, als Anrede:)* Schatz, Schätzchen III
honour ['ɒnə] Ehre II
hook [hʊk] Haken III
hop [hɒp] hüpfen III
hope [həʊp]:
1. hoffen I
2. Hoffnung IV 4 (116)
hopeful ['həʊpfl] zuversichtlich, hoffnungsvoll IV 4 (116)
horn [hɔːn]:
1. Hupe III
blow the horn hupen III
2. Horn IV 1 (17)
horror ['hɒrə] Horror IV 3 (89)
horse [hɔːs] Pferd I
horseback riding ['hɔːsbæk raɪdɪŋ] *(AE)* Reiten IV 3 (89)
hospital ['hɒspɪtl] Krankenhaus II
host [həʊst] Gastgeber/in; Moderator/in III
host family ['həʊst fæməli] Gastfamilie II
host parents *(pl)* ['həʊst peərənts] Gasteltern IV 1 (25)
hostel ['hɒstl] Herberge, Wohnheim III
hot [hɒt] heiß I
hotel [həʊ'tel] Hotel II
hour ['aʊə] Stunde I **… an hour** … pro Stunde III **an hour and a half** eineinhalb Stunden, anderthalb Stunden III **half an hour** eine halbe Stunde III
house [haʊs] Haus I **House of Commons** Unterhaus (des britischen Parlaments) IV 1 (43) **House of Lords** Oberhaus (des britischen Parlaments) IV 1 (43)
how [haʊ] wie I **How are you?** Wie geht's? / Wie geht es dir/euch? I **How do you know …?** Woher weißt/kennst du …? III **How do you like it?** Wie findest du es (sie/ihn)? / Wie gefällt es (sie/er) dir? I **How many …?** Wie viele …? I **How much …?** Wie viel …? I **How much is/are …?** Was kostet/kosten …? I **How old are you?** Wie alt bist du? I **how to do sth.** wie man etwas macht / machen kann / machen soll I **How's things?** *(infml)* Wie geht's? IV 1 (14)
however [haʊ'evə] aber; allerdings; jedoch IV 2 (50)

hub [hʌb] Mittelpunkt, (Verkehrs-) Knotenpunkt IV 1 (28)
hug [hʌg]:
1. hug sb. jn. umarmen II
2. give sb. a hug jn. umarmen II
huge [hjuːdʒ] riesig, sehr groß III
°**Huguenots** *(pl)* ['hjuːgənəʊ] Hugenotten
hum [hʌm] summen; brummen III
human ['hjuːmən]:
1. Mensch III
2. menschlich III
humankind [ˌhjuːmən'kaɪnd] Menschheit IV 4 (110/111)
humble ['hʌmbl] demütig, bescheiden IV 3 (82)
humid ['hjuːmɪd] feucht, feuchtwarm IV 2 (45)
humorous ['hjuːmərəs] humorvoll, witzig IV 1 (17)
humour ['hjuːmə] **(***AE* **humor)** Humor III **sense of humour** (Sinn für) Humor III
hundred ['hʌndrəd]: **a/one hundred** einhundert I
hung [hʌŋ] *siehe* **hang**
hungry ['hʌŋgri]: **be hungry** hungrig sein, Hunger haben I
hunt [hʌnt]:
1. Jagd III
2. jagen III
hunt sb./sth. down auf jn./etwas Jagd machen III
°**hunter** ['hʌntə] Jäger/in
hurricane ['hʌrɪkən], ['hʌrɪkeɪn] Hurrikan, Orkan III
hurry ['hʌri]:
1. eilen; sich beeilen II
hurry up sich beeilen I
2. Eile IV 4 (120)
in a hurry in Eile IV 4 (120)
hurt [hɜːt], **hurt, hurt**:
1. schmerzen, wehtun I
2. verletzen I
be hurt verletzt sein I
hurtful ['hɜːtfl] verletzend IV 2 (57)
husband ['hʌzbənd] Ehemann III
hyphen ['haɪfən] Bindestrich II

I

I [aɪ] ich I **I'm (= I am)** Ich bin I
ice [aɪs] Eis II
ice cream [ˌaɪs 'kriːm] (Speise-)Eis I
ice skating ['aɪs skeɪtɪŋ] Schlittschuhlaufen II
iced tea [ˌaɪst 'tiː] Eistee II
icon ['aɪkɒn] Symbol; Idol; Icon IV 3 (101)
ICT (= Information and Communications Technology) [ˌaɪ siː 'tiː] Informations- und Kommunikationstechnologie I
ID card [ˌaɪ 'diː kɑːd] Personalausweis III
idea [aɪ'dɪə] Idee; Vorstellung I **No idea.** *(infml)* Keine Ahnung. IV 1 (11)
identify [aɪ'dentɪfaɪ] erkennen, (sich) identifizieren IV 3 (108) **identify oneself (as)** sich zu erkennen geben (als) IV 3 (108)
identity [aɪ'dentəti] Identität IV 1 (41)
idiom ['ɪdiəm] Redewendung IV 1 (27)
°**idol** ['aɪdl] Idol
if [ɪf]:
1. wenn, falls I
if-clause Nebensatz mit *if* III
2. ob III
as if als ob III
ignite [ɪg'naɪt] (sich) entzünden; zünden; entfachen IV 2 (65)
ignorance (of/about sth.) ['ɪgnərəns] Unwissenheit (über etwas), Unkenntnis (einer Sache), Ignoranz IV 4 (114)
ignore [ɪg'nɔː] nicht beachten, ignorieren IV 4 (114)
ill [ɪl] krank II
illegal [ɪ'liːgl] illegal, verboten; Illegale/r IV 2 (76)
illness ['ɪlnəs] Krankheit III
illuminate [ɪ'luːmɪneɪt] erleuchten, beleuchten III
illustration [ˌɪlə'streɪʃn] Abbildung, Illustration IV 1 (19)
image ['ɪmɪdʒ] Bild, Abbild; Vorstellung III
imagine sth. [ɪ'mædʒɪn] sich etwas vorstellen I
imitate ['ɪmɪteɪt] imitieren IV 4 (114)
imitation [ˌɪmɪ'teɪʃn] Imitation IV 4 (114)
immediate [ɪ'miːdiət] umgehend, sofortig IV 4 (124)
immediately [ɪ'miːdiətli] sofort III
immigrant ['ɪmɪgrənt] Einwanderer/Einwanderin III
immigrate ['ɪmɪgreɪt] einwandern IV 1 (19)
immigration [ˌɪmɪ'greɪʃn] Einwanderung IV 1 (19)
impact ['ɪmpækt] Einfluss, Auswirkung IV 3 (109)
impatience [ɪm'peɪʃns] Ungeduld IV 3 (86)
impatient [ɪm'peɪʃnt] ungeduldig III
impolite [ˌɪmpə'laɪt] unhöflich III
impoliteness [ˌɪmpə'laɪtnəs] Unhöflichkeit IV 3 (86)
important [ɪm'pɔːtnt] wichtig I
impossible [ɪm'pɒsəbl] unmöglich II
impractical [ɪm'præktɪkl] unpraktisch; nicht praktikabel; unbrauchbar IV 3 (86)
impression [ɪm'preʃn] Eindruck III
improve [ɪm'pruːv] verbessern; sich verbessern III
improvement [ɪm'pruːvmənt] Verbesserung III
in [ɪn] in I **in 1580** im Jahr 1580 I **in England** in England I **in fact** eigentlich, in Wirklichkeit III **in fright** ängstlich, erschrocken III **in front of** vor *(räumlich)* I **in German/English** auf Deutsch/Englisch I **in my opinion** meiner Meinung nach III **in some/many ways** in mancher/vielerlei Hinsicht III **in the attic** auf dem Dachboden I **in the first place** erstens, in erster Linie; überhaupt IV 1 (29) **in the middle** in der Mitte I **in the morning/afternoon/evening** am Morgen / am Nachmittag / am Abend I **in the photo/picture** auf dem Foto/Bild I **in the world** auf der Welt I **in this way** auf diese Weise III **in time** rechtzeitig III **be in** zu Hause sein II **be in** *(infml)* „in" sein *(Mode)* IV 4 (118) **be in trouble** in Schwierigkeiten sein; Ärger kriegen I **come in** hereinkommen I
in-flight ['ɪn flaɪt] während des Fluges, Bord- IV 2 (46)
in-flight magazine ['ɪn flaɪt mægəziːn] Bordmagazin IV 2 (46)
in-flight meal ['ɪn flaɪt miːl] Bordmahlzeit IV 2 (46)
inaccessible (to) [ˌɪnæk'sesəbl] unzugänglich (für), schwer/nicht erreichbar (für) IV 4 (113)
inappropriate [ɪnə'prəʊpriət] unangemessen, unpassend, ungeeignet IV 3 (100)
°**inauguration** [ɪˌnɔːgjə'reɪʃn] Amtseinführung
inch [ɪntʃ] Zoll *(Längenmaß; 2,54 cm)* III
incident ['ɪnsɪdənt] Vorfall, Zwischenfall IV 2 (64)
include [ɪn'kluːd] (mit) einschließen III
included [ɪn'kluːdɪd] inbegriffen III
including [ɪn'kluːdɪŋ] einschließlich; darunter (auch) III
income ['ɪnkʌm] Einkommen IV 1 (28)
low-income einkommensschwach IV 1 (28)
incorrect [ˌɪnkə'rekt] falsch, unrichtig IV 3 (86)
increase ['ɪŋkriːs] Anstieg, Wachstum, Zunahme IV 1 (28)
increase (by) [ɪn'kriːs] steigern, (sich) erhöhen; steigen, zunehmen (um) IV 1 (28)
incredible [ɪn'kredəbl] unglaublich III
independence [ˌɪndɪ'pendəns] Unabhängigkeit II **the Declaration of Independence** die Unabhängigkeitserklärung *(der Vereinigten Staaten im Jahr 1776)* II
independent [ˌɪndɪ'pendənt] unabhängig III
°**index card** ['ɪndeks kɑːd] Karteikarte
Indian ['ɪndiən]:
1. Inder/in; indisch II
2. Indianer/in III
indicate ['ɪndɪkeɪt] anzeigen IV 1 (42)

indigenous (to) [ɪn'dɪdʒənəs] einheimisch (in) III
indigenous people [ɪnˌdɪdʒənəs 'piːpl] Einheimische, Ureinwohner/innen III
°**individual** [ˌɪndɪ'vɪdʒuəl] Einzelne/r, Individuum; Person
indoor ['ɪndɔː] Innen-; Hallen- III
industrial [ɪn'dʌstriəl] industriell, Industrie- IV 2 (58)
industry ['ɪndəstri] Industrie III
inequality [ˌɪnɪ'kwɒləti] Ungleichheit IV 1 (28)
inexpensive [ˌɪnɪk'spensɪv] preiswert IV 4 (119)
infinitive [ɪn'fɪnətɪv] Infinitiv III
influence ['ɪnfluəns]:
1. beeinflussen IV 3 (109)
2. Einfluss IV 3 (109)
influencer ['ɪnfluənsə] Influencer/in IV 4 (119)
influential [ˌɪnflu'enʃl] einflussreich IV 3 (109)
°**inform sb. (about/of sth.)** [ɪn'fɔːm] jn. (über etwas) informieren
informal [ɪn'fɔːml] informell, locker IV 1 (22)
information (about) *(no pl)* [ˌɪnfə'meɪʃn] Information(en) (über) I
Information and Communications Technology (ICT) [ɪnfəˌmeɪʃn ənd kəmjuːnɪ'keɪʃnz teknɒlədʒi] Informations- und Kommunikationstechnologie I
informational [ˌɪnfə'meɪʃənl] Informations- IV 1 (28)
inhabitant [ɪn'hæbɪtənt] Einwohner/in, Bewohner/in IV 1 (19)
injure ['ɪndʒə] (sich) verletzen IV 2 (53)
injury ['ɪndʒəri] Verletzung IV 2 (53)
inland ['ɪnlænd] im Landesinneren, landeinwärts; Binnen- IV 2 (56)
inner ['ɪnə] innere(r, s) IV 1 (28)
innocence ['ɪnəsns] Unschuld IV 2 (64)
innocent ['ɪnəsnt] unschuldig IV 2 (64)
innovate ['ɪnəveɪt] Neuerungen einführen, (neu) einführen IV 4 (124)
innovation [ˌɪnə'veɪʃn] Innovation, Neuerung IV 4 (124)
innovative ['ɪnəveɪtɪv] innovativ IV 4 (124)
innovator ['ɪnəveɪtə] (Er-)Neuerer/(Er-)Neuerin, Wegbereiter/in IV 4 (124)
insect ['ɪnsekt] Insekt IV 2 (52)
inside [ˌɪn'saɪd]:
1. drinnen; nach drinnen I
inside the dome in der Kuppel, innerhalb der Kuppel IV 1 (10)
2. the inside die Innenseite; das Innere III
insignificant [ˌɪnsɪg'nɪfɪkənt] unbedeutend, geringfügig IV 2 (76)
inspire [ɪn'spaɪə] inspirieren, anregen IV 3 (100)
instant ['ɪnstənt] sofortig, unmittelbar IV 4 (129)
instead [ɪn'sted] stattdessen II
instead of [ɪn'sted‿əv] anstelle von, statt III
institution [ˌɪnstɪ'tjuːʃn] Anstalt, Heim; Einrichtung, Institution IV 2 (59)
instruct sb. to do sth. [ɪn'strʌkt] jn. anweisen, etwas zu tun IV 3 (96)
instruction [ɪn'strʌkʃn] Anweisung IV 3 (96)
instructor [ɪn'strʌktə] Lehrer/in, Ausbilder/in IV 3 (96)
instrument ['ɪnstrəmənt] Instrument I
insult ['ɪnsʌlt]:
1. Beleidigung IV 2 (66)
2. insulted beleidigt III
°**integrate** ['ɪntɪgreɪt] (sich) integrieren
intend (to do sth.) [ɪn'tend] beabsichtigen, vorhaben (etwas zu tun) IV 3 (85)
intention [ɪn'tenʃn] Absicht, Vorsatz IV 3 (85)
intentional [ɪn'tenʃənl] absichtlich, vorsätzlich IV 3 (85)
interact [ˌɪntər'ækt] (miteinander) interagieren, kommunizieren IV 3 (99)
interaction [ˌɪntər'ækʃn] Interaktion, Umgang IV 3 (99)
interactive [ˌɪntər'æktɪv] interaktiv IV 3 (99)
interest (in) ['ɪntrəst] Interesse (an) IV 3 (94)
interest sb. ['ɪntrəst] jn. interessieren IV 3 (94)
interested ['ɪntrəstɪd]: **be interested (in)** interessiert sein (an), sich interessieren (für) II
interesting ['ɪntrəstɪŋ] interessant I
interlock [ˌɪntə'lɒk] ineinandergreifen IV 3 (101) **interlock sth. (with sth.)** etwas (mit etwas) verbinden, zusammenfügen IV 3 (101)
intern ['ɪntɜːn] Praktikant/in IV 3 (78/79)
international [ˌɪntə'næʃnəl] international I
internet ['ɪntənet] Internet I **on the internet** im Internet I
internship ['ɪntɜːnʃɪp] Praktikum IV 3 (78/79)
interpret [ɪn'tɜːprɪt] interpretieren; dolmetschen *(gesprochenen Text mündlich wiedergeben)* IV 3 (100)
interpretation [ɪnˌtɜːprɪ'teɪʃn] Interpretation; *(das)* Dolmetschen IV 3 (100)
interpreter [ɪn'tɜːprɪtə] Dolmetscher/in IV 3 (100)
interrupt [ˌɪntə'rʌpt] unterbrechen II
interview ['ɪntəvjuː]:
1. befragen, interviewen IV 2 (64)
2. Interview IV 2 (64)
3. (= job interview) Vorstellungsgespräch IV 3 (78/79)
4. ein Vorstellungsgespräch führen IV 3 (78/79)
into ['ɪntʊ]: **into the kitchen** in die Küche (hinein) I **be into sth.** *(infml)* etwas mögen, auf etwas stehen III
intolerance [ɪn'tɒlərəns] Intoleranz IV 3 (86)
intolerant (of) [ɪn'tɒlərənt] intolerant (gegenüber) IV 3 (86)
intonation [ˌɪntə'neɪʃn] Intonation, Satzmelodie I
introduce sth./sb. (to sb.) [ˌɪntrə'djuːs] etwas/jn. (jm.) vorstellen II
introduction [ˌɪntrə'dʌkʃn] Einleitung, Einführung III
Inuit ['ɪnjuɪt] Inuit *(kanadische Ureinwohner/innen)* III
invade (a country) [ɪn'veɪd] *(in ein Land)* einmarschieren II
invent [ɪn'vent] erfinden IV 1 (21)
invention [ɪn'venʃn] Erfindung IV 1 (21)
inversion [ɪn'vɜːʃn] Umkehrung, Inversion IV 4 (115)
invert [ɪn'vɜːt] umstellen, umkehren IV 4 (115)
°**investment** [ɪn'vestmənt] Anlage, Investition
invitation (to) [ˌɪnvɪ'teɪʃn] Einladung (zu, nach) I
invite sb. (to) [ɪn'vaɪt]:
1. jn. einladen (zu) II
2. jn. auffordern (zu) III
involve [ɪn'vɒlv] mit sich bringen, einbeziehen, beinhalten IV 3 (107)
involved [ɪn'vɒlvd]: **be involved in** beteiligt sein an; etwas zu tun haben mit IV 3 (107) **get involved (in)** sich engagieren (für, bei); sich beteiligen (an) IV 3 (107) **Try not to get involved.** Versuche, dich da rauszuhalten IV 3 (107)
involvement (in) [ɪn'vɒlvmənt] Engagement (für); Beteiligung (an) IV 3 (107)
°**iron** ['aɪən] bügeln **iron-on ...** ... zum Aufbügeln
irregular [ɪ'regjələ] unregelmäßig II
irrelevant (to sb.) [ɪ'reləvənt] irrelevant (für jn.) IV 3 (94)
irresponsible [ˌɪrɪ'spɒnsəbl] verantwortungslos, unverantwortlich IV 3 (86)
is [ɪz] *(er/sie/es)* ist I **Is that you?** Bist du's? / Bist du das? I **The camera is ...** Die Kamera kostet ... I
island ['aɪlənd] Insel I
isn't ['ɪznt]: **he/she/it isn't ... (= he/she/it is not)** er/sie/es ist nicht ...; er/sie/es ist kein/e ... I
issue ['ɪʃuː]:
1. ausgeben, (offiziell) bekannt geben; ausstellen *(z.B. Dokument)* IV 1 (29)
2. Ausgabe, Ausstellung *(z.B. Dokument)* IV 1 (29)
it [ɪt] er, sie, es *(Dinge/Tiere)* I **it's ... (= it is)** er/sie/es ist ... I
°**italics** [ɪ'tælɪks]: **in italics** kursiv (gedruckt)
item ['aɪtəm] Artikel, Gegenstand, Punkt *(auf einer Liste)* IV 4 (119)

°**itinerary** [aɪ'tɪnərəri] Reiseroute, Reiseplan
its name [ɪts] sein Name / ihr Name I
itself [ɪt'self] es/sich selbst/selber III

J

jacket ['dʒækɪt] Jacke, Jackett II
jam [dʒæm] Marmelade I
January ['dʒænjuəri] Januar I
jar [dʒɑː] Glasgefäß IV 4 (128)
jaw [dʒɔː] *(der)* Kiefer IV 2 (48)
jazz [dʒæz] Jazz IV 3 (89)
jazzy ['dʒæzi] *(infml)* auffallend, knallig, poppig IV 4 (119)
jealous (of) ['dʒeləs] neidisch (auf); eifersüchtig IV 3 (86)
jealousy ['dʒeləsi] Eifersucht IV 3 (86)
jeans *(pl)* [dʒiːnz] Jeans I
jeep [dʒiːp] Jeep III
°**jeer** [dʒɪə] höhnischer Zwischenruf, Buhruf
jerk [dʒɜːk] *(infml)* Trottel, Depp III
jersey ['dʒɜːzi] Trikot III
Jew [dʒuː] Jude/Jüdin IV 1 (19)
jewellery *(no pl)* ['dʒuːəlri] (*AE* **jewelry**) Schmuck III
jewels *(pl)* ['dʒuːəlz] Juwelen III
Jewish ['dʒuːɪʃ] jüdisch IV 1 (19)
jigsaw ['dʒɪgsɔː] Puzzle II
job [dʒɒb]:
1. Job, (Arbeits-)Stelle I
2. Aufgabe II
job interview ['dʒɒb_ɪntəvjuː] Vorstellungsgespräch IV 3 (78/79)
join [dʒɔɪn]:
1. **join a club** in einen Klub eintreten; sich einem Klub anschließen I
join in mitmachen III
2. **join sth.** etwas verbinden III
joke [dʒəʊk]:
1. Witz I
2. Witze machen, scherzen IV 1 (27)
joke around herumscherzen IV 1 (27)
You're joking! / You must be joking! Du machst wohl Witze! (= Das kann doch nicht dein Ernst sein!) IV 1 (27)
journey ['dʒɜːni] Reise, Fahrt II
judge [dʒʌdʒ]:
1. Richter/in IV 3 (109)
2. **judge (sb. by ...)** urteilen; jn. beurteilen (nach ...) IV 3 (109)
judo ['dʒuːdəʊ] Judo I
juggle sth. ['dʒʌgl] mit etwas jonglieren II
juggler ['dʒʌglə] Jongleur/in II
juice [djuːs] Saft II
July [dʒu'laɪ] Juli I
jump [dʒʌmp]:
1. Sprung I
2. springen I
jump up hochspringen II
junction ['dʒʌŋkʃn] (Straßen-)Kreuzung III
June [dʒuːn] Juni I
junior ['dʒuːniə]:
1. Junior/in; *(AE) Schüler/in im vorletzten Schuljahr* IV 3 (88)
2. Junioren- I
junior high (school) [ˌdʒuːniə 'haɪ skuːl] *(AE) Schule für Kinder zwischen 12 und 14* IV 3 (80)
junior team ['dʒuːniə tiːm] Jugendmannschaft, Juniorenmannschaft I
just [dʒʌst]:
1. (einfach) nur, bloß I
2. gerade (eben), soeben II
just after ... gleich nachdem ...; kurz nachdem ... II **just then** genau in dem Moment; gerade dann II
3. **just as boring/exciting** genauso langweilig/aufregend III
just like ... genau wie ... II

K

kangaroo [ˌkæŋgə'ruː] (*AusE infml:* **roo)** Känguru IV 2 (45)
kayak ['kaɪæk] Kajak III
kayaking ['kaɪækɪŋ] Kajakfahren III
keen [kiːn]: **be keen on doing sth.** wild darauf sein, etwas zu tun III **be keen on sth.** wild auf etwas sein III
keep [kiːp], **kept, kept**:
1. halten III
keep sth. away from etwas fernhalten von III **keep sth. out of** etwas heraushalten aus III **keep sth. warm/fresh** etwas warm/frisch halten III
keep track of sth. den Überblick behalten bei etwas, etwas im Auge behalten IV 3 (97) **keep up (with sb.)** (mit jm.) Schritt halten IV 1 (32) **keep your distance (from)** Abstand halten (zu/von) IV 1 (33)
2. behalten III
3. aufbewahren III
4. **keep (on) doing sth.** etwas immer wieder / immer weiter tun; etwas ständig tun III
keeper ['kiːpə] (*kurz für* **zookeeper)** Tierpfleger/in IV 2 (66)
kept [kept] *siehe* **keep**
ketchup ['ketʃəp] Ketchup IV 2 (77)
key [kiː] Schlüssel II
key point ['kiː pɔɪnt] Kernpunkt, Hauptpunkt II
keyword ['kiːwɜːd] Schlüsselwort I
°**Kia ora!** [kiː 'ɔːrə] Hallo! *(Begrüßung der Maori, wörtlich etwa: Möge es dir gutgehen!)*
kick [kɪk] treten III
kid [kɪd] *(infml)* Kind; Jugendliche(r) I
kill [kɪl] töten II
kilo ['kiːləʊ] *siehe* **kilogram**
kilogram (= kilo, kg) ['kɪləgræm] Kilo(gramm) (kg) I
kilometre ['kɪləmiːtə], [kɪ'lɒmɪtə] Kilometer II
kind [kaɪnd]:
1. *(adj)* freundlich, nett II
2. *(n)* **a kind of ...** eine Art (von) ... I
3. *(adv)* **kind of scary** *(infml)* irgendwie unheimlich, ganz schön unheimlich III
kindergarten ['kɪndəgɑːtn]:
1. Kindergarten IV 3 (80)
2. *(AE)* Vorschule IV 3 (80)
kindness ['kaɪndnəs] Güte, Freundlichkeit IV 3 (86)
king [kɪŋ] König II
kingdom ['kɪŋdəm] Königreich III
kiss [kɪs] küssen; sich küssen II
kit [kɪt] Ausrüstung I
kitchen ['kɪtʃɪn] Küche I
kitesurfer ['kaɪtsɜːfə] Kitesurfer/in IV 2 (46)
kitesurfing ['kaɪtsɜːfɪŋ] Kitesurfing IV 2 (46)
kiwi ['kiːwi] Kiwi *(Vogel)* IV 2 (76)
kiwi fruit ['kiːwi fruːt], *pl* **kiwi fruit** Kiwi(frucht) IV 2 (76)
knee [niː] Knie II °**take a knee** sich hinknien *(auf einem Knie)*
kneel [niːl], **knelt, knelt** knien II
knelt [nelt] *siehe* **kneel**
knew [njuː] *siehe* **know**
knife [naɪf], *pl* **knives** Messer II
knight [naɪt] Ritter II
knives [naɪvz] *plural of* **knife**
knock [nɒk]:
1. Klopfen; Stoß, Schlag IV 3 (89)
2. **knock (at/on sth.)** (an)klopfen (an etwas) IV 3 (89)
know [nəʊ], **knew, known** wissen; kennen I **know about sth.** sich mit etwas auskennen; über etwas Bescheid wissen I **..., you know.** ..., weißt du. / ..., wissen Sie. I **get to know sb.** jn. kennenlernen IV 4 (116) **How do you know ...?** Woher weißt/kennst du ...? III **I don't know.** Ich weiß (es) nicht. I
knowledge (of/about) ['nɒlɪdʒ] Wissen (von/über), Kenntnis(se) (von/in) IV 3 (94)
known [nəʊn] *siehe* **know** **well known** bekannt II
koala [kəʊ'ɑːlə] Koala(bär) IV 2 (45)
kung fu [ˌkʌŋ 'fuː] Kung Fu I

L

lab [læb] (*infml, kurz für:* **laboratory)** Labor IV 3 (107)
label ['leɪbl]:
1. beschriften; etikettieren II
2. Beschriftung; Schild, Etikett II
laboratory [lə'bɒrətri] (*kurz auch:* **lab)** Labor IV 3 (107)

°**Labour** ['leɪbə] *(short for* the Labour Party*)* die Arbeiterpartei *(in Großbritannien)*
labour ['leɪbə] Arbeit; Arbeitskräfte IV 2 (59)
lack [læk]:
1. lack (of) Mangel (an) IV 2 (48)
for lack of aus Mangel an IV 2 (48)
2. sb. lacks sth. jm. fehlt es an etwas IV 2 (48)
Ladies and gentlemen [ˌleɪdiz‿ən 'dʒentlmən] Meine Damen und Herren / Sehr geehrte Damen und Herren III
°**lady** ['leɪdi] Dame
laid [leɪd] *siehe* **lay**
lain [leɪn] *siehe* **lie**
lake [leɪk] (Binnen-)See I
lamb [læm] Lamm II
lamp [læmp] Lampe I
land [lænd]:
1. Land II
2. landen; an Land gehen II
landing ['lændɪŋ] Landungssteg III
landmark ['lændmɑːk] Wahrzeichen IV 2 (46)
landscape ['lændskeɪp] Landschaft; Landschaftsbild III
language ['læŋgwɪdʒ] Sprache I
lap [læp] Schoß IV 4 (120)
laptop ['læptɒp] Laptop *(tragbarer PC)* III
large [lɑːdʒ] groß I
last [lɑːst]:
1. letzte(r, s) I
last weekend/Friday/... letztes Wochenende / letzten Freitag / ... I **last year's musical** das Musical vom letzten Jahr II
2. zuletzt, das letzte Mal III
3. at last endlich, schließlich I
last (for) [lɑːst] (an)dauern; halten *(von Bestand sein)* IV 1 (24)
late [leɪt] spät I **stay up late** lang aufbleiben II **You're late.** Du bist spät dran. / Du bist zu spät. I
lately ['leɪtli] in letzter Zeit IV 4 (121)
later ['leɪtə] später I **Catch you later.** *(infml)* Bis später dann! IV 1 (11) **See you later.** Bis bald. / Bis nachher. I
Latin ['lætɪn] lateinisch; Latein IV 1 (32)
laugh [lɑːf] lachen I **laugh at sb./sth.** über jn./etwas lachen; jn. auslachen III
laundry ['lɔːndri] Wäsche; Wäscherei IV 4 (122)
laureate ['lɒriət] Preisträger/in IV 3 (109)
law [lɔː] Gesetz III
lawn [lɔːn] Rasen III
lay [leɪ] *siehe* **lie**
lay [leɪ], **laid, laid** legen III
layout ['leɪaʊt] Layout, Gestaltung III
laziness ['leɪzinəs] Faulheit III
lazy ['leɪzi] faul III
lead [liːd], **led, led** führen, leiten III
lead role ['liːd rəʊl] Hauptrolle *(z.B. Film)* IV 2 (62)
leader ['liːdə] Leiter/in III
leadership ['liːdəʃɪp] Führung IV 3 (88)
leadership skills *(pl)* ['liːdəʃɪp skɪlz] Führungseigenschaften, -qualitäten IV 3 (88)
league [liːg] Liga IV 2 (64)
leak [liːk]:
1. Leck *(undichte Stelle)* IV 4 (123)
2. auslaufen, entweichen; sickern IV 4 (123)
lean [liːn] sich lehnen; sich beugen III
learn [lɜːn] lernen I
least [liːst]: **at least** zumindest, wenigstens II
leather ['leðə] Leder III
leave [liːv], **left, left**:
1. (ab)fahren; (weg)gehen I
2. verlassen; zurücklassen I
3. lassen II
leave a message eine Nachricht hinterlassen II **leave sth.** etwas übrig lassen II **leave sth. out** etwas weglassen, auslassen II
led [led] *siehe* **lead**
left [left] *siehe* **leave** **be left** übrig sein III
left [left] linke(r, s); (nach) links I **on the left** links / auf der linken Seite I **right and left** *(infml)* **(***oft auch:* **right, left and centre)** überall; aus allen Richtungen; an allen Ecken und Enden IV 4 (112) **right, left and centre** *(infml)* überall; aus allen Richtungen; an allen Ecken und Enden IV 4 (112)
turn left (nach) links abbiegen II
leg [leg] Bein I **pull sb.'s leg** *(infml)* jn. auf den Arm nehmen *(veräppeln)* IV 1 (27)
legal ['liːgl] legal IV 2 (76)
legend ['ledʒənd] Legende, Sage II
legendary ['ledʒəndri] legendär, berühmt III
leisure centre ['leʒə sentə] Freizeitpark, Freizeitzentrum II
lemon ['lemən] Zitrone IV 4 (120)
length [leŋθ] Länge; Dauer III
less (than) [les] weniger (als) III
lesson ['lesn] (Unterrichts-)Stunde I **before lessons** vorm Unterricht I
let [let], **let, let** lassen I **let alone ...** ganz zu schweigen von ..., geschweige denn ... IV 4 (110/111) **Let me show you ...** Lass mich dir ... zeigen. I **let sb. down** jn. im Stich lassen, enttäuschen IV 2 (64) **Let's ...** Lass(t) uns ... I
letter ['letə]:
1. Brief I
2. Buchstabe I
level ['levl] Grad, Stufe; Niveau, Ebene IV 1 (12)
°**Liberal Democrats** [ˌlɪbərəl 'deməkræts] Liberaldemokratische Partei *(in Großbritannien)*
liberty ['lɪbəti] Freiheit III
library ['laɪbrəri] Bibliothek, Bücherei I
lie [laɪ], **lay, lain** liegen II **lie down** sich hinlegen III
life [laɪf], *pl* **lives** Leben I **way of life** Lebensweise IV 2 (47)
life jacket ['laɪf dʒækɪt] Schwimmweste I
lifeguard ['laɪfgɑːd] Rettungsschwimmer/in; Bademeister/in IV 3 (94)
lifestyle ['laɪfstaɪl] Lebensstil IV 2 (49)
lift [lɪft]:
1. *(BE)* Fahrstuhl, Aufzug, Lift II
2. Mitfahrgelegenheit II
give sb. a lift jn. mitnehmen II
lift sth. [lɪft] etwas heben, hochheben, anheben III **lift sth. up** etwas hochheben IV 1 (32)
light [laɪt]:
1. Licht I
2. *(adv)* **light brown/blue/...** hellbraun/-blau/... III
3. light, lit, lit anzünden II
light sth. up etwas erhellen *(aufleuchten lassen)* II **light up** aufleuchten III
lightning *(no pl)* ['laɪtnɪŋ] Blitz(e) II
a flash of lightning ein Blitz II
like [laɪk] mögen, gernhaben I **I like ...** Ich mag ... I **I like swimming/sailing/...** Ich schwimme/segele/... gern. I **I'd like ... (= I would like ...)** Ich hätte gern ... / Ich möchte ... I **I'd like to go** Ich möchte gehen / Ich würde gern gehen I **I'd like you to ...** Ich möchte/hätte gern, dass du ... II **What would you like to eat?** Was möchtest du essen? I
like [laɪk]:
1. like boys wie Buben I
like that so *(auf diese Weise)* I **like this** so *(auf diese Weise)* I **just like ...** genau wie ... II **What was it like?** Wie war es? II **What's she like?** Wie ist sie? / Wie ist sie so? I
2. *(conjunction; infml)* als ob III
3. She was like: "Stop ..." *(infml)* Und sie so: „Stopp ..." III
likes and dislikes *(pl)* [ˌlaɪks‿ən 'dɪslaɪks] Vorlieben und Abneigungen I
limit ['lɪmɪt]:
1. Grenze, Begrenzung, Beschränkung IV 4 (113)
2. limit sth. (to) etwas beschränken, begrenzen (auf); etwas einschränken IV 4 (113)
limited (to) ['lɪmɪtɪd] beschränkt, begrenzt (auf) IV 1 (42)
line [laɪn]:
1. Zeile I
2. Leine, (Angel-)Schnur III
3. (U-Bahn-)Linie II
4. Reihe III
5. *(AE)* Schlange *(wartender Menschen)* II
be/stand/wait in line *(AE)* Schlange stehen, sich anstellen II

lingua franca [ˌlɪŋgwə 'fræŋkə], *pl.* **lingua francas** Verkehrssprache IV 4 (136)
linguist ['lɪŋgwɪst] Linguist/in, Sprachwissenschaftler/in IV 4 (129)
linguistic [lɪŋ'gwɪstɪk] linguistisch, sprachwissenschaftlich IV 4 (129)
linguistics [lɪŋ'gwɪstɪks] Linguistik *(Sprachwissenschaft)* IV 4 (129)
link [lɪŋk] verbinden, verknüpfen I
linking word ['lɪŋkɪŋ wɜːd] Bindewort III
lion ['laɪən] Löwe I
lip [lɪp] Lippe II
list [lɪst]:
1. Liste I
2. auflisten IV 3 (108)
listen ['lɪsn] zuhören, horchen I **listen to sb.** jm. zuhören I **listen to sth.** sich etwas anhören I °**listen for sth.** auf etwas horchen, *(beim Zuhören)* auf etwas achten
listener ['lɪsənə] Zuhörer/in II
lit [lɪt] *siehe* **light**
°**literal** ['lɪtərəl] wörtlich, buchstäblich
literature ['lɪtrətʃə] Literatur III
litter ['lɪtə]:
1. Müll, Abfall IV 2 (77)
2. Abfälle zurücklassen IV 2 (77)
litter bin ['lɪtə bɪn] Abfalleimer II
little ['lɪtl] klein I **a little** ein bisschen, ein wenig, etwas III
live [lɪv] leben; wohnen I
liveliness ['laɪvlinəs] Lebhaftigkeit IV 3 (86)
lively ['laɪvli] lebendig, lebhaft IV 1 (22)
lives [laɪvz] *plural of* **life**
livestock *(no pl)* ['laɪvstɒk] Vieh IV 2 (77)
living ['lɪvɪŋ] Lebensunterhalt IV 1 (28)
living room ['lɪvɪŋ ruːm] Wohnzimmer I
loads (of ...) [ləʊdz] *(infml)* eine Menge (von ...) IV 1 (22)
lobster ['lɒbstə] Hummer II
local ['ləʊkl] örtlich, Lokal-; am/vom Ort III
location [ləʊ'keɪʃn] Ort, Platz, Lage; Drehort *(z.B. von Filmen)* IV 1 (16)
lock [lɒk]:
1. Schloss *(Türschloss)* IV 4 (124)
2. abschließen *(z.B. Tür)* IV 4 (124)
lock sb. in jn. einsperren IV 4 (124)
locker ['lɒkə] Schließfach, Spind III
log in/out [lɒg] sich ein-/ausloggen III
logbook ['lɒgbʊk] Fahrtenbuch II
°**logical** ['lɒdʒɪkl] logisch
°**LOL (= laugh-out-loud)** [ˌel‿əʊ‿'el] laut lachen(d) *(Internet)*
lonely ['ləʊnli] einsam I
long [lɒŋ] lang(e) I **no longer / not any longer** nicht mehr, nicht länger IV 4 (118)
°**long-necked** ['lɒŋ nekt] langhalsig, mit langem Hals
long shot ['lɒŋ ʃɒt] Totale *(Film)* IV 1 (17)
look [lʊk]:
1. schauen I
look after sb. auf jn. aufpassen; sich um jn. kümmern II **look around (the farm)** sich (auf der Farm) umsehen II **look at** anschauen, ansehen I **look for sth.** etwas suchen I **look forward to sth.** sich auf etwas freuen II **look into sth.** etwas untersuchen, prüfen III **look out for sb./sth.** nach jm./etwas Ausschau halten; auf jn./etwas achten IV 2 (53) **look sth. up** etwas nachschlagen III **look up** hochsehen, aufschauen II
2. **look happy/angry/...** glücklich/wütend/... aussehen I
3. Blick III
have a look (at sth.) nachschauen; einen Blick auf etwas werfen III
lorry ['lɒri] *(BE)* Lastwagen, LKW III
lose [luːz], **lost, lost** verlieren II
lost [lɒst] *siehe* **lose**
lot [lɒt]: **lots of ... / a lot of ...** viel ..., viele ... I **a lot** viel I **That helped us a lot.** Das hat uns sehr geholfen. I
loud [laʊd] laut I **in a loud voice** mit lauter Stimme II
loudspeaker [ˌlaʊd'spiːkə] Lautsprecher; Megaphon III
Love, ... [lʌv] Alles Liebe, ... / Liebe Grüße, ... *(Briefschluss)* II
love [lʌv]:
1. lieben, sehr mögen I
I'd love to ... Ich würde sehr gern ... I
2. Liebe IV 4 (116)
fall in love (with sb.) sich verlieben (in jn.) IV 4 (116) **in love (with)** verliebt (in) IV 4 (116)
lovely ['lʌvli] schön, hübsch, herrlich II
lover ['lʌvə]: **animal lover** Tierfreund/in IV 2 (66)
low [ləʊ] niedrig IV 1 (28) **low-income** einkommensschwach IV 1 (28)
lower ['ləʊə] senken, herabsetzen; sinken lassen IV 2 (48)
lows *(pl)* [ləʊz]: **highs and lows** Höhen und Tiefen IV 4 (112)
loyal ['lɔɪəl] loyal IV 3 (86)
loyalty ['lɔɪəlti] Loyalität IV 3 (86)
luck [lʌk]: **Good luck!** Viel Glück! I
luckily ['lʌkɪli] glücklicherweise III
lucky ['lʌki]: **be lucky** Glück haben I **Lucky you.** Du Glückspilz. II
lunch [lʌntʃ] Mittagessen I **have lunch** zu Mittag essen I **What's for lunch?** Was gibt es zum Mittagessen? I
lunchtime ['lʌntʃtaɪm] Mittagszeit I **at lunchtime** mittags I
luxurious [lʌg'ʒʊəriəs] luxuriös III

M

machine [mə'ʃiːn] Maschine, Gerät III
mad [mæd] verrückt I
madam ['mædəm]: **Dear Sir or Madam** Sehr geehrte Damen und Herren II
made [meɪd] *siehe* **make** **be made of sth.** aus etwas (gemacht) sein II **be made to do sth.** gezwungen werden, etwas zu tun; etwas tun müssen IV 4 (117) **be made up of** bestehen aus IV 2 (76) **be made up of** sich zusammensetzen aus; gebildet sein/werden aus IV 4 (137)
magazine [ˌmægə'ziːn] Zeitschrift I
magic ['mædʒɪk] magisch, Zauber- II
magical ['mædʒɪkl] zauberhaft, wundervoll; magisch III
magnificent [mæg'nɪfɪsnt] prächtig IV 1 (10)
magnitude ['mægnɪtjuːd] Stärke (Erdbeben); Größe, Ausmaß IV 2 (76)
mail [meɪl] E-Mail II
main [meɪn] Haupt- II
main clause ['meɪn klɔːz] Hauptsatz II
mainly ['meɪnli] hauptsächlich, vorwiegend III
maintain [meɪn'teɪn] behaupten; beibehalten, aufrecht erhalten; instand halten, unterhalten IV 4 (124)
major ['meɪdʒə] groß, bedeutend; Haupt- IV 2 (76)
majority [mə'dʒɒrəti] Mehrheit, Mehrzahl III
make [meɪk], **made, made** machen; herstellen I **make (money)** (Geld) verdienen IV 3 (97) **make a wish** sich etwas wünschen I **make eye contact** Blickkontakt herstellen III **make friends** Freunde finden I **make fun of sb./sth.** sich über jn./etwas lustig machen III **make it** es schaffen, Erfolg haben IV 1 (33) **make sb. do sth.** jn. dazu bringen, etwas zu tun IV 4 (117) **make sb. sth.** jn. zu etwas machen II **make sth. up** sich etwas ausdenken III **make sth. up** etwas bilden, ausmachen IV 2 (76) **make sure that ...** sich vergewissern, dass ...; darauf achten, dass ...; dafür sorgen, dass ... II **make the finals** es (bis) zum Finale schaffen IV 1 (33) **make your way (to/through/...)** sich auf den Weg (nach/durch/...) machen IV 4 (127) **I couldn't make your party.** Ich habe es nicht geschafft, zu eurer Party zu kommen. IV 1 (33)
make-up ['meɪk‿ʌp] Makeup II
°**maker** ['meɪkə] Hersteller/in, Produzent/in
malaria [mə'leəriə] Malaria III
male [meɪl] männlich; männliche Person; Männchen IV 4 (116)
mall [mɔːl] (großes) Einkaufszentrum I
mammal ['mæml] Säugetier IV 2 (77)

man [mæn], *pl* **men** Mann I
man-made [ˌmæn 'meɪd] künstlich, Kunst- III
manage ['mænɪdʒ] verwalten; regeln; zurechtkommen mit, fertigwerden mit, kontrollieren *(z.B. Brand)* IV 2 (59)
manage sth. etwas schaffen; etwas zustande bringen III
manager ['mænɪdʒə] Geschäftsführer/in, Manager/in IV 3 (96)
manufacture [ˌmænju'fæktʃə]:
1. herstellen, produzieren, fertigen IV 4 (118)
2. Herstellung, Produktion, Fertigung IV 4 (118)
manufacturing (industry) [ˌmænju'fæktʃərɪŋ] Fertigungsindustrie, verarbeitende Industrie III
many ['meni] viele I **How many ...?** Wie viele ...? I
map [mæp] Landkarte; Stadtplan I **on the map** auf der Landkarte; auf dem Stadtplan I
marathon ['mærəθən] Marathon II
March [mɑːtʃ] März I
marine [mə'riːn] Meeres- IV 2 (45)
marine mammal [məˌriːn 'mæml] Meeressäuger IV 2 (77)
mark [mɑːk]:
1. markieren II
2. **mark sth. up** etwas markieren, kennzeichnen II
marker ['mɑːkə] Marker *(Stift)* IV 4 (119)
market ['mɑːkɪt] Markt I
marmalade ['mɑːməleɪd] Marmelade *(aus Zitrusfrüchten)* I
married (to) ['mærɪd] verheiratet (mit) I **get married (to sb.)** (jn.) heiraten IV 2 (63)
marry ['mæri] heiraten III
mask [mɑːk] Maske II
massive ['mæsɪv] gewaltig, massiv IV 1 (42)
master ['mɑːstə] Meister/in I
master's degree ['mɑːstəz dɪgriː] Master(-Abschluss) IV 3 (108)
match [mætʃ] Spiel, Wettkampf, Match I
match [mætʃ]:
1. (passend) zusammenfügen III
°**match** *(e.g. garments)* *(z.B. Kleidungsstücke)* zusammenstellen, kombinieren, aufeinander abstimmen
2. **match sth.** zu etwas passen III
mate [meɪt] *(infml)* Freund/in, Kumpel IV 2 (48)
material [mə'tɪəriəl] Material, Stoff III
°**math** [mæθ] *(AE)* Mathe(matik)
maths [mæθs] Mathematik I
matter ['mætə]:
1. von Bedeutung sein, wichtig sein IV 4 (118)
It doesn't matter. Es/Das ist egal. IV 4 (118)
2. **no matter what/how/who** (ganz) egal, was/wie/wer IV 1 (42)
What's the matter? Was ist denn?/Was ist los? I °**It's a matter of life and death.** Es entscheidet über Leben oder Tod. / Es geht dabei um Leben und Tod.
maximum (= max) ['mæksɪməm] Maximum; Höchst-, maximal IV 3 (107)
May [meɪ] Mai I
may [meɪ] dürfen II **May I have a word with you?** Kann ich dich/Sie kurz sprechen? II **they may be at home** sie sind vielleicht daheim III
maybe ['meɪbi] vielleicht I
mayor [meə] Bürgermeister/in II
me [miː] mich; mir I **Me too.** Ich auch. I **It's me.** Ich bin's. I
meal [miːl] Mahlzeit, Essen III
mean [miːn] gemein, fies; geizig IV 3 (86)
mean [miːn], **meant, meant**:
1. meinen, sagen wollen II
2. bedeuten II
meaning ['miːnɪŋ] Bedeutung II
°**meaningful** ['miːnɪŋfl] wichtig; bedeutend; bedeutsam; aussagekräftig
meanness ['miːnnəs] Gemeinheit; Geiz IV 3 (86)
meant [ment] *siehe* **mean**
measles *(pl)* ['miːzlz] Masern IV 2 (58)
meat [miːt] Fleisch I
°**meatless** ['miːtləs] fleischlos
medal ['medl] Medaille I
media *(pl)* ['miːdiə] Medien III **social media** *(pl)* soziale Medien III
mediation [ˌmiːdi'eɪʃn] Sprachmittlung, Mediation I
medicine ['medsn], ['medɪsn] Medizin; Arznei II
Mediterranean [ˌmedɪtə'reɪniən] Mittelmeer-, mediterran IV 4 (137)
Mediterranean Sea [ˌmedɪtə'reɪniən] Mittelmeer IV 4 (137)
medium ['miːdiəm] mittelgroß; mittel- III
meet [miːt], **met, met**:
1. treffen, kennenlernen I
Meet your classmates. Triff deine Mitschüler/innen. / Lerne deine Mitschüler/innen kennen. I **Nice to meet you.** Freut mich, dich/euch/Sie kennenzulernen. I
2. sich treffen I
meeting ['miːtɪŋ] Treffen; Zusammenkunft IV 4 (115)
°**melody** ['melədi] Melodie
melt [melt] schmelzen II
member ['membə] Mitglied IV 1 (11)
membership ['membəʃɪp] Mitgliedschaft IV 2 (76)
meme [miːm] (Internet-)Mem III
memorial [mə'mɔːriəl] Denkmal; Gedenk- III
memory ['meməri] Erinnerung II
men [men] *plural of* **man**
mention ['menʃn] erwähnen IV 3 (99)
mentor ['mentə] Mentor/in, Berater/in, Vertrauenslehrer/in IV 3 (78/79)
Merry Christmas! [ˌmeri 'krɪsməs] Frohe Weihnachten! I
mesmerizing ['mezməraɪzɪŋ] fesselnd, hypnotisierend III
mess [mes] Chaos, Unordnung IV 4 (112)
message ['mesɪdʒ]:
1. Nachricht II
leave a message eine Nachricht hinterlassen II
2. Botschaft, Aussage III
3. **message (sb.)** (jm.) eine *(elektronische)* Nachricht schicken/übermitteln IV 1 (14)
messenger ['mesɪndʒə] Kurier/in, Bote/Botin IV 1 (14)
messenger service ['mesɪndʒə sɜːvɪs] Messenger *(Dienst zur Nachrichtenübermittlung im Internet)* IV 1 (14)
messy ['mesi] unordentlich IV 4 (112)
met [met] *siehe* **meet**
metal ['metl] Metall; Metall- III
°**method** ['meθəd] Methode
metre ['miːtə] Meter I
microphone ['maɪkrəfəʊn] Mikrofon IV 4 (112)
microplastics *(pl)* ['maɪkrəʊplæstɪks] Mikroplastik IV 4 (118)
middle ['mɪdl] Mitte I **in the middle** in der Mitte I
middle school ['mɪdl skuːl] *(AE)* Mittelschule *(für 11- bis 14-Jährige)* IV 3 (80)
midnight ['mɪdnaɪt] Mitternacht I
might [maɪt]: **it might be ...** es könnte ... sein, vielleicht ist es ... II
°**migraine** ['miːgreɪn], ['maɪgreɪn] Migräne
mild [maɪld] mild; sanft; leicht *(Schmerzen; Medikamentendosierung)* IV 2 (56)
mile [maɪl] Meile *(ca. 1,6 km)* I **for miles** meilenweit I
milk [mɪlk] Milch I
mill [mɪl] Mühle IV 1 (18)
millennia [mɪ'leniə] *plural of* **millennium**
millennium [mɪ'leniəm], *pl* **milleniums** *or* **millennia** Jahrtausend, Millennium IV 2 (76)
million ['mɪljən] Million I
mind [maɪnd]:
1. aufpassen auf, achten auf IV 1 (27)
2. etwas dagegen haben III
Do you mind ...? Stört es Sie, ...? / Haben Sie etwas dagegen, ...? III **if you don't mind** wenn Sie nichts dagegen haben III
mind [maɪnd] Verstand, Sinn, Geist III
mind map ['maɪnd mæp] Mindmap I
mine [maɪn] meiner, meine, meins II
mine [maɪn]:
1. Bergwerk, Mine III
coal mine Kohlebergwerk III
2. abbauen *(Bodenschätze)* III
3. Mine *(Militär)* III

mineral ['mɪnərəl] Mineral(stoff) IV 2 (58)
mineral water ['mɪnərəl wɔːtə] Mineralwasser IV 2 (58)
minibus ['mɪnibʌs] Kleinbus I
minimum ['mɪnɪməm] Mindest-, minimal; Minimum IV 3 (107)
minimum grade requirement [ˌmɪnɪməm greɪd rɪ'kwaɪəmənt] Mindestanforderung beim Notendurchschnitt *(vergleichbar unserem Numerus Clausus)* IV 3 (107)
minimum wage [mɪnɪməm 'weɪdʒ] Mindestlohn IV 4 (118)
mining ['maɪnɪŋ] Bergbau IV 2 (58)
minor ['maɪnə] weniger bedeutend; gering(er), klein(er) IV 2 (62)
minority [maɪ'nɒrəti] Minderheit III
°**mint** [mɪnt] *(infml)* super, cool
minute ['mɪnɪt] Minute I **a two-minute talk** ein zweiminütiger Vortrag II **Hold on a minute.** Bleib / Bleiben Sie am Apparat. *(am Telefon)* II **Wait a minute.** Warte einen Moment. / Moment mal. I
miracle ['mɪrəkl] Wunder IV 4 (110/111)
mirror ['mɪrə] Spiegel II
miss [mɪs]:
1. vermissen III
2. verpassen I
miss the point nicht verstehen, worum es geht; an der Sache/am Thema vorbeireden/vorbeigehen IV 2 (57)
Miss Bell [mɪs] Frau Bell *(übliche Anrede von Lehrerinnen)* I
missing ['mɪsɪŋ]: **be missing** fehlen II **the missing words** die fehlenden Wörter I
mist [mɪst] (leichter) Nebel, Dunst(schleier) II
mistake [mɪ'steɪk] Fehler II **by mistake** aus Versehen III
mistaken [mɪ'steɪkən]: **be mistaken (about)** sich irren, sich täuschen (in) IV 3 (101)
°**misunderstand** [ˌmɪsʌndə'stænd], **misunderstood, misunderstood** missverstehen
°**misunderstood** [ˌmɪsʌndə'stʊd] *siehe* **misunderstand**
mix [mɪks] Mischung III
°**mixed** [mɪkst] gemischt
mixed bag [ˌmɪkst 'bæg] *etwa:* bunte Mischung I
°**mixed-race (children)** [ˌmɪkst 'reɪs] (Kinder) gemischter Herkunft
mixture ['mɪkstʃə] Mischung IV 1 (19)
°**mob** [mɒb] Gruppe *(Kängurus)*; (Menschen-)Menge, Meute
mobile (phone) [ˌməʊbaɪl 'fəʊn] Mobiltelefon, Handy I
model ['mɒdl] Modell III
°**moderator** ['mɒdəreɪtə] Moderator/in *(bei Debatten)*; Vermittler/in
modern ['mɒdən] modern III
°**module** ['mɒdjuːl] Modul
mom [mɒm], [mɑːm] *(AE)* Mutti, Mama IV 1 (11)
moment ['məʊmənt] Moment I **at the moment** gerade, im Moment I
monarch ['mɒnək] Monarch/in III
monarchy ['mɒnəki] Monarchie IV 1 (43)
Monday ['mʌndeɪ], ['mʌndi] Montag I **on Monday** am Montag I
money ['mʌni] Geld I
monkey ['mʌŋki] Affe I
monotone ['mɒnətəʊn]:
1. monotone Stimme; Monotonie IV 4 (123)
2. monoton, ausdruckslos IV 4 (123)
monster ['mɒnstə] Monster I
month [mʌnθ] Monat I
monthly ['mʌnθli] monatlich III
monument (to) ['mɒnjumənt] Monument, Denkmal (für/zum Gedenken an) IV 1 (24)
mood [muːd] Stimmung, Laune III
moon [muːn] Mond I **full moon** Vollmond II
moonlight ['muːnlaɪt] Mondlicht III
moor [mɔː] Hochmoor II
mop [mɒp]:
1. wischen *(Fußboden)* III
2. Wischmopp III
more [mɔː] mehr I **more beautiful (than)** schöner (als) II **not ... any more** nicht mehr II **one more photo** noch ein Foto; ein weiteres Foto II
morning ['mɔːnɪŋ] Morgen, Vormittag I **Good morning.** Guten Morgen. I **in the morning** morgens, vormittags, am Morgen/Vormittag I **tomorrow morning** morgen früh II
mosquito [məs'kiːtəʊ], *pl* **mosquitos** *or* **mosquitoes** (Stech-)Mücke IV 2 (48)
most [məʊst]: **most people / most of them** die meisten Menschen / die meisten von ihnen II **(the) most beautiful** der/die/das schönste ...; am schönsten II
mostly ['məʊstli] größtenteils, hauptsächlich; meistens IV 3 (108)
moth [mɒθ] Motte; Nachtfalter IV 2 (53)
mother ['mʌðə] Mutter I
motor ['məʊtə] Motor III
mountain ['maʊntən] Berg I
mountain-biking ['maʊntən baɪkɪŋ] Mountainbiken III
mountainous ['maʊntənəs] bergig, gebirgig IV 2 (56)
mourn [mɔːn]: **mourn for (sb./sth.)** trauern um (jn./etwas) IV 2 (58) **mourn sb./sth.** jn./etwas betrauern, beklagen IV 2 (58)
mourning ['mɔːnɪŋ] Trauer IV 2 (58)
mouth [maʊθ] Mund; Maul I
move [muːv]:
1. bewegen; sich bewegen I
2. **move (to)** umziehen (nach) II **move in** einziehen II **move into a house** in ein Haus (ein)ziehen II
3. Zug *(bei Brettspielen)* III
movement ['muːvmənt] Bewegung III
movie ['muːvi] *(bes. AE)* Film II
mozzarella [ˌmɒtsə'relə] Mozzarella IV 4 (120)
°**mozzie** ['mɒzi] *(infml)* (Stech-)Mücke
MP (= Member of Parliament) [ˌem 'piː] Parlamentsangehörige(r), Abgeordnete(r) IV 1 (15)
MP3 player [ˌem piː 'θriː pleɪə] MP3-Player I
Mr Schwarz ['mɪstə] Herr Schwarz I
Mrs Schwarz ['mɪsɪz] Frau Schwarz I
Ms Hancock [mɪz], [məz] Frau Hancock IV 3 (98)
much [mʌtʃ] viel I **How much ...?** Wie viel ...? I **How much is/are ...?** Was kostet/kosten ...? I
mud [mʌd] Schlamm, Matsch II
mug [mʌg] (Tee-/Kaffee-)Becher II
multicultural [ˌmʌlti'kʌltʃərəl] multikulturell IV 1 (19)
multiculturalism [ˌmʌlti'kʌltʃərəlɪzm] Multikulturismus, kulturelle Vielfalt IV 1 (19)
multilingual [ˌmʌlti'lɪŋgwəl] mehrsprachig IV 4 (137)
multilingualism [ˌmʌlti'lɪŋgwəlɪzm] Mehrsprachigkeit IV 4 (137)
°**multiple-choice (question)** [ˌmʌltɪpl 'tʃɔɪs] Multiple-Choice (-Frage)
multiply (by) ['mʌltɪplaɪ] multiplizieren (mit); (sich) vervielfachen, (sich) vermehren IV 4 (110/111)
mum [mʌm] Mama, Mutti I
mural ['mjʊərəl] Wandgemälde IV 1 (18)
museum [mju'ziːəm] Museum I
music ['mjuːzɪk] Musik I
musical ['mjuːzɪkl] Musical II
musician [mju'zɪʃn] Musiker/in III
must [mʌst] müssen I **you mustn't do it** du darfst es nicht tun I
°**mutiny** ['mjuːtəni] Meuterei, Aufstand
my [maɪ] mein, meine, mein I **My birthday is in May.** Ich habe im Mai Geburtstag. I **my name is ...** ich heiße ... I
myself [maɪ'self] ich/mich/mir selbst/selber III
mythical ['mɪθɪkl] mythisch; fiktiv IV 1 (19)
°**mythical beast** [ˌmɪθɪkl 'biːst] Fabelwesen

N

name [neɪm]:
1. Name I
call sb. names jn. beschimpfen, jm. Schimpfwörter nachrufen IV 2 (64) **my name is ...** ich heiße ... I **What's your name?** Wie heißt du? / Wie heißt ihr? I

2. (be)nennen IV 1 (20)
name sb. (as) sth. jn. zu etwas ernennen IV 2 (64)
narration [nə'reɪʃn] Erzählung, Schilderung III
narrative ['nærətɪv] Erzählung, Geschichte IV 2 (71)
narrator [nə'reɪtə] Erzähler/in; Sprecher/in III
narrow ['nærəʊ] schmal, eng II
narrow-minded [ˌnærəʊ 'maɪndɪd] engstirnig IV 2 (77)
nation ['neɪʃn] Nation, Volk III
national ['næʃnəl] national, National- I
national park [næʃnəl 'pɑːk] Nationalpark IV 2 (46)
nationalist ['næʃnəlɪst] Nationalist/in; nationalistisch IV 1 (19)
nationality [ˌnæʃə'næləti] Staatsangehörigkeit, Nationalität IV 1 (30)
°**nationwide** [ˌneɪʃn'waɪd] landesweit, im ganzen Land
native ['neɪtɪv] Mutter- III
Native American [ˌneɪtɪv‿ə'merɪkən] amerikanischer Ureinwohner / amerikanische Ureinwohnerin III
native language [ˌneɪtɪv 'læŋgwɪdʒ] Muttersprache III
native speaker [ˌneɪtɪv 'spiːkə] Muttersprachler/in III
natural ['nætʃrəl] natürlich III
natural history [ˌnætʃrəl 'hɪstri] Naturkunde I
natural world [ˌnætʃrəl 'wɜːld] (Welt der) Natur II
nature ['neɪtʃə] (die) Natur IV 4 (121)
navigate ['nævɪgeɪt] navigieren, den Weg finden (in/durch) IV 2 (62)
°**navigation** [ˌnævɪ'geɪʃn] Navigation
navy ['neɪvi] Marine I
near [nɪə] in der Nähe von, nahe (bei) I **near here** (hier) in der Nähe I
nearby ['nɪəbaɪ]: **a nearby town** eine nahegelegene Stadt II
nearest ['nɪərəst]: **the nearest ...** der/die/das nächstgelegene ... IV 2 (77)
nearly ['nɪəli] fast, beinahe III
necessary ['nesəsəri] notwendig, nötig III
neck [nek] Hals II
need [niːd]:
1. brauchen, benötigen I
need to do sth. etwas tun müssen II
you needn't do it du musst es nicht tun, du brauchst es nicht zu tun I
2. **need (for)** Bedarf (an), Bedürfnis (nach), Notwendigkeit IV 4 (118)
negative ['negətɪv] negativ IV 1 (15)
neighbour ['neɪbə] **(*AE* neighbor)** Nachbar/in II
neighbourhood ['neɪbəhʊd] **(*AE* neighborhood)** Viertel, Gegend, Umgebung; Nachbarschaft IV 1 (22)
neither ['naɪðə], [niːðə]: **Me neither.** Ich auch nicht. III
nephew ['nefjuː], ['nevjuː] Neffe III
nervous ['nɜːvəs] nervös, aufgeregt I
°**net** [net] Netz **slip through the net** durchs Netz gehen
netball ['netbɔːl] Korbball II
°**network** ['netwɜːk] Netz(werk)
never ['nevə] nie, niemals I
new [njuː] neu I
New Year's Eve [ˌnjuː jɪəz‿'iːv] Silvester II
news *(no pl)* [njuːz]:
1. Nachrichten I
2. Neuigkeiten II
newspaper ['njuːspeɪpə] Zeitung III
next [nekst]:
1. als Nächstes III
2. nächste(r, s) I
next year's musical das Musical vom nächsten Jahr II
next to ['nekst tʊ] neben I
nice [naɪs] nett, schön I **Nice to meet you.** Freut mich, dich/euch/Sie kennenzulernen. I
nickname ['nɪkneɪm] Spitzname IV 1 (24)
niece [niːs] Nichte III
night [naɪt] Nacht I **at night** nachts, in der Nacht I
nine [naɪn] neun I
nineteen forties [ˌnaɪntiːn 'fɔːtiz]: **in the 1940s** in den 40er-Jahren (des 20. Jahrhunderts) IV 1 (10)
no [nəʊ]:
1. nein I
2. kein(e) I
No way! auf keinen Fall! / Kommt nicht in Frage! III **No worries.** *(infml)* Kein Problem! / Gern geschehen! III
no one ['nəʊ wʌn] niemand I
nobody ['nəʊbədi] niemand I
nod [nɒd] nicken II
noise [nɔɪz] Geräusch, Lärm I
noisy ['nɔɪzi] laut, lärmend, voller Lärm I
°**nomadic** [nəʊ'mædɪk] nomadisch, Nomaden-
°**nominalize** ['nɒmɪnəlaɪz] substantivieren
°**Nominalized adjectives** substantivierte Adjektive
non- [nɒn] Nicht- IV 4 (136)
none (of ...) [nʌn] keine(r, s) (von ...) III
nonsense ['nɒnsns] Unsinn, Quatsch IV 2 (57)
noon [nuːn] Mittag IV 3 (82)
normal ['nɔːml] normal IV 1 (27)
north [nɔːθ]:
1. (nach) Norden; Nord- I
2. nördlich III
north-east [ˌnɔːθ‿'iːst] Nordosten; nach Nordosten; nordöstlich III
north-west [ˌnɔːθ 'west] Nordwesten; nach Nordwesten; nordwestlich III
northbound ['nɔːθbaʊnd] Richtung Norden III
northern ['nɔːðən] nördlich, Nord- II
nose [nəʊz] Nase I
nostalgic [nɒ'stældʒɪk] nostalgisch IV 1 (19)
nosy ['nəʊzi] **(*auch*: nosey)** neugierig IV 4 (128)
not [nɒt] nicht I **not ... yet** noch nicht I **not even** (noch) nicht einmal II **not till three** erst um drei, nicht vor drei II
note [nəʊt]:
1. Note *(Musik)* III
2. Notiz, Mitteilung I
make notes (on sth.) (sich) Notizen machen (über/zu etwas) *(zur Vorbereitung)* II **take notes** (sich) Notizen machen *(beim Lesen oder Zuhören)* II
3. beachten; *(sich etwas)* notieren IV 4 (115)
°**note sth. down** (sich) etwas notieren; etwas aufschreiben
nothing ['nʌθɪŋ] (gar) nichts I
notice ['nəʊtɪs] (be)merken III
notification [ˌnəʊtɪfɪ'keɪʃn] Benachrichtigung, Mitteilung IV 3 (88)
notify ['nəʊtɪfaɪ] benachrichtigen, mitteilen IV 3 (88)
noun [naʊn] Nomen III
novel ['nɒvl] Roman III
November [nəʊ'vembə] November I
now [naʊ] nun, jetzt I **now that ...** jetzt, wo ... / nun, da ... III
nowhere ['nəʊweə] nirgendwo; nirgendwohin II
nuclear ['njuːkliə] Kern-, Atom-, Nuklear- IV 1 (40)
nuclear power [ˌnjuːkliə 'paʊə] Atomenergie, Kernenergie IV 1 (40)
number ['nʌmbə]:
1. Zahl, Nummer, Ziffer I
2. Anzahl IV 3 (101)
nursery school ['nɜːsəri skuːl] Kindergarten IV 3 (81)

O

o [əʊ] Null *(in Telefonnummern)* I
o'clock [ə'klɒk]: **ten o'clock** 10 Uhr / 22 Uhr I
object ['ɒbdʒɪkt] Objekt, Gegenstand III
obligation [ˌɒblɪ'geɪʃn] Pflicht, Verpflichtung IV 2 (76)
obliged [ə'blaɪdʒd]: **be obliged to do sth.** etwas tun müssen, die Pflicht haben etwas zu tun IV 2 (76)
observation deck [ˌɒbzə'veɪʃn dek] Aussichtsplattform III
occasion [ə'keɪʒn] Gelegenheit; Ereignis, Anlass IV 3 (99)
occasional [ə'keɪʒənl] gelegentliche(r, s) IV 3 (99)
occasionally [ə'keɪʒənəli] gelegentlich, ab und zu IV 3 (99)

occupation [ˌɒkju'peɪʃn] Besetzung; Besatzungszeit III
°**occupy** ['ɒkjupaɪ]:
1. einnehmen; besetzen
2. einnehmen; besetzen; bewohnen IV 2 (76)
occur [ə'kɜː] passieren, vorkommen IV 2 (76)
ocean ['əʊʃn] Ozean I
October [ɒk'təʊbə] Oktober I
of [ɒv], [əv] von I **of all time** aller Zeiten II
of course [əv 'kɔːs] natürlich, selbstverständlich I
off [ɒf]:
1. von … herunter III
Off you go now. Ab mit euch jetzt! / Los mit euch jetzt! III **fall off a bike** vom Fahrrad (herunter)fallen III **run off** wegrennen III **take sth. off** etwas ausziehen III
2. **be off** ausgeschaltet sein, aus sein *(Radio, Licht usw.)* III
offer ['ɒfə]:
1. anbieten II
2. Angebot IV 1 (28)
3. **on offer** im Angebot IV 1 (28)
office ['ɒfɪs] Büro III
official [ə'fɪʃl]:
1. amtlich, Amts- I
2. Beamte(r), Beamtin III
official language [əˌfɪʃl 'læŋgwɪdʒ] Amtssprache IV 2 (76)
offline [ɒf'laɪn] offline, nicht übers/im Internet IV 4 (110/111)
often ['ɒfn], ['ɒftən] oft I
oh [əʊ]: **Oh, it's you.** Ach, du bist es. I **Oh dear!** Oje! II
oil [ɔɪl] Öl III
old [əʊld] alt I **How old are you?** Wie alt bist du? I
old-fashioned [ˌəʊld 'fæʃənd] altmodisch IV 2 (56)
old school ['əʊld skuːl] alt hergebracht, (von)der alten Schule IV 3 (85)
on [ɒn]:
1. auf I
on average im Durchschnitt, durchschnittlich III **on demand** auf Abruf, nach Bedarf III **on earth** auf der Erde II **on Monday** am Montag I **on Monday afternoon** am Montagnachmittag I **on my/your/their/… own** allein II **on the corner of Church Road and London Road** Church Road, Ecke London Road II **on the internet** im Internet I **on the left/right** links/rechts; auf der linken/rechten Seite I **on the map** auf der Landkarte; auf dem Stadtplan I **on the phone** am Telefon II **on the plane** im Flugzeug II **on the radio** im Radio II **on top of each other** übereinander, aufeinander III **on TV** im Fernsehen III **go on a boat trip** einen Bootsausflug machen I
2. **be on** eingeschaltet sein, an sein *(Radio, Licht usw.)*; laufen, übertragen werden *(Programm, Sendung)* III
3. weiter- II
straight on geradeaus weiter II
walk/sail on weitergehen/-segeln II
once [wʌns]:
1. einmal I
2. einst, (früher) einmal II
one [wʌn]:
1. eins I
one another sich (gegenseitig), einander III **one by one** einer nach dem anderen II **one more photo** noch ein Foto; ein weiteres Foto II **one night/day** eines Nachts/Tages II
2. *(pron)* **a white one** ein weißer / eine weiße / ein weißes II
this one diese(r, s) II **two black ones** zwei schwarze II **Which one?** Welche(r, s)? II
oneself [wʌn'self]: **expressing oneself** sich ausdrücken IV 1 (28)
onion ['ʌnjən] Zwiebel III
online [ˌɒn'laɪn] online II
only ['əʊnli]:
1. erst I
2. nur, bloß I
3. *(adj)* **the only …** der/die/das einzige …; die einzigen … II
onto ['ɒntʊ] auf (… hinauf) I **hold onto** sich festhalten an III
open ['əʊpən]:
1. offen, geöffnet I
2. öffnen, aufmachen I
open-minded (about) [ˌəʊpən 'maɪndɪd] offen, aufgeschlossen (gegenüber) IV 2 (77)
opening ['əʊpənɪŋ] Öffnung III
opening times *(pl)* ['əʊpənɪŋ taɪmz] Öffnungszeiten III
opera ['ɒprə] Oper IV 2 (46)
opera house ['ɒprə haʊs] Opernhaus IV 2 (46)
opinion [ə'pɪnjən] Meinung III **in my opinion** meiner Meinung nach III
opinion piece [ə'pɪnjən piːs] Stellungnahme IV 1 (19)
opportunity [ˌɒpə'tjuːnəti] Gelegenheit, Möglichkeit, Chance IV 1 (28)
oppose sth. [ə'pəʊz] etwas ablehnen, gegen etwas sein; sich einer Sache widersetzen IV 2 (50)
opposite ['ɒpəzɪt]:
1. Gegenteil I
2. *(adj)* gegenüberliegende(r, s); entgegengesetzte(r, s) IV 1 (10)
3. *(prep)* gegenüber (von) II
opposition (to) [ˌɒpə'zɪʃn] Widerstand (gegen), Opposition IV 2 (50)
oppress [ə'pres] unterdrücken; bedrücken IV 2 (65)
optimism ['ɒptɪmɪzəm] Optimismus IV 2 (62)
optimistic [ˌɒptɪ'mɪstɪk] optimistisch IV 1 (28)
option ['ɒpʃn] Wahl(möglichkeit), Option IV 3 (81)
optional ['ɒpʃənl] wahlweise, freiwillig IV 3 (81)
or [ɔː] oder I **either … or …** entweder … oder … III
orange ['ɒrɪndʒ]:
1. Orange, Apfelsine II
2. orange(farben) I
°**orchestra** ['ɔːkɪstrə] Orchester
order ['ɔːdə]:
1. anordnen; beauftragen III
2. Reihenfolge I
word order Wortstellung I **in order to do sth.** um etwas zu tun IV 4 (118)
order ['ɔːdə] bestellen II
organic [ɔː'gænɪk] biologisch (angebaut), Bio- IV 4 (122)
organization [ˌɔːgənaɪ'zeɪʃn] Organisation IV 1 (11)
organize ['ɔːgənaɪz] organisieren; ordnen I
organizer ['ɔːgənaɪzə] Organisator/in IV 4 (124)
orientation [ˌɔːriən'teɪʃn] Orientierung IV 3 (88)
origin ['ɒrɪdʒɪn] Ursprung, Herkunft IV 1 (10)
original [ə'rɪdʒənl] Original-; ursprüngliche(r, s) III
other ['ʌðə] andere(r, s) I **each other** sich (gegenseitig), einander III **the other day** neulich IV 4 (115)
otherwise ['ʌðəwaɪz] anderenfalls, ansonsten, sonst; anders IV 3 (88)
our ['aʊə] unser/e I
ours ['aʊəz] unserer, unsere, unseres II
ourselves [ɑː'selvz], [aʊə'selvz] wir/uns selbst/selber III
out [aʊt] heraus, hinaus, nach draußen II **out and about** unterwegs II **out of …** aus … (heraus/hinaus) I **be out** nicht zu Hause sein, nicht da sein II **eight out of ten** acht von zehn(en) IV 2 (58)
outback ['aʊtbæk] *Hinterland Australiens* IV 2 (45)
outdoor ['aʊtdɔː] Außen-, im Freien II
outdoors [ˌaʊt'dɔːz] im Freien, draußen IV 2 (66)
outgoing ['aʊtgəʊɪŋ] kontaktfreudig IV 3 (95)
°**outline** ['aʊtlaɪn] umreißen, grob beschreiben
outlook (on sth.) ['aʊtlʊk] Einstellung (zu etwas); (Zukunfts-)Aussicht(en); Aussicht, Blick IV 4 (121)
outset ['aʊtset]: **at the outset (of sth.)** am Anfang (einer Sache) IV 3 (108)
outside [ˌaʊt'saɪd]:
1. draußen; nach draußen I
2. **outside (of)** außerhalb (von) IV 1 (22)
outside Rosie's Diner vor *Rosie's Diner*; außerhalb von *Rosie's Diner* II

3. the outside die Außenseite, das Äußere III
oval ['əʊvl] oval III
over ['əʊvə]:
1. über I
over 20 people/years über/mehr als 20 Leute/Jahre I **over here** hier herüber; hier drüben II **over there** da drüben, dort drüben II **over to ...** hinüber zu/nach ... I **all over the country / the city / the world** im ganzen Land / in der ganzen Stadt / auf der ganzen Welt II **run over (to)** hinüberrennen (zu/nach) II
2. be over vorbei sein, zu Ende sein I
overboard ['əʊvəbɔːd] über Bord IV 4 (123) **throw sb. overboard** jn. über Bord werfen; *(übertragen)* jn. loswerden IV 4 (123)
°**overcame** [ˌəʊvə'keɪm] *siehe* **overcome**
°**overcome** [ˌəʊvə'kʌm], **overcame, overcome** überwinden; *(Problem)* meistern
overcrowded [ˌəʊvə'kraʊdɪd] überfüllt, übervölkert IV 2 (56)
overlook [ˌəʊvə'lʊk] überblicken; übersehen IV 1 (10)
overthrew [ˌəʊvə'θuː] *siehe* **overthrow**
overthrow [ˌəʊvə'θrəʊ], **overthrew, overthrown** stürzen *(Regierung, Staatsoberhaupt usw.)* III
overthrown [ˌəʊvə'θrəʊn] *siehe* **overthrow**
°**overworked** [ˌəʊvə'wɜːkt] überlastet, überarbeitet
owe [əʊ]: **owe sb. sth.** jm. etwas schulden, schuldig sein IV 4 (119) **owe sth. to sb.** jm. etwas schulden, schuldig sein IV 4 (119)
own [əʊn]:
1. besitzen II
2. my own film/room/... mein eigener Film / mein eigenes Zimmer / ... II
3. on my/your/their/... own allein II
on my/your/their/... own allein II **one of our own** eine/r von uns IV 2 (64)
owner ['əʊnə] Besitzer/in III

P

p [piː] *Abkürzung für „pence", „penny"* I
°**pace** [peɪs] Tempo, Geschwindigkeit; Schritt
pack [pæk] packen; einpacken II
package ['pækɪdʒ]:
1. Verpackung, Schachtel; Paket *(Post)* IV 4 (128)
2. package sth. (up) etwas verpacken IV 4 (128)
packaging ['pækɪdʒɪŋ] Verpackung IV 4 (128)
packet ['pækɪt] Packung, Päckchen II
page [peɪdʒ] Seite I **What page are we on?** Auf welcher Seite sind wir? I
paid [peɪd] *siehe* **pay** **get paid** bezahlt werden III
pain [peɪn] Schmerz(en) IV 1 (32)
paint [peɪnt] (an)streichen; (an)malen II
painted ['peɪntɪd] bemalt, angemalt II
painter ['peɪntə] Maler/in III
painting ['peɪntɪŋ] Gemälde, Bild III
°**dot painting** Punktmalerei; Punktgemälde
pair [peə]:
1. a pair (of) ein Paar I
a pair of trousers eine Hose II
°**2. pair A with B** A und B (einander) zuordnen
palace ['pæləs] Palast, Schloss III
palm tree ['pɑːm triː] Palme III
pancake ['pænkeɪk] Pfannkuchen, Eierkuchen II
°**panel discussion** ['pænl dɪskʌʃn] Podiumsdiskussion
°**panellist** ['pænəlɪst] Diskussionsteilnehmer/in; Mitglied eines Gremiums
panic ['pænɪk] in Panik geraten III
pants *(pl)* [pænts] *(AE)* Hose III
paper ['peɪpə]:
1. Papier; Zeitung I
2. (wissenschaftlicher) Aufsatz IV 3 (108)
parachute ['pærəʃuːt] Fallschirm IV 4 (123)
paper hat ['peɪpə hæt] Papierhut I
parade [pə'reɪd] Parade, Umzug II
paradise ['pærədaɪs] Paradies IV 2 (46)
paragraph ['pærəgrɑːf] Absatz *(in einem Text)* I
paraphrase ['pærəfreɪz]:
1. Umschreibung III
2. umschreiben, mit anderen Worten sagen III
parents *(pl)* ['peərənts] Eltern I
park [pɑːk]:
1. Park I
fun park Vergnügungspark I
2. parken III
parliament ['pɑːləmənt] Parlament I
parliamentary [ˌpɑːlə'mentri] parlamentarisch IV 1 (43)
°**parrot** ['pærət] Papagei
part [pɑːt]:
1. Teil I
part of speech Wortart III **part of the body** Körperteil II **take part (in)** teilnehmen (an) II
2. part with sth. sich von etwas trennen IV 1 (40)
part-time [ˌpɑːt 'taɪm] Teilzeit-, Halbtags- IV 3 (108)
participant [pɑː'tɪsɪpənt] Teilnehmer/in IV 3 (78/79)
participate (in) [pɑː'tɪsɪpeɪt] teilnehmen (an), sich beteiligen (an) IV 3 (78/79)
particular [pə'tɪkjələ] bestimmte(r, s), spezielle(r, s) IV 3 (86) **in particular** insbesondere IV 3 (86)
particularly [pə'tɪkjələli] insbesondere IV 3 (86)
partner ['pɑːtnə] Partner/in I
party ['pɑːti]:
1. Party I
2. Partei IV 1 (42)
pass [pɑːs]:
1. vergehen, vorübergehen *(Zeit)* III
2. pass sth./sb. an etwas/jm. vorbeigehen/vorbeifahren II
pass (a test / an exam) *(einen Test / eine Prüfung)* bestehen, schaffen III
pass a law ein Gesetz verabschieden III
pass sth. around etwas herumgeben, herumreichen II °**pass sth. on (to sb.)** (jm.) etwas weitergeben, weitersagen, weiterleiten
passenger ['pæsɪndʒə] Passagier/in; Fahrgast III
passing grade [ˌpɑːsɪŋ 'greɪd] Note/Zensur, mit der man bestanden hat III
passion ['pæʃn] Leidenschaft IV 4 (119)
passionate ['pæʃənət] leidenschaftlich IV 4 (119) **be passionate about sth.** eine Leidenschaft haben für etwas, etwas leidenschaftlich gern tun IV 4 (119)
passport ['pɑːspɔːt] (Reise-)Pass II
password ['pɑːswɜːd] Passwort III
past [pɑːst]:
1. Vergangenheit I
2. vergangene(r, s), frühere(r, s), ehemalige(r, s) IV 2 (64)
3. vorbei (an), vorüber (an) II
4. half past ten halb elf (10.30 / 22.30) I
quarter past ten Viertel nach zehn (10.15 / 22.15) I
pasta ['pæstə] Pasta *(italienische Bezeichnung für Teigwaren)* IV 4 (128)
pastry ['peɪstri] Pastete; Gebäck IV 3 (82)
pat [pæt]:
1. tätscheln III
2. Klaps, *(ein/das)* Tätscheln III
°**patch** [pætʃ] Flicken; Stück *(z.B. Stoff)*
path [pɑːθ] Pfad, Weg II
°**pathway** ['pɑːθweɪ] Weg
patience ['peɪʃns] Geduld IV 3 (86)
patient ['peɪʃnt] geduldig III
pattern ['pætn] Muster III
pause [pɔːz] innehalten, pausieren; eine Pause einlegen II
pavement ['peɪvmənt] Gehweg, Bürgersteig III
pay (for sth.) [peɪ], **paid, paid** (etwas) bezahlen II
PE (= Physical Education) [ˌpiː‿'iː] Sportunterricht, Turnen I
peace [piːs] Friede, Frieden III

peaceful ['pi:sfl] friedlich II
peak [pi:k] Gipfel II
pebble ['pebl] Kieselstein III
pedestrian [pə'destriən] Fußgänger/in III
pedestrian zone [pə'destrɪən zəʊn] Fußgängerzone II
pen [pen] Kugelschreiber, Stift, Füller I
penal ['pi:nl] Straf-, strafrechtlich IV 2 (58)
pence (p) [pens] *plural of* **penny**
pencil ['pensl] Bleistift I
pencil case ['pensl keɪs] Federmäppchen I
°**penguin** ['peŋgwɪn] Pinguin
peninsula [pə'nɪnsjələ] Halbinsel IV 2 (76)
penny ['peni] Penny I
people ['pi:pl]:
1. Leute, Menschen I
2. *pl* **peoples** Volk IV 1 (19)
pepper ['pepə] Pfeffer I
per cent (%) [pə 'sent] Prozent I
per day/hour [pə], [pɜ:] pro Tag/Stunde III
percentage [pə'sentɪdʒ] Anteil, Prozentsatz IV 4 (122)
perfect ['pɜ:fɪkt] perfekt, ideal I
perform [pə'fɔ:m]:
1. auftreten *(Künstler/in)* III
°2. aufführen; durchführen
performance [pə'fɔ:məns] Aufführung, Vorstellung, Auftritt III
performer [pə'fɔ:mə] Künstler/in *(der/die etwas aufführt)* IV 2 (46)
period ['pɪəriəd] Zeit(raum), Zeitspanne IV 2 (58)
°**periodic table** [ˌpɪəriɒdɪk 'teɪbl] Periodensystem *(Chemie)*
permission [pə'mɪʃn] Erlaubnis III
permit [pə'mɪt]: **permit sb. to do sth.** es jm. erlauben etwas zu tun III **permit sth.** etwas erlauben III
persecution [ˌpɜ:sɪ'kju:ʃn] Verfolgung IV 1 (19)
person ['pɜ:sn] Person I **in person** persönlich IV 3 (95)
personal ['pɜ:sənl] persönlich IV 1 (28)
personal statement [ˌpɜ:sənl 'steɪtmənt] persönliche Beschreibung, Selbstbeschreibung IV 3 (94)
°**personality** [pɜ:sə'næləti] Persönlichkeit; Charakter
°**personalize** ['pɜ:sənəlaɪz] persönlich/individuell gestalten
perspective [pə'spektɪv] Perspektive IV 1 (28) **put sth. in perspective** etw. ins rechte Licht rücken IV 1 (28)
persuade [pə'sweɪd] überreden, überzeugen IV 4 (113)
persuasion [pə'sweɪʒn] Überzeugung(skunst), Überredung(skunst) IV 4 (113)
persuasive [pə'sweɪsɪv] überzeugend IV 4 (113)

pessimism ['pesɪmɪzəm] Pessimismus IV 2 (62)
pessimistic [ˌpesɪ'mɪstɪk] pessimistisch IV 1 (28)
pesticide ['pestɪsaɪd] Schädlingsbekämpfungsmittel, Pestizid IV 4 (118)
pet [pet] Haustier I
petrol ['petrəl] Benzin III
petrol station ['petrəl steɪʃn] Tankstelle III
pharmacy ['fɑ:məsi] Pharmazie; Apotheke IV 3 (108)
°**phase** [feɪz] Phase
PhD [ˌpi:‿eɪtʃ 'di:] Doktor(grad) IV 3 (108)
phone [fəʊn]:
1. Telefon I
answer the phone ans Telefon gehen II **mobile phone** Mobiltelefon, Handy I **on the phone** am Telefon II
2. **phone sb.** jn. anrufen I
phone call ['fəʊn kɔ:l] Anruf; Telefongespräch I
photo ['fəʊtəʊ] Foto I **in the photo** auf dem Foto I **take photos** fotografieren, Fotos machen I
°**photocopy** ['fəʊtəʊkɒpi]:
1. Fotokopie
2. fotokopieren
photograph ['fəʊtəgrɑ:f]:
1. Foto(grafie) IV 2 (47)
2. fotografieren IV 2 (47)
photographer [fə'tɒgrəfə] Fotograf/in IV 2 (47)
photography [fə'tɒgrəfi] Fotografie *(Hobby)* IV 2 (47)
phrase [freɪz] Ausdruck, (Rede-)Wendung I
physical ['fɪzɪkl] körperlich, physisch IV 2 (59)
Physical Education (PE) [ˌfɪzɪkl‿ˌedʒu'keɪʃn] Sportunterricht, Turnen I
piano [pi'ænəʊ] Klavier, Piano I **play the piano** Klavier spielen I
°**pic** [pɪk] **(***infml for* **picture)** Bild
pick [pɪk] pflücken IV 4 (118) **pick sb. up** jn. abholen II **pick sth. up** etwas aufheben *(vom Boden)*, etwas hochheben II
picnic ['pɪknɪk] Picknick I
picture ['pɪktʃə]:
1. Bild I
in the picture auf dem Bild I
°2. **picture sth.** etwas abbilden
pie [paɪ] Obstkuchen; Pastete II
pie chart ['paɪ tʃɑ:t] Tortendiagramm IV 4 (122)
piece [pi:s] Stück III **a piece of …** ein Stück … III
pig [pɪg] Schwein I
pigeon ['pɪdʒɪn] (Stadt-)Taube III
pike [paɪk] Spieß IV 1 (41)
pile [paɪl] Stapel, Haufen III
pilgrim ['pɪlgrɪm] Pilger/in III

°**ping** [pɪŋ] (an)pingen, (an)mailen, eine Nachricht schicken
pink [pɪŋk] pink, rosa I
pipe [paɪp] (Tabaks-)Pfeife III
pipeline ['paɪplaɪn] Pipeline III
pirate ['paɪrət] Pirat/in III
pit [pɪt] Grube, Loch *(im Boden)* IV 2 (77)
pitch [pɪtʃ] Tonhöhe, Stimmlage IV 2 (48)
pity ['pɪti]: **It was a pity that …** Es war schade, dass … III
pizza ['pi:tsə] Pizza I
place [pleɪs] Ort, Platz, Stelle I **in the first place** erstens, in erster Linie; überhaupt IV 1 (29) **take place** stattfinden; spielen, sich abspielen *(Geschichte, Handlung)* I
°**placemat** ['pleɪsmæt] Platzdeckchen
plains *(pl)* [pleɪn]: **plain** Ebene, Flachland III
plan [plæn]:
1. Plan I
2. planen II
plane [pleɪn] Flugzeug II
planet ['plænɪt] Planet I
plant [plɑ:nt]:
1. Pflanze II
2. pflanzen II
plaster ['plɑ:stə] (Heft-)Pflaster II
plastic ['plæstɪk] Plastik, Kunststoff II
plate [pleɪt] Teller I **a plate of …** ein Teller … I
platform ['plætfɔ:m]:
1. Bahnsteig, Gleis II
°2. Plattform
play [pleɪ]:
1. spielen I **play sb.** gegen jn. spielen III **play the piano/guitar/drums** Klavier/Gitarre/Schlagzeug spielen I
2. abspielen *(CD, DVD)* I
3. Theaterstück I
4. Spiel IV 3 (81)
player ['pleɪə] Spieler/in I
please [pli:z] bitte I
pleased [pli:zd] froh, erfreut, zufrieden IV 4 (116) **Pleased to meet you.** Freut mich Sie kennenzulernen. IV 4 (116)
plot [plɒt]:
1. Verschwörung IV 1 (40)
2. sich verschwören IV 1 (40)
plotter ['plɒtə] Verschwörer/in IV 1 (41)
plug [plʌg]:
1. Stecker IV 4 (112)
2. **plug sth. in** etwas einstecken, anschließen IV 4 (112)
plus [plʌs] plus IV 2 (66)
pm [ˌpi:‿'em]: **4 pm** 4 Uhr nachmittags / 16 Uhr I
pocket ['pɒkɪt] Tasche *(Manteltasche, Hosentasche usw.)* II
pocket money ['pɒkɪt mʌni] Taschengeld IV 1 (28)
poem ['pəʊɪm] Gedicht II
poet ['pəʊɪt] Dichter/in IV 4 (129)

poetic [pəʊ'etɪk] poetisch IV 4 (129)
poetry ['pəʊətri] Poesie, Lyrik IV 3 (84)
pogrom ['pɒgrəm] Pogrom *(Ausschreitungen gegen nationale, religiöse oder ethnische Minderheiten)* IV 1 (19)
point [pɔɪnt]:
1. Punkt I
point of view Standpunkt III **from my point of view** aus meiner Sicht III
2. **3.5 (three point five)** 3,5 (drei Komma fünf) III
3. Argument; Standpunkt IV 2 (57)
have a point recht haben, ein gutes Argument haben IV 2 (57) **miss the point** nicht verstehen, worum es geht; an der Sache/am Thema vorbeireden/vorbeigehen IV 2 (57) **take a point** einen Standpunkt verstehen IV 2 (57)
What's your point? Worauf willst du hinaus? IV 2 (57)
point [pɔɪnt]: **point sth. at sb.** etwas auf jn. richten I **point sth. out (to sb.)** (jn.) auf etwas hinweisen III
point to sth. auf etwas zeigen, deuten I
poison ['pɔɪzn]:
1. Gift IV 2 (45)
2. vergiften IV 2 (45)
poisonous ['pɔɪzənəs] giftig IV 2 (45)
police *(pl)* [pə'li:s] Polizei I
police officer [pə'li:s‿ɒfɪsə] Polizist/in I
police station [pə'li:s steɪʃn] Polizeiwache/-revier III
policeman [pə'li:smən] Polizist I
policy ['pɒləsi] Politik, Richtlinie(n), Bestimmung(en) IV 1 (19)
Polish ['pəʊlɪʃ] Polnisch; polnisch I
polite [pə'laɪt] höflich II
politeness [pə'laɪtnəs] Höflichkeit IV 3 (86)
political [pə'lɪtɪkl] politisch IV 1 (43)
politician [ˌpɒlə'tɪʃn] Politiker/in IV 3 (109)
politics ['pɒlətɪks] Politik III
pollute [pə'lu:t] *(die Umwelt)* verschmutzen IV 1 (13)
pollution [pə'lu:ʃn] (Umwelt-)Verschmutzung IV 1 (13)
polyester [ˌpɒli'estə] Polyester IV 4 (118)
°**Pom** [pɒm] *(AusE, infml)* Brite/Britin *(oft abwertend)*
°**Pommy** ['pɒmi] *(AusE, infml)* Brite/Britin *(oft abwertend)*
pony ['pəʊni] Pony II
pool [pu:l] Schwimmbad, -becken I
poor [pɔ:], [pʊə] arm I
pop (music) [pɒp] Pop(musik) II
°**pop** [pɒp] (*short for* **population)** Bevölkerung, Einwohner(zahl)
pope [pəʊp] Papst III
popular (with) ['pɒpjələ] populär, beliebt (bei) I

populate ['pɒpjuleɪt] bevölkern, besiedeln IV 1 (42) °**heavily populated** bevölkerungsreich, dicht besiedelt
population [ˌpɒpju'leɪʃn] Bevölkerung, Einwohner(zahl) III
populous ['pɒpjələs] bevölkerungsreich IV 2 (76)
porch [pɔ:tʃ] Veranda *(AE)*; Vorbau, Vordach *(BE)* III
port [pɔ:t] Hafenstadt I
position [pə'zɪʃn] Position, Standort, Platz; (Arbeits-)Stelle IV 3 (95)
positive ['pɒzətɪv] positiv IV 1 (15)
possibility [ˌpɒsə'bɪləti] Möglichkeit IV 3 (85)
possible ['pɒsəbl] möglich II
°**possum** ['pɒsəm] Opossum
post [pəʊst]:
1. Posting *(auf Blog)*, Blog-Eintrag III
2. **post sth.** etwas posten III
post office ['pəʊst‿ɒfɪs] Postamt II
postcard ['pəʊstkɑ:d] Postkarte I
poster ['pəʊstə] Poster I **study poster** Lernposter II
pot [pɒt] Gefäß; Topf III
potato [pə'teɪtəʊ], *pl* **potatoes** Kartoffel I **roast potatoes** *(pl)* Bratkartoffeln *(im Backofen in Fett gebackene Kartoffeln)* I
pound (£) [paʊnd] Pfund *(britische Währung)* I
pour [pɔ:] gießen II
poverty ['pɒvəti] Armut IV 1 (28)
power ['paʊə] Macht; Kraft, Stärke; Energie, Strom III
powerful ['paʊəfl] mächtig, kräftig, stark III
practical ['præktɪkl] praktisch III
practice ['præktɪs]:
1. Übung I
2. Training; Probe *(Band, Chor)* IV 2 (55)
3. *(AE)* üben, trainieren IV 3 (96)
practise ['præktɪs] üben, trainieren I
predict [prɪ'dɪkt] vorhersagen, voraussagen IV 4 (120)
prediction [prɪ'dɪkʃn] Vorhersage, Voraussage III
prefer sth. to sth. [prɪ'fɜ:] etwas einer Sache vorziehen, etwas lieber tun/haben als etwas III
prejudice (against) ['predʒudɪs] Vorurteil (gegen), Voreingenommenheit (gegenüber) IV 2 (66)
prep school ['prep sku:l] *siehe* **preparatory school**
°**preparation** [ˌprepə'reɪʃn] Vorbereitung; Zubereitung
preparatory school [prɪ'pærətri sku:l] (*kurz auch:* **prep school)**:
1. *Privatschule für Kinder zwischen 7 und 13 Jahren* IV 4 (112)
2. *(AE) (meist private) Schule, die Schüler/innen auf die Universität vorbereitet* IV 4 (112)

prepare (for) [prɪ'peə] sich vorbereiten (auf) I **prepare sth.** etwas vorbereiten I
prescription [prɪ'skrɪpʃn] *(ärztliches)* Rezept II
present ['preznt]:
1. Geschenk I
2. Gegenwart II
present sth. (to sb.) [prɪ'zent] (jm.) etwas präsentieren, vorstellen II
presentation [ˌprezn'teɪʃn] Präsentation, Vorstellung II
°**preserve** [prɪ'zɜ:v] bewahren, erhalten
president ['prezɪdənt] Präsident/in II
presidential election [ˌprezɪˌdenʃl ɪ'lekʃn] Präsidentschaftswahl IV 1 (42)
press [pres] drücken III
pressure ['preʃə] Druck III
pretend [prɪ'tend] so tun, als ob III
pretty ['prɪti]:
1. hübsch II
2. *(adv)* **pretty old/expensive/...** ziemlich alt/teuer/... IV 1 (11)
°**prevent** [prɪ'vent] verhindern, vorbeugen
price [praɪs] (Kauf-)Preis I
pride [praɪd] Stolz IV 2 (49)
primarily [praɪ'merəli] vor allem, hauptsächlich, vorrangig IV 4 (124)
primary school ['praɪməri sku:l] Grundschule IV 3 (80)
prime minister [ˌpraɪm 'mɪnɪstə] Premierminister/in II
prince [prɪns] Prinz II
princess [ˌprɪn'ses] Prinzessin II
principal ['prɪnsəpl] *(AE)* Schulleiter/in IV 4 (112)
print [prɪnt]:
1. Druck; Schrift(art) IV 3 (92)
2. **print sth. (out)** etwas (aus)drucken IV 3 (92)
prison ['prɪzn] Gefängnis I
prisoner ['prɪznə] Gefangene(r) III
private ['praɪvət] privat; persönlich IV 2 (47)
prize [praɪz] Preis, Gewinn II
°**prized** [praɪzd] wertvoll, hoch geschätzt
probable ['prɒbəbl] wahrscheinlich *(Adj.)* III
probably ['prɒbəbli] wahrscheinlich *(Adv.)* II
problem ['prɒbləm] Problem I
produce [prə'dju:s] produzieren, herstellen IV 2 (58)
producer [prə'dju:sə] Produzent/in IV 2 (58)
product ['prɒdʌkt] Produkt IV 2 (58)
production [prə'dʌkʃn] Produktion IV 2 (58)
profession [prə'feʃn] Beruf IV 2 (64)
professional [prə'feʃənl]:
1. professionell, Profi- IV 2 (64)
2. (*infml auch* **pro)** Fachmann/Fachfrau, Profi IV 2 (64)
professor [prə'fesə] Professor/in IV 4 (129)

profile ['prəʊfaɪl] Profil; Beschreibung, Porträt I
profit ['prɒfɪt]:
1. Gewinn *(Profit)* IV 4 (119)
make a profit Gewinn/Profit machen IV 4 (119)
2. **profit (from)** profitieren (von) IV 4 (119)
program ['prəʊgræm] programmieren III
programme ['prəʊgræm] Programm, *(Radio-, Fernseh-)*Sendung I
programmer ['prəʊgræmə] Programmierer/in IV 3 (82)
progress [prə'gres] vorankommen, Fortschritte machen; sich (vorwärts) bewegen; fortschreiten IV 3 (107)
progress *(no pl)* ['prəʊgres] Fortschritt(e) IV 3 (107) **be in progress** im Gange sein IV 3 (107) **make progress** Fortschritte erzielen/machen, vorankommen IV 3 (107)
project ['prɒdʒekt] Projekt II
°**promenade concert** [ˌprɒmənɑːd 'kɒnsət] Promenadenkonzert
°**prominent** ['prɒmɪnənt] bekannt, bedeutend
promise ['prɒmɪs]:
1. versprechen II
2. *(ein/das)* Versprechen III
promote sth. [prə'məʊt] etwas fördern; für etwas werben III
°**prompt** [prɒmpt] Stichwort, Vorgabe
°**Proms** [prɒmz]: **the Proms** die Proms *(pl) (Sommerkonzertreihe in London)*
pronounce [prə'naʊns] aussprechen IV 2 (48)
pronunciation [prəˌnʌnsi'eɪʃn] Aussprache I
proofread ['pruːfred] *siehe* **proofread**
proofread ['pruːfriːd], **proofread, proofread** Korrektur lesen; korrigieren IV 3 (94)
°**property** ['prɒpəti] Eigentum, Besitz
°**pros** *(pl)* [prəʊz]: **the pros and cons** *(pl)* das Für und Wider; die Vor- und Nachteile
protect sb./sth. (from sb./sth.) [prə'tekt] jn./etwas (be)schützen (vor jm./etwas) IV 1 (18)
protection [prə'tekʃn] Schutz IV 3 (88)
protective [prə'tektɪv] schützend, beschützend, Schutz- IV 1 (33)
protest [prə'test] protestieren III
protest ['prəʊtest] Protest III
Protestant ['prɒtɪstənt] Protestant/in; protestantisch III
protester [prə'testə] Demonstrant/in IV 1 (41)
proud (of) [praʊd] stolz (auf) III
prove [pruːv]:
1. nachweisen, beweisen III
2. sich erweisen als IV 2 (58)
°**proven** ['pruːvn] bewiesen; erwiesen; bewährt **sb. is proven guilty** js. Schuld ist erwiesen, jd. wurde für schuldig befunden
provide [prə'vaɪd] (an)bieten, zur Verfügung stellen IV 1 (29) **provide sb. with sth.** jn. mit etwas versorgen, jm. etwas zur Verfügung stellen IV 1 (29)
province ['prɒvɪns] Provinz IV 1 (19)
°**provocative** [prə'vɒkətɪv] provozierend
provoke [prə'vəʊk] provozieren IV 2 (53)
pub [pʌb] Kneipe, Lokal III
public ['pʌblɪk] öffentliche(r, s) III
public holiday [ˌpʌblɪk 'hɒlədeɪ] öffentlicher/gesetzlicher Feiertag IV 2 (58)
publish ['pʌblɪʃ] veröffentlichen IV 1 (43)
pull [pʊl] ziehen I **pull sb.'s leg** *(infml)* jn. auf den Arm nehmen *(veräppeln)* IV 1 (27) **pull sth. out** etwas herausziehen II
pullover ['pʊləʊvə] Pullover II
punctuation [ˌpʌŋktʃu'eɪʃn] Zeichensetzung II
punish ['pʌnɪʃ] bestrafen III
punishment ['pʌnɪʃmənt] Bestrafung, Strafe III
puppet ['pʌpɪt] Marionette, Handpuppe II
purple ['pɜːpl] violett, lila I
purpose ['pɜːpəs] Absicht, Sinn, Zweck, Ziel IV 4 (137) **on purpose** mit Absicht IV 4 (137)
push [pʊʃ] drücken, schieben, stoßen I
put [pʊt], **put, put** legen, stellen, (etwas wohin) tun I **put an end to sth.** einer Sache ein Ende machen, einen Schlussstrich unter etwas ziehen IV 2 (59) **put sth. down** etwas hinlegen III **put sth. on** etwas anziehen *(Kleidung)*; etwas aufsetzen *(Hut, Helm)* II °**put sth. together** etwas zusammenstellen, zusammensetzen
puzzle ['pʌzl] Rätsel II
python ['paɪθən] Python *(Schlange)* IV 2 (53)

Q

qualification [ˌkwɒlɪfɪ'keɪʃn] Qualifikation; (Schul-)Abschluss IV 3 (94)
qualify ['kwɒlɪfaɪ] (sich) qualifizieren IV 3 (78/79)
quarter ['kwɔːtə]:
1. (Stadt-)Viertel III
2. **quarter past ten** Viertel nach zehn (10.15 / 22.15) I
quarter to eleven Viertel vor elf (10.45 / 22.45) I
quarterback ['kwɔːtəbæk] Quarterback *(Schlüsselposition im American Football)* IV 2 (65)
°**quay** [kiː] Kai
queen [kwiːn] Königin I
°**quest (for)** [kwest] Suche (nach), Streben (nach)
question ['kwestʃən] Frage I
question mark ['kwestʃən mɑːk] Fragezeichen II
questionnaire [ˌkwestʃə'neə] Fragebogen III
queue [kjuː]:
1. Schlange, Reihe *(wartender Menschen)* II
2. Schlange stehen, sich anstellen II
quick [kwɪk] schnell II
quiet ['kwaɪət]:
1. ruhig, still, leise I
2. **quiet down** sich beruhigen I
quite [kwaɪt] ziemlich II
quiz [kwɪz] Quiz, Ratespiel I
quote [kwəʊt] Zitat IV 1 (35)

R

rabbit ['ræbɪt] Kaninchen I
race [reɪs]:
1. rasen III
2. Rennen I
race [reɪs] Rasse IV 1 (19)
racial ['reɪʃl] ethnisch, rassisch; Rassen- IV 1 (19)
racism ['reɪsɪzəm] Rassismus IV 2 (64)
racist ['reɪsɪst] Rassist/in IV 2 (64)
radio ['reɪdiəʊ] Radio II **on the radio** im Radio II
raft [rɑːft] Schlauchboot *(wildwassertauglich)*; Floß III
rafting ['rɑːftɪŋ]: **white-water rafting** Wildwasserfahren *(im Schlauchboot)* III
°**rage** [reɪdʒ] wüten, toben
railing ['reɪlɪŋ] Geländer III
railroad ['reɪlrəʊd] *(AE)* Eisenbahn III
railway ['reɪlweɪ] *(BE)* Eisenbahn III
rain [reɪn]:
1. regnen II
2. Regen II
rainbow ['reɪnbəʊ] Regenbogen III
°**rainbow serpent** ['reɪnbəʊ sɜːpənt] Regenbogenschlange
raincoat ['reɪnkəʊt] Regenmantel II
rainfall ['reɪnfɔːl] Niederschlag, Regenfälle IV 2 (54)
rainforest ['reɪnfɒrɪst] Regenwald II
rainy ['reɪni] regnerisch II
raise [reɪz]:
1. (er)heben IV 2 (58)
raise a flag eine Flagge hissen IV 2 (58)
raise one's head den Kopf heben IV 2 (58) **raise one's voice** die Stimme erheben IV 2 (58)
2. **raise money (for)** Geld sammeln (für) II
rally ['ræli]:
1. sich versammeln, sich zusammenscharen IV 4 (124)
2. Versammlung, Kundgebung IV 4 (124)
3. Rallye II
ran [ræn] *siehe* **run**
rang [ræŋ] *siehe* **ring**

range [reɪndʒ]:
1. Bereich, Bandbreite, Palette IV 3 (109)
2. range (from … to …) sich erstrecken, reichen (von … bis …) IV 3 (109)
°**ranger** ['reɪndʒə] *Aufseher/in in einem Nationalpark*
rank (by) [ræŋk] einstufen; anordnen (nach) IV 4 (136)
rap (music) [ræp] Rap IV 4 (121)
rapid ['ræpɪd] rapide, rasch, schnell IV 4 (118)
rapper ['ræpə] Rapper/in IV 4 (110/111)
rare [reə] selten IV 3 (88)
rat [ræt] Ratte I
°**rather** ['rɑːðə]: **I'd rather be …** Ich wäre/würde lieber …
rather than ['rɑːðə ðən] statt, anstatt III
rattlesnake ['rætlsneɪk] Klapperschlange III
raven ['reɪvn] Rabe III
reach [riːtʃ] erreichen III **reach (for)** greifen (nach) III **reach out a hand (to sb.)** die Hand ausstrecken (nach jm.) IV 1 (34) **reach over** die Hand ausstrecken III
°**reachable** ['riːtʃəbl] erreichbar
react (to) [ri'ækt] reagieren (auf) III
reaction (to) [ri'ækʃn] Reaktion (auf) IV 1 (17)
read [red] *siehe* **read**
read [riːd], **read, read** lesen I **read aloud** laut (vor)lesen II °**read out** (laut) vorlesen
reader ['riːdə] Leser/in II
ready ['redi] bereit, fertig I **get ready (for)** sich fertig machen (für); sich vorbereiten (auf) II
real ['riːəl] echt, wirklich II
realistic [ˌriːə'lɪstɪk] realistisch IV 1 (17)
realistically [ˌriːə'lɪstɪkli] realistisch *(Adv.)* IV 1 (17)
reality [ri'æləti] Realität, Wirklichkeit IV 1 (29)
realize sth. ['riːəlaɪz] etwas erkennen; sich einer Sache bewusst werden III
really ['rɪəli] echt, wirklich I **I really care about animals.** Tiere liegen mir sehr am Herzen. / Tiere sind mir sehr wichtig. III
°**realm** [relm] Bereich; Königreich
reason ['riːzn] Grund, Begründung I
rebel ['rebəl] Rebell/in IV 1 (40)
rebellion [rɪ'beljən] Rebellion, Aufstand IV 1 (41)
rebuild [ˌriː'bɪld], **rebuilt, rebuilt** wiederaufbauen III
rebuilt [ˌriː'bɪlt] *siehe* **rebuild**
receive [rɪ'siːv] erhalten, empfangen IV 1 (42)
recent ['riːsnt] aktuell, jüngst; kürzlich geschehen/erfolgt IV 3 (94)
recently ['riːsntli] in letzter Zeit; vor Kurzem IV 1 (19)
recipe ['resəpi] (Koch-)Rezept II
reclaim sth. [rɪ'kleɪm] etwas zurückfordern; etwas zurückerobern IV 2 (59)
recognition [rekəg'nɪʃn] Anerkennung; (Wieder-)Erkennen IV 2 (64)
recognize ['rekəgnaɪz] erkennen; anerkennen III
recommend sth. (to sb.) [ˌrekə'mend] (jm.) etwas empfehlen IV 3 (97)
recommendation [ˌrekəmən'deɪʃn] Empfehlung IV 3 (97)
reconciliation [ˌrekənsɪli'eɪʃn] Versöhnung IV 2 (59)
reconsider [ˌriːkən'sɪdə] (noch einmal) überdenken IV 3 (107)
recorder [rɪ'kɔːdə] Blockflöte II
recreation [ˌriːkri'eɪʃn] Freizeit(beschäftigung); Erholung IV 3 (95)
recycle [riː'saɪkl] recyceln, wiederverwerten IV 4 (119)
recycling [rɪ'saɪklɪŋ] Recycling IV 4 (119)
red [red] rot I **go red** rot werden, erröten II
reduce (by) [rɪ'djuːs] reduzieren, verringern (um) IV 4 (123)
reduction [rɪ'dʌkʃn] Reduzierung, Verringerung IV 4 (123)
reef [riːf] Riff IV 2 (45)
refer to [rɪ'fɜː tə] sich beziehen auf, Bezug nehmen auf III
reference ['refrəns] Bezug (zu) IV 3 (101) **in/with reference to** in/mit Bezug auf IV 3 (101)
°**reflect** [rɪ'flekt] reflektieren, widerspiegeln
°**reflection** [rɪ'flekʃn] **(***BE auch:* **reflexion)** Nachdenken, Überlegung; Spiegelbild, Reflexion
refusal [rɪ'fjuːzl] Ablehnung, (Ver-)Weigerung IV 3 (83)
refuse [rɪ'fjuːz] sich weigern, ablehnen IV 3 (83) **refuse to do sth.** sich weigern / es ablehnen, etwas zu tun IV 3 (83)
region ['riːdʒən] Region II
regional ['riːdʒənl] regional IV 1 (43)
regret [rɪ'gret]:
1. bedauern, bereuen IV 1 (24)
2. *(das)* Bedauern IV 1 (24)
regular ['regjələ] regelmäßig II
rehearsal [rɪ'hɜːsl] Probe *(Theater, Chor, Orchester etc.)* IV 3 (89)
rehearse (for sth.) [rɪ'hɜːs] proben (für etwas) IV 3 (89)
reinforce [riːɪn'fɔːs] (ver)stärken, verfestigen IV 3 (101)
reins *(pl)* [reɪnz] Zügel III
relate [rɪ'leɪt]: **relate sth. to sth.** etwas mit etwas in Zusammenhang bringen; etwas zu etwas in Beziehung setzen IV 4 (129) **relate to sth.** sich auf etwas beziehen IV 4 (129)
related to [rɪ'leɪtɪd tə] verbunden mit; bedingt durch, bezogen auf IV 3 (81)
relation [rɪ'leɪʃn] Beziehung, Verhältnis; Bezug IV 4 (129) **in relation to** in Bezug auf; im Verhältnis zu IV 4 (129)
relationship [rɪ'leɪʃnʃɪp] Beziehung, Verhältnis III
relax [rɪ'læks] sich entspannen, sich ausruhen III
relaxed [rɪ'lækst] entspannt III
release [rɪ'liːs]:
1. veröffentlichen, herausbringen IV 2 (64)
2. Veröffentlichung IV 2 (64)
3. Austritt, Freisetzung IV 4 (118)
4. abgeben, freisetzen IV 4 (118)
5. release a prisoner eine/n Gefangene/n freilassen IV 4 (118)
°**relevance** ['reləvəns] Relevanz, Bedeutung
relevant (to sb.) ['reləvənt] relevant, wichtig (für jn.) IV 3 (94)
reliable [rɪ'laɪəbl] verlässlich, zuverlässig IV 3 (95)
religion [rɪ'lɪdʒən] Religion I
rely on [rɪ'laɪ ɒn] sich verlassen auf IV 3 (95)
remain [rɪ'meɪn] (ver)bleiben III
remember sth. [rɪ'membə]:
1. sich an etwas erinnern I
2. an etwas denken *(etwas nicht vergessen)* II
3. sich etwas merken II
remind sb. [rɪ'maɪnd] jn. erinnern III
remote [rɪ'məʊt] entlegen, abgelegen IV 2 (45)
remote control [rɪˌməʊt kən'trəʊl] **(***kurz auch:* **remote)** Fernbedienung III
remove [rɪ'muːv] entfernen, beseitigen; ausziehen *(Kleidung)* IV 3 (96)
°**renaissance** [rɪ'neɪsns] Renaissance
renewable [rɪ'njuːəbl] erneuerbar; verlängerbar IV 4 (110/111)
repeat [rɪ'piːt] wiederholen II
repeatedly [rɪ'piːtɪdli] wiederholt *(Adv.)* IV 1 (33)
replace (with) [rɪ'pleɪs] ersetzen (durch), austauschen (gegen) IV 4 (129)
replacement [rɪ'pleɪsmənt] *(das)* Austauschen; Ersatz(-) IV 4 (129)
reply (to) [rɪ'plaɪ] antworten (auf); erwidern, entgegnen III
report [rɪ'pɔːt]:
1. berichten III
2. Bericht, Reportage II
reporter [rɪ'pɔːtə] Reporter/in IV 4 (126)
represent [ˌreprɪ'zent]:
1. vertreten, repräsentieren IV 1 (42)
°**2.** darstellen; symbolisieren
representation [ˌreprɪzen'teɪʃn] (Interessens-)Vertretung, Darstellung, Repräsentanz III
representative [ˌreprɪ'zentətɪv] Repräsentant/in, Abgeordnete(r) IV 1 (42)
republic [rɪ'pʌblɪk] Republik III
reputation [ˌrepju'teɪʃn] Ansehen, Ruf, Reputation IV 2 (77)

request [rɪ'kwest] Wunsch, Bitte; Anfrage IV 3 (83)
require [rɪ'kwaɪə] erfordern, benötigen IV 2 (76)
requirement [rɪ'kwaɪəmənt] Voraussetzung, Anforderung IV 2 (76)
rescue ['reskjuː]:
1. retten II
2. Rettung; Rettungs- I
research ['riːsɜːtʃ]: *(no pl)* Recherche, Forschung(en) III
reservation [ˌrezə'veɪʃn] Reservat, Reservation III
reserve [rɪ'zɜːv] Schutzgebiet III
dark sky reserve Lichtschutzgebiet III
reserve sth. [rɪ'zɜːv] etwas reservieren, buchen III
resist [rɪ'zɪst]:
1. Widerstand leisten; widerstehen III
2. sich widersetzen (gegen), sich wehren (gegen) IV 4 (115)
resistance [rɪ'zɪstəns] Widerstand; Resistenz IV 1 (41)
resources *(pl)* [rɪ'sɔːsɪz] Ressourcen; (finanzielle) Mittel IV 4 (118)
respect [rɪ'spekt] respektieren, achten III
respectful (to) [rɪ'spektfl] respektvoll (gegenüber) IV 2 (65)
°**response (to)** [rɪ'spɒns] Reaktion, Antwort (auf)
responsibility [rɪˌspɒnsə'bɪləti] Verantwortung; Zuständigkeit IV 3 (78/79)
responsible [rɪ'spɒnsəbl] verantwortlich II
rest [rest]:
1. Rest III
2. ruhen, sich ausruhen III
restaurant ['restrɒnt] Restaurant I
°**Restoration** [ˌrestə'reɪʃn] Restaurierung (auch: Wiederherstellung der britischen Monarchie im Jahre 1660)
restrict [rɪ'strɪkt] einschränken, beschränken IV 4 (115)
restriction [rɪ'strɪkʃn] Beschränkung, Einschränkung IV 4 (115)
restrictive [rɪ'strɪktɪv] einschränkend IV 4 (115)
restroom ['restruːm] *(AE)* Toilette *(in öffentlichen Gebäuden)* IV 4 (112)
result [rɪ'zʌlt] Ergebnis, Resultat II
retail ['riːteɪl] Einzelhandel; Einzelhandels- IV 4 (122)
return [rɪ'tɜːn]:
1. Rückkehr III
2. *(kurz für:* **return ticket***)* (Hin- und) Rückfahrkarte II
°3. zurückgeben
return ticket [rɪˌtɜːn 'tɪkɪt] (Hin- und) Rückfahrkarte II
°**reveal** [rɪ'viːl] verraten, enthüllen
reverse [rɪ'vɜːs] umkehren, rückgängig machen IV 4 (119)
review [rɪ'vjuː]:
1. Rezension, Besprechung, Kritik III
°2. besprechen, rezensieren; überprüfen
revise [rɪ'vaɪz] überarbeiten; *(Lernstoff)* wiederholen III
revision [rɪ'vɪʒn] Wiederholung *(des Lernstoffs)* II
revolution [ˌrevə'luːʃn] Revolution IV 2 (58)
°**rewarding** [rɪ'wɔːdɪŋ] lohnend
°**rewrite** [riː'raɪt], **rewrote, rewritten** neu schreiben, umschreiben
°**rewritten** [riː'rɪtn] *siehe* **rewrite**
°**rewrote** [riː'rəʊt] *siehe* **rewrite**
°**rhinestone** ['raɪnstəʊn] Strass(stein)
rhyme [raɪm] Reim; Vers I
rhythm ['rɪðəm] Rhythmus III
rich [rɪtʃ] reich I
rid [rɪd]: **get rid of sth.** etwas loswerden IV 4 (115)
ridden ['rɪdn] *siehe* **ride**
ride [raɪd]:
1. Fahrt I
2. Ritt, Ausritt III
ride [raɪd], **rode, ridden**:
1. reiten II
2. fahren I
ride a bike Rad fahren I
riding ['raɪdɪŋ] Reiten I
rifle ['raɪfl] Gewehr IV 4 (124)
right [raɪt]:
1. richtig I
..., right? ..., nicht wahr? II **all right** okay; in Ordnung I **sb. is right** jemand hat Recht I **That's right.** Das stimmt. I °**She'll be right.** *(AusE, infml)* Alles wird gut.
2. Recht IV 2 (64)
civil rights *(pl)* Bürgerrechte IV 2 (64)
3. *(adv)* **right after you** gleich nach dir II
right behind you direkt hinter dir, genau hinter dir II **right now** jetzt gerade II
4. rechts I
right, left and centre *(infml)* überall; aus allen Richtungen; an allen Ecken und Enden IV 4 (112) **right and left** *(infml)* (von) überall(her), aus allen Richtungen IV 4 (112) **on the right** rechts / auf der rechten Seite I **turn right** (nach) rechts abbiegen II
ring [rɪŋ] Ring II
ring [rɪŋ], **rang, rung** klingeln, läuten II
rip [rɪp]:
1. (zer-/ab-)reißen IV 4 (129)
2. Riss IV 4 (129)
°**ripper** ['rɪpə] *(AusE, infml)* klasse, spitze
rise [raɪz] Erhöhung, Anstieg IV 1 (28)
rise [raɪz], **rose, risen**:
1. (sich) erhöhen; höher werden IV 1 (28)
2. sich erheben; (an)steigen; aufsteigen IV 1 (28)
rise up aufragen, emporragen *(Berge, Säulen, Türme, ...)* III
risen ['rɪzn] *siehe* **rise**
risk [rɪsk] Risiko III **take a risk** ein Risiko eingehen III
river ['rɪvə] Fluss I
road [rəʊd] Straße I **at 8 Beach Road** in der Beach Road (Nummer) 8 I **in Beach Road** in der Beach Road I
roar [rɔː] brüllen; tosen, dröhnen III
roast beef [ˌrəʊst 'biːf] Rinderbraten I
roast potatoes *(pl)* [ˌrəʊst pə'teɪtəʊz] Bratkartoffeln *(im Backofen in Fett gebackene Kartoffeln)* I
robotics [rəʊ'bɒtɪks] Robotertechnik, Robotik IV 3 (107)
rock [rɒk]:
1. Fels, Felsen I
2. schaukeln, schwanken III
3. **rock (music)** Rock(musik) II
rocky ['rɒki] felsig, steinig II
rode [rəʊd] *siehe* **ride**
role [rəʊl] Rolle *(in einem Theaterstück, Film)* II
role model ['rəʊl mɒdl] Vorbild IV 2 (62)
role-play ['rəʊl pleɪ] Rollenspiel IV 1 (25)
roll [rəʊl] rollen II
roller coaster ['rəʊlə kəʊstə] Achterbahn III
Roman ['rəʊmən] Römer/in; römisch II
roo [ruː] *(AusE, infml)* Känguru IV 2 (45)
roof [ruːf] Dach II
room [ruːm] Raum, Zimmer I
root [ruːt] Wurzel IV 4 (121)
rope [rəʊp] Seil III
rose [rəʊz] *siehe* **rise**
rose [rəʊz] Rose III
rough [rʌf] rau; grob; hart III
round [raʊnd]:
1. rund III
2. **round ...** um (... herum); in (... umher) IV 1 (11)
round here hier in der Gegend III
roundabout ['raʊndəbaʊt] Kreisverkehr II
route [ruːt] Strecke, Route III
routine [ruː'tiːn] Routine I
row [rəʊ] Reihe III
Royal ['rɔɪəl] *Mitglied der königlichen Familie* IV 1 (15)
royal ['rɔɪəl] königlich II
rubber ['rʌbə] Radiergummi I
rubbish ['rʌbɪʃ]:
1. Müll, Abfall II
2. Unsinn, dummes Zeug IV 2 (57)
rucksack ['rʌksæk] *(BE)* Rucksack I
rude [ruːd] unhöflich; unverschämt III
rudeness ['ruːdnəs] Unhöflichkeit; Unverschämtheit IV 3 (86)
rugby ['rʌgbi] Rugby III
rugby ground ['rʌgbi graʊnd] Rugby-Platz/-Spielfeld III
ruin ['ruːɪn] Ruine II

rule [ruːl]:
1. Regel, Vorschrift II
2. rule sth. etwas beherrschen, über etwas herrschen III
ruler ['ruːlə] Lineal I
run [rʌn], **ran, run:**
1. rennen, laufen I
run after sb. hinter jm. herrennen I
run off wegrennen III
2. verlaufen *(Straße; Grenze)* III
3. run sth. etwas leiten, führen, betreiben *(Firma, Schule)* IV 3 (80)
rung [rʌŋ] *siehe* **ring**
runner ['rʌnə] Läufer/in II
running water [ˌrʌnɪŋ 'wɔːtə] fließend(es) Wasser II
rural ['rʊərəl] ländlich, Land- IV 2 (56)
rush [rʌʃ] eilen, stürzen III
rusty ['rʌsti] rostig; verrostet III

S

sacred (to) ['seɪkrɪd] heilig (für) IV 4 (121)
sad [sæd] traurig I
safari [sə'fɑːri] Safari II
safe [seɪf] sicher, in Sicherheit II
said [sed] *siehe* **say**
sail [seɪl]:
1. segeln I
°**2.** Segel *(Segelboot)*
sailboat ['seɪlbəʊt] *(AE)* Segelboot IV 3 (88)
sailing ['seɪlɪŋ]: **go sailing** segeln; segeln gehen I
sailing boat ['seɪlɪŋ bəʊt] Segelboot I
Saint (= St) [seɪnt] Sankt (St) IV 1 (10)
salad ['sæləd] Salat *(als Gericht oder Beilage)* I **fruit salad** Obstsalat I
sales *(pl)* [seɪlz] Umsatz, Absatz; Verkäufe II
salt [sɔːlt]:
1. Salz III
°**2. salt sth.** etwas salzen
°**saltie** ['sɔːlti] *(AusE, infml)* Salzwasserkrokodil
samba ['sæmbə] Samba I
same [seɪm]: **the same (as)** der-/die-/dasselbe (wie) I
sand [sænd] Sand I
sandcastle ['sændkɑːsl] Sandburg IV 2 (53)
sandwich ['sænwɪtʃ], ['sænwɪdʒ] Sandwich, *(zusammengeklapptes)* belegtes Brot I
sandy ['sændi] Sand-, sandig IV 2 (45)
sang [sæŋ] *siehe* **sing**
sat [sæt] *siehe* **sit**
Saturday ['sætədeɪ], ['sætədi] Samstag I
sauce [sɔːs] Soße IV 2 (77)
sausage ['sɒsɪdʒ] (Brat-, Bock-)Würstchen, Wurst IV 2 (47)

save [seɪv]:
1. retten I
2. save (up) *(z.B. Geld)* sparen III
saw [sɔː] *siehe* **see**
saxophone ['sæksəfəʊn], *infml. auch:* **sax** Saxofon IV 3 (89)
say [seɪ], **said, said** sagen I **Say hello to … for me.** Grüß … von mir. II **It says here: …** Hier steht: … / Es heißt hier: … I
scan sth. (for sth.) [skæn] etwas (nach etwas) absuchen III **scan a text** einen Text schnell nach bestimmten Wörtern/Informationen absuchen II
scare sb. [skeə] jn. erschrecken; jm. Angst machen III
scared [skeəd] verängstigt II
scary ['skeəri] unheimlich, gruselig I
scene [siːn] Szene I
scenic ['siːnɪk] (landschaftlich) schön IV 2 (46)
schedule ['ʃedjuːl], ['skedʒuːl]:
1. (Zeit-)Plan, Programm IV 3 (91)
2. *(AE auch:)* Stundenplan; Fahrplan IV 3 (91)
scholar ['skɒlə] Gelehrte(r) IV 4 (137)
scholarship ['skɒləʃɪp] Stipendium *(finanzielle Hilfe für Schüler/innen, Studierende o.ä.)* IV 3 (88)
school [skuːl] Schule I **at school** in der Schule I **before school** vor der Schule *(vor Schulbeginn)* I **boarding school** Internat II **high school** *(USA) Schule für 14- bis 18-Jährige* III
school bag ['skuːl bæg] Schultasche I
school subject [ˌskuːl 'sʌbdʒɪkt] Schulfach I
science ['saɪəns] Naturwissenschaft I
scientific [ˌsaɪən'tɪfɪk] wissenschaftlich IV 4 (136)
scientist ['saɪəntɪst] Naturwissenschaftler/in III
scone [skɒn] *kleines rundes Milchbrötchen, leicht süß, oft mit Rosinen* I
score [skɔː] ein Tor schießen, einen Treffer erzielen I
scratch [skrætʃ]:
1. Kratzer IV 2 (77)
2. (sich) kratzen; zerkratzen IV 2 (77)
scratch your head (over) sich den Kopf zerbrechen (über) IV 2 (77)
scream [skriːm] schreien II
screen [skriːn] Bildschirm II
scroll [skrəʊl] scrollen IV 4 (112)
°**sculpture** ['skʌlptʃə] Skulptur
sea [siː] Meer I
sea level ['siː levl] Meeresspiegel II
seafood ['siːfuːd] Meeresfrüchte II
seagull ['siːgʌl] Möwe I
seal [siːl] Robbe I
search [sɜːtʃ]:
1. Suche IV 1 (32)
2. search for sth. (nach) etwas suchen IV 1 (32)
season ['siːzn] Saison; Jahreszeit IV 2 (52)

seat [siːt] Sitz, Platz II **take a seat** Platz nehmen III
seated ['siːtɪd]: **be seated** *(auf einem Platz)* sitzen IV 2 (64)
second ['sekənd]:
1. zweite(r, s) I
Second, … Zweitens, … I
2. Sekunde II
second-hand [sekənd 'hænd] second-hand *(gebraucht, aus zweiter Hand)* IV 4 (120)
secondary school ['sekəndri skuːl] weiterführende Schule IV 3 (81)
Secondly, … ['sekəndli] Zweitens … IV 1 (29)
secret ['siːkrət]:
1. Geheimnis IV 2 (62)
2. geheim IV 2 (62)
secretly ['siːkrətli] heimlich, insgeheim IV 2 (62)
section ['sekʃn] Abschnitt, Teilstück III
see [siː], **saw, seen** sehen; besuchen I
see (a doctor) (einen Arzt/eine Ärztin) aufsuchen II **See you later.** Bis bald. / Bis nachher. I **…, you see.** …, weißt du. II **be seeing sb.** mit jm. gehen, mit jm. eine Beziehung haben IV 4 (116) **I see.** Aha! / Verstehe. II
seed [siːd] Samen III
seek (for) [siːk], **sought, sought** suchen (nach); anstreben IV 4 (110/111)
seem (to be/do) [siːm] (zu sein/zu tun) scheinen III
seen [siːn] *siehe* **see**
°**seize** [siːz] beschlagnahmen, konfiszieren, in Besitz nehmen
°**seldom** ['seldəm] selten
select [sɪ'lekt] (aus)wählen IV 3 (106)
selection (of) [sɪ'lekʃn] Auswahl (an) IV 3 (106)
self-employed [ˌself ɪm'plɔɪd] selbstständig, freiberuflich IV 3 (95)
sell [sel], **sold, sold** verkaufen I
semester [sɪ'mestə] *(bes. AE)* Semester IV 3 (80)
semi- ['semi] halb-; Halb- III
semi-automatic [ˌsemi ɔːtə'mætɪk] halbautomatisch IV 4 (124)
senate ['senət] Senat IV 1 (42)
senator ['senətə] Senator/in IV 1 (42)
send [send], **sent, sent** schicken, senden I
senior ['siːniə] Fortgeschrittene(r); Erwachsene(r) *(bei Sport-Teams); Schüler/in im letzten Schuljahr* IV 3 (107)
senior high (school) [ˌsiːniə 'haɪ skuːl] *(AE) Schule für Kinder zwischen 15 und 17* IV 3 (80)
sense (of) [sens] Sinn (für) III **sense of humour** (Sinn für) Humor III
sent [sent] *siehe* **send**
sentence ['sentəns]:
1. Satz I
full sentence ganzer Satz II

2. sentence sb. (to sth.) jn. (zu etwas) verurteilen IV 2 (62)
sentimental [ˌsentɪ'mentl] sentimental IV 4 (114) **sentimental value** ideeller Wert IV 4 (114) **for sentimental reasons** aus Gefühlsgründen IV 4 (114)
sentinel ['sentɪnl] Wache IV 4 (124)
separate ['sepəreɪt] trennen IV 1 (32)
separate ['seprət] getrennt, separat IV 1 (15)
September [sep'tembə] September I
°**sequence** ['siːkwəns] *(richtige)* Reihenfolge, Abfolge
series ['sɪəriːz], *pl* **series** Serie; (Sende-)Reihe IV 2 (62)
serious ['sɪəriəs] ernst; ernsthaft III
seriously ['sɪəriəsli]: **take sth. seriously** etwas ernst nehmen IV 2 (77)
°**serpent** ['sɜːpənt] Schlange
serve [sɜːv]:
1. dienen III
2. servieren *(Essen, Getränke)*; bedienen *(Kundschaft)*; dienen IV 1 (13)
service ['sɜːvɪs]:
1. Dienst(leistung) IV 1 (13)
health service Gesundheitswesen III
social services *(pl)* Sozialwesen, soziale Dienste III
2. Gottesdienst III
set [set] Satz, Set II
set [set], **set, set**:
1. set sth. up etwas aufstellen, aufbauen, errichten; etwas einrichten III
2. untergehen *(Sonne)* III
setting ['setɪŋ] Schauplatz *(z.B. Film/Geschichte)* IV 2 (67)
settle ['setl] sich niederlassen, sich ansiedeln II
settlement ['setlmənt] (Be-)Siedlung IV 2 (58)
settler ['setlə] Siedler/in II
seven ['sevn] sieben I
several ['sevrəl] mehrere, verschiedene II
sexual ['sekʃuəl] sexuell IV 2 (59)
shadow ['ʃædəʊ] Schatten II
shake [ʃeɪk], **shook, shaken** schütteln II
shaken ['ʃeɪkən] *siehe* **shake**
Shall I ...? [ʃæl] Soll ich ...? III
shape [ʃeɪp]:
1. Form, Gestalt III
°**2. shape sth.** etwas formen
°**shaped like a heart** geformt wie ein Herz °**heart-shaped** herzförmig
share [ʃeə]:
1. (An-)Teil IV 4 (122)
2. share sth. (sich) etwas teilen IV 1 (14)
shark [ʃɑːk] Hai I
sharp [ʃɑːp] scharf III
sharpener ['ʃɑːpnə] (An-)Spitzer I
she [ʃiː] sie I
sheep [ʃiːp], *pl* **sheep** Schaf II
°**sheet** [ʃiːt] Blatt, Bogen *(Papier)*
shelf [ʃelf], *pl* **shelves** Regal I
°**shell** [ʃel] Muschel
shelter ['ʃeltə] Unterkunft III
shelves [ʃelvz] *plural of* **shelf**
shift [ʃɪft] (sich) verlagern; (sich) verändern IV 2 (59)
shine [ʃaɪn], **shone, shone** leuchten; scheinen *(Sonne)* III
ship [ʃɪp] Schiff I
shipping ['ʃɪpɪŋ] Schiffstransport, Schifffahrt IV 4 (118)
shirt [ʃɜːt] Hemd II
°**shock sb.** [ʃɒk] jn. schockieren
shocked [ʃɒkt] schockiert, entsetzt II
shocking ['ʃɒkɪŋ] schockierend IV 1 (28)
shoe [ʃuː] Schuh I
shone [ʃɒn] *siehe* **shine**
shook [ʃʊk] *siehe* **shake**
shoot [ʃuːt], **shot, shot** schießen; erschießen III
shooter ['ʃuːtə] Schütze/Schützin IV 4 (127)
shop [ʃɒp]:
1. Laden I
corner shop Laden an der Ecke; Tante-Emma-Laden I
2. einkaufen II
shop assistant ['ʃɒp‿əsɪstənt] Verkäufer/in II
shopper ['ʃɒpə] (Ein-)Käufer/in II
shopping ['ʃɒpɪŋ] Einkaufen I **do the/some shopping** (die) Einkäufe erledigen, einkaufen II **go shopping** einkaufen gehen I
shopping centre ['ʃɒpɪŋ sentə] Einkaufszentrum I
shopping mall ['ʃɒpɪŋ mɔːl] (großes) Einkaufszentrum I
shore [ʃɔː] Ufer *(eines Sees)*, Strand II
short [ʃɔːt] kurz I
short story [ˌʃɔːt 'stɔːri] Kurzgeschichte IV 4 (129)
shortage (of sth.) ['ʃɔːtɪdʒ] Mangel (an etwas), Knappheit IV 2 (59)
°**shorten** ['ʃɔːtn] (ver)kürzen
shorts *(pl)* [ʃɔːts] Shorts, kurze Hose I
shot [ʃɒt]:
1. *siehe* **shoot**
2. Aufnahme, Foto; (Film) Einstellung, Szene III
should [ʃʊd], [ʃəd]: **I should ...** Ich sollte ... II
shoulder ['ʃəʊldə] Schulter II
shout [ʃaʊt] schreien, rufen I
show [ʃəʊ]:
1. Show II
2. show, showed, shown zeigen I
show sb. around (a place) jn. herumführen; jm. einen Ort zeigen IV 3 (89)
show up erscheinen, auftauchen IV 4 (124)
°**showcase** ['ʃəʊkeɪs] präsentieren, zur Schau stellen
shower ['ʃaʊə] Dusche II **have/take a shower** (sich) duschen II
shown [ʃəʊn] *siehe* **show**
°**shrimp** [ʃrɪmp] Shrimp, Krevette
shrub [ʃrʌb] Strauch, Busch III
shrug [ʃrʌg]:
1. Achselzucken IV 3 (82)
2. shrug (your shoulders) mit den Achseln/Schultern zucken IV 3 (82)
shy [ʃaɪ] schüchtern, scheu II
sick [sɪk] krank I **be worried sick** krank vor Sorge sein IV 3 (107) **I feel sick.** Mir ist schlecht. II **I'm going to be sick.** Ich muss mich übergeben. II
sickness ['sɪknəs] Krankheit; Übelkeit II **travel sickness** Reisekrankheit II
side [saɪd] Seite II
sidewalk ['saɪdwɔːk] *(AE)* Gehweg, Bürgersteig III
sigh [saɪ] seufzen III
sight [saɪt] Anblick III **sights** *(pl)* Sehenswürdigkeiten I
sign [saɪn]:
1. Schild; Zeichen I
no sign of ... keine Spur von ... III
2. sign (sth.) (etwas) unterschreiben III
sign up (for) sich anmelden (für) III
signal ['sɪgnəl]:
1. Signal, Zeichen II
2. signalisieren IV 2 (48)
significant [sɪg'nɪfɪkənt] bedeutend, wichtig; signifikant, erheblich IV 2 (76)
silence ['saɪləns] Stille; Schweigen III
silent ['saɪlənt] lautlos, leise; schweigend III
silky ['sɪlki] seidig I
°**silliness** ['sɪlinəs] Dummheit, Albernheit
silly ['sɪli]:
1. albern; blöd I
2. Dummerchen I
°**silver** ['sɪlvə] Silber
similar (to sth./sb.) ['sɪmələ] (etwas/jm.) ähnlich II
°**similarity** [ˌsɪmə'lærəti] Ähnlichkeit, Gemeinsamkeit
simple ['sɪmpl] einfach, unkompliziert III
simplify ['sɪmplɪfaɪ] vereinfachen IV 4 (112)
since [sɪns]:
1. seit III
since 10 o'clock/last week/... seit 10 Uhr/letzter Woche/... III
2. seitdem, inzwischen IV 1 (19)
(ever) since seitdem, seither IV 1 (19)
3. weil, da IV 2 (48)
sincerely [sɪn'sɪəli]: **Yours sincerely** Mit freundlichen Grüßen *(Briefschluss)* IV 1 (23)
sing [sɪŋ], **sang, sung** singen I
singer ['sɪŋə] Sänger/in II
single ['sɪŋgl]:
1. ledig, alleinstehend I
2. *(kurz für:* **single ticket***)* Einzelfahrschein; einfache Fahrkarte II

single-use (product) [ˌsɪŋgl ˈjuːs] (Produkt) zum einmaligen Gebrauch IV 4 (118)
Sir [sɜː]:
1. Sir *(britischer Adelstitel)* IV 1 (10)
2. Dear Sir/Madam Sehr geehrte Damen und Herren II
siren [ˈsaɪrən] Sirene III
sister [ˈsɪstə] Schwester I
sit [sɪt], **sat, sat** sitzen; sich setzen I **sit down** sich hinsetzen I **sit up** sich aufsetzen III
site [saɪt] Ort, Platz, Stelle, Stätte IV 1 (22)
situation [ˌsɪtʃuˈeɪʃn] Situation III
six [sɪks] sechs I
sixth form [ˈsɪksθ fɔːm] *(BE, etwa:)* 12. und 13. Klasse eines Gymnasiums IV 3 (81)
size [saɪz] Größe I **What size tea would you like?** Wie groß soll der/dein Tee sein? II
sizzle [ˈsɪzl] brutzeln, zischen III
skates *(pl)* [skeɪtsˌfiː] Inlineskates I
skating [ˈskeɪtɪŋ]:
1. Inlineskaten, Rollschuhlaufen I
2. *kurz für:* **ice skating** Schlittschuhlaufen II
skill [skɪl] Fertigkeit II **study skills** Lern- und Arbeitstechniken I
skills file [ˈskɪlz faɪl] Übersicht über Lern- und Arbeitstechniken I
skim a text [skɪm] einen Text überfliegen *(um den Inhalt grob zu erfassen)* III
skin [skɪn] Haut; Fell IV 4 (121)
skinny [ˈskɪni] mager, dünn, dürr III
skirt [skɜːt] Rock II
skull [skʌl] Schädel III
sky [skaɪ] Himmel II
skyline [ˈskaɪlaɪn] Skyline; Horizont III
skyscraper [ˈskaɪskreɪpə] Wolkenkratzer III
slang [slæŋ] Slang *(Umgangssprache)* IV 2 (77)
slap [slæp]:
1. Schlag IV 1 (34)
2. schlagen (auf) IV 1 (34)
slap sb.'s face jm. eine Ohrfeige verpassen *(ins Gesicht schlagen)* IV 1 (34)
°**slave** [sleɪv] Sklave/Sklavin
sleep [sliːp]:
1. Schlaf III
2. sleep, slept, slept schlafen I
sleepover [ˈsliːpəʊvə] Pyjama-Party, Schlafparty I
sleepy [ˈsliːpi] schläfrig II
slept [slept] *siehe* **sleep**
slide [slaɪd] Dia; Folie *(Präsentations-software)* IV 1 (16)
°**slip** [slɪp] rutschen, schlüpfen **slip through the net** durchs Netz gehen
slippery [ˈslɪpəri] rutschig, glatt III
slither [ˈslɪðə] gleiten; schlittern III
slow [sləʊ] langsam I **be slow** nachgehen *(Uhr)* III
small [smɔːl] klein I
small talk [ˈsmɔːl tɔːk] Smalltalk *(spontan geführtes Gespräch)* III
smallpox [ˈsmɔːlpɒks] Pocken *(Erkrankung)* IV 2 (58)
smell [smel]:
1. Geruch III
2. riechen I
smell good gut riechen II **smell sth.** an etwas riechen I
smile [smaɪl]:
1. *(ein/das)* Lächeln I
2. lächeln I
smile at sb. jn. anlächeln I
smiley [ˈsmaɪli] Smiley I
smoke [sməʊk]:
1. Rauch III
2. rauchen III
smooth [smuːð] glatt, eben, ruhig IV 4 (123)
smuggle [ˈsmʌgl] schmuggeln I
smuggler [ˈsmʌglə] Schmuggler/in I
smuggling [ˈsmʌglɪŋ] der Schmuggel, das Schmuggeln I
snack [snæk] Snack, Imbiss I
°**snag** [snæg] *(AusE, infml)* (Brat-, Bock-)Würstchen, Wurst
snake [sneɪk] Schlange I
sneeze [sniːz] niesen I
snorkel [ˈsnɔːkl]:
1. Schnorchel IV 2 (53)
2. schnorcheln IV 2 (53)
snow [snəʊ] Schnee II
so [səʊ]:
1. also; deshalb, daher I
2. so cool/nice so cool/nett I
so far bis jetzt; bis hierher II **so that ...** *(oft auch kurz:* **so ...***)* sodass ..., damit ... II
3. So do/can/will/... I. Ich auch. IV 2 (57)
4. So? Und? / Na und? I
5. I think so. Ich glaube ja. IV 1 (25) **I don't think so.** Das glaube/denke ich nicht. IV 1 (25) **If so, ...** Wenn ja, ... / Wenn das der Fall ist, ... IV 1 (25)
so-called [ˌsəʊ ˈkɔːld] sogenannt IV 1 (43)
soccer [ˈsɒkə] Fußball II
social [ˈsəʊʃl] sozial IV 1 (28)
social media *(pl)* [ˌsəʊʃl ˈmiːdiə] soziale Medien III
social services *(pl)* [ˌsəʊʃl ˈsɜːvɪsɪz] Sozialwesen, soziale Dienste III
society [səˈsaɪəti] (die) Gesellschaft IV 2 (59)
sock [sɒk] Socke II
sofa [ˈsəʊfə] Sofa I
soft [sɒft] weich I **in a soft voice** sanft; mit leiser Stimme II
solar panel [ˌsəʊlə ˈpænl] Sonnenkollektor IV 3 (78/79)
sold [səʊld] *siehe* **sell**
soldier [ˈsəʊldʒə] Soldat/in II
solo [ˈsəʊləʊ] Solo- II
solution (to) [səˈluːʃn] Lösung (für) *(Problem, Aufgabe)* IV 1 (29)
solve [sɒlv] lösen *(Rätsel, Problem)*, lüften *(Geheimnis)* IV 1 (29)
some [sʌm], [səm] einige, ein paar; etwas I
somebody [ˈsʌmbədi] jemand I
somehow [ˈsʌmhaʊ] irgendwie III
someone [ˈsʌmwʌn] jemand I
something [ˈsʌmθɪŋ] etwas I
°**sometime** [ˈsʌmtaɪm] irgendwann
sometimes [ˈsʌmtaɪmz] manchmal I
somewhat [ˈsʌmwɒt] ein bisschen, einigermaßen IV 4 (115)
somewhere [ˈsʌmweə] irgendwo, irgendwohin II
son [sʌn] Sohn II
song [sɒŋ] Lied I
°**songline** [ˈsɒŋlaɪn] Traumpfad *(unsichtbare, mythische Landkarte der australischen Ureinwohner/innen)*
soon [suːn] bald I **as soon as** sobald, sowie III **no sooner ... than ...** *(fml)* kaum ..., da ... IV 4 (115)
sophomore [ˈsɒfəmɔː] *Schüler/in im 2. Jahr der amerikanischen High School* IV 3 (88)
sore [sɔː] wund II **have a sore throat** Halsschmerzen haben II
sorrow [ˈsɒrəʊ] Kummer, Leid IV 2 (58)
sorry [ˈsɒri]: **(I'm) sorry.** Tut mir leid. / Entschuldigung. I **I'm sorry about ...** Es tut mir leid wegen ... I
sort (of) [sɔːt] Art (von) IV 3 (107)
some sort of problem irgendwie ein Problem IV 3 (107)
sought [sɔːt] *siehe* **seek**
sound [saʊnd]:
1. Laut I
2. Geräusch; Klang I
3. klingen, sich *(gut usw.)* anhören I
soundtrack [ˈsaʊndtræk] Soundtrack *(Filmmusik)* IV 2 (62)
soup [suːp] Suppe I
°**soup kitchen** [ˈsuːp kɪtʃɪn] Suppenküche *(Armenküche)*
°**source** [sɔːs] Quelle *(auch:* Textquelle)
south [saʊθ] Süden; nach Süden; südlich III
south-east [ˌsaʊθ‿ˈiːst] Südosten; nach Südosten; südöstlich III
south-west [ˌsaʊθ ˈwest] Südwesten; nach Südwesten; südwestlich III
southbound [ˈsaʊθbaʊnd] Richtung Süden III
southern [ˈsʌðən] südlich, Süd- III
souvenir [ˌsuːvəˈnɪə] Andenken, Souvenir II
°**sovereign** [ˈsɒvrɪn] souverän, unabhängig *(Staat)*
soy [sɔɪ] *(AE)* Soja IV 4 (120)
soya [ˈsɔɪə] Soja IV 4 (120)
soya bean [ˈsɔɪə biːn] Sojabohne IV 4 (120)
soybean [ˈsɔɪbiːn] *(AE)* Sojabohne IV 4 (120)
soyburger [ˈsɔɪbɜːgə] Sojaburger IV 4 (120)

space [speɪs] Weltraum; Platz, Raum II
spaghetti [spə'geti] Spaghetti I
Spanish ['spænɪʃ] Spanisch; spanisch I
speak [spiːk], **spoke, spoken** sprechen, reden I **speak out** den Mund aufmachen; sich (kritisch) äußern IV 2 (64) **speak to sb.** mit jm. sprechen II
speaker ['spiːkə] Sprecher/in, Redner/in I
special ['speʃl] besondere(r, s) I
specialize (in) ['speʃəlaɪz] sich spezialisieren (auf) IV 3 (108)
species ['spiːʃiːz], *pl* **species** Art *(Biologie)* IV 2 (66)
specific [spə'sɪfɪk] bestimmte(r, s), spezielle(r, s); genau, präzise IV 4 (110/111)
speculate ['spekjuleɪt] spekulieren, Vermutungen anstellen III
speech [spiːtʃ] *(offizielle)* Rede II
part of speech Wortart III
°**speech bubble** ['spiːtʃ bʌbl] Sprechblase
speed [spiːd] Geschwindigkeit III
spell [spel] buchstabieren I
spelling ['spelɪŋ] Rechtschreibung; Schreibweise II
spend [spend], **spent, spent: spend money (on)** Geld ausgeben (für) III
spend time (on) Zeit verbringen (mit) III
spent [spent] *siehe* **spend**
spider ['spaɪdə] Spinne IV 2 (45)
spin [spɪn], **spun, spun:**
1. spinnen *(Wolle, Garn)* IV 4 (122)
2. **spin around** sich (im Kreis) drehen; herumwirbeln III
spiral ['spaɪrəl] spiralförmig IV 1 (24)
spiral staircase [ˌspaɪrəl 'steəkeɪs] Wendeltreppe IV 1 (24)
°**spiritual** ['spɪrɪtʃuəl] spirituell, geistig-seelisch
splash sb. [splæʃ] jn. nass spritzen III
°**split** [splɪt], **split, split** aufteilen; (sich) trennen; spalten
°**split screen** [ˌsplɪt 'skriːn] geteilter Bildschirm; Bildschirm(auf)teilung
spoke [spəʊk] *siehe* **speak**
spoken ['spəʊkən] *siehe* **speak**
spontaneous [spɒn'teɪniəs] spontan IV 3 (90)
spoon [spuːn] Löffel II
sport [spɔːt] Sport; Sportart I **do sport** Sport treiben I
sports field ['spɔːts fiːld] Sportplatz IV 3 (82)
spot [spɒt] Fleck, Punkt I
spread [spred], **spread, spread** (sich) ausbreiten, verbreiten III
spring [sprɪŋ] Frühling I
spun [spʌn] *siehe* **spin**
square [skweə]:
1. Feld *(auf Brettspiel)* III
2. Kästchen *(auf Papier)* III
3. Platz *(in der Stadt)* II
4. Quadrat III
5. quadratisch III
square kilometre (sq km) [ˌskweə 'kɪləmiːtə] Quadratkilometer (km²) II
squash [skwɒʃ] Kürbis III
squirrel ['skwɪrəl] Eichhörnchen IV 4 (129)
stadium ['steɪdiəm] Stadion IV 2 (64)
staff [stɑːf] Personal, Mitarbeiter/innen IV 1 (26)
stage [steɪdʒ]:
1. Bühne II
°2. Stadium, Phase; Abschnitt, Etappe
3. **stage sth.** etwas veranstalten; etwas inszenieren, etwas aufführen II
staircase ['steəkeɪs] Treppe; Treppenhaus IV 1 (24)
stairs *(pl)* [steəz] Treppe; Treppenstufen II
°**stake** [steɪk]: **have a stake in** einen Anteil haben an, teilhaben an
stall [stɔːl] (Markt-)Stand II
stamp [stæmp]:
1. Stempel II
2. stempeln; (auf)prägen IV 2 (59)
stand [stænd]:
1. Standpunkt, Haltung IV 2 (64)
take a stand (on/for/against sth.) Stellung beziehen (zu/für/gegen etwas) IV 2 (64)
°2. (Markt-/Messe-)Stand
stand [stænd], **stood, stood** stehen; sich (hin)stellen II **stand up** aufstehen I **stand up for/against** eintreten für/gegen, sich einsetzen für/gegen IV 2 (64)
standard ['stændəd] Standard; Standard- III
standardize ['stændədaɪz] standardisieren, normen IV 3 (106)
stank [stæŋk] *siehe* **stink**
star [stɑː]:
1. (Film-, Pop-)Star I
2. Stern III
stare (at sb./sth.) [steə] (jn./etwas an)starren III
start [stɑːt] anfangen, beginnen I
starve [stɑːv] hungern III **be starving** einen Riesenhunger haben III
state [steɪt] Staat I
state [steɪt] darlegen, erklären III
state animal [ˌsteɪt‿'ænɪml] Wappentier II
°**State Opening of Parliament** [ˌsteɪt‿əʊpənɪŋ‿əv 'pɑːləmənt] *(in GB) offizielle Parlamentseröffnung (durch den Monarchen/ die Monarchin)*
statement ['steɪtmənt] Aussage(satz); Feststellung, Behauptung IV 1 (29)
station ['steɪʃn]:
1. Bahnhof II
°2. *(AusE)* Farm
°**statistic** [stə'tɪstɪk] statistische Tatsache, statistische Größe
statistical [stə'tɪstɪkl] statistisch IV 1 (29)
statistics *(pl)* [stə'tɪstɪks] Statistik(en) IV 1 (29)
statue ['stætʃuː] Statue III
status ['steɪtəs] Status IV 4 (117)
stay [steɪ]:
1. bleiben I
2. Aufenthalt IV 2 (46)
3. **stay (at/with)** *(vorübergehend)* wohnen, übernachten (in/bei) II
4. **stay up late** lang aufbleiben II
5. **stay in touch (with sb.)** (mit jm.) Kontakt halten; (mit jm.) in Verbindung bleiben II
°**steady** ['stedi] gleichmäßig, stetig
steal [stiːl], **stole, stolen** stehlen, rauben III
steam [stiːm] Dampf III
steam train ['stiːm treɪn] *Zug mit Dampflok* III
steel [stiːl] Stahl III
steep [stiːp] steil III
steer [stɪə] steuern, lenken I
steering wheel ['stɪərɪŋ wiːl] Lenkrad II
step [step]:
1. Schritt I
take steps Schritte unternehmen, Maßnahmen ergreifen IV 4 (127)
2. Stufe III
3. **step (somewhere)** (irgendwohin) treten *(einen Schritt tun)* IV 3 (78/79)
stick [stɪk] Stock III **glue stick** Klebestift I
stick [stɪk], **stuck, stuck: stick sth. into sth.** etwas in etwas stechen, stecken II
sticky ['stɪki] klebrig II
still [stɪl]:
1. (immer) noch I
2. trotzdem, dennoch II
3. still, ruhig III
°4. Standbild
stilts *(pl)* [stɪlts] Stelzen III
stink [stɪŋk], **stank, stunk** stinken IV 1 (35)
stole [stəʊl] *siehe* **steal**
stolen ['stəʊlən] *siehe* **steal**
stomach ['stʌmək] Magen II
stomach ache ['stʌmək eɪk] Bauchschmerzen, Magenschmerzen IV 3 (96)
stone [stəʊn] Stein II
stood [stʊd] *siehe* **stand**
stop [stɒp]:
1. Halt; Station, Haltestelle II
2. anhalten, stoppen I
3. aufhören II
Stop it! *(infml)* Hör auf (damit)! / Lass das! II
store [stɔː]:
1. Lager III
2. *(AE)* Laden, Geschäft II
storey ['stɔːri], *pl* **storeys** Stock, Stockwerk, Etage III
storm [stɔːm] Sturm, Unwetter, Gewitter II

story ['stɔːri], *pl* **stories**:
1. Geschichte, Erzählung I
2. *(AE)* Stock, Stockwerk, Etage III
straight [streɪt]:
1. gerade II
2. direkt, geradewegs III
straight on geradeaus weiter II
strange [streɪndʒ] seltsam, komisch I
strawberry ['strɔːbəri] Erdbeere II
stream [striːm]:
1. Bach III
2. strömen III
3. streamen III
streaming app ['striːmɪŋ æp] Streaming-App IV 4 (112)
street [striːt] Straße I **at 14 Dean Street** in der Dean Street 14 I **in Dean Street** in der Dean Street I
street artist ['striːt‿ɑːtɪst] Straßenkünstler/in II
strength [streŋθ] Stärke, Kraft III
stress [stres] Betonung I
stress [stres]:
1. Stress, Belastung IV 3 (107)
2. stress sb. (out) jn. stressen, (über)belasten IV 3 (107)
stressful ['stresfl] anstrengend, aufreibend, stressig IV 4 (115)
strict [strɪkt] streng III
strike [straɪk]: **strike, struck, struck** schießen *(Ball, Puck)*; schlagen; treffen IV 1 (32)
string [strɪŋ] Saite III
strong [strɒŋ] stark, kräftig II
strongly ['strɒŋli] heftig, entschieden, voll und ganz IV 2 (57)
struck [strʌk] *siehe* **strike**
structure ['strʌktʃə]:
1. Struktur, Gliederung III
2. strukturieren, aufbauen IV 2 (50)
°**struggle** ['strʌgl] Kampf; Anstrengung, Mühe
stuck [stʌk] *siehe* **stick**
student ['stjuːdənt] Schüler/in; Student/in I
studio ['stjuːdiəʊ] Studio I
study ['stʌdi]:
1. studieren; untersuchen, beobachten; lernen III
2. *(das)* Lernen; Untersuchung, Studie IV 3 (88)
study poster ['stʌdi pəʊstə] Lernposter II
study skills ['stʌdi skɪlz] Lern- und Arbeitstechniken I
stuff [stʌf] *(infml)* Zeug, Kram III
stumble ['stʌmbl] stolpern; torkeln IV 1 (32)
stunk [stʌŋk] *siehe* **stink**
stunning ['stʌnɪŋ] phantastisch, umwerfend IV 2 (45)
stupid ['stjuːpɪd] dumm, blöd III
style [staɪl] Stil III
sub-clause ['sʌb klɔːz] Nebensatz I
sub-heading ['sʌb hedɪŋ] Zwischenüberschrift; Kapitelüberschrift III

subject ['sʌbdʒɪkt]:
1. Schulfach I
2. Thema; *(in E-Mails)* Betreff IV 1 (23)
3. Ziel(person); Gegenstand IV 2 (64)
subscribe to sth. [səb'skraɪb] etwas abonnieren IV 1 (14)
°**substitute sth. with sth.** ['sʌbstɪtjuːt] etwas durch etwas ersetzen
subtitle ['sʌbtaɪtl] Untertitel I
suburb ['sʌbɜːb] Vorstadt, Vorort IV 2 (46)
suburban [sə'bɜːbən] Vorort-, Vorstadt-; vorstädtisch IV 2 (56)
subway ['sʌbweɪ] *(AE)* U-Bahn II
succeed [sək'siːd] Erfolg haben IV 4 (124) **succeed in doing sth.** es schaffen, etwas zu tun IV 4 (124)
success [sək'ses] Erfolg IV 1 (12)
successful [sək'sesfl] erfolgreich II
such [sʌtʃ]: **such a …** so ein/e …; solch ein/e … III **such as** wie zum Beispiel IV 2 (76)
suck [sʌk] *(infml)*: **That sucks!** Das ist echt übel! III
suddenly ['sʌdnli] plötzlich, auf einmal I
suffer (from) ['sʌfə] leiden (an); erleiden III
suffering ['sʌfərɪŋ] *(das)* Leid, Leiden IV 2 (59)
suggest sth. (to sb.) [sə'dʒest] (jm.) etwas vorschlagen III
suggestion [sə'dʒestʃən] Vorschlag III
°**suitable (for)** ['suːtəbl] geeignet, passend (für)
suitcase ['suːtkeɪs] Koffer IV 3 (83)
sum sth. up [ˌsʌm‿'ʌp] etwas zusammenfassen III
°**summarize** ['sʌməraɪz] zusammenfassen
°**summary** ['sʌməri] Zusammenfassung
summer ['sʌmə] Sommer I
summit ['sʌmɪt] Gipfel III
sun [sʌn] Sonne I
Sunday ['sʌndeɪ], ['sʌndi] Sonntag I
sung [sʌŋ] *siehe* **sing**
sunglasses *(pl)* ['sʌnglɑːsɪz] (eine) Sonnenbrille II
sunny ['sʌni] sonnig II
supermarket ['suːpəmɑːkɪt] Supermarkt I
supervise sb. ['suːpəvaɪz] jn. beaufsichtigen IV 3 (78/79)
supervision [ˌsuːpə'vɪʒn] Aufsicht; Beaufsichtigung IV 3 (78/79)
supervisor ['suːpəvaɪzə] Betreuer/in, Leiter/in, Aufsichtsperson IV 3 (78/79)
supply [sə'plaɪ]:
1. Versorgung, Lieferung; Vorrat IV 2 (62)
2. liefern, bereitstellen, zur Verfügung stellen IV 2 (62)

support [sə'pɔːt]:
1. Unterstützung IV 1 (29)
2. unterstützen IV 1 (29)
suppose [sə'pəʊz] glauben, denken, annehmen IV 4 (120) **I suppose** ich denke, ich glaube, ich nehme an IV 4 (120)
Supreme Court [suː'priːm kɔːt] *(AE)* Oberster Gerichtshof IV 3 (109)
sure [ʃʊə], [ʃɔː] sicher I **make sure that …** sich vergewissern, dass …; darauf achten, dass …; dafür sorgen, dass … II °**for sure** ganz sicher, ganz bestimmt
surf [sɜːf] surfen II
surface ['sɜːfɪs] Oberfläche III
surfing ['sɜːfɪŋ] Surfen, Wellenreiten II
surprise [sə'praɪz] Überraschung I
surprised [sə'praɪzd] überrascht I
°**surprising** [sə'praɪzɪŋ] überraschend, verwunderlich
survey ['sɜːveɪ] Umfrage, Studie III
survival [sə'vaɪvl] *(das)* Überleben IV 3 (88)
survive [sə'vaɪv] überleben III
sustain [sə'steɪn] (aufrecht)erhalten IV 4 (110/111)
sustainability [səˌsteɪnə'bɪləti] Nachhaltigkeit IV 4 (110/111)
sustainable [sə'steɪnəbl] nachhaltig, umweltverträglich; zukunftsfähig IV 4 (110/111) **sustainable living** nachhaltige Lebensweise IV 4 (110/111)
swallow ['swɒləʊ] (ver)schlucken IV 1 (34)
swam [swæm] *siehe* **swim**
swamp [swɒmp] Sumpf, Marschland III
°**swan** [swɒn] Schwan
swap [swɒp]:
1. Tausch IV 4 (128)
2. tauschen IV 4 (128)
sweat [swet]:
1. Schweiß IV 1 (34)
2. schwitzen IV 1 (34)
sweet [swiːt] süß II
sweets *(pl)* [swiːts] Süßigkeiten II
swim [swɪm], **swam, swum** schwimmen I
swimmer ['swɪmə] Schwimmer/in I
swimming pool ['swɪmɪŋ puːl] Schwimmbad, Schwimmbecken I
switch [swɪtʃ] Schalter III
sword [sɔːd] Schwert I
swum [swʌm] *siehe* **swim**
syllable ['sɪləbl] Silbe II
symbol ['sɪmbl] Symbol I
°**symbolic (of)** [sɪm'bɒlɪk] symbolisch (für)
synthetic [sɪn'θetɪk]:
1. synthetisch, Kunst- IV 4 (118)
2. Gewebe aus Kunstfasern, synthetisches Gewebe, Kunststoff IV 4 (118)
system ['sɪstəm] System IV 1 (42)

T

T-shirt ['ti: ʃɜ:t] T-Shirt I
table ['teɪbl]:
1. Tisch I
table tennis Tischtennis II
2. Tabelle I
tablet ['tæblət] *(bes. BE)* Tablette II
take [teɪk], **took, taken:**
1. *(Zeit)* brauchen; dauern II
2. nehmen, mitnehmen; (weg-, hin) bringen I
take a risk ein Risiko eingehen III
take a seat Platz nehmen III **take a shower** (sich) duschen II **take a walk** *(bes. AE)* spazieren gehen, einen Spaziergang machen III **take notes** (sich) Notizen machen *(beim Lesen oder Zuhören)* II **take part in sth.** an etwas teilnehmen II **take photos** fotografieren, Fotos machen I **take place** stattfinden; spielen, sich abspielen *(Geschichte, Handlung)* I **take sth. off** etwas ausziehen *(Kleidung)*; etwas absetzen *(Hut, Helm)* II **take sth. out** etwas herausnehmen II
take sth. seriously etwas ernst nehmen IV 2 (77) **take turns** sich abwechseln IV 4 (123) **have what it takes to do sth.** *(infml)* das Zeug dazu haben, etwas zu tun IV 3 (95)
take (on sth.) [teɪk] Einstellung (zu etwas), Sicht(weise) (auf etwas) IV 2 (46)
takeaway ['teɪkəweɪ]:
1. *Restaurant/Imbissgeschäft, das auch Essen zum Mitnehmen verkauft* II
2. *Essen zum Mitnehmen* II
taken ['teɪkən] *siehe* **take**
takeout ['teɪkaʊt] *(AE)* Essen zum Mitnehmen III
talent ['tælənt] Talent, Begabung II
talented ['tæləntɪd] begabt, talentiert II
talk [tɔ:k]:
1. **talk (to)** reden (mit), sich unterhalten (mit) I
2. Vortrag, Referat, Rede I
give a talk (about) einen Vortrag / eine Rede halten (über) I **small talk** Smalltalk *(spontan geführtes Gespräch)* III
talkative ['tɔ:kətɪv] gesprächig IV 2 (47)
tall [tɔ:l] groß *(Person)*; hoch *(Gebäude, Baum)* II
°**tank** [tæŋk] Tank; Aquarium
tap [tæp]:
1. (leichtes) Klopfen III
2. tippen, *(vorsichtig)* klopfen II
°**tap out a rhythm** einen Rhythmus klopfen
task [tɑ:sk] Aufgabe I
taste [teɪst] schmecken I **taste sth.** etwas kosten *(probieren)*; etwas schmecken II
tasty ['teɪsti] lecker II
taught [tɔ:t] *siehe* **teach**
tax [tæks] (die) Steuer III
taxi ['tæksi] Taxi II
tea [ti:]:
1. Tee I
iced tea Eistee II
2. *leichte Nachmittags- oder Abendmahlzeit* II
teach [ti:tʃ], **taught, taught** unterrichten, lehren III **teach sb. to do sth.** jm. beibringen / jn. lehren, etwas zu tun III
teacher ['ti:tʃə] Lehrer/in I
team [ti:m] Team, Mannschaft I
teamwork ['ti:mwɜ:k] Teamwork, Zusammenarbeit IV 3 (88)
tear [teə]:
1. Riss IV 4 (129)
2. **tear, tore, torn** reißen III
tear sth. down etwas abreißen III
tear sth. off etwas abreißen, fortreißen IV 2 (52)
tear [tɪə] Träne II
teaspoon ['ti:spu:n] Teelöffel II
tech [tek] *(infml)* Technik; Technologie IV 3 (91)
technical ['teknɪkl] technisch IV 4 (136)
°**technique** [tek'ni:k] Methode, Technik
technology [tek'nɒlədʒi] Technik(unterricht); Technologie IV 3 (91)
teen [ti:n] Teenager/in II
teenager ['ti:neɪdʒə] Teenager IV 1 (10)
teeth [ti:θ] *plural of* **tooth**
telephone ['telɪfəʊn] Telefon I
telephone box ['telɪfəʊn bɒks] Telefonzelle III
television ['telɪvɪʒn] Fernsehen IV 2 (67)
tell [tel], **told, told: tell (about)** erzählen (von); berichten (über) I **tell sb. (not) to do sth.** jn. auffordern, etwas (nicht) zu tun; jm. sagen, dass er/sie etwas (nicht) tun soll III **tell sb. the way (to …)** jm. den Weg (nach …) beschreiben II
temperature ['temprətʃə] Temperatur, Fieber II **have a temperature** Fieber haben II
ten [ten] zehn I
tend to be/do sth. [tend] dazu neigen etwas zu tun/sein, meistens etwas sein/tun IV 2 (48)
tennis ['tenɪs] Tennis I **table tennis** Tischtennis II
tense [tens] (grammatische) Zeit, Tempus III
tent [tent] Zelt II
term [tɜ:m]:
1. Trimester II
2. Ausdruck, Begriff IV 3 (96)
terminology [ˌtɜ:mɪ'nɒlədʒi] Terminologie, Fachwortschatz IV 3 (108)
terrible ['terəbl] schrecklich, furchtbar II
terrified ['terɪfaɪd] entsetzt IV 4 (116)
be terrified (of sth.) schreckliche Angst (vor etwas) haben IV 4 (116)
terrify sb. ['terɪfaɪ] jm. schreckliche Angst einjagen IV 4 (116)
territory ['terətri] Gebiet, Territorium IV 2 (44)
terrorist ['terərɪst] terroristische(r, s); Terrorist/in III
test [test]:
1. Test I
2. testen, prüfen III
°**testimonial** [ˌtestɪ'məʊniəl] Erfahrungsbericht; Bewertung(en)
text [tekst]:
1. Text I
2. SMS II
3. **text sb.** jm. eine SMS schicken I
text message ['tekst mesɪdʒ] SMS II
textile ['tekstaɪl] Textil- IV 4 (118)
textiles *(pl)* ['tekstaɪlz] Textilien IV 4 (118)
than [ðæn], [ðən]: **bigger than** größer als II
thank ['θæŋk ju:]: **Thank you.** Danke. I
thanks [θæŋks] danke I **thanks to Maya** dank Maya II
that [ðæt]:
1. das (dort) I
that group die Gruppe (dort), jene Gruppe I **That sucks!** *(infml)* Das ist echt übel! III **that's why** deshalb, darum I **that's** das ist I **after that** danach I **Is that you?** Bist du's? / Bist du das? I **like that** so *(auf diese Weise)* I
2. dass I
it shows that … es zeigt, dass … I
Now that … Jetzt, wo … / Nun, da … III **so that …** sodass …, damit … II
3. der, die, das; die *(Relativpronomen)* II
the [ðə]:
1. der, die, das; die I
2. **the more …, the more …** je mehr …, desto mehr … IV 1 (19)
theatre ['θɪətə] Theater I
theft [θeft] Diebstahl IV 2 (58)
their [ðeə] ihr/e *(zu „they")* I
theirs [ðeəz] ihrer, ihre, ihrs II
them [ðem], [ðəm] sie; ihnen I
theme [θi:m] Thema II
themselves [ðəm'selvz] sie/sich selbst/selber *(zu „they")* III
then [ðen] dann I **just then** genau in dem Moment; gerade dann II
theology [θi'ɒlədʒi] Theologie IV 3 (108)
there [ðeə] da, dort; dahin, dorthin I
There are … Es sind … / Es gibt … I
There's … (= There is …) Es ist … / Es gibt … I **Are there any …?** Gibt es (irgendwelche) …? I **over there** da drüben, dort drüben II

therefore ['ðeəfɔː] deshalb, deswegen IV 1 (42)
thermometer [θə'mɒmɪtə] Thermometer II
these [ðiːz] diese (hier) I **these days** heutzutage IV 3 (107)
they [ðeɪ] sie *(Plural)* I **they're ... (= they are)** sie sind ... I
thick [θɪk] dick III
thief [θiːf], *pl* **thieves** Dieb/in I
thieves [θiːvz] *plural of* **thief**
thing [θɪŋ] Sache, Ding I
think [θɪŋk], **thought, thought** denken, glauben I **think (about)** nachdenken (über) I **think of sth.** sich etwas ausdenken; an etwas denken I
third [θɜːd] dritte(r, s) I **Third, ...** Drittens, ... I
Thirdly, ... ['θɜːdli] Drittens ... IV 1 (29)
thirsty ['θɜːsti]: **be thirsty** durstig sein, Durst haben I
this [ðɪs]:
1. dies; diese(r, s) I
this afternoon/evening/... heute Nachmittag/Abend/... II **This is ...** Dies ist ... / Das ist ... I **this one** diese(r, s) II **this time** dieses Mal II **this year's musical** das diesjährige Musical II **like this** so *(auf diese Weise)* I
2. this fast so schnell IV 4 (124)
those [ðəʊz] die ... dort; jene I
though [ðəʊ]:
1. obwohl IV 2 (47)
even though selbst wenn, obwohl *(betont)* IV 1 (42)
2. ... though. ... aber ..., ... trotzdem ... IV 3 (82)
thought [θɔːt]:
1. Gedanke III
2. *siehe* **think**
thousand ['θaʊznd] Tausend, tausend II
thread [θred] Faden IV 4 (110/111)
threat [θret] (Be-)Drohung IV 4 (110/111)
threaten ['θretn] (be)drohen IV 4 (110/111)
three [θriː] drei I
threw [θruː] *siehe* **throw**
thrilled [θrɪld] fasziniert, begeistert IV 3 (86)
throat [θrəʊt] Hals, Kehle II **have a sore throat** Halsschmerzen haben II
through [θruː]:
1. durch I
°**2.** *(AE)* bis (einschließlich)
throughout ... [θruː'aʊt] der/die/das ganze ... (hindurch); überall in ... IV 2 (64)
throw [θrəʊ], **threw, thrown** werfen I **throw sth. away/out** etwas wegwerfen IV 4 (118)
thrown [θrəʊn] *siehe* **throw**
thunder ['θʌndə] Donner II

Thursday ['θɜːzdeɪ], ['θɜːzdi] Donnerstag I
°**tick** [tɪk] ankreuzen, abhaken
ticket ['tɪkɪt]:
1. Eintrittskarte I
2. Fahrkarte I
return ticket (Hin- und) Rückfahrkarte II **single ticket** Einzelfahrschein; einfache Fahrkarte II
ticket office ['tɪkɪt‿ɒfɪs] Fahrkartenschalter; Kasse *(für den Verkauf von Eintrittskarten)* III
tighten ['taɪtn] spannen, festziehen, nachziehen III
till [tɪl] bis I **not till three** erst um drei, nicht vor drei II
time [taɪm]:
1. Zeit; Uhrzeit I
all the time die ganze Zeit II **be in time for the bus** den Bus erreichen; rechtzeitig zum Bus kommen III **feeding time** Fütterungszeit I **of all time** aller Zeiten II **opening times** *(pl)* Öffnungszeiten III **What time is it?** Wie spät ist es? I
2. Mal I
at one time zur selben Zeit, gleichzeitig III **for the first time** zum ersten Mal III **this time** dieses Mal II °**at a time** gleichzeitig, auf einmal; jeweils °**one at a time** einzeln, nacheinander
timeline ['taɪmlaɪn] Zeitstrahl, Zeitleiste III
timer ['taɪmə] Zeitmesser III
timetable ['taɪmteɪbl]:
1. Stundenplan I
2. Fahrplan III
tin [tɪn] Dose II
tiny ['taɪni] winzig III
tip [tɪp] Tipp I
tired ['taɪəd] müde I
°**tiring** ['taɪərɪŋ] anstrengend, ermüdend
titanium [tɪ'teɪniəm] Titan *(Metall)* IV 1 (17)
title ['taɪtl] Titel, Überschrift I
to [tu], [tə]:
1. zu, nach I
to such an extreme that ... in so extremer Form, dass ... / in so extremem Ausmaß, dass ... IV 4 (110/111) **the first European to land ...** der/die erste Europäer/in, der/die ... an Land ging IV 2 (58)
2. um zu II
decide where to go sich entscheiden, wo man hingehen möchte/sollte IV 1 (10) **Nice to meet you.** Freut mich, dich/euch/Sie kennenzulernen. I
3. count to ... zählen bis ... I
from ... to ... von ... bis ... I
4. quarter to eleven Viertel vor elf (10.45 / 22.45) I
toast [təʊst] Toast III
today [tə'deɪ] heute I
toe [təʊ] Zeh II

together [tə'geðə] zusammen I **go together** zusammenpassen, zueinander passen III
toilet ['tɔɪlət] Toilette I
told [təʊld] *siehe* **tell**
tolerance (of/for) ['tɒlərəns] Toleranz (für/gegenüber) IV 1 (19)
tolerant (of/towards) ['tɒlərənt] tolerant (gegenüber) IV 1 (19)
tomato [tə'mɑːtəʊ], *pl* **tomatoes** Tomate I
tomorrow [tə'mɒrəʊ] morgen II
tomorrow morning morgen früh II
tone [təʊn] Ton(höhe) IV 3 (85)
tongue [tʌŋ] Zunge II
tongue-twister ['tʌŋ twɪstə] Zungenbrecher II
tonight [tə'naɪt] heute Nacht, heute Abend III
tonne [tʌn] Tonne *(= 1.000 kg)* IV 4 (122)
tons of ... ['tʌnz‿əv] *(infml)* jede Menge ... IV 2 (47)
too [tuː]:
1. auch I
Me too. Ich auch. I
2. too late/cold/big/... zu spät/kalt/groß/... I
took [tʊk] *siehe* **take**
tool [tuːl] Werkzeug; (Hilfs-)Mittel III
tooth [tuːθ], *pl* **teeth** Zahn II
toothache ['tuːθeɪk]: **have a toothache** Zahnschmerzen haben II
top [tɒp]:
1. Spitze, oberes Ende I
at the top (of) oben, am oberen Ende (von) II **on top of each other** übereinander, aufeinander III
2. Spitzen- I
3. Top, Oberteil I
4. top sth. an der Spitze von etwas stehen; etwas übertreffen, übersteigen IV 2 (62)
topic ['tɒpɪk] Thema, Themengebiet II
topic sentence [ˌtɒpɪk 'sentəns] *Satz, der in das Thema eines Absatzes einführt* III
topping ['tɒpɪŋ] Überzug, Belag; Soße IV 4 (120) **with a cheese topping** mit Käse überbacken IV 4 (120)
torch [tɔːtʃ]:
1. Taschenlampe II
2. Fackel II
tore [tɔː] *siehe* **tear**
torn [tɔːn] *siehe* **tear**
tortoise ['tɔːtəs] (Land-)Schildkröte III
torture ['tɔːtʃə]:
1. Folter IV 1 (41)
2. foltern, quälen IV 1 (41)
total ['təʊtl]: **a total of ...** eine Gesamtsumme von ...; insgesamt III
totally ['təʊtəli] völlig, total III
touch [tʌtʃ]:
1. berühren, anfassen I
2. get in touch (with sb.) (mit jm.) Kontakt aufnehmen; sich (mit jm.) in

Verbindung setzen II
stay in touch (with sb.) (mit jm.) Kontakt halten; (mit jm.) in Verbindung bleiben II
tough [tʌf] (knall)hart; zäh, robust IV 3 (86)
tour [tʊə]:
1. tour (of) Rundgang, Rundfahrt, Reise (durch) I
2. auf Tour(nee) gehen (in/durch), touren (in/durch) IV 2 (62)
tour guide ['tʊə gaɪd] Reiseführer/in IV 1 (24)
tourist ['tʊərɪst] Tourist/in I
tourist (information) office ['tʊərɪst‿ɒfɪs] Touristeninformation, Fremdenverkehrsbüro IV 1 (11)
tourist (information) bureau ['tʊərɪst bjʊərəʊ] *(AE)* Touristeninformation, Fremdenverkehrsbüro IV 1 (11)
touristy ['tʊərɪsti] *(infml)* touristisch IV 1 (22)
towards [tə'wɔ:dz] auf … zu, in Richtung (von) III
tower ['taʊə] Turm I
town [taʊn] Stadt I
toy [tɔɪ] Spielzeug I
track [træk]:
1. (Bahn-)Gleis III
2. keep track of sth. den Überblick behalten bei etwas, etwas im Auge behalten IV 3 (97)
tractor ['træktə] Traktor II
trade [treɪd] Handel III
tradition [trə'dɪʃn] Tradition I
traditional [trə'dɪʃənl] traditionell II
traffic ['træfɪk] Verkehr III
traffic light(s) ['træfɪk laɪt] (Verkehrs-)Ampel III
trail [treɪl] Weg, Pfad III
train [treɪn] Zug I **direct train** durchgehender Zug II **steam train** *Zug mit Dampflok* III
train [treɪn]:
1. train (sb.) trainieren; jn. trainieren II
°2. train (sb.) jn. ausbilden; ausgebildet werden / eine Ausbildung machen
°train (as) ausgebildet werden (zu) / eine Ausbildung machen (zu)
trainer ['treɪnə] Turnschuh I
training ['treɪnɪŋ]:
1. Training(sstunde) I
°2. Ausbildung; Schulung
°trait [treɪt] Wesenszug, Eigenschaft
trance [trɑ:ns] Trance III
transcribe [træn'skraɪb] niederschreiben, aufschreiben; transkribieren IV 4 (112)
transcript ['trænskrɪpt] Niederschrift, Protokoll IV 4 (112)
transfer ['trænsfɜ:] umziehen, (über) wechseln; umsteigen; überweisen *(Geld)* IV 3 (80)
transform [træns'fɔ:m] (sich) verwandeln; umwandeln IV 1 (19)
translate [træns'leɪt] übersetzen II
translation [træns'leɪʃn] Übersetzung III
translator [træns'leɪtə] Übersetzer/in IV 4 (129)
transparency [træns'pærənsi] Folie III
transport ['trænspɔ:t] Verkehrsmittel; Transport(wesen) III
transport [træn'spɔ:t] transportieren, befördern IV 2 (58)
transportation [ˌtrænspɔ:'teɪʃn] *(bes. AE)* Beförderung, Transport(wesen), Verkehr IV 4 (122)
trapped [træpt]: **be trapped** gefangen sein, in der Falle sitzen IV 1 (33)
travel ['trævl]:
1. reisen I
2. *(das)* Reisen IV 4 (110/111)
travel sickness ['trævl sɪknəs] Reisekrankheit II
traveller ['trævələ] Reisende(r) I
treat ['tri:t]:
1. Hochgenuss, besonderes Vergnügen; (besondere) Leckerei IV 1 (19)
2. treat sb. (to sth.) jn. (zu etwas) einladen IV 1 (19)
°treatment ['tri:tmənt] Behandlung
treaty ['tri:ti] (Staats-)Vertrag, Abkommen III
tree [tri:] Baum I
trend [trend]:
1. Trend IV 1 (14)
2. im Trend liegen, angesagt sein IV 1 (14)
trendy ['trendi] modisch, „angesagt" IV 1 (18)
triangular [traɪ'æŋgjələ] dreieckig III
tribe [traɪb] (Volks-)Stamm II
°tribulation [ˌtrɪbju'leɪʃn] Sorge, Plage
trick [trɪk] Kunststück, Trick II
trigger ['trɪgə] auslösen, triggern IV 2 (65)
trio ['tri:əʊ] Trio IV 1 (16)
trip [trɪp] Ausflug; Reise I **go on a boat trip** einen Bootsausflug machen I
trophy ['trəʊfi] Pokal; Trophäe I
tropical ['trɒpɪkl] tropisch, Tropen- III
°tropics *(pl)* ['trɒpɪks] Tropen
trouble ['trʌbl]: **be in trouble** in Schwierigkeiten sein; Ärger kriegen I **get into trouble** in Schwierigkeiten geraten, Ärger kriegen III
trousers *(pl)* ['traʊzəz] Hose II
truck [trʌk] *(bes. AE)* Lastwagen, LKW III
true [tru:] wahr I
trumpet ['trʌmpɪt] Trompete I
trust [trʌst]:
1. Vertrauen IV 1 (33)
2. trauen, vertrauen IV 1 (33)
truth [tru:θ] Wahrheit II
try [traɪ]:
1. Versuch III
2. (aus)probieren; versuchen I
try hard sich anstrengen; sich (große) Mühe geben III **try sth. on** etwas anprobieren III
tube [tju:b]: **the Tube** *(no pl)* die U-Bahn *(in London)* III
Tuesday ['tju:zdeɪ], ['tju:zdi] Dienstag I
tuition [tju'ɪʃn] Unterricht, Anleitung; Studiengebühren IV 3 (109)
tuition fees *(pl)* [tju'ɪʃn fi:z] Studiengebühren IV 3 (109)
tulip ['tju:lɪp] Tulpe II
tuna (fish) ['tju:nə], *pl* **tuna** *or* **tunas** Thunfisch IV 3 (82)
tune [tju:n]:
1. Melodie III
2. stimmen *(Instrument)* III
tunnel ['tʌnl] Tunnel II
turkey ['tɜ:ki] Pute, Truthahn I
turn [tɜ:n]:
1. turn around sich umdrehen I **turn left/right** (nach) links/rechts abbiegen II **turn sth. around** etwas wenden, umdrehen I **turn sth. off** etwas ausschalten II **turn sth. on** etwas einschalten I **turn sth. up/down** etwas lauter/leiser stellen III **turn to sb.** sich jm. zuwenden; sich an jn. wenden II
2. turn red/brown/cold/… rot/braun/kalt/… werden III
turn [tɜ:n]: **(It's) my turn.** Ich bin dran / an der Reihe. I **give sb. his/her turn** jn. auch (mal) drankommen lassen IV 4 (123) **miss two turns** zweimal aussetzen *(im Spiel)* IV 4 (123)
take it in turns (to do sth.) sich (bei/mit etwas) abwechseln IV 4 (123)
take turns (in sth./to do sth.) sich (bei/mit etwas) abwechseln IV 4 (123)
TV [ˌti:'vi:] Fernsehen, Fernsehgerät I **on TV** im Fernsehen III **watch TV** fernsehen I
tweet [twi:t] tweeten, twittern *(Twitter benutzen)* IV 1 (14)
twelve [twelv] zwölf I
twice [twaɪs] zweimal II
twins *(pl)* [twɪnz] Zwillinge I
two [tu:] zwei I
type (of) [taɪp] Typ, Art, Sorte (von) III
°type (in) [taɪp] (ein)tippen
typical (of) ['tɪpɪkl] typisch (für) III

U

umbrella [ʌm'brelə] Schirm, Regenschirm I
uncharted [ˌʌn'tʃɑ:tɪd] unerforscht, unbekannt, auf keiner Landkarte verzeichnet IV 2 (58)
uncle ['ʌŋkl] Onkel I

uncomfortable [ʌn'kʌmftəbl] unbequem, ungemütlich; unangenehm, peinlich IV 4 (115)
°**uncontrolled** [ˌʌnkən'trəʊld] unkontrolliert, ungeregelt
under ['ʌndə] unter I
undergraduate [ˌʌndə'grædʒuət] Student/in *(vor dem ersten Hochschulabschluss)* IV 3 (88)
underground [ˌʌndə'graʊnd] unterirdisch, unter der Erde III
underground ['ʌndəgraʊnd]: **the underground** *(BE)* die U-Bahn II
underline [ˌʌndə'laɪn] unterstreichen II
underlying [ˌʌndə'laɪɪŋ] zugrunde liegend; darunter liegend II
understand [ˌʌndə'stænd], **understood, understood** verstehen I
understood [ˌʌndə'stʊd] *siehe* **understand**
undisturbed [ˌʌndɪ'stɜːbd] ungestört; unberührt IV 2 (58)
unemployed [ˌʌnɪm'plɔɪd] arbeitslos IV 3 (95)
unemployment [ɪm'plɔɪmənt] Arbeitslosigkeit IV 3 (95)
unexpected [ˌʌnɪk'spektɪd] unerwartet IV 2 (53)
unfair [ʌn'feə] unfair III
°**unfinished** [ʌn'fɪnɪʃt] unvollendet
unfortunately [ʌn'fɔːtʃənətli] unglücklicherweise, leider III
unfriendly [ʌn'frendli] unfreundlich I
unhappy [ʌn'hæpi] unglücklich I
uni ['juːni] **(***infml, kurz für:* **university)** Uni(versität) IV 3 (107)
unicorn ['juːnɪkɔːn] Einhorn IV 1 (17)
uniform ['juːnɪfɔːm] (Schul-)Uniform I
unify ['juːnɪfaɪ] (ver)einen, vereinigen IV 2 (58)
unique [ju'niːk] einmalig, einzigartig IV 1 (19)
unit ['juːnɪt] Kapitel, Lektion I
united [ju'naɪtɪd] vereinigt I **United Kingdom (UK)** Vereinigtes Königreich I **United States** Vereinigte Staaten *(von Amerika)* III
university [ˌjuːnɪ'vɜːsəti] Universität II
unkind [ˌʌn'kaɪnd] unfreundlich, herzlos IV 3 (86)
°**unknown** [ˌʌn'nəʊn] unbekannt
unless [ən'les] es sei denn; außer (wenn) IV 4 (127)
unlike [ˌʌn'laɪk] anders als, im Gegensatz zu IV 4 (129)
unload [ˌʌn'ləʊd] entladen III
unlock [ʌn'lɒk] aufschließen, entsperren IV 4 (124)
unnecessary [ʌn'nesəsəri] überflüssig, unnötig IV 4 (112)
unofficial [ˌʌnə'fɪʃl] inoffiziell IV 4 (137)
unpack [ˌʌn'pæk] auspacken III
°**unpaid** [ʌn'peɪd] unbezahlt
unplug sth. [ʌn'plʌg] den Stecker von etwas herausziehen, etwas ausstöpseln IV 4 (112)
unrealistic [ˌʌnrɪə'lɪstɪk] unrealistisch IV 3 (101)
unsubscribe (from) sth. [ˌʌnsəb'skraɪb] etwas abbestellen, kündigen; sich aus einer Mailingliste austragen lassen IV 1 (14)
unsure [ˌʌn'ʃʊə] unsicher IV 2 (48)
until [ən'tɪl] bis II **not until 1912** erst im Jahr 1912; nicht vor 1912 III
unusual [ʌn'juːʒuəl] ungewöhnlich III
up [ʌp] hinauf, herauf; (nach) oben I **up and down** auf und ab; rauf und runter I **up here** hier oben; nach hier oben II **it is up to sb. (to do sth.)** es ist js. Sache / es liegt an jm. (etwas zu tun) IV 4 (137) **What's up?** Was gibt's? / Was ist los? III
up to ['ʌp tə] bis (zu) II
update sth. [ˌʌp'deɪt] etwas aktualisieren, auf den neuesten Stand bringen III
uphill [ˌʌp'hɪl] bergauf III
upload sth. [ˌʌp'ləʊd] etwas hochladen III
upper ['ʌpə] obere(r, s) IV 2 (49)
upset [ʌp'set]:
1. aufgebracht, verärgert III
I felt upset for him. Er tat mir leid. III
2. **upset sb., upset, upset** jn. aufregen, ärgern, erschüttern IV 2 (64)
upstairs [ˌʌp'steəz] oben; nach oben I
upstream [ˌʌp'striːm] flussaufwärts III
°**uptalk** ['ʌptɔːk] *steigende Intonation am Ende von Sätzen (nicht nur von Fragesätzen)*
upwards ['ʌpwədz] nach oben IV 1 (27)
urban ['ɜːbən] städtisch, urban IV 2 (45)
urge [ɜːdʒ]:
1. Drang, Bedürfnis IV 4 (115)
2. **urge sb. to do sth.** jn. drängen, etwas zu tun IV 4 (115)
urgency ['ɜːdʒənsi] Dringlichkeit IV 4 (115)
urgent ['ɜːdʒənt] dringend, eilig IV 4 (115)
US (United States) [ˌjuː‿'es] Vereinigte Staaten *(von Amerika)* III
us [ʌs], [əs] uns I
usage ['juːsɪdʒ] (Sprach-)Gebrauch IV 4 (137)
use [juːz] benutzen, verwenden I
use [juːs] Gebrauch, Verwendung IV 3 (92)
used to ['juːst tə]:
1. **be used to** gewöhnt sein an IV 1 (31)
2. **get used to** sich gewöhnen an III
3. **the trail I used to take** der Weg, den ich (früher immer) genommen habe III
useful ['juːsfl] nützlich, hilfreich IV 4 (122)
user ['juːzə] (Be-)Nutzer/in IV 4 (129)
usual ['juːʒuəl] gewöhnlich, üblich III
usually ['juːʒuəli] meistens, normalerweise, gewöhnlich I

V

vacation [və'keɪʃn] *(AE)* Urlaub II
valley ['væli] Tal II
valuable ['væljuəbl] wertvoll IV 3 (88)
valuables *(pl)* ['væljuəblz] Wertsachen IV 3 (88)
value ['væljuː]:
1. Wert IV 3 (88)
2. wertschätzen, schätzen IV 4 (124)
van [væn] Transporter, Lieferwagen III
variety [və'raɪəti] Variante, Sorte, Art IV 3 (85)
various ['veəriəs] (mehrere) verschiedene IV 2 (58)
vary ['veəri] unterschiedlich sein, verschieden sein III
°**vase** [vɑːz] Vase
vast [vɑːst] riesig, sehr groß IV 2 (56)
vegan ['viːgən]:
1. vegan IV 3 (84)
2. Veganer/in IV 3 (84)
°**veganism** ['viːgənɪzəm] Veganismus
vegetables *(pl)* ['vedʒtəblz] Gemüse I
vegetarian [ˌvedʒə'teəriən]:
1. vegetarisch II
2. Vegetarier/in II
°**vegetarianism** [ˌvedʒə'teəriənɪzəm] Vegetarismus
vendetta [ven'detə] Blutrache; Hetzkampagne IV 1 (40)
verb [vɜːb] Verb III
verse [vɜːs] Vers, Strophe II
version ['vɜːʃn] Version IV 4 (118)
versus ['vɜːsəs] **(v.** *or* **vs.)** gegenüber; gegen *(bei Wettkämpfen)* IV 3 (80)
very ['veri] sehr I
vet [vet] **(***infml, kurz für:***) veterinary surgeon** Tierarzt/Tierärztin III
veterinary ['vetnri], ['vetrənəri] tierärztlich, Tier- IV 3 (108)
veterinary medicine [ˌvetnri 'medsɪn], [ˌvetrənəri 'medsɪn] Tiermedizin IV 3 (108)
veterinary surgeon [ˌvetnri 'sɜːdʒən], [ˌvetrənəri 'sɜːdʒən] **(***kurz auch:* **vet)** Tierarzt/-ärztin IV 3 (108)
vibe [vaɪb] *(infml)* Ausstrahlung, Atmosphäre IV 1 (19)
vibration [vaɪ'breɪʃn] Vibration III
Victorian [vɪk'tɔːriən] viktorianisch; Viktorianer/in IV 1 (8/9)
victory ['vɪktəri] Sieg III
video ['vɪdiəʊ] Video I
video camera ['vɪdiəʊ kæmərə] Videokamera I
view [vjuː]:
1. Ansicht, Meinung III
in my view meiner Meinung nach III
2. **view (of)** Aussicht, Blick (auf) I

3. Aufruf, Klick *(eines Videos im Internet)* IV 4 (124)
view sth. [vjuː] etwas betrachten, etwas anschauen *(auch Film, TV)* IV 3 (100)
viewer ['vjuːə] Zuschauer/in IV 3 (100)
vigorous ['vɪgərəs] energisch, kräftig III
village ['vɪlɪdʒ] Dorf I
violence ['vaɪələns] Gewalt, Gewalttätigkeit IV 1 (28)
violent ['vaɪələnt] gewalttätig; gewaltsam IV 1 (28)
°**violin** [ˌvaɪə'lɪn] Geige, Violine
viral ['vaɪrəl] Virus-, viral IV 4 (124) **go viral** sich *(im Internet)* rasend schnell verbreiten IV 4 (124)
visa ['viːzə] Visum III
viscose ['vɪskəʊz] Viskose IV 4 (122)
visit ['vɪzɪt]:
1. Besuch I
2. besuchen I
visitor ['vɪzɪtə] Besucher/in, Gast I
visual ['vɪʒuəl] visuell; optisch IV 4 (112)
visual materials *(pl)* [vɪʒuəl mə'tɪəriəlz] visuelle Materialien/Hilfsmittel IV 4 (112)
visuals *(pl)* ['vɪʒuəlz] visuelle Materialien/Hilfsmittel IV 4 (112)
°**vitriol** ['vɪtriəl] beißende/giftige Anfeindungen
°**vivid** ['vɪvɪd] lebhaft; leuchtend *(Farben)*
vocabulary [və'kæbjələri] Vokabelverzeichnis, Wörterverzeichnis I
vocational [vəʊ'keɪʃənl] beruflich, Berufs- IV 3 (108)
voice [vɔɪs] Stimme I **in a loud voice** mit lauter Stimme II **in a soft voice** sanft; mit leiser Stimme II
volcanic [vɒl'kænɪk] vulkanisch, Vulkan- IV 2 (76)
volcano [vɒl'keɪnəʊ], *pl* **volcanos** *or* **volcanoes** Vulkan IV 2 (76)
volleyball ['vɒlibɔːl] Volleyball IV 3 (94)
volume ['vɒljuːm] Volumen, Menge; Lautstärke IV 4 (118)
volunteer [vɒlən'tɪə]:
1. freiwillig/ehrenamtlich arbeiten *(unbezahlt)* IV 1 (23)
2. Freiwillige(r), Ehrenamtliche(r) IV 1 (23)
volunteer work freiwillige/ehrenamtliche Arbeit IV 1 (23)
vote [vəʊt]:
1. Stimme *(bei Wahlen)* IV 1 (42)
get the vote das Stimmrecht erhalten IV 1 (42)
2. wählen, zur Wahl gehen; (ab)stimmen IV 1 (42)
vote for/against sb./sth. für/gegen jn./etwas stimmen IV 1 (42)
voter ['vəʊtə] Wähler/in IV 1 (42)
voucher ['vaʊtʃə] Gutschein IV 2 (57)
vowel ['vaʊəl] Vokal, Selbstlaut I

W

wage, *oft auch:* **wages** *(pl)* [weɪdʒ] Lohn, Gehalt IV 4 (118)
waist [weɪst] Taille II
wait (for) [weɪt] warten (auf) I **Wait a minute.** Warte einen Moment. / Moment mal. I **I can't wait to see …** Ich kann es kaum erwarten, … zu sehen. II
waiter ['weɪtə] Kellner IV 4 (120)
waitress ['weɪtrəs] Kellnerin IV 4 (120)
°**waka** ['wɔːkə] Kanu der Maori *(aus der Sprache der Maori)*
wake up [ˌweɪk‿'ʌp], **woke, woken** aufwachen I **wake sb. up** jn. (auf) wecken II
walk [wɔːk]:
1. Spaziergang I
go for a walk einen Spaziergang machen, spazieren gehen I **take a walk** *(bes. AE)* spazieren gehen, einen Spaziergang machen III
2. (zu Fuß) gehen I
walk the dog mit dem Hund rausgehen, den Hund ausführen III
°**walkabout** ['wɔːkəbaʊt]:
1. Bad in der Menge
2. *(AusE)* Buschwanderung *(austr. Ureinwohner/innen)*
walkie-talkie [ˌwɔːki 'tɔːki] Walkie-Talkie IV 1 (21)
walkway ['wɔːkweɪ] Fußweg; Laufgang IV 2 (46)
wall [wɔːl] Mauer; Wand II
°**waltz** [wɔːls] Walzer tanzen (mit)
wander ['wɒndə] herumlaufen; herumirren II
want [wɒnt]: **want sth.** etwas (haben) wollen I **want to do sth.** etwas tun wollen I **I want you to …** Ich möchte, dass du … II
war [wɔː] Krieg III **First/Second World War** *or* **World War I / World War II** erster/zweiter Weltkrieg III
wardrobe ['wɔːdrəʊb] Kleiderschrank IV 4 (119)
warm [wɔːm] warm I
warn sb. (about/against/of sth.) [wɔːn] jn. warnen (vor etwas) IV 4 (121)
warning ['wɔːnɪŋ] Warnung III
warrior ['wɒriə] Krieger/in IV 4 (110/111)
was [wɒz], [wəz] *siehe* **be**
wash [wɒʃ] waschen; wischen III
wash the dishes *(pl)* das Geschirr abwaschen, spülen II
waste [weɪst]: **waste sth. (on sth.)** etwas (für etwas) verschwenden IV 4 (110/111)
watch [wɒtʃ] Armbanduhr I
watch (sth.) [wɒtʃ] sich etwas anschauen; beobachten I **Watch out!** Pass auf! / Vorsicht! I **watch TV** fernsehen I
watcher ['wɒtʃə] Beobachter/in I
water ['wɔːtə] Wasser I
waterfall ['wɔːtəfɔːl] Wasserfall II
waterfront ['wɔːtəfrʌnt] Hafenviertel *(oft modernisiert und zum Wohnviertel umgebaut)* IV 2 (46)
waterhole ['wɔːtəhəʊl] Wasserloch IV 2 (62)
wave [weɪv] Welle II
wave (at sb.) [weɪv] (jm. zu)winken III
way [weɪ]:
1. Weg I
ask sb. the way jn. nach dem Weg fragen II **make your way (to/through/…)** sich auf den Weg (nach/durch/…) machen IV 4 (127) **on the way to …** auf dem Weg zu/nach … I **tell sb. the way (to …)** jm. den Weg (nach …) beschreiben II **that way** dort entlang; in die Richtung II
2. Art und Weise III
by the way übrigens III **in some/many ways** in mancher/vielerlei Hinsicht III **in this way** auf diese Weise III **No way!** Auf keinen Fall! / Kommt nicht in Frage! III
3. **he's way too good/clever/…** *(bes. AE)* er ist viel zu gut/clever/… III
way of life [ˌweɪ‿əv 'laɪf] Lebensweise IV 2 (47)
we [wiː] wir I
weak [wiːk] schwach III
weakness ['wiːknəs] Schwäche IV 3 (99)
°**weapon** ['wepən] Waffe
wear [weə], **wore, worn** tragen *(Kleidung)* I
weather ['weðə] Wetter II
weave [wiːv], **wove, woven** weben IV 4 (110/111)
web [web] Netz IV 4 (110/111)
website ['websaɪt] Website I
wedding ['wedɪŋ] Hochzeit, Trauung III
Wednesday ['wenzdeɪ], ['wenzdi] Mittwoch I
week [wiːk] Woche I
weekend [ˌwiːk'end] Wochenende I
at the weekend am Wochenende I
weekly ['wiːkli] wöchentlich III
weigh [weɪ] wiegen I
weight [weɪt] Gewicht IV 4 (123)
weird [wɪəd] seltsam, komisch III
weirdo ['wɪədəʊ] *(infml)* Spinner/in III
welcome ['welkəm]:
1. **Welcome to Plymouth.** Willkommen in Plymouth. I
2. **You're welcome.** Bitte, gern geschehen. / Nichts zu danken. II
°3. **welcome sb. (to)** jn. begrüßen (in), jn. willkommen heißen (in)
°**welcoming** ['welkəmɪŋ] (gast)freundlich
Well, … [wel] Nun, … / Also, … / Na ja, … I
well [wel]:
1. gut *(Adv.)* II
well known bekannt II **well over a**

year weit über ein Jahr, weit länger als ein Jahr IV 2 (64) **go well** gut laufen, gut gehen II
2. *(gesundheitlich)* gut, gesund II
I don't feel well. Mir geht's nicht gut. / Ich fühle mich nicht gut. II
3. as well auch, ebenso III
... as well as ... sowohl ... als auch ... IV 2 (76)
well behaved [wel bɪ'heɪvd] brav *wohlerzogen* IV 3 (86)
Welsh [welʃ] Walisisch; walisisch I
went [went] *siehe* **go**
were [wɜː] *siehe* **be**
west [west] Westen; nach Westen; westlich III
westbound ['westbaʊnd] Richtung Westen III
western ['westən] westlich, West- III
wet [wet] nass I
°**wetsuit** ['wetsuːt] Taucheranzug, Neoprenanzug
whale [weɪl] Wal I
wharf [wɔːf], *pl* **wharfs** *or* **wharves** Kai IV 2 (46)
wharves [wɔːvz] *plural of* **wharf**
what? [wɒt] was? I **What about ...?** Wie wäre es mit ...? II **What about you?** Und du? / Und was ist mit dir? Und ihr? / Und was ist mit euch? I **What colour ...?** Welche Farbe ...? I **What is the story about?** Wovon handelt die Geschichte? / Worum geht es in der Geschichte? I **What page are we on?** Auf welcher Seite sind wir? I **What programmes ...?** Welche Programme ...? / Welche Art von Programmen ...? I **What size tea would you like?** Wie groß soll der/dein Tee sein? II **What time is it?** Wie spät ist es? I **What was it like?** Wie war es? II **What's for homework?** Was haben wir als Hausaufgabe auf? I **What's for lunch?** Was gibt es zum Mittagessen? I **What's up?** Was gibt's? / Was ist los? III **What's your name?** Wie heißt du? / Wie heißt ihr? I
whatever [ˌwɒt'evə] was (auch) immer III
wheat [wiːt] Weizen IV 1 (18)
wheel [wiːl] Rad II *(kurz für:* **steering wheel***)* Lenkrad II **big wheel** Riesenrad I
when [wen]:
1. als *(zeitlich)* I
2. wenn I
3. wann I
When's your birthday? Wann hast du Geburtstag? I
whenever [ˌwen'evə] wann (auch) immer IV 4 (112)
where [weə] wo / wohin I **Where are you from?** Woher kommst du? I
wherever [weər'evə] wo(hin) (auch) immer; überall, wo(hin) IV 4 (112)
whether ['weðə] ob III
which? [wɪtʃ]:
1. welche(r, s)? *(Fragewort)* I
2. which der/die/das *(Relativpronomen)* II
Which one? Welche(r, s)? II
while [waɪl]:
1. während II
2. a while eine Weile, einige Zeit III
for a while eine Weile, eine Zeit lang III
whisper ['wɪspə] flüstern II
whistle ['wɪsl]:
1. pfeifen II
2. (Triller-)Pfeife III
white [waɪt] weiß I
white water ['waɪt wɔːtə] Wildwasser III
white-water rafting [ˌwaɪt wɔːtə 'rɑːftɪŋ] Wildwasserfahren *(im Schlauchboot)* III
who [huː]:
1. wer I
Who likes Abby? Wer mag Abby? I
2. *(Fragewort Dativ/Akkusativ)* wem; wen II
Who did you tell? Wem hast es erzählt? II **Who does Abby like?** Wen mag Abby? II
3. der, die, das; die *(Relativpronomen)* II
whoever [huː'evə] wer/wen/wem auch immer IV 4 (112)
whole [həʊl] ganze(r, s), gesamte(r, s) II
whose [huːz]:
1. *(Fragewort)* wessen I
2. *(Relativpronomen)* deren, dessen II
cities whose names ... Städte, deren Namen ... II
why [waɪ] warum I **that's why** deshalb, darum I
°**Wi-Fi** ['waɪ faɪ] WLAN, kabellose Datenübertragung
°**wicket** ['wɪkɪt] Wicket *(Tor beim Cricket)*
wide [waɪd] breit II
widespread ['waɪdspred] (weit) verbreitet IV 4 (137)
wife [waɪf], *pl* **wives** Ehefrau III
wild [waɪld] wild I
°**wildfire** ['waɪldfaɪə] Flächenbrand
wildlife ['waɪldlaɪf] Tiere *(in freier Wildbahn)*, Tierwelt IV 2 (45)
will [wɪl]: **we'll miss the girls (= we will miss the girls)** wir werden die Mädchen verpassen II
willing ['wɪlɪŋ]: **be willing to do sth.** bereit sein, etwas zu tun IV 3 (95)
win [wɪn], **won, won** gewinnen I
wind [wɪnd] Wind II
windmill ['wɪndmɪl] Windmühle IV 1 (18)
window ['wɪndəʊ] Fenster I
windy ['wɪndi] windig II
wing [wɪŋ] Flügel III
winner ['wɪnə] Gewinner/in, Sieger/in I
winter ['wɪntə] Winter I
wireless ['waɪələs] drahtlos, Funk- IV 1 (10)
wise [waɪz] weise II
wish [wɪʃ]:
1. wünschen II
I wish it was warmer. Ich wünschte, es wäre wärmer. II
2. Wunsch I
make a wish sich etwas wünschen I
with [wɪð]:
1. mit I
2. bei I
3. be with sb. (on sth.) jn. unterstützen, jm. zustimmen (bei etwas) IV 4 (119)
within [wɪ'ðɪn] innerhalb (von), in IV 1 (13)
without [wɪ'ðaʊt] ohne I
wives [waɪvz] *plural of* **wife**
woke [wəʊk] *siehe* **wake (up)**
woken ['wəʊkən] *siehe* **wake (up)**
woman ['wʊmən], *pl* **women** Frau I
°**wombat** ['wɒmbæt] Wombat *(australisches Beuteltier)*
women ['wɪmɪn] *plural of* **woman**
won [wʌn] *siehe* **win**
wonder ['wʌndə] sich fragen, gern wissen wollen III
wonderful ['wʌndəfəl] wunderbar II
wood [wʊd] Holz II
wooden ['wʊdn] hölzern; Holz- III
wool [wʊl] Wolle IV 2 (58)
woollen ['wʊlən] **(***AE:* **woolen)** Woll- *(aus Wolle)* IV 2 (58)
word [wɜːd] Wort I **May I have a word with you?** Kann ich dich/Sie kurz sprechen? II
word order ['wɜːd‿ɔːdə] Wortstellung I
°**wordle** ['wɜːdl] Anwendung, die beliebige Wörter/Texte zu Wortwolken umformt
wore [wɔː] *siehe* **wear**
work [wɜːk]:
1. arbeiten I
2. funktionieren III
3. Arbeit I
work experience ['wɜːk‿ɪkspɪəriəns] Arbeitserfahrung(en), Praxiserfahrung(en); Praktikum IV 3 (94)
work of art [ˌwɜːk‿əv‿'ɑːt] Kunstwerk III
work-related ['wɜːk rɪleɪtɪd] arbeitsbezogen; arbeitsbedingt IV 3 (81)
workbook ['wɜːkbʊk] Arbeitsheft I
worker ['wɜːkə] Arbeiter/in II
°**workplace** ['wɜːkpleɪs] Arbeitsplatz
worksheet ['wɜːkʃiːt] Arbeitsblatt II
workshop ['wɜːkʃɒp]:
1. Workshop, Lehrgang II
2. Werkstatt III

world [wɜːld] Welt I **world-famous** weltberühmt IV 1 (16) **in the world** auf der Welt I
worldwide ['wɜːldwaɪd] weltweit IV 4 (129)
worn [wɔːn] *siehe* **wear**
worried ['wʌrid] besorgt, beunruhigt I **be worried sick** krank vor Sorge sein IV 3 (107)
worry ['wʌri]:
1. worry (about) sich Sorgen machen (wegen, um) II
2. No worries. *(infml)* Kein Problem! / Gern geschehen! III
worse [wɜːs] schlechter II
worst [wɜːst]: **the worst** der/die/das schlechteste ...; die schlechtesten ... II
worth [wɜːθ] wert III
would [wʊd]:
1. I'd like ... (= I would like ...) Ich hätte gern ... / Ich möchte ... I **it would be ...** es wäre ... II **it would prove ...** es sollte sich als ... herausstellen/erweisen IV 2 (58) **What would you like to eat?** Was möchtest du essen? I **What would you like?** Was hättest du gern? / Was möchtest du? I **You would have liked him.** Du hättest ihn gemocht. III
2. I wouldn't eat .... Ich wollte (früher) nie/nicht ... essen. IV 4 (112)
wove [wəʊv] *siehe* **weave**
woven ['wəʊvn] *siehe* **weave**
write [raɪt], **wrote, written** schreiben I **write sth. down** etwas aufschreiben II
writer ['raɪtə] Schreiber/in; Schriftsteller/in III
written ['rɪtn] *siehe* **write**
wrong [rɒŋ] falsch, verkehrt I **go wrong** schiefgehen III **No, that's wrong.** Nein, das ist falsch. / Nein, das stimmt nicht. I **sb. is wrong** jemand irrt sich; jemand hat Unrecht I **What's wrong with Justin/you?** Was fehlt Justin/dir? / Was ist los mit Justin/dir? II
wrote [rəʊt] *siehe* **write**

Y

yacht [jɒt] Jacht III
year [jɪə]:
1. Jahr I
eighteen-year-old achtzehnjährig; Achtzehnjährige/r IV 3 (106) **this year's musical** das diesjährige Musical II
2. Jahrgang(sstufe) I
yearbook ['jɪəbʊk] Jahrbuch IV 3 (94)
yearly ['jɪəli] jährlich III
yell [jel] schreien III
yellow ['jeləʊ] gelb I
yes [jes] ja I
yesterday ['jestədeɪ], ['jestədi] gestern I
yet [jet]:
1. Have you ... yet? Hast du schon ...? II
2. not ... yet noch nicht I
yoga ['jəʊgə] Yoga I
yoghurt ['jɒgət] Joghurt I
you [juː]:
1. du; Sie; ihr I
2. dir; dich; euch; Ihnen I
3. man III
young [jʌŋ] jung I
your [jɔː], [jə] dein/e; euer/eure; Ihr/e I
yours [jɔːz] deiner, deine, deins; eurer, eure, eures II **Yours, Finn** Dein/Euer Finn *(Briefschluss)* IV 1 (23)
yourself [jɔː'self], [jə'self] dich/dir; (Sie) sich selbst/selber III
yourselves [jɔː'selvz], [jə'selvz] ihr/euch; (Sie) sich selbst/selber III
youth [juːθ] Jugend; Jugend- III
youth hostel ['juːθ hɒstl] Jugendherberge III
°**Yuck!** [jʌk] Igitt!
yummy ['jʌmi] *(infml)* lecker I

Z

zebra ['zebrə] Zebra IV 2 (66)
°**zero** ['zɪərəʊ], *pl* **zeros** Null
zone [zəʊn] Zone II **pedestrian zone** Fußgängerzone II
zoo [zuː] Zoo I
zookeeper ['zuːkiːpə] (*kurz auch:* **keeper)** Tierpfleger/in IV 2 (66)

Countries and continents

Country/Continent	Adjective	Person	People
Marco is from ***Italy****.*	*Pizza is* ***Italian****.*	*Marco is* ***an Italian****.*	***The Italians*** *invented pizza.*
Afghanistan [æf'gænɪstɑːn] *Afghanistan*	Afghan ['æfgæn]	an Afghan	the Afghans
Africa ['æfrɪkə] *Afrika*	African ['æfrɪkən]	an African	the Africans
Asia ['eɪʒə, 'eɪʃə] *Asien*	Asian ['eɪʃn, 'eɪʒn]	an Asian	the Asians
Australia [ɒ'streɪliə] *Australien*	Australian [ɒ'streɪliən]	an Australian	the Australians
Austria ['ɒstriə] *Österreich*	Austrian ['ɒstriən]	an Austrian	the Austrians
Bangladesh [ˌbæŋglə'deʃ] *Bangladesch*	Bangladeshi [ˌbæŋglə'deʃi]	a Bangladeshi	the Bangladeshis
Belgium ['beldʒəm] *Belgien*	Belgian ['beldʒən]	a Belgian	the Belgians
Belize [bə'liːz] *Belize*	Belizean [bə'liːziən]	a Belizean	the Belizeans
Canada ['kænədə] *Kanada*	Canadian [kə'neɪdiən]	a Canadian	the Canadians
China ['tʃaɪnə] *China*	Chinese [ˌtʃaɪ'niːz]	a Chinese	the Chinese
Croatia [krəʊ'eɪʃə] *Kroatien*	Croatian [krəʊ'eɪʃn]	a Croatian	the Croatians
Cyprus ['saɪprəs] *Zypern*	Cypriot ['sɪpriət]	a Cypriot	the Cypriots
Denmark ['denmɑːk] *Dänemark*	Danish ['deɪnɪʃ]	a Dane [deɪn]	the Danes
the **Dominican Republic** [dəˌmɪnɪkən rɪ'pʌblɪk] *die Dominikanische Republik*	Dominican [də'mɪnɪkən]	a Dominican	the Dominicans
Egypt ['iːdʒɪpt] *Ägypten*	Egyptian [i'dʒɪpʃn]	an Egyptian	the Egyptians
England ['ɪŋglənd] *England*	English ['ɪŋglɪʃ]	an Englishman / an Englishwoman	the English
Estonia [e'stəʊniə] *Estland*	Estonian [e'stəʊniən]	an Estonian	the Estonians
Europe ['jʊərəp] *Europa*	European [ˌjʊərə'piːən]	a European	the Europeans
Finland ['fɪnlənd] *Finnland*	Finnish ['fɪnɪʃ]	a Finn [fɪn]	the Finns
France [frɑːns] *Frankreich*	French [frentʃ]	a Frenchman / a Frenchwoman	the French
Germany ['dʒɜːməni] *Deutschland*	German ['dʒɜːmən]	a German	the Germans
(Great) Britain ['brɪtn] *Großbritannien*	British ['brɪtɪʃ]	a Briton ['brɪtn]	the British
Greece [griːs] *Griechenland*	Greek [griːk]	a Greek	the Greeks
Hungary ['hʌŋgəri] *Ungarn*	Hungarian [hʌŋ'geəriən]	a Hungarian	the Hungarians
Iceland ['aɪslənd] *Island*	Icelandic [aɪs'lændɪk]	an Icelander ['aɪsləndə]	the Icelanders
India ['ɪndiə] *Indien*	Indian ['ɪndiən]	an Indian	the Indians
Ireland ['aɪələnd] *Irland*	Irish ['aɪrɪʃ]	an Irishman / an Irishwoman	the Irish
Italy ['ɪtəli] *Italien*	Italian [ɪ'tæliən]	an Italian	the Italians
Jamaica [dʒəmeɪkə] *Jamaika*	Jamaika [dʒəmeɪkən]	a Jamaican	the Jamaicans
Japan [dʒə'pæn] *Japan*	Japanese [ˌdʒæpə'niːz]	a Japanese	the Japanese
Latvia ['lætviə] *Lettland*	Latvian ['lætviən]	a Latvian	the Latvians

Country/Continent	**Adjective**	**Person**	**People**
*Marco is from **Italy**.*	*Pizza is **Italian**.*	*Marco is **an Italian**.*	***The Italians** invented pizza.*
Lithuania [ˌlɪθju'eɪniə] *Litauen*	Lithuanian [ˌlɪθju'eɪniə]	a Lithuanian	the Lithuanians
Malta ['mɔːltə] *Malta*	Maltese [mɔːl'tiːz]	a Maltese	the Maltese
Mexico ['meksɪkəʊ] *Mexiko*	Mexican ['meksɪkən]	a Mexican	the Mexicans
Namibia [nə'mɪbiə] *Namibia*	Namibian [nə'mɪbiən]	a Namibian	the Namibians
the **Netherlands** ['neðələndz] *die Niederlande*	Dutch [dʌtʃ]	a Dutchman / a Dutchwoman	the Dutch
New Zealand [ˌnjuː 'ziːlənd] *Neuseeland*	New Zealand	a New Zealander	the New Zealanders
North America [ˌnɔːθ‿ə'merɪkə] *Nordamerika*	North American [ˌnɔːθ‿ə'merɪkən]	a North American	the North Americans
Northern Ireland [ˌnɔːðən‿'aɪələnd] *Nordirland*	Northern Irish [ˌnɔːðən‿'aɪrɪʃ]	a Northern Irishman / a Northern Irishwoman	the Northern Irish
Norway ['nɔːweɪ] *Norwegen*	Norwegian [nɔː'wiːdʒən]	a Norwegian	the Norwegians
Pakistan [ˌpɑːkɪ'stɑːn] *Pakistan*	Pakistani [ˌpɑːkɪ'stɑːni]	a Pakistani	the Pakistanis
Papua New Guinea [ˌpæpjuə ˌnjuː 'gɪni] *Papua-Neuguinea*	Papua New Guinean [ˌpæpjuə ˌnjuː 'gɪniən]	a Papua New Guinean	the Papua New Guineans
Poland ['pəʊlənd] *Polen*	Polish ['pəʊlɪʃ]	a Pole [pəʊl]	the Poles
Portugal ['pɔːtʃʊgl] *Portugal*	Portuguese [ˌpɔːtʃu'giːz]	a Portuguese	the Portuguese
Russia ['rʌʃə] *Russland*	Russian ['rʌʃn]	a Russian	the Russians
Rwanda [ru'ændə] *Ruanda*	Rwandan [ru'ændən]	a Rwandan	the Rwandans
Scotland ['skɒtlənd] *Schottland*	Scottish ['skɒtɪʃ]	a Scot [skɒt]; a Scotsman / a Scotswoman	the Scots, the Scottish
Serbia ['sɜːbiə] *Serbien*	Serbian ['sɜːbiən]	a Serbian	the Serbians
South America [ˌsaʊθ‿ə'merɪkə] *Südamerika*	South American [ˌsaʊθ‿ə'merɪkən]	a South American	the South Americans
Spain [speɪn] *Spanien*	Spanish ['spænɪʃ]	a Spaniard ['spænɪəd]	the Spanish
Sweden ['swiːdn] *Schweden*	Swedish ['swiːdɪʃ]	a Swede [swiːd]	the Swedes
Switzerland ['swɪtsələnd] *die Schweiz*	Swiss [swɪs]	a Swiss	the Swiss
Turkey ['tɜːki] *die Türkei*	Turkish ['tɜːkɪʃ]	a Turk [tɜːk]	the Turks
Ukraine [juː'kreɪn] *die Ukraine*	Ukrainian [juː'kreɪniən]	a Ukrainian	the Ukrainians
the **United Kingdom** [juˌnaɪtɪd 'kɪŋdəm] *das Vereinigte Königreich*	British ['brɪtɪʃ]	a Briton ['brɪtn]	the British
the **United States of America** [juˌnaɪtɪd ˌsteɪts‿əv‿ə'merɪkə] *die Vereinigten Staaten von Amerika*	American [ə'merɪkən]	an American	the Americans
Vietnam [ˌviːet'næm], [ˌviːet'nɑːm] *Vietnam*	Vietnamese [viːˌetnə'miːz]	a Vietnamese	the Vietnamese
Wales [weɪlz] *Wales*	Welsh [welʃ]	a Welshman/-woman	the Welsh
Zimbabwe [zɪm'bɑːbweɪ, zɪm'bɑːbwi] *Zimbabwe*	Zimbabwean [zɪm'bɑːbwiən]	a Zimbabwean	the Zimbabweans

First names

Abby ['æbi]
Adam ['ædəm]
Aidan ['eɪdn]
Alan ['ælən]
Alex ['ælɪks], ['æleks]
Alyssa [ə'lɪsə]
Amy ['eɪmi]
Andrew ['ændruː]
Angela ['ændʒələ]
Ann, Anne [æn]
Arkady [ɑːr'kʌdi]
Banjo ['bændʒəʊ]
Bashir [bʌ'ʃɪə]
Beau [bəʊ]
Becca ['bekə]
Bernard ['bɜːnəd]
Beyoncé [bi'jɒnseɪ]
Brian ['braɪən]
Bruce [bruːs]
Caleb ['keɪləb]
Carlos ['kɑːlɒs], ['kɑːləs]
Catherine ['kæθrɪn]
Cathy ['kæθi]
Charles [tʃɑːlz]
Charlotte ['ʃɑːlət]
Chris [krɪs]
Christine [krɪ'stiːn]
Christopher ['krɪstəfə]
Colin ['kɒlɪn]
Cooper ['kuːpə]
D'Angelo [di'ændʒələʊ]
Daphne ['dæfni]
Dave [deɪv]
David ['deɪvɪd]
Deborah ['debrə]
Ed [ed]
Elizabeth [ɪ'lɪzəbəθ]
Ella ['elə]
Elvira [el'viːrə]
Emily ['eməli]
Emma ['emə]
Evey ['iːviː]
Fluff [flʌf]
Frank [fræŋk]
Frenchy ['frentʃi]
George [dʒɔːdʒ]
Geraldine ['dʒerəldiːn]
Ghillie ['gɪli]
Gideon ['gɪdiən]
Gordon ['gɔːdn]
Graham ['greɪəm]
Halida ['helɪdə]
Harry ['hæri]
Helen ['helən]
Hercules ['hɜːkjʊliːz]
Hermione [hɜː'maɪəni]
Howard ['haʊəd]
Hugo ['hjuːgəʊ]
Ian ['iːən]
Idris ['ɪdrɪs]
Ignatius [ɪg'neɪʃəs]
Isaac ['aɪzək]
Jaclyn ['dʒæklɪn]
Jade [dʒeɪd]
Jake [dʒeɪk]
James [dʒeɪmz]
Jane [dʒeɪn]
Janine [dʒə'niːn]
Jeff [dʒef]
Jenna ['dʒenə]
Jennie ['dʒeni]
Jennifer ['dʒenɪfə]
Jerry ['dʒeri]
Jessica ['dʒesɪkə]
Jesus ['dʒiːzəs]
Joan [dʒəʊn]
Joey ['dʒəʊi]
John [dʒɒn]
Jonathan ['dʒɒnəθən]
Jones [dʒəʊnz]
Julie ['dʒuːli]
Juliet ['dʒuːliət]
Karen ['kærən]
Kate [keɪt]
Kath [kæθ]
Kay [keɪ]
Kaya ['kaɪə], [keɪə]
Keira ['kɪərə]
Kelvin ['kelvɪn]
Kevin ['kevɪn]
Kiran ['kiːrɑːn], ['kiːræn]
Kyanna [ki'ænə]
Lara ['lɑːrə]
Larry ['læri]
Lauren ['lɔːrən]
Laurence ['lɒrəns]
Lou [luː]
Lukas ['luːkəs]
Mae [meɪ]
Mahatma [mə'hætmə], [mə'hɑːtmə]
Manish [mʌ'niːʃ]
Manisha [mə'niːʃə]
Marcy ['mɑːsi]
Maria [mə'riːə]
Marjory ['mɑːdʒəri]
Mary ['meəri]
Matilda [mə'tɪldə]
Matthew ['mæθjuː]
Maura ['mɔːrə]
Max [mæks]
Maxine [mæk'siːn]
Melanie ['meləni]
Michael ['maɪkl]
Mike [maɪk]
Mina ['miːnə]
Miriam ['mɪriəm]
Morgan ['mɔːgən]
Mourad [mu'rɑːd]
Natalie ['nætəli]
Nate [neɪt]
Nats [næts]
Nikolaos [ˌnɪkə'leɪəs]
Nikolas ['nɪkələs]
Noah ['nəʊə]
Oliver ['ɒlɪvə]
Orpheus ['ɔːrfiːəs]
Ozzie ['ɒzi]
Patrick ['pætrɪk]
Paul [pɔːl]
Pete [piːt]
Peter ['piːtə]
Rebecca [rə'bekə]
Robert ['rɒbət]
Romeo ['rəʊmiəʊ]
Rosamund ['rɒzəmənd]
Rover ['rəʊvə]
Sally ['sæli]
Samantha [sə'mænθə]
Samuel ['sæmjuəl]
Sarah ['seərə]
Sean [ʃɔːn]
Shireen [ʃɪ'riːn]
Simon ['saɪmən]
Siri ['siːrɪ]
Stacey ['steɪsi]
Stephanie ['stefəni]
Steve [stiːv]
Steven ['stiːvn]
Sue [suː]
Susan ['suːzn]
Sylvia ['sɪlviə]
Sym [sɪm]
Symone [sɪ'məʊn]
Thomas ['tɒməs]
Titus ['taɪtəs]
Trevor ['trevə]
Victor ['vɪktə]
Victoria [vɪk'tɔːriə]
William ['wɪliəm]
Willow ['wɪləʊ]
Winona [wɪ'nəʊnə]
Xiuhtezcatl [ˌʃuːtez'kɑːt]
Yannick ['jænɪk]
Yazzie ['jæzi]
Yuma ['juːmə]
Zack [zæk]
Zeki ['zeki]

Family names

Acevedo [ˌæsə'viːdəʊ]
Anderson ['ændəsn]
Barton ['bɑːtn]
Basan ['beɪsæn]
Berkeley ['bɜːkli]
Blunt [blʌnt]
Bowie ['bəʊi]
Bradfield ['brædfiːld]
Brundtland ['brʌndlænd]
Chamberlain ['tʃeɪmbəlɪn]
Chatwin ['tʃætwɪn]
Clive [klaɪv]
Corin ['kɒrɪn]
Costello [kɒ'steləʊ]
Cruz [kruːz]
Dickens ['dɪkɪnz]
Dodds [dɒdz]
Douglas ['dʌgləs]
Elba ['elbə]
Eyers ['aɪəz]
Fawkes [fɔːks]
Fermer ['fɜːmə]
Forchhammer ['fɔːkhæmə]
Freeman ['friːmən]
Galiano [ˌgʌli'ɑːnəʊ]
Gandhi ['gændi]
Gonzalez [gɒn'zɑːlɪz]
Goodes [gʊdz]
Hancock ['hænkɒk]
Hanks [hæŋks]
Harger ['hɑːgə]
Hathaway ['hæθəweɪ]
Haugh [hɔː]
Heimdall ['heɪmdɑːl]
Johnson ['dʒɒnsn]
Kaepernick ['kæpənɪk]
Lee [liː]
Lennon ['lenən]
Lucas ['luːkəs]
Marsden ['mɑːzdən]
Martinez [mɑː'tiːnez]
Mauboy ['maʊbɔɪ]
McCartney [mə'kɑːtni]

McCaughrean [mə'kɔːkreɪn]
McCormick [mə'kɔːmɪk]
McDade [mək'deɪd]
McDonald [mək'dɒnld]
McFadden [mək'fædn]
McNulty [mək'nʌlti]
McPherson [mək'fɜːsn]
Minoff ['maɪnɒf]
Moore [mʊə]
Mundine ['mʌndiːn]
Nobel [nəʊ'bel]
Oates [əʊts]
Obama [əʊ'bɑːmə]
Patel [pə'tel]
Paterson ['pætəsən]
Peberdy ['pebədi]
Pepys [piːps]
Pike [paɪk]
Poppins ['pɒpɪnz]
Portman ['pɔːtmən]
Richardson ['rɪtʃədsən]
Robertson ['rɒbətsən]
Rudd [rʌd]
Scott [skɒt]
Seattle [si'ætl]
Shakespeare ['ʃeɪkspɪə]
Sitsanis [ˌsɪt'sænɪs]
Snyder ['snaɪdə]
Spielberg ['spilbɜːg]
Swan [swɒn]
Trump [trʌmp]
Turner ['tɜːnə]
Utzon ['ʌtzn]
Viñoly ['viːnɒli]
Warren ['wɒrən]
Weaving ['wiːvɪŋ]
Whitlam ['wɪtləm]
Wren [ren]
Zinn [zɪn]

Place names

Adelaide ['ædəleɪd]
Alice Springs [ˌælɪs 'sprɪŋz]
Ayers Rock [ˌeəz 'rɒk]
Banglatown ['bæŋglətaʊn]
Botany Bay [ˌbɒtəni 'beɪ]
Bristol ['brɪstl]
Britannia [brɪ'tæniə]
Brixton ['brɪkstən]
Buckingham Palace [ˌbʌkɪŋəm 'pæləs]
the **Cairngorms** ['keəngɔːmz]
Cairns [keənz]
California [ˌkælə'fɔːniə]
Cambridge ['keɪmbrɪdʒ]
Camden ['kæmdən]
Camp Sakinaw [ˌkæmp 'sækɪˌnɔː]
the **Caribbean** [ˌkærɪ'biːən]
Casuarina [ˌkæzjuə'riːnə]
Chelsea ['tʃelsi]
Chicago [ʃɪ'kɑːgəʊ]
Chinatown ['tʃaɪnətaʊn]
Chisholm ['tʃɪzəm]
Circular Quay [ˌsɜːkjələ 'kiː]
the **Clifton Suspension Bridge** [ˌklɪftən sə'spenʃn brɪdʒ]
Columbia [kə'lʌmbiə]
Coromandel Peninsula [ˌkɒrəʊmændl pə'nɪnsjələ]
the **Daintree** ['deɪntriː]
Darwin ['dɑːwɪn]
Dettifoss ['detɪfɒs]
Edinburgh ['edɪnbrə]
Edisto Island [ˌedɪstəʊ‿'aɪlənd]
Fenchurch Street ['fentʃɜːtʃ striːt]
Florida ['flɒrɪdə]
Fremantle ['friːmæntl]
Fulham ['fʊləm]
Globe Theatre [gləʊb 'θɪətə]
Hackney ['hækni]
Harvard ['hɑːvəd]
Hawaii [hə'waɪi]
Heathrow [ˌhiːθ'rəʊ]
Huntington ['hʌntɪŋtən]
Hyde Park [ˌhaɪd 'pɑːk]
Indiana [ˌɪndi'ænə]
Jordan ['dʒɔːdn]
Kimberley ['kɪmbəli]
Kinchela [kɪn'tʃelə]
Leicester Square [ˌlestə 'skweə]
Manly ['mænli]
Melbourne ['melbən]
Milford Sound Fiord [ˌmɪlfəd saʊnd 'fjɔːd]
Millennium Bridge [mɪˌleniəm 'brɪdʒ]
Mindli ['mɪndli]
Morecambe ['mɔːkəm]
Munich ['mjuːnɪk]
New Malden [ˌnjuː 'mɔːldən]
North Carolina [ˌnɔːθ kærə'laɪnə]
Northern Territory [ˌnɔːðən 'terətri]
Notting Hill [ˌnɒtɪŋ 'hɪl]
Nuneaton [nʌn'iːtn]
Oregon ['ɒrəgən]
Ottawa ['ɒtəwə]
Oxford ['ɒksfəd]
Pacific Islands [pəˌsɪfɪk‿aɪləndz]
Paris ['pærɪs]
Perth [pɜːθ]
Piccadilly Circus [ˌpɪkədɪli 'sɜːkəs]
Princeton ['prɪnstən]
Pudding Lane [ˌpʊdɪŋ 'leɪn]
Queensland ['kwiːnzlənd]
Rapid Creek [ˌræpɪd 'kriːk]
Red Cuillin [ˌred 'kuːlɪn]
Regent's Park [ˌriːdʒənts 'pɑːk]
Richmond ['rɪtʃmənd]
Ross Ice Barrier [rɒs‿'aɪs ˌbæriə]
Rotherhithe ['rɒðəhaɪð]
Saint Ghastly Grim [sənt ˌgɑːstli 'grɪm]
Saint Olave [sənt‿'ɒləv]
San Francisco [ˌsæn frən'sɪskəʊ]
Seething Lane [ˌsiːðɪŋ 'leɪn]
Shaftesbury Avenue [ˌʃɑːftsbri 'ævənjuː]
the **Shard** [ʃɑːd]
Skye [skaɪ]
Spofford ['spɒfəd]
Stamford ['stæmfəd]
Stuart Highway [ˌstjuːət 'haɪweɪ]
Sydney ['sɪdni]
Tampa ['tæmpə]
Tasmania [tæz'meɪniə]
Terra Nova [ˌterə 'nəʊvə]
the **Thames** [temz]
Timor Sea [ˌtiːmɔː 'siː]
Tooting ['tuːtɪŋ]
Torres Strait Islands [ˌtɒrəs streɪt‿'aɪləndz]
Tottenham Court Road [ˌtɒtnəm kɔːt 'rəʊd]
Trafalgar [trə'fælgə]
Uluru ['uːləruː]
Victoria [vɪk'tɔːriə]
Wallaroo [ˌwɒlə'ruː]
Washington ['wɒʃɪŋtn]
Westminster Abbey [ˌwestmɪnstər‿'æbi]
Windrush Square [ˌwɪndrʌʃ 'skweə]
Winton ['wɪntən]
Woolloomooloo [ˌwʊləmə'luː]
Wyrie Swamp [ˌwaɪri 'swɒmp]
Yale ['jeɪl]

Other names

Adobe [ə'dəʊbi]
Aztec ['æztek]
Boudicca ['buːdɪkə]
Brownlow Medal [ˌbraʊnləʊ 'medl]
Duwamish [dʊ'weɪmɪʃ], [dʊ'wɒmɪʃ]
Guardian ['gɑːdiən]
Harrods ['hærədz]
Iceni [aɪ'siːnaɪ]
Iliad ['ɪliəd]
Ludacris ['luːdəkrɪs]
Maori ['maʊri]
Odyssey ['ɒdəsi]
Phoenix ['fiːnɪks]
Polynesian [ˌpɒlɪ'niːʒən]
Rosella [rəʊ'zelə]
Suquamish [su'kwɑːmɪʃ]
Téméraire [ˌtemə'reə]
United Nations (UN) [juˌnaɪtɪd 'neɪʃnz]
Yolngu ['jɒlŋu]
Yothu Yindi [ˌjɒθuː 'jɪndi]

Irregular verbs

infinitive	simple past	past participle	
(to) **be**	**was; were**	**been**	sein
(to) **beat**	**beat**	**beaten**	schlagen; besiegen
(to) **become**	**became**	**become**	werden
(to) **begin**	**began**	**begun**	beginnen, anfangen
(to) **bend**	**bent**	**bent**	sich bücken, sich beugen
(to) **bind** [aɪ]	**bound**	**bound**	(ver)binden
(to) **bite** [aɪ]	**bit** [ɪ]	**bitten** [ɪ]	beißen
(to) **blow sth. out**	**blew**	**blown**	etwas auspusten, ausblasen
(to) **break** [eɪ]	**broke**	**broken**	brechen; zerbrechen
(to) **breed**	**bred**	**bred**	brüten; sich vermehren
(to) **bring**	**brought**	**brought**	(mit-, her)bringen
(to) **build**	**built**	**built**	bauen
(to) **burst** into tears	**burst**	**burst**	in Tränen ausbrechen
(to) **buy**	**bought**	**bought**	kaufen
(to) **catch**	**caught**	**caught**	fangen
(to) **choose** [uː]	**chose** [əʊ]	**chosen** [əʊ]	aussuchen, (aus)wählen; sich aussuchen
(to) **come**	**came**	**come**	kommen
(to) **cost**	**cost**	**cost**	kosten
(to) **creep**	**crept**	**crept**	schleichen; kriechen
(to) **cut**	**cut**	**cut**	schneiden
(to) **dig**	**dug**	**dug**	graben
(to) **do**	**did**	**done** [ʌ]	tun, machen
(to) **draw**	**drew**	**drawn**	zeichnen
(to) **drink**	**drank**	**drunk**	trinken
(to) **drive** [aɪ]	**drove** [əʊ]	**driven** [ɪ]	(mit dem Auto) fahren; (an)treiben
(to) **eat**	**ate** [et, eɪt]	**eaten**	essen
(to) **fall**	**fell**	**fallen**	fallen, stürzen; hinfallen
(to) **feed**	**fed**	**fed**	füttern
(to) **feel**	**felt**	**felt**	fühlen; sich fühlen
(to) **fight**	**fought**	**fought**	(be)kämpfen
(to) **find**	**found**	**found**	finden
(to) **flee**	**fled**	**fled**	flüchten, fliehen
(to) **fly**	**flew**	**flown**	fliegen
(to) **forbid**	**forbade**	**forbidden**	verbieten, untersagen
(to) **forget**	**forgot**	**forgotten**	vergessen
(to) **forgive**	**forgave**	**forgiven**	verzeihen
(to) **freeze**	**froze**	**frozen**	(ge)frieren; zufrieren; einfrieren
(to) **get**	**got**	**got**	bekommen; holen; werden; gelangen
(to) **give**	**gave**	**given**	geben
(to) **go**	**went**	**gone** [ɒ]	gehen
(to) **grind** [aɪ]	**ground**	**ground**	(zer)mahlen
(to) **grow**	**grew**	**grown**	wachsen; anbauen, anpflanzen
(to) **hang**	**hung**	**hung**	hängen
(to) **have**	**had**	**had**	haben
(to) **hear** [ɪə]	**heard** [ɜː]	**heard** [ɜː]	hören
(to) **hide** [aɪ]	**hid** [ɪ]	**hidden** [ɪ]	verstecken; sich verstecken
(to) **hit**	**hit**	**hit**	schlagen
(to) **hold**	**held**	**held**	halten; abhalten *(Veranstaltung)*

infinitive	simple past	past participle	
(to) **hurt**	**hurt**	**hurt**	schmerzen, wehtun; verletzen
(to) **keep**	**kept**	**kept**	behalten; aufheben, aufsparen; aufbewahren
(to) **kneel** [niːl]	**knelt** [nelt]	**knelt** [nelt]	knien
(to) **know** [nəʊ]	**knew** [njuː]	**known** [nəʊn]	wissen; kennen
(to) **lead** [iː]	**led**	**led**	führen, leiten
(to) **leave** [iː]	**left**	**left**	(weg)gehen; abfahren; (zurück)lassen; verlassen
(to) **lend sb. sth.**	**lent**	**lent**	jm. etwas leihen
(to) **let**	**let**	**let**	lassen
(to) **lie**	**lay**	**lain**	liegen
(to) **light** [aɪ]	**lit** [ɪ]	**lit** [ɪ]	anzünden
(to) **lose** [uː]	**lost** [ɒ]	**lost** [ɒ]	verlieren
(to) **make**	**made**	**made**	machen; herstellen
(to) **mean** [iː]	**meant** [e]	**meant** [e]	bedeuten; meinen
(to) **meet** [iː]	**met** [e]	**met**	treffen; sich treffen; kennenlernen
(to) **pay**	**paid**	**paid**	bezahlen
(to) **put**	**put**	**put**	(etwas wohin) tun, legen, stellen
(to) **read** [iː]	**read** [e]	**read** [e]	lesen
(to) **ride** [aɪ]	**rode**	**ridden** [ɪ]	reiten; (Rad) fahren
(to) **ring**	**rang**	**rung**	klingeln, läuten
(to) **rise** [aɪ]	**rose**	**risen** [ɪ]	(an)steigen, aufsteigen; (sich) erhöhen
(to) **run**	**ran**	**run**	rennen, laufen
(to) **say** [eɪ]	**said** [e]	**said** [e]	sagen
(to) **see**	**saw**	**seen**	sehen
(to) **seek (for)**	**sought**	**sought**	suchen (nach); anstreben
(to) **sell**	**sold**	**sold**	verkaufen
(to) **send**	**sent**	**sent**	schicken, senden
(to) **set sth. up**	**set**	**set**	etwas errichten, aufbauen; etwas arrangieren
(to) **shake**	**shook**	**shaken**	schütteln
(to) **shine**	**shone** [*BE:* ɒ, *AE:* əʊ]	**shone** [ɒ, əʊ]	scheinen *(Sonne)*
(to) **shoot** [uː]	**shot** [ɒ]	**shot** [ɒ]	schießen; erschießen
(to) **show**	**showed**	**shown**	zeigen
(to) **shut (down)**	**shut**	**shut**	schließen
(to) **sing**	**sang**	**sung**	singen
(to) **sit**	**sat**	**sat**	sitzen; sich setzen
(to) **sleep**	**slept**	**slept**	schlafen
(to) **slide** [aɪ]	**slid** [ɪ]	**slid** [ɪ]	gleiten, rutschen; schieben
(to) **speak** [iː]	**spoke**	**spoken**	sprechen
(to) **speed up**	**sped**	**sped**	beschleunigen
(to) **spend**	**spent**	**spent**	*(Zeit)* verbringen; *(Geld)* ausgeben
(to) **spin**	**spun**	**spun**	spinnen *(Wolle, Garn)*
(to) **split**	**split**	**split**	aufteilen; (sich) trennen; spalten
(to) **spread** [e]	**spread** [e]	**spread** [e]	ausbreiten, verbreiten; sich ausbreiten, verbreiten
(to) **stand**	**stood**	**stood**	stehen; sich (hin)stellen
(to) **steal**	**stole**	**stolen**	stehlen
(to) **stick**	**stuck**	**stuck**	stechen, stecken
(to) **stink**	**stank**	**stunk**	stinken
(to) **strike**	**struck**	**struck**	schießen *(Ball, Puck)*; (zu)schlagen; treffen

Irregular verbs

infinitive	simple past	past participle	
(to) **swear** [eə]	**swore**	**sworn**	schwören
(to) **swim**	**swam**	**swum**	schwimmen
(to) **take**	**took**	**taken**	(mit)nehmen; (weg-, hin)bringen; dauern
(to) **teach**	**taught**	**taught**	unterrichten, lehren
(to) **tear (down)** [teə]	**tore**	**torn**	(ab)reißen
(to) **tell**	**told**	**told**	erzählen, berichten
(to) **think**	**thought**	**thought**	denken, glauben
(to) **throw**	**threw**	**thrown**	werfen
(to) **tread** [e]	**trod**	**trodden**	treten
(to) **understand**	**understood**	**understood**	verstehen
(to) **upset**	**upset**	**upset**	aufregen, ärgern, erschüttern
(to) **wake up**	**woke up**	**woken up**	aufwachen; (auf)wecken
(to) **wear** [eə]	**wore** [ɔː]	**worn** [ɔː]	tragen *(Kleidung)*
(to) **weave** [iː]	**wove** [əʊ]	**woven** [əʊ]	weben
(to) **win**	**won** [ʌ]	**won** [ʌ]	gewinnen
(to) **write**	**wrote**	**written**	schreiben

Partner B

4 Which is the oldest?

p. 21

b) Partner B: Ask the questions about 2 and 4.

Liverpool Cathedral was started …

1

Liverpool Cathedral

start 1907
finish 1978

Cologne Cathedral

start 1248
finish 1880

2

Mona Lisa

paint

Portrait of Ludwig van Beethoven

paint

3

Berlin Underground

open 1902

London Underground

open 1863

4

Treasure Island

write

Oliver Twist

write

5

Lift

invent
1852

Escalator

invent
1895

Titelbild

S.I: Cornelsen/ London Tower Bridge: Mauritius images/ Alamy/Sergio Nogueira; Boot: stock.adobe.com/ chrisdorney; Amerikan. Flagge: stock.adobe.com/moonrun; S.II & III (Karte) : Carlos Borrell Eiköter, Berlin.

Fotos/Abbildungen

Action Press (S.52: un.li./ NEWSPIX); **Adobe Stock/ stock.adobe.com** (S.42: karenfoleyphoto; S.44 E: bennymarty; S.52 un.re.: krishnadasekm; S.52 ob.re.: BlueOrange Studio; S.54 E: mOai99; S.54 A: Rita Kochmarjova; S.54 D: Robert Kneschke; S.84 B: zsv3207; S.84 C: tlovely; S.84 F: anyaberkut; S.84 A: Nightman1965; S.102: wikornr; S.147 E: mOai99; S.147 A: Rita Kochmarjova; S.147 D: Robert Kneschke; S.166 un.: Miriam Dörr; S.172 ob.: pressmaster; S.236 Spiders: Henrik Larsson); **Bridgeman Images** (S.4 ob.re.: Look and Learn; S.5 oben & S.40 un.: Protester wearing a Guy Fawkes mask , trademark of the Anonymous movement and based on a character in the film V for Vendetta ; Paris France; S.9 B mi.li.: Look and Learn; S.154 2 ob. ; S.154 2 un.: A. Dagli Orti / De Agostini Picture Library; S.154 4 ob.: Lebrecht Authors; S.340 2 ob.; S.340 2 un.: A. Dagli Orti / De Agostini Picture Library; S.340 4 ob.: Lebrecht Authors); **CartoonStock** (S.86: Mike Flanagan); **ClipDealer GmbH** (S.84 E: Axel Bueckert; S.136 ob.re.: kbuntu); **dpa Picture-Alliance** (S.16 : Valettea-AGF; S.52 mi.re.: Dave Hunt; S.52 mi.li.: picture-alliance/AAP; S.59 re.); **Bonnie Glänzer** (S.159; S.164); **Imago sportfotodienst GmbH** (S.65: / ZUMA Press); **Imago Stock & People GmbH** (S.18 4: ZUMA Press; S.40 ob.: ZUMA Press; S.41 un.: United Archives; S.53 ob.li.: Ardea; S.59 li.: imago images); **Interfoto e.k.** (S.8 C: Illustrated London News Ltd; S.9 D un.re.: Austrian Archives; S.53 un.li.: Hans and Judy Beste; S.76 un.mi.: David Wall; S.154 4 un.: Mary Evans; S.340 4 un.: Mary Evans); **Murdo Macleod** (S.130 Bild von Zeki Basan); **Mauritius Images** (S.10 un.li.: Marcus Davidson; S.10 ob.re.: Travel Collection; S.11 un.li.: Graham Prentice; S.18 6: Paul Gapper; S.25 : Stockbroker RF; S.37 B: Marcus Davidson; S.37 C: Travel Collection; S.37 A: Graham Prentice; S.41 ob.: S Swenson; S.45 D: Konrad Wothe; S.46 ob.: tbkmedia.de; S.59 mi.: Bill Bachman; S.64 : Hugh PETERSWALD; S.68 : Ryan Jorgensen; S.77: alamy stock photo/Roger Sedres; S.107 un.re.: Richard Wayman; S.125 un.re.: Gary Roberts; S.166 ob.: Picture Partners); **Panther Media GmbH** (S.19 : Markus Mainka); Uwe Tröger (S.47 Bild von Philip Fleischauer); **SEI/Shroders.com** (S.122 Grafiken : https://www.schroders.com/de/insights/ economics/the-material-consequences-of-choosing-sustainable-fashion/); **Shutterstock.com** (S.4 un.li.: ChameleonsEye; S.4 ob.li.: pisaphotography; S.5 unten: Korawee; S.6 ob.li.: Gal Sharony; S.6 un.re.: Ben Carlson; S.6 un.li.: MikeDotta; S.7 ob.re.: Julien_j; S.8 A: Engel Ching; S.10 ob.li.: Victor Moussa; S.10 un.re.: Alex Cimbal; S.11 ob.li.vorne: mimagephotography; S.11 Smiley: Ricardo Romero; S.11 ob.li.hinten: f11photo; S.11 un.re.: FenlioQ; S.14 : littleWhale; S.15 : Matt Gibson; S.18 5: Willy Barton; S.18 2: stockfour; S.18 3: Meik; S.18 1 vorne: mimagephotography; S.18 1 hinten: Rocketclips, Inc.; S.20 : arboursabroad; S.21 ob.li.: Patryk Kosmider; S.21 ob.re.: DJ Cockburn; S.24 unten: pcruciatti; S.24 ob.li.: Alizada Studios; S.24 ob.re.: Bikeworldtravel; S.26 re.: TristanBM; S.26 li.: 2p2play; S.27 ob.: Antonio Guillem; S.31 : yvonnestewarthenderson; S.36 un.: 470images; S.37 D: FenlioQ; S.39 : Luis Molinero; S.43 ob.li.: Maximumvector; S.43 ob.re.: octopusaga; S.44 B: FiledIMAGE; S.45 A ob.: iwbrooks; S.45 F: Chang-Min Ok; S.45 G: f11photo; S.45 C: Dan Breckwoldt; S.46 un.: Leah-Anne Thompson; S.51 un.li.: Peter Vanco; S.51 un.re.: travellight; S.51 mi.: Chris Ison; S.53 un.re.: mark higgins; S.53 ob.re.: Angelica Glen; S.54 C: Aleksey Sagitov; S.54 F: NatUlrich; S.54 B: GLRL; S.58 li.: Charles Lewis/Axiom Design; S.58 mi.: Bika Ambon; S.58 re.: Holli; S.60 vorne ob.: dedoma; S.61 un.: structuresxx; S.61 ob.: stockpexel; S.62 : Featureflash Photo Agency; S.63 li.: Maurizio De Mattei; S.63 re.: EA Given; S.66 un.: pruit phatsrivong; S.74 : ChameleonsEye; S.75 un.: Korawee; S.75 ob.: ArliftAtoz2205; S.76 un.li.: DmitrySerbin; S.76 un.re.: Al Teich; S.78 C: goodluz; S.78 A: Gal Sharony; S.79 G: Dmytro Zinkevych; S.79 F: ESB Professional; S.79 B: MAD_Production; S.79 D: Syda Productions; S.81 : Monkey Business Images; S.82 : Charles Brutlag;S.84 D: PHOTO FUN; S.88 : FamVeld; S.89 mi.re.: Juri Pozzi; S.95 re.: Gregory E. Clifford; S.95 li.: Julien_j; S.96 : Janna Golovacheva; S.100 mi.mi.: linear_design; S.100 mi.re.: Cihan Terlan; S.100 un.re.: TeaGraphicDesign; S.100 un.li.: Mr. Rashad; S.100 oben: fizkes; S.100 mi.li.: OLYVIA; S.107 ob.re.: Maximumvector; S.107 un.li.: Syda Productions; S.107 ob.li.: octopusaga; S.109 : Spiroview Inc; S.110 A: MikeDotta; S.110 C: Sundry Photography; S.111 D : Ken Wolter; S.111 B: Syda Productions; S.112 re.: Vjom; S.112 li.: rui vale sousa; S.113 2: Nejron Photo; S.113 5: Fleur_de_papier; S.113 7: Motortion Films; S.113 8: Jevanto Productions; S.113 1: Monkey Business Images; S.113 6: Motortion Films; S.113 4: vector_ic; S.113 3: littlenySTOCK; S.114 re.: Roman Samborskyi; S.114 li.: Alex_Po; S.114 ob.: Milos Luzanin; S.114 un.: FERNANDO BLANCO CALZADA; S.119 ob.: Yuriy Golub; S.119 un.: In Green; S.125 ob.re.: Mark Dozier; S.125 ob.li.: Katherine Welles; S.127 : Alexandros Michailidis; S.129 : cybrain; S.132 un.: Ivan Marc; S.132 ob.: Fractal Pictures; S.132 mi.: Solveig Been; S.136 mi.: ViChizh; S.137 : pjhpix; S.140 mi.: Smirnof; S.140 ob.: Dubova; S.140 un.: Undrey; S.141 un.: Rus Limon; S.141 ob.: Irina Ippolitova; S.143 : Kichigin; S.147 C: Aleksey Sagitov; S.147 F: NatUlrich; S.147 B: GLRL; S.153 : Alexandros Michailidis; S.154 5 un.: Ekkachai; S.154 3 ob.: PHOTOCREO Michal Bednarek; S.154 1 un.: Taras Vyshnya; S.154 5 ob.: Carsten Reisinger; S.154 1 ob.: Claudio Divizia; S.154 3 un.: Mario Hagen; S.156 : sarahdesign; S.157 : AVAVA; S.175 un.: Cartoonresource; S.172 un.: Creaktiva; S.185 : phloxii; S.222 : ValentinT; S.224 re.: Fotos593; S.224 li.: robmoffat; S.225 un.: Happy cake Happy cafe; S.225 ob.: symbiot; S.225 mi.: 5 second Studio; S.228 : ANTONIO TRUZZI; S.229 : macgyverhh; S.233 : Vaternam; S.234 ob.: Stepan Bormotov; S.234 un.: hjochen; S.236 un.: e X p o s e;

S.236 stunning: Phil Date; S.237 li.: tagstiles.com – S. Gruene; S.237 re.: Miroslav Hlavko; S.238 un.: frank60; S.238 ob.: Lawkeeper; S.239 un.: denisik11; S.240 : Ermolaev Alexander; S.241 un.: a40757; S.241 mi.: Dudarev Mikhail; S.241 ob.: Melinda Fawver; S.242 : withGod; S.248 re.: andamanec; S.248 li.: Nagel Photography; S.248 mi.: Eric Isselee; S.250 un.: Chinch; S.250 ob.: Svietlieisha Olena; S.251 : deepspace; S.252 ob.: aslan ozcan; S.252 un.: sianc; S.253 : Slavun; S.255 ob.li.: AnikonaAnn; S.255 un.re.: Nikiti; S.255 ob.re.: Shebeko; S.255 un.li.: lunamarina; S.256 ob.: Pixel-Shot; S.256 un.: Daniel Fung; S.257 : eddo; S.259 : ykokamoto; S.260 li.: Joseph Sohm; S.260 re.: Domenic Gareri; S.262 : Standard Studio; S.266 un.: Matej Kastelic; S.266 ob.: Radha Design; S.269 un.: YegoeVdo22; S.269 ob.: Evgeny Karandaev; S.276 : David Pereiras; S.278 un.: Moving Moment; S.278 mi.: Juris Kraulis; S.278 ob.: Thawornnurak; S.279 walter: worradirek; S.279 lap: Budimir Jevtic; S.279 lemon: AlenKadr; S.279 root: IvanDbajo; S.280 : Ico Maker; S.281 ob.: Paul Michael Hughes; S.281 un.: VladKK; S.282 : SolidMaks; S.283 : AlenKadr; S.285 : nelik; S.340 5 un.: Ekkachai; S.340 3 ob.: PHOTOCREO Michal Bednarek; S.340 1 un.: Taras Vyshnya; S.340 5 ob.: Carsten Reisinger; S.340 1 ob.: Claudio Divizia; S.340 3 un.: Mario Hagen).

Filmstills

ACTV (S.67 A bis F: © 2007 Film Finance Corporation Australia Limited, New South Wales Film and Television Office and CAAMA, Central Australian Aboriginal Media Association (Aboriginal Corporation)); **Crooked Letter Films, NY** (S.167); **Interfilm Berlin Management GmbH** (S.17 : Cool Unicorn Bruv / Ninian Doff, UK; S.93 : Aviary/ Corrie Chen; S.117 un. & ob.: Walter Woodman & Patrick Cederberg); **Koloro-Design, Julia Hintz** (S.43); **Rockfinch Ltd** (S.99).

Illustrationen

Stefan Bachmann (S.139); **Roland Beier** (S.239; S.272); **Carlos Borrell Eiköter, Berlin** (Karte: S.II; S.III; S.8: mi.li.); **Tobias Dahmen, Utrecht / www.tobidahmen.de** (S.27: mi.re.; S.27: mi.li.; S.57); **Michael Fleischmann** (S.182: un.; S.189: ; S.191: li.; S.191: re.; S.195: ; S.200: ; S.202: ; S.205: li.; S.205: re.; S.236: ob.); **Eric Gira, Berlin** (S.8 mi.mi. ; S.36 ob. ; S.48 ob.re. ; S.56 ob.re. ; S.60 Hintergr. ; S.61 Hintergr. ; S.76 Hintergr. ; S.77 Hintergr. ; S.78 E ; S.78 E ; S.78 un.li. ; S.89 Smiley; S.106 Hintergr. ; S.107 Hintergr. ; S.108 Vorne & Hintergr. ; S.109 Hintergr. ; S.118 ; S.120 ; S.122 Mitte; S.136 Hintergr. ; S.137 Hintergr.); **Sapna Richter** (S.72: re.; S.72: li.; S.128: re.; S.128: li.; S.168: ; S.174: ; S.175: ob.); **M.B.Schulz, Düsseldorf** (S.49: A bis D; S.83; S.126 S.181; S.182: ob.; S.184).

Texte

S.32-35 Jonathan Eyers: The Thieves of Pudding Lane, Bloomsbury 2014; S.130-131 Guardian News & Media Ltd 2020/ Zeki Basan; S.138 Elizabeth Acevedo: The Poet X, HarperTeen 2018; S.140-141 Fuck You Dave/Halla!Halla! Publishing/Late 80's Music/Hunger/Big Dreams Aps/ StefMusic/Then We Take The World/Thou Art the Hunger/ WC Music Corp./Westside Independent Music Publishing LLC/Neue Welt Musikverlag GmbH, Hamburg / Text: Chris Brown / Lukas Forchhammer / Morten Jensen / Stefan Forrest / Morten Pilegaard / David Labrel; S.142-145 Geraldine McCaughrean: The White Darkness, Oxford University Press 2005.

TEXT — PRESENTATION

CONTENT	
✓	You covered the important points in the task.
√	The information was interesting/new.
√	You gave examples/details.
√	You gave your opinion.
√	You gave arguments for your opinion.
✎	*Your story had a plot.*[2]
	You described the characters.
	…

✓ Choose criteria[1] for your feedback.

✎ Add other criteria you need, e.g. for feedback on a story.

Text:

STRUCTURE	
√	Your introduction said what the text is about.
√	You used paragraphs.
√	Each paragraph had a new idea.
√	You had a conclusion.
✎	…

LANGUAGE	
√	You used different adjectives and adverbs.
√	You joined sentences with linking words.
√	You used special vocabulary for the topic.
√	Your spelling was correct.
√	Your grammar was correct.
✎	…

Presentation:

STRUCTURE	
√	You introduced the topic.
√	Your presentation had a clear structure.
√	You showed your main points on a poster/…
√	You summed up at the end.
√	You invited us to ask questions.
✎	…

DELIVERY	
√	You seemed relaxed.
√	You made eye contact.
√	You used notes.
√	You spoke clearly.
√	You explained your pictures.
✎	…

TIPS

1 Use the criteria you chose to assess your classmate's work.

2 Give details when you say what a classmate did/didn't do well.
Always start with something positive.

Where	What
In the first paragraph you …	*wrote a good introduction ….*
At the end of your presentation you …	*didn't ask if we had questions /…*

3 Suggest how your classmate could do better.
You could try to *use more linking words like* ***and*** *or* ***because*** */use more pictures / …*

[1] **criteria** *(pl)* [kraɪˈtɪəriə] Kriterien [2]**plot** [plɒt] Handlung

Giving feedback to your classmates: Phrases

You can use emoticons (😃 ...) when you assess a classmate's work.

CONTENT	😃	🙂	😐	☹
You covered the important points in the task.	✓			
The information was interesting/new/...			✓	
You gave examples/details/...				

The phrases below can help you when you give feedback and make suggestions.

😃

Your introduction / ideas / pictures / ... was / were brilliant! / clever! / interesting! / ...

I really liked the way you structured your text. / summed up at the end. / explained your pictures. / ....

Here's an example of what I liked.

🙂

Your introduction / ideas / pictures / ... was / were quite good. / quite interesting. / mostly OK. / ...

You structured your text / explained your pictures / summed up / ... quite well.

Here's an example of what you did well. / could improve.

😐

Some of your ideas / examples / pictures / ... were quite good. / interesting. / all right. / ...

Your introduction / grammar / ... was OK, but ...

You didn't (always) use linking words. / speak very clearly. / ...

I don't think you checked your text very carefully. / gave very good examples. / used enough adjectives. / ...

Maybe you could join up these sentences. / use captions under your pictures. / ...

☹

You forgot to / You didn't cover the important points. / use paragraphs. / introduce your subject. / sum up at the end. / ...

You almost never used linking words. / gave examples. / made eye contact with us. / ...

I don't think you did enough research. / spent much time on your text. / had a good conclusion. / ...

If I were you I would start a new paragraph here. / write the conclusion again. / ...